Introduction to Environmental Law and Policy

Protecting the Environment
Through Law

Introduction to Environmental Law and Policy

Protecting the Environment Through Law

Christina M. Valente
Villanova University
U.S. Environmental Protection Agency, Philadelphia

William D. Valente
Villanova University

West Publishing Company
Minneapolis/St. Paul   New York   Los Angeles   San Francisco

PRODUCTION CREDITS

Artwork   Alice B. Thiede and William A. Thiede, Cartographics
Composition   Parkwood Composition

Production, Prepress, Printing and Binding by West Publishing Company.

 TEXT IS PRINTED ON 10% POST CONSUMER RECYCLED PAPER

WEST'S COMMITMENT TO THE ENVIRONMENT

In 1906, West Publishing Company began recycling materials left over from the production of books. This began a tradition of efficient and responsible use of resources. Today, up to 95 percent of our legal books and 70 percent of our college and school texts are printed on recycled, acid-free stock. West also recycles nearly 22 million pounds of scrap paper annually—the equivalent of 181,717 trees. Since the 1960s, West has devised ways to capture and recycle waste inks, solvents, oils, and vapors created in the printing process. We also recycle plastics of all kinds, wood, glass, corrugated cardboard, and batteries, and have eliminated the use of Styrofoam book packaging. We at West are proud of the longevity and the scope of our commitment to the environment.

DISCLAIMER

This book was written by the authors in a private capacity. The United States Environmental Protection Agency has given no official endorsement, either express or implied, to the views or opinions contained herein.

British Library Cataloguing-in-Publication Data. A catalogue record for this book is available from the British Library.

COPYRIGHT © 1995   By WEST PUBLISHING COMPANY
                    610 Opperman Drive
                    P.O. Box 64526
                    St. Paul, MN 55164-0526

Printed in the United States of America

02 01 00 99 98 97 96 95 8 7 6 5 4 3 2 1 0

Library of Congress Cataloging-in-Publication Data

Valente, Christina M.
  Introduction to environmental law and policy: protecting the
environment through law / Christina M. Valente, William D. Valente.
     p. cm.
  Includes index.
  ISBN 0-314-04356-X (hardbound)
  1. Environmental law—United States.   2. Environmental policy—
United States.   I. Valente, William D.   II. Title.
KF3775.V35   1995
344.73'046—dc20   94-36479
[347.30446]   CIP

To

Elizabeth J. Valente

Educator, Counsellor, Confidante

Preface

Contemporary environmental law, both domestic and international, is comprised largely of laws, regulations, court decisions, and treaties made since the early 1960s. The National Environmental Policy Act of 1970 (NEPA) was the first promulgation of a comprehensive national policy on the environment. Legislative enactments which constitute the core of U.S. environmental law soon followed. Among them are statutes addressing chemical wastes, pesticides, hazardous wastes, cleanups of hazardous sites, and water and air quality. Courts have also been active in carrying forward environmental reforms by resolving disputes on the interpretation and constitutionality of environmental laws. Of the thirty-five court opinions featured in this book, eleven were rendered by the U.S. Supreme Court since 1985, and all others but two were decided after 1980. The last two decades have also witnessed major advances in creating international law on the environment, the most salient being the agreements forged at the second Earth Summit in Rio de Janeiro in 1992.

Given the novelty, diversity, and complexity of environmental law, it is not surprising that colleges and universities have begun only recently to offer undergraduate courses on environmental law and policy. The task of creating these courses is far from simple. While literature on the environment is burgeoning, much of it addresses discrete environmental issues or the special needs of professionals—scientists, engineers, administrators, and lawyers—who work within the environmental arena. Needless to say, such literature is often highly technical or unsuitably narrow in scope for use in undergraduate courses.

This book seeks to fill the evident need for introductory course materials which can impart a working knowledge of current environmental regulation and of the processes and institutions which shape environmental law and policy. It also aims to foster a general understanding of the principal strategies and mechanisms available to policymakers in light of societal, economic and institutional factors, which influence and limit governmental efforts to protect the environment. Such a survey of the framework of environmental regulation is not only desirable, but is also a necessary prelude to meaningful advanced study of specialized aspects of environmental law and policy. This text focuses on federal law, although related state and local law is discussed, particularly in areas of overlap or conflict with federal law.

Preparing a text suitable for college use presented obvious challenges. Environmental law is pervasively interdisciplinary, yet students will naturally approach the subject from the outlooks of their respective disciplines. Our goal has been to present a text which allows teachers to make good use of the varied insights of undergraduates in different "majors" while promoting a common exploration of environmental solutions. This requires an adequate mix of materials on the scientific, economic, political, and legal issues that coalesce in environmental law. It also compels a simplification of the technical aspects of environmental decisionmaking, lest students be driven to focus on fine distinctions at the expense of larger issues. Our classroom experience with the text materials has been enormously helpful in addressing these concerns, but there is ample room for differing opinions on the optimal mix and emphasis of text materials. We therefore continue to invite criticisms and suggestions on the content and organization of this book.

The organization of the book is fairly straightforward. The first three chapters sketch the historical and institutional background against which modern environmental law developed and lay the framework for understanding the substantive law that is covered in remaining chapters. Chapter 1 explores the evolution of environmental problems and movements. Chapter 2 delves into the operations and strictures of the federal governmental and legal systems wherein environmental regulations are created and enforced. Chapter 3 examines the requirements of the National Environmental Policy Act (NEPA) and also introduces the concept of regulatory mechanisms which are reflected in substantive environmental laws.

Chapters 4 through 6 deal with pollutant-specific laws that seek to manage prospectively the hazards associated with chemicals, pesticides and hazardous wastes. Chapter 7 explores the thorny political and economic issues associated with environmental remediation and cleanup by examining the operation of the Superfund law, whose broad sweep potentially reaches practically every business activity and use of real property today.

Chapters 8 and 9 switch the focus from pollutant specific legislation to regulatory schemes designed to protect the overall quality of environmental media, namely air and water. The complexity and difficulties of setting and achieving realistic standards to limit environmental degradation and improve environmental quality come into sharp relief in these chapters.

The final two chapters survey law and policy related to federal and tribal lands and the global environment. Chapter 10 explores environmental regulation of public lands, governmental facilities, and Native American reservations, as well as the difficulties of reconciling the regulatory authority of some federal agencies with the operational independence of others. Chapter 11 looks at barriers to effective protection of the international environment, especially in the creation and enforcement of just, comprehensive, internationally applicable standards.

Certain pervasive themes run through many of the chapters. A constant refrain is the need to promote sustainable development policies to ensure that worldwide natural resource exploitation is consistent with global environmental health, human welfare, and fairness among nations and regions. The dynamics of regional and socioeconomic conflicts within and among nations are considered in the context of the global marketplace and international treaties. Another theme that echoes throughout is the need to evaluate the effectiveness of regulatory mechanisms and to choose wisely from among them. Efficiency must be balanced by fairness in the allocation of the costs and benefits of environmental protection among different segments of society. The historical tensions between effectiveness, efficiency, and fairness come into sharp focus in the text's comparisons of technology-driven regulation, based upon cost and availability of pollution control technologies, with technology-forcing mechanisms which rely upon human and environmental health-based standards. In the same vein, disputes over the reliability and usefulness of cost-benefit analyses for structuring environmental regulation highlight the benefits and drawbacks of alternative regulatory mechanisms. Hopefully, the recurrence of these central themes in different chapter settings will enhance student understanding of fundamental issues in governmental regulation and international cooperation.

A brief explanation of featured source materials may be in order: We have relied heavily upon government statistics in the text but wherever doubts exist as to the reliability or comprehensiveness of such information, we have presented alternative sources of information as well. Excerpts of the statutes covered in Chapters 3 through 8 appear in appendices to those chapters. Other relevant statutes, case law, and treaties appear in the text of all chapters. We have liberally reprinted abstracts from publications of Congress, the Environmental Protection Agency, the Council on Environmental Quality, and other federal offices so that the views of governmental agencies are presented in their own words. The court opinions which appear in most chapters were selected to elucidate the operation of environmental statues and to present the predominant issues associated with protection of the environment through law. They represent the latest, most authoritative pronouncements available through the end of the 1993–94 term of the U.S. Supreme Court. Unless otherwise indicated, footnotes and dissenting and concurring opinions are omitted from case abstracts.

As Congress continues to consider proposed amendments and reauthorizations of the laws covered in this text, and as lawsuits continue to work their way towards judicial decision, important, ongoing changes can be expected. In this continually evolving field, no book on environmental law can present the last word for very long without periodic updates and supplements. The authors expect to prepare supplementary materials as needed to keep the text current, accurate, and reliable.

Christina M. Valente

William D. Valente

Acknowledgments

We acknowledge our indebtedness to the institutions, government agencies, scholars and authors whose studies and publications made the preparation of this text possible. While we cannot list those sources fully, our citations to them in the text and endnotes are evidence of their contributions. We express our special thanks to the following individuals and organizations.

At Villanova University, we received invaluable assistance from Dean Steven P. Frankino, the Director and staff of the Law Library, our colleagues at the Law School and the Political Science Department, and our student research assistants. The patient assistance of faculty secretary, Joan DeLong, greatly eased our burdens through the trying stage of manuscript preparation.

From Christina Valente's colleagues at the Philadelphia regional offices of the Environmental Protection Agency, we gained distinctive insights into current environmental problems and fresh legal developments for which we are grateful.

At West Educational Publishing Company, the progress and quality of this publication were greatly enhanced by the efficient assistance of acquiring editor Elizabeth Hannan, developmental editor Patty Bryant, production editor Mary Verrill, and promotions manager Ann Hillstrom. We are also indebted to the following reviewers of various draft chapters for their thoughtful criticisms and suggestions: Professors Mark W. Anderson, Lois J. Bruinooge, William Green, David Hoch, Mary C. Keifer, Penny Lynn, Don McCabe, Marlene McGuirl, David Sadosky, Dennis L. Soden, and Mary Urisko.

Brief Contents

Contents

Table of Cases

The boldface cases represent U.S. Supreme Court cases.

PART I

INTRODUCTION TO ENVIRONMENTAL LAW AND POLICY

The study of environmental law can proceed from various viewpoints and motivations and can serve varying purposes. Whatever one's purpose in pursuing the topic, comprehension of U.S. environmental law and policy proceeds from basic understandings of: (a) particular environmental problems and issues; (b) the system of law within which statutes to protect the environment are designed, enacted, administered, and enforced; and (c) the various models of regulation that can be fashioned within the U.S. legal system to address targeted environmental problems. The three chapters of Part I survey these basic subjects.

CHAPTER 1

Overview of Modern Environmental Problems

Outline

Protection of the environment has been the focus of growing public attention and debate since the 1960s, and concern for the environment has soared in this final decade of the twentieth century. People of many backgrounds and political persuasions profess to be environmentally aware and manifest concern for the state of the environment. Although most people in the United States would agree in principle that some laws for protecting the environment are necessary and valuable, disagreement persists as to the issues environmental law should address, the levels of environmental protection which are necessary and desirable, and the manner in which the political and legal systems should protect or restore the environment. In exploring these issues, it is helpful first to appraise the practical and philosophical environmental issues that contemporary societies confront.

1.1 Practical Reasons for Studying Environmental Law and Policy

The study of environmental law and policy is not a narrow discipline, useful only to those who are planning careers in business, law, or government. Human welfare and the state of the environment are inextricably linked, and most human enterprises interact with the environment, for better or worse. In the United States, environmental law has developed to the point where it now impacts a broad spectrum of social, economic, and personal activities. For these reasons, it is important and practical to cultivate an awareness and understanding of environmental issues. Knowledge of the fundamentals of environmental law and policy lays the groundwork for understanding current and future environmental issues.

Many career fields and professions now require specialized knowledge of environmental science or law. In other career fields, such expertise is not a strict prerequisite, but the individual who has such a background will experience greater success or have more career options. Naturally, a person who wishes to practice environmental law or to provide environmental engineering and consulting services must have a specialized background in environmental law and regulation. But those considering other careers should not ignore the importance of the basic and applied sciences, the social sciences, and the humanities in the formulation and administration of environmental law and policy.

- *''Hard'' sciences* such as chemistry, physics, geology, and biology and subspecialties such as climatology and toxicology inform the study of environmental quality and its effects on human health, the origin and transport of environmental pollutants and exposure pathways for humans and other organisms, global phenomena such as warming and ozone depletion, and many other environmental conditions.
- *Applied sciences,* such as engineering contribute to the search for environmental solutions, such as improved pollution-control technologies, source reduction of pollutants through changes in manufacturing techniques, and pollution prevention through genetically engineered products such as pest-resistant plant hybrids.
- *The social sciences* such as economics, history, and political science provide tools needed for developing effective regulatory programs, for assuring their passage into law, and for effective administration thereafter. These tools include economic analysis of the projected costs and benefits of proposed environmental regulations, political analysis of constituencies and special interests that will favor or oppose particular kinds of regulation, and historical research into the efficacy and unintended results of previous legal and regulatory regimes—an inquiry that has been too often neglected.
- *The humanities* illuminate the relationships between human beings and the natural world and the ethical, spiritual, aesthetic, and social dimensions of environmental policies.

Given the wide range of disciplines that contribute to current knowledge of the environment and environmental issues, it is not surprising that college and university curriculums are being supplemented by additional courses whose most obvious feature is the addition of the single word *environmental*.[1]

Industries, business, and consumers are daily affected by environmental laws and regulations in the United States. Obviously, lawyers, agricultural scientists, environmental engineers, and people who work in the chemical industry must have knowledge of environmental laws and regulations, but so must persons engaged in many other occupations. Environmental laws regulate such small businesses as gas stations, dry cleaners, and distributors of various products and such institutions as colleges, hospitals, and banks as well as more visible sources of environmental harm such as petrochemical companies and electrical utilities. The insurance industry, the legal profession, and real estate agents must be aware of environmental laws and regulations that affect their clients and their own earnings. Cities, towns, and other local governments operate facilities that are covered by environmental regulations, such as municipal landfills, power stations, and schools. Therefore, employees, executives, and professionals in all of these fields as well as government officials need to have a general background in the nature and structure of environmental law. This knowledge will also benefit those who plan to pursue specialized training in environmental law or science, as well as those who wish to protect themselves from environmental hazards in the workplace.

Knowledge of environmental regulations can benefit consumers and citizens:

- To avoid liability for the costly cleanup of hazardous substances by investigating the former uses of a property purchased for residential or business use;
- To make informed decisions when purchasing imported fruits and vegetables, which may pass customs inspection even though they contain residues of dangerous pesticides whose use is banned in the United States;
- To make informed decisions when purchasing lawn and garden pesticides and fertilizers or lawn care services;
- To purchase products that do not contribute to the thinning of the ozone layer;
- To dispose of such dangerous household products as batteries and motor oil safely; and
- To promote environmental legislation that incorporates effective regulatory mechanisms.

Environmental law affects everyone—at home, in the workplace, as citizens, as inhabitants of the planet. Understanding how environmental laws work and what they regulate is not merely useful; it is vital.

1.2 Environmental Concerns: From the Practical to the Philosophical

The lack of consensus concerning the proper objectives of environmental law and policy stems largely from differing assessments of the present state of the environment. Some experts believe that we are currently facing an environmental crisis of the highest order; that the environment is being—or has already been—degraded to a point where neither natural nor human forces can restore it. Other experts believe that the dimensions of our environmental problems are not nearly so monumental. Most experts agree, however, that human management of the environment has been less than optimal and that serious environmental concerns, both local and global in scale, necessitate some form of governmental intervention. In the following excerpt, a former EPA Administrator who later became chairman of the World Wildlife Fund surveys the more salient environmental issues facing the United States and other nations:

> Despite numerous victories, the United States is losing the battle: Global environmental problems . . . climate change, loss of biodiversity, stratospheric ozone depletion, for instance—are placing both human and natural systems at risk. The air . . . threatens to deteriorate further as improvements in auto emissions controls are overwhelmed by the sheer numbers of cars and miles driven. . . . Disposal and cleanup of . . . waste . . . pose ever greater difficulties. . . . Encroaching land development is displacing and undermining critical ecosystems . . . and threatens . . . natural areas and biological diversity. Large areas of natural forests and other public lands . . . are not managed sustainably. Farmlands are suffering from . . . excessive use of chemicals. Aquifers . . . are being consumed and contaminated at an alarming rate. . . .
>
> * * *
>
> . . . [T]his litany of environmental ills . . . by no means complete, is a product of *today's* level of economic activity and human population. . . . [C]onsider tomorrow. Over the next 50 years . . . economic activity in the United States is projected to *quadruple* and global population to at least double.[2]

For the sake of discussion, environmental concerns can be roughly divided into two broad categories: pollution and natural-resource depletion. The two categories are by no means separate, however. For example, since pollution of a resource makes it unavailable for other uses, it is, therefore, also a form of depletion. In addition, certain global issues, such as climate change, do not fall neatly into either category. The current trend, one that is more holistic and interdisciplinary, is to think of environmental law as regulating the use, distribution, and availability of resources. This perspective permits more fluent incorporation of related subjects such as land use, zoning, resource management, and private property rights into an analysis of environmental law. However, public environmental regulation and management in the United States has traditionally created a dichotomy between regulating pollution and managing natural resources. For this reason, the two concerns are discussed in separate subsections here. Finally, aesthetic, ethical, and spiritual concerns relating to the environment are considered in this section. Although these concerns have only occasionally been directly targeted by legislative initiatives,[3] environmental laws nonetheless reflect environmental ethics.

Pollution's Impact on Human Health and Economic Interests

The individual and synergistic effects of pollution on human health and economic interests are myriad and startling. Pollution affects people in every segment of society—consumers, factory and agricultural workers, urban residents, property owners—though in differing degrees and in different ways. Many polluting chemicals and technologies came into use after World War II. Other pollution-causing agents, such as fossil fuels, have been used for centuries.

The worldwide, widespread use of pesticides in agriculture leaves residues in many foodstuffs that consumers purchase every day. Farmworkers who must work in recently sprayed fields and factory workers who are exposed to chemicals during manufacturing processes face heightened risks to life and health, including the increased occurrence of serious birth defects, sterility, and various cancers.

Inadequate controls on emissions from industrial smokestacks and automobiles pose increased risks of lung cancer and other respiratory illnesses to urban residents. Hazardous substances released into soil and ground water contaminate drinking-water supplies in many parts of the United States and the world.

Chlorofluorocarbons (CFCs; the compounds used as coolants in refrigerators and air conditioners and as propellants in aerosol-spray cans) escaping into the environment are almost universally blamed for damaging the earth's protective ozone layer, which shields humans and other organisms from harmful ultraviolet rays. Emissions from industries, power plants, and automobiles, the so-called greenhouse gases, may be producing dramatic changes in climate and weather worldwide. Many scientists believe that these climate changes could lead to droughts, and to a rise in sea level, which will cause salt water intrusions. These are but a few examples of the inescapable and seemingly intractable problems human beings face as a result of environmental degradation.

Health considerations aside, environmental quality affects economic and property interests of all kinds. Discharges of untreated human sewage, storm-sewer runoff, hazardous medical wastes, mercury and other toxic substances into lakes, oceans, and streams have ravaged fisheries and spawning grounds. Those discharges have also despoiled recreational areas and adversely affected tourist industries on the East and West Coasts, in the Great Lakes area, and elsewhere. The careless use and disposal of hazardous substances and petroleum products have caused serious economic losses to property owners, developers, industries, banks, and insurance companies—losses that are passed on to taxpayers and consumers. In cases of large-scale contamination, repercussions may be felt throughout the banking industry, the stock markets, and the regional and national economies.

Natural Resource Damage and Depletion: The Challenges Posed by Overpopulation and Excessive Consumption

Equally significant are the difficulties faced by burgeoning human populations of natural resource depletion, a less apparent but equally critical aspect of environmental degradation. Like all other organisms, human beings are dependent upon the ecosystems that sustain their physical needs. When necessary resources are depleted, ecosystems are no longer self-sustaining, and the survival of dependent organisms is threatened.

A well-publicized example of a resource depletion crisis is the diminishing availability of usable water worldwide. Even the world's wealthiest countries, which possess large-scale water purification capabilities, have already experienced or are projected to experience serious water shortages. In many areas of the less-industrialized nations of South America, Asia, and Africa, safe drinking water is simply not available to a majority of the population. Pollution, salinization, and depletion of water supplies are often directly attributable to human activities such as deforestation, excessive pumping, and overgrazing undertaken without sufficient regard for the environmental impacts.

Another major concern is soil damage, which threatens the world's food supply. A recent United Nations study found that more than a tenth of the world's fertile soil (an area the size of India and China combined) has been damaged since 1945. The study cites overgrazing, farming practices, deforestation, urbanization, and pollution as the primary causes of soil damage.

Depletion of the earth's ozone layer also can be viewed as a form of natural resource depletion. CFCs and other substances that break down the ozone layer are themselves nontoxic. When they are released into the atmosphere, however, they cause a thinning of the ozone layer. The overall effect is actually a "consumption" of the ozone layer, a valuable natural resource.

The causes of resource depletion are complex and interrelated. Excessive depletion of a natural resource occurs when a population consumes a resource faster than it can be replenished or replaced. Population growth increases the competition for limited resources and decreases the availability of those resources. It can also escalate existing environmental crises exponentially. Although worldwide population growth is often cited as the primary reason for resource depletion, this is, in fact, not the case. *Disproportionate* consumption by a small percentage of the world's population is a far more important cause. A mere 20 percent of the world's population consumes 80 percent of the world's resources: 75 percent of its commercial energy, 90 percent of its traded hardwoods, 81 percent of its paper, 80 percent of its iron and steel, and 70 percent of its milk and meat. The world's population may double by the year 2025, but even if 90 percent of that growth occurs in developing countries, its impact on resource consumption will actually be less than that exerted by the 10 percent added in developed countries, assuming that the consumption patterns of the early 1990s continue.[4] Nevertheless, population growth magnifies the effects of resource depletion on marginal ecosystems. In this excerpt, Shridath Ramphal explains how poverty induces population growth and accelerates environmental degradation:

> . . . [T]here is no avoiding the reality that burgeoning populations in poor countries will strain their natural resources beyond tolerable limits.
>
> For a family on the edge of survival, it makes sense to have several children in the hope that some will survive to support the rest. But when many families act in the same way, the result is far more people than resources can sustain . . . In Kenya, . . . which suffers acutely from land hunger, urban unemployment, and environmental stress, a woman now produces nearly seven children on average. The population could quadruple to nearly 100 million in 35 years if the present rate of growth continues. In Bangladesh, where almost every acre of cultivable land is already used, and millions live on flood-prone mudbanks, facing imminent disaster, the population is expected to double from 100 million to 220 million over the same period, even assuming a halving of the birthrate. Increases in population pressure of this order contribute to many of the world's most acute environmental problems, including deforestation and desertification. They widen and deepen poverty, which in turn keeps birthrates high. Poverty, in a perverse but historically predictable way, restrains the demographic transition to smaller families.[5]

Demographers have established that a population's birthrate declines as the standard of living of the majority of the population rises. Where the dominant market structure distributes wealth and resources unevenly among different human populations, the populations increase or decrease for reasons directly linked to the distribution of resources.

The structure of the international market economy also contributes to resource depletion by favoring ecologically unsound practices in poorer countries. Two examples of this are tariffs and foreign debt. Most industrialized countries levy higher import duties (sometimes doubly high) on value-added or finished products than on raw materials. Such tariffs encourage developing nations to export raw materials rather than manufactured or processed goods. Raw materials do not generate as much profit as finished products. Exporting countries must sell more of the raw product than of finished products using those same raw materials to generate the same income. In this way, tariff structures serve to escalate resource depletion in marginal economies.

Developing nations' efforts to repay of loans made to them in past decades has also induced ecologically unsound practices. Efforts to repay foreign loans have led poor nations to turn to cash-crop and beef exports in order to raise hard currency. As a consequence, land that has long been used for subsistence agriculture or sustainable forestry is being turned over to monoculture (single-crop agriculture) and grazing. Not only does this fuel the cycle of dependency, but it can also have devastating ecological consequences, as Carrie Meyer explains occurred in Costa Rica:

> Almost 70 percent of Costa Rica's total land area is suitable only for forests; yet because of rapid deforestation during the past two decades, today less than 40 percent of the land is under forests. Once the forests were cut, soils that had sustained them were quickly lost. Between 1970 and 1989, an estimated 2.2 billion metric tons of soil were eroded in Costa Rica. . . . Costa Rica's land policies, economic subsidies, and the government's handling of the debt crisis of the early 1980s can be directly linked to the destruction of the forestlands, as those policies encouraged the nation's rapidly growing and poor population to move out onto the forested, or "frontier," lands.
>
> Among the policies that led to Costa Rica's troubles were incentives provided to cattle ranchers, such as subsidized credit and preferential exchange rates, to encourage them to produce beef for export. . . . [B]eef exports increased over 500 percent, and forests were cut to make grazing lands for the beef. Between 1963 and 1984, pastureland almost doubled, rising to 54 percent of the country's land area. However, . . . only about 10 percent of Costa Rica's territory is suitable for pasture, implying that forests were squandered and soil resources washed away as steep and fragile slopes became pastureland. Pastures also encroached on good agricultural land. . . .
>
> The "debt crisis" that hit Costa Rica in the early 1980s brought burgeoning unemployment and plummeting real wages, and pushed many more landless peasants toward the frontiers in search of substinence. . . .[6]

Industrialized nations also employ technologies and policies that are far from ecologically sound, even though they are not compelled to do so for survival. The United States remains dependent on the world's oil supplies despite the availability of energy sources that do not have the same detrimental effects on climate and air quality. Furthermore, the United States' use of energy is highly inefficient; if the United States were as energy-efficient as Japan, for example, it would spend $230 billion dollars a year on energy instead of $450 billion.

National forest and rangeland management have provided other examples of ecologically detrimental U.S. policy. For decades the Forest Service and the logging industry carried out massive clear-cutting of public forests without adequate efforts to replenish hardwood species and to preserve biotic diversity. Clear-cutting not only depletes the supply of renewable lumber resources, but also causes soil erosion and water runoff and destroys wildlife habitats. The U.S. Bureau of Land Management's below-market rates for grazing rights continues to encourage overgrazing on public lands. Overgrazing makes forage less available for wildlife and often results in permanent soil damage and erosion.

Current uses of U.S. public lands and forests do not yet threaten human survival as does overconsumption in poorer nations, but they do raise issues of economic and environmental fairness. Such uses permit certain segments of society to derive economic benefit from publicly owned natural resources, without regard for adverse ecological consequences or for the availability of those resources for other public uses.

Aesthetic, Ethical, and Spiritual Implications of the Human Relationship to the Environment

Thus far, we have focused on the impact of environmental quality upon human physical and material needs. Now we briefly survey the aesthetic, ethical, and spiritual dimensions of human interaction with the environment.

Human societies almost universally recognize aesthetic values in the natural environment. In mainstream U.S. culture, such aesthetic values translate into common desires to breathe fresh air; to be surrounded by "natural objects" such as flowers, trees, and birds; to cultivate gardens; and to visit areas of great natural beauty. Millions of Americans vacation in scenic areas each year; the popularity of the National Park system demonstrates the importance of wilderness in the national psyche. But American culture has also defined nature as a place where the human presence is not evident, where the dichotomy between "man" and "nature" that underlies Western culture is confirmed.

Traditional Western philosophical and religious traditions view human beings as having dominance over nature. From this understanding of the human relationship with nature, two dramatically different viewpoints have emerged. The first is that human dominance entails a moral obligation to engage in careful stewardship of the environment, to conserve natural resources, and to guard against extinction of species. The second viewpoint is that humans may use nature for their sole benefit, regardless of the consequences to other species. Both viewpoints embody an *anthropocentric* (human-centered) perspective.

Not all cultural and religious traditions incorporate a human—nature dualism. Native American cultures, for example, generally regard humans and all other living things as interdependent. Within this tradition, every human action that touches the earth or another organism requires concomitant measures to maintain the harmonious balance of nature.

Deep ecologists hold as a matter of philosophical belief the view that humans have obligations to protect and maintain the balance of nature. These obligations stem from the interdependence of humans and other organisms in the larger ecosystem. Hence, human enjoyment and convenience must be considered within the context of what is good for the earth. Many regard human degradation of the environment as problematic or iniquitous quite apart from its tangible or intangible human consequences. This philosophy is referred to as an *ecocentric* perspective.

U.S. environmental law and policy have not explicitly or consistently espoused any identifiable environmental ethic. However, the protection of human health and, to a lesser extent, economic interests have generally taken precedence. With few exceptions, the development of U.S. environmental law and policy has proceeded from an anthropocentric perspective, as opposed to an ecocentric one.

1.3   Basic Principles of Ecology Affecting Environmental Decision Making

Although this book focuses on the study of environmental protection through law, some explanation of the basic principles of ecology is necessary in order to illuminate fundamental issues in environmental law and policy. Ecology is a branch of science that examines the natural environment by pinpointing relationships among organisms, populations of organisms, and ecosystems. In order to formulate environmental policies that will have the desired effects, it is necessary to understand how organisms, including humans, relate to each other and to their environments.

To stress the importance of ecology as a foundation for the study of environmental law and policy is not to suggest that ecological knowledge is immutable. All sciences are subject to "revolutions" in which accepted "truths" are reevaluated and newly discovered "truths" are incorporated.[7] Even so, current scientific thought (encompassing areas of debate as well as agreement) is the framework within which societies must approach environmental issues. Thus even as environmental technology continues to be refined in response to new knowledge gained through research, certain broad ecological hypotheses hold sway and command near-universal acceptance.

One of these universally accepted principles is that of ecosystem interdependence, which Zachary Smith discusses in his 1992 book, *Environmental Policy Paradox*:

> An *ecosystem* is any group of plants, animals, and nonliving things interacting within their external environment. Typically, ecologists study individual organisms (the life cycle of the individual, its requirements, and its functioning in the environment); populations of organisms (including questions such as stability, decline, or growth in populations); communities of organisms; or the ecosystem as a whole (including the biogeochemical cycles of carbon, oxygen, hydrogen, soil minerals, and energy).
>
> Ecosystems may appear to be independent units that have little interaction with their external environment. Some ecologists describe them as "a watershed in New Hampshire, a Syrian desert, the Arctic icecap, or Lake Michigan." Yet ecosystems are open in the sense that they interact with everything else in the environment. In fact, the earth itself is an ecosystem, commonly referred to as the ecosphere or biosphere.
>
> The earth, like all ecosystems, receives energy from the sun. Otherwise, there is very little interaction between the earth and the external environment. Consequently, with the reception of energy from the sun, the resources that the planet started with are the same as those that exist today (although constantly changing form). This is why some use the term "Spaceship Earth" to describe the earth's relationship with the external environment. Like a spaceship, the planet must work with what it has. When certain resources are exhausted or converted into a form in which they are no longer useful to humans, they are lost forever.[8]

Barry Commoner's Four Laws of Ecology

In his classic work, *The Closing Circle*, biologist and environmental activist Barry Commoner advanced four laws of ecology

1. Everything is connected to everything else.
2. Everything must go somewhere.
3. Nature knows best.
4. There is no such thing as a free lunch.

Regarding his first law, Commoner explains that the multiple interconnected parts that make up an ecosystem interact upon each other. He uses as an example the fresh-water ecosystem comprised of fish, organic wastes, bacteria of decay, inorganic products, and algae, explaining that the system is destroyed when the natural balance is upset by excessive pollution. In discussing his second law, Commoner stresses the indestructibility of matter, however it is altered by human processes, and the damage caused when toxic substances are deposited in nature, "where they do not belong." His third law, that nature "knows best," is resisted by the human urge to control nature. Commoner points out that humans cannot force nature to absorb human-made wastes and poisons beyond its capacity to do so without harming the ecosphere. He suggests, therefore, that humans should consider the signs of environmental overload in determining the prudent limits of polluting discharges around the planet.

Commoner's fourth law is a conclusion based upon the first three:

> Because the global ecosystem is a connected whole . . . anything extracted from it by human effort must be replaced. Payment of this price cannot be avoided; it can only be delayed.[9]

By this law, the generation of economic benefit through environmental degradation, for example, will subsequently result in other costs: damaged or depleted natural resources, environmental remediation, medical care for environmental illnesses, property damage, and lost profits in other economic sectors.

Barry Commoner's four laws of ecology demonstrate how environmental issues arise from every kind of human endeavor because all life on earth is interconnected. Everything that enters the environment remains in the environment, whether for good or ill, in altered forms and composition. This tenet of ecology should be a central consideration in all environmental decision-making.

Aldo Leopold and the Biotic Pyramid

Aldo Leopold provides a different perspective on ecological interdependence. In *A Sand County Almanac*, Leopold describes his "circuit of life" model, a biotic pyramid within which life-sustaining energy flows upward from the land base through food chains of energy-absorbing plants, insects, birds, rodents, and larger organisms:

> When a change occurs in one part of the circuit, many other parts must adjust themselves to it. . . . Man's invention of tools has enabled him to make changes of unprecedented violence, rapidity and scope . . . [T]he less violent the manmade changes, the greater the probability of successful readjustment in the pyramid.[10]

Leopold's thesis is that the escalation of environmental exploitation to satisfy human desires will, over time, alter the natural biotic pyramid and its capacity to support human life.

1.4   The Environmental Movement

The common perception of the environment as an integrated ecosystem (or, at least, an interrelated series of ecosystems) that needs protection from further degradation is a relatively recent phenomenon. It is only within the past century or two that citizens and governments in Western cultures have undertaken significant efforts to protect the environment. Only within this century have large groups of people recognized the global implications of pollution and resource depletion. Earlier "movements," such as the turn-of-the-century conservation movement, though sensitive to environmental values, were primarily motivated by the desire to preserve natural resources for public enjoyment. In contrast, today's environmental movement is also concerned with ecological systems and sustainability.

Although some major environmental disasters have precipitated federal and state government responses to particular environmental threats, the primary stimulus for governments' attention to a growing list of environmental hazards has been the agitation of environmental activists.These activists have included laypersons, some members of the scientific, medical, and public-health communities, and segments of the mass media.

The Four Stages of Environmentalism

In a 1992 article on environmental equity, David Morris traced the evolution of the environmental movement through four stages:

> Over the past century, environmentalism has moved through four distinct stages, all of which are found in the environmental movement today.
>
> The American conservation movement began in the late 19th century as a reaction to the devastation of what had once been considered an inexhaustible wilderness. "Wilderness preservation" was its rallying cry. Its legacy is our national park system. Today wilderness advocates—hikers, anglers, hunters—still represent the vast majority of environmentalists.
>
> The second stage of environmentalism was sparked by *Silent Spring*, Rachel Carson's exposé of the dangers of DDT, which spurred activists in the '60s and '70s to widen their focus from preservation to protection. They targeted materials hazardous to human health: DDT, PCBs, mercury, lead, and other heavy metals. The rallying cry of second-stage environmentalists is "toxic reductions." Their legacy includes much of our current environmental legislation along with federal and state protection agencies and the idea of environmental impact statements.
>
> In the 1980s the discovery of the hole in the ozone layer over Antarctica and growing concern about global warming ushered in a third phase of environmentalism. In a sharp break with the past, stage-three environmentalism does not target just toxic materials. CFCs, leading culprits in the ozone layer hole, are not toxic. Rather than focusing on immediate dangers to this generation, the goal of third-stage environmentalists is to protect future generations from the dangers of exceeding nature's ability to restore itself. "Sustainability" is the rallying cry of this new breed.
>
> This new environmentalism's reach is much broader than that of previous stages. It targets not only the small proportion of substances we produce that directly threaten human health, but also other environmentally damaging materials—oil, natural gas, and coal, for example—that make up the underpinnings of industrial society. While earlier environmental efforts generally opposed development, this one may possibly be the most pro-development movement in history, for it argues that complete reconstruction of our agricultural, manufacturing, and transportation systems is needed to create a sustainable society.
>
> Even as we still grapple with the implications of all three stages of environmentalism, especially the new visions of sustainable development, the fourth stage of environmentalism is upon us. Beginning in the late 1990s, it is likely that most of the world's new greenhouse-gas emissions will come from developing nations in the Southern Hemisphere, home to the vast majority of the world's population. (On a per-capita basis, however, developing nations will still produce only a fraction of the greenhouse gases that Northern developed nations do.) How the world confronts this new phenomenon may constitute the principal environmental challenge of the 1990s.

The fourth-stage environmentalists who are just beginning to speak up argue that the principle of sustainability must be accompanied by an emphasis on equity. As Florentin Krause of the California-based International Project for Sustainable Energy Paths explains, "Ecological destruction in the Third World is inextricably linked to [its] history of colonization."

Anil Agarwal and Sunita Naritain of the Center for Science and Environment in New Delhi insist that "it is patently immoral to equate the emissions of carbon dioxide from American, European, or, for that matter, New Delhi automobiles with the survival emissions of methane from the minuscule paddy fields or few head of cattle owned by a poor west Bengal or Thai farmer."

This rift between North and South has prompted many developing nations to propose an environmental summit in Malaysia, which will serve as an alternative to the U.N.-sponsored Earth Summit to be held in Brazil in June 1992, which they view as dominated by the developed world. Forty-one nations from Latin America, Africa, and Asia currently plan to attend the protest session.

Fourth-stage environmentalists' proposal for dealing with the threat of global warming is to combine equity and sustainability by establishing a global quota for emission of gases causing the greenhouse effect and allocating to each human inhabitant of the planet an equal share. Remember, greenhouse gases like carbon dioxide, methane, and nitrous oxide are part of the natural system. Unlike DDT, they are not poisons that can be banned. The danger stems not from the nature of the emissions, but from their quantity. Environmentalists want to limit emissions, not abolish them.

Giving every human being an equal share in nature's regenerative capacity would dramatically change the relationships between North and South. Since Third World countries generate only a fraction of the greenhouse gases on a per capita basis that developed countries do, they would be allowed to increase their generation; industralized countries would have to drastically curtail theirs. Some environmentalists advocate creating a world market for emission rights. Since we all share the same atmosphere, developed countries would have the choice of either investing in measures to reduce their own emissions or purchasing emission "rights" from developing countries, whichever is the least expensive method of reducing emissions. Revenues generated from the sale of emission rights would be invested in sustainable development in poorer countries.

Almost 100 years after Gifford Pinchot and John Muir galvanized the nation to address the problem of disappearing wilderness, environmentalism continues to mature and broaden its scope. In the 1990s, the twin issues of global warming and global equity may offer the greatest challenge of all.[11]

Individual and Organized Initiatives

The true extent of citizen involvement on a wide range of environmental issues that affect homes, workplaces, recreation, and basic needs remains unclear:

> Are Americans really becoming "green" or are they just talking "green"? . . . A look at some recent polling information from the Roper Organization . . . reveals some trends. . . . Americans are more concerned about the environment than [they are about] many other "traditional" issues. . . . Another 1992 poll shows that 58 percent of Americans say they return beer or soda bottles or cans to stores or recycling centers on a regular basis. . . . Forty-three percent recycle newspapers (up from 20 percent three years ago), and 35 percent sort their garbage (up from 14 percent). Twelve percent avoid products from companies they feel aren't environmentally responsible, a proportion that has held steady since 1989.[12]

Carol Grunewald Rifkin observes that there has been a recent backlash against the environmental movement, but that this backlash indicates the inroads which ''green'' politics have made into the public psyche.[13] The extent to which the environmental movement is being taken seriously as a political force demonstrates how broad-based it has become.

This was not always the case. Until recently, environmentalism was the province of the well-educated, white, upper-middle class. Fewer than twenty large national organizations dominated the movement, which focused on legislative and judicial battles. The face of environmentalism is changing, however, as minorities, feminists, labor leaders, and others form coalitions to pursue common environmental objectives. Green parties now appear on the ballot in several states. Grassroots environmentalists are focusing attention at the state and local levels, as it becomes increasingly clear that national legislation is not sufficiently protective. Besides attempting to change the law, they are also using consumer boycotts and direct-confrontation tactics to change corporate policies.

Divergent socioeconomic interests give rise to conflicting views of what kinds of environmental regulation are desirable and feasible and who should bear their cost. Competing interests often make any choice unpalatable to lawmakers. Faced with difficult choices, legislators often avoid taking any action whatsoever. Alternately, they may seek compromise solutions that satisfy no one. Without clear mandates, government officials tend to delay taking any action. In response to this, environmental organizations and individuals have often originated reform initiatives. These initiatives have not been limited to the political sphere; through organized and individual efforts, employees, consumers, and investors have learned that they can influence corporate environmental policies as well.

Promotion of Environmental Equity

The disproportionate environmental burdens borne by some segments of society—notably the poor and racial and ethnic minorities—under current environmental laws was not effectively addressed by the environmental movement until recent years. Disproportionate environmental treatment acutely affects the health and lives of large population groups. The Executive Director of the Natural Resources Defense Council, a large, influential environmental public-interest group, outlines the problems and sources of environmental inequity in the United States and the nation's failure to extend environmental protection to all persons equally:

> The statistics are plentiful and they are frightening. Three out of four toxic waste dumps are sited in predominantly African American or Latino communities. Two million tons of radioactive uranium tailings have been dumped on [the tribal lands of] Native Americans. Three hundred thousand Latino farm laborers suffer from pesticide-related illnesses. . . .
>
> Statistics like these reflect a nationwide pattern of disproportionate environmental impact on people of color and the poor. This pattern stems from a profound flaw in the structure of the U.S. economy: Polluters do not absorb the costs of the environmental degradation they create, and society as a whole does not confront the problems and solve them. Instead, the problems are displaced. . . . [I]t is far easier for state governments to disregard the lead poisoning of poor children than to test and treat them as federal law requires. What this means is that we are building our economy on the backs of people of color and the poor.
>
> . . . The fact of disproportionate impact demands a disproportionate effort. Federal and state governments must direct a disproportionate share of cleanup funds and other environmental funding to these communities. . . .

. . . We [the environmental organizations] have been criticized by environmental justice advocates, and there is much to criticize. . . . The history is well-documented: The mainstream environmental movement grew out of a white, middle-class effort to preserve the world's natural wonders. . . .

The [mainstream] movement began with wilderness conservation, and there is no question that, in its early life, its work and vision only rarely encompassed the protection of human beings. But . . . this is a movement that has matured far beyond its origins. . . . [F]or mainstream environmentalists today the two critical issues— environmental violation of the Earth and environmental violation of its human inhabitants— are inextricably linked. . . .[14]

The lack of environmental justice and equity, particularly with respect to the storage, use, disposition, and location of toxic materials and of dump sites, has given rise to the "environmental equity" movement, which seeks to redress the disparate impacts of environmental management upon particular population groups. Aimed at developing a more just system of distributing environmental benefit and burden, the movement is gaining increasing acceptance and support in civil, professional, and political circles. The Clinton administration EPA Administrator, Carol Browner, committed her support to the principle of environmental equity, as did the governing body of the American Bar Association in an August 1993 resolution. In spite of this growing acceptance of the need for "environmental equity," the current law does not provide adequate means for its achievement. The enduring challenge is to devise the legal means that will assure some reasonable degree of environmental equity.

Sustainable Development

In recent years, the international environmental movement has focused on promoting sustainable development in recognition of the earth's limited capacity to absorb pollution and loss of natural resources while still providing the base for viable habitats and economic development. Destruction of the natural environment has already ravaged the basis for human welfare and survival in some parts of the world.

A central goal of the second Earth Summit (officially titled the *1992 United Nations Conference on Sustainable Development*) was to fashion structures that will promote sustainable development. The conference produced few concrete results in this area, however.[15] Environmentally blind economic activity will in time destroy the economy itself, which depends upon natural resources and processes. Referring to the organization of the 1992 United Nations conference, then EPA administrator Reilly noted:

We did so in recognition of the potential dangers to human survival and the impediments to economic opportunity that come from poisoning of our Earth, the disruption of our planet's natural systems, the degradation of human and ecological health, and the depletion of our productive natural resources. The Rio Conference was intended to promote better integration of nations' environmental goals with their economic aspirations.[16]

The principle of sustainable development implicates the need to coordinate economic development with protection of environmental quality:

Sustainable development has been succinctly stated as the interdependence and synthesis of the environment and economics; i.e., "that environmental quality and economic health are inextricably linked—that the economic well-being of the Earth's people depends directly on the continued health of its natural resources."

. . .

The choice between crisis and sustainable development is one our nation shares with the rest of the world. . . . As the world's single largest economy, the largest user of natural resources, the largest producer and consumer of energy, and the largest producer of carbon dioxide pollution, the United States has not just a special responsibility to exercise world leadership, but a particularly high stake in meeting environmental challenges of the future.[17]

1.5   Addressing Environmental Problems through Law

The major avenue for improving environmental conditions in the United States continues to be legislation and governmental regulation. Despite the need for improved approaches to environmental administration, however, the progress of reform in environmental law and policy has been snail-paced. The reasons for this merit examination.

The Anglo-American Tradition of Private Property Rights

Environmental law is fundamentally concerned with the allocation of resources. Laws that place restrictions on polluting activities ultimately affect the distribution and use of the resources, such as air and water, that they are intended to protect. In order to understand the environmental regulatory process and the conflicts it confronts, it is necessary to understand the legal context in which environmental regulation occurs. Certain aspects of the U.S. system of law significantly impact the choice of legal mechanisms for achieving environmental protection. This subsection very briefly surveys two features of U.S. law that provide the greatest challenges to fashioning effective legal means for protecting the environment.

The United States legal system is primarily based upon the traditional English common law (judge-made law) and is often referred to as the *Anglo-American common law system*. Two aspects of this common law system have tremendous impact on environmental regulation: the preeminence of private property rights and the adversarial nature of the Anglo-American justice system.

The protection of private property is a primary focus of Anglo-American law. Much of the common law actually developed in order to protect the rights of landowners and other property holders, since private ownership of property was the basis for the entire economic system in England and later in the United States. Protection of private property rights remains an integral part of the current capitalist economic system.

Under the common law, an owner of real property (land) had the right to use his or her property as he or she saw fit, provided such use did not interfere with others' "use and enjoyment" of their property. In the United States, it has always been the rule, rather than the exception, that landowners were permitted to use all of the natural resources—land, minerals, water, air—to which their property gave them access, generally without restriction. As a corollary, they have also been allowed to pollute those resources with few legal restrictions. The environmental or ecological ramifications of property owners' uses of their property were usually of no consequence under the common law.

One restriction the law placed on this right to use one's property as one saw fit was that an owner was not allowed to carry out an activity using the property if pollution resulting from it directly and adversely impacted a neighbor's enjoyment of his or her own property. (Some of these causes of action are discussed more fully in Chapter 2.) However, the law protected a polluter's neighbors only because the neighbors themselves owned property, which gave them rights of use and enjoyment.

Traditionally, there was no legal recognition of an individual's right to breathe clean air or have access to clean water. Environmental rights, such as they were, could only be derived from ownership of real property. Even today, an individual-rights-oriented approach to environmental protection is barely nascent in U.S jurisprudence. For instance, although the Pennsylvania Constitution guarantees every state citizen the right to a clean and healthful environment, the Pennsylvania Supreme Court has ruled that this constitutional provision is unenforceable. The failure to enforce that provision indicates that the law does not yet fully accept the notion that an individual, regardless of property ownership, has rights to a healthy environment.

The vast majority of environmental laws in the United States, including those discussed in this book, are regulatory (designed to protect the public interest generally) rather than rights-oriented (created to protect the interests of individuals). Essentially, environmental regulatory law, like many other forms of government regulation, has been grafted onto a system of law in which protecting the property rights of individuals is preeminent. Indeed, environmental laws seek to correct some of the problems inherent in a legal system that assumes property owners have the right to use and to pollute the natural resources to which their properties give them access without preventing degradation of the ecosystem of which their property is an integral part. This traditional bias in favor of economic growth, rather than ecological stability, persists. The assumption underlying U.S. environmental law is that, in the absence of explicit restrictions, property owners may continue to carry out environmentally detrimental activities. The law generally places limits on polluting activities, rather than prohibiting them completely.

The system of public controls for protecting the environment that was grafted onto the common law has created considerable conflicts between the traditional rights of use and enjoyment arising from land ownership and the protection of the ecosystem of which land is an integral part. Public environmental law often seeks controls that will deprive landowners of some of the rights recognized under the common law system. Regulation of the use of wetlands, discussed in Chapter 8, is a primary example of this conflict.

The second aspect of Anglo-American law that creates considerable difficulties in environmental protection is the *adversarial system* of adjudication. Under the U.S. system of justice, lawsuits are adjudicated (heard and decided) by a court in order to determine the rights of two parties to the dispute vis-à-vis each other. The court's sole function is to make a decision based upon the evidence presented by the two sides. In contrast to the *inquisitorial system* of courts in most Continental European countries, U.S. courts do not make their own inquiries into the facts of a dispute or perform their own investigations of matters before them. It is up to the adversaries in the dispute to present evidence that proves their contentions.

The adversarial system is not particularly well-suited to the adjudication of environmental disputes, many of which are *polycentric*; that is, more than two parties' rights are implicated, the interests of these parties do not fall neatly into two opposing camps. Appropriate solutions for multifaceted environmental problems require consideration and mediation of the concerns of many parties, including some who are not parties to the lawsuit but who will nonetheless be affected by the outcome. The *Boomer* case illustrates the inadequacy of common-law causes of action, such as the law of nuisance, to adjudicate environmental disputes.

BOOMER ET AL. V. ATLANTIC CEMENT COMPANY

New York Court of Appeals, 1970
26 N.Y.2d 219, 257 N.E.2d 870, 309 N.Y.S.2d 312

Bergan, J.

* * *

The public concern with air pollution arising from many sources in industry and in transportation is currently accorded ever wider recognition accompanied by a growing sense of responsibility in State and Federal Governments to control it. Cement plants are obvious sources of air pollution in the neighborhoods where they operate.

But there is now before the court private litigation in which individual property owners have sought specific relief from a single plant operation. The threshold question . . . is whether the court should resolve the litigation between the parties now before it as equitably as seems possible; or whether, . . . it should channel private litigation into broad public objectives.

A court performs its essential function when it decides the rights of parties before it. Its decision of private controversies may sometimes greatly affect public issues. . . . But this is normally an incident to the court's main function to settle controversy. . . .

Effective control of air pollution is a problem presently far from solution even with the full public and financial powers of government. In large measure adequate technical procedures are yet to be developed, and some that appear possible may be economically impracticable.

It seems apparent that the amelioration of air pollution will depend on technical research in great depth; on a carefully balanced consideration of the economic impact of close regulation; and of the actual effect on public health. It is likely to require massive public expenditure and to demand more than any local community can accomplish and to depend on regional and interstate controls.

A court should not try to do this on its own as a by-product of private litigation, and it seems manifest that the judicial establishment is neither equipped . . . nor prepared to lay down and implement an effective policy for the elimination of air pollution. This is an area beyond the circumference of one private lawsuit. . . .

The cement making operations of defendant have been found . . . to have damaged the nearby properties of plaintiffs in these two actions. That court, . . . accordingly found defendant maintained a nuisance. . . . The trial judge had made a simple, direct finding that "the discharge of large quantities of dust upon each of the properties and excessive vibration from blasting deprived each party of the reasonable use of his property and thereby prevented his enjoyment of life and liberty therein." The judge continued, however: ". . . Although the Supreme Court has the power to grant and enforce an injunction, equity forbids its employment in this instance. The defendant's immense investment in the Hudson River Valley, its contribution to the Capital District's economy and its immediate help to the education of children in the Town of Coeymans through the payment of substantial sums in school and property taxes leads me to the conclusion that an injunction would produce great public . . . hardship." The total damage to plaintiffs' properties is, however, relatively small in comparison with the value of defendant's operation and with the consequences of the injunction which plaintiffs seek. . . .

The rule in New York has been that such a nuisance will be enjoined although marked disparity be shown in economic consequence between the effect of the injunction and the effect of the nuisance.

The problem of disparity in economic consequence was sharply in focus in Whalen v. Union Bag & Paper Co., 101 N.E. 805. A pulp mill entailing an investment of more than a million dollars polluted a stream in which plaintiff, who owned a farm, was "a lower riparian owner." The economic loss to plaintiff from this pollution was small. This court, reversing the Appellate Division, reinstated the injunction . . . against the argument of the mill owner that in view of "the slight advantage to plaintiff and the great loss that will be inflicted on defendant" an injunction should not be granted. . . .

* * *

This result at Special Term and at the Appellate Division is a departure from a rule that has become settled; but to follow the rule literally in these cases would be to close down the plant at once. This court is fully agreed to avoid that immediately drastic remedy; the difference in view is how best to avoid it.

One alternative is to grant the injunction but postpone its effect to a specified future date to give opportunity for technical advances to permit defendant to eliminate the nuisance; another is to grant the injunction conditioned on the payment of permanent damages to plaintiffs which would compensate them for the total economic loss to their property present and future caused by defendant's operations. For reasons which will be developed the court chooses the latter alternative.

The parties could settle this private litigation at any time if defendant paid enough money and the imminent threat of closing the plant would build up the pressure on defendant. If there were no improved techniques found, there would inevitably be applications to the court at Special Term for extensions of time to perform on showing of good faith efforts to find such techniques.

Moreover, techniques to eliminate dust and other annoying by-products of cement making . . . will depend on the total resources of the cement industry nationwide and throughout the world. . . .

For obvious reasons the rate of the research is beyond control of defendant. If at the end of 18 months the whole industry has not found a technical solution a court would be hard put to close down this one cement plant if due regard be given to equitable principles.

On the other hand, to grant the injunction unless defendant pays plaintiffs such permanent damages as may be fixed by the court seems to do justice between the contending parties.

* * *

It seems reasonable to think that the risk of being required to pay permanent damages to injured property owners by cement plant owners would itself be a reasonable effective spur to research for improved techniques to minimize nuisance.

The power of the court to condition on equitable grounds the continuance of an injunction on the payment of permanent damages seems undoubted. . . .

The present cases and the remedy here proposed are in a number of other respects rather similar to Northern Indiana Public Service Co. v. W. J. & M. S. Vesey, 200 N.E. 620 decided by the Supreme Court of Indiana. The gases, odors, ammonia, and smoke from the Northern Indiana company's gas plant damaged the nearby Vesey greenhouse operation. An injunction and damages were sought, but an injunction was denied and the relief granted was limited to permanent damages "present, past, and future." . . .

Thus it seems fair to both sides to grant permanent damages to plaintiffs which will terminate this private litigation.

* * *

Although the Trial Term has found permanent damages as a possible basis of settlement of the litigation, on remission the court should be entirely free to examine this subject. It may again find the permanent damage already found, or make new findings.

The orders should be reversed, without costs, and the cases remitted to Supreme Court, Albany County to grant an injunction which shall be vacated upon payment by defendant of such amounts of permanent damage to the respective plaintiffs as shall for this purpose be determined by the court.

* * *

The Evolution of Public Controls

Private efforts alone cannot remedy or reverse environmental degradation. Problems arising from the distribution and use of natural resources are too complex, multifaceted, and polycentric to be resolved by isolated private solutions. As Garrett Hardin pointed out in *Tragedy of the Commons*,[18] the supply of resources useful to humans is not inexhaustible and it may be destroyed by improper or excessive exploitation as people strive to maximize output and gain. The waste products humans return to the environment—chemicals, fumes, heat wastes, sewage—if unchecked, also threaten environmental resources and habitats upon which humans and other organisms depend for survival. Whether dealing with overutilization or degradation of resources, Hardin notes, individuals tend to ignore the cumulative adverse impacts of their actions.

> The rational man finds that his share of the cost of the wastes he discharges into the commons is less than the cost of purifying his wastes before releasing them.

> Since this is true of everyone, we are locked into a system of "fouling our own nest," so long as we behave only as independent, rational, free enterprisers.[19]

The only currently workable approach to this problem is to develop government regulation that will protect the environment for the benefit of society. That regulation can take many forms, running the gamut from command-and-control legislation to taxes that force the market system to account for the negative environmental impacts of irrational socioenvironmental behavior. At least for the present, responsibility for structuring responsible human interaction with the natural environment lies in the public domain.

The need for government monitoring of human activity that affects the environment is not seriously disputed. What remain controversial are the extent to which society should protect the environment, the costs society is willing to bear for environmental protection, and the way society should distribute the costs. Perhaps the issue is better framed in other terms: who has a right to degrade the environment; how should those rights be defined; and who should suffer from and pay for environmental damage?

A persistent issue in environmental regulatory efforts is how protective criteria should be set. Determining an appropriate level of protection is a function of three factors:

1. acceptability of risk,
2. cost, and
3. technological feasibility.

Three questions underlie the development of virtually all regulatory mechanisms:

1. Who should be authorized to make these critical determinations?
2. What guidelines should constrain the decision maker?
3. Who should bear the cost of the mandated protection?

Some environmental statutes have spelled out answers to these questions in their wording, but most statutes have have left these important determinations to regulatory agencies. Answering such questions often requires the use of evolving scientific tools and technologies.

In a market-oriented economic system, the incentive to fund the scientific research necessary for promoting environmental protection is highly diffused. Although advances in environmental protection benefit everyone, few legal and economic incentives exist to make acquisition of useful knowledge and sound technologies profitable for particular individuals, institutions, or industries.

Technological development of the means for preventing and remediating environmental problems is far from advanced, at least in relation to the magnitude of the problems. Development of environmental remediation technologies has not kept pace with the degradation caused by technological developments in manufacturing, transportation, agriculture, and energy generation. For instance, only very costly, inefficient, and ineffective methods exist for treating many of the hazardous wastes created by industrial processes. Nor have effective controls been implemented to minimize the billions of pounds of toxic air emission released yearly. Not surprisingly, industries that have invested heavily in their existing technologies tend to discourage the development of environmentally superior technologies that might render their existing plants obsolete and thus uncompetitive. The automobile industry, for example, has repeatedly thwarted efforts to develop an alternative to the combustion engine that would be more environmentally sound.

Regulation on the Frontiers of Scientific Knowledge and Technology

The insufficiency of scientific knowledge about environmental problems and potential solutions engenders uncertainty and political disagreements about how the law can best regulate environmental matters. Furthermore, the acquisition of environmental information is often colored by the special interests and perspectives of whomever is gathering that information. The slow progress of environmental reform reflects the difficulty of acquiring three interdependent kinds of knowledge:

1. scientific data and information about the nature of various ecosystems, the human influences within them, and the global consequences of injury to them;
2. effective, practical technologies for countering the causes and the effects of environmental damage; and
3. legal mechanisms that effectively promote:
   a. development of needed scientific, engineering, and economic solutions;
   b. implementation of appropriate safeguards for activities and products that endanger the environment; and
   c. monitoring and compliance enforcement of legal standards.

Acquiring these kinds of knowledge requires the cooperation of institutions engaged in many disciplines—the pure and applied sciences, engineering, economics, history, and law. It requires expenditure of considerable resources. Whether governmental or private entities should fund the necessary research is a matter of considerable debate.

Because of the vast amount of human knowledge and the speed with which it accumulates, only limited numbers of individuals can receive the specialized education and experience necessary for becoming experts in any particular field. In highly industrialized societies, technological expertise is held by a relatively small group of highly educated professionals. Detailed technical information is usually inaccessible to the general population, not only because it is not widely disseminated, but also because it is beyond the grasp of those who do not have specialized knowledge. Most legislators have a background in law; they are rarely knowledgeable about the availability and costs of specialized pollution-prevention or environmental-remediation technologies. This lack of knowledge makes it difficult for legislators to fashion public controls that will accommodate the development of environmentally sound technologies as well as provide adequate environmental protection. Yet this is what meaningful regulation on the frontiers of scientific knowledge encompasses.

Compounding the problem of lack of expertise are political pressures from special interests across the spectrum. Legislators must satisfy the concerns of their constituents and campaign contributors. Many business contributors have a stronger interest in maintaining the status quo than in the development of technologies that are environmentally more sound.

As later chapters of this book illustrate, lawmakers have enacted significantly different regulatory schemes for different kinds of environmental hazards. Some schemes have stemmed from technological and cost considerations. Other schemes reflect lawmakers' perceptions of the environmental hazards as justifying more burdensome technological requirements.

Regulatory choices in the environmental area are numerous. A particular regulation may

- permit continuation of the status quo;
- require installation of particular control technologies;
- prohibit certain kinds of activities;
- authorize designated government officials to impose flexible controls at their discretion on a case-by-case basis;
- set limits on pollution outputs; or
- give polluting sources "pollution allowances" that can be bought and sold.

The choice of regulatory options often depends directly upon perceptions of the feasibility and desirability of mandating particular control technologies or limits on pollution outputs.

Legislators' lack of technological expertise not only complicates regulatory choices, but it also engenders unintended results at times. A common pitfall is for a regulatory scheme to discourage, rather than foster, technological developments. If the law sets a particular standard of technology as a regulatory requirement, it discourages research and development of technologies that could be more efficient or effective for reducing pollution or conserving resources. Conversely, if the law enforces quantitative emissions limits, it encourages the development of the most efficient technology to satisfy those specified limits. The downside is that such laws are difficult to administer. Thus, law and technology interact to advance or to impede optimal solutions to environmental problems.

The Network of Environmentally Related Statutes

Since the early 1970s, federal, state, and local governments have enacted an impressive body of environmental laws. Nationally, expenditures on environmental programs have grown to average more than 2 percent of the gross national product annually.[20] The laws that directly and indirectly affect the environment are too numerous and too varied in their design and details for them to be reviewed even generally in this book. A comprehensive list of environmentally significant statutes appears in the Appendix of Environmental Statutes. Figure 1.1 summarizes the varying objectives and approaches of federal statutes regarding wastes. It portrays the complexity, range, and overlap in this one subfield of environmental law.

The major federal statutes examined in this book deal with toxic and hazardous substances, waste disposal, protection of air and water quality, and management of publicly owned resources and lands. Some of these statutes have overlapping coverage with each other, with state environmental laws, and with non-environmental statutes on trade, worker safety, and public health.[21]

Although various government agencies are charged with implementing the numerous federal laws concerning the environment and with regulating resource use, the Environmental Protection Agency (EPA) is the primary agency to which Congress and the Executive Branch have entrusted the administration of environmental laws. State and local laws and agencies also play significant roles in environmental regulation. Many federal environmental statutes specifically authorize or oblige the states to take measures to carry out federal environmental mandates. In addition, state and local laws impose environmental protection measures over and above those provided by federal law. The fact that state environmental laws are not canvassed in this book does not diminish their importance.

■ **Figure 1.1** Major Federal Laws Regarding Waste

Statute	Waste Management Objective	Pollutants/Wastes Covered*	Regulatory Approach	Basis for Controls	Primary Transfers to Another Medium
Clean Water Act; 33 U.S.C. § 1251 et seq.	Protect and improve surface water quality	All discharges to surface waters, including 126 priority toxic pollutants	Effluent limitations; water quality standards	Technology and cost	Sludge to land; air emissions from treatment plant and sludge incineration
Marine Protection, Research, and Sanctuaries Act; 16 U.S.C. § 1401 et seq.	Limit dumping into ocean	All wastes except oil and sewage in the ocean	All dumping prohibited unless permitted.	Potential damages of dumping; cost; availability	
Safe Drinking Water Act; 40 U.S.C. § 300f–300j 10 (Supp. 1977); P.L. 99-339	Protect public drinking water supply	Contaminants found in drinking water and wastes injected into deep wells	Drinking-water quality standards; proper construction and operation of injection wells	Health risks; cost of treatment technology	
Clean Air Act; 42 U.S.C. § 7401 et seq.	Protect and improve air quality	All emissions to air	Air quality standards and emissions limitations	Health risks and environmental damages	Sludge and incinerator residues to land
Resource Conservation and Recovery Act; 42 U.S.C. § 6901 et seq.	Control hazardous and solid wastes; encourage waste reduction and recycling	Hazardous and solid wastes	Waste tracking system and management standards for treatment, storage, and disposal facilities	Risk and cost	Air through incineration; water through sewage treatment plants
Comprehensive Environmental Response, Compensation, and Liability Act; 42 U.S.C. § 9601 et seq.; P.L. 99-499	Clean-up abandoned hazardous waste sites; emergency response	All hazardous wastes found at sites	Site cleanup	Risk and cost	Air through volatilization, incineration, and dust
Surface Mining Control and Reclamation Act; 30 U.S.C. § 1201 et seq.	Control pollution from surface coal mines	Surface coal mining wastes	Management practices	Potential damages and cost	Releases to water
Nuclear Waste Policy Act; 42 U.S.C. § 10101 et seq.	Control disposal of high-level radioactive wastes	Commercial high-level radioactive waste	Prohibit disposal except in geological repositories	Performance and design standards	
Low-Level Radioactive Waste Policy Act; 42 U.S.C. § 2021b et seq.	Control disposal of low-level radioactive waste	Commercial low-level radioactive waste	Performance standards for waste disposal facilities through interstate compacts	Performance and design standards	
Uranium Mill Tailings Radiation Control Act; 42 U.S.C. § 7901 et seq.	Manage uranium mill tailings	Uranium mill tailings	Standards for remedial action	Health and environmental impact; technology	Air from dust
Toxic Substances Control Act; 15 U.S.C. § 2601 et seq.	Prevent unreasonable risk from chemical substances	Wastes from the production or use of industrial chemical substances	Limitations on manufacture, use, and disposal of industrial chemical substances	Risk and cost	

*Includes all substances that could be controlled under the acts.

Source: Conservation Foundation, *State of the Environment* (1987), pp. 426–427. Copyright © 1987 by World Wildlife Fund. Reprinted with permission.

Some strands of commercial law, primarily those relating to insurance, lending, and bankruptcy, also intersect with the operation of environmental laws, predominately with the Superfund law. Their effects on environmental liabilities are reviewed in Chapter 7.

The development of international environmental laws presents unique regulatory and legal issues. They are the subject of Chapter 11. International relations is itself an extensive and specialized topic, but the growing importance of international environmental law to the welfare of all peoples demands at least a general acquaintance with it.

■ Chapter 1 Endnotes

1. See, for example, "Green Field: Environmental Engineers Command High Pay, Choice Assignments," *The Wall Street Journal*, 21 October 1991, p. B1; and "Environmental Courses in MBA Study," *The New York Times*, 13 March 1990, p. D2.

2. R. E. Train, "A Call for Sustainability to Ensure Our Future Survival," 18, *EPA Journal* No. 8 (September/October 1992).

3. Exceptions might be said to include the Endangered Species Act and certain laws relating to national parks.

4. S. Ramphal, "Beyond Mere Survival," 19, *EPA Journal* No. 2 (April–June 1993).

5. Ibid.

6. G. Meyer, "Deforestation and the Frontier Lands," 19, *EPA Journal* No. 2 (April–June 1993).

7. See, for example, Thomas Kuhn, *The Structure of Scientific Revolutions* (1970).

8. Z. Smith, *The Environmental Policy Paradox* (Prentice Hall 1992), pp. 1–2.

9. Barry Commoner, *The Closing Circle* (Alfred A. Knopf, 1971), p. 46.

10. A. Leopold, *A Sand County Almanac* (1968), pp. 214–220.

11. David Morris, "The Four Stages of Environmentalism," *UTNE Reader*, pp. 157–159 (March/April 1992). David Morris is Vice President of the Washington, D.C. and Minneapolis-based Institute for Self-Reliance. Copyright © Institute for Local Self-Reliance. Used with permission.

12. F. Allen and G. Seksciensi, "Greening at the Grassroots," 18, *EPA Journal* No. 4 (1992), pp. 52–53.

13. C. G. Rifkin, "Voting Green," *UTNE Reader*, September/October 1992.

14. J. H. Adams, "The Mainstream Environmental Movement," 18, *EPA Journal* No. 1 (March/April 1992).

15. See the discussion of the Earth Summits in Chapter 11.

16. W. Reilly, "The Road from Rio," 18, *EPA Journal* No. 11 (September/October 1992).

17. R. E. Train, "Call for Sustainability," n. 2 supra, p. 7.

18. G. Hardin, "Tragedy of the Commons," 162, *Science* 1243 (1968).

19. Ibid.

20. R. E. Train, "Call for Sustainability," n. 2, supra.

21. For discussions of federal–state law overlaps, see Chapters 2, 8, and 9 of this book.

CHAPTER 2

Environmental Regulation in the American Legal System

Outline

2.1 Overview of the U.S. Legal System

The study of U.S. environmental law requires a basic familiarity with the structure and operation of the U.S. legal system. In the United States, environmental law is primarily public and regulatory in nature. This means that governmental agencies are generally responsible for enforcing laws to protect the environment. However, there also exist some private causes of action, available to individuals who suffer injuries resulting from environmental contamination.

The field of law that governs the actions of governmental agencies and the enforcement of public regulatory laws, including environmental laws, is called *administrative law*. An understanding of the fundamental principles of administrative law is therefore highly relevant to the study of environmental law. *Constitutional law* is another field of law that informs the study of environmental law. Constitutional law defines the powers of the federal and state governments and the relationships between individuals and governmental entities. It describes how the legal system is "constituted"; it specifies the limits of governmental power and the latitude of governmental discretion in administration of environmental laws.

Environmental law, like all law, has two basic components: substantive and procedural. The *substantive components* of environmental law indicate what is permissible and what is prohibited—which actions must be taken and which must be avoided. The *procedural components* outline the processes and standards by which the government is to administer and enforce the law as well as the rights of citizens to seek enforcement of environmental laws. General administrative and constitutional law principles which apply to many legal subjects also define how the government is to administer environmental laws and how the courts are to interpret those laws and adjudicate environmental disputes.

In contrast to substantive laws, which change over time, legal principles which outline how law is created and specify the processes by which it is to be administered and interpreted remain relatively constant. For example, the constitutional law that creates and controls the authorities of the United States as a national government and those of the fifty state governments is only rarely changed by constitutional amendment. Similarly, administrative law, which governs the operations of government agencies, also remains relatively unchanged, though it can be altered by legislation. This chapter surveys administrative and constitutional law in explaining the manner in which governmental and judicial authority is exercised to protect the environment.

Protecting human health and the environment through law requires provisions that:

1. establish the legislative policies and directives to be implemented,
2. prescribe the methods for executing those policies and directives, and
3. prescribe mechanisms for resolving disputes over the meaning and validity of those laws and the actions of officials under them.

Under the federal Constitution these essential functions are performed by the three branches of government: Congress; the Executive Branch, which includes administrative agencies such as the Environmental Protection Agency (EPA); and the courts. The Constitution specifies that Congress is responsible for making laws, the Executive Branch for administering and enforcing them, and the courts for adjudicating legal disputes. The Constitution does so, however, only in broad terms:

> While the Constitution . . . divides all power conferred upon Federal Government into "legislative Powers," Art. I, § 1, the "executive Power," Art. II, § 1, and "the judicial Power," Art. III, § 1, it does not attempt to define these terms. To be sure, it limits the jurisdiction of federal courts to "Cases" and "Controversies," but an executive inquiry can bear the name "controversy" . . . . Obviously, then, the Constitution's central mechanism of separation of powers depends largely upon common understanding of what activities are appropriate to legislatures, to executives, and to courts.[1]

Although the Constitution vests "all legislative Powers" (policymaking power) in Congress, "the executive Power" (the power to enforce laws) in the presidency, and "the judicial Power" (the power to resolve disputes) in the federal courts, it does not spell out how each branch should proceed, either with respect to its internal organization and procedures or with respect to the other two branches of government. To some degree, each branch of government retains discretion in determining its internal operations, but supplemental rules are needed to assure that each branch fulfills its constitutional role in a manner that does not intrude upon the authority of the other branches or upon the rights of citizens. This supplemental law describes *how* the law is to be enforced, as distinguished from substantive law, which describes *what* the law requires of its subjects. The law governing the proceedings of government agencies, other than courts, is hereafter referred to as *administrative law* and the law on court proceedings that review disputed agency decisions is hereafter referred to as *judicial review*. The requirements of administrative law and judicial review exert a strong influence on environmental regulatory programs. The success or failure of these programs often depends upon whether they are properly structured so as to satisfy governing principles of administrative law and judicial review.

2.2   Administrative Agencies: Microcosms of the Federal System

As parts of the executive branch, administrative agencies are charged with administering and enforcing the law. In the process of doing so, however, they perform functions similar to those of the other two branches of government. Administrative agencies monitor compliance with statutes and bring enforcement actions against violators; these duties are consistent with the executive function of enforcing the law. In order to enforce the law, however, administrative agencies must often interpret congressional legislation which is written in very general terms. Indeed, legislation often mandates that the executive branch or particular administrative agencies promulgate (issue) regulations pursuant to the statute. Thus, administrative agencies serve as auxiliary policymakers in a quasi-legislative capacity.

Administrative agencies also perform an adjudicative or quasi-judicial function. Legislation often authorizes administrative agencies to conduct their own hearings in order to determine whether the law they administer has been violated. Administrative agencies may have the option of bringing certain enforcement actions in an administrative forum, rather than a judicial forum. Officials who are members of the executive branch are designated to hear and adjudicate administrative cases. The three kinds of functions administrative agencies perform are explained in the following subsections.

The Regulatory Function

Over the years, and particularly since 1970, Congress has enacted a series of statutes to impose substantive controls on specified activities that endanger the environment and has vested primary authority to carry out these enactments in the Environmental Protection Agency (EPA). Under virtually all of these environmental statutes, Congress authorizes EPA to promulgate rules and regulations to carry out the general mandates of these statutes. Such regulatory schemes are necessary for transforming broad legislative directives into precise requirements and prohibitions for the many entities affected by environmental legislation, for clarifying the meaning of ambiguous legislative provisions, and for implementing and enforcing statutes. Agency regulations include: implementing regulations, interpretive rules, and other rule-making. The legal force and effect of these regulations are the same, but they serve different purposes.

Implementing Regulations

Under particular statutory directives and general administrative law principles, EPA and other administrative agencies promulgate implementing regulations that specify how legislation will be administered and enforced. When the legislation specifically or implicitly requires the agency to issue regulations for making the statute effective, agencies promulgate implementing regulations. These regulations flesh out broad statutory mandates and specify how the statute will affect various segments of the regulated community, what sorts of actions will be required to comply with the law, and how the agency will enforce the law.

Interpretive Rules

Interpretive rules are proposed and adopted by EPA and other administrative agencies in order to clarify what Congress intended under a particular statute. Normally, such rules are not issued pursuant to an express statutory directive but when the need for them arises under general administrative law principles. For instance, sometimes a question arises as to whether Congress intended to subject a particular industry to liability under an environmental statute. In that case, EPA may issue an interpretive rule outlining the agency's interpretation of the statute. Under general principles of administrative law, an agency's interpretation of a statute it administers is subject to great deference. Therefore, interpretive rules have a significant impact on the administration and enforcement of environmental statutes.

Rule-Making

EPA and other agencies also engage in rule-making for purposes specifically mandated by statutes. Agencies issue such rules only when circumstances or facts warrant them. For instance, the Toxic Substances Control Act, which is covered in Chapter 5, requires that EPA propose and adopt rules for the testing of potentially harmful substances about which too little is known.

When they are promulgated according to applicable procedural requirements, agency rules and regulations have the full force of law. Consequently, litigants often challenge the validity of EPA's rules and regulations by asserting that the agency failed to promulgate them properly. If a court finds that EPA did improperly promulgate a rule or regulation, it can overturn or invalidate the rule, sometimes with far-reaching consequences.

As a general rule, but subject to specific exemptions, an agency must take three basic steps before a rule can be legally effective:

1. The agency must publish a notice of the proposed rule.
2. The agency must provide an opportunity, usually through public hearing, for interested parties to present comments and objections to the proposed rule.
3. The agency must consider the interested parties' comments and objections prior to officially adopting the rule.

Interested parties may petition the agency at any time to issue a new rule or to amend or repeal an existing rule.

This excerpt from *Shell Oil Company v. EPA*[2] illustrates the procedural pitfalls that can invalidate an agency's rule-making. Shell Oil and others challenged EPA's promulgation of two rules under the Resource Conservation and Recovery Act as amended (RCRA),[3] which governs the treatment, storage, and disposal of hazardous waste. (RCRA is the subject of Chapter 6.) The D.C. Circuit Court of Appeals vacated the rules because of EPA's failure to provide adequate notice and opportunity for comment.

SHELL OIL CO. V. EPA

950 F.2d 741 (D.C. Cir. 1991)

Before Buckley, Williams and Thomas, Circuit Judges.

In these . . . cases, petitioners challenge both the substance of several rules promulgated by the Environmental Protection Agency pursuant to the Resource Conservation and Recovery Act of 1976 and its compliance with the Administrative procedure Act's rulemaking requirements.

. . . [p]etitioners challenge two rules that categorize substances as hazardous wastes, the "mixture rule," . . . and the "derived-from" rule, ... They argue that the EPA failed to provide adequate notice and opportunity for comment when it promulgated the mixture and derived-from rules, and that the rules exceed the EPA's statutory authority.

* * *

Finally, the Environmental Defense Fund challenges the EPA's "permit-shield" provision, a regulation that, with some exceptions, exempts a facility from enforcement proceedings for statutory violations if it is in compliance with its permit conditions.

We agree with petitioners that the EPA failed to give sufficient notice and opportunity for comment in promulgating the "mixture" and "derived-from" rules and the leachate monitoring requirement. . . . As for the permit-shield provision, all parties agree that it cannot trump the citizen's statutory right to sue. As applied to the Agency, however, the regulation lies well within the limits of the EPA's enforcement discretion.

I. BACKGROUND

The EPA promulgated the disputed rules in order to implement the Resource Conservation and Recovery Act ("RCRA"), . . . [RCRA] gave the EPA until April 21, 1978 to develop and promulgate criteria for identifying characteristics of hazardous waste and to list particular wastes as hazardous. . . .

It further required the EPA to promulgate regulations "as may be necessary to protect human health and the environment" respecting the practices of generators, transporters, and those who own or operate hazardous waste treatment, storage, or disposal facilities. . . . RCRA required the EPA to promulgate standards governing permits for [hazardous waste] facilities . . . .

On February 17, 1977, the EPA published a Notice of Intent to Develop Rulemaking, ... on May 2, 1977, it published an Advance Notice of Proposed Rulemaking, ... In addition, it circulated for comment several drafts of regulations, met with experts and representatives of interested groups, and held public hearings. This process culminated in the publication, on December 18, 1978, of proposed regulations . . . .

This proposal elicited voluminous comment, and the EPA held five large public hearings. . . .

The EPA published its "[r]evisions to final rule and interim final rule" on May 19, 1980. . . .

More than fifty petitions were brought to challenge these final rules. . . .

Consolidated petitioners assert that the regulations proposed on December 18, 1978 did not foreshadow the inclusion of the mixture and derived-from rules in the final rule's definition of "hazardous waste." . . . Thus, they assert, they were deprived of adequate notice and opportunity for comment. They also claim that the EPA exceeded its statutory authority by including the two rules in the final definition of hazardous waste. . . . The Environmental Defense fund asserts that the issuance of the permit-shield rule, . . . was arbitrary and capricious and that the rule is outside the scope of the statute. . . .

II. DISCUSSION

A.   Principles Governing Judicial Review

The Administrative Procedure Act ("APA") governs judicial review of final regulations promulgated under RCRA. . . .

In issuing regulations, the EPA must observe the notice-and-comment procedures of the

APA . . . and the public-participation directive of RCRA. . . . The relationship between the proposed regulation and the final rule determines the adequacy of notice. A difference between the two will not invalidate the notice so long as the final rule is a "logical outgrowth" of the one proposed. If the deviation from the proposal is too sharp, the affected parties will not have had adequate notice and opportunity for comment. . . .

RCRA defines the scope of the EPA's regulatory discretion: In formulating rules, the clearly expressed intent of Congress binds agencies as it binds courts. Where congressional intent is ambiguous, however, an agency's interpretation of a statute entrusted to its administration is entitled to deference, so long as it is reasonable. . . .

B. The Mixture and Derived-From Rules

The mixture and derived-from rules are to be found in the definition of "hazardous waste" that appears in the final rules. . . . Petitioners protest that these provisions had no counterpart in, and were not a logical outgrowth of, the proposed regulations; thus, the promulgation of the rules violated the notice-and-comment requirements of RCRA and the APA. We agree.

* * *

4. *The Mixture Rule*

The mixture rule requires that a waste be treated as hazardous if

[I]t is a mixture of solid waste and one or more hazardous wastes . . . .
    . . . Once classified as hazardous, then, a mixture must be so treated until delisted.

The EPA acknowledged at the outset that the mixture rule was "a new provision," and that it had no "direct counterpart in the proposed regulations." . . . Nevertheless, it added the rule for purposes of clarification and in response to questions raised during the comment period . . .

Although admitting that it had failed to say so in the proposed regulations, the EPA stated that it had "intended" to treat waste mixtures . . . as hazardous. It then presented the mixture rule as necessary to close "a major loophole . . ."

* * *

While the EPA admits that the mixture rule lacks a clear antecedent in the proposed regulations, it nonetheless argues that the rule merely clarifies the intent behind the proposal that listed wastes remain hazardous until delisted: As industry could not have reasonably assumed that a generator could bring a listed waste outside the generic listing description simply by mixing it with a nonhazardous waste, the rule cannot be seen as a "bolt from the blue." . . .

5. *The Derived-From Rule*

The derived-from rule provides that

[a]ny solid waste generated from the treatment, storage or disposal of a hazardous waste, including any sludge, spill residue, ash, emission control dust or leachate (but not including precipitation run-off), is a hazardous waste.

. . . The EPA's justifications for the derived-from rule resemble those for the mixture rule.
    . . . The EPA acknowledged, however, that the rule was a new provision, "added both in response to comment and as a logical outgrowth . . ."

6. *Adequacy of Notice*

Although the EPA acknowledges that neither of the two rules was to be found among the proposed regulations, it nevertheless argues that they were foreseeable—and, therefore, the notice adequate—because certain of the comments received in response to the rulemaking appeared to anticipate both the mixture and the derived-from rules. We are unimpressed by the scanty evidence marshaled in support of this position.

* * *

An agency, of course, may promulgate final rules that differ from the proposed regulations. To avoid "the absurdity that . . . the agency can learn from the comments on its proposals only at the peril of starting a new procedural round of commentary," . . . we have held that final rules need only be a "logical outgrowth" of the proposed regulations. . . . But an unexpressed intention cannot convert a final rule into a "logical outgrowth" that the public should have anticipated. Interested parties cannot be expected to divine the EPA's unspoken thoughts. . . . The reasons given by the EPA in support of its contention that interested parties should have anticipated the new rules are simply too insubstantial to justify a finding of implicit notice.

While it is true that such parties might have anticipated the potential for avoiding regulation by simply mixing hazardous and nonhazardous wastes, it was the business of the EPA, and not the public, to foresee that possibility and to address it in its proposed regulations. Moreover, while a comment may evidence a recognition of a problem, it can tell us nothing of how, or even whether, the agency will choose to address it. The comments the EPA cites strike us as sparse and ambiguous at best. Some address similar concerns, but none squarely anticipates the rules.

Even if the mixture and derived-from rules had been widely anticipated, comments by members of the public would not in themselves constitute adequate notice. Under the standards of the APA, "notice necessarily must come—if at all—from the Agency." . . . Although we have held that comments raising a foreseeable possibility of agency action can be a factor in providing notice. . . . [H]ere, the ambiguous comments and weak signals from the agency gave petitioners no such opportunity to anticipate and criticize the rules or to offer alternatives. Under these circumstances, the mixture and derived-from rules exceed the limits of "logical outgrowth."

The EPA's argument also fails to take into account a marked shift in emphasis between the proposed regulations and the final rules. Under the EPA's initial regulatory strategy the

EPA planned to identify and quantitatively define all of the characteristics of hazardous waste. . . .

. . . As a consequence, listing was to "play [the] largely supplementary function" of increasing the "certainty" of the process. . . .

The final rules, however, place a heavy emphasis on listing. As a consequence, the final criteria for listing are "considerably expanded and more specific" than those proposed. . . .

Whatever the basis for this shift in strategy, it erodes the foundation of the EPA's argument that the mixture rule was implicit in the proposed regulations. . . . We conclude, therefore, that the mixture rule was neither implicit in nor a "logical outgrowth" of the proposed regulations.

Similarly, while the derived-from rule may well have been the best regulatory approach the EPA could devise, . . . it was not a logical outgrowth of the proposed regulations. The derived-from rule is not implicit in a system based upon testing wastes for specified hazardous characteristics—the system presented in the proposed regulations. . . .

* * *

E. Permit-Shield Provision

The Environmental Defense Fund ("EDF") challenges the EPA's "permit as shield" provision that, with some exceptions, protects holders of RCRA permits from enforcement actions for violations of the underlying statute. The provision currently reads:

Compliance with an RCRA permit during its term constitutes compliance for purpose of enforcement, with . . . RCRA . . . .

. . . We conclude that the EDF's citizen-suit challenge does not present a case or controversy requiring resolution, and its remaining challenges lack merit.

1. *Statutory and Regulatory Background*

RCRA requires owners and operators of hazardous waste treatment, storage, or disposal facilities to obtain a permit before commencing operations. . . . Before granting a permit, the EPA must determine that the facility meets the requirements of [RCRA] . . . and its implementing regulations. . . . The EPA described the permit-shield rule as a binding principle under which it "will not take enforcement action against any person who has received a final RCRA permit except for noncompliance with the conditions of that permit." . . . According to the Agency, the shield applies not only to the EPA enforcement actions, but also to enforcement actions brought by States and by citizens through RCRA's citizen-suit provision. Although the permit-shield rule lacks explicit statutory authorization, the Agency asserts that the rule furthers the objectives of the RCRA permit program by protecting owners and operators of waste facilities against otherwise "unavoidable uncertainty as to the standing of their operations under the law," . . . .

2. Conflict with Citizen-Suit Provision

The EDF first challenges the permit-shield provision on the ground that it conflicts with RCRA's citizen-suit provision, which states:

> . . . any person may commence a civil action on his own behalf—
>
> > (1)(A) against any person . . . who is alleged to be in violation of any permit, standard, regulation, condition, requirement, prohibition, or order which has become effective pursuant to this chapter . . .

. . . The EDF contends that by restricting citizens to enforcement actions based on permit violations, the permit-shield provision expressly contravenes the statute's broad grant of authority to citizens to enforce violations of any "standard, regulation, condition, requirement, prohibition, or order." . . .

We do not decide the merits of the EDF's challenge. The EPA represents that although it believes its permit system will narrow the opportunities for citizen suits, "the Agency does not maintain that the shield precludes [such] suits." . . . Although the EPA appears to have taken a different position when it first promulgated the rule, it has evidently changed its mind. Therefore, as we do not have an actual controversy before us, we do not decide whether the permit provision could lawfully bar "citizen suits." . . . ("Article III of the Constitution limits federal courts to the adjudication of actual, ongoing controversies. . . .").

3. Conflict with EPA's Enforcement Authority

The parties dispute whether Congress has directly spoken to the question whether the EPA can limit its own enforcement actions to violations of permits, and, if not, whether the EPA nonetheless acted unreasonably by issuing the permit-shield rule.

The EDF argues that RCRA requires the EPA to do more than simply enforce permit provisions:

> [W]henever . . . the Administrator determines that any person has violated or is in violation of *any* requirement of [RCRA] the Administrator may issue an order assessing a civil penalty for any past or current violation, requiring compliance . . . or the Administrator may commence a civil action. . . .

. . . According to the EDF, Congress's use of the broad phrase "any requirement" demonstrates that it intended the EPA to bring enforcement actions for all violations of RCRA's standards, even when those standards are not incorporated into a permit. . . . As courts should "give effect, if possible, to every word that Congress has used in a statute," . . . the EDF concludes, the shield provision must fall.

The EDF's . . . argument is unavailing. Although the provision authorizes the EPA to enforce violations of "any requirement," it does not require that the EPA do so. On the contrary, the provision's use of the permissive word "may" guarantees the EPA's discretion in the civil enforcement arena. . . .

The Supreme Court pointed out . . . that agencies are generally free to set their own enforcement agendas. In the Court's words, "an agency's decision not to prosecute or enforce, whether through civil or criminal process, is a decision generally committed to an agency's absolute discretion." . . . The Court noted that agency discretion with respect to enforcement decisions is generally desirable because

> an agency decision not to enforce often involves a complicated balancing of a number of factors which are peculiarly within its expertise. Thus, the agency must not only assess whether a violation has occurred, but whether agency resources are best spent on this violation or another, whether the agency is likely to succeed if it acts, whether the particular enforcement action requested best fits the agency's overall policies, and, indeed, whether the agency has enough resources to undertake the action at all.

. . . In short, in its view, "[t]he agency is far better equipped than the courts to deal with the many variables involved in the proper ordering of its priorities." . . .

The Court adds, however, that

Congress may limit an agency's exercise of enforcement power if it wishes, either by setting substantive priorities, or by otherwise circumscribing an agency's power to discriminate among issues or cases it will pursue.

. . . Here, as we indicated in rejecting EDF's argument that the plain language of the statute required us to set the shield provision aside, we see no congressional constraints on the EPA's exercise of enforcement discretion.

* * *

. . . the EPA explains that it plans to include all of the applicable statutory requirements in each permit and to enforce each permit fully. RCRA permits are subject to full public notice and comment. . . . Therefore, members of the public can ensure that proposed permits include all the requisite terms by submitting comments and participating in public hearings, . . . and by seeking administrative, . . . and judicial . . . review of each final permit. Next, the EPA points out that it can cure mistakes occurring in final permits by modifying or revoking and reissuing them, or by terminating them if it finds that the permittee misrepresented or

failed to disclose material facts in the permit issuance process. . . . or that "the permitted activity endangers human health or the environment and can only be regulated to acceptable levels by permit modification or termination." Finally, the EPA stresses that the shield provision in no way limits its enforcement authority to respond to instances where the "handling, storage, treatment, transportation or disposal of any solid waste or hazardous waste may present an imminent and substantial endangerment to health or the environment." . . .

Notwithstanding the permit-shield provision, then, the EPA retains sufficient flexibility to properly carry out its statutory responsibilities. Moreover, the insulating effect of the provision is limited both in scope and duration. The shield rule does not apply to self-implementing statutory provisions or to the regulatory restrictions on land disposal, and it can only preclude enforcement of standards omitted by mistake for up to ten years, the maximum permit term. We therefore uphold the permit-shield rule as a reasonable, self-imposed constraint on the Agency's enforcement discretion.

* * *

The Enforcement Function

The second primary function of an administrative agency such as EPA is to administer and enforce those statutes for which Congress has made it responsible. EPA is responsible for enforcing most environmental legislation, although other federal agencies—such as the Department of the Interior, the Department of Justice, and the Army Corps of Engineers—also enforce some statutory provisions relating to environmental protection.

The enforcement function of administrative agencies encompasses many related roles. In administering and enforcing environmental laws, EPA is responsible for

- monitoring compliance with regulations;
- taking legal action against violators;
- assessing penalties;
- ordering, instituting, and overseeing environmental cleanups;
- devising policies that encourage compliance and pollution prevention;
- setting programmatic enforcement priorities; and
- allocating available resources.

EPA also authorizes state programs to undertake enforcement actions pursuant to federal law and oversees the state programs to ensure that they comply with fundamental requirements.

Like other administrative agencies, EPA has several enforcement mechanisms to choose from when it takes legal action against violators of environmental laws. All agencies' enforcement capabilities derive from legislative authorization. Under the various federal environmental statutes, EPA is authorized to:

- assess penalties for the purpose of deterring future violations,
- refer matters for criminal prosecution,
- order cleanups and other corrective actions,
- enjoin future violations, and in some cases, recoup monies it has expended in remediating environmental contamination.

Many environmental statutes give EPA the option to pursue legal remedies in either an administrative or judicial forum. For instance, EPA can file either an administrative or a judicial complaint against an environmental violator. Likewise, EPA can either issue an administrative cleanup order or petition a court to issue an order. In order to bring a judicial case, however, EPA must first refer the matter to the Department of Justice, which is responsible for litigating the action on its behalf. Because EPA and the Department of Justice do not always possess the same institutional interests, priorities, or view of a case, their views on when and how cases should be litigated sometimes conflict. The more salient conflicts over case administration arise with respect to violations of environmental laws by other federal agencies, criminal cases, and matters before bankruptcy tribunals. Some of these conflicts are explored in subsequent chapters.

Whether EPA utilizes administrative or judicial remedies depends upon the nature of the violation and the circumstances of each case. Generally, administrative actions entail simpler hearing procedures and can be resolved more quickly. If a violator fails to comply with an administrative order or to pay a penalty assessed by an administrative forum, however, EPA may have to seek judicial enforcement.

Judicial actions require referral to the Department of Justice, can take much longer to resolve, and require more agency resources. Nevertheless, the courts have enforcement powers that EPA lacks. These include the abilities to hold recalcitrant parties in contempt and to enforce judgment liens on property. The pros and cons of administrative and judicial enforcement actions must be weighed in light of the nature of the violation, the characteristics of the violator, the precedential importance of the case, and the relative likelihood of a successful outcome in an administrative or judicial tribunal.

The Adjudication Function

The third primary function of administrative agencies is to adjudicate disputes arising over applications and interpretations of agency regulations. We have already noted that administrative agencies are often empowered to institute administrative (as opposed to judicial) enforcement actions. As a general rule, due process requires that one who is subject to any sort of enforcement action, including an administrative complaint, be granted a hearing on request. If the agency has chosen to take administrative enforcement action, the hearing takes place before an administrative hearing officer—sometimes called an *administrative law judge* or *presiding officer*. Although administrative hearing officers are officials of the agency bringing the action, they are charged with being neutral decision-makers. They perform the administrative agency's adjudicative function.

Under most environmental statutes, EPA may bring administrative complaints for the assessment of penalties and the issuance of compliance or cleanup orders. If a respondent (the violator responding to the enforcement action) requests a hearing, an administrative law judge (ALJ) hears the case. EPA's own regulations and the Administrative Procedure Act govern how these hearings are conducted, including the manner in which the parties may present or rebut evidence, the types of procedural motions the parties may make, and the rules of decision under which the ALJ must issue rulings. A party that is not satisfied with the decision of the ALJ may appeal the case to the EPA's Environmental Hearing Board. Thereafter, further appeals must be brought in a judicial forum.

At first blush, it would appear patently unfair and even absurd that an official of the agency bringing a legal action is responsible for ruling on the merits of the case. However, administrative hearing officers are protected from undue influence by fellow agency officials by fairly stringent bureaucratic mechanisms. Agencies usually cultivate the independence and neutrality of their hearing officers in order to maintain the integrity of a process that benefits the agencies by providing a relatively expeditious means of penalizing and rectifying violations. Agency officials are aware that if the administrative hearing process appears to be biased or corrupt, legislators may repeal the statutory authorization for them, which would deprive their agency of the more expeditious adjudicative tools the administrative forums provide. Thus the long-term benefits of maintaining the integrity of administrative hearing processes usually outweigh any short-term benefits that might be achieved by unfairly influencing administrative hearings. Likewise, administrative hearing officers themselves have a significant institutional stake in the fairness and integrity of the administrative hearing process.

2.3   The Role of the Courts: Judicial Review

Judicial review is the process by which parties petititon courts to overturn agency actions. It has been aptly described as a part of the administrative process:

> This court has been assigned special responsibility for determining challenges to EPA's . . . standards. This judicial review rests on the premise that agency and court "together constitute a partnership in furtherance of the public interest, and are collaborative instrumentalities of justice. The court is in a real sense part of the total administrative process."[4]

Courts may exercise judicial review of both substantive and procedural aspects of agency decisions. When a court exercises substantive review, it ascertains whether the agency is enforcing a statute according to congressional intent. When a court reviews procedural aspects of agency action, it passes on the validity of agency proceedings without regard to the substance of the agency's decision. For example, the National Environmental Protection Act (NEPA), the subject of Chapter 3, does not prescribe substantive environmental rules, but merely requires compliance by federal agencies with NEPA procedures. Even so, NEPA is a fertile source of challenges to governmental programs, because it authorizes judicial review of citizens' complaints that federal agencies have failed to conduct Environmental Impact Studies for proposed actions which adversely affect the environment. NEPA contains no substantive provisions by which the actions of federal agencies are to be evaluated by the courts, but courts may invalidate an agency's actions if the agency has failed to follow NEPA's procedural requirements.

> The reviewing court probably cannot reverse a substantive decision [of an agency] on its merits . . . . but if the decision was reached procedurally without individualized consideration and balancing of environmental factors . . . it is the responsibility of the courts to reverse.[5]

The authority of courts to pass on the validity of the government's exercise of power was established early in U.S. legal history. In the words of a famous jurist in a landmark Supreme Court decision:

> It is emphatically the province . . . of the judicial department to say what the law is.[6]

This authority "to say what the law is" gives courts the last say on the validity of agency actions. Regardless of whether courts exercise judicial review on substantive or procedural grounds, they have a significant impact on the actions and programs of administrative agencies.

Under the judicial review power, courts also have the power to determine when and how courts will hear petitions for review. These "justiciability" issues may be stated as follows:

- Which parties are entitled to bring lawsuits to challenge agency actions?
- At what point in the agency decision-making process will courts entertain suits to review agency action?
- What is the scope of issues that courts will consider in reviewing agency actions?
- What degree of scrutiny will courts bring to bear in reviewing agency actions?
- What standards will courts utilize in reviewing agency action?

The most prominent doctrines governing these questions are the standing doctrine, exhaustion of administrative remedies, scope of review, and standard of review. There are other judicial grounds, not discussed here, under which courts may refuse to hear cases. For instance, when a court sees that a case raises a "political" question, it leaves the exclusive decision to another branch of government.

Who May Sue?: The Standing Doctrine

The standing doctrine limits the access of individuals and groups to judicial review and often frustrates attempts by citizens and organizations to prevent or preclude environmental law violations. Not everyone who is dissatisfied with the actions of an administrative agency has standing to sue, no matter how valid their substantive objections. To demonstrate standing to sue, a party must have a valid procedural basis to bring the claim. Standing status may be granted by statute or by court-fashioned rules when statutory standing does not exist. Where legal relief is not sought by parties that have standing, the refusal of courts to hear environmental grievances remains a major barrier to legal redress for environmental law violations, whether committed by government agencies or by private entities.

Judicial Standing

In the absence of a statute explicitly conferring standing, a court will hear a case only if the petitioner possesses a concrete—as opposed to philosophical—interest in the matter and the court is capable of fashioning a valid remedy. The judicial standing requirement thus has two prongs. First, a petitioner must prove that agency action has caused injury-in-fact. This means that the petitioner must have some "personal stake" in the challenged agency action or be threatened with an actual injury by it. Second, the petitioner must satisfy the court that the relief sought is something the court has the authority to grant. Failure to show either of these elements is a bar to suit unless Congress has conferred standing by statute.

The standing requirement is independent of the validity of the complaint as a substantive matter, and a court never proceeds to consider the "merits" of the claim if the petitioner lacks standing to sue. For example, when two environmental groups in New England sued to force EPA to comply with a law requiring it to evaluate 840 federal hazardous waste sites across the nation, the court denied them standing to seek relief despite the fact that EPA was almost certainly in violation of the law. The court refused to hear the case, because the sites neither affected the petitioners personally nor were located in their vicinity.[7]

The standing doctrine arises from Article III of the U.S. Constitution, which gives courts jurisdiction to hear cases and controversies. If a party cannot demonstrate injury-in-fact, courts have held that there is no actual case or controversy that confers jurisdiction. The primary practical justification for the judicial standing doctrine is the notion that a party who is not materially affected by a legal violation should not be able to require courts and other parties to expend resources litigating the matter. There is also a perception that because courts cannot rectify every legal violation that citizens may uncover, they should concentrate on situations where a concrete injury to the petitioner is demonstrated.

The standing doctrine does not consider the seriousness of the merits of a case but, rather, focuses upon the nexus perceived to exist between the party seeking redress and the issue raised. The standing doctrine also implicitly refuses to recognize that a group or individual willing to stake the considerable effort and expense required to file a lawsuit perforce perceives that it does in fact have a concrete interest to vindicate.

Early environmental standing cases, such as the *Sierra Club* case opinion excerpted here, seemed to indicate that environmental standing could be conferred once individual members of a public-interest group alleged harm to their own interests.

SIERRA CLUB v. MORTON

405 U.S. 727, 31 L. Ed. 2d 636, 92 S. Ct. 1361 (1972)

[The U.S. Forest Service, which is charged with maintaining national forests, approved a plan whereby Walt Disney Enterprises would develop an extensive recreational complex in Mineral King Valley, a designated game refuge that is part of the Sequoia National Forest in California's Sierra Nevada mountains. The Sierra Club brought suit to have the court enjoin the development. Over the objection that the Sierra Club lacked standing to sue, the trial court granted the injunction. On further appeal, the Circuit Court of Appeal held that the Club lacked standing. On final appeal to the United States Supreme Court, the following opinion was rendered on the issue of standing.]

* * *

II

The first question presented is whether the Sierra Club has alleged facts that entitle it to obtain judicial review of the challenged action. Whether a party has a sufficient stake in an otherwise justiciable controversy to obtain judicial resolution of that controversy is what has traditionally been referred to as the question of standing to sue. Where the party does not rely on any specific statute authorizing invocation of the judicial process, the question of standing depends upon whether the party has alleged such a "personal stake in the outcome of the controversy," . . . as to ensure that "the dispute sought to be adjudicated will be presented in an adversary context and in a form historically viewed as capable of judicial resolution." . . . Where, however, Congress has authorized public officials to perform certain functions according to law, and has provided by statute for judicial review of those actions under certain circumstances, the inquiry as to standing must begin with a determination of whether the statute in question authorizes review at the behest of the plaintiff.

The Sierra Club relies upon § 10 of the Administrative Procedure Act (APA), 5 U.S.C. § 702, which provides:

"A person suffering legal wrong because of agency action, or adversely affected or aggrieved by agency action within the meaning of a relevant statute, is entitled to judicial review thereof."

. . . But, in Data Processing Service v. Camp, 397 U.S. 150, . . . we held more broadly that persons had standing to obtain judicial review of federal agency action under § 10 of the APA where they had alleged that the challenged action had caused them "injury in fact," and where the alleged injury was to an interest "arguably within the zone of interests to be protected or regulated" by the statutes that the agencies were claimed to have violated.

* * *

. . . neither Data Processing nor Barlow addressed itself to the question, . . . as to what must be alleged by persons who claim injury of a noneconomic nature to interests that are widely shared. That question is presented in this case.

III

The injury alleged by the Sierra Club will be incurred entirely by reason of the change in the uses to which Mineral King will be put, and the attendant change in the aesthetics and ecology of the area. Thus, . . . the complaint alleged that the development "would destroy or otherwise adversely affect the scenery, natural and historic objects and wildlife of the park and would impair the enjoyment of the park for future generations." We do not question that this type of harm may amount to an "injury in fact" sufficient to lay the basis for standing under § 10 of the APA. Aesthetic and environmental well-being, like economic well-being, are important ingredients of the quality of life in our society, and the fact that particular environmental interests are shared by the many rather than the few does not make them less deserving of legal protection through the judicial process. But the "injury in fact" test requires more than an injury to a cognizable interest. It requires that the party seeking review be himself among the injured.

The impact of the proposed changes in the environment of Mineral King will not fall indiscriminately upon every citizen. The alleged injury will be felt directly only by those who use Mineral King and Sequoia National Park. . . . The Sierra Club failed to allege that it or its members would be affected in any of their activities or pastimes by the Disney development. Nowhere in the pleadings or affidavits did the Club state that its members use Mineral King for any purpose, much less that they use it in any way that would be significantly affected by the proposed actions of the respondents.

The Club apparently regarded any allegations of individualized injury as superfluous, on the theory that this was a "public" action involving questions as to the use of natural resources, and that the Club's long-standing concern with and expertise in such matters were sufficient to give it standing as a "representative of the public." This theory reflects a misunderstanding of our cases involving so-called "public actions" in the area of administrative law.

* * *

The trend of cases arising under the APA and other statutes authorizing judicial review of federal agency action has been toward recognizing that injuries other than economic harm are sufficient to bring a person within the meaning of the statutory language. . . . We noted this development with approval in Data

Processing, 397 U.S., at 154, 25 L. Ed. 2d at 188, in saying that the interest alleged to have been injured, "may reflect 'aesthetic, conservational, and recreational' as well as economic values." But broadening the categories of injury that may be alleged in support of standing is a different matter from abandoning the requirement that the party seeking review must himself have suffered an injury.

Some courts have indicated a willingness to take this latter step by conferring standing upon organizations that have demonstrated "an organizational interest in the problem" of environmental or consumer protection. Environmental Defense Fund v. Hardin, 138 U.S. App. D.C. 391, 395, 428 F.2d 1093, 1097. It is clear that an organization whose members are injured may represent those members in a proceeding for judicial review. . . .

* * *

The requirement that a party seeking review must allege facts showing that he is himself adversely affected does not insulate executive action from judicial review, nor does it prevent any public interests from being protected through the judicial process. It does serve . . . to put the decision as to whether review will be sought in the hands of those who have a direct stake in the outcome. That goal would be undermined were we to construe the APA to authorize judicial review at the behest of organizations or individuals who seek to do no more than vindicate their own value preferences through the judicial process.

* * *

As we conclude that the Court of Appeals was correct in its holding that the Sierra Club lacked standing to maintain this action, we do not reach any other questions presented in the petition, ...

* * *

In the years following the *Sierra Club* decision, the Supreme Court further constricted the circumstances under which standing in environmental public interest cases would be granted. In a 1990 decision, the Supreme Court dismissed a suit by the National Wildlife Federation to enjoin a Bureau of Land Management decision to reclassify public lands so that private entities could stake mining claims thereon.[8] Some of the tracts of land the Bureau sought to open for mining claims were large tracts in remote wilderness areas. Federation members stated that they had used and enjoyed federal lands in the vicinity of lands the Bureau was seeking to open for mining. On the basis of individual affidavits, the Federation alleged that the Bureau's decision was unlawful and would have a detrimental impact on its members, harming their recreational use and aesthetic enjoyment of areas that would be adversely affected by nearby mining activity. Nonetheless, the Court ruled that the Federation did not state *with sufficient specificity* how its members would actually be affected by the land reclassification. First, the Court found that no sufficient injury was alleged, because Federation members did not indicate that the contemplated agency action would interfere with their actual use of the precise acreage the Bureau's decision would open for mining. Second, the Court found that the programmatic decisions by the Bureau were rules of general applicability and not specific agency actions; it concluded that the Federation's challenge would not be ripe (ready for court review) until the Bureau had taken further specific actions or neglected to take actions that would actually harm citizens' interests.

The decision in the *Wildlife Federation* suit places nearly insurmountable barriers, both practical and strategic, to citizens' suits challenging federal-land management decisions. For a plaintiff to allege that he or she uses or enjoys specific acreage within a large remote, tract of land that is subject to federal-agency action might well require extensive land surveys and costly analyses of ecosystem impacts of the contemplated federal action. In the environmental context, a narrow view of standing ignores the interconnectedness of ecological systems and the likelihood that an environmental injury will have a detrimental impact somewhere. The requirement that a citizen challenge only the specific agency action that threatens injuries, rather than general programs comprised of many actions that could reasonably be said to affect citizen interests, is also an extremely elusive and burdensome one. The Court in the *Wildlife Federation* opinion provided no guidance as to when an agency action is general and programmatic (and thus immune to challenge) and when it constitutes specific and final action (which is not immune to challenge). The decision invites courts to categorize agency actions as general in order to limit access to judicial review. The net result is to make governmental actions undertaken as part of a comprehensive program virtually unreviewable for alleged substantive violations of law.

Another Supreme Court decision that followed in 1992[9] further narrowed the circumstances in which judicial environmental standing would be found. In the 1992 case, Defenders of Wildlife brought suit to challenge the federal government's interpretation that the Endangered Species Act (ESA) does not apply to federally funded programs outside U.S. borders. Defenders of Wildlife alleged that the Secretary of the Interior failed to comply with the ESA requirement that federal agencies pursue consultations with interested parties in order to ensure that federal programs do not jeopardize the continued existence of endangered species or of the habitats supporting them. In attempting to establish injury-in-fact, the Defenders of Wildlife alleged that the lack of consultation by the Interior Secretary had contributed to an increased rate of extinction of certain endangered species in other countires, thereby injuring its members' ability to observe the species in their natural habitats. The Defenders group submitted affidavits by two of its members stating that they had observed certain threatened species in their native habitats in the past and hoped to observe them again, but that the U.S.-funded projects would destroy the special habitats before observers would be able to return.

While acknowledging that observation of animal species for aesthetic purposes is a recognized interest sufficient for standing purposes, the Court found the affidavits insufficient in that neither of the affiants had immediate plans to travel to observe the endangered species. The Court opinion stated that to confer standing, a party must allege "imminent" injury to the recognized interest. The *Defenders* opinion effectively expanded the injury-in-fact requirement to require that the injury be "imminent."

In addition to proving an *imminent injury in fact* to the petitioner's *specific interests* that is caused by a *specific, as opposed to programmatic, agency decision,* a petitioner must also satisfy the court that the relief it seeks is practical and would effectively redress the petitioner's injury. In both of the cases discussed here, the Court also found that the remedies sought would not be sufficient to redress the alleged injuries.

Barriers to standing apply to industry groups as well as environmentalists. Following the *Wildlife Federation* and *Defenders of Wildlife* decisions, timber purchasers and their employees sued the Forest Service to overturn its decision to restrict timber harvesting in an endangered bird's habitat areas. They asserted that the forest service decision violated several federal substantive and procedural statutes.[10] Without reaching the legality of the Forest Service action, the federal appeals court dismissed the suit for lack of standing to sue. It found that the timber purchasers' allegation of economic injury from the removal of a timber supply source was too speculative and that the company employees' claims of aesthetic interests were too ill-defined. Although the petitioners alleged that the Forest Service failed to follow statutory procedures in restricting the timber cutting area, the Court found the grievance to be too general and indirect to confer standing. Since there was no statutory grant of standing, the failure to meet judicial-standing requirements barred the suit.

Statutory Standing

Citizen oversight of environmental programs may be particularly valuable in situations where EPA resists or delays taking enforcement action or where EPA's enforcement efforts are hampered by other governmental agencies or by the regulated industries. Therefore, Congress has sometimes expressly authorized citizen suits as a means of enforcing compliance with environmental laws. In the absence of judicial standing, a lack of statutory standing would leave the courts powerless to rectify legal violations and would materially diminish the incentive for government agencies and regulated entities to comply with applicable laws and regulations.

The nature and scope of statutory standing varies from statute to statute. Congress has not granted citizens standing to sue under all environmental laws nor under all provisions of statutes that do contain some standing provisions. Nor have the courts found statutory standing to exist under all circumstances when a statuatory provision generally authorizes it. For example, the Clean Water Act (the subject of Chapter 8) has been construed to authorize citizen suits to remedy present or future injuries, but not to rectify wholly past injuries.[11] In contrast, the Clean Air Act (the subject of Chapter 9) does not impose the same limitation on citizens' suits. The extent of statutory standing, therefore, depends upon judicial interpretation of the particular provisions of each environmental statute.

When May a Party Sue?: Exhaustion of Administrative Remedies and Notice Requirements

Exhaustion of Administrative Remedies

When the law provides for administrative remedies, courts generally require that those remedies be exhausted before they undertake judicial review. For instance, if the law allows for public comment and administrative hearing on a proposed agency action, a party is not permitted to mount a judicial challenge to the proposed action until it has utilized administrative proceedings. The exhaustion doctrine serves several purposes:

- to avoid unnecessary interruptions of administrative processes,
- to afford agency experts the opportunity to respond to comments and to resolve issues, and
- to encourage full development of an administrative record of relevant facts and arguments to inform a reviewing court's decision.[12]

Courts do not apply the exhaustion doctrine where it would not serve these purposes or where it might unduly prejudice a suing party. When a party can demonstrate that its pursuit of administrative relief would be futile, the exhaustion doctrine does not apply. Likewise, when the agency cannot provide an adequate remedy for the complaint, or when delays in administrative hearing would cause irreparable injury to an aggrieved party, exhaustion of administrative remedies is not required.

Congress has supplemented the judicial doctrine of exhaustion in some environmental statutes by provisions that expressly preclude judicial review until the EPA has the opportunity to consider and rule upon challenges or objections to its actions. As with statutory standing, legislative exhaustion rules are not universal, and their existence and scope must be determined from the provisions of each statute.

Notice Requirements

Somewhat related to the exhaustion doctrine are the notice requirements found in many environmental statutes, which bar a party from bringing suit until it has given advance notice of its intent to sue to the affected parties and appropriate government agencies. In a typical case,[13] the plaintiff was denied judicial hearing on a complaint under the Resource Conservation and Recovery Act (RCRA) because it failed to give the EPA, the alleged violator, and the interested state agency written notice of its intent to sue, as required by the statute. The purposes of notice requirements are to give the alleged violator the opportunity to avoid a suit by remedying the violation and to give the EPA and the interested state agency the opportunity to initiate enforcement proceedings.

Other Limitations: Scope and Standard of Review

Courts limit the scope and extent of their review of agency actions as a matter of institutional competence and economy. In the many cases where the core issues involve statutory interpretation, the court's dominant task is to interpret and apply the law according to Congressional intent. Courts are generally not authorized to make environmental policy or to substitute their judgments for those of Congress or administrative agencies. Although judge-made common law principles may affect environmental claims, they are not central to Congressionally created schemes of regulation. Where Congress has vested EPA with primary responsibility for interpreting, administering, and enforcing its statutes, courts will defer to EPA's expertise and judgments unless those judgments are found to be patently erroneous. This is especially true where Congress has expressed the intention that agency determinations be subject only to limited judicial review. The major doctrines by which courts confine their review of agency actions are those relating to the scope of review and the standards of review.

Scope of Review

Scope of review refers to the kinds of administrative actions a court will examine. Before a court reviews a challenged agency position or action it must decide which EPA actions or inactions Congress intended to subject to, or insulate from, judicial review. Where Congress has not prescribed the scope of review in express terms, courts may find guidance as to the appropriate scope of review in the legislative history or design of the statute in question. If no such guidance is available, the court will infer the appropriate scope of review from statutes of similar design or purpose or from prior judicial decisions. Nevertheless, a court generally determines the scope of review by interpreting the intent of the governing statute, rather than by making an independent judicial choice. Scope of review can range from a full rehearing of the entire case to an examination of only those issues raised and considered in the administrative record of agency proceedings. Unless there are compelling circumstances, a court will usually confine its review to the agency's written record documenting the reasons for its decision.

Standards of Review

Once a court has decided which issues fall within its proper scope of review, it must determine which standard of review is appropriate. The standard of review fixes the degree of scrutiny the court will exercise in examining a challenge to an agency action. In many cases, the court must determine the appropriate standard of review as an issue in itself. The standard of review a court utilizes often materially influences its treatment of issues presented by the case and the case's outcome.

Rules for determining the applicable standard of review are found in various places. The statute under which an issue arises may expressly mandate the standard of review. If the statute gives no guidance, courts look to the Administrative Procedures Act or to judge-made rules adopted by other courts in similar cases.

The appropriate standard of review depends partly on the nature of the dispute and partly on the extent to which the applicable statute assigns particular questions to agency determination. Different standards of review are warranted in different cases, because government agencies such as EPA perform a wide variety of governmental functions. The appropriate standard of review assures that EPA observes legal standards applicable to each distinct function without impinging upon its statutory authority, discretion, or its expertise in the field.

Standards of review range from a complete judicial reassessment of all factual and legal findings in the case to a mere determination of whether the agency acted in an arbitrary and capricious fashion. The former standard is called *de novo* review and is rather rare in judicial review of administrative actions. It is far more common for courts to respect the wide latitude agencies have been given for interpreting the statutes they administer. Courts also defer to the agency's expertise in its subject-matter area. For these reasons, courts refrain from overturning an agency decision unless the decision

1. is clearly without foundation in law,
2. is arbitrary and capricious, or
3. is not supported by substantial evidence.

Courts are considered competent to exercise review for pure errors of law (errors that do not involve issues of fact, opinion, or agency discretion) inasmuch as they are peculiarly suited to detect errors in legal interpretation. Agency decisions that rest upon administrative fact findings, properly promulgated policy directives, or enforcement discretion, however, require a different weighing of relative input by EPA and the courts. In such cases, primary decisional competence and responsibility rests with the agency, and courts provide only a limited review of the record so as to ensure that the agency's decision is warranted by the facts and the evidence.

When exercising limited review, courts generally employ one of two standards: the "abuse of discretion" standard or the "substantial evidence" rule. Under the *abuse of discretion standard*, a court accepts the agency's fact findings and determines only whether the agency exercised its statutory discretion reasonably. Using this standard, a court overturns an agency decision only when it finds that the agency acted arbitrarily or capriciously. The abuse of discretion standard is particularly appropriate where the decision in question involves specialized knowledge or expert judgments on the part of the agency.

The *substantial evidence rule* calls for a different kind of judicial scrutiny. Under this standard, courts review the evidence in the record and determine whether it justified the agency findings. Although they still defer to administrative appraisals of evidence, they do so to a lesser degree—particularly where the evidence supporting the agency decision is conflicting. Under the substantial evidence rule, courts scrutinize evidence with less deference than they give to agency discretion, and they evaluate the record *independently* to decide if there was substantial evidence to support the administrator's findings. Here the focus is primarily on the factual foundations for agency action, rather than on agency judgment. Even in these cases, however, courts uphold the agency's decision if they find substantial evidence to support the agency's findings. The test is not whether the court would have read the evidence differently had it conducted the hearing itself, but only whether substantial evidence justified the agency's finding.

The Artful Words: **Shall** *and* **May**

One factor that affects the appropriate standard of review is whether the governing statute requires an agency to take certain action as a matter of duty or permits it to act at its own discretion. Many agency decisions are, by statute, "committed to agency discretion." Where the statute clearly distinguishes "duty" from "discretion," however, statutory mandates govern. Words such as *may, shall* or *must* are significant statutory clues courts use to determine whether the agency is obligated or merely authorized to take particular action. However, courts do not universally seize upon verbiage as an indication of legislative intent. They also look at the structure of the statute as a whole and other expressions of legislative intent.

The term *may* is generally interpreted to denote that Congress intended action to be "committed to agency discretion." When the statute says that an agency "may" undertake a certain action, judicial review is limited to the narrow question of whether there has been an abuse of discretion or a reliance on insufficient supporting evidence. Since the essence of discretion is judgment, a court will uphold a discretionary decision it finds to be reasonable, even if, acting independently, it would have arrived at a different conclusion.

Where the governing statute contains the imperative term *shall,* courts interpret it to impose an obligation that the agency has no discretion to ignore. As a general rule, aggrieved parties may compel an agency to act only if the statute mandates that the agency "shall" perform that duty. In many circumstances, a statute imposes a duty to act only after the agency has made certain threshold findings. Under these circumstances, the agency is *not required to make* the threshold findings that would trigger the mandatory obligation; thus the agency retains a broad degree of discretion despite the legislature's use of the word *shall.*

2.4 The Role of State Environmental Law

Virtually all states have followed Congress's lead by enacting their own environmental laws and by establishing state agencies for implementing those laws as well as federal environmental laws. Most state statutes leave in place the older body of state "common law" that entitles injured parties to bring private lawsuits against parties who wrongfully injure them. The concurrent existence of federal and state environmental laws, on one hand, and of state statutory and common-law remedies for environmental injuries, on the other hand, raises "choice of law" issues that courts must decide.

Common Law Remedies for Environmental Injuries

Prior to the enactment of statutory remedies, common law doctrines provided virtually the only legal recourse for individuals who suffered environmental injuries. As opposed to environmental statutes, which are generally "public" law enactments that regulate the actions of individuals for the benefit of the public at large, the common law gives rise to "private" causes of action for individuals who have suffered injuries as a result of another individual's actions. The common law is judge-made law and it encompasses the law of contracts, trespass, torts, and nuisance. These common law causes of action provide remedies not available to individuals under environmental statutes and they are largely unaffected by public law statutes.

Common law principles are of continued importance even where comprehensive public environmental regulation exists:

> Although many of today's environmental controversies involve public law statutes and regulations, in functional terms the common law made by judges and private litigants . . . continues to play a critical role in environmental law.
>
> Each year many environmental cases involving localized pollution are filed under common law theories. These local cases undoubtedly make up the numerical majority of environmental cases generally. Even so, when an oil tanker disaster strikes the waters and shores of a coastal state, or a chemical factory's dump-site poisons land and groundwater, the major remedies litigated by injured parties are likewise based almost entirely on common law. After the wreck of the *Exxon-Valdez*, for example, the lawsuits filed by the State of Alaska and its citizens relied on tort and public trust theories to respond to that vast catastrophe. The common law is a fertile hunting ground for environmental lawyers trying to get a handle on some of the most modern ecological problems and underscores the critical role played by private litigation in U.S. environmental law.
>
> The common law also provides the conceptual underpinning for most statutes and regulations. Legislatures and agencies rely on the continued existence of common law to fill gaps in public law and to guide courts and agencies in their interpretation of statutes and rules. . . .
>
> Many fundamental issues raised in environmental law . . . will continue to be raised first in the common law realm. Questions of proof, uncertainty, balances of risk, fault, and other liability issues, foreseeability, standards of care, technological feasibility, causation, long-term residual injuries, remedies, practical deterrence, enforceability . . . all these are found first in the common law. Despite the existence of innumerable federal and state environmental statues and reams of administrative regulations, the common law of environmental protection remains vigorous and important.[14]

The need for both private law and public law relating to the environment is obvious. Although the private relief afforded by the common law remains important for individuals injured by environmental pollution, the common law cannot fully address or adequately remedy major environmental wrongs.

In a common law suit, a party suffering an environmental injury must shoulder a heavy burden of proof and produce factual evidence that is often beyond that party's practical reach. In a toxic tort action, for example, a plaintiff must generally show that the defendant acted in an unreasonable fashion or caused the release of polluting substances onto the plaintiff's property and that the defendant's activities, and not those of a third party, caused injury to the plaintiff's health or property. The plaintiff must also prove the extent of damages it suffered and show the actual, as opposed to speculative, monetary value of the damages. Collecting this kind of evidence can be prohibitively expensive, particularly where more than one possible source of pollution must be traced in order to determine which is responsible for the plaintiff's injury. Proving that the defendant's activities directly contributed to an illness such as cancer can be enormously difficult if other environmental or genetic factors may also have played a role. Furthermore, such injuries to health may not appear until many years after exposure, when responsible parties, such as corporate defendants, may no longer be financially viable or extant.

Moreover, monetary remedies do not prevent recurring future injury from the polluting source or assure compensation for future as well as past damages. Thus, a homeowner whose well water is contaminated by one or more nearby sources not only has the daunting task of proving culpability, but has no real assurance that the polluting activities will cease. The need to bring successive lawsuits for each new toxic invasion is hardly a satisfactory solution for one suffering environmental injuries. Even if a property owner obtains a restraining order against future activities by a polluting source, courts are ill equipped to monitor conditions continually. As illustrated by the *Boomer* opinion excerpted in this subsection, common law remedies are ineffective in preventing or deterring large-scale industrial pollution.

In enacting environmental statutes, legislators can opt to shift some of the burden of proof in environmental litigation from the injured parties to the polluters. Of equal significance are statutory schemes that create or authorize administrative agencies to monitor and enforce environmental laws at public expense. Governmental agencies such as EPA are better equipped to provide ongoing oversight of environmental safety than are individual judges, whose authority extends only to the parties in a particular case. Agency regulations provide a more comprehensive means of regulating the activities of large classes of potential polluters than are court orders, which bind only parties before the court. The *Boomer* case excerpt reprinted here briefly analyzes some of the problems associated with common law remedies for environmental injuries and expounds on the manifest need for public law solutions.

BOOMER ET AL. V. ATLANTIC CEMENT COMPANY

New York Court of Appeals, 1970
26 N.Y.2d 219, 257 N.E.2d 870, 309 N.Y.S.2d 312

Bergan, J. . . .

The public concern with air pollution arising from many sources in industry and in transportation is currently accorded ever wider recognition accompanied by a growing sense of responsibility in State and Federal Governments to control it. Cement plants are obvious sources of air pollution in the neighborhoods where they operate.

But there is now before the court private litigation in which individual property owners have sought specific relief from a single plant operation. The threshold question . . . is whether the court should resolve the litigation between the parties now before it as equitably as seems possible; or whether, . . . it should channel private litigation into broad public objectives.

A court performs its essential function when it decides the rights of parties before it. Its decision of private controversies may sometimes greatly affect public issues. . . . But this is normally an incident to the court's main function to settle controversy; . . . .

Effective control of air pollution is a problem presently far from solution even with the full public and financial powers of government. In large measure adequate technical procedures are yet to be developed and some that appear possible may be economically impracticable.

It seems apparent that the amelioration of air pollution will depend on technical research in great depth; on a carefully balanced consideration of the economic impact of close regulation; and of the actual effect on public health. It is likely to require massive public expenditure and to demand more than any local community can accomplish and to depend on regional and interstate controls.

A court should not try to do this on its own as a by-product of private litigation and it seems manifest that the judicial establishment is neither equipped . . . nor prepared to lay down and implement an effective policy for the elimination of air pollution. This is an area beyond the circumference of one private lawsuit. . . .

The cement making operations of defendant have been found . . . to have damaged the nearby properties of plaintiffs in these two actions. That court, . . . accordingly found defendant maintained a nuisance. . . . The trial judge had made a simple, direct finding that "the discharge of large quantities of dust upon each of the properties and excessive vibration from blasting deprived each party of the reasonable use of his property and thereby prevented his enjoyment of life and liberty therein." The judge continued, however: ". . . Although the Supreme Court has the power to grant and enforce an injunction, equity forbids its employment in this instance. The defendant's immense investment in the Hudson River Valley, its contribution to the Capital District's economy and its immediate help to the education of children in the Town of Coeymans through the payment of substantial sums in school and property taxes leads me to the conclusion that an injunction would produce great

public . . . hardship." The total damage to plaintiffs' properties is, however, relatively small in comparison with the value of defendant's operation and with the consequences of the injunction which plaintiffs seek. . . .

The rule in New York has been that such a nuisance will be enjoined although marked disparity be shown in economic consequence between the effect of the injunction and the effect of the nuisance.

The problem of disparity in economic consequence was sharply in focus in Whalen v. Union Bag & Paper Co., 101 N.E. 805. A pulp mill entailing an investment of more than a million dollars polluted a stream in which plaintiff, who owned a farm, was "a lower riparian owner." The economic loss to plaintiff from this pollution was small. The court, reversing the Appellate Division, reinstated the injunction . . . against the argument of the mill owner that in view of "the slight advantage to plaintiff and the great loss that will be inflicted on defendant" an injunction should not be granted.

* * *

This result at Special Term and at the Appellate Division is a departure from a rule that has become settled; but to follow the rule literally in these cases would be to close down the plant at once. This court is fully agreed to avoid that immediately drastic remedy; the difference in view is how best to avoid it.

One alternative is to grant the injunction but postpone its effect to a specified future date to give opportunity for technical advances to permit defendant to eliminate the nuisance; another is to grant the injunction conditioned on the payment of permanent damages to plaintiffs which would compensate them for the total economic loss to their property present and future caused by defendant's operations. For reasons which will be developed the court chooses the latter alternative.

The parties could settle this private litigation at any time if defendant paid enough money and the imminent threat of closing the plant would build up the pressure on defendant. If there were no improved techniques found, there would inevitably be applications to the court at Special Term for extensions of time to perform on showing of good faith efforts to find such techniques.

Moreover, technique to eliminate dust and other annoying by-products of cement making . . . will depend on the total resources of the cement industry nationwide and throughout the world.

For obvious reasons the rate of the research is beyond control of defendant. If at the end of 18 months the whole industry has not found a technical solution a court would be hard put to close down this one cement plant if due regard be given to equitable principles.

On the other hand, to grant the injunction unless defendant pays plaintiffs such permanent damages as may be fixed by the court seems to do justice between the contending parties. . . .

It seems reasonable to think that the risk of being required to pay permanent damages to injured property owners by cement plant owners would itself be a reasonable effective spur to research for improved techniques to minimize nuisance.

The power of the court to condition on equitable grounds the continuance of an injunction on the payment of permanent damages seems undoubted. . . .

The present cases and the remedy here proposed are in a number of other respects rather similar to Northern Indiana Public Service Co. v. W. J. & M. S. Vesey, 200 N.E. 620 decided by the Supreme Court of Indiana. The gases, odors, ammonia, and smoke from the Northern Indiana company's gas plant damaged the nearby Vesey greenhouse operation. An injunction and damages were sought, but an injunction was denied and the relief granted was limited to permanent damages "present, past, and future." . . .

Thus it seems fair to both sides to grant permanent damages to plaintiffs which will terminate this private litigation.

* * *

Although the Trial Term has found permanent damages as a possible basis of settlement of the litigation, on remission the court should be entirely free to examine this subject. It may again find the permanent damage already found, or make new findings.

The orders should be reversed, without costs, and the cases remitted to Supreme Court, Albany County to grant an injunction which shall be vacated upon payment by defendant of such amounts of permanent damage to the respective plaintiffs as shall for this purpose be determined by the court.

* * *

One primary focus of the common law has been the protection of private property rights. Many common law causes of action, such as trespass, were available only to property holders who suffered environmental injuries. Under common law principles, the right to use and enjoy one's property gave rise to common law causes of action for environmental pollution that impaired the owner's use and enjoyment. In many circumstances, one could sue for environmental injuries only by proving that the polluter's activities interfered with the use and enjoyment of one's property.

In contrast, the focus of most federal environmental regulatory statutes is the protection of public health and the environment. These statutes do not give specific rights to individuals and they rarely authorize private causes of action. However, the zone of interests protected by federal environmental regulation is broader than that protected by the common law. One need not demonstrate injury to a property interest in order to benefit from the protections afforded by public environmental regulation.

Federal environmental legislation has been superimposed on common law principles. Not surprisingly, some of its requirements and prohibitions are at odds with the uses and enjoyments of property the common law protects. Many environmental statutes forbid practices that were permitted at common law and impinge upon certain economic uses of property. These conflicts between the common law protection of private property and statutory protection of the environment for the public good are examined in later chapters.

Federal-State Law Conflicts: The Preemption Doctrine

Dual federal and state environmental regulatory schemes present opportunities both for fruitful collaboration and for occasional conflicts. The nature of federal and state law interactions vary with specific environmental laws and programs. One common issue with overlapping federal and state laws that converge on the same activity is whether such laws are consistent with each other or give rise to a federal-state law conflict. Laws that are consistent can generally be enforced concurrently. Federal and state laws that are inconsistent with each other give rise to a conflict. In such a case, federal law "preempts," or displaces, state law under the Supremacy Clause of the U.S. Constitution (Article VI), which reads:

> The Constitution and Laws of the United States . . . shall be the supreme Law of the Land; and the Judges in every State shall be bound thereby, any Thing in the . . . Laws of any State to the Contrary notwithstanding.

The effect of the Supremacy Clause was settled in the early years of the republic when the Supreme Court ruled that it renders invalid any state law or regulation that interferes with or is contrary to federal law.[15] In many cases, federal and state laws can be enforced concurrently without difficulty, even though they may impose somewhat different compliance standards. In other cases, however, state law requirements may impede or defeat the purposes of federal laws. The determination of consistency or conflict can often be made only on a case-by-case basis, but certain general principles apply. Specifically, state law is preempted by federal law where

- it conflicts with a federal statute,
- it impinges on a subject that is reserved to exclusive federal control under the U.S. Constitution (even if Congress has not legislated in the reserved area), or
- Congress has acted to "occupy the field" of legislation to the exclusion of all other laws.

In any of these cases, state law cannot be enforced.

An example of *constitutional reservation* of exclusive federal control was found when New Jersey passed a statute to forbid importation of wastes from other states. That law was struck down as unconstitutional, because it attempted to control interstate commerce, a subject reserved exclusively to Congress by the Commerce Clause of the Constitution. Other examples of *Congressional reservation* of exclusive federal authority appear in federal laws dealing with atomic energy and nuclear wastes. Congress has expressly reserved the authority to regulate in these areas.

Preemption can also occur where the Constitution and Congress have not expressly reserved a subject to exclusive federal regulation. *Implied reservation* was found to invalidate an Illinois statute requiring state licensing of workers at hazardous waste facilities. The Supreme Court struck down the Illinois law on the ground that Congress had impliedly occupied the field of worker safety by enacting the federal Occupational Safety and Health Act (OSHA) and thereby excluded state regulation.[17] The courts determine whether the Constitution or Congress has reserved a particular area for sole federal regulation.

Where no constitutional reservation exists and Congress has not expressly declared the intention to prevent state or local regulation, the courts must interpret a statute to determine if Congress intended to preempt state legislation. To aid in this interpretation, the Supreme Court has consistently adopted a *prima facie* (on its face) rebuttable presumption against preemption. In other words, unless there is an express Congressional reservation or the general scheme of a federal law is so pervasive that it manifests Congress's intent to occupy the field, federal legislation on a particular subject will not be deemed to exclude supplementary state laws:

> [W]e start with the assumption that the historic police powers of the States were not to be superseded by the Federal Act unless that was the clear and manifest purpose of Congress.[18]

It is nevertheless true that this presumption against preemption can be overcome, even where Congress has not clearly addressed the question.

Federal preemption is not necessarily an all-or-nothing issue. In reviewing overlapping federal and state environmental regulatory schemes, courts often find that a particular federal law or regulation preempts only a particular part of a state law or regulation. Thus, as the Supreme Court ruled under the Clean Water Act, the preemption doctrine goes no further than is necessary for preserving the purposes and effects of federal law. Hence it will not defeat those parts of state or local laws that do not undercut federal law:

> Our conclusion that Vermont nuisance law is inapplicable to a New York point source does not leave respondents [Vermont shoreline residents] without a remedy. The CWA [Clean Water Act] precludes only those suits that may require standards of effluent control that are incompatible with those established by . . . the Act. . . . [N]othing in the Act bars aggrieved individuals from bringing a nuisance claim pursuant to the law of the source state [New York].[19]

Interstate Environmental Issues

The control of in-migration of pollution and toxic materials from other states is a major concern of state governments. The U.S. Constitution forbids individual states from excluding, burdening, or discriminating against interstate or foreign commerce, even for the laudable goal of protecting their own citizens, unless Congress has empowered them to do so. This is true even where that commerce involves the transport and disposition of hazardous wastes.[20] States are even more powerless to exclude pollution from other states that is borne through the air and interstate waterways, such as acid rain and industrial wastewater discharges.

The lack of legal jurisdiction and fiscal resources to regulate interstate pollution has been addressed only nominally by federal enactments such as the Clean Air Act (CAA) and Clean Water Act (CWA), which require individual states to collaborate, adopt, and coordinate environmental programs as part of the federal regulatory scheme. EPA has generally been unwilling to enforce CWA and CAA provisions to prevent interstate polluting discharges and has been unable to devise other effective means to minimize interstate pollution. States, therefore, usually lack the legal means to prevent environmental damage emanating from external sources.

2.5   International Law and the Global Environment

Environmental degradation across national boundaries and throughout the planet cannot be adequately remedied by individual countries' isolated efforts. Environmental pollution ravages the natural resources of all nations as well as shared international resources such as the oceans and ocean fisheries. Without formal international agreements and general acceptance of international law obligations, nations have no means of effectively coordinating their protection efforts and no assurance that other nations will avoid damaging global environments and resources.

The American Law Institute's *Restatement of Foreign Relations* (3d) advocates that international law incorporate a general principle obligating each nation to:

> ... take such measures as may be necessary, to the extent practicable ... to ensure that activities within its jurisdiction ... conform to generally accepted international ... standards for the prevention ... of injury to the environment of another state .... [21]

To date, international law has not firmly established such a broad principle of nuisance liability, which is akin to the one enunciated in the *Boomer* opinion. Express written treaties and agreements furnish more promising avenues than do attempts to promote universal, broad principles of unwritten international law. The trend of international efforts has been toward reliance on such written agreements.

Even where nations have arrived at specific environmental agreements, enforcement has been complicated by the nature of national sovereignty. In the event of a dispute, the agreement's effectiveness often depends upon the signatory nations' willingness to subject themselves to some external tribunal, such as the International Court of Justice. Many nations, the United States among them, are unwilling to subject themselves or their nationals to international tribunals consistently. National and international organizations continue to attempt to develop new strategies and mechanisms for overcoming these difficulties.

Other serious obstacles to achieving international consensus on environmental strategies arise from conflicting opinions and desires of industrialized nations and poorer, Third World nations. Many poor nations are saddled with foreign debt and cannot afford to forego economic activities that damage the international environment. Their leaders argue that the industrially developed nations should underwrite and subsidize the international conservation and protection measures that they espouse. They also argue that developed countries should underwrite the bulk of environmental protection costs, since it is they who have contributed the most to environmental degradation through their past and present exploitation and consumption of the world's natural resources.

The conflicting first and third world views on the ability and responsibility of different nations to fund international environmental efforts reflect the same basic problems of resource use and distribution that were discussed in Chapter 1. In order to pay their international obligations, especially loans owed to international banks and monetary institutions, Third World countries must engage in cash-producing activities that are among the most environmentally damaging, such as single-crop agriculture, cattle grazing, and excessive timber cutting. Another disincentive for these nations to adopt and enforce environmental protection legislation is the high probability that enforcement would hinder their industrial development and foreign investment by multinational corporations. Foreign investment is often viewed as indispensable for creating new industry and jobs in many poor nations. To many of these countries, the alternative to environmentally unsound development efforts would appear to be large-scale starvation of their population.

Problems of creating and enforcing a system of international law to deal with environmental problems not amenable to local solution are explored further in Chapter 11.

■ Chapter 2 Endnotes

1. *Lujan v. Defenders of Wildlife,* 112 S. Ct. 2135, 2136 (1992).
2. 950 F.2d 741 (D.C. Cir., 1991).
3. 42 U.S.C. § 6901 *et seq.*
4. *Kennecott Copper Corp. v. Environmental Protection Agency,* 462 F.2d 846, 848–849 (D.C. Cir. 1972).
5. *Calvert Cliffs' Coordinating Committee v. AEC,* 449 F.2d 1109, 1115 (D.C. Cir. 1971).
6. *Marbury v. Madison,* 1 Cranch (5 U.S.) 137 (1803).
7. *Conservation Law Foundation of New England, Inc. v. Reilly,* 950 F.2d 38 (1st Cir. 1991).
8. *Lujan v. National Wildlife Federation,* 497 U.S. 871 (1990).
9. *Lujan v. Defenders of Wildlife,* 112 S. Ct. 2135 (1992).
10. *Region 8 Forest Service Timber Purchasers v. Alacock,* 993 F.2d 800 (11th Cir. 1993).
11. *Gwaltney of Smithfield, Ltd. v. Chesapeake Bay Foundation,* 484 U.S. 49 (1987).
12. See *McKart v. United States,* 395 U.S. 185, 193–194 (1969).
13. *Hallstrom v. Tillamook County,* 493 U.S. 20 (1989).
14. Z. Plater, R. Abrams, and W. Goldfarb, *Environmental Law and Policy: Nature, Law, and Society* (West Publishing Co., 1991), p. 101.
15. *Gibbons v. Ogden,* 22 U.S. (9 Wheat.) § 1 (1824).
16. *City of Philadelphia v. New Jersey,* 437 U.S. 617 (1978).
17. *Gade v. National Solid Waste Management Assoc.,* 112 S. Ct. 2374 (1992).
18. *Rice v. Santa Fe Elevator Corp.,* 331 U.S. 218, 230 (1947).
19. *International Paper Co. v. Ouellette,* 479 U.S. 481, 497 (1987).
20. See Chapter 6.
21. American Law Institute, *Restatement of Foreign Relations (3d),* § 601(3).

CHAPTER 3

Mechanisms and Models of Environmental Regulation

Outline

3.1 Historical Approaches to Federal Environmental Legislation

Before the Environmental Protection Agency (EPA) came into existence in 1970, the responsibilities for administering laws regarding the environment were distributed among various federal agencies. The Department of Agriculture, for

53

instance, originally had responsibility for enforcing the Federal Insecticide, Fungicide, and Rodenticide Act of 1947. In December 1970, then-President Nixon, by Reorganization Order Number 3, created EPA and transferred to it many of the environmental regulatory functions previously assigned to other federal departments. Congress has since vested EPA with the authority to enforce a wide range of environmental laws and regulations. Nonetheless, other federal agencies, such as the Department of the Interior, the Army Corps of Engineers, the Department of Justice, and the Occupational Health and Safety Administration, retain responsibility for administering some provisions of federal law which deal with the environment. For instance, although the EPA administers the Comprehensive Environmental Response, Compensation, and Liability Act (CERCLA; see Chapter 7), the Department of the Interior (DOI) retains primary jurisdiction under CERCLA for recovery for injuries to publicly owned natural resources. Under other environmental statutes, DOI and its Bureau of Land Management, rather than EPA, retain responsibility for management of public lands and natural resources despite the overwhelming environmental ramifications of the many uses of federal lands. Thus, the consolidation of authority for enforcing environmental laws within EPA is far from absolute. In fact, early in the Clinton administration, DOI's role in environmental matters was increased somewhat.

The history of federal environmental law is one of experimentation. Congress has experimented with three variables: the subject matter, or scope, of legislation; the governmental entity to which functions are delegated; and the choice of regulatory schemes or mechanisms. The first variable, scope, pertains to what is to be regulated; it is discussed in this section. The second, delegation of functions, concerns who is to have regulatory authority; it is covered in section 3.2. The third variable, the choice of regulatory mechanism, concerns how regulation is to be accomplished. Discussion of the factors that must be considered and the types of mechanisms that can be employed appear in sections 3.3 and 3.4, respectively.

Congressional approaches to the scope of regulation have varied markedly. Early environmental legislation sought to protect the quality of environmental media, air and water in particular. Several statutes passed in the mid seventies and the eighties addressed specific kinds of pollutants. The emerging regulatory trend is toward multimedia environmental protection, an approach that considers the interrelationships among environmental media. The following sections examine the evolution of subject-matter approaches to federal environmental legislation.

NEPA: A Patchwork Approach

The National Environmental Policy Act (NEPA) was the first of a series of modern federal laws explicitly directed toward protecting the environment. Signed into law on January 1, 1970, NEPA declared as a matter of national policy that the federal government was to "use all practical means . . . to create and maintain conditions in which man and nature can exist in productive harmony." NEPA created the President's Council on Environmental Quality (CEQ) to

- oversee federal-agency compliance with NEPA,
- help mediate interagency disputes,
- conduct studies on the environment,
- advise the President on environmental matters, and
- prepare and publish annual reports for the President and the Congress.

The annual CEQ reports, entitled *Environmental Quality,* contain useful official reports and data on changes and trends in environmental conditions and on the progress and deficiencies of federal environmental programs. In its early years, the CEQ was effective in advancing proposals that spurred the enactment of major laws to protect the environment. It also issued some environmental regulations prior to the full organization of the Environmental Protection Agency. Since then, the function of issuing regulations has largely been passed on to the EPA.

As of late 1993, the future of the CEQ was mired in doubt. The Clinton administration's plan to elevate EPA to cabinet-level status also called for the CEQ to be abolished and for its functions to be transferred to a new Office of Environmental Policy (OEP) within the White House. Congresspersons, including the Chairs of the House Energy and Commerce Committee and the Merchant Marine and Fisheries Committee, objected to the Clinton plan because the OEP would lack a statutory mandate and could therefore be abolished at any time, unlike the CEQ, which has specific statutory duties under NEPA. While legislation was held up over this controversy, the Clinton administration reduced the CEQ staff from thirty-two to three without effectuating a transfer of CEQ responsibilities. Of the three CEQ staff members remaining, none had the authority to release necessary operational funds to other agencies from the CEQ's interagency management fund. In addition, the remaining staff was insufficient to fulfill the Council's NEPA oversight and annual report responsibilities. It remains to be seen whether and to what extent the CEQ will survive if EPA is elevated to cabinet-level status.

NEPA does not regulate specific kinds of pollution or prescribe specific substantive standards relating to the environment. Rather, it sets forth more generalized procedural requirements, such as mandating that federal agencies evaluate the environmental impact of federal projects. It also enunciates broad, but unenforceable, policy goals:

> The sweeping policy goals announced in . . . NEPA are . . . realized through a set of "action forcing" procedures that require that agencies take a "hard look" at environmental consequences . . . and that provide for broad dissemination of relevant environmental information. . . . [I]t is now well settled that NEPA itself does not mandate particular results, but simply prescribes the necessary process.[1]

NEPA's major requirement is that federal agencies perform an environmental assessment (EA) of the impact of their actions and adopt measures to minimize the adverse effects of their actions on the environment. Before taking actions that would significantly affect the environment, a federal agency must prepare and publish an environmental impact statement (EIS) outlining the environmental effects of the proposed action. On the basis of environmental impact studies conducted as part of the EIS requirement, federal agencies must consider all available means of minimizing the harmful environmental effects of their actions. Each federal agency is required to make good-faith attempts to quantify the extent of environmental harms posed by its proposed actions or programs, to weigh the costs and benefits of alternative courses of action, and to consider less environmentally harmful alternatives for carrying out its primary mission. NEPA does not prohibit a federal agency from engaging in environmentally damaging activities, provided that it has considered other means of accomplishing its primary goal and has weighed the costs and benefits of each potential alternative.

An agency may avoid preparation of an EIS if it concludes from its EA that its proposed actions would have no significant impact on the environment. Hundreds of lawsuits challenging agency decisions not to prepare an EIS have been brought under NEPA. In some instances where agencies have performed EISs, lawsuits have been brought to challenge their validity and adequacy.

NEPA thus furnishes a mechanism, albeit one of questionable effectiveness, for public oversight and public input into environmentally sensitive government actions. The EIS requirement may serve to heighten official awareness of environmental issues and encourage decisionmakers to account for the environmental implications of agency actions, to consider less environmentally harmful alternatives, and to minimize injury to the environment. In many instances, no alternative exists that will yield the same perceived benefits as the proposed action while minimizing environmental harms. In other cases, environmentally sounder alternatives exist, but they are far more costly and thus less desired by the federal agency that is committing funds to the project.

Most NEPA suits have been initiated not by government authorities, but by citizens and environmental organizations. Although NEPA lacks adequate enforcement mechanisms, it does provide an avenue for public participation in the evaluation of environmental impacts of governmental activities. The *Heckler* opinion illustrates typical issues that arise under NEPA.

FOUNDATION ON ECONOMIC TRENDS V. HECKLER

756 F.2d 143 (1985)

J. Skelly Wright, Circuit Judge:

Almost 14 years ago, soon after passage of the National Environmental Policy Act (NEPA), ... this court faced the challenge of ensuring that the Act's "important legislative purposes, heralded in the halls of Congress, [were] not lost or misdirected in the vast hallways of the federal bureaucracy." *Calvert Cliffs' Coordinating Committee v. USAEC,* 449 F.2d 1109, 1111 (D.C. Cir. 1971). This case poses a no less formidable challenge: to ensure that the bold words and vigorous spirit of NEPA are not similarly lost or misdirected in the brisk frontiers of science.

For this appeal presents an important question at the dawn of the genetic engineering age: what is the appropriate level of environmental review required of the National Institutes of Health (NIH) before it approves the deliberate release of genetically engineered, recombinant-DNA-containing organisms into the open environment? . . .

I. BACKGROUND

This case arises against a backdrop of the National Environmental Policy Act, the emergence of genetic engineering, and federal attempts to regulate genetic engineering.

A. National Environmental Policy Act

On January 1, 1970 the National Environmental Policy Act became law. Recognizing "the profound impact of man's activity on the interrelation of all components of the natural environment," . . . Congress sought to "fulfill the responsibilities of each generation as trustee of the environment for succeeding generations," . . . The major "action-forcing" provision of NEPA is the requirement that "all agencies of the Federal government" prepare a detailed environmental analysis for "major Federal actions significantly affecting the quality of the human environment." . . .

Congress mandated that this detailed statement, long known as an Environmental Impact Statement (EIS), include such considerations as "the environmental impact of the proposed action," "any adverse environmental effects which cannot be avoided should the proposal be implemented," and "alternatives to the proposed action." . . . on Environmental Quality (CEQ), an entity created by NEPA, issued regulations establishing that, . . . the agency should support each finding of "no significant impact" with a "concise public document" called an "environmental assessment" (EA) . . .

The environmental assessment must "[b]riefly provide sufficient evidence and analysis for determining whether to prepare an environmental impact statement or a finding of no significant impact." . . . CEQ regulations apply to all federal agencies. . . .

Two fundamental principles underlie NEPA's requirements: federal agencies have the responsibility to consider the environmental effects of major actions significantly affecting environment, and the public has the right to review that consideration. . . .

NEPA's dual mission is thus to generate federal attention to environmental concerns and to reveal that federal consideration for public scrutiny.

In passing NEPA Congress emphasized its particular concern with the role of new technologies and their effect on the environment. . . . The legislative history reveals an underlying concern with "[a] growing technological power . . . far outstripping man's capacity to understand and ability to control its impact on the environment." . . . One of NEPA's main functions was to bolster this capacity to understand and control the effects of new technology. . . .

B. Genetic Engineering

Genetic engineering is an important development at the very cusp of scientific advances. More than a decade ago scientists discovered a method for transplanting deoxyribonucleic acid (DNA), the principal substance of genes. . . . genetic engineering provides the ability to control these fundamental processes of life and evolution. DNA segments can be recovered and cloned from one organism and inserted into another. The result is known as "recombinant DNA." . . .

Recombinant DNA technology has been limited primarily to small organisms, usually bacteria. This production of new bacteria through altering genetic material has been confined to the laboratory; organisms with recombinant DNA have never been released into the general environment.

Broad claims are made about both the potential benefits and the potential hazards of genetically engineered organisms. Use of recombinant DNA may lead to welcome advances in such areas as food production and disease control. At the same time, however, the environmental consequences of dispersion of genetically engineered organisms are far from clear. . . . "The potential environmental risks associated with the deliberate release of genetically engineered organisms into an ecosystem are best described as 'low probability, high consequence risk': that is, while there is only a small possibility that damage could occur, the damage that could occur is great." *The Environmental Implications of Genetic Engineering*, Report by Subcommittee on Investigations & Oversight to House Committee on Science & Technology, 98th Cong., 2d Sess. 9 (1984) (hereinafter cited as *Genetic Engineering Report*), JA 167.

C. Federal Oversight of Genetic Engineering

Spurred by scientists . . . NIH began efforts to oversee genetic engineering in the mid-1970's. Federal oversight of deliberate release experiments falls into four periods: (1) NIH's 1976 standards, which prohibited deliberate release of organisms containing recombinant DNA; (2) NIH's 1978 revision, which gave the NIH Director power to approve deliberate release experiments; (3) the NIH Director's approval of three such experiments in the early 1980's; and (4) the District Court's injunction prohibiting the University of California experiment and enjoining NIH approval of all other deliberate release experiments.

* * *

In 1974 scientists . . . voluntarily called for a moratorium on certain kinds of experiments until an international meeting could be convened to consider the potential hazards of recombinant DNA molecules. . . . And in February 1975 NIH, the National Science Foundation, and the National Academy of Sciences sponsored an international conference . . . to review the questions posed by the possibility of genetic engineering.

Finally, in the summer of 1976 the NIH Director announced the Guidelines that would govern NIH-supported genetic research experiments. In broad terms, the Guidelines permitted certain laboratory experiments to go forward under carefully specified conditions; certain other types of experiments were flatly prohibited. . . .

Significantly, NIH prepared an EIS to accompany its Guidelines, JA 244—the only EIS NIH has ever completed on the subject of genetic engineering. The EIS did not specifically refer to deliberate release experiments; such experiments were banned. The EIS did, however, note that dispersion of organisms with recombinant DNA molecules loomed as a potential environmental hazard from the permitted experiments: . . .

2.   The 1978 revision: permission to waive the prohibition against deliberate release.   In 1978 the NIH Director undertook an effort to revise the Guidelines . . . Most importantly for this appeal, the 1978 revision allowed the NIH Director authority to grant exceptions to the five absolute prohibitions in the Guidelines—including the prohibition on deliberate release of organisms containing recombinant DNA into the environment. . . .

NIH announced that the standard governing the use of this waiver authority would be the standard generally applicable to the Director's exercise of his duties: "[T]he Director shall weigh each proposed action, . . . to determine that it . . . presents no significant risk to health or the environment." . . . The Director further stated that his "waiver decisions [would] include a careful consideration of the potential environmental impact, and certain decisions may be accompanied by a formal assessment or statement. This must be determined on a case-by-case basis." 43 Fed.Reg. at 33051, JA 442.

On the subject of deliberate release experiments in particular, the Director suggested that clear standards might be necessary to guide his waiver discretion: . . . .

NIH did not prepare an EIS to accompany its 1978 revision. . . .

3.   Approval of deliberate release experiments. The 1978 revision was the last significant revision of NIH's guidelines regarding deliberate release experiments. A 1982 revision was largely semantic, ...

Although the guidelines have not changed, NIH's role has begun to change dramatically. For, with the maturation of genetic engineering technology, NIH has been faced with applications for approval of deliberate release experiments.

The NIH Director, acting on the advice of RAC, has approved three deliberate release experiments at institutions receiving NIH funds for recombinant DNA research. On August 7, 1981 the Director approved a request by Dr. Ronald Davis of Stanford University to field-test corn plants containing recombinant DNA molecules. . . . The goal was to increase the corn's dietary value by improving its ability to store protein. However, the field tests were never conducted because feasibility problems developed. . . .

On April 15, 1983 the Director approved a request by Dr. John Sanford of Cornell University to field-test tomato and tobacco plants with recombinant DNA. . . . The goal was to prove that pollen could serve as a "vector" for insertion of recombinant DNA. Again, however, due to feasibility problems, the experiment never went forward. . . .

On June 1, 1983 the Director gave final approval to the experiment at issue on appeal—the request by Drs. Nickolas Panopoulos and Steven Lindow of the University of California at Berkeley to apply genetically altered bacteria to plots of potatoes, tomatoes, and beans in northern California. 48 Fed.Reg. 24549 (June 1, 1983), JA 522. . . . Because of the cancellation of the previous two experiments, the Panopoulos-Lindow experiment would be the first NIH-approved deliberate release experiment actually to be conducted.

In February 1984 a congressional subcommittee report sharply criticized NIH's method of reviewing deliberate release experiments. The report concluded that "the current regulatory framework does not guarantee that adequate consideration will be given to the potential environmental effects of a deliberate release." *Genetic Engineering Report* at 10, JA 168. In particular, "the RAC's ability to adequately evaluate the environmental hazards posed by deliberate releases is limited by both its expertise and its jurisdiction." *Id.* The subcommittee report recommended a moratorium on deliberate release approvals until an interagency review panel was established to consider the potential environmental effects of each deliberate release experiment. . . .

4.   The injunction. In September 1983 three public interest organizations and two individuals filed suit against the three federal officials ultimately responsible for NIH deliberate release decisions; they later added Regents of the University of California as a defendant. . . . On May 18 the District Court issued an injunction enjoining the University of California experiment and NIH approval of other deliberate release experiments. The District Court found that plaintiffs were likely to succeed in showing that NIH should have completed at least a more complete environmental assessment, and perhaps an EIS, before approving the University of California experiment; it also found them likely to succeed in showing that NIH should have completed an Environmental Impact Statement in connection with both its 1978 policy change and its imminent "program" of deliberate release approvals.

* * *

II. STANDARD OF REVIEW

Two principles guide our analysis of this appeal: the standard for judicial review of an agency decision not to prepare an EIS and the standard for appellate review of a District Court decision to grant an injunction.

A. Review of an Agency Decision Not to Prepare an EIS

That courts must play a cardinal role in the realization of NEPA's mandate is beyond dispute. As the Supreme Court recently emphasized, the critical judicial task is "to ensure that the agency has adequately considered and disclosed the environmental impact of its actions and that its decision is not arbitrary or capricious." *Baltimore Gas & Electric, supra,* 462 U.S. at 97–98, 103 S.Ct. at 2253. . . . Although the "agency commencing federal action has the initial and primary responsibility for ascertaining whether an EIS is required," . . . . the courts must determine that this decision accords with traditional norms of reasoned decisionmaking and that the agency has taken the "hard look" required by NEPA. . . .

B. Review of an Injunction

We review the decision to grant an injunction as an exercise of the District Court's discretion. . . .

III. THE UNIVERSITY OF CALIFORNIA EXPERIMENT

The University Regents raise objections about the District Court's view that the envi-

ronment assessment of the University of California experiment was inadequate. . . . The federal appellants claim not to appeal the part of the injunction that applies to the U.C. experiment, but they continue to insist that the only flaw in NIH's environment assessment is that NIH did not publish the results of its environmental review in a document titled "Environmental Assessment." . . .

A. The Adequacy of the Environmental Review

1. The proposed experiment. On September 17, 1982 Drs. Lindow and Panopoulos, scientists at Berkeley, submitted a request for NIH approval of an experiment that would involve deliberate release of genetically altered organisms in the open environment. . . . Lindow and Panopoulos proposed to apply the genetically altered bacteria to various crops, including potatoes, tomatoes, and beans. By changing the bacteria's genetic composition, Lindow and Panopoulos hoped that the bacteria would change from frost-triggering bacteria to non-frost-triggering bacteria; . . . . The ultimate goal was to protect the crops from frost and thus to extend their growing season. Such non-frost-triggering bacteria occur in nature as products of natural mutation, but Lindow and Panopoulos apparently hoped that the genetically engineered organisms would be more stable than the natural mutants. . . .

2. NIH review. NIH announced the Lindow-Panopoulos request for approval, ... No comments were received. At the RAC meeting on October 25, 1982 RAC members raised questions about the number of sites, the lack of adequate information, and the possible effects on rainfall. . . . The Director decided to postpone approval and suggested further consideration.

Lindow and Panopoulos resubmitted their proposal with some modifications, ... On April 11, 1983, after some discussion, RAC voted to recommend approving the proposal. . . .

The Director then approved the experiment. . . .

3. NEPA compliance. NIH's consideration of the Lindow-Panopoulos experiment falls far short of the NEPA requirements. And, despite the government's apparent belief, the deficiency is not a question of which document contains the environmental analysis. Rather, the deficiency rests in NIH's complete failure to consider the possibility of various environmental effects.

Neither the government nor the University seriously disputes that an environmental assessment is necessary. . . .

The most glaring deficiency in NIH's review . . . is its treatment of the possibility of dispersion of recombinant-DNA-containing organisms. As noted, NIH's only EIS on genetic engineering specifically identified dispersion as one of the major environmental concerns associated with recombinant DNA research. The consequences of dispersion of genetically altered organisms are uncertain. Some observers believe that such dispersion would affect the environment and the climate in harmful ways. *See, e.g., Genetic Engineering Report* at 9, JA 167 . . . .

Thus the problem of dispersion would seem to be one of the major concerns associated with the Lindow-Panopoulos experiment, the first experiment that would actually release genetically engineered organisms in the open environment. Yet in the minutes of the RAC meeting—the only document on appeal that records *any* NIH consideration of the environmental impact of dispersion— . . . is the following statement: according to a RAC evaluator, "Although some movement of bacteria toward sites near treatment locations by insect or aerial transport *is possible*, the numbers of viable cells transported has been shown to be very small; and these cells are subject to biological and physical processes limiting survival." RAC Minutes (April 11, 1983), JA 715 (emphasis added). In this sentence, which was taken almost verbatim from the Lindow-Panopoulos proposal, the RAC evaluator thus conceded the possibility of aerial or insect transport, but merely commented that the number of viable cells would be small, and that they were subject to processes limiting survival. Remarkably, therefore, RAC completely failed to consider the possible environmental impact from dispersion of genetically altered bacteria, however small the number and however subject to procedures limiting survival.

In light of this complete failure to address a major environmental concern, NIH's environmental assessment utterly fails to meet the standard of environmental review necessary before an agency decides not to prepare an EIS. . . . An environmental assessment that fails to address a significant environmental concern can hardly be deemed adequate for a reasoned determination that an EIS is not appropriate. . . .

Appellants also contend that the adequacy of the environmental assessment can be divined from the NIH Director's final approval—and his accompanying statement of "no significant risk," . . . . This contention also reveals a fundamental misunderstanding about the adequacy of an environmental assessment. Simple, conclusory statements of "no impact" are not enough to fulfill an agency's duty under NEPA. . . .

It should be stressed that this inquiry . . . is ultimately relevant to the agency's determination that its proposed federal action will not have a "significant impact" on the environment—and thus no EIS is required. . . . it is notable that NIH never directly addressed the question whether an EIS should be prepared. Such an inquiry is, of course, the ultimate purpose of an environmental assessment. . . .

To reiterate, NIH must first complete a far more adequate environmental assessment of the possible environmental impact of the deliberate release experiment than it has yet undertaken. That assessment must "provide sufficient evidence and analysis for determining whether to prepare an environmental impact statement or a finding of no significant impact." 40 C.F.R. § 1508.9(a)(1). . . . Instead, NIH must attempt to evaluate seriously the risk that emigration of such organisms from the test site will create ecological disruption. Second, until NIH completes such an evaluation the question whether the experiment requires an EIS remains open. The University of California experiment clearly presents the possibility of a problem identified by NIH in its EIS as a potential environmental hazard. This fact weighs heavily in support of the view that an EIS should be completed, unless NIH can demonstrate either that the experiment does not pose the previously identified danger, or that its assessment of the previously identified danger has changed through a process of reasoned decisionmaking. Nor is it sufficient for the agency merely to state that the environmental effects are currently unknown. Indeed, one of the specific criteria for determining whether an EIS is necessary is "[t]he degree to which the possible effects on the human environment are highly uncertain or involve unique or unknown risks." 40 C.F.R § 1508.27(b)(5).

Thus we approve the District Court's determination that, as a matter of law, plaintiffs are likely to prevail in showing that NIH's environmental assessment of the University of California experiment—and its discharge of its statutory duty to consider the propriety of an EIS—was wholly inadequate. . . .

NEPA applies only to final agency action. As the *Public Citizen v. U.S. Trade Representative* opinion illustrates, courts may find that an agency action is not final and thus avoid ruling on the thornier issue of whether an EIS is required.

PUBLIC CITIZEN V. U.S. TRADE REPRESENTATIVE

5 F.3d 549 (D.C. Cir. 1993)

Mikva, Chief Judge:

Appellees Public Citizen, Friends of the Earth, Inc., and the Sierra Club (collectively "Public Citizen") sued the Office of the United States Trade Representative, claiming that an environmental impact statement was required for the North American Free Trade Agreement; ("NAFTA"). The district court granted Public Citizen's motion for summary judgment and ordered that an impact statement be prepared "forthwith." . . . the government contends that the Trace Representative's preparation of NAFTA without an impact statement is not "final agency action" under the Administrative Procedure Act ("APA") and therefore is not reviewable by this court. Because we conclude that NAFTA is not "final agency action" under the APA, we reverse the decision of the district court . . .

I.   BACKGROUND

In 1990, the United states, Mexico, and Canada initiated negotiations on the North American Free Trade Agreement. NAFTA creates a "free trade zone" encompassing the three countries by eliminating or reducing tariffs and "non-tariff" barriers to trade on thousands of items of commerce. After two years of negotiations, the leaders of the three countries signed the agreement on December 17, 1992. NAFTA has not yet been transmitted to Congress. If approved by Congress, NAFTA is scheduled to take effect on January 1, 1994.

Negotiations on behalf of the United States were conducted primarily by the Office of the United States Trade Representative ("OTR"). OTR, located "within the Executive Office of the President," is the United States' chief negotiator for trade matters. OTR "report[s] directly to the President and the Congress and [is] responsible to the President and the Congress for the administration of trade agreements . . ." . . .

Under the Trade Acts and congressional rules, NAFTA is entitled to "fast-track" enactment procedures which provide that Congress must vote on the agreement, without amendment, within ninety legislative days after transmittal by the President. The current version of NAFTA, once submitted, will therefore be identical to the version on which Congress will vote. President Clinton has indicated, however, that he will not submit NAFTA to Congress until negotiations have been completed on several side agreements regarding, among other things, compliance with environmental laws.

II.   DISCUSSION

The National Environmental Policy Act ("NEPA") requires federal agencies to include an EIS "in every recommendation or report on proposals for legislation and other major Federal actions significantly affecting the quality of the human environment. . . ." . . . In drafting NEPA, however, Congress did not create a private right of action. Accordingly, Public Citizen must rest its claim for judicial review on the Administrative Procedure Act. Section 702 of the APA confers an action for injunctive relief on persons "adversely affected or aggrieved by agency action within the meaning of a relevant statute." . . . Section 704, however, allows review only of "*final* agency action." . . . The central question in this appeal then is whether Public Citizen has identified some agency action that is final upon which to base APA review.

In support of its argument that NAFTA does not constitute "final agency action" within the meaning of the APA, the government relies heavily on *Franklin v. Massachusetts,* —U.S. —, 112 S.Ct. 2767, 120 L.Ed.2d 636 (1992). *Franklin* involved a challenge to the method used by the Secretary of Commerce to calculate the 1990 census. . . . After receiving the Secretary's report, the President must transmit to Congress the number of Representatives to which each state is entitled under the method of equal proportions. . . . The Supreme Court held that APA review was unavailable because the final action under the reapportionment statute (transmittal of the apportionment to Congress) was that of the President, and the President is not an agency. . . . The *Franklin* Court found that although the Secretary had completed her decisionmaking process, the action that would directly affect the plaintiffs was the President's calculation and transmittal of the apportionment to Congress, not the Secretary's report to the President. . . .

This logic applies with equal force to NAFTA. Even though the OTR has completed negotiations on NAFTA, the agreement will have no effect on Public Citizen's members unless and until the President submits it to Congress. . . . The Trade Acts involve the President at the final stage of the process by providing for him to submit to Congress the final legal text of the agreement, a draft of the implementing legislation and supporting information. . . . The President is not obligated to submit any agreement to Congress, and until he does there is no final action. If and when the agreement is submitted to Congress, it will be the result of action by the President, action clearly not reviewable under the APA.

The district court attempts to distinguish *Franklin* by noting that . . . NAFTA is no longer a "moving target" because the "final product . . . will not be changed before submission to Congress." . . . The district court goes on to say that NAFTA "shall" be submitted to Congress. . . . This distinction is unpersuasive. NAFTA is just as much a "moving target" as the census report in *Franklin* because in both cases the President has statutory discretion to exercise supervisory power over the agency's action. It is completely within the President's discretion, for example, to renegotiate portions of NAFTA before submitting it to Congress or to refuse to submit the agreement at all. In fact, President Clinton has conditioned the submission of NAFTA on the successful negotiation of side agreements on the environment, labor, and import surges. . . .

Finally, Public Citizen argues that applying *Franklin* in this case would effectively nullify NEPA's EIS requirement because often "some other step must be taken before" otherwise final agency actions will result in environmental harm. . . . In support of this position, it catalogs a number of cases in which courts have reviewed NEPA challenges to agency actions that require the involvement of some other governmental or private entity before becoming final. . . . though we acknowledge the stringency of *Franklin's* "direct effect" requirement, we disagree that it represents the death knell of the legislative EIS. *Franklin* is limited to those cases in which the President has final constitutional or statutory responsibility for the final step necessary for the agency action directly to affect the parties. . . . Similarly, the requirement that the President, and not OTR, initiate trade negotiations and submit trade agreements and their implementing legislation to Congress indicates that Congress deemed the President's involvement essential to the integrity of international trade negotiations. When the President's role is not essential to the integrity of the process, however, APA review of otherwise final agency actions may well be available.

The government advances many other arguments opposing the preparation of an EIS, including weighty constitutional positions on the separation of powers and Public Citizen's lack of standing, as well as the inapplicability of NEPA to agreements executed pursuant to the Trade Acts in general, and NAFTA in particular. It also suggests that the judicial branch should avoid any conflict with the President's power by exercising the "equitable discretion" given it by § 702 of the APA. We need not and do not consider such arguments . . . .

The ultimate destiny of NAFTA has yet to be determined. Recently negotiated side agreements may well change the dimensions of the conflict that Public Citizen sought to have resolved by the courts. More importantly, the po-

litical debate over NAFTA in Congress has yet to play out. Whatever the ultimate result, however, NAFTA's fate now rests in the hands of the political branches. The judiciary has no role to play.

. . . The President's actions are not "agency action" and thus cannot be reviewed under the APA. The district court's grant of summary judgment in favor of Public Citizen is, therefore,

Reversed.

* * *

Many federal courts have exhibited hostility toward NEPA suits. As a result of courts' unwillingness to find NEPA violations, the number of EIS preparations by federal agencies continues to drop:

> During 1990 a total of 85 legal cases were filed against federal departments and agencies on the basis of NEPA, with 11 cases resulting in injunctions. . . . The most common complaint continued to be "No environmental impact statement when one should have been prepared." . . . The second most common complaint, "Inadequate environmental impact statement" . . . . In 1991, the number of . . . [EISs] . . . dropped slightly from 1990. Federal agencies filed 456 EISs, continuing a downward trend over the past decade.[2]

The CEQ's cumulative tabulation of NEPA litigation from 1970 to 1990 indicated a consistent pattern of infrequent success of NEPA suits.[3] In those 20 years, not a single U.S. Supreme Court decision upheld a citizens' suit under NEPA.

A primary reason for the failure of many NEPA suits is that under judicial standards of review, federal agencies have considerable discretion in performing the EIS's required cost-benefit analyses. An agency has a strong incentive to highlight the benefits of a project that will carry out its institutional mission and to downplay the environmental impacts that are not its primary concern. Those conducting cost-benefit analyses are required to quantify, or appraise, the values of things for which there are no satisfactory measures of market value, such as human lives. Comparisons of potential alternatives yield varying mixes of costs and benefits and they necessarily incorporate subjective value judgements. Since cost-benefit analyses can rarely be performed with absolute precision, courts do not apply a high level of scrutiny to them.

In addition to the likely failure of potential NEPA suits, other factors tend to influence government agencies not to find adverse potential environmental impacts that would require an EIS. Since the law vests the initial decision of whether an environmental impact study is required for a particular activity in the very same agency that desires to pursue that activity, there is an inherent incentive to avoid preparing an EIS that would delay and could thwart the agency's agenda. Agencies are also disinclined to expend the time and money necessary for preparing EISs. They thus have a vested interest in reaching a finding of no significant impact (FONSI).

Some commentators argue that NEPA has become a "paper tiger" and that it requires federal agencies only to generate documentation that will give the appearance that they have considered the environmental impacts of their actions. Nevertheless, even if its major effect is to increase transaction costs and impose delays upon federal-agency action, NEPA still generates potentially beneficial side effects. NEPA can serve to increase an agency's burden of promoting an environmentally detrimental project. It can also promote the generation or collection of data, which is indispensable for public oversight. Often such data could not be generated or collected by citizens' groups themselves due to resource limitations or a lack of timely access. To paraphrase one commentator, information in the environmental field is political capital. In giving the public advance notice and information on potentially harmful government actions, NEPA facilitates the application of political pressure or resort to the courts. The prospect of adverse public reaction and its consequent costs, delays, and potential frustrations at later stages tends to deter imprudent agency actions and to increase the negotiating leverage of citizens who are pressing for sounder environmental alternatives.

NEPA's regulatory approach is "patchwork," rather than comprehensive. Congress passed NEPA in 1969 in the face of upcoming elections as a response to growing public concern for the environment that can be traced at least partly to the publication of Rachel Carson's *Silent Spring*. NEPA's legislative history and its general unenforceability reflect Congressional and presidential hesitancy or unwillingness to undertake more than token efforts for environmental protection at the time. Initially, for instance, NEPA granted individuals the inalienable right to a healthful environment—which may have made standing a far less thorny issue for environmental plaintiffs. As legislators and then-President Nixon became concerned about the ramifications of the proposed law, NEPA was watered down to its present form. To a certain extent, NEPA's broad, unenforceable policy proclamations, its applicability to every kind of government endeavor, and its lack of implementing provisions in the final legislation also reflect the nation's inexperience with environmental regulation. The need for bolder legislation soon became apparent, however, and this led to enactment of more substantive statutes. Those statutes are examined in later chapters of this book.

All environmental laws share the ultimate goals of preserving human health and protecting environmental resources, but the subject matter they address and the regulatory mechanisms they employ vary from statute to statute. The following subsections discuss the subject matter approaches of federal environmental laws and regulations.

Regulation of Specific Environmental Media: Air and Water Quality

Two major early environmental statutes, the Clean Water Act (CWA) and the Clean Air Act (CAA), seek to protect the environment by regulating pollution of specific environmental media. These enactments address most kinds of pollution affecting water and air. Each statute sets standards to proscribe or limit activities that pollute or degrade the quality of the particular medium, although the regulatory mechanisms they employ for setting and enforcing the environmental quality standards are quite distinct. In enacting media-specific regulatory laws, Congress faces two fundamental issues:

■ how to establish enforceable standards for banning or limiting pollution and
■ whether standards for limiting polluting emissions should be national in scope or should be set by state and local authorities.

With respect to the first issue, pollution limitations under the CWA and the CAA have historically been set in one of two ways: either by mandating that pollution be reduced to levels achievable by using the best available technology (technology-based limitations) or by enforcing standards that reduce overall pollution to levels that will not harm human health or the environment (health-based standards). The legislative histories of the CWA and the CAA illustrate how Congress has time and again grappled with the issue of whether limitations on pollution should reflect the availability of technologies that make compliance feasible or should force the development of new technologies in order to meet health-based standards.

With respect to the issue of national versus local emissions standards, Congress has struck different balances between federal and state or local control in various amendments to the CWA and the CAA. Today, most media-specific regulatory standards are national in scope, but states have considerable input in determining the mix of controls that will be placed on various polluting entities for achievement of the national standards.

Targeting Specific Kinds of Pollutants: Toxic and Hazardous Substances and Wastes

Several major federal statutes govern the production, use, disposal, and cleanup of toxic and hazardous substances and wastes. These statutes deal with the aftermath of the sharp increases since World War II in the synthesis, use, and disposal of chemical substances. Pollutant-specific statutes examined in depth in later chapters include the Federal Insecticide, Fungicide, and Rodenticide Act (FIFRA); the Toxic Substances Control Act (TSCA); the Resource, Conservation, and Recovery Act (RCRA); and the Comprehensive Environmental Compensation, Recovery, and Liability Act (CERCLA); popularly known as the ''Superfund'' law.

Pollutant-specific legislation can focus on preventing releases of toxic substances or on cleaning up substances after they have been released into the environment. FIFRA, TSCA, and RCRA are examples of legislation that *prospectively* addresses the risks posed by toxic and hazardous substances and wastes and attempts to minimize them. FIFRA deals specifically with pesticides; TSCA, with other chemical substances; and RCRA, with hazardous wastes. CERCLA focuses on *remediating* environmental harms resulting from past activities. Although other statutes, such as RCRA, contain ancillary provisions that mandate environmental remediation, such cleanups are CERCLA's principal focus.

Pollutant-specific statutes that prospectively regulate toxic substances may or may not require formal risk assessment, but they necessarily result in some allocation of risks and regulatory burdens. Where no risk assessment procedures are explicitly mandated, environmental and health risks fall by default upon the public. Some prospective pollutant-specific legislation also distinguishes between newly developed synthetic substances and those in use prior to regulation. This yields statutory designs of varying comprehensiveness and effectiveness.

Pollutant-specific remedial statutes specify how cleanups are to be conducted and how the costs are to be distributed among parties responsible for or suffering from environmental contamination. Parties that caused the contamination, parties that own contaminated property, and the tax-paying public are all potential sources of revenues for performing environmental cleanups. The efficacy of pollutant-specific remedial legislation often depends as much upon who is required to undertake cleanups as upon the kinds of cleanups envisioned by the statute. Although it is seldom the primary intent of remedial statutes such as CERCLA, an incidental effect of them is to deter conduct that causes environmental contamination or degradation in the future.

Focusing on particular chemicals and wastes has regulatory benefits and drawbacks. Under pollutant-specific legislation, the regulatory agency's jurisdiction is typically more clearly demarcated than under other subject-matter approaches. The limited subject matter of a pollutant-specific statute permits regulatory efforts to be centered upon the peculiar properties of that particularly harmful substance or waste. Pollutant-specific regulatory tools, such as licensing, registration, permitting, and risk assessment give EPA access to information necessary for effective regulation. On the other hand, regulatory programs that focus on particular substances or wastes are costly to administer. In addition, they do not necessarily encourage the development of better technologies or give the implementing agency latitude to address the greatest threats to public health and the environment.

Multimedia (Polluter-Specific) Regulation: An Emerging Trend

Environmental scientists and regulators have come to recognize the interrelatedness of the environmental media—air, soil, and water—and now realize that efforts to clean up one part of the environment can lead to environmental problems elsewhere. The cycle of migration of pollutants in the three environmental media is graphically expressed in Figure 3.1.

Without an assessment of the multi-media effects of legislation, unintended consequences can result. For example, a statute that prohibits land disposal of a particular substance may encourage its discharge into water or its incineration, which may lead to water contamination or air pollution. The alternatives can be more detrimental than what is prohibited. The only way to prevent unintended regulatory consequences is to analyze the potential effects of legislation on all environmental media and then to assess the risks from a multimedia perspective.

A difficulty inherent in media- or pollutant-specific regulation is its failure to allocate resources to address the greatest threats first. For example, EPA has been criticized for devoting far too many resources to hazardous substance cleanups, which only marginally reduce risks to human health, while expending too few resources on such problems as indoor air pollution and lead poisoning, which have far greater consequences for larger numbers of people. Media- and pollutant-specific statutes generally mandate that the agency prioritize the risks posed by specific kinds of pollutants, but they give little guidance for prioritizing enforcement with respect to laws addressing other risks. This problem is complicated by disparate funding mechanisms for enforcing the various statutes.

There is a rising awareness that regulators can enforce environmental laws more efficiently by employing a multimedia perspective. However, multimedia enforcement is complicated by the existing structure of regulatory agencies, which have traditionally been subdivided into specialized divisions for enforcing particular statutes. For instance, since most federal environmental statutes are media- or pollutant-specific, EPA has separate offices or divisions for managing hazardous wastes, air quality, and so forth. The need for coordination among these offices and divisions in order to assess the overall effectiveness of environmental enforcement poses administrative challenges and complicates budgeting of the agency's resources. Nonetheless, environmental regulatory agencies are

■ **Figure 3.1**   Exposure Pathways to Humans

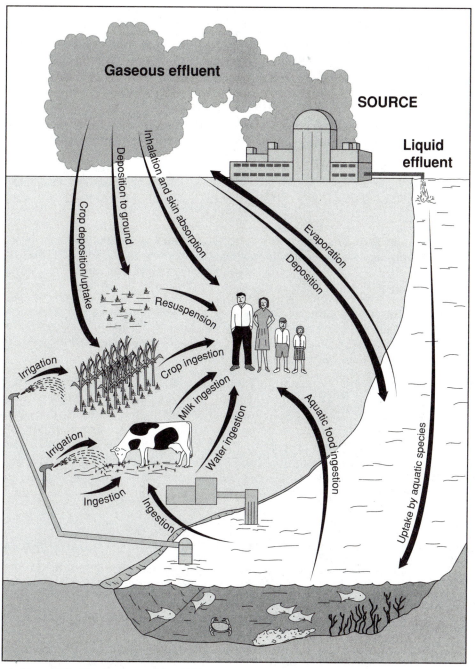

Source: Adapted from EPA, *Risk Assessment,* (May 1992) cover.

beginning to recognize the value of coordinating their efforts across various media, even where their respective statutory obligations are placed in specialized
divisions. Thus, regional EPA offices are now attempting to focus on the entire
environmental impact of, for example, a petrochemical concern or a manufacturing plant. Instead of making several separate inspections under different stat-

utes, EPA can send a multidisciplinary team to the site to perform a multimedia inspection pursuant to all applicable statutes. EPA can then initiate all the necessary administrative or judicial actions at the same time, assigning a group of individuals with varying specialties to the case. By pooling resources and factual information concerning the facility, EPA can eliminate duplication of effort and use available information most efficiently. Most importantly, input from agency personnel with expertise in several disciplines helps to ensure that the agency does not select a remedy that has unintended detrimental impacts. The CEQ has endorsed a multimedia enforcement perspective:

> Since passage of the National Environmental Policy Act of 1969, the trends in environmental law enforcement have been toward more criminal enforcement, greater self-reporting within the regulated community, and increased overall federal enforcement activity. In 1991 these trends, which continued undiminished, were supplemented by the emerging trends of market incentives and multimedia enforcement. . . .
>
> * * *
>
> Historically most environmental enforcement has been media-specific, focusing on air *or* land *or* water in specific locations. However, in 1991 the federal government continued a move toward multimedia initiatives linking enforcement actions under several statutes to address violations adversely affecting more than one environmental medium. For example, in July 1991 [the Department of Justice] DOJ and the Environmental Protection Agency (EPA) joined forces to file 36 enforcement actions against major sources of lead emissions under six environmental statutes, including the Clean Air Act, the Clean Water Act, the Resource Conservation and Recovery Act (RCRA), and the Comprehensive Environmental Response, Compensation, and Liability Act (CERCLA, or Superfund).[4]

In addition to instituting multimedia enforcement techniques, EPA has begun to develop multimedia regulations. So-called cluster rules address the quality of more than one environmental medium and implement more than one regulatory statute, the common tie being their applicability to a particular industry category. For instance, EPA proposed a cluster rule for the paper industry in late 1993 that implements provisions of the CWA and CAA for reducing discharges of dioxin and other pollutants. Besides the potential environmental benefits, this kind of multimedia regulation is seen as less burdensome by the affected industries and may lead to greater compliance.

3.2   Participants in the Making of Environmental Law

Enactment of legislation is the beginning, not the end, of the process by which environmental laws evolve. Once legislation has been enacted, administrative agencies issue implementing regulations, interpretive rules, and policy statements, and then courts interpret the law and related regulations and rule on their validity. Public-interest and industry groups lobby legislators, comment on the proposed regulations, and mount judicial challenges to the law and regulations. All of these entities—federal and state agencies, courts, public-interest groups, and industry lobbyists—contribute to the development and evolution of federal environmental laws.

The Structure and Role of the Environmental Protection Agency

The Environmental Protection Agency was created as a federal agency by President Nixon during a 1970 governmental reorganization. As an office within the executive branch, EPA is charged with administering federal environmental statutes. Although it is an independent agency, its Administrator is appointed by and serves at the will of the President and can be removed at any time. In 1993, the Clinton administration proposed that the EPA Administrator be elevated to cabinet-level status. Legislation to do so has stalled and may not be passed.

Congress may, by statute, directly delegate authority to the EPA Administrator and vest EPA with responsibility for administering particular laws. This ensures that EPA, and not another federal agency, will govern the administration of the statute. Alternatively, Congress may delegate authority for enforcing an environmental law to the President, who in turn may delegate that authority to the EPA or to another administrative agency within the executive branch.

EPA is organized into one national headquarters office (HQ), based in the Washington, D.C. area, and ten regional offices. At headquarters, Assistant Administrators supervise implementation and administration of environmental statutes and perform broad administrative and policy functions affecting many agency programs. Various HQ offices develop national policy, propose and promulgate administrative rules and regulations for implementing environmental legislation, and issue interpretive and policy directives and guidance to the regional offices. Each regional office is headed by a Regional Administrator. Regional offices monitor compliance with and enforce environmental laws and regulations and approve and oversee federally mandated state programs and permits. Assistant and Regional Administrators are political appointees.

Due to its multifarious responsibilities, EPA can be viewed as a microcosm of the federal system of government. As described in Chapter 2 and illustrated in Figure 3.2, EPA performs policy-making, executive, and adjudicative functions similar to those vested in the three branches of the federal government.

■ **Figure 3.2**   EPA Functions

Regulation	Adjudication	Enforcement
Regulation	Informal dispute resolution	File administrative complaints
Rule-making		or
Statutory interpretation	Administrative hearings	Referral to DOJ for judicial action
Policy-making	Appeals to the Administrator	

The Role of the Federal Courts

Federal courts play a significant role in the evolution and implementation of environmental laws and regulations. The role of the federal courts is twofold. First, courts decide which parties are entitled to judicial review of environmental laws and agency decisions under doctrines of standing to sue, exhaustion of administrative remedies, and other legal principles (see Chapter 2). Second, federal courts interpret environmental laws to determine if EPA has administered the statutes according to Congressional intent and within the parameters of the authority granted by Congress. In interpreting environmental statutes, some of which are vague or ambiguous, federal courts must supply meaning to unclear provisions or fill in gaps in the legislative scheme. This filling in of gaps and interpreting of ambiguities affects the very substance of environmental law.

Other Participants in the Regulatory Process

The constellation of environmental statutes includes laws not administered by the EPA. Other federal, state, and local agencies also have responsibilities for administering of environmental laws. EPA's statutory authority sometimes overlaps that of another federal, state, or local agency. These jurisdictional complications affect EPA's ability to enforce the laws entrusted to its oversight. As Madonna and Breslin have stated:

> Enforcement of environmental laws in the United States is accomplished through the use of a complex maze of civil, criminal, and administrative remedies lodged within numerous divisions, departments and elements of [*author's addition: federal,*] state, county, and local governments. As a consequence of the failure to coordinate . . . enforcement efforts, multiple remedies have been unartfully utilized in numerous jurisdictions, resulting in an ineffective "system" of environmental enforcement.[5]

Other participants in the federal environmental regulatory process include states, which are authorized to administer federal statutes; other federal agencies, such as the Office of Management and Budget (OMB) and the Department of Justice (DOJ); citizens' groups; and even regulated industries. These entities can sometimes aid and other times hinder EPA's achievement of its regulatory goals.

The States

Under several federal environmental statutes, states are authorized to promulgate and enforce regulations to operate in lieu of a federal program within state boundaries. To obtain authorization, a state must demonstrate to the satisfaction of EPA that its own regulations are at least as stringent as the parallel federal regulations. EPA still has responsibility for overseeing state programs and can step in and take enforcement action if a state fails to do so. It is generally in EPA's interest to approve states' requests for authorization; the ability of states to enforce laws for which EPA is responsible frees EPA's resources for other tasks. The authorization process is generally an arduous one, however; states rarely promulgate regulations that match federal ones exactly, and it is often difficult to determine if a state's regulations are less stringent or different in scope.

Other Federal Agencies

Other federal agencies having regulatory functions under federal environmental laws EPA administers include the Office of Management and Budget (OMB), the Department of Justice (DOJ), the Department of the Interior (DOI), the Department of Energy (DOE), and others. OMB must approve proposed environmental regulations before they can be promulgated in order to ensure compliance with the Paperwork Reduction Act, and various executive orders. In some cases, OMB has withheld approval for so long that EPA has been unable to meet its statutory deadlines. During the Bush administration, for example, OMB allegedly delayed action on regulations with which the White House did not agree for political reasons. This was the case with implementing regulations EPA was required to promulgate pursuant to the 1990 Clean Air Act Amendments.

The Justice Department is an important participant in the enforcement of environmental laws and regulations. EPA cannot itself litigate in judicial forums; it must refer judicial cases to DOJ for filing. DOJ essentially acts as EPA's legal counsel in such matters and can provide additional resources for litigation of environmental cases. Sometimes, however, DOJ's institutional priorities differ from EPA's. DOJ serves as counsel for several federal agencies whose goals and objectives may not be shared by EPA. DOJ has its own resource limitations and it must set priorities according to the demands of its docket. It may not be as willing as EPA to stake considerable resources on a lawsuit involving novel legal issues and it may be more willing than EPA to settle cases where litigative risk is higher. In these instances, EPA's objectives may be subsumed by its reliance on DOJ to litigate its cases. Some of these issues are examined in Chapters 6, 7, and 10.

EPA must also work with the Department of the Interior, which has primary responsibility for managing federal lands and resources, in which many environmental issues are implicated. Under the CERCLA statute, for example, the DOI has primary responsibility for recovery of damages for injury to natural resources, and EPA has the responsibility to recover costs expended for environmental cleanups. The two functions are closely connected, and DOI and EPA must work together to ensure that cleanup actions chosen by EPA also protect and preserve publicly owned natural resources.

Many of the Department of Energy's nuclear programs have a significant impact on the environment. DOE's oversight of federal nuclear programs, for example, sometimes conflicts with EPA's enforcement of environmental laws. At federal nuclear-weapons facilities, DOE and EPA have clashed over their respective jurisdictions to address certain releases of hazardous and nuclear substances. This conflict most often arises when EPA undertakes enforcement actions or cleanups at sites contaminated by both hazardous substances or wastes and nuclear wastes. The overlapping jurisdictions of DOE and EPA are discussed in Chapters 6, 7, and 10.

Citizens' Groups and Regulated Industries

Citizens' groups play a significant public oversight role in the environmental regulatory and enforcement process. Environmental public interest groups such as the Natural Resources Defense Council, the Sierra Club, and Ralph Nader's Public Interest Research Groups (PIRGs) monitor regulatory and enforcement activities, keep abreast of proposed EPA regulations, and bring citizens' suits to enforce environmental laws against polluters and EPA itself. These groups, whose members number in the millions, have the expertise and resources to accomplish what the average citizen cannot: to gather the most current information on EPA's activities and to challenge the agency when it fails to comply with its statutory obligations. Many environmental public interest groups have become mainstream players in the regulatory process; EPA seeks their advice when it promulgates regulations and considers implementation of new policies. Environmental public interest groups now participate in regulatory negotiations (sometimes called *reg-negs*), a process by which EPA actually negotiates the substance of new regulations with interested parties. Industry groups also participate in reg-negs and they regularly comment on proposed regulations affecting the industries which they represent. By considering the input of interested parties early in the process of promulgating new regulations, EPA can sometimes avoid litigation challenging the validity of its regulatory actions.

3.3 Factors in Creation and Enforcement of Environmental Laws

In addition to defining the subject matter of environmental legislation and allocating responsibility for its administration, Congress must also fashion, from among many alternatives, regulatory mechanisms for achieving its goals. It must decide which risks to health and the environment to regulate, how to allocate regulatory burdens, and what incentives and deterrents to use. Institutional factors such as political feasibility and implementation costs also are relevant considerations. The following excerpt explains three major regulatory approaches to environmental protection and compares their benefits and drawbacks.

The common law enforcement problem with respect to pollution is, in part anyway, the same as with respect to consumer fraud: the individual injury may be too slight to justify the expense of litigation to the victim. Again, improvements in the common law machinery are possible, but again, the emphasis has been placed on public regulation instead.

There are three approaches in the public regulation of pollution. The first is for the legislature or an administrative agency to prescribe the specific measures that the polluter must take to avoid the sanctions of the law (or, what is the same thing, to entitle him to a subsidy). For example, a municipality might be required to install a certain kind of sewage treatment plant, a steel mill to build its smokestacks four feet higher, automobile manufacturers to install a particular type of emission control device. Specification of the particular method of pollution control discourages the search for the most efficient method. In the deliberations before the legislature or agency leading to the formulation of the standard, the affected industry has an incentive to propose the cheapest pollution-control method, regardless of its efficacy, and to deny the existence of any more costly devices (even if they are more efficient because of the amount of pollution eliminated). Once the specified measure is adopted, the industry has no incentive to develop better devices unless they also happen to be cheaper. Worse, the members of the industry have an incentive to collude to withhold from the legislature or agency information concerning the technical and economic feasibility of pollution control and even, as alleged in recent antitrust actions against the automobile manufacturers, to conspire to delay the development of pollution control technology.

A second approach is to establish the level of pollution emissions deemed tolerable, to compel the polluters, under penalty of injunction or fine, not to exceed that level, but to leave the choice of method to the industry. This is a better approach than the first, but it is not so simple or efficient as it seems. When enforcement is attempted, the industry will argue that the cost of compliance is prohibitive—meaning disproportionate to the benefits from reduced pollution. Such an argument cannot be ignored unless society wants to reduce pollution below efficient levels. It then becomes necessary to weigh the benefits of reduced pollution against the cost of reduction—an analysis similar to that in a common law nuisance case. And the dangers of collusion mentioned above remain under this approach.

The third approach, not yet employed in this country but a great favorite of economists, is to tax pollution. The tax rate for each pollutant would be set equal to the estimated costs imposed by the pollutant. A firm subject to a pollution tax would compare its tax costs with the costs of reducing the tax by installing pollution control equipment, reducing its output, or otherwise changing its operations to reduce pollution. If a net tax saving would be possible through one of these measures, it would adopt it; otherwise it would pay the tax and continue to pollute.

This approach is actually quite similar to the imposition of strict liability in tort. The tax corresponds to the damages (costs) of the victims of pollution. The polluters are required to pay those costs (though, under the tax approach, not to the victims) whether or not there are methods of pollution control that would avert them at less cost. This gives polluters an incentive to search for and to adopt cost-justified pollution preventives, but not to adopt any methods of pollution control that cost more than the value they create by reducing pollution.

One problem with this approach is the difficulty of quantifying the costs of pollution—a necessary step in fixing the tax rate. But this is a problem common to all methods of pollution control, so it is not an objection to the tax approach as compared with others. A second problem is that the approach makes no provision for those situations, which may be quite common, where the cheapest pollution avoider is the victim (by installing air conditioning, living farther from the factory, etc.). The polluter will spend on pollution control an amount equal to the estimated tax saving even though victims could have reduced pollution costs by the same amount at lower cost. Third, if we assume that much, if not most, pollution is and will remain cost justified—that it would be prohibitively costly to have absolutely clear air and clean water—then the major effect of the tax will not be to reduce pollution, but to increase the tax bills of polluting enterprises. The tax is in the nature of an excise tax, since it is roughly proportional to output. Excise taxes are regressive. To assure the overall proportionality or progressivity of the tax system, the imposition of comprehensive pollution taxes would require compensating changes elsewhere in the tax system. These changes might not be made; or [they] might be made at great cost. Fourth, the tax approach eliminates private enforcement of pollution standards.[6]

Interrelatedness of Means and Ends

A close connection exists between the means used in environmental legislation and the ends that are achieved. For instance, a statute that mandates reductions in emissions based on the use of particular control technologies will tend to deter the development of more effective pollution-control technologies. If pollution reductions using current technologies are sufficient to protect health and the environment at projected rates of production, then the means are appropriate for achieving the desired goal. If on the other hand, a fundamental aim of the statute is to achieve progressively greater reductions in emissions levels, the means may not be suitable. Similarly, a statute that requires a permit for certain activities will tend to limit the number of companies operating in the field and it may drive out smaller, more innovative companies. If the goal of the legislation is to discourage or limit activities not deemed to be essential or socially valuable, the law will have the desired effect. But if the goal is to encourage the use of more environmentally sound technologies, permit requirements may have the undesired effect of reducing the healthy competition among firms that spurs development of new technologies.

These are but two instances in which the means used actually shape the ends that are achieved. In order to draft legislation that effectuates the desired goals, legislators must anticipate all potential short- and long-term effects of the regulatory means that may be used.

Legislative Practicalities

Before major federal legislation is enacted, a large variety of industry lobbyists, public interest groups, and state and local government representatives descend upon the Capitol. Lawmakers concerned with the views of these constituencies—and with their political support—are open to the views and influence of such lobbying and they typically try to accommodate as many views as possible. The truism that politics is the art of the possible is particularly apt for the politics of environmental regulation, which has involved a great deal of "punting" to the EPA. In seeking to avoid difficult political choices and controversies, Congress has often simply enunciated vague standards and left to EPA the task of devising more precise and exacting regulations. Some proponents and opponents of environmental legislation have seemed to approve of this tactic of foregoing clarity, since it offers them the hope of "winning the day" when the law is later interpreted in an administrative or judicial forum.

In contemplating proposed legislation, lawmakers attempt to anticipate not only its chances of enactment, but also what changes and amendments are likely to be inserted during debate and conference. In order to accommodate different interests, legislators often pass laws that contain strong declarations of goals but weak substantive requirements or enforcement mechanisms. One strategy for satisfying competing interests is the inclusion of statutory exemptions. Once legislation is passed on a particular subject, Congress is not likely to "revisit" it for some time, even in the face of substantial dissatisfaction. In most cases, the political climate prevailing at the time an environmental statute is enacted has a more lasting influence on that law than the political reaction to it.

The selection of enforcement mechanisms also involves an appraisal of institutional practicalities. In order to avoid criticism of government spending, legislators often fail to appropriate the funds necessary for administering and enforcing their mandate. This can result in the tasks envisioned by the legislation being deferred indefinitely, and the blame for failing to act on pressing issues being shifted to administrative agencies.

Administrative Costs

The costs of administering and enforcing a particular regulatory model—in itself and in relation to the benefits it attains—determine the success or failure of many regulatory schemes. No matter how great a law's potential benefits, the costs of administering it must not be so great that the implementing agency cannot carry out the necessary oversight and enforcement. If a regulatory scheme's perceived costs exceed its perceived benefits, regulators can expect to be criticized for wasting taxpayer dollars on petty initiatives.

The incentives a statute provides for agencies to take timely action also influence a statute's effectiveness. If a statute leaves the agency little discretion and specifies a means of compelling agency action (for instance, by authorizing citizens' suits), agency personnel are more likely to pursue statutory mandates energetically—if only to avoid the expense of defending against citizens' suits. It is, however, very difficult for agencies to allocate resources most effectively if their discretion has been statutorily curtailed. Statutes that permit an agency to recoup its costs or to collect fines and penalties from the regulated community for the agency's own coffers generally promote vigorous agency enforcement activities. Such regulatory schemes can, however, foster conflicts of interest, in that agency personnel may be subtly pressured to pursue recovery of funds, rather than to promote environmental goals.

Statutory incentives for the regulated community to comply with environmental standards can also lower administrative burdens, but they may be costly in other ways. Incentives such as tax credits and research grants for developing and implementing better environmental practices and technologies may be less costly for the agency to administer than assessments of penalties, but they require the budgeting of additional funds or the foregoing of potential tax revenues. These examples illustrate that most regulatory devices have advantages and disadvantages which lawmakers must consider in relation to their legislative goals in order to design optimum models of regulation.

Risk Assessment

Every form of governmental regulation involves some form of risk assessment, whether implicit or explicit. For instance, a prohibition on particular activities implies the legislative judgment that the risks those activities pose are greater than the benefits they achieve. Conversely, legislative failure to regulate certain activities indicates the judgment that their benefits are greater than their risks. Whether or not a risk assessment is performed consciously is largely irrelevant; the presence or absence of formal risk assessment procedures nonetheless operates to encourage or discourage certain behaviors and to generate certain levels of risk.

The base formula for assessing risk is the magnitude, or severity, of the harm magnified by its probability. As described by EPA, risk assessment consists of:

> the identification of potential adverse effects to humans or ecosystems resulting from exposure to environmental hazards. The risk involved (probable injury, disease, functional deficits, or death) may be expressed in quantitative terms or in qualitative terms. The process for human health risk assessment often involves the following steps: 1) hazard identification . . . 2) dose-response assessment—determination of the relationship between the level of exposure and the probability of occurrence of adverse effects 3) exposure assessment . . . [and] 4) risk characterization—description of the nature and often the magnitude of risk, including the accompanying uncertainty. . . .
>
> The fact that exposure to many potential hazards can occur simultaneously and in varying degree dictates that the risk assessment process is complex. . . . Observed facts, estimations, and extrapolations are all used to establish estimates and their uncertainties to support planning and decision making.
>
> Risk assessment is frequently used in developing regulations to protect the public . . . . Because there are general gaps in risk assessment data sets, efforts to compare and evaluate environmental risk will always rely on professional judgment.[7]

Environmental statutes establish risk-assessment procedures in one of three ways.

1. Some statutes obligate EPA to determine and appraise the risks. An example is the Clean Air Act, which directs EPA to set national air-quality standards based upon the health and environmental effects of certain pollutants.

2. Some statutes direct the regulated community to assess the risks connected with its enterprises. For instance, FIFRA requires pesticide manufacturers and distributors to demonstrate that the effects of their products do not exceed a certain legally established threshold of risk.

3. Some statutes incorporate a legislative determination of risk. As an example, legislation that bans or phases out the use of chlorofluorocarbons is presumably based upon a determination that the risks they pose are unacceptable.

The absence of legislative controls is also evidence of an assessment that the risks posed by unregulated activities are politically acceptable.

Formal risk assessment is a tool or method for identifying and measuring potential harms; it does not, in itself, alleviate harm or yield a solution. Following assessment of the risks implicated by alternative courses of action, decisions must be made as to what level of risk is acceptable and in what way risks should be distributed among various entities. This process, sometimes called *risk manage-*

ment, is value-charged. Nor can risk assessments always proceed in purely objective fashion. Risk assessments are often made precisely because there exists incomplete knowledge of potential harms and costs. As the CEQ has noted:

> Despite the work of scientists in and out of government, current environmental indicators are not as comprehensive and meaningful as needed. They tend to be indirect measures, such as discharge quantities [of pollutants] . . . rather than more direct measures of ecological or human impacts. Ongoing research will improve the usefulness of environmental indicators. . . .[8]

Whenever unknown or unquantifiable variables exist—and they exist at virtually every stage of the environmental-risk-assessment process—the people carrying out a risk assessment must decide how conservative their estimates of potential harms should be. The perspectives of those performing the risk assessment and those for whom the risk assessments are being performed, inevitably color the risk assessment process. It is not surprising, therefore, that industry assessments of environmental risks—particularly those that would be costly to mitigate—are less likely to conclude that the potential risks are as numerous, harmful, or probable as are assessments made by public interest groups advocating greater environmental protection.

Cost–Benefit Analyses

Since the early eighties, the use of formal cost-benefit analysis in federal environmental regulation has been actively promoted by some and harshly criticized by others. Detractors are not so much opposed to the notion of regulatory cost-benefit analysis itself as to the manner in which the analyses are commonly performed and their underlying assumptions. The uses and limits of economic analyses in environmental regulation are discussed in this excerpt from CEQ's 1991 Report.

> Environmental economics is an integrative tool—a science that seeks the optimal balance of costs and benefits of policies that affect the environment. Economists generally approach environmental issues by developing least-cost, market-based approaches to achieve a target level of environmental quality. . . . The application of environmental economics is handicapped, however, by incomplete information about causes and effects of environmental conditions. Economists often face difficulties in measuring environmental changes, natural resource values, and the well-being of society. Even so, the use of environmental economics to bring harmony among various goals has continued to grow in recent years.

> CONDITIONS AND TRENDS

> In the United States and in the increasingly intertwined global economy, large flows of income are associated with the environment. Benefits and costs are spread throughout the economy. For example, industries which earn profits directly from natural resources, such as agriculture, forestry, fisheries, and minerals, account for close to $200 billion in the $5.7 trillion U.S. economy. These direct, quantifiable links between the environment and the economy are augmented by indirect effects, such as the potential loss of crop productivity resulting from air pollution, the ripple effect of regulatory costs, and the way that environmental issues influence consumer decisions.

> . . . The majority of pollution control expenditures are made by the private sector, with the largest expenditures in the chemical, petroleum, primary metals, food, and paper industries. . . .

> The federal government itself spends billions of dollars on resource and environmental management. . . .

The federal government also earns revenues from environmental and natural resources management. In 1991 the government collected over $8.4 billion in revenues from activities such as the following:

- Leasing and extraction of oil, natural gas, timber, grazing, and water resources on federal lands;
- Taxes on chlorofluorocarbons;
- Penalties from oil spill and Superfund prosecutions.

Government receipts more distantly related to federal environmental purposes or natural resources management run ito the tens of billions of dollars from sources such as gasoline, diesel, and cigarette taxes. . . .[9]

Over the years, federal environmental regulation has been criticized as being inefficient. Critics often claim that the expenditures industries must make for pollution control under environmental laws outweigh the benefits achieved. Quantified cost-benefit analyses proceed from the assumption that costs and benefits can be quantified with reasonable precision and in a manner that is satisfactory to most people. Experience often belies this assumption, however, in part because of the difficulties of accurately quantifying environmental and health risks.

The largest difficulty in conducting cost-benefit analyses of environmental regulations is that of quantifying the benefits of regulation. Furthermore, the entire detrimental environmental impact of the activity to be regulated is seldom known, making any cost-benefit comparison highly speculative. Even if all the dangers are known, the costs of many kinds of environmental harm, such as human deaths and the extinction of species, are impossible to quantify in any objective manner.

Perhaps most importantly, the market system does not distribute environmental costs among the individuals who benefit from polluting activities. Aside from the problems of quantification, environmental harms often flow to different segments of the population than do the associated economic benefits. Cost-benefit comparisons normally consider the overall costs and benefits to the society at large and not to specified groups or individuals. Thus the use of cost-benefit analyses to determine whether to institute regulations for protecting human health often raise questions of fairness and equity. Obviously, those who are exposed to health and environmental risks so that others derive economic gain will take a jaundiced view of cost-benefit analyses which criticize regulations as being overprotective.

Moreover, quantifying the costs and benefits related to various forms of regulation may entail so much time and expense that the knowledge gained does not justify the effort. A question always exists as to the most appropriate way to distribute the costs of conducting cost-benefit analyses, which are an integral part of many regulatory processes.

As a result of then-President Reagan's Executive Order requiring the use of cost-benefit methods by federal agencies, EPA incorporates cost-benefit analyses in its regulatory programs to decide, at least to a certain extent, how to allocate resources and assign regulatory priorities. EPA's use of cost-benefit methods has led to charges that it has adopted a different set of regulatory standards and priorities than those Congress prescribed by statute.

Incentives and Deterrents

Penalties for violating environmental laws must be large enough to induce the regulated community to comply with the law. Though this principle would appear to be self-evident, many regulatory programs have failed to take economic incentives into account. Under former versions of the Clean Air Act, for instance, the maximum statutory penalty for businesses violating applicable emissions standards was often lower than their cost of complying with the act by installing smokestack-scrubbing equipment. EPA recognized some time ago that some penalties it negotiated in settling administrative actions under various statutes were lower than the economic savings the violators had derived by avoiding or delaying compliance with the law. These settlements essentially rewarded environmental violations. As a consequence, EPA's later policies have contained specific guidelines that, under most circumstances, mandate the agency to assess penalties higher than the violator's estimated economic benefit of avoiding or delaying compliance.

Penalties must also discourage would-be violators from taking the chance that their violations will go undetected. Given the government's limited resources, the odds of uncovering certain types of violations are fairly slim. Beyond that, regulatory agencies must have sufficient resources to enforce deterrents and withstand efforts by well-financed recalcitrant violators to wear down the agency through costly, protracted legal proceedings.

Environmental Equity

The disproportionate environmental burdens borne by some segments of society—notably the poor and racial and ethnic minorities—under federal environmental laws has not been effectively addressed by environmental movements and reforms until very recently. Disproportionate environmental treatment acutely affects the health and lives of minorities and the poor. The executive director of the Natural Resources Defense Council, one of the largest and most influential environmental public-interest groups, outlined the problems and sources of environmental inequity and the failure to extend environmental protection to all persons equally in the United States.

> The statistics are plentiful and they are frightening.
> Three out of four toxic waste dumps are sited in predominantly African American or Latino communities. Two million tons of radioactive uranium tailings have been dumped on Native Americans. Three hundred thousand Latino farm laborers suffer from pesticide-related illnesses. . . .
> Statistics like these reflect a nationwide pattern of disproportionate environmental impact on people of color and the poor. This pattern stems from a profound flaw in the structure of the U.S. economy: Polluters do not absorb the costs of the environmental degradation they create, and society as a whole does not confront the problems and solve them. Instead, the problems are displaced. . . . [I]t is far easier for state governments to disregard the lead poisoning of poor children than to test and treat them as federal law requires. What this means is that we are building our economy on the backs of people of color and the poor.
> . . . The fact of disproportionate impact demands a disproportionate effort. Federal and state governments must direct a disproportionate share of clean-up funds and other environmental funding to these communities. . . .
> . . . We [the environmental organizations] have been criticized by environmental justice advocates, and there is much to criticize . . . . The history is well-documented: The mainstream environmental movement grew out of a white, middle-class effort to preserve the world's natural wonders. . . .
> The [mainstream environmental] movement began with wilderness conservation, and there is no question that, in its early life, its work and vision only rarely

encompassed the protection of human beings. But . . . this is a movement that has matured far beyond its origins. . . . [F]or mainstream environmentalists today the two critical issues—environmental violation of the Earth and environmental violation of its human inhabitants—are inextricably linked. . . .[10]

The lack of environmental justice and equity—particularly with respect to the storage, use, disposition, and location of toxic materials and dump sites—gave rise to the "environmental equity" movement, which seeks to redress the disparate impacts of environmental management upon different population groups. The environmental equity movement aims to develop a more just system of distributing environmental benefit and burden and it has gained increasing acceptance and support in civic, professional, and political circles. While the environmental equity ideal has gained a measure of public acceptance, current environmental laws usually do not provide the means for its achievement. The enduring challenge is to devise legal means that will ensure that certain segments of society are not inequitably burdened by the effects of environmental degradation.

3.4   Overview of Selected Regulatory Mechanisms

Federal environmental statutes incorporate a wide variety of regulatory mechanisms intended to influence behavior and to achieve their specific goals. Most federal statutes utilize a combination of mechanisms, some of which are more effective for particular purposes than others. Comparisons of the scope of regulation and the regulatory mechanisms employed by various environmental statutes can yield useful information about the effectiveness of particular regulatory mechanisms in differing circumstances. The task of developing optimum regulatory schemes is common to all government efforts, but it is particularly challenging in environmental regulation. In this field, legislators must cope with a myriad of political, social, and economic factors in designing regulatory schemes which influence the behavior of many public and private entities in a wide variety of circumstances.

Given the enormity of the challenge, it is not surprising that many schemes of environmental regulation have not achieved their stated goals. Federal environmental law contains many examples of regulatory mechanisms that have produced wholly unintended and destructive environmental consequences. When a regulation fails to achieve its intended goals, it is usually because of one or more of these reasons:

- Inadequate resources have been devoted to implementing or enforcing it.
- The mechanism is poorly tailored to the prevailing economic, social, or political conditions.
- Inappropriate considerations have influenced critical policy choices and assessments.

Environmental law is a relatively new field, and the U.S. experience since 1970 may be instructive. Most current statutes are the result of trial-and-error ground-breaking legislation. It is apparent that Congress has sometimes failed to anticipate the effects of its legislation and has not adequately examined the results of prior legislation when undertaking new legislative ventures.

Comparing the relative merits and disadvantages of various regulatory mechanisms is essential to improve the scope and effectiveness of environmental law. Before considering the major Federal environmental statutes in depth in the following chapters, it will be useful to examine the regulatory mechanisms they employ. Virtually none of the major federal environmental statutes employs a single regulatory model. Practically every statute employs a mix of regulatory mechanisms. The basic environmental regulatory mechanisms are explained in the following subsections, and the federal statutes most closely associated with them are identified.

Regulation through Notice, Licensing, and Permitting

Mechanisms such as permits, registration, licensing, and notification concerning particular activities or substances provide regulatory agencies with three important tools:

- Information concerning the identified environmental hazards,
- A framework for assessing the risks and comparing the costs and benefits posed by these hazards, and
- Means of enforcing restrictions on these hazards.

Permits, registrations, and notification provisions operate *prospectively;* that is, they are attempts to *prevent* environmental harms arising from potentially hazardous activities or from the creation, use, and disposal of potentially harmful substances. These kinds of regulatory mechanisms are employed in:

Federal Insecticide, Fungicide, and Rodenticide Act (FIFRA)
Toxic Substances Control Act (TSCA)
Resource Conservation and Recovery Act (RCRA)
Clean Water Act (CWA)
Clean Air Act (CAA)

Technology-Forcing and Source-Reduction Mechanisms

A common regulatory practice for achieving improvements in the quality of environmental media such as air and water is to limit overall polluting emissions. The regulatory scheme may, for example, impose limitations on emissions at a level determined not to harm public and environmental health or it may mandate emissions reductions as a specific percentage of the current rate. Consistent enforcement of such regulatory schemes will tend to force the development of better "end-of-the-pipe," technological controls on the pollutants being emitted or the reduction of emissions at their source through the use of different raw materials, a reconfiguration of production processes, or changes in consumption patterns. Technology mechanisms and source reduction do not result, however, from regulatory schemes that mandate the use of currently available technologies or minimum technological requirements based upon the currently available technologies.

Examples of technology-forcing regulation are found in Clean Air Act provisions for limiting certain polluting emissions to levels at or below those that are protective of humans, plants, and animals.

Technology-Driven Regulation

Regulatory schemes that set permissible levels of polluting emissions at rates achievable with currently available technology are described as "technology-driven." A technology-driven regulation may specify the use of a particular existing technology or its requirements may be based upon whatever reductions are possible using currently available technology. Although this kind of regulation provides greater specificity in the articulation of compliance requirements, it provides little incentive for the development of more effective pollution-control technologies.

The most salient example of technology-driven regulation is the CWA's National Pollution Discharge Elimination System (NPDES).

Cost Distribution Mechanisms

Virtually all environmental statutes distribute the costs of environmental protection implicitly or explicitly. In some statutes, however, the means of distributing the costs is a principal object of the legislation, rather than a by-product of other regulatory mechanisms. This is particularly true of the Comprehensive Environmental Response, Liability, and Compensation Act (CERCLA), which is based on the "polluter pays" principle. CERCLA's regulatory scheme is designed not only to provide mechanisms for cleaning up hazardous substance sites, but also to distribute liability for the cleanups among certain classes of parties.

Direct Financial Inducements: Taxes, Credits, and "Marketplace" Approaches

Most environmental statutes provide for some financial deterrents to environmentally harmful behavior. For instance, civil and criminal penalties for violations of environmental requirements function as deterrents to actions the legislature has proscribed as environmentally harmful. Penalties are necessary for ensuring compliance with environmental laws. They are not, however, necessarily set at levels sufficient to counteract the market's failure to discourage pollution and depletion of commonly-held resources or to counteract the economic benefits derived by some individuals and firms from environmentally harmful activities.

Other regulatory mechanisms, such as pollution taxes, more directly influence the behavior of firms in the marketplace. When set at proper levels, these mechanisms deter environmentally harmful activities by making them more costly. Such mechanisms force the market to account for the social and ecological costs of environmental degradation in the prices of goods and services. The purest form of regulation for accomplishing these objectives is the imposition of taxes on polluting emissions at levels that account for market externalities. According to former EPA Administrator Russell Train,

> The most efficient way to achieve environmental progress is to harness market forces. Here, the role of public policy is to send the right signals to the economy—"getting the prices right" and making the marketplace work for, instead of against, environmental protection. Available tools include social-cost pricing, taxes, and removing or instituting subsidies . . . .[16]

The chief drawback of market-oriented regulation is that it is exceptionally difficult and costly to set pollution taxes and other financial deterrents at levels that properly account for the social and ecological costs of environmental degradation. Monitoring and enforcing compliance with marketplace mechanisms also pose special difficulties. Although market-oriented mechanisms that encourage more environmentally sound behaviors and technologies are still largely untried, interest in them is growing.

A modified form of market-incentive regulation is the provision for trading pollution allowances in the 1990 Clean Air Act Amendments.

Appendix—Chapter 3

Selected Statutory Sections—National Environmental Policy Act (Codified at 42 U.S.C. § 4321 *et seq.*)

NEPA § 2 Congressional Declaration of Purpose

The purposes of this [Act] are: To declare a national policy which will encourage productive and enjoyable harmony between man and his environment; to promote efforts which will prevent or eliminate damage to the environment and biosphere and stimulate the health and welfare of man; to enrich the understanding of the ecological systems and natural resources important to the Nation; and to establish a Council on Environmental Quality.

NEPA § 101 Congressional Declaration of National Environmental Policy

(a) The Congress, recognizing the profound impact of man's activity on the interrelations of all components of the natural environment, particularly the profound influences of population growth, high-density urbanization, industrial expansion, resource exploitation, and new and expanding technological advances and recognizing further the critical importance of restoring and maintaining environmental quality . . . declares that it is the continuing policy of the Federal Government, in cooperation with State and local governments, and other concerned public and private organizations, to use all practicable means and measures, including financial and technical assistance, . . . to create and maintain conditions under which man and nature can exist in productive harmony, and fulfill the social, economic, and other requirements of present and future generations of Americans.

(b) . . . it is the continuing responsibility of the Federal Government to use all practicable means, consistent with other essential considerations of national policy, to improve and co-

ordinate Federal plans, functions, programs, and resources to the end that the Nation may—

(1) fulfill the responsibilities of each generation as trustee of the environment, . . .
(2) assure for all Americans safe, healthful, productive, and esthetically and culturally pleasing surroundings;
(3) attain the widest range of beneficial uses of the environment without degradation, risk to health or safety, . . .
(4) preserve important historic, cultural, and natural aspects of our national heritage, . . .

* * *

(6) enhance the quality of renewable resources and approach the maximum attainable recycling of depletable resources. . . .

NEPA § 102 Cooperation of Agencies; Reports; Availability of Information; Recommendations: International and National Coordination of Efforts

The Congress authorizes and directs that, to the fullest extent possible: (1) the policies, regulations, and public laws of the United States shall be interpreted and administered in accordance with the policies set forth in this Act, and (2) all agencies of the Federal Government shall—

. . .

(C) include in every recommendation or report on proposals for legislation and other major Federal actions significantly affecting the quality of the human environment, a detailed statement by the responsible official on—

(i) the environmental impact of the proposed action,

(ii) any adverse environmental effects which cannot be avoided

(iii) alternatives to the proposed action,

* * *

Prior to making any detailed statement, the responsible Federal official shall consult with and obtain the comments of any Federal agency which has jurisdiction by law or special expertise with respect to any environmental impact involved. . . .

* * *

(F) recognize the worldwide and long-range character of environmental problems and, where consistent with the foreign policy of the United States, lend appropriate support to initiative, resolutions, and programs designed to maximize international cooperation in anticipating and preventing a decline in the quality of mankind's world environment;

(G) make available to States, counties, municipalities, institutions, and individuals, advice and information useful in restoring, maintaining, and enhancing the quality of the environment;

* * *

(I) assist the Council on Environmental Quality established by title II of this Act.

NEPA § 201   Reports to Congress; Recommendations for Legislation

The President shall transmit to the Congress annually beginning July 1, 1970, an Environmental Quality Report . . . .

NEPA § 202   Establishment; Membership; Chairman; Appointments

There is created in the Executive Office of the President a Council on Environmental Quality (hereinafter referred to as the "Council"). The Council shall be composed of three members who shall be appointed by the President to serve at his pleasure, by and with the advice and consent of the Senate. . . .

NEPA § 204   Duties and Functions

It shall be the duty and function of the Council—

(1) to assist and advise the President in the preparation of the Environmental Quality Report required by section 201;

(2) to gather timely and authoritative information concerning the conditions and trends in the quality of the environment . . . to analyze and interpret such information for the purpose of determining whether such conditions and trends are interfering, or are likely to interfere, with the achievement of the policy set forth in title I of this Act, and to compile and submit to the President studies relating to such conditions and trends;

(3) to review and appraise the various programs and activities of the Federal Government . . . . to make recommendations to the President with respect thereto;

(4) to develop and recommend to the President national policies to foster and promote the improvement of environmental quality . . .

(5) to conduct investigations, studies, surveys, research, and analyses relating to ecological systems and environmental quality; . . .

* * *

(7) to report at least once each year to the President on the state and condition of the environment; . . .

■   Chapter 3 Endnotes

1. *Robertson v. Methow Valley Citizens' Council,* 109 S. Ct. 1835, 1846 (1989).
2. CEQ, *Environmental Quality,* 1991, p. 141.
3. CEQ, *Environmental Quality,* 1991, pp. 142–150.
4. CEQ, *Environmental Quality,* 1991, pp. 81–82.
5. S. Madonna and K. Breslin, "The Environmental Prosecutor," III *Villanova Env. Law J.* (No. 1 1992), p. 47 (correction sticker).

6. R. Posner, *Economic Analysis of Law* (1972), pp. 159–161. Copyright © 1992 Little, Brown and Company. Used with permission.

7. EPA, *Risk Assessment,* 1 (1992).

8. CEQ, *Environmental Quality,* 1991, p. 43.

9. Ibid., pp. 57–58.

10. J. H. Adams, "The Mainstream Environmental Movement," 18 *EPA Journal,* no. 1 (March/April 1992), pp. 25–26.

11. Russell E. Train, "A Call for Sustainability to Ensure Our Future Survival," 18 *EPA Journal,* no. 84 (September/October 1992), p. 9.

PART II

REGULATING USES OF SPECIFIC SUBSTANCES

One approach to protecting the environment is to regulate the sources and disposition of specific classes of pollutants. Chapters 4, 5, and 6 consider three important statutes that employ this approach to regulate pesticides, synthetic chemicals, and industrial and household wastes, respectively. Although these three statutes share the common goal of minimizing pollution, they utilize different models of regulation and thus present an opportunity to compare the relative merits and disadvantages of their respective regulatory schemes.

CHAPTER 4

The Federal Insecticide, Fungicide, and Rodenticide Act (FIFRA)

A Registration and Licensing Model

Outline

4.1 Historical Background of FIFRA

Pesticides are produced to control or exterminate unwanted plants, animals, insects, fungi and other pests; they are designed to be toxic and, of necessity, are environmentally hazardous in some respects. The Federal Insecticide, Fungicide, and Rodenticide Act (FIFRA) defines *pest* and *pesticide* broadly:

> The term, pest, means any . . . insect, rodent, nematode, fungus, weed, or . . . any other form of . . . plant or animal life or virus, bacteria or other micro-organism . . . which the [EPA] Administrator declares to be a pest and a term, pesticide means . . . any substance or mixture . . . intended for preventing, destroying, repelling, or mitigating any pest, and . . . any substance or mixture intended for use as a plant regulator, defoliant or desiccant. . . .

Over the years, it has become increasingly clear that many pesticides adversely affect numerous organisms other than those they are intended to control. Particular pesticides damage human health and natural resources in various ways: they poison farmworkers who come into direct contact with them, contaminate food products by their residues, destroy other plants and animals, and deplete the earth's ozone layer. Pesticide products such as Benlate, methyl bromide, and alar have become familiar news topics and have been the subject of legal proceedings brought by farmers and environmentalists to challenge their production, labeling or uses.

Recognizing the Dangers Posed by Pesticides

The revelations in Rachel Carson's book *Silent Spring* (1962) concerning the effects of unrestricted use of pesticides heightened public awareness of the ecological devastation wrought by pesticide poisons. Among other things, Carson showed the damaging effects of pesticides that accumulate and persist in plant and animal tissues and spread throughout the food chain. Today it is generally acknowledged that bioaccumulation can threaten the health of humans who are part of and dependent upon the many food chains affected by pesticides.

From a broader ecological perspective, it has become equally evident that even a single toxic substance, such as the insecticide DDT, can interfere with reproductive processes and contribute to the extinction of entire species. According to EPA, more than half of all plant and animal species on the Endangered Species List are in jeopardy because of chemical pesticide poisoning. Any breakdowns of balances within natural ecosystems may have grave ramifications, the dimensions of which are often unknown.

By the early 1990s, 26 widely used, registered pesticides had been found to be carcinogenic. Other pesticides had been found to cause life-threatening or crippling birth defects. Farmworker exposure to pesticides has resulted in abnormally high incidences of serious birth defects. In some California farmworker communities, for example, the United Farm Workers found the rate of leukemia in children to be eight times the national average.

In urban and suburban communities, the use of lawn pesticides and pest extermination products in homes, offices, and apartment buildings engenders concern and controversy. Many individuals complain of debilitating allergic reactions to some pesticide products; others are concerned about the unknown effects of periodic and/or chronic exposure to them.

Pesticides also threaten the global environment. One widely used pesticide, methyl bromide, for example, damages the earth's ozone layer:

> Every time he uses the potent pesticide methyl bromide to kill the worms on his walnuts, farmer Mark Gibson worries that he is also destroying a small chunk of the planet's ozone layer. . . . But for Gibson . . . methyl bromide is a matter of economic survival. One of the most widely used pesticides on Earth, it is applied on such crops as alfalfa and wheat . . . . In cities, the odorless and highly poisonous gas is also the chemical of choice for [exterminating] . . . termites. But . . . pressure is mounting to ban the pesticide because of the discovery that it is one of the most potent causes of ozone depletion. . . . It breaks down ozone about 40 times as quickly as . . . chlorofluorocarbons or CFCs. . . . Methyl bromide . . . also has a checkered history of causing residential deaths . . . and some experts suspect, birth defects. . . . [T]he Environmental Protection Agency is considering banning methyl

bromide because of its destructive effect on the ozone layer. [A] U.N. study group recently added the pesticide to its list of ozone depleting chemicals that should be banned by 1995.[1]

Improper pesticide formulation can also cause major crop damage. The on-going controversy surrounding the fungicide Benlate, developed by the Du Pont corporation, is illustrative. In response to growing complaints of plant damage, Du Pont withdrew Benlate from the market in 1991 and over the next year and a half voluntarily paid complaining growers about $500 million. Subsequently Du Pont scientists concluded that Benlate does not cause crop damage, and the company refused to pay such claims. Literally hundreds of lawsuits alleging crop damage from Benlate were filed against Du Pont throughout the country. Most of the cases were still awaiting trial in 1993. A Georgia trial was settled before completion for far less than the plaintiffs' claim, apparently because the plaintiffs believed it would be difficult to prove that Benlate caused the claimed plant damage. But a jury in Arkansas later found Du Pont liable to Benlate users in an amount exceeding $10 million for actual and punitive damages. It will take years for the numerous cases to work their way through trial and appeals courts. The proceedings in the Georgia case, however, produced revelations of a serious dispute between Du Pont and EPA concerning their respective understandings of the nature and testing of Benlate.[2] The ultimate resolution of the question of Benlate's safety will fall to private lawsuits, rather than to the EPA.

The full effects of pesticides in the atmosphere, soil, and ground water may not be discovered until years after their introduction into the environment, and eradication of unwanted pesticides from the environment takes even longer than that. Even though DDT was banned in the United States in 1972, for example, almost all Americans have traces of it in their body tissues.

Unanticipated hazards are also coming to light in the fast-growing, relatively young biotechnology industry. The *Heckler* case, discussed in Chapter 3, illustrates the complexity of regulating genetic engineering under various federal statutes, including FIFRA. Although EPA has ample statutory grounds to regulate micro-bial products under FIFRA, development of regulatory programs for addressing the novel problems presented by biotechnology will take years.[3] Moreover, EPA's limited resources will no doubt cause significant and risky delays in biotechnology regulation.

Overall, chemical pesticides cost Americans over $8 billion per year, according to government figures. These costs are incurred for the following: medical treatment for pesticide-related health problems, increased reliance on chemicals as pest resistance develops, cleanup of the water supply, and enforcement of governmental pesticide regulations. Ironically, the largest cost is attributable to the vicious cycle that results when predators of the targeted undesirable pests are eliminated by the substances being used for pest control.

Expanding Uses of Pesticides

Recent studies indicate that approximately 2.5 billion pounds of pesticides are used each year in the United States, not only in fields, lakes, and forests, but also in homes, offices, schools, and hospitals. As pest organisms develop resistance to pesticides, increasingly toxic new pesticides or increased amounts of existing pesticides must be used. The scale of pesticide use in the United States is reported in the following excerpt:

The United States is the largest single user of pesticides in the world. By EPA's own estimate, each year U.S. farmers use about 1.2 billion pounds of pesticides at an expenditure of $4.6 billion. More than 600 active ingredients are combined with other ingredients to form approximately 35,000 different commercial formulations. Yet, full evaluation of their hazards lags far behind the development of new products. Less than 10 percent of the products·in current use have been fully tested for potential health effects; of the 600 active ingredients in these products, EPA was recently able to provide full safety assurance for only six.[4]

Regulation of pesticides poses a twofold challenge. The first challenge is to render pesticide *content* reasonably safe. The second, and still more significant challenge is to render pesticide *use* reasonably safe by prescribing standards and procedures for their applications. Even a product of reasonably safe content can be dangerous when it is improperly used or applied. These twin concerns of safe content and safe use are the primary objects of federal pesticide regulation.

Legislative History and Overview of FIFRA

Early federal pesticide legislation (the Insecticide Act of 1910) was mainly concerned with pesticide effectiveness; only incidentally did it address environmental impact. A pesticide-registration requirement was adopted as an attempt to ensure that pesticides lived up to their producers' claims of effectiveness against targeted pests. The fact that the law assigned authority for overseeing pesticide registration to the Department of Agriculture (USDA) implies that pest control took priority over environmental protection.

It is known today, however, that pesticides can and do cause far-reaching environmental and ecological degradation. Unlike hazardous waste dumps, which can be cleaned up, albeit at great cost, it is virtually impossible to clean up pesticide residues once they are dispersed into the environment and have accumulated in the tissues of plants and animals. These factors and the destructive ecological effects of extensive pesticide use dictate stringent regulation of the manufacture, distribution, and application of pesticide products. Nevertheless, such comprehensive and effective regulation has yet to be achieved.

Congress enacted FIFRA in 1947 in order to broaden the original purpose of pesticide registration to include protection of the environment. Under this new act, however, the Secretary of Agriculture still had no legal authority to refuse registration and no regulatory authority to prevent the use of a pesticide or its production in contravention of its labeling. Moreover, the USDA had little incentive to cancel a pesticide's registration for environmental reasons, since its primary mission is to promote agriculture, which often relies heavily on pesticide application. By later amendments to FIFRA (principally in 1970, 1972, and 1988), Congress transferred responsibility for pesticide registration from the Department of Agriculture to the Environmental Protection Agency, which had been established in 1970. FIFRA provided that pesticides developed after 1972 must, *before being commercially produced or sold for the U.S. market,* meet the requirement that they will not have unreasonable adverse effects on public health or the environment.

In 1992, the EPA, for the first time in 18 years, also issued new final rules (four years after their initial proposal) to protect farmworkers from pesticide poisoning which is a major hazard in agricultural work. An estimated 300,000 agricultural workers were being poisoned each year, approximately 1,000 of them fatally.[5] The rules, which also apply to workers in nurseries and forests, specify worker training and warning, protective equipment, quarantining of freshly sprayed areas, and decontamination and emergency measures. The new rules have been controversial. Migrant workers' rights groups have criticized them as being too lenient. In addition, EPA must rely upon state agricultural departments to enforce the rules. Such departments have often been criticized for siding with agribusiness in disputes between growers and farmworkers.

4.2   Structure and Workings of FIFRA

Major FIFRA Provisions

Under FIFRA, EPA performs multiple functions; namely, testing pesticides that are already on the market, registering new pesticides, reregistering old pesticides, and licensing applicators of pesticides that are classified for restricted use. One court distilled EPA duties as follows:

> . . . to regulate the introduction of potentially harmful pesticides into the environment [by] (1) the establishment of registration and labeling requirements for "economic poisons" [now known as *pesticides*] under FIFRA, . . . and (2) the establishment of tolerance limits for shipment . . . of crops "adulterated" by pesticide residues.[6]

The major prohibition of FIFRA is that a manufacturer or importer may not sell a pesticide product for use within the United States unless it meets FIFRA's requirements for registration or reregistration. To qualify for registration under FIFRA, a pesticide must carry labeling that contains adequate information about it, directions for its use, and warnings sufficient to safeguard humans, animals, and vegetation. When "an economic poison [pesticide] is such that a label with adequate safeguards cannot be written, it may not be registered or sold . . . ."[7] In sum, if a product cannot be applied or used with adequate safety under proper labeling, FIFRA forbids its sale or use within the United States.

The FIFRA prohibition against the sale of unregistered pesticides applies only within U.S. boundaries. FIFRA's provisions on exported pesticides are considerably less stringent. Pesticide products that do not qualify for FIFRA registration may be manufactured within the United States for foreign sale and distribution. Shipments of exported pesticides that do not qualify for FIFRA registration must be labeled as not registered for use in the United States, and the purchaser must receive a written notification of this. Currently, the United States exports approximately 380 million pounds of registered and unregistered pesticides worth an estimated $2 billion each year. The EPA's enforcement activity is insignificant in relation to the volume of pesticide exports: enforcement actions for illegal pesticide exports netted $635,000 in penalties for the combined years of 1990 and 1991.

By placing upon pesticide producers the initial burden of applying for registration and submitting the required form of labeling for EPA approval, FIFRA relieves EPA of responsibility for preliminary investigation of proposed pesticide products. It does not, however, lighten EPA's considerable burdens of reviewing and determining the effects of submitted compounds and evaluating the adequacy of their proposed labeling and directions for use. Since completion of the registration process may take a considerable period of time, FIFRA permits the EPA Administrator to register a product *conditionally*, pending final EPA review and determination.

Neither does the registration system relieve EPA of the burden of investigating the safety of older pesticides. With respect to "old pesticides"—that is, the approximately 50,000 pesticides that were registered before 1972—FIFRA permitted their continued sale until the EPA initiated a reregistration process. Congress originally set a deadline of 1976 for EPA completion of the reregistration scheme but later extended it to 1984. EPA was also unable to attain the 1984 deadline due to the huge number of active ingredients in older pesticides that had to be reviewed and to the agency's limited resources available for that task. In 1988, Congress again extended the reregistration deadline through amendments that call for EPA to reregister old pesticides at the rate of nine per year. As of early 1994, most "old pesticides" had still not been reviewed by EPA. The U.S. General Accounting Office estimated in 1988 that EPA could not complete the reregistration process before the year 2024.

The specific FIFRA provisions that deal with reregistration are complex, and they need not be detailed here. It suffices to note that although FIFRA directs the EPA Administrator to pursue reregistrations and to cancel obsolete registrations, EPA has not kept pace with FIFRA's registration or cancellation mandates. As a result, many pesticides, old and new, remain on the market without sufficient evaluation of their effects on human health and the environment.

Once a pesticide is registered, FIFRA permits EPA to *cancel* or *reclassify* that pesticide if it should prove to pose a significant harm. Unfortunately, FIFRA's cancellation procedures and conditions are so cumbersome that, as a practical matter the EPA cannot effectuate cancellation of a registration number whenever warranted. Thus, the goal of FIFRA's cancellation provisions is often defeated by practical considerations. This is unfortunate, since the dangerous effects of a particular pesticide may not be ascertained until years after it has been registered. When EPA does propose to cancel a registration, it must submit that proposal to a scientific review panel, and unless the pesticide poses an "imminent hazard," EPA must grant an administrative hearing if the registrant facing cancellation requests it. Since the proposed cancellation cannot take place until such hearings and subsequent appeals have run their course, the registrant can delay cancellation for long periods by simply demanding a hearing. In the case of an "imminent hazard," EPA may suspend registration immediately pending the outcome of cancellation proceedings. However, EPA's burden of justifying suspension is considerably weightier, and that option is rarely used. The excerpts from the *Environmental Defense Fund* case that appears later in the chapter illustrate the administrative impediments to registration cancellations.

An even greater barrier to cancellation or suspension of a pesticide registration is the FIFRA requirement that EPA, with certain exceptions, must indemnify parties for the economic losses they suffer by reason of suspension or cancellation of the registration.[8] Such indemnification claims have run into the tens of millions of dollars; claims for three suspended pesticides 2,4,5-T/silvex, ethylene dibromide (EDB), and dinoseb were estimated to total $70 million. Prior to 1988, EPA was also required to pay the costs of disposing of cancelled pesticides, at a price tag of $195 million for those three pesticides. Congress made a tepid effort in 1988 to lessen the chilling effect of these financial burdens by transferring the source of indemnity payments from EPA's budget to the Federal Judgment Fund, an arm of the Executive Branch, and by placing responsibility for disposal upon the pesticide industry. Those changes did little to remove the economic deterrent to registration cancellation, and EPA officials have acknowledged that these indemnity costs, combined with the time delays and administrative burdens of cancellation procedures, have deterred EPA from seeking registration suspensions or cancellations.

In addition to determining the safety of active pesticide ingredients, EPA must also investigate the toxicity of inert ingredients. In its 1991 report to Congress, the EPA Office of the Inspector General criticized EPA's performance on this front:

> EPA had not promptly reviewed about 1,300 inert ingredients in pesticides of unknown toxicity to determine whether they pose potential adverse effects to human health and the environment. Inert ingredients in pesticides serve as a solvent, thickener, or propellant to make them more effective or usable. EPA issued an Inerts Strategy in 1987 classifying inerts into four categories: (1) those of unknown toxicity (1,300), (2) those known to be toxic (56), (3) those potentially toxic (68), and (4) those generally recognized as having no toxic effect (300). The Strategy did not detail how EPA would address those inerts of unknown toxicity even though they were the largest category. As a result of EPA's action, the toxic inert ingredients identified in the Inerts Strategy had been removed from most of the 1,228 products previously containing these inert ingredients. However, EPA had not completed several other actions intended to reduce the risk from pesticides containing toxic inert ingredients, including completing the review of 68 inerts identified as potentially toxic for reclassification as toxic or generally safe.[9]

EPA also has the authority to set maximum limits, called *tolerances*, on pesticide residues in food products. Other federal agencies are charged with enforcing those limits:

> . . . EPA sets maximum legal . . . tolerances for pesticides on food or feed crops. The Department of Agriculture enforces pesticide tolerances for meat and poultry, and the Food and Drug Administration in the Department of Health . . . enforces tolerances for all other food products. . . .[10]

In determining how to set limits on pesticide residues in food products, EPA must comply with other federal statutes as well as with FIFRA. The *Les v. Reilly* opinion illustrates the overlap of federal laws governing pesticides.

LES V. REILLY

968 F.2d 985 (9th Cir. 1992)

SCHROEDER, Circuit Judge:

Petitioners seek review of a final order of the Environmental Protection Agency permitting the use of four pesticides as food additives although they have been found to induce cancer. Petitioners challenge the final order on the ground that it violates the provisions of the Delaney clause, 21 U.S.C. § 348(c)(3), which prohibits the use of any food additive that is found to induce cancer.

Prior to 1988, EPA regulations promulgated in the absence of evidence of carcinogenicity permitted use of the four pesticides at issue here as food additives. In 1988, however, the EPA found these pesticides to be carcinogens. Notwithstanding the Delaney clause, the EPA refused to revoke the earlier regulations, reasoning that, although the chemicals posed a measurable risk of causing cancer, that risk was "de minimis."

We set aside the EPA's order because we agree with the petitioners that the language of the Delaney clause, its history and purpose all reflect that Congress intended the EPA to prohibit all additives that are carcinogens, regardless of the degree of risk involved.

BACKGROUND

The Federal Food, Drug, and Cosmetic Act (FFDCA), ... is designed to ensure the safety of the food we eat by prohibiting the sale of food that is "adulterated." ... Adulterated food is in turn defined as food containing any unsafe food "additive." ... A food "additive" is defined broadly as "any substance the intended use of which results or may reasonably be expected to result ... in its becoming a component ... of any food." ...

Before 1988, the four pesticide chemicals with which we are here concerned—benomyl, mancozeb, phosmet and trifluralin—were all the subject of regulations issued by the EPA permitting their use. In October 1988, however, the EPA published a list of substances, including the pesticides at issue here, that had been found to induce cancer. ... As known carcinogens, the four pesticides ran afoul of a special provision of the FFDCA known as the Delaney clause, which prescribes that additives found to induce cancer can never be deemed "safe" for purposes of the FFDCA. ...

* * *

DISCUSSION

The issue before us is whether the EPA has violated ... the Delaney clause, by permitting the use of carcinogenic food additives which it finds to present only a de minimis or negligible risk of causing cancer. The Agency acknowledges that its interpretation of the law is a new and changed one. From the initial enactment of the Delaney clause in 1958 to the time of the rulings here in issue, the statute had been strictly and literally enforced. ...

The language is clear and mandatory. ... The statute provides that once the finding of carcinogenicity is made, the EPA has no discretion. ...

* * *

The Agency asks us to look behind the language of the Delaney clause to the overall statutory scheme governing pesticides, which permits the use of carcinogenic pesticides on raw food without regard to the Delaney clause. Yet section 402 of the FFDCA, ... expressly harmonizes that scheme with the Delaney clause by providing that residues on processed foods may not exceed the tolerance level es-

tablished for the raw food. ... If pesticides which concentrate in processed foods induce cancer in humans or animals, they render the food adulterated and must be prohibited.

The legislative history, too, reflects that Congress intended the very rigidity that the language it chose commands. The food additive Delaney clause was enacted in response to increasing public concern about cancer. ...

The part that chemical additives play in the cancer picture may not yet be completely understood, but enough is known to put us on our guard. ...

* * *

The EPA contends that the legislative history shows that Congress never intended to regulate pesticides, as opposed to other additives, with extraordinary rigidity .... The Agency is indeed correct that the legislative history of the food additive provision does not focus on pesticides, and that pesticides are regulated more comprehensively under the Federal Insecticide, Fungicide, and Rodenticide Act (FIFRA). ... Nevertheless, the EPA's contention ... is belied by the events prompting passage of the provision into law: FDA approval of Aramite was the principal impetus for the food additive Delaney clause and Aramite was itself a regulated pesticide. Thus, Congress intended to regulate pesticides as food additives ....

Finally, the EPA argues that a de minimis exception to the Delaney clause is necessary in order to bring about a more sensible application of the regulatory scheme. It relies particularly on a recent study suggesting that the criterion of concentration level in processed foods may bear little or no relation to actual risk of cancer. ... The EPA in effect asks us to approve what it deems to be a more enlightened system than that which Congress established. The EPA is not alone in criticizing the scheme established by the Delaney clause. ... Revising the existing statutory scheme, however, is neither our function nor the function of the EPA. ...

The EPA's refusal to revoke regulations permitting the use of benomyl, mancozeb, phosmet and trifluralin as food additives ... is contrary to the provisions of the Delaney clause prohibiting food additives that induce cancer. The EPA's final order is set aside.

New proposals for redressing deficiencies in pesticide regulation were made to Congress by officials of the Clinton administration in September 1993. They are discussed in Section 4.3.

States are permitted by FIFRA to regulate the sale or use of federally registered pesticides by state law so long as state regulations do not conflict with federal law requirements. The determination of whether particular state regulations are consistent with or preempted by FIFRA is left for courts to decide, but courts have issued conflicting opinions on the extent to which state labeling regulations are permissible under FIFRA. In the *Ferebee* case, reported below, the federal circuit court for the District of Columbia found that state laws that imposed monetary sanctions for improper *use* of pesticides are consistent with FIFRA and are not preempted by federal law. A different federal court later ruled that state-law labeling requirements were "preempted" by FIFRA.[11] The courts of two states interpreted FIFRA as barring state law damage suits for pesticide mislabeling.[12] These case differences must await further clarification by the Supreme Court of the United States.

Municipalities may also regulate pesticides through local ordinance. Dissatisfied with the results of federal and state regulatory efforts, many municipalities undertook further regulation, often in the form of restricting application of pesticides in certain locations and by certain methods. In the *Mortier* case, excerpts of which appear in the following subsection, the Supreme Court ruled that FIFRA did not preclude a third layer of local pesticide regulation, so long as the municipal law is consistent with FIFRA requirements.

Illustrative FIFRA Cases

Excerpts from three cases illustrate the principal features of FIFRA's regulatory scheme.

ENVIRONMENTAL DEFENSE FUND, INC. v. ENVIRONMENTAL PROTECTION AGENCY

465 F.2d 528 (D.C. Cir. 1972)

[Suit to challenge failure of EPA to suspend registrations for toxic pesticides aldrin and dieldrin after initiating proceedings to cancel their registration. The court found EPA findings as to the benefits of the pesticides deficient, but returned the case for further EPA proceedings. These excerpts from its opinion discuss the cumbersome procedural requirements and complex criteria applied by EPA in the registration, cancellation, and suspension of economic poisons, as well as the legal principles by which courts limit their oversight of EPA decisions.]

Leventhal J.

* * *

Petition to review EPA's failure to suspend registrations of economic poisons. The Court of Appeals, . . . held that where EPA initiated proceeding for cancellation of registrations of certain economic poisons but did not order immediate suspension, and EPA made inadequate findings as to benefit but stated that its suspension decisions would be reexamined on receipt of scientific advisory committee's report, reviewing court would remand entire record.

* * *

Aldrin and dieldrin are "economic poisons" under the definition in § 2 of FIFRA, . . . and hence are required to be registered with EPA before they may be distributed in interstate commerce, . . . An economic poison may lawfully be registered only if it is properly labeled—not "misbranded." . . . If an economic poison is such that a label with adequate safeguards cannot be written, it may not be registered or sold in interstate commence, 7 U. S. C. § 135(a)(5).

The burden of establishing the safety of a product . . . remains at all times on the applicant and registrant. Whenever it appears that a registered economic poison may be or has become "misbranded," the Administrator is required to issue a notice of cancellation.

* * *

In § 4 of FIFRA, . . . Congress has provided extensive safeguards for those whose FIFRA registrations are challenged. Whenever an application for registration is refused, the applicant may request that the matter be referred to an advisory committee . . . . of experts as determined by the Administrator, or may file objections and request a public hearing. The same options are available in case of a notice of cancellation of registration; . . . .

In case the committee is requested, the statute provides that the committee shall submit a report and recommendation as to registration as soon as practicable . . . but not later than 60 days unless the period is extended by the Administrator for another 60 days. Within 90 days after receipt of the committee's report the Administrator shall make his determination as to registration, by issuing an order with findings of fact. Then the applicant or registrant has 60 days to file objections and request a public hearing for the purpose of receiving material evidence. The Administrator is required to take action—as soon as possible, but not more than 90 days, after completion of the hearing—by issuing an order granting, denying, or canceling the registration, or requiring modification of the claims or labeling.

Hence a substantial time, likely to exceed one year, may lapse between issuance of notice of cancellation and final order of cancellation. . . . In addition, there is the possibility that a cancellation order might be stayed pending court review . . . .

The elaborate procedural protection against improvident cancellations emphasizes the importance of the immediate suspension provision available under § 4 of FIFRA, for use when appropriate:

Notwithstanding any other provision of this section the Administrator may, when he finds that such action is necessary to prevent an imminent hazard to the public, by order, suspend the registration of an economic poison immediately. . . .

Because of the potential for delay, and consequent possibility of serious and irreparable environmental damage from an erroneous decision on suspension, a refusal to suspend is a final order reviewable immediately. . . .

B. Recent Decisions Concerning DDT

We now turn to recent decisions concerning EPA's administration of the pesticide control statutes in light of our expanding national commitment to environmental rehabilitation. In EDF v. Hardin, . . . we held that EDF had standing to challenge official determinations under the FIFRA as representative of those "adversely affected" by the environmental impact of DDT. We concluded that the Secretary of Agriculture's failure to act on EDF's request for suspension of DDT registrations for an appreciable time was reviewable as "tantamount to an order denying suspension," 428 F.2d at 1099.

* * *

Some three months later EDF again sought review of the EPA's explicit refusal either to order suspension or to issue notices of cancellation for all uses of DDT . . . The findings accompanying the EPA's refusal to issue notices of cancellation clearly demonstrated recognition that a "substantial question" existed as to the safety of DDT. Since "that is the standard for the issuance of cancellation notices under the FIFRA," 439 F.2d at 595, we remanded the case again, with instructions to issue notices for all DDT registrations "and thereby commence the administrative process."

* * *

Since the Administrator again had not explained the reasons for his refusal to suspend, we asked "once more . . . for a fresh determination on that issue." *id.* at 596. We left the Administrator free to explain his decision in terms of the general considerations at work in pesticide suspension cases or by discussion of the factors specifically relevant to DDT that influenced his decision.

* * *

We emphasized, . . . that the "FIFRA confers broad discretion on the [Administrator] . . . not merely to find facts, but also to set policy in the public interest." . . . We indicated our reluctance to override his apparent reservation of suspension authority as "an emergency power," to be exercised or not only after careful consideration of "both the magnitude of the anticipated harm, and the likelihood that it will occur."

II. EPA's Reasons for Declining to Order Immediate Suspension of Aldrin and Dieldrin Registrations

1.   The Decisions Taken by the EPA Administrator

The EPA initiated an administrative investigation . . . for aldrin and dieldrin that resulted in cancellation of registrations for certain uses. On December 2, 1970, the EDF addressed a petition to the Administrator requesting the suspension and eventual cancellation of registrations for all products containing aldrin and dieldrin. . . . On March 18, 1971, he issued his Statement of Reasons . . . [and] the decision to issue notices of cancellation for all registrations for those substances, and also the decision not to order interim suspension of registrations pending administrative decision.

EPA's decision to issue notices of cancellation "merely sets in motion the administrative process" and is not a reviewable order. . . . As to EDF's petition for suspension of registrations, the Administrator accepted the alternative . . . to develop suspension criteria case-by-case. . . .

2.   General Approach of EPA Statement of Reasons

* * *

The EPA points out that the final decision on registration depends on a balance struck between benefits and dangers to the public health and welfare from the product's use, and comments that the concept of safety of the product is under evolution and refinement in the light of increasing knowledge.

Suspension

The EPA's Statement points out that whereas a notice of cancellation is appropriate whenever there is "a substantial question as to the safety of a product," immediate suspension

is authorized only in order to prevent an "imminent hazard to the public," and to protect the public by prohibiting shipment of an economic poison "so dangerous that its continued use should not be tolerated during the pendency of the administrative process." The EPA described its general criteria for suspension as follows: . . .

The type, extent, probability and duration of potential or actual injury to man, plants and animals will be measured in light of the positive benefits accruing from, for example, use of the responsible economic poison in human or animal disease control or food production.

General Standards

* * *

EPA points out that, in general, economic poisons, including those under present consideration, are "ecologically crude"—that is, by reason of technology limitations, are toxic to non-target organisms as well as to pest life. Thus continued registration for particular ecologically crude pesticides "are acceptable only to the extent that the benefits accruing from use of a particular economic poison outweigh" the adverse results of effects on nontarget species. EPA cites "dramatic steps in disease control" and the gradual amelioration of "the chronic problem of world hunger" as examples of the kind of beneficial effect to be looked for in balancing benefits against harm for specific substances.

* * *

The immense difficulties of achieving a comprehensive solution to pesticide control are manifest from the Administrator's Statement of Reasons. It records that there are nearly 45,000 presently outstanding pesticide registrations for "hundreds" of substances in use over approximately five percent of the total land area of the United States. Available data show wide variety among individual substances both as to effectiveness against target species and as to potential harm to non-target species. Laboratory tests with some substances have raised serious questions regarding carcinogenicity that "deserve particular searching" because carcinogenic effects are generally cumulative and irreversible when discovered. Threats presented by individual substances vary not only as to observed persistence in the environment but also as to environmental mobility—which in turn depends in part on how a particular pesticide is introduced into the environment, either by ground insertion or by dispersal directly into the ambient air or water.

Based on the discussion of these general considerations, the EPA concludes that individual decisions on initial or continued registration must depend on a complex administrative calculus, in which the "nature and magnitude of the foreseeable hazards associated with use of a particular product" is weighed against the "nature of the benefit conferred" by its use.

3.   Discussion of Aldrin and Dieldrin

* * *

We set forth the paragraphs pertinent to the dangers of aldrin and dieldrin . . . because they provide perspective for the questions we must consider.

> The questions raised concerning the safety of these products are similar to those encountered with DDT . . . . Some studies indicate that dieldrin alone, or in possibly synergistic combination with DDT, has an equivalent potential for adverse effect on non-target predatory wildlife resulting from its low level toxicity intensified by its mobility and concentration up certain food chains. The scientific data also indicate that dieldrin, again like DDT, has an affinity for storage in the fatty tissue of a number of animals, including humans. There are also similar carcinogenic data developed in the laboratory from high dosage rates of dieldrin administered to test animals. . . .

Denial of Suspension

The Administrator's reasons for denial of suspension, as to aldrin and dieldrin, appear in the following paragraphs of the Statement:

> [B]ecause the vast majority of the present use of these products is restricted to ground insertion, which presents little foreseeable damage from general environmental mobility, . . . the delay inherent in the administrative process does not present an imminent hazard.

* * *

It is significant to note that no residues of either aldrin or dieldrin are now permitted on corn, eggs, milk, poultry, or animal fats shipped in interstate commerce. Because of the use patterns of aldrin and dieldrin, these products constitute the major sources whereby these substances would find their way into human food chains. During the pendency of the administrative process hereby initiated, this Agency will take no action to grant any residue tolerances for these foodstuffs . . . .

III.   The EDF's Contentions . . .

The EDF's petition . . . has two prongs: First, it challenges the sufficiency of the analysis of the relevant factual data. Secondly, it contends that the Administrator has failed to provide a consistent statement of reasons for the refusal to suspend.

A.   Contentions as to EPA Conclusions of Limited Nature of Immediate Harm

1.   EDF first disputes the EPA's three factual conclusions, underlying its conclusion of non-imminency of harm. . . . The EDF characterizes these conclusions as "irrational" in light of the data before the agency—in other words argues that they have no fair support in the record. We do not agree. . . . We cannot accept the proposition. . . . that the Administrator's findings regarding harm were insufficient because controverted by respectable scientific authority. It was enough at this stage that the . . . record contained respectable scientific authority supporting the Administrator.

2.   The EPA's one-sentence discussion of carcinogenicity of aldrin and dieldrin presents a harder question. EDF made a non-trivial showing with respect to carcinogenicity, a matter we have emphasized in the past. . . .

. . . The EPA asks us not to consider the aldrin-dieldrin discussion, standing alone, but to take it as incorporating, by reference, the more detailed carcinogenicity discussion in the Administrator's DDT section. . . .

On the other hand, candor compels us to say that when the matter involved is as sensitive and fright-laden as cancer, even a court scrupulous . . . in deference to administrative latitude is beset with concern when the cross-reference is so abbreviated. All the Statement of Reasons says, after noting that dieldrin, like DDT, has an affinity for storage in the fatty tissue of animals, is this:

> There are also similar carcinogenic data developed in the laboratory from high dosage rates of dieldrin administered to test animals.

Such transfer and extrapolation may well be sound, but it is not necessarily sound, or obvious, . . . and the matter is important enough to warrant the care of explicitness.

We need not decide this question for, as will appear, the record must go back to EPA for other reasons. Even assuming this problem alone would not have required a remand, we do not think it unduly burdensome to ask EPA to explicate, . . . the nature and extent of incorporation of its DDT statement on carcinogenicity.

B.   Claim Based on Lack of EPA Identification of Benefits to Offset Possible Dangers

* * *

We are not clear that the FIFRA requires separate analysis of benefits at the suspension stage. We are clear that the statute empowers the Administrator to take account of benefits or their absence as affecting imminency of hazard. The Administrator's general decision to follow that course cannot be assailed as unreasonable. . . .

The suspension decision is not ordinarily one to be made in a matter of moments, or even hours or days. The statute contemplates at least the kind of ventilation of issues commonly had prior to decisions by courts . . . .

Judicial doctrine teaches that a court must consider possibility of success on the merits, the nature and extent of the damage to each of the parties . . . to differentiate between uses of the product. Aldrin and dieldrin are apparently not viewed by the EPA as uniform in their benefit characteristics for all their uses. The Administrator had previously stopped certain uses of the pesticides in question in house paints and in water use. . . . Even assuming the essentiality of aldrin and dieldrin, and of the lack of feasible alternative control mechanisms for cer-

tain uses, there may be no corresponding benefit for other uses, which may be curtailed during the suspension period.

Flexibility as to Limits

. . . EPA has flexibility not only to confine suspensions to certain uses, but also to order conditional suspensions for uses, available only if certain volumes or limits are not exceeded. . . .

Analysis of Limited Short-Run Harm

We do not say there is an absolute need for analysis of benefits. It might have been possible for EPA to say that although there were no significant benefits from aldrin-dieldrin the possibility of harm—though substantial enough to present a long-run danger to the public warranting cancellation proceedings—did not present a serious short-run danger that constituted an imminent hazard. EPA's counsel offers this as a justification for its action.

If this is to be said, it must be said clearly, so that it may be reviewed carefully. . . . But we must caution against any approach to the term "imminent hazard," used in the statute, that restricts it to a concept of crisis. It is enough if there is substantial likelihood that serious harm will be experienced during the year or two required in any realistic projection of the administrative process. It is not good practice for an agency to defend an order on the hypothesis that it is valid even assuming there are no benefits, when the reality is that some conclusion of benefits was visualized by the agency. This kind of abstraction pushes argument—and judicial review—to the wall of extremes, when realism calls for an awareness of middle ground.

Articulation of Criteria

Our comments according EPA substantial policy choice and discretion are not to be taken as mere lip service . . . that is undercut by the need we find for better articulation. We recognize that EPA's functions are difficult and demanding and are impressed by the thoughtfulness and range of EPA's general approach; . . . Our own responsibility as a court is as a partner in the overall administrative process— acting with restraint, but providing supervision. We cannot discharge our role adequately unless we hold EPA to a high standard of articulation. . . .

Environmental law marks out a domain where knowledge is hard to obtain and appraise, even in the administrative corridors; in the courtrooms, difficulties of understanding are multiplied. But there is a will in the courts to study and understand what the agency puts before us. . . . The court's concern is for elucidation of basis, not for restriction of EPA's latitude.

IV.   PROVISION FOR FURTHER CONSIDERATION

We are not vacating the action before us. At argument we were informed of the delibera-

tions of the aldrin-dieldrin scientific advisory committee, and it is public knowledge that its report has recently been filed. . . .

The EPA proposes to study the committee's analyses and recommendations. We think it in the interest of justice, . . . that the record be remanded to the EPA for considerations at the same time of this opinion. This remand leaves the EPA with latitude, . . . to continue, vacate or modify its order on the question of suspension of aldrin and dieldrin.

WISCONSIN PUBLIC INTERVENOR v. MORTIER

111 S. Ct. 2476 (1991)

[Suit by Mortier and others seeking a court ruling that a town ordinance and regulations that restricted aerial pesticide spraying to certain land areas was unlawful and thus prohibited by FIFRA. Mortier argued that local pesticide regulation was inconsistent with FIFRA and therefore barred. The lower courts agreed, but the Supreme Court reversed their decision, and held that the local pesticide regulation was lawful and not precluded by FIFRA. The following excerpts from the Supreme Court opinion outline the general scheme of FIFRA regulation and the concurrent state and local authority to regulate pesticides.]

Justice White delivered the opinion of the Court.

This case requires us to consider whether the Federal Insecticide, Fungicide, and Rodenticide Act, (FIFRA), . . . pre-empts the regulation of pesticides by local governments. We hold that it does not.

* * *

FIFRA was enacted in 1947 to replace the Federal Government's first effort at pesticide regulation, the Insecticide Act of 1910, ... Like its predecessor, FIFRA as originally adopted "was primarily a licensing and labeling statute." . . . In 1972, growing environmental and safety concerns led Congress to undertake a comprehensive revision of FIFRA . . . The 1972 amendments significantly strengthened FIFRA's registration and labeling standards.

. . . the revisions further insured that FIFRA "regulated the use, as well as the sale and labeling, of pesticides; regulated pesticides produced and sold in both intrastate and interstate commerce; [and] provided for review, cancellation, and suspension of registration." . . . An additional change was the grant of increased enforcement authority to the Environmental Protection Agency (EPA), which had been charged with federal oversight of pesticides since 1970. . . . In this fashion, the 1972 amendments "transformed FIFRA from a labeling law into a comprehensive regulatory statute." . . .

As amended, FIFRA specifies several roles for state and local authorities. The statute, for example, authorizes the EPA Administrator to enter into cooperative agreements with the States to enforce FIFRA provisions. . . .

. . . FIFRA requires manufacturers to produce records for inspection "upon request of any officer or employee of the Environmental Protection Agency or of any State or political subdivision, duly designated by the Administrator." . . . Of particular relevance to this case, § 24(a) specifies that States may regulate the sale or use of pesticides so long as the state regulation does not permit a sale or use prohibited by the Act. . . .

* * *

II

Under the Supremacy Clause, U.S. Const. Art. VI, cl. 2, state laws that interfere with, or are contrary to the laws of congress, made in pursuance of the constitution" are invalid. . . . Congress' intent to supplant state authority in a particular field may be expressed in the terms of the statute. . . . Absent explicit pre-emptive language, Congress' intent to supersede state law in a given area may nonetheless be implicit if a scheme of federal regulation is "so pervasive as to make reasonable the inference that Congress left no room for the States to supplement it, if "the Act of Congress . . . touch[es] a field in which the federal interest is so dominant that the federal system will be assumed to preclude enforcement of state laws on the same subject," or if the goals "sought to be obtained" and the "obligations imposed" reveal a purpose to preclude state authority. . . . When considering pre-emption, "we start with the assumption that the historic police powers of the States were not to be superseded by the Federal Act unless that was the clear and manifest purpose of Congress." *Rice, supra,* 331 U.S., at 230, 67 S.Ct. at 1152.

Even when Congress has not chosen to occupy a particular field, pre-emption may occur to the extent that state and federal law actually conflict. Such a conflict arises when "compliance with both federal and state regulations is a physical impossibility." . . . or when a state law "stands as an obstacle to the accomplishment and execution of the full purposes and objectives of Congress," . . . .

* * *

III

Applying these principles, we conclude that FIFRA does not pre-empt the town's ordinance either explicitly, implicitly, or by virtue of an actual conflict.

A

As the Wisconsin Supreme court recognized, FIFRA nowhere expressly supersedes local regulation of pesticide use. . . .

* * *

We agree that neither the language of the statute nor its legislative history, standing alone, would suffice to pre-empt local regulation. . . . Mere silence, in this context, cannot suffice to establish a "clear and manifest purpose" to pre-empt local authority. . . .

Even if FIFRA's express grant of regulatory authority to the States could not be read as applying to municipalities, it would not follow that municipalities were left with no regulatory authority. . . .

. . . The exclusion of political subdivisions cannot be inferred from the express authorization to the "State[s]" because political subdivisions are components of the very entity the statute empowers. . . .

* * *

B

Likewise, FIFRA fails to provide any clear and manifest indication that Congress sought to supplant local authority over pesticide regulation impliedly. In particular, we reject the position . . . that the 1972 amendments transformed FIFRA into a comprehensive statute that occupied the field of pesticide regulation, ...

* * *

. . . While the 1972 amendments turned FIFRA into a "comprehensive regulatory statute," . . . the resulting scheme was not "so pervasive as to make reasonable the inference that Congress left no room for the States to supplement it." . . . To the contrary, the statute leaves ample room for States and localities to supplement federal efforts . . . .

FIFRA nowhere seeks to establish an affirmative permit scheme for the actual use of pesticides. It certainly does not equate registration and labeling requirements with a general approval to apply pesticides throughout the Nation without regard to regional and local factors like climate, population, geography, and water supply. Whatever else FIFRA may supplant, it does not occupy the field of pesticide regulation in general or the area of local use permitting in particular. . . .

* * *

C

Finally, like the EPA, we discern no actual conflict either between FIFRA and the ordinance before us or between FIFRA and local regulation generally. Mortier does not rely, nor could he, on the theory that compliance with the ordinance and FIFRA is a "physical impossibility." . . .

* * *

We hold that FIFRA does not pre-empt the town of Casey's ordinance regulating the use

of pesticides. The judgment of the Wisconsin Supreme Court is reversed, and the case is remanded for proceedings not inconsistent with this opinion.

* * *

FEREBEE V. CHEVRON CHEMICAL CO.

736 F.2d 1529 (D.C. Cir. 1984)

[Suit by agricultural worker against the manufacturer of the herbicide paraquat, alleging that his long-term skin exposure to dilute solutions of paraquat caused him to contract pulmonary fibrosis and that the manufacturer, knowing of the link between paraquat exposure and lung disease, wrongfully failed to provide a proper warning and labeling concerning the use of its product. Upon the worker's death before trial, the action was continued by his estate and expanded to cover claims of his surviving minor children. The manufacturer defended on the ground that the EPA had found its product labeling adequate under FIFRA, and that it could not be held negligent or liable for negligent labeling. In upholding the jury verdict for the claimants, the court made important observations regarding differing federal and state purposes and standards for pesticide regulation and the possible differing legal obligations imposed by those laws upon producers and users of dangerous pesticides.]

Mikva, Circuit Judge

* * *

Chevron's argument misunderstands the nature of the determination made by EPA and misconceives the relation between federal and state law. The fact that EPA has determined that Chevron's label is adequate *for purposes of FIFRA* does not compel a jury to find that the label is also adequate *for purposes of state tort law* as well. The purposes of FIFRA and those of state tort law may be quite distinct. FIFRA aims at ensuring that, from a cost-benefit point of view, paraquat as labeled does not produce "unreasonable adverse effects on the environment." State tort law, in contrast, may have broader compensatory goals; conceivably, a label may be inadequate under state law if that

label, while sufficient under a cost-benefit standard, nonetheless fails to warn against any significant risk. In addition, even if the ultimate purposes of federal and state law in this area are the same, a state (acting through its jurors) may assign distinct weight to the elements which go into determining whether a substance as labeled is of sufficient net benefit as to warrant its use. To approve use and sale of paraquat, for example, EPA was required to assess *inter alia* the health risks from use of paraquat, to assign a cost value to those risks, and to estimate the benefit to society at large from use of the chemical. Unless Congress intended to preempt states from considering these issues, a question we address below, there is no reason a state need strike the same balance on these difficult questions as EPA. Assignment of values to such "soft" variables as human health is among the most difficult tasks faced in a regulatory society, *see* NATIONAL ACADEMY OF SCIENCES, DECISION MAKING FOR REGULATING CHEMICALS IN THE ENVIRONMENT 41 (1975), and a state may choose to tip the scales more heavily in favor of the health of its citizens than EPA is permitted to by FIFRA. . . .

. . . Unless FIFRA preempts a state from making these choices, a state jury may find a product inadequately labeled despite EPA's determination that, for purposes of FIFRA, the label is adequate. EPA's determination may be taken into account by the jury, and the jury was instructed in this case that it was permitted to do so, but absent preemption the jury need not give that determination conclusive weight.

That brings us to the heart of Chevron's preemption claim: that FIFRA *does* preempt states from reconsidering such questions and that state tort suits of the sort at issue here are completely preempted by the Act. Chevron's position is grounded upon a section of FIFRA which provides that a state "shall not impose or continue in effect any requirements for labeling . . . in addition to or different from those required under this subchapter." 7 U.S.C. § 136v(b). Chevron argues that a damage action based on the inadequacy of a label has a regulatory aim—to assure that adequate labels are used—and that it is precisely this regulatory aim that FIFRA explicitly preempts.

Damage actions typically, however, can have *both* regulatory and compensatory aims.

* * *

Imposition of such a dual obligation upon a manufacturer is permissible under the Act. While FIFRA does not allow states directly to impose additional labeling requirements, the Act clearly allows states to impose more stringent constraints on the *use* of EPA-approved pesticides than those imposed by the EPA: "A State may regulate the sale or use of any federally registered pesticide or device in the State, but only if and to the extent the regulation does not permit any sale or use prohibited by this subchapter." 7 U.S.C. § 136v(a).

* * *

. . . Given this provision, Maryland might well have the power to ban paraquat entirely. We need not decide that issue, however, to hold that, if a state chooses to restrict pesticide use by requiring that the manufacturer compensate for all injuries or for some of these injuries resulting from *use* of a pesticide, federal law stands as no barrier. . . .

Moreover, tort recovery in a case such as this one may also promote legitimate regulatory aims. By encouraging plaintiffs to bring suit for injuries not previously recognized as traceable to pesticides such as paraquat, a state tort action of the kind under review may aid in the exposure of new dangers associated with pesticides. Successful actions of this sort may lead manufacturers to petition EPA to allow more detailed labeling of their products; alternatively, EPA itself may decide that revised labels are required in light of the new information that has been brought to its attention through common law suits. In addition, the specter of damage actions may provide manufacturers with added dynamic incentives to continue to keep abreast of . . . injuries stemming from use of their product. . . .

* * *

4.3 Appraisal of FIFRA's Regulatory Scheme

Registration Requirements and the Distribution of Regulatory Burdens

In 1990 the President's Council on Environmental Quality summarized the FIFRA's enforcement problems as follows:

> Over the years, FIFRA enforcement has changed focus from assuring that insecticides, fungicides and rodenticides actually kill pests to assuring that they do not at the same time harm human health and the environment. This midstream change has placed EPA in what some call "the FIFRA trap." To suspend or cancel a pesticide, EPA must employ a "tortuous mechanism" fraught with "procedural obstacles" that may account for the current decline in FIFRA enforcement actions. In 1972 EPA took 860 . . . actions against FIFRA violators. These figures rose . . . in 1976, and then fluctuated to the 1989 figure of 443 actions. In 1985, the states initiated 8,899 FIFRA administrative orders; in 1989 that number had declined to 6,698. The figures suggest that it may have been simpler to enforce regulations requiring pesti-

cides to kill pests than it is to insure that the same pesticides do not pollute the environment.[13]

With respect to registration of new pesticides, FIFRA effects a somewhat more rational allocation of the costs of assessing environmental risks than it does for "old" pesticides, those registered before 1972. By placing the initial and primary responsibility for developing product data and ascertaining environmental effects on the manufacturer, FIFRA spreads at least some of the regulatory costs to the parties who benefit from a product—namely, the manufacturer and the consumers to whom those costs are passed on through product pricing. These costs include the expenditures for research of a pesticide's environmental impact. In this respect, FIFRA presents a major contrast to the Toxic Substance Control Act (discussed in Chapter 5), which places the cost and primary burden of determining environmental risks of producing or using new chemicals upon the federal government and the taxpaying public, rather than upon producers and users. Even so, the FIFRA registration process does not impose all costs of assessing environmental impacts upon pesticide manufacturers and consumers. EPA must still evaluate data submitted pursuant to a registration statement. And FIFRA's registration mechanism provides no funding mechanism for the costs of remediating environmental degradation discovered after the pesticide has been registered and marketed.

With regard to *old* pesticides—that is, those registered before 1972—FIFRA places far more onerous initial burdens on EPA. One might question if this difference in regulatory burdens is rational and desirable, as pesticides that have been on the market for decades are likely to be less pest-specific and potentially more damaging than new products. Many older pesticides are broad-spectrum products (effective against various insects or microorganisms) designed at a time when efforts to dominate nature were not as informed by the notion of preserving ecosystems' natural balances or as concerned about long-term effects upon ecosystems and human health.

The apparent simplest means of resolving the prevailing disparities between registration provisions for new and old pesticides would be to adopt uniform registration rules for all pesticides, but that approach has spawned considerable political opposition from manufacturers and agribusiness. Agribusiness, the petrochemical industry, and the food industry have heavy economic stakes in the manufacture and availability of older pesticides and have effectively lobbied against further legislative or regulatory restrictions on them. Since FIFRA requires EPA to conduct cost-benefit analyses in developing new regulations, those who oppose new restrictions on old pesticides predictably argue that, upon proper analysis, the costs and benefits of pesticide withdrawals do not warrant new restrictive regulation. The *Environmental Defense Fund* case excerpted in section 4.2 exemplifies this conflict.

Although consumer, farmworker, and environmentalist groups have sought legislative reforms, they have also resorted to extralegal actions, such as boycotts of pesticide-affected produce, and have promoted the production of organic foods.[14] The impact of consumer measures has been somewhat blunted, however, by a lack of public information concerning risks posed by pesticides and by the higher cost and limited availability of organically produced food items. Traditionally, only a small segment of the population has had access to organic products and could afford to pay the higher prices for them. Over time, however, demand for organic foods has grown markedly, and many small farmers are now utilizing alternative pest-management means in order to satisfy the market.

Recourse to state law to rectify deficiencies in federal law also has inherent legal and economic limitations. States are not as well-equipped as the federal government to regulate pesticides; many lack the resources and expertise necessary for making effective, timely assessments of numerous pesticides and the impacts of widespread use. States also lack jurisdiction to regulate across state lines, of course. Interested industries lobby against state regulatory schemes not only on the basis of stringency, but also because their lack of uniformity makes complying with them costly and confusing. Perhaps most importantly, state legislatures tend to be driven by their own near-term needs, such as jobs and revenue from regulated industries. State legislatures are not inclined to enact stricter laws that may precipitate business relocations, job losses, and shrinking of the tax base.

This is not to say that state and local pesticide regulations are without value, but only to recognize that individual states cannot solve problems that are national in scope. Indeed, as the *Mortier* and *Ferebee* cases illustrate (see section 4.2), state and local laws can, within their geographic territories, provide significant supplementary remedies that are not found in federal law.

Another serious gap in FIFRA's scheme of regulation is the disparate treatment of pesticides that are produced for export to other nations. As pointed out earlier, FIFRA's registration requirements for domestically marketed pesticides do not apply to exports. This allows many unregistered (and unregisterable) pesticides to be lawfully exported under FIFRA. FIFRA's registration exceptions for pesticides produced for export raises many practical as well as ethical considerations.

Fruits and vegetables grown with pesticides not allowed to be used in the United States are imported into the country for human consumption. Governmental tests routinely indicate much higher levels of illegal pesticide residues in imported produce than in domestically grown products. Because such goods are perishable, import shipments are not routinely held at the docks until lab results are available, and the national food distribution network makes it virtually impossible for government officials to track imported produce once it has left the port of entry. Ironically, some of the pesticides that contaminate imported produce are manufactured in the United States for export only.

Some U.S.-produced and exported pesticides that are unregisterable under FIFRA also reenter the United States via contamination of rivers, ground water, and air. This international movement of pesticides in the form of imports, exports, and transboundary environmental contamination constitutes a "circle of poison" that FIFRA's current export provisions fail to address.

On September 21, 1993, EPA Administrator Carol Browner, along with several high officials of the Agriculture Department, the Food and Drug Administration, and the White House staff, in an attempt to resolve or mitigate some of these deficiencies in current pesticide regulations, proposed to Congress several changes in the laws and regulations governing pesticides.[15] The aims of those proposals are

1. To require, within a seven-year period, that pesticide manufacturers resubmit their products for government approval under a standard of "reasonable certainty of no harm to consumers of food," a standard that would apply to both raw and processed foods. If adopted, this change would induce the EPA and other federal agencies to expedite pesticide review and thereby remedy the lack of deadlines for EPA review under current law. It would also replace the stricter, but largely ignored, test of the Delaney Clause for food products and substitute a more flexible "rule of reason."

2. To have all government approvals of pesticides expire within 15 years unless they are explicitly renewed by EPA and other governing agencies. If adopted, this change, like the first item, would also close a loophole of current law and assure that unreviewed pesticides would be outlawed after 15 years, even if the lack of required review and renewal were due to EPA's default in making such review.

3. To empower the EPA to "phase out" the use of a pesticide under a relaxed standard of evidence that the pesticide poses a likely, even if not proven, risk to humans or the environment, rather than confining EPA to current suspension and cancellation process. If adopted, this proposal would substantially broaden EPA's grounds and leeway to remove a dangerous pesticide from the market gradually. Such gradual phaseouts would lessen the degree of economic loss and of opposition by adversely affected parties, as well as skirt the procedural obstacles to outright pesticide cancellations.

4. To effectuate EPA cancellations of a previously registered pesticide without having to grant, await or complete any administrative hearing for the affected registrant. If adopted, this proposal would avoid the procedural barriers and delays that have effectively forestalled cancellation of pesticide registrations.

These proposals will undoubtedly encounter opposition by interest groups and their supporters in Congress. The agricultural chemical industry and agribusiness in general contribute more than $6.5 million per year to congressional campaigns and constitute a powerful lobby against stricter pesticide legislation. However, these proposals do signal a recognition that the current system of regulation needs improvement.

Disproportionate Impact and Environmental Equity

Current pesticide regulation raises acute questions of fairness and has drawn sharp criticism from environmental equity advocates. The following article presents the case of environmental inequity with regard to farmworkers:

> While many people are aware of the dangers of pesticide residues in food and the detrimental effects of pesticides on the environment, few appreciate the serious health hazards that pesticides pose to farmworkers and their families. The fact is that farmworkers are disproportionately affected by the pesticides that characterize agriculture in the United States.
>
> * * *
>
> Those who suffer most directly from the chemical dependency of U.S. agriculture are farmworkers, who are working in the fields while some of the most toxic substances known to humans are sprayed. The World Resources Institute has estimated that as many as 313,000 farmworkers in the United States may suffer from pesticide-related illnesses each year. Another source estimates that 800 to 1,000 farmworkers die each year as a direct consequence of pesticide exposure.
>
> Ninety percent of the approximately two million hired farmworkers in the United States are people of color. . . . Farmworkers are intentionally excluded from the Occupational Safety and Health Act (OSHA), which governs health and safety standards in the workplace [as well as from the two major statutes which govern wage and labor standards].
>
> * * *
>
> Not being covered by OSHA, . . . farmworkers are forced to petition EPA. . . . But such petitioning offers few formal legal remedies, leaving farmworkers virtually unprotected against pesticide hazards. Under [FIFRA] . . . , "reentry" times (the in-

terval that must elapse between the application of a pesticide and workers' reentry into the fields) have been set for just 12 pesticides. Moreover, there is no provision to assure that these regulations . . . are enforced.

In fact, it is not uncommon to see farmers spraying while workers are in the field. [One study] reported that 48 percent of more than 400 farmworkers interviewed had been sprayed at least once while harvesting. Seventy-five percent of the workers surveyed said they had experienced one or more symptoms of pesticide poisoning while at work. . . . [M]any growers do not provide workers with protective masks or gloves and do not inform workers when and what chemicals are being used.

. . . . In 1986, EPA found that [the insecticide] parathion caused poisoning among all categories of workers who came in contact with it. In addition, EPA admitted that parathion was associated with unacceptable risks to farmworkers and that poisonings occurred even under the most stringent protective conditions. . . . Nevertheless, it is still legally used on nine major crops in the United States.

Parathion is only one of many acutely toxic pesticides belonging to the organophosphate family. These pesticides came into wide use approximately 20 years ago, when environmental awareness called for limitations on persistent pesticides [many of which belong to another group of pesticides called organochlorines, and which have been associated with cancer, reproductive malfunctions, birth defects and developmental growth problems]. The organophosphates, on the other hand, degrade much faster and therefore reduced the risk for wildlife and for consumers.

However, for farmworkers the switch from organochlorines to organophosphates meant exposure to more acutely toxic pesticides, since many of these rapidly degradable pesticides (parathion is one of them) are characterized by acute toxicity, which can cause dizziness; vomiting; irritation of the eye, upper respiratory tract, and skin; and death. There is an irony here that has not escaped the attention of farmworkers: The new wave of environmental consciousness, which forced welcome changes in production technologies, may have actually made things more precarious for farmworkers.

. . . In the past, EPA has operated under the assumption that these chemicals are essential for high productivity in U.S. agriculture. This notion was recently challenged by a 1989 report of the National Research Council, which concluded that low-input agriculture was not significantly less productive than chemically intensive agriculture. . . . Pesticides are not the only option for pest control. Integrated Pest Management, for example, is a strategy that combines alternative methods of pest control . . . to achieve a significant reduction in chemical pesticide applications.

. . . Chemical pesticides have not been all that successful . . . and . . . alternatives are already available which could lead to a new agriculture. Such an agriculture— call it sustainable or ecological or low-input or simply rational—is now on the horizon. The time seems ripe to reject the anachronistic notion that chemical poisons must be part and parcel of modern agriculture and redefine the meaning of "modern" to include the health and safety of farmworkers, farmers, consumers, and the environment.[16]

Alternative Pest Management

It is undisputed that U.S. agriculture is highly dependent on chemical pesticides. The debate arises over the extent to which chemical methods are desirable or necessary as a matter of sound agricultural policy and competitiveness. Contamination of ground water, surface water, soil, and air is one unfortunate byproduct of chemical pesticide use; damage to nontargeted animals and plants and to human health is another. Moreover, more than 400 insect species have developed immunities to pesticides developed to control them; these species must be treated with increasingly toxic chemicals in order to achieve the same level of control.

To avoid the problems associated with chemical pesticides, some scientists and farmers are using a variety of nonchemical pest-control methods, often referred to as *alternative pest-management techniques.* The use of such methods in conjunction with chemical pesticides is referred to as *integrated pest management.* Such efforts have historically been underfunded by Congress, but they are now growing in popularity.

Five alternative pest-management methods predominate today:

- *Biological treatment:* Every serious gardener is aware of the value of certain insects, such as ladybugs, in controlling less desirable populations, such as aphids. Numerous other insect, bacterial, and viral agents can be used to control unwanted pests through predation or parasitic activity.
- *Sterilization:* Several methods can be used to sterilize pest populations. They include radiation, hormonal treatments, and releasing sterile mating competitors into the target population.
- *Reproduction inhibition:* Insect breeding cycles can be interrupted through the use of pheromones and attractants that confuse mating insects and prevent actual mating from occurring.
- *Genetic alteration:* Hybridization and more sophisticated forms of genetic engineering can enhance the natural pest resistance of certain crops or introduce pest-resistant genetic material into different species.
- *Cultural control:* Also referred to as *mechanical techniques,* cultural controls range from eliminating crop residues, which harbor dormant insect populations, to cultivating complementary crops whose own defenses (such as odors or toxins) serve to prevent infestation of the primary crop. Monoculture and its attendant crop concentration tend to attract pests; therefore, growing different crops together or rotating crops provides a measure of protection against unwanted pests.

Many farmers who have turned to alternative or integrated pest-management techniques have maintained or increased yields while saving considerable sums of money. The U.S. Office of Technology Assessment estimates that a national commitment to integrated pest management could diminish pesticide use by up to 75 percent without crop loss, yielding significant environmental benefits. Nevertheless, while it is clear that society's return on investment in integrated pest management could be substantial, individual farmers have legitimate fears about implementing such techniques on their own. Although biological controls are highly reliable, implementation of any new method requires some fine tuning, and farmers are naturally reluctant to put an entire crop at risk. Therefore, a commitment of public resources to provide incentives or insurance to those who are willing to utilize such techniques may be necessary in order to promote the adoption of alternative pest management on a nationwide scale.

■ Policy Issues and Questions

1. Should pesticide laws provide greater incentives for the use of nonchemical alternative pest management? How could FIFRA be structured to provide such incentives in an efficient, cost-effective manner? In a manner that would be politically feasible?

2. Should EPA, in the FIFRA registration process, regard the availability of alternative, nonchemical forms of pest management as a factor that lessens the overall benefit of a chemical pesticide?

3. When engaging in the cost-benefit analyses of potential pesticide regulations, should EPA place greater emphasis on determining the societal health and economic benefits of pesticide use, as distinguished from the economic costs of limiting pesticide production, distribution, and use? What specific factors do you think EPA should consider in making the cost-benefit analysis mandated by FIFRA? Which factors should receive priority in evaluating a health or environmental risk?

4. Should EPA give more weight to the costs and benefits of a pesticide to particular groups in society than to the overall costs and benefits? Should the costs or benefits to particular groups be considered as part of the general social costs or benefits? Should some kinds of costs to individuals or to particular groups be given greater priority and weight than benefits and costs to society at large? Does FIFRA's mandate that economic factors be considered rule out EPA's consideration of social justice issues?

5. Should environmental laws and regulations provide specific protections for groups that typically experience disproportionate impacts from environmental pollutants or environmental degradation? Would legislation that provides environmental protection commensurate with disproportionate impact be special-interest legislation or a legally defensible form of equal protection of the law?

6. John H. Adams has argued that protection of the environment and protection of human beings are inextricably linked. Does it necessarily follow that protecting human health also protects the environment and vice versa? What paradigms of thought or regulation, if any, might reconcile those interests?

7. Some pesticides, such as the organophosphates, may protect the majority of people but harm a particular minority group, such as farmworkers. Is every individual entitled to a minimum right to environmental protection as a constitutional or civil rights matter?

8. Do you think a majority of Americans care if the produce they consume is harvested by farmworkers at a risk of pesticide damage to their health? Why or why not?

9. Many fruits and vegetables sold in U.S. supermarkets are imported from countries where growers commonly use pesticides whose use is illegal in the United States. Should consumers have a legal right to know the health effects (to themselves? to others?) of pesticides used on the produce they purchase? Should FIFRA require consumer labeling of pesticides used in the production and distribution of imported food? Of all food?

■ Problem Set Exercises

The hypothetical Tully Corporation provides the basis for the problem set questions on the environmental statutes presented here and in subsequent chapters. Your purpose in using the problem set questions should be to review and test your understanding of the major provisions and overall regulatory structure of the particular environmental statutes and to identify salient features and characteristics of specific regulatory schemes. Once you have identified the features of a regulatory scheme and noted its practical operation, you should be able to draw some conclusions about the scheme's effectiveness and relative costs.

Tully Corporation is a multimillion dollar chemical manufacturer that operates a single plant in the city of Cedarville, situated on the Elk River within Deer Valley. Cedarville is Deer Valley's only large city, and the area is economically dependent on Tully Corporation, which employs 70 percent of the valley's work force. In recent years, residents of Cedarville have become aware of some serious environmental problems in their area, including a higher-than-average incidence of Seward's syndrome, a rare form of cancer.

Tully Corporation presently manufactures Exterminant A-1, a pesticide that was registered in 1970. It also has plans to manufacture a new pesticide product called Mordor.

1. If Tully has not yet registered Mordor, can it legally sell Mordor to retailers?
2. What must Tully include in its registration application for Mordor? Must Tully demonstrate that it is effective?
3. What environmental factors must the EPA Administrator consider in deciding whether to register Mordor?
4. If Mordor is found to be as effective as Tully claims, and "when used in accordance with widespread and commonly recognized practice it will not generally cause unreasonable adverse effects on the environment," does the EPA Administrator have any discretion to refuse to register Mordor?
5. If a pesticide similar to Mordor is presently on the market, will Tully obtain registration of Mordor more easily?
6. If Mordor's use on wheat and barley crops would have unreasonable adverse effects on the environment, must the EPA Administrator deny registration for Mordor?
7. If the EPA Administrator decides not to register Mordor, what must the Administrator provide Tully?
8. One of Tully's competitors alleges that Exterminant A-1 interrupts the breeding cycles of certain waterfowl in areas where it is used. What, if anything, is Tully required to do under FIFRA?
9. Assume that Mordor is registered only for restricted uses and that Mordor's packaging clearly states that Mordor is not to be used for residential purposes. Happy Harper at Happy's Lawn Hut sells Mordor to Ella Browning, a homeowner, without asking Ms. Browning how she intends to use it. Ms. Browning sprays her lawn with Mordor. What legal actions could EPA take against Ms. Browning? Against Ms. Harper?

Appendix—Chapter 4

Selected Statutory Sections—Federal Insecticide, Fungicide, and Rodenticide Act (Codified at 7 U.S.C.A. § 136 *et seq.*)

Selected FIFRA provisions are excerpted here for the purposes of demonstrating the general workings of the statute and assisting you as you complete the problem sets. The full text of the statute is much too long and detailed to justify including it here. Where the content or wording of a particular provision is unduly complex, the authors have paraphrased the provision, indicating the paraphrase by enclosing it in brackets.

FIFRA § 2   Definitions

(t) **Pest** . . . means . . . any insect, rodent, nematode, fungus, weed, or . . . any other form of . . . plant or animal life or virus, bacteria or other micro-organism . . . which the Administrator declares to be a pest . . . .

(u) **Pesticide** . . . means . . . any substance or mixture . . . intended for preventing, destroying, repelling, or mitigating any pest, and . . . any substance or mixture intended for use as a plant regulator, defoliant or desiccant . . . .

(l) **Imminent hazard** means a situation which exists when the continued use of a pesticide during the time required for cancellation proceeding would be likely to result in unreasonable adverse effects on the environment . . . .

(q) **Misbranded.**—(1) A pesticide is misbranded if

(A) its labeling bears any . . . representation . . . which is false or misleading; . . .

(B) . . . it is contained in a package . . . which does not conform to the standards estab - lished by the [EPA] Administrator . . . ; . . .

(D) its label does not bear the [assigned] registration number; . . .

(F) . . . the labeling . . . does not contain directions for use which . . . if complied with . . . are adequate to protect health and the environment; . . .

(G) . . . the label does not contain a warning or caution statement which may be necessary . . . [and] adequate to protect health and the environment; . . .

(2)(B) the labeling does not contain a statement of the use classification under which the product is registered; or . . .

(D) . . . the pesticide contains any substance . . . in quantities highly toxic to man unless the label shall bear . . . the skull and crossbones; the word "poison" prominently in red . . . and a statement of a practical treatment . . . in case of poisoning by the pesticide. . . .

(bb) **Unreasonable adverse effects on the environment.** . . . means any unreasonable risk to [humans] or the environment, taking into account the economic, social, and environmental costs and benefits of the use of any pesticide.

(ff)(1) **Outstanding data requirement.** . . . means a requirement for any study, information or data that is necessary to make a determination [as to whether the pesticide shall be registered].

FIFRA § 3   Registration of Pesticides

(a) Except as otherwise provided . . . , no person . . . may distribute or sell to any person any pesticide that is not registered . . . .

(c)(1) **Procedure for registration.** . . . Each applicant . . . shall file with the Administrator a statement which includes . . .

(C) a complete copy of the labeling of the pesticide, a statement of all claims to be made for it, and any directions for its use;

(D) the complete formula of the pesticide;

(E) a request that the pesticide be classified for general use or for restricted use, or for both; and

(F) . . . a full description of the tests made and the results thereof upon which the claims are based. [However, data previously used to support an original registration or amendment adding a new use shall not, without the permission of the original data submitter, be considered by the EPA Administrator to support an application by another person for ten years following the initial registration.]

(c)(2)(A) **Data submission.** The Administrator shall publish guidelines specifying the kinds of information which will be required to support the registration of a pesticide . . . .

(c)(3) [The Administrator shall, as expeditiously as possible, review the data after receipt of an application and either register the pesticide or notify the application that the requirements for registration are not satisfied. In the case of a pesticide that is substantially similar in composition and labeling of a currently registered pesticide, the Administrator shall notify the applicant within 90 days of receipt of a complete application of approval or denial.]

(c)(5) **Approval of registration.**—The Administrator shall register a pesticide if [she] determines that . . . —

(A) its composition . . . warrant[s] [its] proposed claims;

(B) its labeling . . . compl[ies] with . . . requirements . . . . ;

(C) it will perform its intended function without unreasonable adverse effects on the environment; and

(D) when used in accordance with widespread and commonly recognized practice it will not generally cause unreasonable adverse effects on the environment.

The Administrator shall not make lack of essentiality a criterion for denying registration of any pesticide.

(c)(6) **Denial of registration.**—[If the Administrator determines that the criteria for registration are not met, he or she shall inform the applicant of the reasons and factual basis for this determination, and the applicant shall have 30 days to correct the conditions, after which the Administrator may refuse registration.]

(c)(7) [The Administrator may conditionally register or amend registration of a pesticide that is identical or substantially similar to a registered pesticide without a § 3(c)(5) evaluation if the Administrator determines that the new

pesticide and proposed use differ only in ways that would not significantly increase the risk of unreasonable adverse effects.]

(d) **Classification of pesticides.**—[The Administrator may classify a pesticide for general use or for restricted use. If the Administrator determines that a pesticide] may generally cause, without additional regulatory restrictions, unreasonable adverse effects on the environment, including injury to the applicator, the Administrator shall classify the pesticide, . . . , for restricted use . . . . [Author's note: *Restricted use* means that only a certified applicator trained in the application of pesticides can legally apply the pesticide.]

FIFRA § 4 Reregistration of Registered Pesticides

[The Administrator is required to reregister pesticides first registered prior to November 1, 1984, by listing active ingredients that will be reregistered, identifying outstanding data requirements and approving or denying reregistration.]

(i) **Fees**

(i)(7) If two or more registrants are required to pay any fee . . . with respect to a particular active ingredient, the fees for such active ingredient shall be apportioned among such registrants on the basis of the market share in United States sales for the [preceding] three calendar years . . . .

FIFRA § 6 Administrative Review; Suspension

(a)(2) **Information.**—If at any time after the registration of a pesticide the registrant has additional factual information regarding unreasonable adverse effects on the environment of the pesticide, the registrant shall submit such information to the Administrator.

(b) **Cancellation and change in classification.**—If it appears to the Administrator that a pesticide or its labeling or other material does not comply with [FIFRA] or, when used in accordance with commonly recognized practice, generally causes unreasonable adverse effects on the environment, the Administrator may issue a notice of [her] intent either—

(1) to cancel its registration or to change its classification together with the reasons (includ-

ing the factual basis) for the Administrator's action, or

(2) to hold a hearing to determine whether or not its registration should be canceled or its classification changed. [The Administrator shall consider, among other factors, the impact of such notice on agricultural commodities production and prices, retail food prices, and the agricultural economy. Prior to sending such notice, the Administrator shall provide the Secretary of Agriculture with a copy of the proposed notice and an analysis of its expected impact on the agricultural economy.]

(c) **Suspension.**—

(1) **Order.**—If the Administrator determines that action is necessary to prevent an imminent hazard during the time required for cancellation or change in classification proceedings, the Administrator may, by order, suspend the registration of the pesticide immediately. . . . The registrant shall then have an opportunity . . . for an expedited hearing before the Administrator on the question of whether an imminent hazard exists.

FIFRA § 12   Unlawful Acts

(a)(1) . . . [I]t shall be unlawful for any person . . . to distribute or sell to any person—

(A) any pesticide which is not registered . . . or whose registration has been canceled or suspended . . . ;
(E) any pesticide which is adulterated or misbranded . . . ;
(F) any device which is misbranded.

(a)(2) It shall be unlawful for any person—

(B) to refuse to [submit required reports or records]; . . .
(F) to distribute or sell, or to make available for use, or to use any [restricted pesticide for purposes not permitted by the registration];
(G) to use any . . . pesticide in a manner inconsistent with its labeling;

[to violate any suspension or cancellation order.]

FIFRA § 15   Indemnities

(a)(1) [If the Administrator suspends and thereafter cancels registration of a pesticide, the Administrator shall make an indemnity payment to any person who owned any quantity of the pesticide immediately before the notice to the registrant and who suffered losses by reason of cancellation or suspension. The indemnity payment shall be determined by the cost of the pesticide, not exceeding the fair market value.]

FIFRA § 17   Imports and Exports

(a) **Pesticides and devices intended for export.** . . . [N]o pesticide or device or active ingredient used in producing a pesticide intended solely for export to a foreign country shall be deemed in violation of [FIFRA] [if packaged properly and if] the foreign purchaser has signed a statement acknowledging that the purchaser understands that such pesticide is not registered for use in the United States and cannot be sold in the United States . . .

■   Chapter 4 Endnotes

1. See, "U.S., U.N. Consider Ban on Pesticides," *The Philadelphia Inquirer,* 20 September 1992, p. A4. See also "New Rule to Protect Agricultural Workers from Pesticide," 18, *EPA Journal,* no. 4, (1992), p. 3.
2. See, "EPA Says Du Pont 'Mischaracterized' Agency's Concern on Benlate Fungicide," *The Wall Street Journal,* 8 September 1993, p. A2; and "Du Pont Found Liable by Jury in Benlate Case," *The Wall Street Journal,* 7 September 1993, p. A3.
3. See G. Jaffe, "Inadequacies in the Federal Regulation of Biotechnology," 11 *Harvard Environmental Law Review* 491 (1987); and R. Harlow, "The EPA and Biotechnology Regulation: Coping with Scientific Uncertainty," 95 *Yale Law Journal,* 553 (1986).

4. I. Perfecto and B. Velasquez, "Farm Workers: Among the Least Protected," 18 *EPA Journal,* no. 1 (1992), p. 13.

5. "EPA Sets Rules for Pesticides," *The Wall Street Journal,* 14 August 1992, p. B8.

6. *Environmental Defense Fund, Inc. v. Environmental Protection Agency,* 465 F.2d 528 (D.C. Cir. 1972).

7. Ibid.

8. FIFRA § 15(a).

9. *EPA Office of the Inspector General Report to Congress: Highlights of Fiscal Year 1991* (U.S. Government Printing Office, December 1991).

10. CEQ, *Environmental Quality* (1990), p. 160.

11. *Arkansas-Platte and Gulf v. Wan Waters & Rogers,* 959 F.2d 158 (10th Cir. 1992).

12. *King v. E. I. du Pont de Nemours,* 806 F. Supp. 1030 (D. Me. 1992) and *Davidson v. Velsicol Chem. Corp.,* 108 Nev. 591 (1992).

13. CEQ, *Environmental Quality* (1990), pp. 159, 160.

14. Defined as "food produced with the use of feed or fertilizer of plant or animal origin without employment of chemically formulated fertilizers, growth stimulants, antibiotics, or pesticides" in *Webster's Ninth New Collegiate Dictionary.*

15. "Pesticide Rules Seek New Tests," *The Wall Street Journal,* 22 September 1993, p. B6.

16. I. Perfecto and B. Velasquez, "Farm Workers: Among the Least Protected," *EPA Journal* 18, no. 1 (March/April 1992).

Chapter 5

The Toxic Substances Control Act (TSCA)

A Premanufacture Notice and Governmental Risk Assessment Model

Outline

5.1 Historical Background

In 1972, following the post-war manufacturing revolution in synthetic chemicals, Congress enacted the Toxic Substances Control Act (TSCA) in order to establish a system for identifying and appraising the effects of existing and new substances on human health and the environment. Congress placed the administration of that system with EPA.

The Problem of New Chemical Substances

Many new chemical substances were developed and used in the United States after World War II. In *The Closing Circle*, Barry Commoner explains that the pollution problems that worsened in that period resulted, not from increased production or consumption of basic goods and services, but from changes in the technology of production. Using statistical data on the U.S. economy from 1946 to 1971 (the year *The Closing Circle* was published), Commoner shows that production for satisfying basic needs such as food, clothing, and housing kept pace with increases in population, but that the kinds of goods produced to meet those needs changed radically:

New production technologies have displaced old ones. Soap powder has been displaced by synthetic detergents; natural fibers (cotton and wool) have been displaced by synthetic ones; steel and lumber have been displaced by aluminum, plastics, and concrete . . . returnable bottles have been displaced by nonreturnable ones. . . . On the farm, while per capita production has remained about constant, the amount of harvested acreage has decreased; in effect, fertilizer has replaced land. Older methods of insect control have been displaced by synthetic insecticides . . . and for controlling weeds, the cultivator has been displaced by the herbicide spray. Range-feeding of livestock has been displaced by feedlots. . . .

[T]he "average American" now consumes, each year, about as many calories, protein, and other [nutrients] . . . uses about the same amount of clothes and cleaners; occupies about the same amount of newly constructed housing . . . as he did in 1946. However, his food is now grown on less land with much more fertilizer and pesticides than before; his clothes are more likely to be made of synthetic fibers . . . he launders with synthetic detergents rather than soap; he lives and works in buildings that depend more heavily on aluminum, concrete, and plastic than on steel and lumber; the goods he uses are increasingly shipped by truck rather than rail . . . . He is more likely to live and work in air-conditioned surroundings. . . .

To provide the raw materials needed for the new synthetic fibers, pesticides, detergents, plastics, and rubber, the production of synthetic organic chemicals has also grown very rapidly. . . . [This has led to a nearly 4,000% increase in mercury consumption between 1946 and 1971.] Chemical products, along with cement for concrete and aluminum . . . use rather large amounts of electric power. Not surprisingly, then, that item, too has increased considerably . . . .

. . . A good deal of the mystery and confusion about the sudden emergence of the environmental crisis can be removed by pinpointing, pollutant by pollutant, how the postwar technological transformation of the United States economy has produced . . . at a rate about ten times faster than the growth of GNP, the rising levels of environmental pollution.[1]

Besides contributing to increases in recognized environmental pollution, some of the new post-war synthetic chemical substances created unforeseen dangers to human health and the environment. Large quantities of the new chemical substances were used and released to the environment without knowledge of their biological and ecological consequences. Commoner uses the example of polyvinyl plastics in explaining how a new chemical substance used for a variety of purposes can result in widespread exposure of humans and other natural organisms with unforeseen harm.

In the 1950s, the plastics industry developed new types of flexible, synthetic materials—polyvinyl plastics—with good wearing properties. They found a ready market in automobile upholstery, so that within a decade the interiors of nearly every American car contained yards of the new plastic . . . . [The material was also used in food packaging, medical and dental equipment, water hoses, and clothing. Polyvinyl plastic also replaced glass items used to store and transfuse blood, because it was unbreakable. Such equipment was used in military hospitals in Vietnam, where the] new medical phenomenon "shock lung," a sometimes fatal disorder, [was] noticed in wounded after transfusion, especially of long-stored blood. The effect was reported in medical journals in 1959, but [was] not related to the transfusion process.

[In 1970, a researcher was having difficulty producing cultures of embryonic chicken heart cells.] After some effort he discovers the cause: some toxic material is leaching out of polyvinyl containers into his culture medium, killing the cells. He soon informs a colleague [who is concerned because] this same material may be leaching from polyvinyl blood transfusion equipment. Material incorporated into the polyvinyl plastic in the manufacturing process, which is designed to make it flexible, readily enters stored blood. He finds the plasticizer and its metabolic break-down products in the blood, urine, and tissues of patients receiving blood that has been stored in polyvinyl bags. He finds, too, that the plasticizer causes blood platelets to become sticky and clot—a condition that probably explains "shock lung" . . . .

Meanwhile, back in the scientific journals, . . . that issue has been raised[;] one can find earlier studies which show that plastics contain not only plasticizers having toxic effects, but also other additives, known as "stabilizers," that are usually even more hazardous . . . .

[Further research, established that some of the plasticizing and stabilizing materials] have significant effects on cell growth. . . . [Researchers discovered that phthalic acid derivatives used in the formation of polyvinyl chloride plastics caused embryonic defects and congenital damage to the central nervous system of developing chicken embryos] . . . .

. . . What our experience with the plasticizer problem reveals is something much more serious than the harm that it might engender. It reminds us of our ignorance—that we are hardly aware of the potential hazards from hundreds of similar substances that have so quickly become ubiquitous in our environment.[2]

Several laws passed prior to the 1972 Toxic Substances Control Act—such as the federal Food, Drug, and Cosmetics Act—addressed some of the potential exposure problems of synthesized substances. Before TSCA, however, no federal law had established systematic means for identifying and studying the effects of particular chemical substances on both human health and the environment.

Legislative History and Overview

The task of developing a strategy for assessing the health and environmental impacts of the many synthetic chemical substances that came into use after World War II was not easy. Congress was aware of the difficulty of regulating such substances. Its concern is evident in this excerpt from a report of a House of Representatives committee:

Chemicals have become . . . an enduring part of our environment. They are in our air, our water, and our soil. They are used in our manufacturing processes, and they are essential components for consumer and industrial goods. Production and use of chemicals have surged in the recent past. . . . Society reaps enormous benefits from chemicals. However, . . . as the number of chemicals . . . is greatly increased, the risk of producing chemicals that can cause grave and irreversible environmental damage or health problems is also increased. This vast volume of chemicals have, for the most part, been released into the environment with little or no knowledge of their long-term . . . effects. . . . It is often many years after exposure to a harmful chemical before the effects of its harm become visible. By that time it may be too late to reverse the effects. . . .[3]

In order to identify when new chemical substances are being manufactured, used, or sold TSCA requires, among other things, that manufacturers and distributors of covered substances notify EPA of their intent to manufacture or distribute them. TSCA also contains mechanisms by which EPA, upon determining that a substance is potentially harmful, may require that it be tested and that data concerning its chemical characteristics, including workplace hazards, be submitted to EPA. TSCA further authorizes EPA to prohibit or control the conditions under which substances it has identified as potentially harmful are manufactured and used and to require the producers or distributors to publish the characteristics and dangers of such substances that it has permitted to be manufactured or sold.

TSCA has been described as a "gap-filling" law, in that it extends to manufacturing activities and substances that are not reached by the other major environmental statutes, such as those dealing with disposal of hazardous waste or with air or water quality.

5.2   Structure and Workings of TSCA

Outline of Major Statutory Provisions

This section provides brief descriptions of TSCA's major requirements. Fuller excerpts of selected TSCA provisions appear in the chapter Appendix.

Subchapter I—Control of Toxic Substances

Definitions [*TSCA § 3*]:   This section sets forth definitions of terms used in the act and provides a general idea of the scope of what is covered in this subchapter.

Premanufacture Notice [*TSCA § 5*]:   At the heart of TSCA's regulatory scheme is the premanufacture notice requirement—the process by which manufacturers and distributors must notify EPA when they produce or distribute a new synthetic substance for a "significant new use."

Testing Requirements [*TSCA § 4*]:   In order to assess the effects of a chemical substance, EPA must, after reaching certain threshold findings, require manufacturers or distributors to submit data concerning health and environmental effects of the substance's manufacture or distribution.

Permissible Regulatory Action [*TSCA § 5(e)*]:   Pending development of information about health and environmental effects of a chemical substance, the EPA Administrator has discretion to prohibit or limit its manufacture, processing, distribution, use, or disposal.

Mandatory Regulatory Actions [*TSCA § 4(a)*]:   When the Administrator determines that the manufacture, distribution, use, or disposal of a substance "may present an unreasonable risk of injury to health or the environment" and there is insufficient data to predict reasonably those effects, TSCA requires the Administrator to promulgate a rule for testing the substance and submission of data concerning its health and environmental effects. The Administrator may promulgate the same sort of testing rule for an "old" substance that is being put to a "significant new use" that could cause the substance to enter the environment in substantial quantities or create significant human exposure.

Priority List [*TSCA § 4(e)*]:   This section requires that a committee be established to publish and update a list of substances to which the Administrator must give priority consideration.

Required Actions [*TSCA § 4(f)*]:   Any time that the Administrator receives information indicating "that there may be a reasonable basis to conclude that a chemical substance . . . presents or will present a significant risk of serious or widespread harm to human beings from cancer, gene mutations, or birth defects," he or she must take action to reduce the risk or publish a determination that the risk is not unreasonable.

Regulation [*TSCA § 6*]:   The Administrator is required to regulate chemical substances for which "there is a reasonable basis to conclude" that manufacture, distribution, use, or disposal "presents or will present an unreasonable risk of injury to health or the environment." The Administrator must promulgate regulations protecting against the risk "using the least burdensome requirements."

Imminent Hazards [TSCA § 7]:   The Administrator may institute civil lawsuits against manufacturers, distributors, users, or disposers of "imminently hazardous" chemical substances or articles containing those substances. A court may order seizure of the substances and may grant other remedies which are necessary for protecting human health or the environment from the unreasonable risk associated with substances identified as imminently hazardous.

Record Keeping [TSCA § 8]:   This section requires manufacturers, distributors, and users of chemical substances to keep records, according to rules promulgated by the Administrator, of significant adverse reactions to health or the environment from those substances. The Administrator may also require those who conduct or are aware of health and safety studies to submit them to EPA. The Administrator must maintain an inventory of all chemical substances that are manufactured or processed in the United States.

Subchapter II—Asbestos Hazard Emergency Response

This subchapter requires EPA to promulgate regulations that address the risks posed by asbestos in schools and public buildings.

Subchapter III—Indoor Radon Abatement

This subchapter requires radon studies and includes mechanisms for financial and technical assistance in addressing the dangers posed by high indoor radon levels.

Summary

Figure 5.1 summarizes the EPA obligations and powers in administering the TSCA statute. The first column denotes the section of the statute under which the Administrator's duty or authority arises. The second column indicates the statutory section's scope of application. The third column states the threshold findings that trigger EPA action under the statutory section, and the last column contains miscellaneous notes for certain sections.

As the table shows some statutory powers are to be exercised in a discretionary fashion, while others are mandatory. It should be remembered that even in cases where the Administrator has a mandatory obligation to take action pursuant to a threshold finding, he or she has the discretion to decide whether to make the threshold finding. Therefore, some mandatory duties are predicated upon a prior discretionary finding.

Illustrative TSCA Cases

The *Chemical Manufacturers Association v. U.S. EPA* opinion illustrates the workings of TSCA Subchapter I, which specifies the circumstances under which EPA may order testing of a chemical substance. It also illustrates the administrative

■ **Figure 5.1**   EPA Duties under TSCA Subchapter I (15 U.S.C. § 2601 *et seq*)

Section and Subject/ Type of Duty	Applies To	Threshold Finding	Miscellaneous
§ 5(a)(1) Premanufacture notice (MANDATORY) and § 5(a)(2) Significant new use rule (MANDATORY)	All new chemical substances* and significant new uses	No findings of risk	Factors for significant new use: projected volume manufacturing; change in type or form of human or environmental exposure; increase in magnitude or duration of exposure; anticipated methods of manufacture, distribution, and disposal
§ 4(a) Testing rule (MANDATORY)	All chemical substances (old as well as new)	May present unreasonable risk; insufficient data; and testing necessary	——
§ 4(c) Exemptions/ reimbursement	All chemical substances	——	——
§ 5(e) Priority list	All chemical substances	——	——
§ 5(e) Pending regulation (to prohibit or limit manufacture, etc. before testing rule information available) (DISCRETIONARY)	All chemical substances	Information insufficient to permit reasoned evaluation; *and* may present unreasonable risk *or* is or may be significant human or environmental exposure	——
§ 5(e)(1)(C) Manufacturer may object and thus stop an order from taking effect until court orders it	——	——	——
§ 4(f) Regulation to prevent or reduce cancer, gene mutations, or birth defects (MANDATORY)	All chemical substances	Reasonable basis to conclude is or will be significant risk of serious or widespread harm from cancer, gene mutation, birth defects	180 days to act or publish finding that risk is not unreasonable
§ 6 Regulation of hazardous substances (MANDATORY)	All chemical substances	Reasonable basis to conclude that manufacture, etc., presents or will present unreasonable risk to health or environment	Must use least burdensome regulation and consider risk/benefit/economics

*As defined in § 3(9).

difficulties inherent in a regulation that places the initial burden of generating health and environmental information about new products and technologies upon the government.

CHEMICAL MFRS. ASS'N. v. U.S. EPA

859 F.2d 977 (D.C. Cir. 1988)

Wald, Chief Judge:

Petitioners, Chemical Manufacturers Association and four companies that manufacture chemicals (collectively, "CMA"), seek to set aside a rule promulgated by the Environmental Protection Agency ("EPA" or "the Agency"). This Final Test Rule was promulgated under section 4 of the Toxic Substances Control Act ("TSCA" or "the Act"), . . . The Final Test Rule required toxicological testing to determine the health effects of the chemical 2-ethylhexanoic acid ("EHA"), and it continues to impose on exporters of EHA a duty to file certain notices with EPA.

We uphold EPA's interpretation of TSCA as empowering the Agency to issue a test rule on health grounds where it finds a more-than-theoretical basis for suspecting that the chemical substance in question presents an "unreasonable risk of injury to health." This, in turn, requires the Agency to find a more-than-theoretical basis for concluding that the substance is sufficiently toxic, and human exposure to it is sufficient in amount, to generate an "unreasonable risk of injury to health." We hold, further, that EPA can establish the existence and amount of human exposure on the basis of inferences drawn from the circumstances under which the substance is manufactured and used. EPA must rebut industry-supplied evidence attacking those inferences only if the industry evidence succeeds in rendering the probability of exposure in the amount found by EPA no more than theoretical or speculative. The probability of infrequent or even one-time exposure to individuals can warrant a test rule, so long as there is a more-than-theoretical basis for determining that exposure in such doses presents an "unreasonable risk of injury to health." Finally, we hold that the Agency correctly applied these standards in this case and that its findings are supported by substantial evidence. Consequently, we affirm the Final Test Rule.

I. BACKGROUND

A.   Statutory Structure

TSCA provides for a two-tier system for evaluating and regulating chemical substances to protect against unreasonable risks to human health and to the environment. Section 6 of the Act permits EPA to regulate a substance that the Agency has found "presents or will present an unreasonable risk of injury to health or the environment." . . . Section 4 of the Act empowers EPA to require testing of a suspect substance in order to obtain the toxicological data necessary to make a decision whether or not to regulate the substance under section 6.

* * *

EPA is empowered to require testing where it finds that the manufacture, distribution, processing, use or disposal of a particular chemical substance "may present an unreasonable risk of injury to human health or the environment." . . . The Agency's interpretation of this statutory standard for testing is the central issue in this case.

One of the chief policies underlying the Act is that—

adequate data should be developed with respect to the effect of chemical substances and mixtures on health and the environment and that the development of such data should be the responsibility of those who manufacture and those who process such chemical substances and mixtures.

. . . The statute establishes an Interagency Testing Committee, comprised of scientists from various federal agencies, to recommend that EPA give certain chemicals "priority consideration" for testing.

* * *

The companies that manufacture and process the substance are to conduct the tests and submit the data to the Agency. . . . Costs of testing are to be shared among the companies, either by agreement or by EPA order in the absence of agreement. . . .

A test rule promulgated under section 4 is subject to judicial review in a court of appeals, pursuant to section 19(a) of TSCA, 15 U.S.C. § 2618(a). A test rule may be set aside if it is not "supported by substantial evidence in the rule-making record . . . taken as a whole." . . .

B.   Facts and Prior Proceedings

EHA is a colorless liquid with a mild odor. It is used exclusively as a chemical intermediate or reactant in the production of metal soaps, peroxy esters and other products used in industrial settings. EHA itself is totally consumed during the manufacture of these products; as a result, no products offered for sale to industry or to consumers contain EHA. . . .

The Interagency Testing Committee first designated EHA for priority consideration for health effects tests on May 29, 1984. . . . The Committee based its recommendation in part on the structural similarity of EHA to chemicals known to cause cancer in test animals and on its finding that insufficient information existed concerning the chronic health effects of EHA. . . . Subsequently, EPA held two public meetings on EHA. . . . During these meetings, EPA sought information on a variety of issues relating to EHA uses, production and human exposure.

* * *

EPA issued a proposed test rule on May 17, 1985. . . . The rule proposed a series of tests to ascertain the health risks of EHA, and it set out proposed standards for the conduct of those tests.

. . . EPA based the Proposed Test Rule on a finding that EHA "may present an unreasonable risk" of subchronic toxicity (harm to bodily organs from repeated exposure over a limited period of time), oncogenicity (tumor formation) and developmental toxicity (harm to the fetus).

* * *

The Proposed Test Rule also addressed the question of whether humans are exposed to EHA, a question of critical importance to this case. The Agency acknowledged that, since no finished products contain EHA, consumer exposure is not a concern. It likewise discounted the dangers of . . . exposure to EHA vapors. . . .

The Agency based its Proposed Test Rule solely on the potential danger that EHA will come in contact with the skin of workers. As evidence of potential dermal exposure, the Agency noted that approximately 400 workers are engaged in the manufacture, transfer, storage and processing of 20 to 25 million pounds of EHA per year. . . . Further, rebutting claims by industry representatives that gloves are routinely worn during these activities, EPA noted that worker hygiene procedures "can vary widely throughout the industry," that workers are not required by existing federal regulations to wear gloves, and that the industry had not monitored work sites for worker exposure to EHA. . . .

* * *

CMA criticized the toxicology studies cited by EPA and sought to show that the use of gloves by employees of companies working with EHA prevented human exposure to the chemical, thus rendering any test rule invalid.

* * *

EPA published the Final Test Rule for EHA on November 6, 1986. The rule required a 90-day subchronic toxicity test, a developmental toxicity test, and a pharmacokinetics test. . . . The Agency rebutted industry claims of non-exposure by criticizing the methodology of the Glove Use Survey and the Glove Permeability Study. . . . The Final Test Rule also addressed the industry critique of the prior toxicology studies on EHA. Acknowledging some weaknesses in the studies, EPA nonetheless asserted that they "add to the weight of evidence" supporting findings of potential toxicity and thus helped to justify further testing. . . .

The pharmacokinetics study required by the rule entailed the oral and dermal administration of EHA to experimental animals, at low and high doses. . . .

All studies were to be conducted in accordance with EPA standards. Results were to be submitted by certain deadlines, the last of which was 18 months after the effective date of the Final Test Rule; hence, the last deadline was June 20, 1988.

* * *

The last of the required test data were submitted to EPA on June 20, 1988.

* * *

III.   STATUTORY INTERPRETATION

* * *

The parties both accept the proposition that the degree to which a particular substance presents a risk to health is a function of two factors: (a) human exposure to the substance, and (b) the toxicity of the substance. . . . They also agree that EPA must make some sort of threshold finding as to the existence of an "unreasonable risk of injury to health." The parties differ, however, as to the manner in which this finding must be made. Specifically, three issues are presented.

The first issue is whether, under section 4 of TSCA, EPA must find that the existence of an "unreasonable risk of injury to health" is more probable than not in order to issue a test rule. . . .

The second issue is whether, once industry has presented evidence tending to show an absence of human exposure, EPA must rebut it by producing direct evidence of exposure.

* * *

The third issue is whether the Agency was authority to issue a test rule where any individual's exposure to a substance is an isolated, non-recurrent event. * * *

We will explore each of these three issues in turn. In each instance, we must examine the statute itself and its legislative history to determine whether Congress addressed the particular point in question. If this court ascertains that Congress has directly spoken to the precise question at issue, then both the court and EPA "must give effect to the unambiguously expressed intent of Congress." . . . If, however, the statute is silent or ambiguous with respect to the specific issue, the court is left to decide only whether the Agency's construction of the statute is a reasonable one.

. . . Congressional silence is deemed an implicit delegation of power to an agency to make policy choices consistent with the statutory purpose. . . .

* * *

A.   Required Finding of "Unreasonable Risk"

As to the first issue in this case, the standard of probability of an unreasonable risk to health, we find that Congress did not address the precise question in issue. Examining the EPA interpretation . . . we find it to be reasonable and consistent with the statutory scheme and legislative history. Consequently, we uphold the Agency's construction of TSCA as authorizing a test rule where EPA's basis for suspecting the existence of an "unreasonable risk of injury to health" is substantial—i.e., when there is a more-than-theoretical basis for suspecting that some amount of exposure takes place and that the substance is sufficiently toxic at that level of exposure to present an "unreasonable risk of injury to health."

1.   Text and Structure of the Statute

Both the wording and structure of TSCA reveal that Congress did not expect that EPA would have to document to a certainty the existence of an "unreasonable risk" before it could require testing. . . .

2.   Legislative History

The legislative history of TSCA compels a further conclusion. . . . it shows the reasonableness of EPA's conclusion that "unreasonable risk" need not be established to a more-probable-than-not degree.

A House Report on the version of the bill that eventually became TSCA underscores the distinction between the section 6 standard and the section 4 standard. To issue a test rule, EPA need not find that a substance actually does cause or present an "unreasonable risk."

* * *

. . . According to that report, the word "may" in section 4 was intended to focus the Agency's attention on chemical substances *"about which there is a basis for concern, but about which there is inadequate information to reasonably predict or determine the effects of the substance or mixture on health or the environment."* . . . The Conference Committee Report reemphasized that the statutory language focused the Agency's attention on substances "about which there is a basis for concern." . . .

These indications of congressional intent illustrate that EPA's reading of TSCA is a permissible one. . . .

* * *

Of course, it is also evident from the legislative history that Congress did not intend to authorize EPA to issue test rules on the basis of mere hunches. The House Report states:

> [T]he term "may" . . . does not permit the Administrator to make a finding respecting probability of a risk on the basis of mere conjecture or speculation, i.e., it may or may not cause a risk.

* * *

Congress obviously intended section 4 to empower EPA to issue a test rule only after it had found a solid "basis for concern" by accumulating enough information to demonstrate a more-than-theoretical basis for suspecting that an "unreasonable risk" was involved in the use of the chemical.

* * *

3.   Interpretations in Other Circuits

We note that EPA's interpretation of section 4 is consistent with the views of the only other two courts of appeals that have examined its "may present" language. *See Ausimont U.S.A., Inc. v. EPA,* 838 F.2d 93 (3d Cir. 1988); *Shell Chemical Co. v. EPA,* 826 F.2d 295 (5th Cir. 1987).

* * *

CMA cites other cases interpreting language identical or similar to the "may present" term of section 4 as requiring a more-probable-than-not finding of risk. These opinions are of scant assistance, however, because in the main they involve provisions authorizing the regulation or prohibition of substances, rather than mere testing. Such interpretations can hardly be transplanted into the statutory scheme of TSCA, where Congress has self-consciously created a lower threshold for testing rules than for rules regulating chemical substances. . . .

B.   Use of Inferences versus Direct Evidence of Exposure

The second issue in the case is whether EPA must produce direct evidence documenting human exposure in order to rebut industry-submitted evidence casting doubt on the existence of exposure.

. . . EPA concedes that exposure is a necessary component of "unreasonable risk of injury to health." . . . The Agency argues, however, that it can issue a test rule where the existence of exposure is inferred from the circumstances under which the substance is manufactured and used. So long as industry evidence attacking those inferences fails to negate the Agency's more-than-theoretical basis for inferring the existence of exposure, EPA claims, a test rule is warranted. After a careful search of the legislative materials, we conclude that Congress did not address this particular issue. Applying the second prong of *Chevron,* however, we conclude that the Agency's construction of section 4 is a reasonable one and therefore uphold it.

Reasonableness of Agency Interpretation

CMA does not contest the proposition that the use of inferences to establish exposure is reasonable as a general matter. . . . CMA challenges only the Agency's reliance on inferences in the face of industry evidence attacking its initial exposure finding. . . . In light of our preceding decision on the quantum of proof necessary for a test rule, however, we see no reason to require EPA to come up with additional evidence of exposure when the industry challenges its initial finding unless the industry evidence effectively reduces the basis for an exposure finding to the realm of theory, speculation and conjecture. . . . At any rate, we have concluded that a standard less rigorous than a more-probable-than-not standard is reasonable and consistent with the intent of Congress. Accordingly, we find EPA's interpretation of section 4 as not requiring direct evidence of exposure to be reasonable and consistent with the statutory scheme.

C.   Recurrent versus Rare Exposure

The third statutory issue is whether section 4 of TSCA authorized EPA to issue a test rule where any individual's exposure to a chemical is likely to be a rare, brief event. CMA contends that only recurrent exposure warrants a test rule. EPA maintains that it can issue a test rule in the absence of recurrent exposure, where there is a more-than-theoretical basis for suspecting that infrequent or single-dose exposure presents an "unreasonable risk of injury to health." We find no indication in the statute or its history that Congress addressed this particular issue, but once again turning to the second prong of *Chevron*, we deem reasonable the Agency's construction of section 4 as permitting a test rule even where exposure is not recurrent.

* * *

In *Corrosion Proof Fittings* the court was unusually candid about what a cost-benefit analysis under TSCA entails. In discussing risks to human health, many courts utilize numerical formulations that obscure the real issue in many environmental cost-benefit analyses: how much a human life is worth in dollars. The court in *Corrosion Proof Fittings* purports to meet that issue head-on.

CORROSION PROOF FITTINGS v. EPA

947 F.2d 1201 (5th Cir. 1991)

[Following EPA issuance of a "final rule" under TSCA that banned the manufacture, importation, processing, and distribution of asbestos products, interested parties sued to overturn the final rule on the grounds that the EPA did not properly follow and apply the TSCA standards and procedures for its rule and that it failed to justify the ban by substantial evidence. For reasons explained in this opinion, the court upheld the petitioners' objections, vacated the EPA rule, and sent the case back to EPA for further proceedings.]

Jerry A. Smith, Circuit Judge:

IV. THE LANGUAGE OF TSCA

A. Standard of Review

Our inquire into the legitimacy of the EPA rulemaking begins with a discussion of the standard of review governing this case. EPA's phase-out ban is a TSCA § 6(a) rulemaking. TSCA provides that a reviewing court "shall hold unlawful and set aside" a final rule promulgated under § 6(a) "if the court finds that the rule is not supported by substantial evidence in the rulemaking record . . .

Substantial evidence requires "something less than the weight of the evidence, and the possibility of drawing two inconsistent conclusions from the evidence does not prevent an administrative agency's finding from being supported by substantial evidence." . . . Thus, even if there is enough evidence in the record to support the petitioners' assertions, we will not reverse if there is substantial evidence to support the agency's decision. . . .

Contrary to the EPA's assertions, the arbitrary and capricious standard found in the APA and the substantial evidence standard found in TSCA are different standards, even in the context of an informal rulemaking. . . . "The substantial evidence standard mandated by [TSCA] is generally considered to be more rigorous than the arbitrary and capricious standard normally applied to informal rulemaking." . . . and "afford[s] a considerably more generous judicial review" than the arbitrary and capricious test. . . .

. . . In evaluating whether the EPA has presented substantial evidence, we examine (1) whether the quantities of the regulated chemical entering into the environment are "substantial" and (2) whether human exposure to the chemical is "substantial" or "significant." . . . An agency may exercise its judgment without strictly relying upon quantifiable risks, costs, and benefits, but it must "cogently explain why it has exercised its discretion in a given manner" and "must offer a 'rational connection between the facts found and the choice made.'" . . .

We note that . . . we give all agency rules a presumption of validity, and it is up to the challenger to any rule to show that the agency action is invalid. . . . The burden remains on the EPA, however, to justify that the products it bans present an unreasonable risk, no matter how regulated. . . . Finally, . . . because TSCA instructs the EPA to undertake the least burdensome regulation sufficient to regulate the substance at issue, the agency bears a heavier burden when it seeks a partial or total ban of a substance than when it merely seeks to regulate that product. . . .

B.   The EPA's Burden under TSCA

TSCA provides, in pertinent part, as follows:

(a) Scope of regulation—If the Administrator finds that there is a *reasonable basis* to conclude that the manufacture, processing, distribution in commerce, use, or disposal of a chemical substance or mixture, or that any combination of such activities, presents or will present an *unreasonable risk of injury* to health or the environment, the Administrator shall by rule apply one or more of the following requirements to such substance or mixture to the extent necessary *to protect adequately* against such risk using the *least burdensome* requirements. . . . .

We conclude that the EPA has presented insufficient evidence to justify its asbestos ban. We base this conclusion upon two grounds: the failure of the EPA to consider all necessary evidence and its failure to give adequate weight to statutory language requiring it to promulgate the least burdensome, reasonable regulation required to protect the environment adequately. Because the EPA failed to address these concerns, . . . we are compelled to return the regulation to the agency for reconsideration.

1.   *Least Burdensome and Reasonable*

TSCA requires that the EPA use the least burdensome regulation to achieve its goal of minimum reasonable risk. This statutory requirement can create problems in evaluating just what is a "reasonable risk." . . .

In this case, the EPA banned, for all practical purposes, all present and future uses of asbestos—a position the petitioners characterize as the "death penalty alternative," as this is the *most* burdensome of all possible alternatives. . . . TSCA not only provides the EPA with a list of alternative actions. . . . The regulations thus provide for EPA regulation ranging from labeling the least toxic chemicals to limiting the total amount of chemicals an industry may use. Total bans head the list as the most burdensome regulatory option.

. . . Since, both by definition and by the terms of TSCA, the complete ban of manufacturing is the most burdensome alternative . . . the EPA's regulation cannot stand if there is any other regulation that would achieve an acceptable level of risk as mandated by TSCA.

* * *

The EPA considered, and rejected, such options as labeling asbestos products, thereby warning users and workers . . . and stricter workplace rules. EPA also rejected controlled use of asbestos in the workplace and deferral to other government agencies charged with worker and consumer exposure to industrial and product hazards, such as OSHA, the CPSC, and the MSHA. The EPA determine that deferral to these other agencies was inappriate because no other authority could address all the risks posed "throughout the life cycle" by asbestos. . . .

Much of the EPA's analysis is correct and the EPA's basic decision to use TSCA as a comprehensive statute designed to fight a multi-industry problem was a proper one that we uphold today on review. What concerns us, however, is the manner in which the EPA conducted some of its analysis. TSCA requires the EPA to consider, along with the effects of toxic substances on human health and the environment, "the benefits of such substance[s] or mixture[s] and the availability of substitutes for such uses," as well as "the reasonably ascertainable economic consequences of the rule, after consideration for the effect on the national economy, small business, technological innovation, the environment, and public health." . . .

* * *

Thus it was not enough for the EPA to show, as it did in this case, that banning some asbestos products might reduce the harm that could occur from the use of these products. If that were the standard, it would be no standard at all, for few indeed are the products that are so safe that a complete ban of them would not make the world still safer.

* * *

Upon an initial showing of product danger, the proper course for the EPA to follow is to consider each regulatory option, beginning with the least burdensome, and the costs and benefits of regulation under each option. The EPA cannot simply skip several rungs, as it did in this case, for in doing so, it may skip a less-burdensome alternative mandated by TSCA. Here, although the EPA mentions the problems posed by intermediate levels of regulation, it takes no steps to calculate the costs and benefits of these intermediate levels. . . .

. . . The EPA did not calculate the risk levels for intermediate levels of regulation, as it believed that there was no asbestos exposure level for which the risk of injury or death was zero. Reducing risk to zero, however, was not the task that Congress set for the EPA in enacting TSCA. . . .

2. *The EPA's Calculations*

Furthermore, we are concerned about some of the methodology employed by the EPA in making various of the calculations that it did perform. . . .

* * *

Although various commentators dispute whether it ever is appropriate to discount benefits when they are measured in human lives, we note that it would skew the results to discount only costs without according similar treatment to the benefits side of the equation. . . .

* * *

Of more concern to us is the failure of the EPA to compute the costs and benefits of its proposed rule past the year 2000, and its double-counting of the costs of asbestos use. In performing its calculus, the EPA only included the number of lives saved over the next thirteen years, and counted any additional lives saved as simply "unquantified benefits." . . . The EPA and intervenors now seek to use these unquantified lives saved to justify calculations as to which the benefits seem far outweighed by the astronomical costs. For example, the EPA plans to save about three lives with its ban of asbestos pipe, at a cost of $123–227 million (*i.e.,* approximately $43–76 million per life saved). Although the EPA admits that the price

tag is high, it claims that the lives saved past the year 2000 justify the price. . . .

. . . While TSCA contemplates a useful place for unquantified benefits beyond the EPA's calculation, unquantified benefits never were intended as a trump card allowing the EPA to justify any cost calculus, no matter how high.

* * *

Unquantified benefits can, at times, permissibly tip the balance in close cases. They cannot, however, be used to effect a wholesale shift on the balance beam. Such a use makes a mockery of the requirements of TSCA that the EPA weigh the costs of its actions before it chooses the least burdensome alternative.

We do not today determine what an appropriate period for the EPA's calculations would be, as this is a matter better left for agency discretion. . . . We do note, however, that the choice of a thirteen-year period is so short as to make the unquantified period so unreasonably large that any EPA reliance upon it must be displaced.

* * *

We also note that the EPA appears to place too great a reliance upon the concept of population exposure. While a high population exposure certainly is a factor that the EPA must consider . . . the agency cannot count such problems more than once. For example, in the case of asbestos brake products, the EPA used factors such as risk and exposure to calculate the probable harm of the brakes, and then used, as an *additional* reason to ban the products, the fact that the exposure levels were high. . . . the EPA's redundant use of population exposure to justify its actions cannot stand.

3. *Reasonable Basis*

In addition to showing that its regulation is the least burdensome one necessary to protect the environment adequately, the EPA also must show that it has a reasonable basis for the regulation. 15 U.S.C. § 2605(a). . . .

Most problematical to us is the EPA's ban of products for which no substitutes presently are available. In these cases, the EPA bears a tough burden indeed to show that under TSCA a ban is the least burdensome alternative. . . .

As the EPA itself states, "[w]hen no information is available for a product indicating that cost-effective substitutes exist, the estimated cost of a product ban is very high." . . . Because of this, the EPA did not ban certain uses of asbestos, such as its use in rocket engines and battery separators. The EPA, however, in several other instances, ignores its own arguments and attempts to justify its ban by stating that the ban itself will cause the development of low-cost, adequate substitute products.

As a general matter, we agree with the EPA that a product ban can lead to great innovation, and it is true that an agency under TSCA, . . . "is empowered to issue safety standards which require improvements in existing technology or which require the development of new technology." . . . As even the EPA acknowledges, however, when no adequate substitutes currently exist, the EPA cannot fail to consider this lack when formulating its own guidelines. . . .

We note that the EPA does provide a waiver provision for industries where the hoped-for substitutes fail to materialize in time. . . .

The EPA uses this provision to argue that it can ban any product, regardless of whether it has an adequate substitute, because inventive companies soon will develop good substitutes. The EPA contends that if they do not, the waiver provision will allow the continued use of asbestos in these areas, just as if the ban had not occurred at all.

The EPA errs, however, in asserting that the waiver provision will allow a continuation of the status quo. . . . By its own terms, the exemption shifts the burden onto the waiver proponent to convince the EPA that the waiver is justified. . . .

The EPA thus cannot use the waiver provision to lessen its burden when justifying banning products without existing substitutes. . . .

We also are concerned with the EPA's evaluation of substitutes even in those instances in which the record shows that they are available. The EPA explicitly rejects considering the harm that may flow from the increased use of products designed to substitute for asbestos, even where the probable substitutes themselves are known carcinogens. . . . The agency thus concludes that any "[r]egulatory decisions about asbestos which poses well-recognized, serious risks should not be delayed until the risk of all replacement materials are fully quantified." . . .

This presents two problems. First, TSCA instructs the EPA to consider the relative merits of its ban, as compared to the economic effects of its actions. The EPA cannot make this calculation if it fails to consider the effects that alternate substitutes will pose after a ban.

Second, the EPA cannot say with any assurance that its regulation will increase workplace safety when it refuses to evaluate the harm that will result from the increased use of substitute products. . . . The EPA's explicit failure to consider the toxicity of likely substitutes thus deprives its order of a reasonable basis. . . .

* * *

In short, a death is a death, whether occasioned by asbestos or by a toxic substitute product, and the EPA's decision not to evaluate the toxicity of known carcinogenic substitutes is not a reasonable action under TSCA. . . .

4.   Unreasonable Risk of Injury

The final requirement the EPA must satisfy . . . is that it only take steps designed to prevent "unreasonable" risks. In evaluating what is "unreasonable," the EPA is required to consider the costs of any proposed actions. . . .

* * *

While Congress did not dictate that the EPA engage in an exhaustive, full-scale cost-benefit analysis, it did require the EPA to consider both sides of the regulatory equation, and it rejected the notion that the EPA should pursue the reduction of workplace risk at any cost. . . .

Even taking all of the EPA's figures as true, and evaluating them in the light most favorable to the agency's decision . . . the agency's analysis results in figures as high as $74 million per life saved. For example, the EPA states that its ban of asbestos pipe will save three lives over the next thirteen years, at a cost of $128–227 million ($43–76 million per life saved), depending upon the price of substitutes; that its ban of asbestos shingles will cost $23–34 million to save 0.32 statistical lives ($72–106 million per life saved); that its ban of asbestos coatings will cost $46–181 million to save 3.33 lives ($14–54 million per life saved); and that its ban of asbestos paper products will save 0.60 lives at a cost of $4–5 million ($7–8 million per life saved). . . .

While we do not sit as a regulatory agency that must make the difficult decision as to what an appropriate expenditure is to prevent someone from incurring the risk of an asbestos-related death, we do note that the EPA . . . basically ignored the cost side of the TSCA equation. The EPA would have this court believe that Congress thought that spending $200–300 million to save approximately seven lives (approximately $30–40 million per life) over thirteen years is reasonable.

* * *

The EPA's willingness to argue that spending $23.7 million to save less than one-third of a life reveals that its economic review . . . was meaningless. As . . . our review of EPA case law reveals, such high costs are rarely, if ever, used to support a safety regulation. If we were to allow such cavalier treatment of the EPA's duty to consider the economic effects of its decisions, we would have to excise entire sections and phrases from the language of TSCA. . . . we decline to do so.

V.   SUBSTANTIAL EVIDENCE REGARDING LEAST BURDENSOME, ADEQUATE REGULATION

TSCA provides that a reviewing court "shall hold unlawful and set aside" a final rule promulgated under section 6(a) "if the court finds that the rule is not supported by substantial evidence in the rulemaking record . . . taken as a whole." . . . The substantial evidence standard "afford[s] a considerably more generous judicial review" than the arbitrary or capricious test, *Abbott Laboratories,* 387 U.S. at 143, 87 S. Ct. at 1513, and "imposes a considerable burden on the agency and limits its discretion in arriving at a factual predicate." *Mobil Oil Corp. v. FPC,* 483 F.2d 1238, 1258 (D.C. Cir. 1973).

We have declared that the EPA must articulate an "understandable basis" to support its TSCA action with respect to each substance or application of the substance banned. *Chemical Mfrs. Ass'n.* 899 F.2d at 357. To make a finding of unreasonable risk based upon this assessment, the "EPA must balance the probability

that harm will occur from the activities against the effects of the proposed regulatory action. . . .

* * *

VI.   CONCLUSION

In summary, of most concern to us is that the EPA has failed to implement the dictates of TSCA . . . before it impose a ban on a product, it first evaluate and then reject the less burdensome alternatives laid out for it by Congress. While the EPA spent much time and care crafting its asbestos regulation, its explicit failure to consider the alternatives required of it by Congress deprived its final rule of the reasonable basis it needed to survive judicial scrutiny.

Furthermore, the EPA's adoption of the analogous exposure estimates . . . after public comment was concluded, . . . was unreasonable and deprived the petitioners of the notice that they required in order to present their own evidence on the validity of the estimates and its data bases. By depriving the petitioners of their right to cross-examine EPA witnesses on methodology and data . . . the EPA also violated the dictates of TSCA.

Finally, the EPA failed to provide a reasonable basis for the purported benefits of its proposed rule by refusing to evaluate the toxicity of likely substitute products that will be used to replace asbestos goods. While the EPA does not have the duty under TSCA of affirmatively seeking out and testing all possible substitutes, when an interested party comes forward with credible evidence that the planned substitutes present a significant, or even greater, toxic risk than the substance in question, the agency must make a formal finding on the record that its proposed action still is both reasonable and warranted under TSCA.

We regret that this matter must continue to take up the valuable time of the agency, parties and, undoubtedly, future courts. The requirements of TSCA, however, are plain, and the EPA cannot deviate from them to reach its desired result. We therefore . . . VACATE the EPA's proposed regulation, and REMAND to the EPA for further proceedings in light of this opinion.

* * *

Corrosion Proof Fittings does not evaluate to which individuals costs and benefits, as calculated by EPA, flow. Rather, it speaks in terms of generic deaths ("a death is a death") and dollar amounts. The court's analysis suggests that in enacting TSCA, Congress was as concerned with the operating losses of individual businesses as with human lives. A different interpretation of TSCA is that Congress required the cost-benefit analyses as a means of ensuring that regulation would not threaten the survival of entire industries. Cost-benefit analyses tend to obscure distinctions between business income and profits. The assumption underlying *Corrosion-Proof Fittings* is that business savings from lack of regulation are as socially beneficial as protecting human lives. In practice, however, business savings through nonregulation do not necessarily benefit society at large, but sometimes benefit only a small segment of the population. In many cases, those individuals benefitting from lack of regulation are not those exposed to the greatest environmental harms caused by unregulated industries.

5.3 Appraisal of TSCA's Regulatory Scheme

The Burden Placed on Governmental Regulators

The task of regulating the thousands of new synthetic chemicals being developed in laboratories across the country is indeed formidable. The expectation that the EPA Administrator would promulgate rules governing the testing of all potentially harmful substances (as defined by section 4 of TSCA) proved unrealistic. Of the more than 2,300 *new substances* for which premanufacture notice had been submitted and that, presumably, had undergone EPA premanufacture review by 1992, EPA had limited or halted production of only 13 of them. For *existing chemicals,* EPA's record is even worse.

In 1991, EPA once again came under sharp criticism for its failure to pursue the regulation of potentially harmful chemical substances aggressively. In that year's report to Congress, the EPA Inspector General highlighted some deficiencies in EPA regulations:

> EPA's Office of Toxic Substances (OTS) had regulated few existing chemicals thought to pose a significant risk to humans. There are over 60,000 existing chemicals in the Toxic Substances Control Act (TSCA) inventory, of which about 10,000 potentially pose a health risk. OTS had not followed established guidelines for designating chemicals for priority review if data indicates a chemical may pose a substantial risk from cancer, genetic mutations, or birth defects. Also, OTS had not developed adequate procedures to expedite ongoing priority reviews. As a result, it took years for OTS to review and determine if a chemical posed an unreasonable risk to health or the environment. Since January 1, 1977, the effective date of TSCA, only four existing chemicals had been regulated (PCBs, CFCs, dioxin, and asbestos).[4]

Part of the difficulty lies with the administrative rule making process, which is lengthy and open to challenges at numerous stages. For instance, the Administrator's duty to regulate a new chemical substance only arises when he or she determines that the manufacture of a substance would present "an unreasonable risk of injury to health or the environment." But the threshold determination as to what constitutes an "unreasonable risk" is itself a basis for a legal challenge, as was seen in the *Corrosion Proof Fittings* case.

In contrast to the pesticide statute (FIFRA), the subject of Chapter 4, TSCA's premanufacture notice provision places the burden on the EPA to determine initially whether a new chemical substance might be harmful to the environment and to promulgate rules requiring testing. Instead, Congress could have required that the manufacturer assess a chemical's dangers and prove that it is relatively safe prior to manufacture.

The Difficulties of Regulating at the Frontiers of Scientific Knowledge

TSCA, in particular, and hazardous substance law, generally, represent attempts by legislators to deal with the scientific uncertainty surrounding the manufacture and use of chemical substances whose effects are not known or fully understood. In spite of this lack of knowledge, the intent of TSCA is that scientific determinations of the risks of particular substances be made.

The underlying dilemma in any society's attempt to regulate (or not regulate) the production and use of a new chemical substance is intensified by the fact that in many cases no one can reasonably ascertain its effects until exposure has occurred. Even if experimentation with humans were permitted and carried out, in many cases it would be impossible to anticipate or to replicate all of the interacting variables that might render the chemical toxic in differing circumstances. It is equally difficult to evaluate a new substance's impact in various ecosystems.

When science cannot predict with reasonable certainty the risks associated with a new substance or technology, society must decide if it will require that its potential risks be evaluated and, if so, by whom. If the associated risks are not systematically evaluated, unknown persons will be exposed to the potential hazards of the new product or process—which is a form of uncontrolled experimentation. The exposed persons may include consumers, manufacturing employees, or persons who derive no benefit whatsoever from the new substance or technology.

If a society decides to require evaluation of risks, it can place the burden on the manufacturer or on government. Manufacturers pass their costs for this on to consumers of the new product. Government must pass the costs on to taxpayers, many of whom will derive no benefit from the product. How society chooses to evaluate risks is reflected in its particular scheme of regulation, regardless of whether it explicitly addresses the distribution of risks and costs. The regulatory scheme also specifies the extent to which the properties of a new chemical substance must be demonstrated. In some cases the burden is shared, though unevenly, by the regulator and the regulated entity. In the United States, for example, TSCA and FIFRA are both examples of this scheme. However, TSCA places a much larger burden for risk evaluation on the government than does FIFRA, which divides the burden more equally.

Questions that must be considered include the magnitude of the hazards posed by the substance under specified conditions and the probability that those dangers will occur under those conditions. In addition, the new substance's potential usefulness must be considered. Societies are more willing to tolerate higher risks with substances they view as highly useful. In a complex, heterogenous society, however, the individuals who benefit the most from production or use of a chemical substance are seldom the persons who face the greatest risks from it.

Cost-benefit analyses and determinations of the degree of knowledge a society desires about new technologies are not made in a vacuum and, as a practical matter, cannot be made jointly by all citizens. Those judgments are often made by individuals whose interests may differ from those who are ultimately affected by them. A society's regulatory policy is thus influenced not merely by what questions are asked, but also by who is empowered to answer them.

Scientific judgments at the frontiers of knowledge are also necessarily influenced by other social and political considerations. For instance, short of performing experiments on humans, scientists must extrapolate the possible effects of a chemical substance upon humans from studies of its effects on other animal species. In making these extrapolations, scientists incorporate value judgments concerning how cautious, how "conservative," the society should be in its attempt to protect human health. Even if scientists could accurately quantify risks to humans (morbidity and mortality rates), science cannot make judgments as to whether the benefits to some persons justify the risks to others. Science alone cannot quantify the value of human life or of the environment.

■ Policy Issues and Questions

1. Under TSCA, what incentives and disincentives do chemical manufacturers and distributors have for undertaking rigorous analyses of the health and environmental effects of new chemical substances or new uses of existing substances? What can be expected to be a manufacturer's main consideration in deciding whether to manufacture a new chemical substance?

2. What is the principal purpose of the mandate that EPA establish standards for developing test data; to ensure that EPA would have valid data, or to ease the burden on the regulated industries? Does it make sense to have manufacturers with a profit motive provide the information on which EPA will rely in determining whether to regulate the manufacture of a substance? What, if any, alternatives are there to this arrangement?

3. Does TSCA fail adequately to address hidden costs of manufacturing and using chemical substances whose effects are unknown? If so, what kinds of costs?

4. Under TSCA, who bears the burden of determining the safety of a chemical substance? How is the burden distributed? Is there a correlation between the allocation of this burden and the contemplated benefits of the substance's use? Does the answer to this question depend on the perspective of the person being asked? Does it matter whether one is a consumer of the product, a chemical plant employee, a company shareholder, or governor of the state in which the manufacturing plant is located?

5. Do some individuals who derive neither consumer nor economic benefit from the manufacture of a chemical substance nonetheless have to pay for it? In what ways? Discuss the efficiency and the ethical implications of this. Does TSCA require EPA to account for these costs? Can you think of a different regulatory scheme that might better address these issues?

6. Is cost-benefit analysis for determining acceptable levels of a health or environmental risk the *only* way, or the *optimal* way to regulate activities that have environmental impacts? Could and should assumptions other than social cost-benefit analysis be incorporated into environmental regulatory schemes?

■ Problem Set Exercises

Problem set questions should be answered by referring to the statutory sections in the chapter appendix.

Tully Corporation's Household Division manufactures paints, solvents, and other chemicals for home use, while its Farm Division specializes in the development and manufacture of pesticides and fertilizers. Among other products, Tully is presently manufacturing Junipox, a solvent, and Exterminant A-1, a pesticide. It has plans to manufacture a new household solvent, Solvor, as well as a pesticide, Mordor.

Answer the following questions based upon the statutory provisions excerpted in the chapter appendix and upon the cases presented in this chapter.

1. Which of the substances—Junipox, Exterminant A-1, Solvor, and Mordor—are subject to regulation under TSCA? Why or why not?
2. What must Tully do before it manufactures Solvor and Mordor to ensure compliance with TSCA? Why?
3. Assuming that EPA has issued a rule requiring testing of the chemical substance in Solvor, what must Tully submit with its premanufacture notice?
4. What finding must EPA make about the chemical substance in Solvor before issuing a test rule?
5. Suppose that EPA prescribes a test rule for the active ingredient in Solvor and that another manufacturer has plans to manufacture a solvent with the same active ingredient as Solvor. What are Tully's options for complying with EPA's test rule?
6. What actions may EPA take while the health and environmental effects of Solvor are being evaluated? What must EPA determine about Solvor in order to regulate the product before it has received test data?
7. Assuming that EPA has sufficient information at its disposal, what must EPA determine about Solvor in order to restrict its manufacture, use, or disposal? How does the case law interpret TSCA in this regard? Must EPA issue a test rule before regulating a substance?
8. EPA issues a section 6 rule prohibiting the manufacture of Solvor for household use based upon test data indicating that inhalation of freshly sprayed Solvor poses a risk of upper-respiratory-tract irritation in household pets. Tully objects and files suit. What standard of review would a court employ to decide the case? What is the standard enunciated by TSCA?
9. What sorts of actions must EPA take if it finds that there is a reasonable basis for concluding that the manufacture or use of Solvor will present an unreasonable risk of injury to health or the environment? May EPA take other discretionary actions as well?
10. Assume that for political reasons, the EPA Administrator does not wish to issue a test rule for a significant new use of an existing chemical substance. How might the Administrator avoid a situation in which he or she would be required to issue a test rule under section 4 of TSCA?
11. If EPA does nothing within 90 days after Tully submits premanufacture notice, may Tully begin production of Solvor?
12. Suppose that no test rule or regulation regarding Solvor has yet been issued and that Tully has decided to distribute a new product, Solvor-Wipes, a household cleansing product. The Administrator learns that small quantities or residues of the active ingredient in Solvor-Wipes can cause seizure disorders in children if it is accidentally ingested or absorbed through the skin. What can the Administrator do to abate this imminent hazard? What relief might a federal district court order?
13. What must a testing rule for Solvor include? Why are standards for the development of test data necessary?

Appendix—Chapter 5

Selected Statutory Sections—Toxic Substances Control Act (Codified at 15 U.S.C. § 2601 *et seq.*)

Significant TSCA provisions are excerpted here for the purposes of demonstrating the general workings of the statute and assisting you to complete the problem set questions. The authors have paraphrased those provisions that are particularly complicated, indicating it with brackets. The entire text of the statute is much longer and more involved than what is presented here.

SUBCHAPTER I—CONTROL OF TOXIC SUBSTANCES

TSCA § 3   Definitions

(2)(A) . . . the term "chemical substance" means any organic or inorganic substance of a particular molecular identity, including (i) any combination of such substances occurring . . . as a result of a chemical reaction or occurring in nature . . .

(2)(B) Such term does not include—
(ii) any pesticide . . . [and certain other substances that are governed by other federal laws, such as tobacco, nuclear material, food, and drug products].

(12) The term "standards for the development of test data" means a prescription of—
(A) the
(i) health and environmental effects, and
(ii) information relating to toxicity, persistence and other characteristics which affect health and the environment, for which test data . . . are to be developed and any analysis that is to be performed . . . , and
(B) to the extent necessary to assure that data . . . are reliable and adequate—
(i) the manner in which such data are to be developed,
(ii) the specification of any test . . . methodology to be employed in the development of such data . . . .

TSCA § 4   Testing of Chemical Substances
(a) **Testing requirements**
If the Administrator finds that—

(1)(A)(i) the manufacture, distribution . . . , processing, use, or disposal of a chemical substance . . . may present an unreasonable risk of injury to health or the environment,

(ii) there are insufficient data . . . upon which the effects of such manufacture, distribution . . . , processing, use, or disposal of such substance . . . on health or the environment can reasonably be determined or predicted, and

(iii) testing of such substance . . . is necessary to develop such data; or

(B)(i) a chemical substance . . . is or will be produced in substantial quantities and (I) it enters or may reasonably be anticipated to enter the environment in substantial quantities or (II) there is or may be a significant or substantial human exposure to such substances . . .

(ii) there are insufficient data . . . upon which the effects of the manufacture, distribution. . . , processing, use, or disposal of such substance . . . on health or the environment can reasonably be determined or predicted, and

(iii) testing of such substance . . . is necessary to develop such data;

the Administrator shall by rule require that testing be conducted on such substance . . . to develop data with respect to the health and environmental effects for which there is an insufficiency of data . . . and which are relevant to a determination that the manufacture, distribution. . . , processing, use, or disposal of such substance . . . does or does not present an unreasonable risk of injury to health or the environment.

(b) Testing requirement rule

(1) A [testing] rule shall include—

(A) identification of the chemical substance . . . for which testing is required . . .

(B) standards for the development of test data for such substance . . . , and

(C) with respect to chemical substances which are not new . . . , a specification of . . . [a reasonable period of time] within which the persons required to conduct testing shall submit [the required data] to the Administrator. . . .

(3)(B) [Any person who manufactures or processes or intends to manufacture or process a substance subject to a testing rule is required to conduct tests and submit data on that substance.]

(c) Exemption [from testing]

(2) [The Administrator may grant an exemption from the testing rule requirements if data on the same chemical substance have already been submitted pursuant to a testing rule or if the data would duplicate data already submitted or being developed.]

(3)(A) If [a person has been granted an exemption from conducting tests and submitting test data] on the basis of . . . previously submitted test data . . . the Administrator shall order the person granted the exemption to provide . . . reimbursement . . .

(i) to the person who previously submitted such test data, for the portion of the costs incurred by such person in complying with the requirement to submit such data, and

(ii) to any other person who has been required . . . to contribute with respect to such costs . . . .

(e) Priority list

(1)(A) [There is a committee that recommends which chemical substances the Administrator should give priority consideration for promulgation of testing rules.] In making such a recommendation . . . the committee shall consider . . .—

(i) the quantities [of the substance which are or will be] manufactured,

(ii) the quantities [of the substance that enter] or will enter the environment,

(iii) the number of individuals who are or will be exposed to the substance . . . in their places of employment and the duration of such exposure,

(iv) the extent to which human beings are or will be exposed to the substance . . . ,

(v) the extent to which the substance . . . is closely related to a chemical substance which is known to present an unreasonable risk of injury to health or the environment,

(vi) the existence of data concerning the effects of the substance or mixture on health or the environment, . . .

[The committee shall submit a list of substances set forth] in the order in which the committee determines the Administrator should [make a testing requirement finding]. . . . [T]he committee shall give priority attention to those chemical substances known [or suspected] to cause or contribute to cancer, gene mutations, or birth defects . . .

(B) At least every six months after [the committee submits its initial list], the committee shall make such revisions in the list as it determines to be necessary and shall transmit them to the Administrator together with the committee's reasons for revision. [The initial list and subsequent revisions must be published in the Federal Register, and the Administrator must give interested persons an opportunity to comment.] Within [a year of a substance's inclusion on the committee's list], the Administrator shall . . . either initiate a rulemaking proceeding . . . or . . . publish in the Federal Register the Administrator's reason for not initiating such a proceeding.

(f) Required actions

Upon receipt of—

(1) any test data required to be submitted . . . , or

(2) any other information available to the Administrator, which indicates to the Administrator that there may be a reasonable basis to conclude that a chemical substance . . . presents or will present a significant risk of serious or

widespread harm to human beings from cancer, gene mutations, or birth defects, the Administrator shall, within [180 days of receipt of the data or information], initiate appropriate action [under TSCA sections 5, 6, or 7] to prevent or reduce to a sufficient extent such risk or publish in the Federal Register a finding that such risk is not unreasonable.

TSCA § 5   Manufacturing and Processing Notices

(a) **[Pre-manufacture notices]**

(1) . . . no person may

(A) manufacture a new chemical substance . . . or

(B) manufacture or process any chemical substance for a use which the Administrator has determined . . . is a significant new use

unless such person submits to the Administrator, at least 90 days before such manufacture or processing a notice . . . of such person's intention to manufacture or process such substance . . .

(2) A determination by the Administrator that a use of a chemical substance is a significant new use . . . shall be made by a rule promulgated after a consideration of all relevant factors, including —

(A) the projected volume of manufacturing . . .

(B) the extent to which a [new] use changes the type or form of exposure of human beings or the environment to a chemical substance,

(C) the extent to which a [new] use increases the magnitude and duration of exposure of human beings or the environment to [the] substance, and

(D) the reasonably anticipated . . . methods of manufacturing, processing, distribution . . . , and disposal of [the] chemical substance.

(b) **Submission of test data**

(1)(A) [If a person is required to submit pre-manufacture notice and test data pursuant to a testing rule, the person shall submit the data at the same time he or she submits the notice.]

(e) **Regulations pending development of information**

(1)(A) If the Administrator determines that—

(i) the information available to the Administrator is insufficient to permit a reasoned evaluation of the health and environmental effects of a chemical substance . . . ; and

(ii)(I) in the absence of sufficient information . . . , the manufacture, processing, distribution . . . , use, or disposal of such substance . . . may present an unreasonable risk of injury to health or the environment, or

(II) such substance is or will be produced in substantial quantities, and such substance either enters or may reasonably be anticipated to enter the environment in substantial quantities or there is or may be significant or substantial human exposure to the substance,

the Administrator may issue a proposed order . . . to prohibit or limit the manufacture, processing, distribution . . . , use, or disposal of such substance or to prohibit or limit any combination of such activities . . .

(C) If a manufacturer or processor of a chemical substance subject to a proposed order . . . files with the Administrator . . . objections specifying . . . the provisions of the order deemed objectionable . . . , the proposed order shall not take effect. [The Administrator may, but is not required to, bring an action in federal court for an injunction to prohibit or limit manufacture, processing, distribution, use, or disposal of the substance.]

TSCA § 6   Regulation of hazardous substances and mixtures

(a) **Scope of Regulation**

If the Administrator finds that there is a reasonable basis to conclude that the manufacture, [etc.,] of a chemical substance . . . presents or will present an unreasonable risk of injury to health or the environment, the Administrator shall by rule apply one or more of the following requirements . . . to the extent necessary to protect adequately against such risk using the least burdensome requirements:

(1) A requirement . . . prohibiting the manufacturing, [etc.,] of such substance . . . or limiting the amount of such substance . . . which may be manufactured, [etc.].

(2) A requirement—

(A) prohibiting the manufacture, [etc.,] of such substance . . . for (i) a particular use or (ii) a particular use in a concentration in excess of a level specified by the Administrator . . . , or

(B) limiting the amount of such substance . . . which may be manufactured, processed, or distributed in commerce [for a particular use or use in a concentration in excess of the specified level].

(3) A requirement that such substance . . . or any article containing such substance . . . be marked with or accompanied by clear and adequate warnings and instructions with respect to its use, distribution in commerce, or disposal . . . .

(4) A requirement that manufacturers and processors of such substance . . . make and retain records of the processes used to manufacture or process such substance . . . and monitor or conduct tests which are reasonable and necessary to assure compliance with the any rule [issued by the Administrator under TSCA § 6].

(5), (6) [A requirement prohibiting or regulating any manner or method of commercial use or disposal of the substance or any article containing the substance by manufacturers or other persons who use or dispose of the substance or article for commercial purposes.]

(7) A requirement directing manufacturers or processors of such substance . . . (A) to give notice of such unreasonable risk of injury to distributors in commerce of such substance . . . and, to the extent reasonably ascertainable, to other persons in possession of such substance . . . or exposed to such substance . . . (B) to give public notice of such risk of injury, . . .

Any requirement (or combination of requirements) imposed . . . may be limited . . . to specific geographical areas.

(c) **Promulgation of [regulatory rules]**

(1) . . . The Administrator shall consider . . . —

(A), (B) [the effects of such substance . . . on health and the environment and the magnitude of the exposure of human beings and the environment to such substance . . . ,]

(C) the benefits of such substance or mixture for various uses and the availability of substitutes for such uses, and

(D) the reasonably ascertainable economic consequences of the rule, after consideration of the effect on the national economy, small business, technological innovation, the environment, and public health.

(e) **Polychlorinated biphenyls**

[With certain limited exceptions, no person is allowed to manufacture or distribute PCBs after June 1, 1979.]

SUBCHAPTER II—ASBESTOS HAZARD EMERGENCY RESPONSE

TSCA § 201   Congressional findings and purposes

[Congress found that EPA's rule on school board inspection for, and notification of, the presence of friable asbestos-containing material in school buildings included neither standards for identifying asbestos-containing material nor a requirement that response actions with respect to friable asbestos be carried out in a safe and complete manner. The purpose of this subchapter is to establish federal regulations requiring inspection for asbestos and implementation of appropriate response actions in the nation's schools and to require the Administrator to conduct a study to learn the extent of the danger to human health and the environment posed by asbestos in public and commercial buildings.]

TSCA § 202   Definitions

(6) Friable asbestos-containing material

The term "friable asbestos-containing material" means any asbestos-containing material applied on ceilings, walls, . . . , piping, duct work, . . . which may be crumbled, pulverized, or reduced to powder by hand pressure. . . .

TSCA § 203   EPA Regulations

[The EPA Administrator shall promulgate regulations that:

1. prescribe procedures for determining whether asbestos is present in a school building;
2. define the appropriate response action in situations where there is damage or potential damage to friable asbestos-containing material;
3. describe response actions using the least burdensome methods that protect human health and the environment, taking into account local circumstances, use and occupancy patterns, and short- and long-term costs;
4. require school boards to develop an asbestos management plan for school buildings, to begin implementation by October 1989, and to complete implementation of such plans in a timely fashion.]

TSCA § 204   Requirements if EPA fails to promulgate regulations

(a) **In general**

(1) **Failure to promulgate**

If the Administrator fails to promulgate [§ 203 regulations] within the prescribed period—

... each [school board] shall carry out the requirements described in [the following subsections] in accordance with [EPA's] most current guidance document. ...

(b), (c), (d) [School boards are required to conduct inspections for asbestos, implement operation and maintenance, and develop and complete asbestos management plans, using accredited personnel and maintaining safety procedures, within specified time periods. This provision outlines the management plan re-

quirements, including an ambient interior concentration standard for asbestos fibers.]

TSCA § 208   Emergency Authority

(a) **Emergency action**

(1) **Authority**

Whenever—

(A) the presence of airborne asbestos or the condition of friable asbestos-containing material in a school building . . . poses an imminent and substantial endangerment to human health or the environment, and

(B) the local educational agency is not taking sufficient action (as determined by the Administrator or the Governor [of the State] to respond to the airborne asbestos or friable asbestos-containing material,

the Administrator or the Governor of a State is authorized to act to protect human health or the environment.

(b) **Cost recovery**

The Administrator or the Governor of a State may seek reimbursement for all costs of an emergency action . . . in [federal court].

SUBCHAPTER III—INDOOR RADON ABATEMENT

TSCA § 301   National goal

The national long-term goal of the United States with respect to radon levels in buildings is that the air within buildings in the United States should be as free of radon as the ambient air outside of buildings.

[Most of the provisions of this subchapter concern studies and educational programs on the dangers of radon and provide financial and technical assistance for addressing high radon levels in buildings.]

■ Chapter 5 Endnotes

1. From *The Closing Circle: Nature, Man, and Technology* by Barry Commoner. Copyright © 1971 Alfred A. Knopf, Inc. Reprinted by permission of Alfred A. Knopf, Inc. (1971), pp. 142–146.
2. Ibid., pp. 229–231. Copyright © 1971 Alfred A. Knopf, Inc. Reprinted by permission of Alfred A. Knopf, Inc.
3. *Report of the House Interstate and Foreign Commerce Committee on the Toxic Substance Control Act,* H.R. Rep. No. 94-1341 (1976).
4. *Highlights of the EPA Office of the Inspector General Report to Congress for Fiscal Year 1991.*

CHAPTER 6

Resource Conservation and Recovery Act (RCRA)

Solid Waste Tracking and Treatment: Cradle-to-Grave Waste Regulation

Outline

6.1   Historical Background of RCRA

Defining Waste

A generic definition of *waste* is something that is no longer useful. Although we usually think of waste in terms of garbage, or perhaps sewage, waste also occurs as unwanted by-products of manufacturing processes and as leakage from containers used to store useful materials. The Resource Conservation and Recovery Act (RCRA) was enacted for regulating the disposal and treatment of many kinds of wastes: household trash, referred to as *municipal waste*; hazardous waste, waste that is generally considered particularly dangerous; petroleum products that have leaked from underground storage tanks; solvents that have been expended in cleaning machinery; and spent chemicals.

Although RCRA is the nation's primary statute for dealing with waste, it does not regulate every kind of waste produced in the United States. For instance, Congress excluded from RCRA regulation domestic sewage and industrial discharges, both of which require Clean Water Act permits. Radioactive, or nuclear, wastes are not primarily regulated by RCRA.

Nuclear wastes result from the testing of nuclear weapons and the generation of energy in nuclear reactors. RCRA is not the primary mechanism for regulation of nuclear wastes[1] because they are supposed to be regulated under the Atomic Energy Act, which is administered by the Department of Energy. However, *mixed wastes,* those consisting of intermixed hazardous and radioactive wastes, are regulated by EPA under RCRA. Even though RCRA is not the primary mechanism for regulating radioactive wastes, some issues related to them are addressed in this chapter in discussions of the challenges posed by waste regulation in technologically advanced and highly industrialized societies.

The definition of *solid waste* is central to the RCRA regulatory scheme. Nevertheless, determining whether certain materials are "solid" wastes can be difficult, as any environmental lawyer can attest. The general definition is that a solid waste is a "discarded material" that is a "solid, liquid, semisolid, or contained gaseous material."[2] Thus, according to the law, a "solid waste" need not be in solid form.

RCRA and its implementing regulations include in the definition of *solid waste* not only materials that we commonly think of as discarded or abandoned but also materials that are "recycled" or "inherently wastelike."[3] The universe of "solid waste" includes materials that are disposed of, burned or incinerated, accumulated, stored, or treated before *or instead of* being abandoned. Although materials that are going to be recycled are considered solid wastes, materials that are going to be used or reused as ingredients in the same industrial process to make a product or as a substitute for commercial products are *not* considered solid waste. Materials that will be burned to produce energy are considered solid wastes if they fit the definition otherwise.

In order to be considered a "waste," a substance must either be intentionally disposed of or be spilled or placed in some routine fashion, even though spillage or placement was not intended as a means of disposal. A common example is a solvent that is used for rinsing machine parts and is allowed to spill onto the soil on a regular basis. The regularity of the spillage establishes that "disposal" is occurring even though disposal is not the primary intention.

"Hazardous waste" is a subset of "solid waste." In other words, all hazardous wastes are solid wastes, but not all solid wastes are hazardous wastes. To be considered a "hazardous waste," a material must first satisfy the definition of "solid waste."

RCRA defines *hazardous waste* as a solid waste that:

> because of its quantity, concentration, or physical, chemical, or infectious characteristics may—(A) cause, or significantly contribute to an increase in mortality or an increase in serious irreversible, or incapacitating reversible, illness; or (B) pose a substantial present or potential hazard to human health or the environment when improperly treated, stored, transported, or disposed of, or otherwise managed.

Note that this definition of "hazardous waste" takes into account the possibility that the material may pose a threat if it is disposed of improperly. The fact that disposal in a particular case may mitigate the threat of improper disposal does not exclude the material in question from the definition of "hazardous waste."

Under the implementing regulations that EPA is required to promulgate under RCRA,[4] a solid waste qualifies as a "hazardous waste" either by listing or by characteristic. *Listed hazardous wastes* are those that EPA places on a list that RCRA requires it to publish. Most of these are industrial or commercial wastes. A listed waste may be denoted by its chemical makeup when the composition is known. For those whose precise chemical makeup is unknown or varies widely, the waste may be denoted by an identification of the industrial process that produces it.

Characteristic hazardous wastes are wastes that exhibit one or more of four hazardous characteristics:

1. *ignitability* (e.g., a liquid with a low flash point);
2. *corrosivity* (i.e., a substance having a very low or very high pH)
3. *reactivity* (e.g., explosives)
4. *toxicity* (e.g., a substance that leaches particular metals or organic materials above specified concentrations)

Some listed hazardous wastes have been listed solely because they consistently display one of these hazardous characteristics.

Whereas characteristic hazardous wastes are considered hazardous for as long as they display a hazardous characteristic, listed hazardous wastes are considered hazardous until they are "delisted," even if they no longer display any hazardous characteristic. "Delisting" is the process whereby a person petitions EPA to exclude from RCRA regulation a waste that is generated at a specific facility. The petitioner must show that the waste does not meet any of the four hazardous criteria or any of the criteria under which it was initially listed. Normally, this situation arises when the processes at the facility for which delisting is sought are unique in some way.

Certain wastes which are otherwise hazardous are excluded from regulation as hazardous wastes. For instance, *household waste* is excluded from the RCRA definition of hazardous waste regardless of whether it exhibits one or more of the hazardous characteristics or falls under a listed category. Also, facilities that generate and store only very small quantities of waste identified as hazardous at any one time may be exempt from RCRA hazardous waste regulation.

The Mounting Problems of Accumulating Waste

In the late 1980s the Council on Environmental Quality (CEQ) reported on the accumulation of solid waste since World War II.

> Per capita waste production in the United States is greater than in any [other] country in the world. Collectively, this nation produces 160 million tons of garbage a year. . . . Americans are producing more solid waste than ever. . . and have fewer places to put it.
>
>   . . . In 1960 Americans generated municipal type solid waste at the rate of 2.65 pounds per person per day. By 1986, that figure climbed to 3.58 pounds, and the trend is up [to 4 pounds per person in 1988]. . . . While the amount of trash has grown, facilities to handle it have become scarcer. In 1978, there were approximately 20,000 municipal landfills. . . . Today less than 6000 are still in use. By 1993 about a third of these will be filled. Many more will be closed due to inadequate safety or environmental practices. . . . A large number of existing . . . landfills do not meet current . . . standards for safe design and operation. . . . More than half . . . make no attempt to control water pollution resulting from the runoff of rain from their sites. The cost of trash disposal is going up. . . . The issues discussed above apply mainly to municipal solid waste. . . . Most solid waste, however, is industrial, agricultural, and mining. Municipal type wastes are estimated at 160 million tons. Industrial wastes are measured in the billions of tons. The Environmental Protection Agency estimates that industries generate 7.6 billion tons per year of solid waste. . . . Oil and gas producers generate two to three billion tons per year; mining . . . about 1.4 billion tons.[5]

Municipal wastes consist mostly of paper, yard wastes, food and packaging such as glass, metal, and plastics. Industrial waste contains many substances that by themselves or in mixture with other wastes are hazardous and toxic. Household and industrial wastes formerly were intermixed in common dumpsites, and in some cases still are, although RCRA hazardous waste regulations now generally prohibit that practice. The CEQ report also noted the dimensions of the problem of disposing of these wastes:

> Twenty-two percent of the sites on the . . . National Priorities List, which includes the sites posing the greatest chemical hazards to public health and the environment, are municipal waste landfills. Most of these were developed prior to the imposition of state and federal regulations, and often received wastes that today are considered hazardous. . . . Uncertainty exists as to the overall risk . . . posed by landfills. . . . The siting of new waste facilities and the choice of waste processing technologies have ignited heated controversies in almost every city and county in the land. Some of the controversy is just an outgrowth of the . . . NIMBY, or not-in-my-back-yard, phenomenon. Much of it grows out of concerns . . . about the side effects of technologies and the inadequacies of regulation.[6]

The options for disposing of ever-increasing quantities of municipal solid waste by means other than landfilling are limited. For instance, a solution often proposed in communities facing a shortage of landfill space is incineration, a technology that has its own set of risks:

> As of 1988, the Council on Environmental Quality reported that ten to fifteen percent of American solid waste was disposed of by combustion in about 134 municipal trash burning facilities, but that the volatile economics of waste combustion impeded expansion of combustion facilities. As air pollution control standards become stricter, so do the costs of trash combustion which generate both air pollutants and residual ash that contain toxic substances and harmful particulates. The high cost of installing equipment to avoid air pollution and to dispose of combustion ash remains a serious impediment to the growth of combustion technology.[7]

The hazards of current incineration technology cannot be overemphasized. First, certain extremely toxic pollutants, such as mercury, are not capable of being reduced at incineration temperatures that destroy other harmful constituents. Therefore, they escape into the atmosphere during combustion, even when state-of-the-art pollution-control technologies are utilized.

Second, disposal of incineration ash presents a thorny quandary. Consider the following "odyssey of a poison ship."

> When Joseph Poalino, a Philadelphia waste contractor, struck a deal to get rid of 200,000 tons of ash from the city's garbage incinerators in early 1986, he clearly believed there was money to be made. The municipal docks were piled high with huge mounds of the gray refuse, lining the Schuylkill River like a vast dunescape. But as more and more landfills [that would accept the ash] . . . closed down and citizens began to protest the gritty ash blowing through their neighborhoods, Pa-olino realized he had a problem.
>
> Frustrated and faced with a massive backlog of the toxic ash, he then came up with what seemed a brilliant solution—hire a ship and find a dumpsite overseas.
>
> That ship, the *Khian Sea*, would create an international scandal as it hauled Phi-ladelphia's incinerated trash around the world. The ship was to spend twenty-seven months wandering the seas like a gypsy, with "more lives than a cat and more names than a Spanish duke," as [one reporter] put it.[8]

The *Khian Sea* carried 15,000 tons of ash, a month's worth of Philadelphia's incinerator refuse. The EPA later revealed that the ash was laced with lead, chro-mium, arsenic, and dioxin—in concentrations greater than those found at Times Beach, Missouri, a town that was evacuated for that reason in 1983. The ash was so corrosive that it actually ate away at the ship's cargo bays. Between 1986 and 1988, the *Khian Sea* sailed to the Bahamas and throughout the Caribbean seeking a disposal location. It off-loaded 4,000 tons of ash in Haiti, before the newly elected government stopped it, and then returned to the Delaware Bay in March 1988. Against Coast Guard orders to remain in port due to its inoperative sonar and radar, it continued its journey that spring, going first to Yugoslavia for repairs and then through the Suez Canal into the Red Sea and the Indian Ocean. The ship arrived in Singapore in November 1988 minus its cargo.

In criminal indictments returned by a Delaware grand jury in July 1992, two executives of the vessel's shipping agent were charged with lying to a grand jury in 1990 when they were asked if they knew where the ash had been disposed. The ship's captain testified that, pursuant to the explicit and repeated instructions of his superiors, the crew dumped 11,000 tons of ash into the Atlantic and Indian Oceans. He also testified that he had been instructed by the operating company's president to falsify records and to lie about the disposal location.

Due to growing recognition that both incineration and land disposal pose sig-nificant environmental problems, more consideration has been given to attacking the problem from the other direction; that is, reducing the amount of waste that must be disposed. There are two general ways to reduce overall quantities of waste:

1. *Source reduction*, reducing the amount of waste that is generated at the source; and
2. *Resource recovery*, reusing and recycling materials that would otherwise re-main as waste.

Source reduction requires improved design and use of materials in ways that minimize the quantity and toxicity of wastes remaining after production and use. Thus, source reduction entails using smaller amounts of less toxic materials and extending their useful life before discarding them—such as, for example, developing longer-lasting auto and truck tires. For many products and purposes, source reduction is favored because it is financially attractive. In other instances, though, producers resist developing and implementing source-reduction techniques and technologies because they involve higher short-term costs. The cost of research and development for less wasteful products and perceived consumer preferences for "throw-away" packaging tend to deter greater source reduction efforts by industry. In such instances, private interests often run counter to responsible environmental policy. It is clear, therefore, that private efforts alone will not solve waste management problems.

For similar reasons, many business and institutional interests opt against resource recovery through recycling. For example, when paper pulp is in short supply and demand for waste paper is high, communities and businesses energetically promote paper recycling programs. When the cost of pulp decreases, however, recycling becomes more costly and declines. As one writer noted, recycling is good for the environment, but the challenge is how to make it pay in the short term. The long-term social benefits of recycling—namely, economical use of increasingly costly landfill space and preservation of natural resources—are not generally accounted for by individuals seeking to maximize their own gains. To the extent that regulation can affirmatively promote recycling by engineering market systems which confer economic incentives for environmentally responsible behavior, recycling will become a viable option. Until this occurs, however, regulation of a negative, restraining nature (such as by requiring a specified percentage of recycled material in new products) may be required. The cost factors affecting recycling obviously vary with products and their markets, variations that can only be addressed by carefully tailored regulations.

Given that most of our waste has not historically been reduced at the source or recovered for reuse, and that the huge economic and environmental costs of disposal are ultimately paid by the general public, comprehensive government involvement in waste regulation is appropriate and necessary. In many cases only government regulation, and not private markets, can create economic incentives to reduce waste accumulation. Where such incentives are not available, only government can strike a balance between conflicting public and private interests through laws that oblige public and private institutions to contribute to environmental solutions. This is particularly true for the management of hazardous wastes, which pose far greater dangers and are far costlier to remediate once careless disposal has occurred.

Nevertheless, governmental authority was not energetically employed in the area of waste management until the discoveries at Love Canal in Niagara Falls, New York, propelled Congress into action in 1978:

> The focus changed . . . when then-President Carter declared a state of emergency in a neighborhood near Love Canal, where long-buried chemicals were seeping into homes and high incidents of health effects . . . were reported. The event triggered the discovery of thousands of other dumpsites, alarming the public and mobilizing the Administration and the Congress. . . . "What our political system takes to move it is galvanizing events. And when Love Canal came along, bingo. That was a tremendously galvanizing event."[9]

After Love Canal, the evident dangers of hazardous waste in open dumps and landfills hastened the passage of environmental laws to address hazardous waste issues.

Despite governmental and social recognition of the solid waste crisis, the volume of municipal solid waste continues to grow. The good news is that recycling also is on the rise, at least for municipal solid waste. The Director of EPA's Office of Solid Waste traced these developments in a 1992 article:

> We're glad to report that recycling has increased substantially nationwide. In 1990, Americans generated 195 million tons of municipal solid waste. Of this total, 33 million tons were recovered for recycling or composting. That amounts to a 17 percent recycling rate, compared to 13 percent in 1988. . . .
>
> Between 1985 and 1990, the amount of material recovered from municipal solid waste more than doubled. The amount of yard debris that was collected for municipal composting increased dramatically during the 1988–1990 period, rising from 2 percent to 12 percent. If current trends continue, recovery of materials for recycling and composting is expected to rise from the current 17 percent to about 20–30 percent in 1995 (EPA's goal is to reduce and recycle 25 percent of municipal waste by the end of 1992) and then up to about 25–35 percent by the end of the century.
>
> In 1988, Americans produced about 4 pounds per person per day (ppd) of garbage. In 1990, the rate increased 4.3 ppd, an 8 percent increase since 1988. EPA projects that the amount of garbage generated in the United States will increase to about 4.5 ppd by the year 2000.
>
> The new data also shows that 16 percent of garbage was managed by combustion in 1990, up from 14 percent in 1988, and that the remaining 67 percent was landfilled, down from 73 percent in 1988. . . .[10]

History and Overview of Solid and Hazardous Waste Regulation

Congressional concern over the effects of the postwar revolution in production of synthetic chemicals and the mounting solid and hazardous waste problem led it in 1976 to enact the Toxic Substances Control Act (TSCA; the subject of Chapter 5) as well as the Resource Conservation and Recovery Act (RCRA). RCRA overhauled the Solid Waste Disposal Act of 1965 and the Resource Recovery Act of 1970, which had sought primarily to reduce solid waste generation and to increase recycling, respectively. However, RCRA stressed the goal of protecting human health and the environment and provided a much more comprehensive regulation scheme. Its broad sweep has been summarized as follows:

> The new law continued [the older] provisions on solid waste and resource recovery . . . and it closed most open dumps; it redefined solid waste to include hazardous waste and ordered EPA to require "cradle to grave" tracking of hazardous waste and controls on hazardous waste facilities. The Act required standards to be set for hazardous waste treatment, storage, and disposal facilities . . . "requiring such additional qualifications as to ownership, continuity of operation, training for personnel, and financial responsibility . . . as may be necessary or desirable."[11]

Subtitle C of RCRA contains provisions for managing hazardous waste. It authorizes "cradle to grave" regulation of all phases of hazardous-waste generation and disposal with separate and specific provisions for:

1. waste generators;
2. waste transporters; and
3. owners and operators of facilities for waste treatment, storage, and disposal.

EPA was slow to implement Subtitle C and, indeed, was forced by lawsuit and court order in 1980 to issue regulations to identify hazardous wastes and to prescribe standards for their disposal.

Over time, experience with the RCRA regulations indicated that additional restrictions were needed to stem the dangers posed by active treatment, storage, and disposal facilities. In 1984, Congress substantially amended RCRA to achieve these purposes:

- To subject smaller generators of hazardous waste (who were exempt from the original 1976 law) to RCRA regulation;
- To require EPA to regulate underground storage tanks;
- To require EPA to develop and impose standards for treating different classes of hazardous waste;
- To direct EPA to prohibit land disposal of untreated hazardous waste no later than the deadline set by the amendments (five and a half years), unless EPA could show that a particular land disposal operation would protect human health and the environment.

It is important to note that RCRA Subtitle C is directed primarily to management of active facilities that store, treat, or dispose of hazardous wastes and not to the cleanup of abandoned or inactive sites that have been contaminated by hazardous constituents. To provide mechanisms for the cleanup of abandoned, as well as active sites, Congress had enacted the Comprehensive Environmental Response, Compensation, and Liability Act, popularly known as *Superfund*, in 1980.[12] The Superfund law (the subject of Chapter 7) is a necessary complement to RCRA, which only regulates facilities engaged in routine or intentional disposal and is only occasionally useful in addressing problems at older, abandoned sites.

6.2 Structure and Workings of RCRA

Outline of Major Statutory Provisions

The statutory locations of some of RCRA's major requirements are given in this subsection. Excerpts of selected RCRA provisions appear in the appendix to this chapter.

Solid Waste (Subtitle D)

Subtitle D contains provisions for state and regional solid waste plans to encourage the use of environmentally sound technologies for conserving energy and resources. It also authorizes promulgation of regulations concerning landfills. Two sections are particularly worthy of note:

Landfills

Criteria For Sanitary Landfills	§ 4004
Upgrading of Open Dumps	§ 4005

Hazardous Waste (Subtitle C)

Subtitle C regulates the management of hazardous waste. Subtitle C and its implementing regulations: define hazardous waste; enunciate standards that apply to parties who generate, transport, and treat or dispose of hazardous waste; outline the requirements of the manifest system, by which all hazardous wastes are tracked from the point of generation to the ultimate point of disposal; establish a permit system for those who treat, store, or dispose of hazardous wastes; and authorize federally approved state programs. The following provisions are central to the establishment of hazardous waste management standards:

Identification and Listing of Hazardous Wastes

Listing	§ 3001 (a)
Identifying Characteristics	§ 3001 (b)
Small-Quantity Generators	§ 3001 (d)
Delisting Procedures	§ 3001 (f)
Household Waste Exclusion	§ 3001 (i)

The Manifest System: Record Keeping and Tracking of Wastes

Generators	§ 3002
Transporters	§ 3003
Owners/Operators of Treatment, Storage, and Disposal Facilities (TSDs)	§ 3004 (a)

Acceptable Disposal Methods

Land Ban: Restrictions on Landfilling Wastes

Liquids	§ 3004 (c)
Hazardous Wastes	§ 3004 (d)
Solvents and Dioxins	§ 3004 (e)
Underground Injection	§ 3004 (f)
Additional Land Ban	§ 3004 (g)
Variances	§ 3004 (h)
No Disposal, No Storage	§ 3004 (j)
Dust Suppression	§ 3004 (l)
Treatment Standards	§ 3004 (m)
Minimum Technological Requirements	§ 3004 (o)
Financial Responsibility	§ 3004 (t)

Corrective Action

Onsite	§ 3004 (u)
Offsite	§ 3004 (v)

The Permit System

Standards, Issuance, and Revocation	§ 3005 (a)–(d)
Interim Status	§ 3005 (e)
Notification of Hazardous Waste Activity	§ 3010 (a)
Research and Development	§ 3005 (g)
Waste Minimization	§ 3005 (h)

State Authorization

State authorization	§ 3006

Civil and Criminal Enforcement

A number of provisions authorize EPA or an authorized state program to take legal actions to enforce standards relating to hazardous waste and to require corrective action to clean up hazardous waste spills:

Criminal Penalties

Criminal Violations	§ 3008 (d)
Knowing Endangerment	§ 3008 (e)

Enforcement

Compliance Orders	§ 3008 (a) (1)
Permit Revocation	§ 3008 (a) (3)

Penalties	§ 3008 (c)
Interim-Status Corrective Action	§ 3008 (h)(1)
Substantial Hazard	§ 3013
Imminent and Substantial Endangerment	§ 7003
Citizens' Suits	§ 7002

Underground Storage Tanks (Subtitle I)

Subtitle I regulates underground storage tanks used for storing petroleum products and hazardous substances.

Underground Storage Tanks

Definitions	§ 9001
Notification	§ 9002
Release Detection	§ 9003
Corrective Action	§ 9003 (h)
Inspection and Monitoring	§ 9005
Enforcement Orders/Penalties	§ 9006

Illustrative RCRA Cases

The three cases excerpted in this subsection illustrate the general workings of the RCRA Subtitle C and how it affects hazardous-waste generators, transporters, and treatment, storage, and disposal facilities.

SHELL OIL CO. v. EPA

950 F.2d 741 (D.C. Cir. 1991)

Before BUCKLEY, WILLIAMS, and THOMAS, Circuit Judges.

Consolidated petitioners challenge two rules that categorize substances as hazardous wastes . . . ; the "mixture" rule, which classifies as a hazardous waste any mixture of a "listed" hazardous waste with any other solid waste, and the "derived-from" rule, which so classifies any residue derived from the treatment of hazardous waste. They argue that the EPA failed to provide adequate notice and opportunity for comment when it promulgated the mixture and derived-from rules, and that the rules exceed the EPA's statutory authority.

I. BACKGROUND

The EPA promulgated the disputed rules in order to implement the Resource Conservation and Recovery Act ("RCRA") . . . RCRA created a "cradle-to-grave" system for tracking wastes from their generation to disposal. The statute consists of two main parts: one governs the management of non-hazardous solid waste; the other, hazardous waste. . . .

An enacted, Subtitle C of RCRA required the EPA to establish a comprehensive national system for safely treating, storing, and disposing of hazardous wastes. It defined "hazardous waste," in part, as a "solid waste" which may "pose a substantial present or potential hazard to human health or the environment when improperly treated, stored, transported, or disposed of, or otherwise managed." . . . It gave the EPA until April 21, 1978 to develop and promulgate criteria for identifying characteristics of hazardous waste and to list particular wastes as hazardous. . . . It further required the EPA to promulgate regulations "as may be necessary to protect human health and the environment" respecting the practices of generators, transporters, and those who own or operate hazardous waste treatment, storage, or disposal facilities. . . .

RCRA prohibited treatment, storage, or disposal of hazardous waste without a permit and required the EPA to promulgate standards governing permits for facilities performing such functions. . . .

On February 17, 1977, the EPA published a Notice of Intent to Develop Rulemaking, . . . and on May 2, 1977, it published an Advance Notice of Proposed Rulemaking, . . . In addition, it circulated for comment several drafts of regulations . . . and held public hearings. This process culminated in the publication, on December 18, 1978, of proposed regulations covering most of the statutorily required standards. . . .

This proposal elicited voluminous comment, and the EPA held five large public hearings. The EPA failed to issue final regulations by the April 1978 statutory deadline; several parties sued the Agency to compel it to do so.

The EPA published its "[r]evisions to final rule and interim final rule" on May 19, 1980 . . . It noted that time pressures had had an effect on the new regulations: Because of limited information, the Agency was unable to avoid underregulation and overregulation. . . .

More than fifty petitions were brought to challenge these final rules. In 1982, we deferred briefing on these challenges to allow the parties to pursue settlement discussions . . . We did not stay the rules, however, which have remained in effect. Most of the issues have been resolved by settlement, by subsequent statutory or regulatory revision, or by the failure of petitioners to pursue them. The issues presented here are those that the EPA identified as unlikely . . . to be settled. . . .

Consolidated petitioners assert that the regulations proposed on December 18, 1978, did not foreshadow the inclusion of the mixture and derived-from rules in the final rule's definition of "hazardous waste." Thus, they assert, they were deprived of adequate notice and opportunity for comment. They also claim that the EPA exceeded its statutory authority by including the two rules in the final definition of hazardous waste. . . .

II. DISCUSSION

A. Principles Governing Judicial Review
The Administrative Procedure Act ("APA")

governs judicial review of final regulations promulgated under RCRA. . . . In issuing regulations, the EPA must observe the notice-and-comment procedures of the APA . . . and the public-participation directive of RCRA. . . . The relationship between the proposed regulation and the final rule determines the adequacy of notice. A difference between the two will not invalidate the notice so long as the final rule is a "logical outgrowth" of the one proposed. If the deviation from the proposal is too sharp, the affected parties will not have had adequate notice and opportunity for comment. . . .

RCRA defines the scope of the EPA's regulatory discretion: In formulating rules, the clearly expressed intent of Congress binds agencies as it binds courts. Where congressional intent is ambiguous, however, an agency's interpretation of a statute entrusted to its administration is entitled to deference, so long as it is reasonable. . . .

B. The Mixture and Derived-From Rules

The mixture and derived-from rules are to be found in the definition of "hazardous waste" that appears in the final rules. That definition includes as hazardous all wastes resulting from mixing hazardous and other wastes and from treating, storing, or disposing of hazardous wastes, until such time as the wastes are proven nonhazardous. Petitioners protest that these provisions had no counterpart in, and were not a logical outgrowth of, the proposed regulations; thus, the promulgation of the rules violated the notice-and-comment requirements of RCRA and the APA. We agree.

1. Statutory Background

To become subject to RCRA's comprehensive regulatory system, a material must be a hazardous waste, which RCRA defines, in part, as:

a solid waste, or combination of solid wastes, which because of its quantity, concentration, or physical, chemical, or infectious characteristics may—

. . . . . .

(B) pose a substantial present or potential hazard to human health or the environment when improperly treated, stored, transported, or disposed of, or otherwise managed. . . .

To determine what materials fall within that definition, the EPA must promulgate criteria for the identification and listing of hazardous wastes. The statute provides the EPA with specific instructions for identifying and listing hazardous waste:

(a) Criteria for identification or listing

. . . the Administrator shall, after notice and opportunity for public hearing, . . . develop and promulgate criteria for identifying the characteristics of hazardous waste, and for listing hazardous waste, . . . taking into account toxicity, persistence, and degradability in nature, potential for accumulation in tissue, and other related factors such as flammability, corrosiveness, and other hazardous characteristics. Such criteria shall be revised from time to time as may be appropriate.

(b) Identification and listing

. . . the Administrator shall promulgate regulations identifying the characteristics of hazardous waste, and listing particular hazardous wastes . . . Such regulations shall be based on the criteria promulgated under subsection (a) of this section . . .

* * *

Although the EPA initially identified nine possible characteristics as potentially hazardous, it decided to rely on only four of them—ignitability, corrosivity, reactivity, and toxicity—in its proposed section 250.13, because only these could be tested reliably and inexpensively. . . . Because solid wastes that present a hazard but do not display one of these four characteristics remained subject to RCRA, the EPA proposed to list such wastes specifically, . . .

* * *

. . . and to treat any waste once listed as hazardous until a person managing the waste filed a delisting petition and demonstrated to the EPA that the waste did not pose a hazard . . .

3.   The Final Rules

The final rules defined a hazardous waste more broadly than did the proposed regulations. . . .

A number of interested parties had challenged the listing of classes of wastes in the

proposed regulations as an unwarranted expansion of the statutory phrase "particular wastes," which, they asserted, required the listing of specific wastes only. . . . The EPA nevertheless retained the proposed scheme in its final rules, stating that its use of classes was justified by the complexity of the factors bearing on hazard and the impossibility of defining a numerical threshold level for hazardous characteristics. . . .

4.   The Mixture Rule

The mixture rule requires that a waste be treated as hazardous if

[i]t is a mixture of solid waste and one or more hazardous wastes. . . . Once classified as hazardous, then, a mixture must be so treated until delisted.

The EPA acknowledged at the outset that the mixture rule was "a new provision," and that it had no "direct counterpart in the proposed regulations." . . . Nevertheless, it added the rule for purposes of clarification and in response to questions raised during the comment period . . . .

Although admitting that it had failed to say so in the proposed regulations, the EPA stated that it had "intended" to treat waste mixtures containing Subpart D wastes as hazardous. It then presented the mixture rule as necessary to close "a major loophole in the Subtitle C management system." . . . Otherwise, generators of hazardous waste "could evade [those] requirements simply by commingling [Subpart D] wastes with nonhazardous solid waste" to create a waste that did not demonstrate any of the four testable characteristics but that posed a hazard for another reason. . . . The Agency explained that although the mixture rule might include waste with concentrations of Subpart D wastes too low to pose a hazard, the delisting process and the possibility of segregating waste to avoid the problem mitigated the burden of the rule. Finally, the EPA invoked the practical difficulties of its task to justify the rule's adoption:

Because the potential combinations of listed wastes and other wastes are infinite, we have been unable to devise any workable, broadly applicable formula which would distinguish between those waste mixtures which are and are not hazardous. . . .

While the EPA admits that the mixture rule lacks a clear antecedent in the proposed regulations, it nonetheless argues that the rule merely clarifies the intent behind the proposal that listed wastes remain hazardous until delisted: As industry could not have reasonably assumed that a generator could bring a listed waste outside the generic listing description simply by mixing it with a nonhazardous waste, the rule cannot be seen as a "bolt from the blue." . . .

5. The Derived-From Rule

The derived-from rule provides that

[a]ny solid waste generated from the treatment, storage or disposal of a hazardous waste, including any sludge, spill residue, ash, emission control dust or leachate (but not including precipitation run-off), is a hazardous waste.

* * *

The EPA's justifications for the derived-from rule resemble those for the mixture rule. Arguing that the products of treatment, storage, or disposal of listed hazardous wastes usually continue to pose hazards, the EPA defends the rule as "the best regulatory approach we can devise," given the fact that "[w]e are not now in a position to prescribe waste-specific treatment standards which would identify those processes which do and do not render wastes or treatment residues nonhazardous." . . . The EPA acknowledged, however, that the rule was a new provision, "added both in response to comment and as a logical outgrowth of [another proposed rule].

6. Adequacy of Notice

Although the EPA acknowledges that neither of the two rules was to be found among the proposed regulations, it nevertheless argues that they were foreseeable—and, therefore, the notice adequate—because certain of the comments received in response to the rulemaking appeared to anticipate both the mixture and the derived-from rules. We are unimpressed by the scanty evidence marshaled in support of this position. . . .

The EPA also draws attention to a response it made before the close of the comment period to a question posed by the American Mining Congress in which the Agency indicated that the delisting procedure would permit generators to remove wastes from the RCRA system. This, apparently, is supposed to have alerted interested parties that delisting would be the only means of exit from regulation. But examination of the precise words that the EPA used reveals a different message. The EPA stated that "[de]listing provides a means . . . to demonstrate that that waste does not belong in the system at all." . . . This response concerned the exclusion from regulation of wastes included by initial regulatory error, not the deregulation of wastes that have ceased to be hazardous.

The EPA's remaining evidence of implied notice is equally unimpressive. . . .

An agency, of course, may promulgate final rules that differ from the proposed regulations. To avoid "the absurdity that the agency can learn from the comments on its proposals only at the peril of starting a new procedural round of commentary" . . . we have held that final rules need only be a "logical outgrowth" of the proposed regulations. . . . But an unexpressed intention cannot convert a final rule into a "logical outgrowth" that the public should have anticipated . . . The reasons given by the EPA in support of its contention that interested parties should have anticipated the new rules are simply too insubstantial to justify a finding of implicit notice.

While it is true that such parties might have anticipated the potential for avoiding regulation by simply mixing hazardous and nonhazardous wastes, it was the business of the EPA, and not the public, to foresee that possibility and to address it in its proposed regulations. Moreover, while a comment may evidence a recognition of a problem, it can tell us nothing of how, or even whether, the agency will choose to address it. . . .

Even if the mixture and derived-from rules had been widely anticipated, comments by members of the public would not in themselves constitute adequate notice. Under the standards of the APA, "notice necessarily must come—if at all—from the Agency." . . .

* * *

The EPA's argument also fails to take into account a marked shift . . . between the proposed regulations and the final rules. Under the EPA's initial regulatory strategy, the EPA planned to identify and quantitatively define all of the characteristics of hazardous waste. . . . As a consequence, listing was to "play [the] largely supplementary function" of increasing the "certainty" of the process. . . . Thus, the proposed regulations imposed, as a generator's principal responsibility, the duty to test wastes for hazardous characteristics and suggested that if the required tests failed to reveal a hazard, the waste would not need to be managed as hazardous.

The final rules, however, place a heavy emphasis on listing . . .

Whatever the basis for this shift in strategy, it erodes the foundation of the EPA's argument that the mixture rule was implicit in the proposed regulations. A system that would rely primarily on lists of wastes and waste-producing processes might imply inclusion of a waste until it is formally removed from the list. The proposed regulations, however, did not suggest such a system. Rather, their emphasis on characteristics suggested that if a waste did not exhibit the nine characteristics originally proposed, it need not be regulated as hazardous.

Similarly, while the derived-from rule may well have been the best regulatory approach the EPA could devise, . . . it was not a logical outgrowth of the proposed regulations. The derived-from rule is not implicit in a system based upon testing wastes for specified hazardous characteristics—the system presented in the proposed regulations . . .

* * *

Because the EPA has not provided adequate notice and opportunity for comment, we conclude that the mixture and derived-from rules must be set aside and remanded to the EPA. . . .

* * *

Although RCRA addresses resource recovery from nonhazardous solid wastes, it is silent as to how the extraction of any recoverable value is to be handled once a material falls within the EPA's exclusive jurisdiction as hazardous

waste. Yet, one purpose of the statute is to conserve useful resources, . . . and such recovery must be incident to the management of hazardous wastes.

* * *

Thus, we are faced with the question of whether the absence of the words "resource recovery" from the statutory definition of "treatment." . . . requires the EPA to recede from its clear regulatory role in the management of hazardous wastes . . . when useable resources are being salvaged from them. . . .

The EPA insists that . . . to assert that hazardous materials may be removed from this "cradle-to-grave" regulatory system whenever resources are recovered from hazardous wastes, would create a paradoxical system. . . .

. . . Yet, resource recovery and recycling activities pose the same kinds of dangers that treatment and storage do. . . . As the EPA noted in promulgating the final rules, such a system could significantly undermine the entire regulatory structure. Excluding resource recovery from hazardous wastes from Subtitle C jurisdiction

> would make the regulatory program largely unworkable and create a major regulatory loophole not intended by the Act. Without a manifest system (or its functional equivalent) there would be no way of assuring that wastes which were intended to be used, reused, recycled or reclaimed were in fact delivered to their intended destination. . . .

* * *

Under *Chevron,* if we determine that Congress has not spoken to the precise question at issue, we

> must assume that Congress implicitly delegated to the agency the power to make policy choices that represent[ ] a reasonable accommodation of conflicting policies that were committed to the agency's care by the statute.

. . . Although Subtitle C is silent on the question of resource recovery from hazardous waste, its structure and its broad grant of authority to the EPA to manage the problem of hazardous waste make it unclear, at the very least, whether Congress intended to exempt resource recovery from what is otherwise a comprehensive mandate to regulate hazardous wastes. . . .

Under such circumstances, *Chevron* requires us to defer to the EPA's construction of its authority under Subtitle C so long as it "is reasonable and consistent with the statutory purpose." . . . As Subtitle C, read as a whole, provides broad authority to the EPA to fashion rules to govern the management of hazardous wastes, it would seem entirely reasonable for the EPA to conclude that it has the authority to regulate the extraction of resources from the wastes committed to its care.

* * *

Given the structure of Subtitle C and the power delegated to the EPA, we find the Agency's regulation of resource recovery from hazardous wastes to be permissible . . . Further, we believe the EPA acted reasonably in incorporating resource recovery within the regulatory definition of treatment. . . . Thus, we deny the AMC's petition challenging the EPA's authority to regulate resource recovery.

* * *

2. Final Rules

The final rules required only groundwater monitoring at landfills and surface impoundments. . . . Unlike the proposed regulations, they did not require leachate monitoring at these facilities because of the "technical problems" associated with its implementation. . . .

* * *

In contrast, the final rules required that land treatment facilities utilize soil-core and leachate, as well as groundwater, monitoring systems. . . . According to the EPA, all three testing systems were necessary "to accurately determine whether the complex processes involved in land treatment are, in fact, occurring, and whether contaminants are migrating to ground water." The EPA explained that it was requiring both types of unsaturated zone monitoring because they perform complementary functions: . . .

The EPA also explained why leachate monitoring was required at land treatment facilities, despite its rejection of such a requirement for landfills and surface impoundments:

[Leachate] monitoring is more easily achieved at land treatment sites than at landfills or surface impoundments. . . .

We conclude that the EPA did not adequately forewarn parties that leachate monitoring might be imposed. As both the proposed regulations and final rules reveal, the three types of proposed monitoring requirements are quite different: Leachate and groundwater monitoring test different subterranean zones (unsaturated and saturated, respectively), and soil-core and leachate monitoring perform different analyses within the same zone. A proposal to require one type of monitoring does not imply an intent to require another, nor does a proposal to require one kind of monitoring at landfills and surface impoundments imply an intent to require the same kind at land treatment facilities.

B.   Permit-Shield Provision

The Environmental Defense Fund ("EDF") challenges the EPA's "permit as shield" provision that, . . . protects holders of RCRA permits from enforcement actions for violations of the underlying statute." The provision currently reads:

Compliance with an RCRA permit during its term constitutes compliance for purpose of enforcement, with Subtitle C of RCRA . . .

* * *

2.   Conflict with Citizen-Suit Provision

The EDF first challenges the permit-shield provision on the ground that it conflicts with RCRA's citizen-suit provision, which states:

Except as provided in subsection (b) or (c) of this section, any person may commence a civil action on his own behalf—
(1)(A) against any person . . . who is alleged to be in violation of any permit, standard, regulation, condition, requirement, prohibition, or order which has become effective pursuant to this chapter. . . .

. . . The EDF contends that by restricting citizens to enforcement actions based on permit violations, the permit-shield provision expressly contravenes the statute's broad grant of authority to citizens to enforce violations of any "standard, regulation, condition, requirement, prohibition, or order." . . .

We do not decide the merits of the EDF's challenge. The EPA represents that although it believes its permit system will narrow the opportunities for citizen suits, "the Agency does not maintain that the shield precludes [such] suits." . . .

3. Conflict with EPA's Enforcement Authority

The parties dispute whether Congress has directly spoken to the question whether the EPA can limit its own enforcement actions to violations of permits, and, . . . whether the EPA nonetheless acted unreasonably by issuing the permit-shield rule.

The EDF argues that RCRA requires the EPA to do more than simply enforce permit provisions:

* * *

. . . We therefore uphold the permit-shield rule as a reasonable, self-imposed constraint on the Agency's enforcement discretion.

III. Conclusion

Because the EPA failed to provide adequate notice and opportunity for comment with regard to the mixture and derived-from rules and with regard to the leachate monitoring requirement, we vacate these rules and remand them to the Agency. . . . Finally, we find the permit-shield regulation, as applied to the enforcement activities of the EPA, to fall within the Agency's discretion under RCRA.

The petitions for review are therefore granted in part and denied in part.

■   **United States v. Northeastern Pharmaceutical**   ■

810 F.2d 726 (8th Cir. 1986)

McMILLIAN, Circuit Judge.

Northeastern Pharmaceutical & Chemical Co. (NEPACCO), Edwin Michaels and John W. Lee appeal from a final judgment entered in the District Court for the Western District of Missouri finding them and Ronald Mills jointly and severally liable for response costs incurred by the government . . . relative to the cleanup of the Denney farm site . . .

The United States cross-appeals from that part of the district Court judgment denying recovery of response costs incurred before December 11, 1980, and finding appellants and Mills were not liable for response costs pursuant to the Resource Conservation and Recovery Act of 1976 (RCRA). . . . For reversal the government argues the district court erred in (1) finding the government could not recover response costs incurred before the effective date of CERCLA, December 11, 1980, and (2) finding appellants and Mills were not liable for response costs under RCRA. . . .

For the reasons discussed below, we affirm in part, reverse in part, and remand for further proceedings consistent with this opinion.

I. Facts

NEPACCO was incorporated in 1966 under the laws of Delaware, . . . Although NEPACCO's corporate charter was forfeited in 1976 for failure to maintain an agent for service of process, NEPACCO did not file a certificate of voluntary dissolution with the secretary of state of Delaware. In 1974 its corporate assets were liquidated, and the proceeds were used to pay corporate debts and then distributed to the shareholders. Michaels formed NEPACCO, was a major shareholder, and was its president. Lee was NEPACCO's vice-president, the supervisor of it manufacturing plant located in Verona, Missouri, and also a shareholder. Mills was employed as shift supervisor at NEPACCO's Verona plant.

From April 1970 to January 1972 NEPACCO manufactured the disinfectant hexachlorophene at its Verona plant. . . . Michaels and Lee knew that NEPPACO's manufacturing process produced various hazardous and toxic byproducts. . . . Occasionally, however, excess waste byproducts were sealed in 55-gallon drums and then stored at the plant.

In July 1971 Mills approached NEPACCO plant manager Bill Ray with a proposal to dispose of the waste-filled 55-gallon drums on a farm owned by James Denney located about seven miles south of Verona. Ray visited the Denney farm and discussed the proposal with Lee; Lee approved the use of Mills' services and the Denney farm as a disposal site. In mid-July 1971 Mills and Gerald Lechner dumped approximately 85 of the 55-gallon drums into a large trench on the Denney farm (Denney farm site) that had been excavated by Leon Vaughn. Vaughn then filled in the trench. Only NEPACCO drums were disposed of at the Denney farm site.

In October 1979 the Environmental Protection Agency (EPA) received an anonymous tip that hazardous wastes had been disposed of at the Denney farm. Subsequent EPA investigation confirmed that hazardous wastes had in fact been disposed of at the Denney farm and that the site was not geologically suitable for the disposal of hazardous wastes. Between January and April 1980 the EPA prepared a plan for the cleanup of the Denney farm site and constructed an access road and a security fence. During April 1980 the EPA conducted an on-site investigation, exposed and sampled 13 of the 55-gallon drums, which were found to be badly deteriorated, and took water and soil samples. The samples were found to contain"alarmingly" high concentrations of dioxin, TCP and toluene.

In July 1980 the EPA installed a temporary cap over the trench to prevent the entry and run-off of surface water and to minimize contamination of the surrounding soil and groundwater. The EPA also contracted with Ecology & Environment, Inc. for the preparation of a feasibility study for the cleanup of the Denney farm site. Additional on-site testing was conducted. In August 1980 the government filed an initial complaint against

NEPACCO, the generator of the hazardous substance; Michaels and Lee, the corporate officers responsible for arranging for the disposal of the hazardous substances; Miller, the transporter of the hazardous substances; and Syntex, the owner and lessor of the Verona plant, seeking injunctive relief and reimbursement of response costs pursuant to RCRA . . . In September 1993 the feasibility study was completed.

In the meantime the EPA had been negotiating with Syntex about Syntex's liability for cleanup of the Denney farm site. In September 1980 the government and Syntex entered into a settlement and consent decree. Pursuant to the terms of the settlement, Syntex would pay $100,000 of the government's response costs and handle the removal, storage and permanent disposal of the hazardous substances from the Denney farm site. The EPA approved Syntex's proposed cleanup plan, and in June 1981 Syntex began excavation of the trench. In November 1981 the site was closed. The 55-gallon drums are now stored in a specially constructed concrete bunker on the Denney farm. The drums as stored do not present an imminent and substantial endangerment to health or the environment; however, no plan for permanent disposal as been developed, and the site will continue to require testing and monitoring in the future.

In August 1982 the government filed an amended complaint adding counts for relief pursuant to CERCLA . . . . The trial was conducted during October 1983. The district court filed its memorandum opinion in January 1984.

II. DISTRICT COURT DECISION

The district court found that dioxin, hexachlorophene, TCP, TCB and toluene have high levels of toxicity at low-dose levels and are thus "hazardous substances" within the meaning of RCRA. . . . The district court also found there was a substantial likelihood that the environment and human beings would be exposed to the hazardous substances that had been disposed of at the Denney farm site. . . . A state geologist testified the Denney farm site is located in an area in which substances rapidly move through the soil and into the groundwater and, although no dioxin had been found in the water in nearby wells, dioxin had been found as far as 30 inches beneath the soil in the trench. . . .

A.   RCRA Findings

The district court held that RCRA § 7003(a), . . . requires a finding of negligence in order to hold past off-site generators and transporters liable for response costs . . . and thus RCRA did not apply to past non-negligent off-site generators and transporters of hazardous substances.

* * *

IV.   RCRA

A.   Standard and Scope of § 7003 Liability

As an alternative basis for recovery of the response costs incurred before December 11, 1980, the government argues on cross-appeal that it can also recover its response costs pursuant to RCRA § 7003(a). The district court . . . held that under RCRA § 7003(a), (prior to 1984 amendments discussed below), proof of fault or negligence was required in order to impose liability upon past off-site generators and transporters. . . . Because the government did not allege or prove negligence, the district court found no liability under RCRA § 7003(a), (prior to 1984 amendments). The government argues that the standard of liability under RCRA § 7003(a), initially enacted and as amended in 1984, is strict liability, not negligence, and that liability under RCRA can be imposed even though the acts of disposal occurred before RCRA became effective in 1976. We agree.

RCRA was initially enacted in 1976, ... In November 1984, after the district court's January 1984 decision in the present case, RCRA was again amended by the Hazardous and Solid Waste Amendments of 1984, . . . We have considered the 1984 amendments and the accompanying legislative history and, . . . we believe the 1984 amendments support the government's arguments about RCRA's standard and scope of liability and retroactivity.

The critical issue is the meaning of the phrase "contributing to." Before its amendment in 1984, RCRA § 7003(a) . . . imposed liability upon any person "contributing to" "the handling, storage, treatment, transportation or disposal of any solid or hazardous waste" that

"may present an imminent and substantial endangerment to health or the environment." . . .

Then, in November 1984, Congress passed and President Reagan signed the 1984 amendments, which were described as "clarifying" amendments and specifically addressed the standard and scope of liability of § 7003(a). As amended in 1984, RCRA § 7003(a), . . . now provides in pertinent part:

> Notwithstanding any other provision of this chapter, upon receipt of evidence that the *past or present* handling, storage, treatment, transportation of disposal of any solid waste or hazardous waste may present an imminent and substantial endangerment to health or the environment, the Administrator may bring suit on behalf of the United States in the appropriate district court [to immediately restrain any person] *against any person (including any past or present generator, past or present transporter, or past or present owner or operator of a treatment, storage, or disposal facility) who has contributed or who is* contributing to such handling, storage, treatment, transportation or disposal [to stop] *to restrain such person from* such handling, storage, treatment, transportation, or disposal [or to take such other action as may be necessary] *to order such person to take such other action as may be necessary, or both.*

As amended, RCRA § 7003(a), . . . specifically applies to *past* generators and transporters. Section 7003 focuses on the abatement of conditions threatening health and the environment and not particularly human activity. Therefore, it has *always reached those persons who have contributed in the past or are presently contributing to the endangerment, including but not limited to generators, regardless of fault or negligence.* The amendment, by adding the words "have contributed" is merely intended to clarify the existing authority. Thus, for example, *nonnegligent generators whose wastes are no longer being deposited or dumped at a particular site may be ordered to abate the hazard to health or the environment posed by the leaking of the wastes they once generated and which have been deposited on the site.* The amendment reflects the longstanding view that generators and other persons involved in the handling, storage, treatment, transportation or disposal of hazardous wastes must share in the responsibility for the abatement of the hazards arising from their activities. The section was intended and is intended to abate conditions resulting from past activities. . . .

* * *

Thus, following the 1984 amendments, past off-site generators and transporters are within the scope of RCRA § 7003(a). . . .

Appellants argue, however, that the 1984 amendments should not be applied to them because the 1984 amendments are not merely clarifying amendments but instead substantively changed the existing law. We disagree. First, Congress itself expressly characterized the 1984 amendments as "clarifying" amendments. Second, as part of the legislative history of the 1984 amendments, Congress expressly stated what its intention had been when it initially passed the RCRA in 1976, even though the 1976 legislative history contained no specific discussion of the standard and scope of liability of § 7003(a).

Although this is not legislative history as such, the views of subsequent Congresses on the same of similar statutes are entitled to some weight in the construction of previous legislation. Although the views of subsequent Congresses cannot override the unmistakable intent of the enacting one, this is not a problem in this case because there was no absolutely "unmistakable intent" of Congress concerning section 7003. To the extent that the precise intent of the enacting Congress may be obscure, the views of subsequent Congresses should be given greater deference than they would be otherwise enntitled to receive.

* * *

B. Retroactivity

. . . Appellants argue that because RCRA . . . is prospective in focus and was not enacted until 1976, RCRA cannot be retroactively applied to impose liability on them for acts that occurred in 1971. A similar retroactivity argument was raised in *United States v. Price* . . . The defendants in *United States v. Price* had argued that RCRA could not be applied retroactively to impose liability on them for disposing of toxic

wastes in 1972. The *Price* court rejected the retroactivity argument, stating

[t]he gravamen of a section 7003 action is not defendants' dumping practices, which admittedly ceased with respect to toxic wastes in 1972, but the present imminent hazard posed by the continuing disposal . . . to include "[t]he . . . leaking . . . of any solid waste or hazardous waste into or on any land or water,"] of contaminants into the groundwater [or into the environment]. Thus, the statute neither punishes wrongdoing nor imposes liability for injuries inflicted by past acts. Rather, as defendants themselves argue, its orientation is essentially prospective. When construed in this manner, the statute is simply not retroactive. It merely relates to current and future conditions.

* * *

We reverse that part of the district court judgment holding that RCRA does not apply to past non-negligent off-site generators and transporters.

C. Individual Liability under RCRA § 7003(a), 12 U.S.C.A. § 6973(a) (West Supp. 1986)

. . . RCRA is applicable to past non-negligent off-site generators. The government argues Lee and Michaels are individually liable as "contributors" under RCRA § 7003(a). We agree. . . .

RCRA § 7003(a) . . . imposes strict liability upon "any person" who is contributing or who has contributed to the disposal of hazardous substances that may present an imminent and substantial endangerment to health or the environment. As defined by statute, the term "person" includes both individuals and corporations and does not exclude corporate officers and employees. . . . More importantly, imposing liability upon only the corporation, but not those corporate officers and employees who actually make corporate decisions, would be inconsistent with Congress' intent to impose liability upon the persons who are involved in the handling and disposal of hazardous substances. . . . Thus, Lee and Michaels can be held individually liable if they were personally involved in or directly responsible for corporate acts in violation of RCRA. . . . We hold Lee and Michaels are individually liable as ''contributors'' under RCRA § 7003(a). . . . Lee actually participated in the conduct that violated RCRA; he personally arranged for the transportation and disposal of hazardous substances that presented an imminent and substantial endangerment to health and the environment. Unlike Lee, Michaels was not personally involved in the actual decision to transport and dispose of the hazardous substances. As NEPACCO's cor-

porate president and as a major NEPACCO shareholder, however, Michaels was the individual in charge of and directly responsible for all of NEPACCO's operations, including those at the Verona plant, and he had the ultimate authority to control the disposal of NEPACCO's hazardous substances. . . .

In summary, we hold . . . Lee and Michaels individually liable for contributing to an imminent and substantial endangerment to health and the environment in violation of RCRA § 7003(a). . . .

U.S. Environmental Protection Agency and Supporters to Oppose Pollution, Inc. v. Environmental Waste Control, Inc., doing business as Four County Landfill, Steven W. Shambaugh, James A. Wilkins, West Holding Company, Inc.

917 F.2d 327 (7th Cir. 1990)

Cudahy, Circuit Judge. The Environmental Protection Agency, together with an environmental intervener, Supporters to Oppose Pollution, Inc., brought suit against Environmental Waste Control (and its owners and operators) in connection with a hazardous waste landfill operated by Environmental Waste Control in Indiana. The district court found against Environmental Waste Control, ordered the offending landfill permanently closed and assessed civil fines amounting to almost $3,000,000. Environmental Waste Control appeals. We affirm.

I. Factual Background

This appeal arises from an enforcement action brought by the United States, on behalf of the Environmental Protection Agency (the ''EPA''), to enforce hazardous waste requirements under the Resource Conservation and Recovery Act (''RCRA''), 42 U.S.C. §§ 6901–87, at Environmental Waste Control's County Landfill (the ''Landfill'') in Fulton County, Indiana. . . .

RCRA establishes a comprehensive federal program governing the generation, transportation, storage and treatment of hazardous

wastes ''to minimize the present and future threat to human health and the environment.'' 42 U.S.C. § 6902(b). 42 U.S.C. §6925(a) requires that a hazardous waste facility be operated only in accordance with a permit. Recognizing that the EPA could not issue permits to all applicants before RCRA's effective date, Congress provided that a facility in existence as of November 19, 1980, could obtain ''interim status,'' allowing it to continue operating until final action on its permit application. 42 U.S.C. § 6925(e); . . . To obtain interim status, a facility is required to file a limited ''Part A application,'' and is then ''treated as having been issued a permit.'' . . . An interim status facility must comply with the standards set forth in 40 C.F.R. pt. 265, which, among other things, mandates that such a facility have a ''groundwater monitoring program capable of determining the facility's impact on the quality of ground water in the uppermost aquifer underlying the facility'' and also requires that an interim status facility meet certain financial responsibility requirements.

Following the submission of the ''Part A application,'' a facility must file a ''Part B application'' to obtain a permit. . . . Upon successful completion of the Part B process, a hazardous waste permit is issued, and the facility must comply with this permit and the regulatory standards set forth in 40 C.F.R. pt. 264.

In 1984, Congress passed the Hazardous and Solid Waste Amendments (the "HSWA") to RCRA. The HSWA were adopted in response to concerns about widespread ground-water contamination from interim status facilities. The HSWA provide, in part, that all land disposal facilities granted interim status, . . . would automatically lose that status on November 8, 1985, unless the facility: (A) applied for a final Part B permit determination before November 8, 1985; and (B) certified that it was "in compliance with applicable groundwater monitoring and financial responsibility requirements." 42 U.S.C. § 6925(e)(2). RCRA also requires the owners and operators of hazardous waste landfills to comply with minimum technology requirements which mandate the installation of two or more liners and a leachate collection system for the lateral expansion of interim status landfills with respect to waste received after May 8, 1985. . . . When the EPA determines that there has been a release of hazardous waste from an interim status facility, the EPA may seek corrective action. 42 U.S.C. § 6928(h)(1). Accordingly, the EPA filed suit against EWC in federal court, alleging basically: (1) that the Landfill had lost its interim status by failing to comply with the applicable financial responsibility and groundwater monitoring requirements; (2) that EWC had violated RCRA's minimum technology requirements; . . . (3) that the Landfill's groundwater monitoring system did not comply with the applicable regulations; and (4) that hazardous waste or hazardous waste constituents had been released at the Landfill, thereby permitting the court to order a corrective measure study. The EPA sought civil penalties and an order closing the Landfill, at least temporarily. The Supporters to Oppose Pollution ("STOP"), the environmental intervenor, joined the EPA's claims, but asked for a permanent, instead of temporary, closing of the Landfill. STOP also brought additional claims relating to the Landfill's alleged release of hazardous waste into the environment.

. . . The district court essentially found: that the Landfill had lost it interim status as of November 8, 1985 because, as of that date, it had not fully complied with the required financial assurance and groundwater monitoring standards; . . . that EWC had failed to maintain an adequate monitoring system and had illegally disposed of hazardous wastes in cells lacking liners; . . . and that, as a result of EWC's violations, there was a release of hazardous wastes which contaminated groundwater underlying the Landfill and which had the potential for contaminating nearby private drinking wells. . . . The district court assessed civil penalties of nearly $3,000,000 against EWC. The district court also ordered EWC to undertake certain corrective measures and, most importantly, permanently enjoined the operation of the Landfill.

EWC appeals on the grounds that: (1) a permanent injunction was improper; (2) the Four County Landfill should not have lost its interim status; (3) its current groundwater monitoring system is fully adequate, and (4) the corrective action plan mandated by the district court was inappropriate for the conditions existing at the Four County Landfill. We affirm the judgment of the district court in all respects.

II. LEGAL ANALYSIS

A. The Propriety of the Permanent Injunction

* * *

EWC first contends that RCRA does not authorize permanent closure in *interim status* cases. We are puzzled how EWC can seriously advance this argument. First, it should be noted that the district court held that EWC "has not argued that permanent closure is not an available remedy." . . . Hence, in all likelihood, EWC has waived this argument. Regardless, the text of the relevant statute plainly allows for a permanent injunction in interim status cases such as this one.

EWC's next contention, that the district court did not properly balance the competing equities, is simply incorrect. The record shows that the district court, in fact, went to great pains to outline the reasons (which included threats to the environment) for its decision to permanently enjoin the operation of EWC's landfill. . . . Moreover, it is clear that the district court specifically undertook to balance the benefit to the public against the harm to the public in this case. . . . ("The risk to the public of any continued operation of the Four County Landfill by EWC greatly outweighs any harm from permanent closure.") As the Supreme Court noted in *Amoco Production Co. v. Gambell,* 480 U.S. 531, 545 (1987):

> Environmental injury, by its nature, can seldom be adequately remedied by money damages and is often permanent, or at least of long duration, *i.e.,* irreparable. If such injury is sufficiently likely, therefore, the balance of harms will usually favor the issuance of an injunction to protect the environment.

Hence, the record shows that the district court did balance the competing equities . . . notwithstanding that it may not have even been required to undertake such a balance. It is an accepted equitable principle that a court does not have to balance the equities in a case where the defendant's conduct has been willful. . . .

For all the foregoing reasons, we find that the district court's decision to issue a permanent injunction against EWC was correct. . . .

B. The Loss of Environmental Waste Control's "Interim Status"

EWC contends that the Four County Landfill never lost its interim status, . . . because (1) EWC's insurance complied with all applicable regulations as of November 8, 1985, or, in the alternative, because the district court should have considered good faith a defense not the failure to carry the required amount of insurance; and (2) because EWC was actually in compliance with the applicable hazardous waste groundwater monitoring requirements as of November 8, 1985. . . .

. . . Because we find that EWC failed to carry the required amount of insurance and because good faith is not an adequate defense to compliance with these financial regulations, EWC lost its interim status as of November 8, 1985. We therefore need not address EWC's allegations concerning whether the Landfill met the

groundwater monitoring standards required of interim status facilities as of November 8, 1985.

* * *

EWC initially challenges the district court's ruling that the EPA's interim status regulations required total coverage for sudden and non-sudden occurrences of $4,000,000 per occurrence and $8,000,000 in the aggregate. The relevant financial responsibility regulations are set forth in 40 C.F.R. § 265.147. Subpart (a) requires, with respect to hazardous waste treatment, storage or disposal facilities, that:

> [t]he owner or operator must have and maintain liability coverage for sudden accidental occurrences in the amount of at least $1 million per occurrence with an annual aggregate of at least $2 million, exclusive of legal defense costs.

Subpart (b) applies to surface impoundments, landfills or land treatment facilities and requires that:

> [t]he owner or operator must have and maintain liability coverage for nonsudden accidental occurrences in the amount of at least $3 million per occurrence with an annual aggregate of at least $6 million, exclusive of legal defense costs.

* * *

EWC contends that the requirements "nowhere expressly stated that a total of $4 million per occurrence and $8 million annual aggregate was required for a combined limits policy." . . . (EWC carried an insurance policy which covered only $3,000,000 per occurrence and had an annual aggregate of $6,000,000.) But we think that the requirements were clear. The separate subparts applied to different types of occurrences. Each subpart had to be satisfied. Aggregation was therefore required. . . .

EWC argues, however, that the 1988 amendment to these regulations, which explicitly calls for aggregation of the interim status insurance requirements, and the 1981 draft of the regulations (which also contained an aggregation provision that was later deleted) support its theory that aggregation was not required *until* the 1988 amendment. Appellants' Brief at 33-36. We do not agree. . . . In sum, we think that the language of this regulation was sufficiently clear to preclude a presumption that the 1988 amendments were meant to change rather than clarify, existing law. Indeed the 1988 rule states that it is merely, "specifying more clearly" the aggregate coverage mechanisms

* * *

C.   The Adequacy of EWC's Groundwater Monitoring System

The district court held that the groundwater monitoring system at the Landfill did not meet the required standards as of November 8, 1985. . . . In this regard, the district court noted that

[t]he purpose of a hazardous waste landfill's groundwater monitoring system is to detect immediately the migration of hazardous waste or hazardous waste constituents from the waste management area into the environment so that any necessary corrective or remedial action can be taken. Among the major threats a hazardous waste landfill may pose to pubic health and the environment is the potential that hazardous constituents may escape and contaminate the groundwater beneath the facility.

* * * *

The design, construction, and depth of [the Landfill's] groundwater monitoring wells have prevented EWC and its consultants from learning the extent and permeability of the uppermost aquifer. . . . One cannot design a meaningful groundwater monitoring system without knowing the location of the uppermost aquifer and direction of the groundwater flow. EWC has not acquired that knowledge.

The thrust of EWC's complaint on appeal seem to be that the district court erred in not admitting newly obtained data into evidence or, in the alternative, that the district court erred in finding EWC's groundwater monitoring system to be inadequate. Whether EWC's groundwater monitoring system complied with federal law is a question of fact which will not be disturbed unless clearly erroneous. . . . The new data proffered by EWC came too late. Moreover, the evidence in the record was sufficient to sustain the court's extensive findings. . . .

D.   The District Court's Corrective Action Plan

Finally, EWC contends that the corrective action plan imposed by the district court was inappropriate for the conditions existing at the Landfill. Again, we disagree. The assessment of penalties is committed to the informed discretion of the trial court, and will be reversed only upon a showing that the district court abused its discretion. . . . EWC has offered us no sound reason which would justify a finding that the district court abused its discretion in deciding on the corrective action plan and other remedies. . . .

As to other matters raised by EWC, they have been considered and have been found to be without merit.

6.3   Appraisal of RCRA's Regulatory Scheme

Impact of Cradle-to-Grave Regulation on Waste Management

RCRA is prospective, rather than retrospective, legislation. Rather than putting off the costs of cleaning up toxic-waste dumpsites until years after the wastes are generated, RCRA seeks to assess and allocate hazardous-waste disposal costs of products and services more rationally.

The real cost of manufacturing any product includes the harmful effects caused by waste by-products generated in producing it. If the manufacturer is forced to absorb the costs of disposing of these by-products by environmentally sound technologies, its waste management costs will be reflected in the price of the product or service. This gives businesses an incentive to reduce waste and allows consumers to decide realistically whether the product or service is worth the added waste cost component. Thus, consumers' choices in the marketplace can be based on more realistic assessments of what goods and services actually cost to produce and deliver.

Indeed, only if each manufacturer or consumer in the waste management cycle is required by law to pay a rough approximation of its proportionate share of waste-management costs can pollution costs be accounted for in the market system, rather than treated as an externality. In any other scheme, some individuals and businesses profit from increased harm to human health and environmental degradation while others who live or work in polluted areas will bear the costs without benefiting in any substantial way from the pollution-causing product or service.

To summarize, cradle-to-grave regulation serves a twofold purpose: it forces businesses to dispose of waste in a more environmentally sound (and in the long term, less-expensive) manner, and it effects a more timely, market-oriented allocation of pollution-prevention and waste-management costs. Such a system treats waste management as a current, rather than an extraordinary, business expense. The hope is that this "cradle-to-grave" control of wastes will ultimately encourage businesses and consumers to adopt such rational alternatives as resource recovery and recycling.

Regulation of Municipal Landfills and Incinerator Ash

The number of municipal landfills allowed to operate under current RCRA regulations is rapidly diminishing. Municipal landfill regulation developed in response to studies that revealed that 25 percent of the country's worst toxic-waste disposal sites were former municipal landfills, and that fewer than 25 percent of currently active landfills were systematically being checked for leakage or were lined with barriers to prevent ground-water contamination from such leakage.

In September 1991, EPA promulgated Solid Waste Disposal Facility Criteria[13] with the intended multiple purposes of preventing pollution, detecting and cleaning up toxic wastes at municipal landfills, and minimizing financial hardship for affected municipalities, while allowing states some flexibility in implementing the criteria. Nevertheless, compliance with the proposed standards for landfill design, ground-water monitoring, and financial assurance was beyond the financial means of many small communities—which account for about half of the covered active 6,000 landfills. Unless they are relieved of those costs, some municipalities will be forced to close their landfills and use the services of larger, regional landfills.

The EPA provided conditional exemptions for some small municipal landfills. These exemptions provide relief from RCRA's requirements regarding landfill design, financial assurance, corrective action, operations, and closure, but not from ground-water monitoring requirements,[14] if the municipality can show that:

- the landfill receives less than 20 tons of waste daily;
- there is no evidence of ground-water contamination;
- the municipality has no alternative regional waste management outlet *or* it annually experiences an interruption of surface transportation for three consecutive months that prevents access to a regional facility;
- the landfill receives no more than 25 inches of precipitation annually.

A municipality that does not qualify for, or that declines, the exemption must close a noncompliant landfill. In doing so, it will incur the burdensome costs of landfill closure and maintenance for 30 years in the manner specified by EPA, as well as costs associated with correcting contaminant releases from the closed landfill. Further, municipalities, unlike the federal and state governments, are not exempt from RCRA provisions that require assurance of financial ability to comply with RCRA standards. Many municipalities' immediate reaction was to avoid planning for either closure or compliance and to wait for adoption of a final EPA rule and for state implementation of the rule.

In September 1991, the EPA proposed standards of management for active, new, and closed landfills.[15] The Final Rule was adopted in October 1993. The rule aims to prevent leaching of toxic materials from trash dumps into ground water and aquifers that supply much of the nation's drinking water. With regard to *active landfills,* the rule requires that operators:

- install the necessary equipment and procedures for monitoring the ground water at the landfill semiannually,
- monitor the migration of underground contaminants at the landfill,
- clean up any ground water that is found to be polluted by the landfill, and
- cover the dump daily with soil in order to avoid pest infestation of the site.

With regard to *new landfills,* and expansions of existing landfills, the rule requires that these be constructed to prevent leakage or migration of contaminants by using insulating soil and plastic liners and a system of collection pipes for capturing leaking materials for proper disposition. With regard to *closed dumps,* the rule requires annual monitoring of ground water and that any discovered contamination be cleaned up. As adopted, the rule would be phased in over a period of years, which still leaves improved municipal landfill regulations in the interim to voluntary state and local initiatives. If the rule is challenged, its beneficial effects may be delayed even longer.

The EPA's new technological standards do not address the need to assure future landfill capacity once the dwindling existing landfill capacity is exhausted. Solving that problem has largely been left to the states. As indicated by the Supreme Court decisions reported in the next section, however, states' efforts to conserve their landfill capacity by excluding wastes from other states, are barred to a substantial extent by federal law.

Concerning the pressures to compromise on enforcement standards, either to relieve regulatory or budgetary pressures on local governments or to avoid standards that ultimately impact heavily on industrial facilities, one report concluded that:

> . . . the purported aim of preventing ground water contamination has been diminished by the lengthy delay in promulgation of the [final implementation] rule and the absence of specific criteria for state implementation. . . . [T]he new regulatory approach appears to rubberstamp the programs of a majority of states while granting exemptions and waivers for those unable to comply. Until a formal State Implementation Plan is promulgated, many states will view the new standards as mere legislative gloss on currently existing programs.[16]

Similar uncertainty exists regarding disposal of incinerator ash from the burning of municipal solid waste. During the late eighties and early nineties, EPA took contradictory positions, and the federal courts issued conflicting rulings, as to whether municipal incinerator ash should be regulated as a hazardous substance under RCRA. Requiring that the ash, which often contains hazardous substances, be treated as hazardous waste would increase disposal costs tenfold. In 1993 the Supreme Court decided that municipal incinerator ash is hazardous under RCRA if it contains hazardous constituents.[17] Until the uncertainty is laid to rest, however, municipalities face the dilemma of planning for future capacity. Comparisons of the costs of incineration with those of other disposal options cannot realistically be made without knowing if incinerator ash must be treated and disposed of as an RCRA hazardous waste.[18]

The need to arrive at some settled scheme of municipal landfill and incinerator ash regulation encompasses more than eliminating current hazards. The shortage of landfill capacity requires new waste disposal facilities, but state and local governments can be expected to move slowly on new landfills without some assurance that their plans will satisfy future federal guidelines. Political difficulties and budgetary shortfalls already deter state and local governments from siting new landfills. The uncertainty about future federal regulation provides one more excuse for local authorities not to press for permanent solutions. All participants in the regulatory process agree that implementing RCRA demands complex, time-consuming studies and consultations and that ongoing review and adjustments of the adopted regulations are necessary. The fact remains, however, that without reasonably stable, consistent standards and regulations, practical solutions to municipal waste disposal will remain unattainable.

Hazardous Waste Export

As the world's leading producer of hazardous waste—more than 500 million tons per year—the United States is also a top exporter of hazardous waste. Worldwide, more than 2.2 million tons of toxic wastes cross international borders annually.[19] The saga of the *Khian Sea*, described in section 6.1, is just one of many instances in which hazardous waste has been exported from an industrialized nation under shameful conditions. The bulk of these industrial wastes end up in underdeveloped countries where environmental regulation is ineffectual, technological means for coping with the wastes are nonexistent, and the population is most at risk. Extreme poverty, greed, nonrepresentational forms of government, and ignorance explain why large numbers of people in the Third World become sick or die each year due to improper hazardous-waste disposal.

The international trade in environmentally harmful substances and wastes—such as domestically banned pesticides and hazardous and radioactive wastes—results from a lack of regulation at national and international levels. RCRA's export provisions and extraterritorial nonenforcement do little to stem the damage caused by the disposal of U.S. wastes in other countries.

RCRA's hazardous-waste-export provisions (RCRA § 3017) require that an individual or business that intends to export hazardous waste notify the EPA Administrator; describe the waste to be exported, its destination, and the manner of disposal there; and provide the address of the ultimate treatment, storage, or disposal facility. The Administrator and the Secretary of State are required to send a copy of the notification to the government of the receiving country and to advise that government that U.S. law prohibits export if the receiving country objects to receiving the waste. These procedures may be bypassed if an international agreement exists. The Administrator may promulgate other standards for export. In recognition of growing international environmental problems posed by such exports to countries where treatment standards are lax or nonexistent, EPA has considered further restrictions on hazardous waste export.

Although RCRA's export provisions may be sufficiently protective when waste is exported to an industrialized nation that has sophisticated treatment and disposal standards, RCRA does not ensure that waste generated in the United States and exported elsewhere will be subject to standards that are protective of human health and the environment. Since other countries have the prerogative to accept or ban the import of hazardous wastes, RCRA on its own accomplishes little more than to ensure that the receiving country's government is notified of an incoming shipment.

RCRA's export provisions do not take into account the truism that environmental contamination does not respect national boundaries. Once a hazardous waste is exported to a country whose standards are low or poorly enforced, its disposition there may not only threaten the regional population but may also adversely affect the global environment. From this perspective, RCRA's export provisions are inadequate to protect even the U.S. environment and population. The United States already suffers the consequences of failing to subject domestically generated waste to RCRA's treatment and disposal standards; hazardous substances dumped in Mexico by U.S. companies contaminate U.S. air and waters.

A further crimp on a global approach to hazardous-waste regulation is a ruling by a New York federal district court that RCRA's civil penalty provisions do not apply extraterritorially. In a *case of first impression* (the first case to decide on an issue), a New York corporation sued a Delaware corporation under RCRA section 7002, a citizens' suit provision that permits a private plaintiff to sue a transporter of waste for acts that may present an imminent and substantial endangerment to health or the environment. The court ruled that the plaintiff could not prevail because the waste, though generated in the United States and transported under a contract made in the United States, was exported.

Underground Storage Tank Program

Two million underground storage tanks (USTs) are used in the United States to store petroleum, heating oil, waste oil, and other substances at refineries, service stations, and institutions. Many of the owners or operators of these USTs are not large companies (such as petrochemical concerns, which are accustomed to government regulation), but small businesses, such as corner gas stations, that may be unaware of their regulatory obligations. Unlike larger businesses, many "mom and pop" service-station operators lack the resources to acquire environmental-protection technology for guarding against the spills and leaks from underground tanks that are now known to be common at service stations. Even where a major oil company owns a station's petroleum storage tanks, the franchisee who owns and operates the business is usually responsible for tank maintenance. Effective regulation of a group that includes many small businesses requires EPA to devise ways for reaching and informing those businesses of their obligations and to provide assistance in complying with EPA regulations.

The disparities that exist between large and small businesses in the same "regulatory universe"[20] sometimes lead to enforcement problems. In the case of USTs for petroleum products, large oil companies often place ownership, as well as operation, of underground storage tanks in their franchisees, many of whom are unsophisticated businesspersons with little bargaining power in negotiating franchise agreements. These companies thus attempt to shield themselves from RCRA liability for replacing old tanks, installing the required leak-detection devices, and cleaning up leaks and spills.

Had Congress more closely considered these business facts in developing and enacting RCRA Subtitle I (Underground Storage Tanks), it could have required that EPA take enforcement action against petrochemical franchisers, which have the capabilities and resources for installing more effective protection and remediation technologies. Instead, the burden of complying with UST installation, monitoring, release-detection, and cleanup requirements often falls on service-station owner-operators, who are least able to comply and are least financially capable of undertaking corrective action when a leak of petroleum or waste oil does occur.

As written, UST regulations sometimes invite deceptive practices, if not outright fraud, by savvy companies seeking to avoid potential liability. For instance, implementation of the requirement that older underground storage tanks have release-detection equipment appears to have spurred some oil companies to sell older tanks to service-station owner-operators at prices indicating that the sellers' primary motive was to avoid liability for past or future leakage. The contracts for most of these sales state that, to the best of the seller's knowledge, the tanks are not corroded and are structurally sound, even though no inspection was conducted. An unprotected, bare steel tank that has been in the ground thirty years is almost certain to have pitting, rusting, or holes. Despite the potentially fraudulent nature of these sales, EPA generally lacks the authority to bring an enforcement action for leaks against anyone other than the present owner, who may be unable to pay for the necessary cleanup.

6.4   Selected Issues in Waste Management

The Politics of Trash: Landfill and Incinerator Siting

Across the nation, communities large and small are attempting to cope with two hot issues: where to put their trash and how to deal with other people's trash. For New York and New Jersey, which together generate more solid waste than the other 48 states combined, the challenge is to find new or less costly landfill space, often in the Midwest. For Midwestern states, the challenge is to find ways to restrict the amount of out-of-state trash coming into their landfills. For the urban and rural poor, the challenge is to avoid having landfills or incinerators placed in their communities or, alternatively, to strike deals that will establish landfills in their communities that will provide jobs and services but not jeopardize their health and quality of life.

Landfill and incinerator siting issues are complex. This subsection and the next one focus on the economics and politics of interstate trash disposal, respectively. A later subsection discusses the legal barriers that restrict communities' and states' abilities to forbid the dumping of out-of-state trash within their borders.

Population density in the United States varies widely, as do land values, which tend to be higher where the population is denser. Areas with larger populations, such as the Northeast, naturally produce more garbage, and these are the same areas where landfill space has become increasingly limited. Old dumps are filling up, and available land for new facilities is scarce and costly. In addition, the new

EPA requirements for municipal landfills discussed earlier are forcing many older landfills to close. Elizabeth Royte described the problem in a 1992 article:

> [B]y the mid-1990s, one half of the 6,500 municipal landfills still operating in the United States are expected to reach capacity. (Since 1978, 14,000 landfills have closed.) Already the Fresh Kills landfill on Staten Island, the nation's largest city dump, turns away 10,000 of the 27,000 tons New York City generates each day. When it peaks at 505 feet, within the decade, Fresh Kills will be almost as tall as the Washington Monument.
>
> . . . [The new EPA municipal landfill requirements] carry a big price tag [upwards of $10 million to construct], and so, for most small communities, up-to-snuff dumps have become prohibitively expensive. Nationally, the solution would appear to be fewer but larger landfills; in relative terms, giant dumps are cheaper to build than small ones. To these strategically placed, privately run sites will be trucked, or hauled by rail, garbage from surrounding regions, even from out of state.[21]

Reflecting the interstate disposal trend, in densely populated New Jersey only 11 of the 300 landfills that existed there in the 1970s remained open in 1991. According to the National Solid Waste Management Association, about 15 million tons of trash crossed state lines in 1989, more than half of it originating in New Jersey and New York. In a span of three years, the percentage of out-of-state trash disposed of in Indiana rose from nearly zero to more than twenty percent.[22]

As Midwestern landfills take spiraling amounts of out-of-state trash, local residents resent the stench of garbage and the heavy, 24-hour-per-day tractor-trailer traffic in their neighborhoods. They also worry about the safety of their drinking water. Because many landfills are privately owned and states cannot absolutely bar out-of-state trash, affected residents are often powerless to prevent an existing landfill from expanding its capacity in order to accommodate more trash from outside the area.

As for new landfill projects, private companies seeking to maximize profit are likely to locate new landfills in sparsely populated areas, such as in the Midwest or the rural South where land is available and inexpensive. To avoid community opposition, a company may seek an area whose residents lack political clout and that needs new revenues and industry—for instance, in a county suffering high unemployment and a diminished tax base due to business dislocation or closures. The latter scenario was the subject of an investigation by Elizabeth Royte for the article quoted above.

Residents of some poor communities are forced to live with the risks. One unemployed man dismissed the risks fatalistically: "We're gonna die anyhow. We'll starve to death."[23] Not all residents of communities under extreme economic duress take that view, however. Many of them express legitimate fears that such potentially harmful materials as municipal waste and incinerator ash containing high levels of lead, cadmium, mercury, and arsenic may be buried in these landfills. Royte's study suggests that even less-rational fears and prejudices regarding out-of-state waste, particularly from the Northeast, may tip the scales against local acceptance.

Aside from economic issues, some commentators condemn landfill and incinerator siting practices as being racist and elitist. Robert Bullard wrote of these objections in a 1992 article:

> Despite the numerous laws, mandates, and directives by the federal government to eliminate discrimination, . . . [EPA] has made few attempts to address discrim-

inatory environmental practices. People of color (African Americans, Latinos, Asians, and Native Americans) have borne a disproportionate burden in the siting of municipal landfills, incinerators, and hazardous waste treatment, storage, and disposal facilities. . . .

. . . African Americans, no matter what their educational or occupational achievement or income level, are exposed to greater environmental threats in their neighborhoods because of their race. . . . Institutional racism influences local land use policies, industrial facility siting, and where people of color live, work, and play.

. . . Waste generation is directly correlated with per capita income, but few garbage dumps and toxic waste sites are located in affluent suburbs. . . .

The first major empirical study that linked municipal solid waste siting with the race of surrounding residents was conducted in 1979 and chronicled in *Invisible Houston: The Black Experience in Boom and Bust.* From the early 1920s to the late 1970s, all of the city-owned municipal landfill and six of the eight garbage incinerators were located in African American neighborhoods.

From 1970 to 1978, three of the four privately owned landfills that were used to dispose of Houston's garbage were located in African American neighborhoods. Although African Americans made up only 28 percent of Houston's population, 82 percent of the solid waste sites (public and private) were located in African American neighborhoods.

. . . As recently as 1991, Residents Involved in Saving the Environment, or RISE (a biracial community group), challenged the King and Queen County (Virginia) board of supervisors for selecting a 420-acre site in a mostly African American community for a regional landfill. From 1969 to 1990, all three of the county-run landfills had been located in mostly African American communities.

Siting inequities are not unique to facilities where household garbage is dumped. The findings I recently published in *Dumping in Dixie* revealed that African Americans bear a disparate burden in the siting of hazardous waste landfills and incinerators in South Louisiana's "Cancer Alley" and Alabama's "blackbelt." The nation's largest commercial hazardous waste landfill, the "Cadillac of dumps," is located in Emelle, Alabama. African Americans make up 90 percent of Emelle's population and 75 percent of the residents in Sumter County. The Emelle landfill receives wastes from Superfund sites and from all 48 contiguous states.

. . .[A] 1983 U.S. General Accounting Office (GAO) study . . . found four off-site commercial hazardous waste landfills in EPA's Region 4 (Alabama, Florida, Georgia, Kentucky, Mississippi, North Carolina, South Carolina, and Tennessee). Three of the four landfills were located in mostly African American communities, although African Americans made up only one-fifth of the population in the region.

. . . In 1992, African Americans still make up about one-fifth of the population in the region. However, the region's two currently operating off-site commercial hazardous waste landfills are located in zip codes where African Americans are a majority of the population.

* * *

Siting inequities are national in scope. The Commission for Racial Justice's landmark *Toxic Wastes and Race* study found race to be the single most important factor (i.e., more important than income, home ownership rate, and property values) in the location of abandoned toxic waste sites. The 1987 study also found that: . . .

- Three of the five largest commercial hazardous waste landfills are located in predominately African American or Latino communities and account for 40 percent of the nation's total estimated landfill capacity in 1986. . . .

* * *

. . . A 1990 Greenpeace report, *Playing with Fire*, confirmed what many environmental justice activists had suspected all along:

* * *

- Communities where incinerators are proposed have minority populations 60 percent higher than the national average.
- Average income in communities with existing incinerators is 15 percent less than the national average.
- Property values in communities that host incinerators are 38 percent less than the national average.
- In communities where incinerators are proposed, average property values are 35 percent lower than the national average.

Native American lands have become prime targets for waste disposal proposals. More than three dozen reservations have been targeted for landfills and incinerators. Because of the special quasi-sovereign status of Indian nations, companies have attempted to skirt state regulations.

In 1991, the Choctaws in Philadelphia, Mississippi, defeated a plan to locate a 466-acre hazardous waste landfill in their midst. In the same year, a Connecticut company proposed to build a 6,000-acre municipal landfill on the Rosebud reservation in South Dakota . . . The Good Road Coalition, an alliance of grass-roots groups, blocked the proposal . . .[24]

Congress has the power to address some issues on landfill siting. For example it may permit a state to limit the amount of out-of-state waste it will accept or to charge higher fees for disposal of it. States may not do such things without express Congressional authority, however. Other issues are not as easily solved by legislation, such as the fact that the nation's trash usually finds its way to the poorest communities, portending greater health risks for residents whose health is already affected adversely by a lower standard of living. Only environmental policies such as recycling and source reduction can ultimately mitigate the problems of landfill siting.

The Economics of Trash: Municipal Waste Management

In light of the increasing costs of trash disposal and decreasing landfill space, many municipalities face the dilemma of choosing between two alternatives, each of which carries significant risks. On the one hand, a city may choose to make a long-term contract with a private waste disposal company in order to assure a future outlet for its trash, to fix future disposal costs and to avoid exposure to unpredictable price increases. The drawback is that if improved technology and business competition subsequently produce significant drops in market prices for waste disposal, the city will be bound for the contract term to the higher costs or to a contractor who may prove to be inept or unreliable.

On the other hand, a city may, in order to avoid relying upon private businesses and to gain greater cost control, choose to build and operate its own incinerator plant. In that event, the city must confront the health and environmental risks of combustion of wastes and the problem of disposing of incinerator ash, which itself contains hazardous wastes. From an economic perspective, the costs of constructing and operating an incinerator for a given volume of trash (i.e., cost per ton) in compliance with environmental laws should not be greater than the unit cost of using outside businesses. But the cost-effectiveness of the municipality's incinerator operation would be vulnerable to the same contingencies that affect private contractors—namely, the requirements of future environmental regulations and the possible development of more cost-effective disposal technologies. Municipal incineration is thus subject to the same economic and environmental risks that affect private contractors.

Many municipalities that have opted for long-term, fixed-price contracts with private disposal companies have found themselves locked into excessively high costs after market forces have produced unanticipated drops in contractor charges for waste disposal. On the other hand, some municipalities that have chosen to build their own incineration plants have found that, to be cost-effective, the plant had to have a large capacity and usage greater than what they and other municipal customers could provide. Many small municipalities could not construct incinerator plants of economically viable size, and those that could have sought economies of scale by relying on incineration business from neighboring municipalities. Once they are in this contracting business, however, municipal plants face the same market risks and competition for customers that private businesses do. There is no guarantee that, without some legal compulsion, a neighboring municipality will refrain from giving its trash business to a private competitor at some time in the future.

The need to ensure the minimal stream of trash for economic viability has produced an ironic turnabout by some municipalities and counties experiencing unused incineration capacity. These entities have sought to restrain the removal by private haulers of trash from the municipality and to capture it—like a valuable commodity—for disposal (for a fee) at their government plants. A number of states have accordingly passed laws authorizing local governments, through various licensing schemes, to control and direct the flow of trash to specific disposal sites within the respective jurisdiction. Due to this shift in market economics, some municipalities that once sought to export their trash because they lacked landfill capacity now insist that all locally generated trash be disposed of locally.[25] Although this scenario of trash retention efforts may be an exceptional, rather than the dominant, trend, it highlights the economic vagaries of trash management and suggests that solutions to the problems may not exist in rapidly changing marketplaces.

Such restraints on trash export raise a constitutional issue that is considered in the next subsection; namely, whether trash-flow control amounts to an unconstitutional restraint on interstate commerce.

Commerce Clause Issues

The business of waste hauling and disposal is considered "commerce" within the coverage of the Commerce Clause of the U.S. constitution. The Commerce Clause vests Congress with supreme authority to regulate interstate commerce, which includes the power to permit or prohibit interstate commerce activity that it deems good or bad for the nation's economy. Even where Congress has remained silent, the Commerce Clause still operates to prevent states from regulating businesses in ways that discriminate against or burden interstate transport and disposal of wastes. Thus, unless Congress expressly acts to regulate that activity—for example, by permitting states to limit entry and deposit of out-of-state wastes—the states remain powerless to resolve their own waste disposal problems. Two U.S. Supreme Court decisions clarify these Commerce Clause restraints.

FORT GRATIOT SANITARY LANDFILL V. MICHIGAN DEPT. OF NATURAL RESOURCES

112 S. Ct. 2019 (1992)

Justice STEVENS delivered the opinion of the Court.

In *Philadelphia v. New Jersey,* 437 U.S. 617, 618, 98 S. Ct. 2531, 2532, 57 L.Ed. 2d 475 (1978), we held that a New Jersey law prohibiting the importation of most "'solid or liquid waste which originated or was collected outside the territorial limits of the State'" violated the Commerce Clause of the United States Constitution. In this case petitioner challenges a Michigan law that prohibits private landfill operators from accepting solid waste that originates outside the county in which their facilities are located. Adhering to our holding in the *New Jersey* case, we conclude that this Michigan statute is also unconstitutional.

I

In 1978 Michigan enacted its Solid Waste Management Act (SWMA). That Act required every Michigan county to estimate the amount of solid waste that would be generated in the county in the next 20 years and to adopt a plan providing for its disposal at facilities that comply with state health standards. . . .

On December 28, 1988, the Michigan Legislature amended the SWMA. . . . Those amendments (Waste Import Restrictions) . . . provide:

"A person shall not accept for disposal solid waste . . . that is not generated in the county in which the disposal area is located unless the acceptance of solid waste . . . that is not generated in the county is explicitly authorized in the approved county solid waste management plan." . . .

In February, 1989, petitioner submitted an application to the St. Clair County Solid Waste Planning Committee for authority to accept up to 1,750 tons per day of out-of-state waste at its landfill. . . . In that application petitioner promised to reserve sufficient capacity to dispose of all solid waste generated in the county in the next 20 years. The planning committee denied the application. *Ibid.* In view of the fact that the county's management plan does not authorize the acceptance of any out-of-county waste, the Waste Import Restriction in the 1988 statute effectively prevent petitioner from receiving any solid waste that does not originate in St. Clair County.

Petitioner therefore commenced this action seeking a judgment declaring the Waste Import Restrictions unconstitutional and enjoining their enforcement. Petitioner contended that requiring a private landfill operator to limit its business to the acceptance of local waste constituted impermissible discrimination against interstate commerce. . . .

* * *

Before discussing the rather narrow issue that is contested, it is appropriate to identify certain matters that are not in dispute. . . . No issue relating to hazardous waste is presented, and there is no claim that petitioner's operation violated any health, safety, or sanitation requirement. Nor does the case raise any question concerning policies that municipalities or other governmental agencies may pursue in the management of publicly owned facilities. The case involves only the validity of the Waste Import Restrictions as they apply to privately owned and operated landfills.

* * *

As we have long recognized, the "negative" or "dormant" aspect of the Commerce Clause prohibits States from "advanc[ing] their own commercial interests by curtailing the movement of articles of commerce, either into or out of the state." . . . A state statute that clearly discriminates against interstate commerce is therefore unconstitutional "unless the discrimination is demonstrably justified by a valid factor unrelated to economic protectionism." . . .

* * *

The Waste Import Restrictions enacted by Michigan authorize each of its 83 counties to isolate itself from the national economy. Indeed, unless a county acts affirmatively to permit other waste to enter its jurisdiction, the statute affords local waste producers complete protection from competition from out-of-state waste producers who seek to use local waste disposal areas. In view of the fact that Michigan has not identified any reason, apart from its origin, why solid waste coming from outside the county should be treated differently from solid waste within the county, the foregoing reasoning would appear to control the disposition of this case.

III

Respondents Michigan and St. Clair County argue, however, that the Waste Import Restrictions . . . do not discriminate against interstate commerce on their face or in effect because they treat waste from other Michigan counties no differently than waste from other States. Instead, respondents maintain, the statute regulates evenhandedly to effectuate local interests and should be upheld because the burden on interstate commerce is not clearly excessive in relation to the local benefits. . . . We disagree, for our prior cases teach that a State (or one of its political subdivisions) may not avoid the strictures of the Commerce Clause by curtailing the movement of articles of commerce through subdivisions of the State, rather than through the State itself.

* * *

Nor does the fact that the Michigan statute allows individual counties to accept solid waste from out of state qualify its discriminatory character. . . . Similarly, in this case St. Clair County's total ban on out-of-state waste is unaffected by the fact that some other counties have adopted a different policy.

* * *

IV

Michigan and St. Clair County also argue that this case is different from *Philadelphia v. New Jersey* because the SWMA constitutes a comprehensive health and safety regulation rather than "economic protectionism" of the State's limited landfill capacity. . . .

* * *

. . . We may assume that all of the provisons of Michigan's SWMA prior to the 1988 amendments adding the Waste Import Restrictions could fairly be characterized as health and safety regulations with no protectionist purpose, but we cannot make that same assumption with respect to the Waste Import Restrictions themselves. Because those provisions unambiguously discriminate against interstate commerce, the State bears the burden of proving that they further health and safety concerns that cannot be adequately served by nondiscriminatory alternatives. Michigan and St. Clair County have not met this burden.

Michigan and St. Clair County assert that the Waste Import Restrictions are necessary because they enable individual counties to make adequate plans for the safe disposal of future waste. Although accurate forecasts about the volume and composition of future waste flows may be an indispensable part of a comprehensive waste disposal plan, Michigan could attain that objective without discriminating between in- and out-of-state waste. . . .

Of course our conclusion would be different if the imported waste raised health or other concerns not presented by Michigan waste. . . . In this case, in contrast, the lower courts did not find—and respondents have not provided—any legitimate reason for allowing petitioner to accept waste from inside the county but not waste from outside the county.

For the foregoing reasons, the Waste Import Restrictions unambiguously discriminate against interstate commerce and are appropriately characterized as protectionist measures that cannot withstand scrutiny under the Commerce Clause. . . .

* * *

CHEMICAL WASTE MANAGEMENT, INC. V. HUNT

112 S. Ct. 2009 (1992)

[When this case was decided, landfills for hazardous waste existed in only 16 states. Chemical Waste Management, Inc., operated a facility for the treatment, storage, and disposal of hazardous waste at the largest of these facilities, which was located in Alabama, doing so under a permit issued by the EPA under the RCRA and TSCA statutes. Most of the waste (90%) at that facility had been generated in states other than Alabama. Alabama enacted a disposal fee for out-of-state hazardous wastes, and Chemical Waste Management brought suit to challenge the fee as a violation of the Commerce Clause of the United States Constitution. This opinion excerpt deals with the Commerce Clause issue.]

Justice WHITE delivered the opinion of the Court.

* * *

The parties do not dispute that the wastes and substances being landfilled at the Emelle facility "include substances that are inherently dangerous to human health and safety and to the environment. Such waste consists of ignitable, corrosive, toxic and reactive wastes which contain poisonous and cancer causing chemicals and which can cause birth defects, genetic damage, blindness, crippling and death." . . . From 1985 through 1989, the tonnage of hazardous waste received per year has more than doubled, increasing from 341,000 tons in 1985 to 788,000 tons by 1989. Of this, up to 90% of the tonnage permanently buried each year is shipped in from other States.

Against this backdrop Alabama enacted Act No. 90-326 (the Act). Ala. Code §§ 22-30B-1 to 22-30B-18 (1990 and Supp. 1991). Among other provisions, the Act includes . . . a "cap" that generally limits the amount of hazardous wastes or substances that may be disposed of in any 1-year period. . . . Finally, the Act imposes the "additional fee" at issue here, which states in full:

"For waste and substances which are generated outside of Alabama and disposed of at a commercial site for the disposal of hazardous waste or hazardous substances in Alabama, an additional fee shall be levied at the rate of $72.00 per ton." . . .

. . . In addition to state law claims, petitioner contended that the Act violated the Commerce, Due Process, and Equal Protection Clauses of the United States Constitution, and was preempted by various federal statutes. . . .

. . . Because of the importance of the federal question and the likelihood that it had been decided in a way conflicting with applicable decisions of this Court, . . . we granted certiorari limited to petitioner's Commerce Clause challenge to the additional fee. . . .

II

No State may attempt to isolate itself from a problem common to the several States by raising barriers to the free flow of interstate trade. Today, in *Fort Gratiot Sanitary Landfill, Inc. v. Michigan Dept. of Natural Resources,* ___ U.S. ___, 112 S. Ct. 2019, ___ L.Ed. 2d ___ (1992), we have also considered a Commerce Clause challenge to a Michigan law prohibiting private landfill operators from accepting solid waste originating outside the county in which their facilities operate. In striking down that law, we adhered to our decision in *Philadelphia v. New Jersey,* 437 U.S. 617, 98 S. Ct. 2531, 57 L.Ed. 2d 475 (1978), where we found New Jersey's prohibition of solid waste from outside that State to amount to economic protectionism barred by the Commerce Clause: . . .

The Act's additional fee facially discriminates against hazardous waste generated in States other than Alabama, and the Act overall has plainly discouraged the full operation of petitioner's Emelle facility. Such burdensome taxes imposed on interstate commerce alone are generally forbidden: "[A] State may not tax a transaction or incident more heavily when it crosses state lines than when it occurs entirely within the State." . . . Once a state tax is found to discriminate against out-of-state commerce, it is typically struck down without further inquiry. . . .

The State, however, argues that the additional fee imposed on out-of-state hazardous waste serves legitimate local purposes related to its citizens' health and safety. Because the additional fee discriminates both on its face and in practical effect, the burden falls on the State "to justify it both in terms of the local benefits flowing from the statute and the unavailability of nondiscriminatory alternatives adequate to preserve the local interests at stake." . . . "At a minimum such facial discrimination invokes the strictest scrutiny of any purported legitimate local purpose and of the absence of nondiscriminatory alternatives." . . .

The State's argument here does not significantly differ from the Alabama Supreme Court's conclusions on the legitimate local purposes of the additional fee imposed, which were:

> . . . (1) protection of the health and safety of the citizens of Alabama from toxic substances; (2) conservation of the environment and the state's natural resources; (3) provision for compensatory revenue for the costs and burdens that out-of-state waste generators impose by dumping their hazardous waste in Alabama; (4) reduction of the overall flow of wastes traveling on the state's highways, which flow creates a great risk to the health and safety of the state's citizens." 584 So. 2d, at 1389.

These may all be legitimate local interests, and petitioner has not attacked them. But only rhetoric, and not explanation, emerges as to why Alabama targets *only* interstate hazardous waste to meet these goals. . . . The [trial] Court finds under the facts of this case that the only basis for the additional fee is the origin of the waste." App. to Pet. for Cert. 83a–84a. In the face of such findings, invalidity under the Commerce clause necessarily follows, for "whatever [Alabama's] ultimate purpose, it may not be accomplished by discriminating against articles of commerce coming from outside the State unless there is some reason, apart from their origin, to treat them differently." . . . The burden is on the State to show that "the *discrimination* is demonstrably justified by a valid factor unrelated to economic protectionism," . . . .

Ultimately, the State's concern focuses on the volume of the waste entering the Emelle facility. Less discriminatory alternatives, however, are available to alleviate this concern, not the least of which are a generally applicable per-ton additional fee on *all* hazardous waste disposed of within Alabama, . . . or a per mile tax on *all* vehicles transporting hazardous waste across Alabama roads. . . . or an even-handed cap on the total tonnage landfilled at Emelle, . . . which would curtail volume from all sources. To the extent Alabama's concern touches environmental conservation and the health and safety of its citizens, such concern does not vary with the point of origin of the waste, and it remains within the State's power to monitor and regulate more closely the transportation and disposal of *all* hazardous waste within its borders. . . . In sum, we find the additional fee to be "an obvious effort to saddle those outside the State" with most of the burden of slowing the flow of waste into the Emelle facility. . . . "That legislative effort is clearly impermissible under the Commerce Clause of the Constitution."

* * *

Carefully tailored regulations may allow a state or local government to accomplish purposes that are generally forbidden by the Commerce Clause, such as preventing waste that is generated elsewhere from being incinerated in a particular area. In the *Medical Waste Assoc.* case, a municipality was able to avoid violating the Commerce Clause by enacting an ordinance that affected only one facility, albeit one that was unique to the region.

■   ■

MEDICAL WASTE ASSOC. v. MAYOR AND CITY COUNCIL

966 F.2d 148 (4th Cir. 1992)

[Medical waste facility operator brought action challenging a zoning ordinance that limited it to medical waste generated within the city. The court held that an ordinance that limited one facility in the city to waste generated within the city did not violate the commerce clause.]

* * *

Commerce Clause

The Commerce Clause limits the extent to which states may seal off their borders from the flow of interstate commerce. Indeed, the Supreme Court in *City of Philadelphia v. State of New Jersey* . . . held that a state may not close off its boundaries to an article of commerce regardless of the nature of that commerce. In that case, the Court struck down a New Jersey statute which prevented all out-of-state trash from being accepted by landfills within the State of New Jersey. In so doing, the Court set out a two tier test for analyzing statutes which impact interstate commerce:

* * *

Thus, where simple economic protectionism is effected by state legislation, a virtual *per se* rule of invalidity has been erected (citation omitted). The clearest example of such legislation is a law that overtly blocks the flow of intestate commerce at a State's borders (citations omitted). But, where other legislative objectives are credibly advanced and there is no patent discrimination against interstate trade, the Court has adopted a much more flexible approach, . . .

In *Pike v. Bruce Church, Inc.* the Court set out a less restrictive test commonly referred to as the *Pike* balancing test. Under that test, "[w]here [a] statute regulates evenhandedly to effectuate a legitimate local public interest, and its effects on interstate commerce are only incidental, it will be upheld unless the burden imposed on such commerce is clearly excessive in relation to the putative local benefit." Therefore, when a statute does not fall within the *per se* rule of *City of Philadelphia*, the *Pike* test will apply to determine whether the statute passes muster under the Commerce Clause.

We believe that the *per se* rule of *City of Philadelphia* does not apply to the case at bar for several reasons. First, and most importantly, Ordinance 323 on its face doe not discriminate against out-of-state waste being brought into the City of Baltimore. Unlike the statute in *City of Philadelphia*, which banned all out-of-state trash from entering the entire State of New Jersey, the statute in question here bans medical waste from only *one facility* within a city. We believe that to fall within the purview of the *per se* rule enunciated in *City of Philadelphia*, a statute must, either on its face or in its practical effect, discriminate against waste entering a political subdivision such as a city, county or state. Merely excluding out-of-state waste from *one facility* within a region will not result in a *per se* violation unless the exclusion has the practical effect of restricting waste from entering the political subdivision involved.

Second, under the "market participant" exception . . . the City of Baltimore could have built and operated the medical waste facility itself and reserved the entire capacity of the facility for its residents. We believe that by adopting a rule incorporating a "single facility" exception to the *per se* rule of *City of Philadelphia*, we reconcile the "market participant" rule with the practical way that cities and counties solve regional waste problems. Specifically, by adopting a rule which allows a city to restrict a single facility's use to its residents, we allow a city to use private capital to solve a regional problem which might otherwise be too costly as a credit impairment for the city to undertake on its own. Indeed, forcing a city to choose between building a waste facility itself, or allowing waste from outside the region to overwhelm a privately built facility, could result in regional waste problems remaining unsolved.

The Ninth Circuit, confronted with a situation almost parallel to this case, also concluded that the *per se* rule did not apply when the restriction against out-of-state waste involved a single facility. *See Evergreen Waste Systems, Inc. v. Metropolitan Serv. Dist*, 820 F.2d 1482 (9th Cir. 1987). In *Evergreen*, the Metropolitan Service District, a municipal entity which operated a single landfill, adopted an ordinance barring from that landfill waste from outside its three county district. . . .

In conclusion, we agree with the district court that the case before us is "remarkably similar" to *Evergreen* and agree with that court that a "single facility" exception to the broad *per se* rule of *City of Philadelphia* is appropriate. Having found that the statute is not a *per se* violation of the Commerce Clause, we now analyze Ordinance 323 under the *Pike* balancing test. Accordingly, we turn to whether the ordinance (1) effectuates a legitimate local public interest, (2) has only an incidental effect on interstate commerce, and (3) does not impose a burden on commerce that is clearly excessive in relation to the putative local benefits. . . . Without pause, we agree with the district court that the ordinance satisfied these criteria and, therefore, is constitutional.

Certainly, the purpose of the ordinance, which was to meet emergency regulations and to prevent medical waste from polluting Chesapeake Bay and the landfills of Baltimore, "effectuates a legitimate local public interest." Creating a regional facility limited to a specific geographical area ensures that all of the waste from that area will be properly disposed of. Any burden on interstate commerce that might exist, of which plaintiff has offered no evidence, is only of an incidental nature and is not "clearly excessive" in light of the proper disposal of a whole region's infectious and non-infectious medical waste. Moreover, as previously noted, Ordinance 323 involves only one facility in one city in Maryland. If demand so requires, Ordinance 323 does not prohibit another incinerator from being built nor preclude the City Council from allowing a second facility in Baltimore to expand. This Court concludes that Ordinance 323 satisfies the *Pike* balancing test and, that the ordinance is constitutional.

Source Reduction and Recycling

Various proposals have been advanced for managing municipal and solid waste from a marketplace perspective. Some of these, such as those described in the following article, advocate marketplace incentives to encourage source reduction and recycling efforts.

* * *

Waste disposal imposes costs on society, including the expense of collecting the waste and building and operating disposal facilities. The possible environmental and health effects of leakage from landfills and emissions from incinerators are hotly debated, and many communities have encountered strong resistance to siting new disposal facilities. . . .

Although waste disposal imposes costs on society, the activities that generate waste also provide benefits. For example, packaging keeps food clean and may help in its preparation. Being able to dispose of waste easily is also a valued benefit. Setting out trash for pickup is quicker and easier than finding another use for it in the home, composting it in the backyard, or taking it to a recycling center.

Ideally, the costs and benefits of disposal would be taken into account when deciding how much to change consumption patterns to reduce waste, to recycle, or to compost. Economic incentives may play a key role in helping society balance these costs and benefits. Three types of incentives that might be useful in achieving this balance are household charges, combination disposal tax and reuse subsidies, and recycling credit systems.

Most households pay for waste disposal services through their local property taxes or by a fixed fee to a private collector. Under this flat-fee system, they don't have a monetary incentive to change their consumption behavior or to increase their recycling and composting efforts.

Some communities have begun to charge households according to each bag or can of trash that they discard. These "unit-based pricing" programs encourage households to weigh the convenience of waste disposal against the charge for an additional bag or can. Under these programs, households can save money by buying goods with less packaging, or by recycling and composting their waste. A study of three unit-based pricing programs in Perkasie, Pennsylvania; Ilion, New York; and Seattle, Washington, found that such programs may significantly decrease the amount of waste sent to the landfill or incinerator.

Unit-based pricing programs hold much promise, but there are some important concerns. They may, for example, create an incentive to illegally dispose of waste. Tracking illegal disposal is very difficult, . . . but anecdotal evidence indicates that some people in unit-based pricing programs are illegally burning waste, dumping it in vacant lots, and disposing of it at public facilities, private dumpsites, or in surrounding communities. EPA is investigating the effects of unit-based pricing and will provide guidance about the types of communities where it may be effective. For example, suburban communities may be better suited for unit-based pricing than rural areas where illegal dumping would be easier. Communities with predominantly single-family housing may be better suited than areas with multifamily housing, where monitoring the waste generated by individual families is more difficult.

Under a combination disposal tax and reuse subsidy policy, producers would be taxed according to the cost of disposing of the goods that they produce, and importers would be taxed for the cost of disposing of the goods they import. This would encourage them to reduce the amount or the toxicity of waste associated with their products. In addition, firms that use recycled materials (referred to as end users) would receive a subsidy, thereby encouraging increased recycling.

Idaho has established a combination disposal tax and reuse subsidy program for tires. The state imposes a $1 surcharge on all tires sold; the revenue is used to subsidize recycling. Firms that retread tires receive up to $1 per reprocessed tire; other end users of old tires receive $25 per ton.

A disposal tax would encourage producers to reduce the amount of waste associated with their products as long as the cost of doing so were less than the tax. Likewise, the reuse subsidy would encourage end users to use recycled materials as long as the cost of doing so were less than the subsidy. Provided that the government set the disposal tax and reuse subsidy so that each were equal to the benefit that society received from reduced waste disposal, this policy would provide an incentive for firms to balance the costs and benefits of waste disposal.

An advantage of this policy is that it would not create an incentive for illegal disposal. However, its application is limited: To administer a set of taxes and subsidies on all consumer products would not be feasible. The policy could be targeted at items that had the potential for increased recycling and were particularly problematic components of the waste stream, such as old car batteries, tires, and used oil.

Under a recycling credit system, the government would set a target for a product, and producers and importers would be responsible for ensuring that the required percentage of the product was recycled. . . . For example, if a 50-percent recycling target was set for newspapers, for every ton of newspapers it sold, *Hometown Daily* would have to buy half-a-ton's worth of newspaper recycling credits. It would buy them from companies, such as cardboard container producers, that used old newspapers in their production processes. Firms that could use old newspapers would have an increased incentive to do so.

An advantage of a credit system over one that mandates the recycled content level of individual products is that it produces an incentive for firms that can reuse the old product at the least cost of doing so. For example, a system that mandated content level would require that old newspapers go into making new newspapers. Under a credit system, however, old newspapers would go into whichever products could use them most cheaply. Because of this, a recycling credit system would help to ensure that the recycling target set by the government is achieved at the lowest cost to society.

. . . The government must take care, therefore, to set the target at a level where the cost of meeting it is equal to the benefits received. In other words, the increased cost of using the additional amount of recycled materials must be balanced by the decreased cost of disposal.

Congress has considered using a recycling credit system for a variety of items, including tires, used oil, and old newspapers. Like the combination disposal tax and reuse subsidy policy, a recycling credit system would be feasible for a limited number of items.[26]

Federal Facilities

Federal agencies, such as the Departments of Energy and Defense, operate nuclear plants, military bases, and other facilities throughout the country that are subject to numerous environmental laws, including those relating to the hazardous waste, which they produce in large quantities. The environmental compliance record of these facilities has received increasing criticism in recent years. At a few, such as The Rocky Flats nuclear-weapons production facility in Colorado, massive, illegal mismanagement of hazardous and nuclear wastes was the order of the day, and resulted in devastating environmental contamination.

The diverse issues related to federal facilities' compliance with environmental laws include:

- the extent to which EPA and the states may assess penalties and issue compliance orders to federal facilities,
- the institutional and political barriers faced by those seeking to enforce environmental laws against federal agencies,
- the programs or policies that are most effective in achieving compliance at federal facilities, and
- the detrimental example set for private industry by some federal agencies' irresponsible environmental management and chronic disregard of environmental laws.

A significant percentage, perhaps a majority, of environmental violations are perpetrated by federal-government agencies. A leading sponsor of the Federal Facilities Compliance Act noted that more than half of the federal facilities nationwide were in violation of waste disposal laws at the time. After years of attempts by the Bush Administration to block similar legislation, Congress in September 1992 enacted a law requiring federal installations to comply with state and federal laws in disposing of hazardous and nuclear waste. The law, known as the Federal Facilities Compliance Act, mandates that the Department of Energy (DOE), within three years' time, reach agreements with states on disposal strategies for nuclear and hazardous wastes at facilities it oversees. The three-year grace period was included in order to meet DOE objections that nuclear- and mixed-waste disposal technologies were not available at the time of the enactment. The Act leaves open the question of whether states may impose fines on the federal government for violating state environmental laws and for violating federal laws, such as RCRA, that are enforced in many states under federally approved state-run programs.[27]

The Nuclear Waste Crisis

Although nuclear waste is not usually subject to regulation under RCRA, the subject of this chapter, it is discussed here because it is a significant waste management issue. A Worldwatch Institute report estimates that more than 80,000 tons of high-level nuclear waste exist worldwide, not including tens of thousands of tons of nuclear weapons and radioactive medical and industrial waste. The report notes that U.S. reactors annually produce about 67 times the amount of plutonium that would cause lung cancer in everyone on earth.

Nuclear wastes are classified according to their source and their level of radioactivity. The most radioactive of nuclear wastes is spent uranium fuel rods, byproducts of nuclear power generation. Spent fuel from the approximately 110 U.S. nuclear power plants poses the most intractable high-level nuclear waste problem. (The rods are actually much more radioactive after their useful life is over.) Neither recycling nor reclamation technologies have proven feasible, due to the overwhelming energy they require and the dangers they pose. Measured by radioactivity, spent fuel accounts for 90 percent of the accumulated nuclear waste in the United States. In the early 1990s more than 20,000 metric tons of spent fuel and other nuclear waste was in "temporary" storage in cooling pools at 82 nuclear power facilities across the country. By the year 2000, the amount is expected to be 40,000 metric tons.

Societies that use nuclear technology thus face the dilemma of developing safe storage means for ever-increasing amounts of spent fuel and other high-level nuclear wastes. Monica Bauerlien discussed some proposed solutions in a 1992 *Utne Reader* article:

> The U.S. Department of Energy (DOE) selected Yucca Mountain, Nevada, as the national "permanent repository for nuclear waste." But after 10 years of research and more than $1 billion dollars, DOE still hasn't drilled a single hole into Yucca Mountain—mostly because of opposition from Nevadans and their state government, who have been able to show potential risks in the project. By now, DOE has pushed back its deadline for the dump from 1998 to 2010, and many believe Yucca Mountain will never open.
>
> Meanwhile, nuclear waste keeps piling up at the country's 110 nuclear reactors, mostly in indoor water pools originally designed to hold small quantities for a few years. . . . [U]tility organizations estimate that within the next 10 years, about half of the nation's nuclear power plants will have to find [other places] to put their waste or shut down; as a result, power companies have begun to create their own on-site nuclear waste dumps. The preferred technology is called "dry-cask storage," which means keeping the waste in giant outdoor steel cans.
>
> . . . [A]t least 67 of the nation's current 110 nuclear plants will have to close and be dismantled within the next 30 years, adding uncounted tons of radioactive debris to the nuclear waste stream. The Bush administration [has proposed] that most reactors get "relicensed" for another 30 years beyond their original lifespan, but that idea carries its own set of safety and environmental problems.[28]

The Yucca Mountain project's problems are numerous, among them its location: Yucca Mountain lies between two earthquake faults and is only twelve miles from a geologically young volcano. Another DOE high-level nuclear waste project, the Waste Isolation Pilot Plant (WIPP) near Carlsbad, New Mexico, has similar problems.

WIPP was authorized in 1979 as a permanent home for high-level waste such as plutonium-contaminated materials, equipment, and protective clothing from the nation's nuclear weapons factories. Since the 1940s, such military nuclear wastes have been temporarily stored in rusting, poorly labeled drums stacked in open trenches. WIPP is an immense underground repository carved from salt bed formations at a cost of $1 billion. When it is completed, it will be the world's first repository.

Although high-level nuclear waste remains radioactive for 240,000 years, EPA's regulations require that facilities such as WIPP not leak appreciably for only 10,000 years. Attempting to design and mark a repository that will remain intact for even 10,000 years is a formidable challenge.

WIPP's location is a massive salt-bed formation, the remains of a 200 million-year-old inland sea located near Carlsbad, New Mexico. Salt-bed formations generally indicate that a site is dry (otherwise, the salt would dissolve), and the risk of wastes leaching into ground water and migrating off-site is reduced if the disposal site remains dry. The rationale for burial in salt formations is that the salt will surround the buried wastes and hold them in a geologically stable state.

In 1975, the site originally selected for the WIPP repository was discovered to be situated directly above a vast pressurized brine reservoir. After selecting a second location and beginning construction there, a probe for pressurized brine released several million gallons of it. Yet another location was selected, and it too may lie over the brine reservoir. Alan Burdick, senior editor of *The Sciences,* describes the potential dangers of situating nuclear waste in the salt-bed formations near the brine reservoir:

> [The location ultimately chosen] placed WIPP in a stratum of salt thought to contain significant amounts of brine. The DOE itself estimates that within twenty years of burial, the thousands of soft steel drums [that contain plutonium-contaminated wastes] will corrode and their contents be laid naked. Exposed to the brine, the waste gradually will decompose to slurry, threatening to leach out through the hairline cracks that lace the [salt] bed. Moreover, as it decomposes, the nuclear slush will generate copious amounts of gas, which would enlarge the cracks. Exactly how much and what kinds of gases would be generated are hard to predict, however, since no one can say with precision what many of the drums contain. In any event, if the repository is as airtight as engineers promise, the gas will become trapped and pressurized, a condition that could push the [radioactive] slurry through WIPP's minute pores.
>
> . . . Designed to remain intact for millennia, WIPP would not surprise its critics if it sprung a leak within a century. [This would pose] another problem. One highly touted advantage of salt beds is their self-healing properties: the tomb walls slowly will close around the waste and encase it, inert. The advantage becomes a liability, however, if the waste turns to slurry: it will be virtually impossible to get at the stuff if something goes wrong.
>
> . . . In any event, WIPP is only a partial solution. To contain the volume of plutonium-contaminated waste currently in retrievable storage would require three WIPPs; to hold the nation's entire backlog of military and commercial waste, ten.[29]

After WIPP is full, sometime around 2030, it will be sealed and its surface buildings razed. Burdick's article raises another major challenge: how to mark the site as dangerous so that people in future millenia will understand that excavating or disturbing it would be deadly. As Burdick points out, repositories such as WIPP will outlast by far any institutional history or widespread comprehension of any current modern language. Pictogrammatic and sculptural representations could well be misunderstood as art or civic or religious monument and thus might invite, rather than deter, excavation by future generations.

Low-level radioactive wastes have less radioactivity and shorter decay times than high-level wastes. However, they can also be lethal. Many low-level radioactive waste generators—various industries, hospitals, and research institutions as well as the federal government—are finding it increasingly difficult to dispose of. In 1985, however, only three U.S. disposal sites existed for the millions of cubic feet of low-level radioactive waste generated each year. That year Congress passed legislation that contained three incentive provisions to compel states to create their own sites or to make arrangements with other states for disposing of low-level radioactive waste generated within their borders. Two of the provisions were upheld as constitutional, but the third provision was struck down by the Supreme Court as unconstitutional under the Tenth Amendment.[30] That provision would have required any state that lacks disposal capacity or other arrangements for disposing of radioactive waste (a) to take title to and possession of the waste at the request of its owner or generator and (b) to be liable for any damages incurred by the generator or owner if the state failed to take title. The problem of low-level waste disposal has been largely left by Congress with the states.

In addition to the challenges posed by the need for safe disposal of wastes generated by nuclear facilities, the United States is faced with the huge expense of cleaning up nuclear weapons facilities and restoring the environment at nuclear-waste disposal sites. The Department of Energy estimated in 1990 that it will cost $30 billion to clean up its nearly 100 nuclear weapons plants. That estimate exceeded the previous year's estimate by 60 percent. Figure 6.1 shows the estimated annual cleanup costs of each DOE field office. Figure 6.2 shows the Office of Technology Assessment cost estimates for restoration projects at various facilities.

Although most radioactive wastes are regulated under the Atomic Energy Act, "mixed" wastes—those that contain both radioactive and hazardous components—are subject to RCRA regulation as well.[31] Many mixed wastes are generated by nuclear power plants, universities, medical facilities, and industrial plants. Disposal capacity for mixed wastes is almost nonexistent, and many generators have merely been storing such wastes indefinitely. However, a 1993 court decision held that lack of disposal capacity did not render generators immune from RCRA's prohibitions against indefinite storage and stressed that RCRA's technology-forcing aspects would be undermined by allowing indefinite storage of hard-to-treat wastes.[32]

■ **Figure 6.1**   Nuclear Weapons Facilities Cleanup Costs*

DOE Regional Field Office	1990	1991	1992	1993	1994	1995
Albuquerque	$ 256	$ 360	$ 807	$ 802	$ 751	$ 661
Chicago	28	62	73	61	73	68
Headquarters	76	143	379	529	526	398
Idaho	300	369	718	657	601	520
Nevada	11	24	67	88	127	122
Oak Ridge	417	567	1,214	1,408	1,637	1,634
Richland	430	627	1,302	1,385	1,514	1,460
Rocky Flats	136	89	167	193	196	189
San Francisco	48	51	138	161	127	90
Savannah River	475	585	822	777	888	872
Technology Development	186	206	280	353	359	359
Total	$2,363	$3,083	$5,967	$6,414	$6,800	$6,372

*Costs shown in millions of dollars.

Source: ENR, 12 July 1990, p. 8. Data from U.S. Department of Energy.

■ Figure 6.2 Restoration-Project Cost Ranges

Type of Project	Cost Range, in Millions			
	Cost	*Project*	*Cost*	*Project*
Installation of ground-water monitoring well (per foot)	$ 150	Pinellas	$ 417	Hanford
Annual sample analysis (per well)	1,333	LLNL	20,500	INEL
Excavation of soil and sludge (per cubic yard)	8	Savannah River	260	Oak Ridge
Off-site soil disposal (per ton)	110	Pinellas	146	Kansas City
Installation of ground-water recovery well (per foot)	159	Savannah River	400	LLNL
Cap installation (per square foot)	5	Oak Ridge	8	Oak Ridge

Source: U.S. Congress, Office of Technology Assessment, *Complex Cleanup: The Environmental Legacy of Nuclear Weapons Production,* OTA-O-484 (Washington, D.C., February 1991), p. 59.

■ Problem Set Exercises

On the site of Tully's operations, a two-square-mile area known as "the Trench" is used for dumping waste and by-products resulting from the firm's research and production operations. Tully employees incinerate solid wastes and pile the ashes in mounds. Liquid wastes are placed in steel drums, which are then buried in the Trench. Most of these wastes are hazardous wastes under RCRA, but Tully has not applied for an RCRA permit, nor does it maintain any records of its waste disposal activities.

1. Which sections of the RCRA statute is Tully violating by its waste disposal activities?
2. Under what circumstances would these violations be considered criminal? What is the distinction between the two kinds of criminal intent in the statute, and which is punished more severely?
3. What would Tully need to have done to qualify for interim status?

Many of the drums buried in the Trench have corroded and are now leaking. There is no covering on the ash heaps to prevent the ash from becoming airborne, nor are there any liners to prevent the ash from leaching into the soil and ground water.

4. Assuming that Tully has never qualified for interim status, under which sections of RCRA could the EPA Administrator take action to compel Tully to clean up the Trench?
5. Assuming instead that Tully did become an interim-status facility, under which provision would the Administrator take action? Why would the Administrator choose one applicable provision over another?

6. What types of fines will Tully face if it does not comply with the Administrator's orders?

7. Assume that Tully applied for a permit and became an interim-status facility. If EPA wants to ensure that the Trench is cleaned up before it issues a permit to Tully for treatment, storage, or disposal activities, under what statutory sections may the Administrator take action?

8. Tully uses underground storage tanks to store petroleum near the Trench. What must the firm do to ensure that its use of these tanks does not violate RCRA?

Not all of Tully's wastes are dumped in the Trench. Some are hauled away by an independent contractor, Nelson Enterprises, which is under instructions to haul them to ABC Limited.

9. What are the record-keeping and manifest obligations of Nelson and ABC? Which of these enterprises is obligated to secure a permit under RCRA?

10. Suppose that Nelson's operator backs the truck into a telephone pole and damages one of the drums containing hazardous waste, causing the waste to leak out onto the ground. Would this subject Nelson to treatment, storage, and disposal liability under RCRA?

11. Suppose Nelson Enterprises fails to take the waste to ABC Limited as it is instructed to do. Instead, Mr. Nelson, who is having cash-flow difficulties, pockets the money entrusted to him to pay ABC and places the drums on an abandoned lot near his home. He plans to take the drums to ABC when he gets a little spare cash in the future. Has Mr. Nelson undertaken storage activities? Does he need a permit under RCRA?

Appendix—Chapter 6

Selected Statutory Sections—Resource Conservation and Recovery Act (Codified at 42 U.S.C. § 901 *et seq.*)

SUBCHAPTER III   HAZARDOUS WASTE MANAGEMENT

RCRA § 3001   Identification and listing of hazardous waste

(a) *Criteria for identification or listing* . . . [T]he Administrator shall . . . develop and promulgate criteria for identifying the characteristics of hazardous waste, and for listing hazardous waste, . . . taking into account the toxicity, persistence, and degradability . . . potential for accumulation in tissue, and other related factors, such as flammability, corrosiveness, and other hazardous characteristics. . . . (i) *Clarification of household waste exclusion.* A . . . facility recovering energy from the mass burning of municipal solid waste shall not be deemed to be treating, storing, disposing of, or otherwise managing hazardous wastes . . . if—

(1)(A) such facility receives and burns only—

   (i) household waste . . . and

   (ii) solid waste from commercial or industrial sources that does not contain [listed or identified] hazardous waste . . . and

  (B) does not accept [listed or identified]hazardous wastes, and

(2) the owner or operator of such facility has established . . . appropriate notification or inspection procedures to assure that hazardous wastes are not received at . . . such facility.

RCRA § 3002   Standards applicable to generators of hazardous waste

(a) *In general* . . . the Administrator shall promulgate regulations establishing such standards applicable to generators of hazardous waste . . . as may be necessary to protect human health and the environment. Such standards shall establish requirements respecting—

(1) recordkeeping practices that accurately identify the quantities of such [generated] hazardous waste . . . [its] constituents . . . which are significant in quantity or in potential harm to human health or the environment, and [its] disposition

* * *

(3) use of appropriate containers . . .

(4) furnishing of information on the general chemical composition of such hazardous waste to persons transporting, treating, storing, or disposing of such wastes;

(5) use of a manifest system and . . . other reasonable means necessary to assure that all such . . . hazardous waste . . . is designated for [proper handling] . . . in, and arrives at, facilities . . . for which a permit has been issued . . .

(6) submission of reports . . . setting out—

  (A) the quantity and nature of hazardous waste that he has generated during the year;

  (B) the disposition of all hazardous waste . . . ;

  (C) the efforts undertaken . . . to reduce the volume and toxicity of waste generated; and

  (D) the change in volume and toxicity of waste actually achieved during the year in question in comparison with previous years . . . .

(b) *Waste Minimization* . . . the manifest required [by subsection 5 above] . . . shall contain a certification . . . that

(1) the generator . . . has a program in place to reduce the volume . . . and toxicity of such waste to the degree determined by the generator to be economically feasible; and

(2) the proposed method of treatment, storage and disposal is ... [a currently available] practicable method ... which minimizes the present and future threat to human health and the environment.

RCRA § 3003   Standards applicable to transporters ...

(a) *Standards* ... the Administrator ... shall promulgate regulations establishing such standards applicable to transporters of hazardous waste ... as may be necessary to protect human health and the environment. Such standard shall include ...
  (1) recordkeeping concerning ... waste transported, and their source and delivery points;
  (2) transportation ... only if properly labelled;
  (3) compliance with the manifest system ...;
  (4) transportation of all such hazardous waste only to the ... facilities which the shipper designates on the manifest form ....

RCRA § 3004   Standards applicable to owners and operators ...

(a) *In general* ... the Administrator shall promulgate regulations establishing ... performance standards, ... for the treatment, storage, or disposal [of hazardous waste] ... as may be necessary to protect human health and the environment. ... [T]he Administrator shall, ... distinguish ... between requirements appropriate for new facilities and for facilities [already] in existence .... Such standards shall include ... requirements respecting—
  (1) maintaining records of all hazardous wastes ... which is treated, stored, or disposed of ... ;
  (2) satisfactory reporting, monitoring, and inspection and compliance with the manifest system ... ;
  (3) treatment, storage or disposal of all such waste ... pursuant to such ... practices as may be satisfactory to the Administrator;
  (4) the location, design, and construction of such ... facilities; ... and

(5) contingency plans ...
(6) the maintenance ... of such facilities and requiring ... qualifications as to [such] ownership, ... operation, training for personnel and financial responsibility ... as may be necessary or desirable; ...
(7) compliance with the ... permits [and regulations] for treatment, storage, or disposal.

(c) *Liquids in landfills*
  (1) ... the placement of bulk or noncontainerized liquid hazardous waste ... in any landfill is prohibited.
  (2) ... the Administrator shall promulgate final regulations which—
    (B) minimize the presence of free liquids in containerized hazardous waste to be disposed of in landfills.
  (3) ... the placement of any liquid which is not a hazardous waste in a [treatment, storage or disposal] landfill ... is prohibited unless the owner or operator ... demonstrates ... or the Administrator determines that—
    (A) the only reasonable alternative ... is placement in a landfill ... which contains ... hazardous waste; and
    (B) the placement [of hazardous waste] in ... [the] landfill will not present a risk of contamination of any underground source of drinking water.

(d) *Prohibitions on land disposal of specified wastes*
  (1) ... the land disposal of [land-restricted] hazardous wastes ... is prohibited unless the Administrator determines the prohibition ... is not required in order to protect human health and the environment for as long as the waste remains hazardous, taking into account
    (A) the long-term uncertainties associated with land disposal,
    (B) the goal of managing hazardous waste ...
    (C) the persistence, toxicity, mobility and propensity to bioaccumulate of such hazardous waste ...
  For the purposes of this paragraph, a method of land disposal may not be determined to be protective of human health and the environment ... unless ... it has been demonstrated to the Administrator, to a reasonable degree of certainty, that there

will be no migration of hazardous constituents from the disposal unit . . . as long as the wastes remain hazardous.

(2) [land-restricted wastes include]:

   (A) Liquid hazardous wastes . . . containing free cyanide [above specified concentrations].

   (B)(i) to (viii) Liquid hazardous wastes . . . containing the following metals . . . or compounds [above-specified concentrations] arsenic, cadmium, chromium, lead, mercury, nickel, selenium, thallium. . . .

   (D) Liquid hazardous wastes containing [above-specified concentration of polychlorinated byphenils, halogenated organic compounds].

   (E) Hazardous wastes containing [above-specified concentration of halogenated organic compounds].

(e) *Solvents and dioxins*

   (1) . . . the land disposal of [solvents and dioxins] . . . is prohibited unless the Administrator determines the prohibition . . . is not required . . . to protect human health and the environment, for as long as the waste remains hazardous . . .

(f) *Disposal into deep injection wells; . . .*

   (2) . . . [D]isposal . . . into deep injection wells . . . shall [be prohibited if] . . . it may reasonably be determined that such disposal may not be protective of human health and the environment . . . .

(g) *Additional land disposal prohibition determinations*

   (1) . . . The Administrator shall submit a schedule to Congress for—

   (A) reviewing all [listed] hazardous wastes . . .

   (B) taking action [to prohibit land disposal of listed hazardous wastes if not protective of human health and the environment;]

   (2) The Administrator shall base the schedule on a ranking of . . . wastes considering their inherent hazard and their volume . . .

   (4) The schedule . . . shall require that the Administrator . . . promulgate regulations . . .

   (A) for at least one-third of all [listed] hazardous wastes [within 45 months after Nov. 8, 1984] . . .

   (B) for at least two-thirds of all such [listed] hazardous wastes [within 55 months after Nov. 8, 1984] . . .

   (C) for all such [listed] wastes . . . [within 66 months after Nov. 8, 1984] . . .

   (6)(A) If the Administrator fails . . . to promulgate regulations . . . for any hazardous waste . . . included in . . . the schedule . . . such hazardous waste may be disposed of in a landfill . . . only if—

   (i) such facility is in compliance with . . . minimum technological requirements; and

   (ii) . . . the generator has certified to the Administrator . . . that the use of such landfill . . . is the only practical alternative to treatment currently available. . . .

   (C) If the Administrator fails to promulgate regulations . . . for any hazardous waste . . . [within the required time schedule] such hazardous waste shall be prohibited from land disposal.

(h) *Variance from land disposal prohibitions*

   (3) The Administrator . . . may . . . grant an extension of the [land ban] effective date . . . for up to one year, where the applicant demonstrates that there is a binding contractual commitment to construct or otherwise provide . . . alternative disposal capacity but due to circumstances beyond the control of such [variance] applicant such alternative capacity cannot . . . be made available by such effective date. . . .

(j) *Storage of hazardous waste prohibited from land disposal*

   . . . [T]he storage of [land-disposal-restricted hazardous waste] is prohibited unless such storage is solely for the purpose of the accumulation of such quantities . . . as are necessary to facilitate proper recovery, treatment or disposal.

(l) *Ban on dust suppression*

The use of waste or used oil or other material, which is contaminated . . . with dioxin or any other hazardous waste . . . for dust suppression or road treatment is prohibited.

(m) *Treatment standards . . .*

   (1) . . . [T]he Administrator shall . . . promulgate regulations specifying those . . . meth-

ods . . . of treatment . . . which substantially diminish the toxicity of the waste or substantially reduce the likelihood of migration of hazardous constituents from the waste . . .

(2) If such . . . waste has been treated . . . by a method specified in regulations promulgated under this section, such waste . . . may be disposed of in a land disposal facility. . . .

(o) *Minimum technological requirements*

(1) The regulations . . . shall be revised from time to time to take into account improvements in the technology of control and measurement. . . . [Such] regulations shall require . . .

(A) for each new landfill . . . or each . . . replacement of an existing landfill . . . and each lateral expansion of an existing landfill . . .

(i) the installation of two or more liners and a leachate collection system . . . between such liners; and

(ii) ground water monitoring

(B for each incinerator . . . attainment of the minimum destruction and removal efficiency required by regulations . . . .

(2) [Exceptions to the preceding section allowed] . . . if . . . the Administrator finds . . . that alternative design and operating practices, together with location characteristics, will prevent the migration of any hazardous constituents into the ground water or surface water . . . as effectively as such liners and leachate collection systems.

(4) (A) . . . [T]he Administrator shall . . . promulgate standards requiring that new landfill units, waste piles, underground tanks and land treatment units for the storage, treatment or disposal of . . . waste . . . shall be required to utilize approved leakage detection systems. . . .

(t) *Financial responsibility provisions*

(1) Financial responsibility required by . . . this section may be established by any one . . . of the following: insurance, guarantee, surety bond, letter of credit, or qualification as a self-insurer. . . .

(u) *Continuing releases at permitted facilities*
Standards . . . under this section . . . and a permit issued . . . by the Administrator or a State

shall require corrective action for all releases of hazardous waste or constituents from any waste management unit . . . seeking a permit . . . regardless of the time at which waste was placed in the unit. Permits . . . shall contain schedules of compliance for such corrective action . . . .

(v) *Corrective action beyond facility boundary*
. . . [T]he Administrator shall . . . require that corrective action be taken beyond the facility boundary where necessary to protect human health and the environment unless the owner or operator . . . demonstrates that despite . . . best efforts, the owner or operator was unable to obtain the necessary permission to undertake such action. . . .

RCRA § 3005   Permits for treatment, storage, or disposal of hazardous waste

(a) *Permit requirements* . . . [T]he Administrator shall promulgate regulations requiring each person owning or operating an existing facility or planning to construct a new facility . . . to have a permit issued pursuant to this section. . . . [T]he treatment, storage or disposal of any such hazardous waste and the construction of any new facility . . . is prohibited except in accordance with such a permit.

(b) *Requirements of permit application.* Each application for a permit . . . shall contain information as may be required under regulations promulgated by the Administrator including . . .—

(1) estimates   with   respect   to   the composition, quantities, and concentrations of any hazardous waste . . . and any other solid waste, proposed to be disposed of, treated, transported or stored and the time, frequency, or rate of which such waste is proposed to be disposed of, treated, transported or stored and

(2) the site at which such hazardous waste . . . will be disposed of, treated, transported or stored.

(c) *Permit issuance*

(1) Upon determination by the Administrator . . . of compliance [with RCRA requirements] by a facility for which a permit

is applied . . . the Administrator . . . shall issue a permit for such facilities. . . .

(3) Any permit . . . shall be for a fixed term, not to exceed 10 years . . . . Review of any application for a permit renewal shall consider improvements in the state of . . . technology . . . .

(d) *Permit revocation.* Upon determination by the Administrator . . . of noncompliance by a facility . . . the Administrator . . . shall revoke such permit.

(e) *Interim status.*

(1) Any person who—

(A) owns or operates a . . . facility required to have a permit . . . which

(ii) is in existence on the effective date of . . . changes . . . that render the facility subject to . . . a permit [requirement]

(B) has complied with the [minimum technology regulation] requirements . . .

(C) has made an application for a permit . . .

shall be treated as having been issued such permit until such time as final administrative disposition of such application is made, unless . . . that final administrative disposition has not been made because of the failure of the applicant to furnish information reasonably required . . . in order to process the application. . . .

(g) *Research, development and demonstration permits*

(1) The Administrator may issue a research, development and demonstration permit for any . . . facility which proposes to utilize an . . . experimental . . . treatment technology . . . for which permit standards . . . have not been promulgated. . . . Such permits—

(B) shall provide for . . . the receipt . . . by the facility of only those types and quantities of hazardous waste which the Administrator deems necessary for the purpose of determining the efficacy and . . . capabilities of the technology . . . and the effects of such technology . . . on human health and the environment. . . .

(C) shall include such requirements as the Administrator deems necessary to protect human health and the environment, and such requirements as the Administrator deems necessary regarding testing and providing of information with respect to the operation of the facility.

(3) The Administrator may order an immediate termination of all operations . . . at any time he determines that termination is necessary to protect human health and the environment.

(h) *Waste minimization*

. . . it shall be a condition of any permit issued . . . that the permittee certify . . . no less than annually, that—

(1) the generator . . . has a program in place to reduce the volume or quantity and toxicity of such waste to the degree determined by the generator to be economically practicable; and

(2) the proposed method of treatment, storage or disposal is that practicable method currently available . . . which minimizes the present and future threat to human health and the environment.

RCRA § 3006   Authorized State hazardous waste programs

(b) *Authorization of State program.* Any state which seeks to administer and enforce a hazardous waste program . . . may develop and . . . submit to the Administrator an application . . . for authorization of such program. . . . [A] . . . State is authorized to carry out [its] program in lieu of the Federal program . . . and to issue and enforce permits for the storage treatment or disposal of . . . hazardous waste . . . unless . . . the Administrator notifies such State that such program may not be authorized and he finds (1) that such program is not the equivalent of the Federal program . . . , (2) such program is not consistent with the Federal or State programs . . . in other states, or (3) such program does not provide adequate enforcement of compliance with the requirements of this [Subtitle C] subchapter. . . .

(c) *Interim Authorization.*

(1) ... The Administrator shall, if the ... State program ... [is] substantially equivalent to the Federal program ... grant an interim authorization to the State ....

(3) Pending ... authorization of a State program ... which reflects the amendments made by the Hazardous and Solid Waste Amendments of 1984, the State may enter into agreements with the Administrator under which the State may assist in the administration of the requirements [imposed by] ... such amendments. ...

(4) ... [U]ntil [a State] program is amended to reflect the ... Hazardous and Solid Waste Amendments of 1984 and such program amendments receive ... authorization, the Administrator shall have the authority ... to issue or deny permits affected by ... the Hazardous and Solid Waste Amendments of 1984. ...

(d) *Effect of State Permit.* Any action taken by a State under [an authorized] hazardous waste program ... shall have the same force and effect as actions taken by the Administrator ....

(e) *Withdrawal of authorization.* Whenever the Administrator determines ... that a State is not administering ... a program in accordance with [RCRA] requirements ... he shall notify the State and, if ... corrective action is not taken within a reasonable time, ... the Administrator shall withdraw authorization ....

(f) No State program may be authorized ... unless—
   (1) such program provides for the public availability of information ... regarding facilities and sites [treating, storing, and disposing of] hazardous waste; ...

RCRA § 3008   Federal enforcement

(a) *Compliance orders*
   (1) ... [W]henever ... the Administrator determines that any person has violated [this subchapter C] ... the Administrator may issue an order assessing a civil penalty for any past or current violation, requiring compliance ... or both, the Administrator may commence a civil action [lawsuit] ... for appropriate relief, including a temporary or permanent injunction.

(3) Any [penalty assessment or corrective action] order ... may include a suspension or revocation of any permit issued by the Administrator or a State .... Any penalty assessed ... shall not exceed $25,000 per day of noncompliance for each violation ....

(d) *Criminal penalties*
Any person who [knowingly]
   (1) ... [T]ransports ... any hazardous waste ... to a facility which does not have a permit ...
   (2) ... [T]reats, stores, or disposes of any hazardous waste
     (A) ... without a permit ... ; or
     (B) in knowing violation of any material condition or requirement of ... [such] permit; [or]
     (C) in knowing violation of any material condition or requirement of any applicable interim status regulations ... ;
   (3) knowingly omits material information or makes any false material statement ... in any application, label, manifest, ... permit or other document ... used for ... compliance with regulations ...
   (4) [k]nowingly destroys, alters, conceals, or fails to file any record ... or other document required to be maintained or filed ... ;
   (5) knowingly transports without a manifest ... any hazardous waste or any used oil ... required to be accompanied by a manifest;
   (6) knowingly exports a hazardous waste ... without the consent of the receiving country or ... in a manner ... not in conformance with [an international] ... agreement; or
   (7)(A)(B) knowingly ... handles any used oil in knowing violation of any ... permit ... or in knowing violation of any material ... requirements of [this Subchapter C]

shall, upon conviction, be subject to a fine of not more than $50,000 for each day of violation, or imprisonment not to exceed two years ... or both. If the conviction is for a violation committed after a first conviction . . . under this paragraph, the maximum punishment . . . shall be doubled with respect to both fine and imprisonment.

(e) *Knowing endangerment.* Any person who knowingly transports, treats, stores, disposes of or exports any hazardous waste . . . or used oil . . . in violation of [this law] . . . who knows . . . that he thereby places another person in imminent danger of death or serious bodily injury, shall upon conviction be subject to a fine of not more than $250,000 or imprisonment for not more than fifteen years, or both. A defendant that is an organization shall . . . be subject to a fine of not more than $1,000,000.

(h) *Interim status corrective action*

(1) Whenever . . . the Administrator determines that there is . . . a release of hazardous waste into the environment from [an interim status] facility . . . , the Administrator may issue an order requiring corrective action . . . .

RCRA § 3013   Monitoring, analysis, and testing

(a) *Authority of Administrator.* If the Administrator determines . . . that —

(1) the presence of any . . . waste at a facility or site . . . ; or

(2) the release of any such waste from such . . . facility or site may present a substantial hazard to human health or the environment, he may issue an order requiring the owner or operator . . . to conduct such monitoring, testing, analysis, and reporting . . . as the Administrator deems reasonable to ascertain the nature and extent of such hazard.

(b) *Previous owners or operators.* In the case of any facility or site not in operation . . . if the Administrator finds that the owner . . . could not reasonably be expected to have actual knowledge of the presence of hazardous waste . . . and of its potential for release, he may issue an order requiring the most recent previous owner or operator of such facility or site who could reasonably be expected to have such actual knowledge to [conduct the required testing and reporting] . . . .

SUBCHAPTER IV—STATE OR REGIONAL SOLID WASTE DISPOSAL PLANS

RCRA §4004   Criteria for sanitary landfills

(a) . . . [t]he Administrator shall promulgate regulations . . . for [criteria to classify] . . . sanitary landfills and . . . open dumps . . . . At a minimum, such criteria shall provide that a facility may be classified as a sanitary landfill and not an open dump only if there is no reasonable probability of adverse effects on human health or the environment from disposal of solid waste at such facility. . . .

(b) *Disposal required to be in sanitary landfills.* . . . [E]ach State plan shall prohibit the establishment of open dumps . . . .

RCRA § 4005   Upgrading of open dumps

(a) *Closing or upgrading of existing open dumps.* . . . [A]ny . . . disposal of solid waste or hazardous waste which constitutes the open dumping of [such] . . . waste is prohibited . . . .

SUBCHAPTER VII—MISCELLANEOUS PROVISIONS

RCRA § 7003   Imminent hazard

(a) *Authority of Administrator.* Notwithstanding any other provision of this chapter, upon receipt of evidence that the past or present handling . . . of any solid waste or hazardous waste may present an imminent and substantial endangerment to health or the environment, the Administrator may bring suit . . . against any person . . . who has contributed or . . . is contributing to such handling . . . to restrain such person from such handling . . . to order such person to take such other action as may be necessary. . . . The Administrator may also . . . take other action . . . including . . . issuing such orders as may be necessary to protect public health and the environment.

SUBCHAPTER IX—REGULATION OF UNDERGROUND STORAGE TANKS

RCRA § 9001   Definitions and exemptions

For purposes of this subchapter—

(1)(A)(B)(I) . . . "underground storage tank" means any one or combination of tanks (including pipes connected thereto) which is used to contain an accumulation of regulated substances, and the volume of which . . . is 10 per centum or more beneath the surface of the ground. Such term does not include any— . . . farm or residential tank used for storing motor fuel for noncommercial purposes; tanks for storing . . . heating oil [for use at the premises]; . . . storage tank situated in an underground area (such as a basement . . .) if the storage tank is situated upon or above the surface of the floor.

(2) The term "regulated substance" means—

    (A) any [hazardous substance as defined in the Superfund (CERCLA) statute *and* not elsewhere regulated under RCRA];

    (B) petroleum.

(4) The term "operator" means any person in control of, or having responsibility for, the daily operation of the underground tank.

RCRA § 9002   Notification

(a) *Underground storage tanks*

    (1) . . . [E]ach owner . . . shall notify the State or [designated] agency of the existence of such [underground storage] tank, specifying the age, size, type, location and uses of such tank.

RCRA § 9003   Release, detection, prevention, and correction regulations

(a) *Regulations* The Administrator . . . shall promulgate release, detention, prevention and correction regulations applicable to all owners and operators of underground storage tanks as may be necessary to protect human health and the environment.

(b) Distinctions in regulations. . . . [T]he Administrator may . . . take into consideration factors including . . . location . . . , soil and climate conditions, uses . . . , history of maintenance, age of the tanks . . . hydrogeology, water table, size of the tanks, . . . the technical capability of . . . owners and operators, and . . . the materials of which the tank is fabricated.

(c) *Requirements.* The regulations [hereunder] . . . shall include . . . the following . . .

    (1) requirements for maintaining a leak detection system, an inventory control system together with tank testing . . . designed to identify releases in a manner consistent with the protection of human health and the environment;

    (2) requirements for maintaining records of any . . . [such] system;

    (3) requirements for reporting of releases and corrective action . . . , ;

    (4) requirements for taking corrective action in response to a release from an underground storage tank;

    (5) requirements for the closure of tanks to prevent future releases . . . ; and

    (6) requirements for maintaining evidence of financial responsibility for taking corrective action and compensating third parties for . . . injury and . . . damage caused by . . . accidental releases from operating an underground storage tank.

(d) *Financial responsibility*

    (1) (C) In establishing classes and categories for [financial responsibility] . . . the Administrator may consider the following factors . . .

        (i) The size, type, location, storage and handling capacity of underground storage tanks . . .

        (ii) The likelihood of release and the potential extent of damage from any release . . .

        (iii) the economic impact . . . on the . . . owners and operators of each such class, . . . particularly relating to the small business segment of the petroleum marketing industry.

(e) *New tank performance standards*

The Administrator shall . . . issue performance standards for . . . tanks brought into use . . . after the effective date of such standards. The performance standards for new . . . tanks shall include . . . design, construction, installation, release detection, and compatibility standards.

(g) *Interim prohibition*

(1) Until the effective date of the standards promulgated by the Administrator . . . no person may install an underground storage tank . . . unless such tank . . .

(A) will prevent releases due to corrosion or structural failure for . . . the life of the tank;

(B) is cathodically protected against corrosion, constructed of noncorrosive material, steel clad with a noncorrosive material, or designed . . . to prevent the release . . . of any stored substance; and

(C) the material used in . . . the tank is compatible with the substance to be stored.

(h) *EPA Response Program for Petroleum*

(4) Corrective Action Orders. The Administrator is authorized to issue orders to the owner or operator of an underground storage tank to carry out [corrective action] . . . .

(5) Allowable corrective actions. The corrective actions . . . may include . . . relocation of residents and alternative household water supplies. . . .

(6)(A) Recovery of costs. Whenever costs have been incurred by the Administrator, or by a State . . . for undertaking corrective actions or enforcement action . . . the owner or operator of such tank shall be liable . . . for such costs.

(C) Effect on liability.

(i) No transfers of liability. No indemnification . . . or similar agreement or conveyance shall be effective to transfer from the owner or operator of any underground storage tank or from any person who may be liable . . . under this subsection, to any other person the liability imposed under this section. . . .

RCRA § 9004   Approval of State programs

(a) *Elements of State program.* . . . [A]ny State may submit an underground storage tank . . . program for review and approval by the Administrator. . . . A State program may be approved . . . under this section only if the State demonstrates that the State program . . . provides for adequate enforcement of compliance with [regulations promulgated by the Administrator and used in federal enforcement] . . . .

(b) (1) *Federal standards.* A State program . . . may be approved only if the requirements . . . are no less stringent than the corresponding requirements [of the federal program] . . . .

RCRA § 9006   Federal enforcement

(a) *Compliance orders*

(1) . . . whenever . . . the Administrator determines that any person is in violation [of this subchapter] . . . [he] . . . may issue [a compliance] order requiring compliance . . . for appropriate relief . . . .

(3) If a violator fails to comply with an order . . . he shall be liable for a civil penalty of not more than $25,000 for each day of continued noncompliance.

(d) *Civil penalties*

(1) Any owner who knowingly fails to notify or submits false information . . . shall be subject to a civil penalty not to exceed $10,000 for each tank for which notification is not given or for which false information is submitted.

(2) Any owner or operator . . . who fails to comply with

(A) any requirement or standard promulgated by the Administrator . . . ;

(B) any requirement . . . of [an approved] State program . . .

shall be subject to a civil penalty not to exceed $10,000 for each tank for each day of violation.

■ ## Chapter 6 Endnotes

1. See RCRA § 1006(a).
2. RCRA § 1004(27).
3. See 40 C.F.R. (Code of Federal Regulations) § 261.2(a)(2).
4. See RCRA § 3001(a).
5. CEQ, *Environmental Quality,* (1987–1988) pp. 2–6.
6. Ibid., pp. 3–4.
7. Ibid., pp. 32–33.
8. Bill Moyers and the Center for Investigative Reporting, *Global Dumping Ground* (Seven Locks Press, 1990).
9. Quoting former EPA administrator, D. Costle in *U.S. Environmental Laws,* (Bureau of National Affairs, Inc., 1988), pp. 277–278.
10. S. Lawrence, "Recycling Is Picking Up," *EPA Insight,* (September 1992).
11. *U.S. Environmental Laws,* supra, p. 277.
12. Comprehensive Environmental Response, Compensation, and Liability Act, 42 U.S.C. § 101 *et seq.*
13. 40 C.F.R. Parts 257–258 (1991).
14. Because of a federal court decision, EPA's final rule did not grant the exemption from ground-water monitoring that it had initially proposed for these operators.
15. *Philadelphia Inquirer,* 12 Sept. 1992, p. 3A.
16. "The New Federal Standards for Municipal Solid Waste Landfills," 3 *Villanova Environmental Law Journal* 401, 402 (1992).
17. *City of Chicago v. Environmental Defense Fund,* 114 S. Ct. 1588 (1994).
18. EPA placed an indefinite moratorium on the construction of new incineration facilities in 1993; however, existing incinerators were allowed to continue to operate.
19. These figures and other information in this subsection are drawn from an extensively researched report on the international trade in hazardous substances and wastes, *Global Dumping Ground,* an expanded companion volume to the PBS "Frontline" program of the same name, written by Bill Moyers and the Center for Investigative Reporting. See endnote 8.
20. That is, the universe of businesses regulated under one regulatory program.
21. E. Royte, "Other People's Garbage," *Harper's,* June 1992.
22. "As Eastern Landfills Reach Capacity, States Send Garbage West," *The Wall Street Journal,* 26 April 1991, p. A1.
23. Royte, supra, "Other People's Garbage."
24. R. Bullard, "In Our Backyards," 18 *EPA Journal,* March/April 1992, pp. 11, 12.
25. *See C & A Carbone, Inc. v. Town of Clarkstown,* 114 S. Ct. 1677 (1994); S. Stranahan, "New Economics of Trash: More Is Better," *The Philadelphia Inquirer,* 10 October 1993, pp. A1, A20.
26. T. Dinan, "Solid Waste: Incentives that Could Lighten the Load," 18 *EPA Journal,* May/June 1992, pp. 12–14.
27. For a more detailed discussion of issues related to federal-facility compliance with environmental laws, see Chapter 10.
28. M. Bauerlien, "Plutonium Is Forever: Is There Any Sane Place to Put Nuclear Waste?" *Utne Reader,* No. 52 (July/August 1992).
29. A. Burdick, "The Last Cold War Monument," *Harper's* (August 1992).
30. *New York v. United States,* 112 S. Ct. 2408 (1993).
31. *Edison Electric Institute v. EPA,* 996 F.2d 326 (D.C. Cir. 1993).
32. Ibid.

PART III

REMEDIATING ENVIRONMENTAL CONTAMINATION

The single statute covered in this part is one of the most important and well-known of the federal environmental statutes. Its primary aim is to provide mechanisms for cleaning up environmental contamination which has already resulted from past industrial waste disposal practices. The statute (called CERCLA, the acronym for its full title) provides unique funding mechanisms and sources for cleanups which derive from the basic principle that a polluter should pay for the consequences of its polluting activities. This approach has engendered considerable resistance from industries and municipalities which have been subjected by CERCLA to liability for expensive cleanups of environmental contamination.

CHAPTER 7

The Comprehensive Environmental Response, Compensation, and Liability Act (CERCLA)

Large-Scale Environmental Remediation

Outline

7.1 Historical Background and Overview of CERCLA

History of CERCLA's Enactment and Amendment

The Comprehensive Environmental Response, Compensation, and Liability Act, as amended (CERCLA), commonly known as "the Superfund law," was originally enacted in 1980. The immediate impetus for CERCLA legislation resulted from environmental disasters at abandoned hazardous-waste dumpsites, such as those at Love Canal near Niagara Falls, New York, and at other, less spectacular but no less significant sites across the country. It was the very real specter of hazardous substances leaching from abandoned dumpsites and contaminating the land on which people live and the water they drink that spurred Congress to enact CERCLA.

In the late 1970s, authorities investigated the high incidence of miscarriages, birth defects, liver cancer, and seizure-inducing childhood diseases in a residential subdivision built over an 80-foot by 3,300-foot trench (the Love Canal) into which a chemical company had dumped highly toxic substances for 11 years. The study found that 82 toxic chemical substances had leaked through the canal's "impermeable" clay cap and into basements, yards, and shallow aquifers. A thousand families were evacuated from the area. This tragedy was one of a string of environmental disasters whose discovery revealed hitherto-unknown effects of technologies and chemical substances developed after World War II. Moreover, it demonstrated the perils posed by using new technologies without regard for their potential dangers. In particular, it showed that many industries had failed to investigate adequately the new chemicals' potential health and environmental effects once they are released into the environment. The industrial practices that resulted in the Love Canal disaster are by no means purely historic; similar dangers attend the continuing creation of nuclear and other wastes for which safe disposal methods have not yet been developed.

After enactment, CERCLA directed EPA to effect cleanups at sites (called *facilities*) that release or threaten to release *hazardous substances* into the environment by taking appropriate *response actions to abate any actual or threatened release of hazardous substances* and to abate conditions that present an *imminent and substantial endangerment* to public health or the environment.[1] CERCLA empowers EPA to order responsible parties to undertake necessary cleanup measures or to conduct cleanups itself when responsible parties either refuse or are unable to obey its cleanup orders. Under those circumstances, EPA finances such cleanups out of monies from the Superfund, a fund partially underwritten by taxes on the petrochemical industry. If EPA cleans up a site itself, it is authorized by CERCLA to recover its expenditures from parties who are considered liable under CERCLA; recovered funds are then returned to the Superfund. In addition, CERCLA provides mechanisms whereby parties that share liability under CERCLA for a particular site can recover part of their cleanup expenditures by demanding "contribution" from other responsible parties.

In 1986, following complaints of inadequate EPA action and numerous lawsuits challenging EPA's interpretation of various CERCLA provisions, Congress amended CERCLA to expedite hazardous-site cleanup schedules, to augment the Superfund, and to strengthen mechanisms for recovering cleanup costs from responsible parties. These amendments, called the *Superfund Amendment and Reauthorization Act (SARA)* also clarified certain liability issues, created an "innocent landowner" defense, and incorporated into legislation several important early court decisions.

CERCLA employs a distinctive approach to environmental regulation through its mechanisms for remedying past conditions:

> Superfund is a major departure from the environmental statutes of the 1970s which were, at heart, forward looking acts which sought to reduce and prevent future pollution by establishing standards for permissible discharges based on the . . . rulemaking of an administrative agency. . . . Superfund does not look forward but is focused from the present backward, seeking to abate immediate threats or releases of hazardous substances, and most importantly, to clean up past releases. . . . It works by establishing liability for the cost of cleanup.[2]

The sheer number of sites awaiting cleanup under CERCLA indicates how monumental are the environmental problems facing the nation:

> As of June 1986, EPA ha[d] inventoried 24,269 abandoned hazardous waste sites across the United States. . . . In 1986, the Superfund Amendments provided $8.5 billion to that fund for cleaning up waste sites, as well as 500 million for underground storage tanks. To qualify for cleanup under Superfund, a site must be placed on the National Priorities List . . . or be designated for an emergency removal action. . . . [A]s of mid-1987, just 13 of these 951 sites had been cleaned up. . . . The Office of Technology Assessment estimated in a 1985 report that the NPL [National Priorities List, an inventory of the most dangerous sites to be cleaned up] might eventually contain as many as 10,000 sites.[3]

The *Twentieth Annual Report of the President's Council on Environmental Quality* reported a 1989 inventory in which EPA identified 27,000 hazardous substance sites nationwide, of which 1,077 appeared on the National Priorities List. A later study by the Rand Institute for Civil Justice found that only 5 percent of the 1236 sites on the National Priorities List had been cleaned up by 1990.[4]

EPA's administrative enforcement actions and referrals to the Department of Justice for civil actions number in the hundreds each year. For instance, EPA has annually issued somewhat more than 200 administrative cleanup orders and referred more than 100 judicial cases to complete remedial work. In 1989, for the first time, private parties undertook more remedial actions (pursuant to consent decrees with the United States) than did the government under the Superfund program.

Common Law and State Statutory Remedies for Environmental Injury

Besides the sheer magnitude of the hazardous waste cleanup problem, another factor urging CERCLA's enactment was the lack of adequate remedies for environmental injury under the common law. Virtually the only recourse under the common law for injuries from improper releases of hazardous substances is a private tort lawsuit against a responsible party for monetary damages through a trespass, negligence, or nuisance claim. The common law does not recognize any general right to protection from environmental injury as such, nor does it provide efficient mechanisms to redress environmental injury.

Indeed, the common law places heavy burdens of proof upon a party injured by environmental contamination. For example, in order to recover money compensation for an injury, the suing party (the *plaintiff*) at common law must prove: (1) that the party sued (*the defendant*) committed a wrong, (2) that the defendant (and not someone else) caused the plaintiff's injury, and (3) the monetary loss due to the proven injury. A plaintiff who fails to prove any one of these elements cannot recover anything for his or her injuries.

In addition, failure to bring suit (no matter how compelling the case) within the time limit set by state "statutes of limitation" will defeat a claim for environmental injuries. These statutes of limitation seldom account for the peculiarities of environmental injuries, which may not be apparent until many years after the pollution occurs. Thus, these statutes may bar plaintiffs from bringing suit even before they learn they have suffered an injury.

Additional factors render common law remedies unavailable for many environmental injuries. Litigation costs are prohibitively high for many individuals, particularly when a causal relationship is difficult to establish and expert witnesses must be paid 'o investigate and prove the relationship. In environmental trespass, nuisance, and negligence suits, these costs exert a powerful deterrent for private plaintiffs. In addition, legal fees are not recoverable from the wrongdoer under the U.S. system.

Even if a suing party prevails, he or she can only recover compensation for past injury, and not for continuing or future injury from the same polluting source. This means that in the absence of extraordinary circumstances that would merit an injunction, a suing party would have to start a new round of lawsuits for each successive injury. Without statutory authorization, courts are usually reluctant to enjoin admittedly harmful conduct if they perceive that the social or economic costs of injunctive relief are high. Hence, when a business argues that it cannot survive without polluting, courts tend to decide that the environmental injury and its attendant costs are lesser evils than closing down the polluting business and causing job losses and economic dislocations. Without legislation explicitly directing that corrective action be carried out to remediate hazardous sites, the common law leaves courts with too few weapons and too little incentive to devise enduring solutions for pollution injuries.

An example can serve to illustrate the limits on common law remedies. A private water well is found to be contaminated by one or more hazardous substances coming from one or more sources, such as, perhaps, a nearby manufacturing plant or waste dump. Under common law, the homeowner must ascertain and identify the contaminants that are polluting the well and then establish how and from where they migrated to the well. The owner may lack the technical know-how and the financial means to trace and fingerprint the sources of the contamination. Indeed, that task might be impossible even for a well-financed team of scientists, which few homeowners could afford to employ. Ground water can carry contaminants from many sources and from great distances, and the well contamination may result from a mingling or interaction of different substances. Even if the contamination can be traced to its source, the homeowner must still prove that a specific injury has occurred. If the contaminants are carcinogenic, the homeowner may not know for many years whether she or others who have used the well water will develop cancer. In other words, the injury may be speculative, and speculative damages cannot be recovered under traditional common law principles.

Finally, the passage of time alone can work to defeat effective private remedies at common law. Where pollution has occurred and remained undetected for a long period, the responsible party or parties may have died, moved away, gone bankrupt, or disappeared during that interval. As one study concluded,

> . . . [A]lthough causes of action do exist for some plaintiffs, . . . a private litigant faces substantial substantive and procedural barriers in a personal injury action for hazardous waste exposure, particularly where the individual claims are relatively small.[5]

Before enactment of CERCLA, states had not made great inroads in providing statutory and regulatory mechanisms for remediating toxic dumpsites. States are now enacting legislation that has the same goals as CERCLA, but that employs different enforcement mechanisms. Pennsylvania, for example, enacted a state superfund law that is generally modeled on the federal law but is quite different from it in some respects.

Although state statutes focused on protecting the environment provide broader relief than do personal suits at common law, they cannot resolve the nationwide causes and effects of hazardous substance releases. There are several reasons for this. First, a hazardous substance may be released at any time in its "chain" of generation, storage, transport, and disposal, and the chain of those activities extends back and forth across state boundaries. Second, the necessary technical, monetary and enforcement resources for effective oversight of hazardous-substance management far exceed the resources available to individual states. Third, state governors and administrators have strong incentives to attract and keep industries and jobs in order to protect their states' tax bases. Particularly in times of decreased federal assistance and tight state budgets, short-term economic concerns tend to overshadow environmental issues at the state level. Moreover, state legislators rely on businesses and local industries for campaign contributions. This provides a disincentive to passage of strong environmental-protection measures.

Although CERCLA leaves many state environmental laws intact, states cannot alone achieve the goal of cleaning up hazardous substances that have been released into the environment. The large number and geographical dispersion of hazardous-substance releases, and the huge costs and technological problems encountered in cleaning them up require a comprehensive, nationally coordinated approach akin to that attempted by the drafters of CERCLA.

Scope of CERCLA's Coverage

CERCLA is mainly concerned with "hazardous substances," a class of identified substances deemed to be particularly dangerous to human health and the environment. These substances, many of which are used in industrial and manufacturing operations, appear on a list promulgated by EPA. The basis for EPA enforcement action under CERCLA is usually its determination that one or more of the identified hazardous substances (or, sometimes, other pollutants or contaminants) has been released, or is likely to be released, into the environment. Such releases have usually occurred at dumpsites where drums of chemicals, municipal waste, incinerator ash, or other wastes have been deposited.

Unlike laws aimed at preventing harmful waste disposal, CERCLA deals primarily with correcting hazardous conditions created by past waste-disposal practices. Even so, CERCLA's liability provisions, which determine who is responsible to pay for cleaning up hazardous substances, have the incidental, but nevertheless significant, effect of deterring irresponsible waste disposal in the future.

The legal definition of *hazardous waste* was examined in Chapter 6 within the discussion of the scope of RCRA. The definition of ''hazardous substance'' is equally crucial to the scope of CERCLA's coverage. Under CERCLA, ''hazardous substances'' include all substances listed as hazardous or toxic under other environmental statutes, specifically:

- an imminently hazardous chemical substance or mixture with respect to which EPA has taken action under the Toxic Substance Control Act;
- a hazardous waste, either listed or characteristic, under the Resource Conservation and Recovery Act; and
- a hazardous air pollutant under the Clean Air Act.

Hazardous substances also include any element, compound, mixture, solution, or substance designated by the EPA as a hazardous substance pursuant to CERCLA. The complete list of hazardous substances appears in the *Code of Federal Regulations,* a compilation of regulations promulgated by federal agencies, including EPA. By 1992, EPA had listed more than 700 substances that fall within CERCLA's scope. However, Congress excluded natural gas and oil and related products from CERCLA coverage,[6] even though some of them may be more dangerous to health and the environment than some of the listed substances. This exclusion of petroleum products is discussed in section 7.4.

In addition to hazardous substances, CERCLA also contains provisions for cleaning up certain pollutants and contaminants. Boron, for instance, is considered a pollutant but not a hazardous substance, even though ingesting sufficient quantities of it can damage human health. Certain provisions of CERCLA apply only to ''hazardous substances'' and not to ''pollutants'' and ''contaminants.'' Due to the highly technical implications of this distinction, this chapter focuses on ''hazardous substances'' only.

CERCLA requires the government to identify and rank sites where hazardous substances are being released and to prioritize cleanup efforts in accordance with the National Contingency Plan. Once ranked, the nation's worst Superfund sites appear on the National Priorities List. EPA can either order the responsible parties to clean up a Superfund site (*facility*) or perform the cleanup itself and then seek to recover the costs of doing so from those parties. Responsible parties usually include:

- the present owner or operator of the facility;
- the owner or operator of the facility at the time the hazardous substances were disposed there;
- any party who arranged for the disposal of the hazardous substances (usually referred to as the *generator*), and
- any party who selected the disposal site and accepted the hazardous substances for transportation to it.

The court in the *Kelley* case summarized EPA's authority under CERCLA.

■   ■

KELLEY AND STATE OF MICHIGAN v. ENVIRONMENTAL PROTECTION AGENCY

15 F.3d 1100 (D.C. Cir. 1994)

Opinion: Silberman, Circuit Judge: Petitioners challenge an EPA regulation limiting lender liability under CERCLA. We hold that EPA lacks statutory authority to restrict by regulation private rights of action arising under the statute. . . .

I.

Congress enacted the Comprehensive Environmental Response, Compensation and Liability Act (CERCLA), . . . in 1980 to "provide for liability, compensation, cleanup, and emergency response for hazardous substances released into the environment and the cleanup of inactive hazardous waste disposal sites." . . . The statute provides several mechanisms to further these objectives. . . . 105 requires the President to promulgate and publish a National Contingency Plan (NCP) to direct actions in response to a hazardous contamination and to prescribe the procedures for those actions. . . . The President in turn has delegated primary authority under section 105—and much of CERCLA—to EPA. See Exec. Order No. 12,580 @ 1(b)(1), ... Under section 104, the President (again, EPA by delegation, see Exec. Order No. 12,580 @ 2(g)) may undertake direct remedial actions—either by employing agency personnel or through private contracting—to clean up a contaminated site and may fund the cost of such actions through the Hazardous Waste Superfund, ... The government may then bring cost recovery actions under section 107 of CERCLA against responsible parties to replenish the funds expended. . . .

Alternatively, where "there may be an imminent and substantial endangerment to the public health or welfare or the environment," EPA may order parties to clean up the hazardous waste and remedy its effects. . . . Those who receive and comply with such orders are entitled to reimbursement of their reasonable costs if they are not liable under section 107, or—even if liable—if they establish on the administrative record that the cleanup action ordered was arbitrary and capricious or otherwise unlawful. . . . EPA also may assess civil penalties for noncompliance with certain CERCLA provisions and bring an action in federal district court to collect such penalties. . . .

* * *

Congress gave EPA the authority to decide whether to order a cleanup or to go ahead and perform the cleanup itself in order that the needed cleanups could proceed without being delayed by litigation. Courts have interpreted CERCLA to bar preenforcement review; that is, they have ruled that a party that has received a cleanup (*abatement*) order may not, before fulfilling the obligations of the order, challenge EPA's selection of a "response action" or its determination of liability. Congress's intent was to prevent further environmental damage during the time EPA would need to ascertain who was liable and to collect the cleanup costs from them. Hence the Superfund motto: "Cleanup first: litigate later." As we shall see, this goal has not always been achieved.

When liable parties cannot be found or are unable or unwilling to carry out CERCLA-mandated cleanups, the Superfund is available to fund cleanups performed by EPA. The Superfund is funded by monies from several sources: fees charged for disposing of hazardous substances at qualified disposal facilities, special taxes on the petrochemical and chemical industries, and Congressional appropriations. After EPA has cleaned up a site using Superfund monies and recovered the cleanup costs from the responsible parties, the recovered amounts are credited to the Superfund. In this way, the Superfund is maintained as a sort of continuous, revolving charge account for cleanups.

7.2 Structure and Workings of CERCLA

This section examines the elements of the CERCLA cleanup scheme. The first four subsections survey the nuts and bolts of its operation. The fifth subsection outlines the major statutory provisions; it can serve as a road map to the statute in answering the problem set exercises at the end of the chapter. The sixth subsection provides four cases that illustrate the major features of the statute. The last two subsections describe specific exemptions from CERCLA liability and significant interpretive problems associated with them.

The National Priorities List: Identifying Sites for Cleanup

CERCLA requires the President to develop and implement a *National Contingency Plan (NCP)* to protect public health, welfare, and the environment against actual or threatened releases of hazardous substances.[7] The NCP serves as the foundation for implementing all CERCLA provisions. All EPA decisions and actions must be consistent with the NCP.

By Executive Order, the President delegated CERCLA's administrative functions to the EPA and its Administrator. These functions include the powers to enforce CERCLA and to promulgate detailed regulations regarding its proper interpretation, performance, and enforcement. In 1990, the EPA published a revised NCP.[8] The NCP requires identification of active and abandoned hazardous-substance sites and maintenance of a *National Priorities List (NPL)* that ranks those sites. The procedures for identifying, listing, prioritizing and cleaning up hazardous waste sites nationwide were specifically devised to circumvent political pressure and other factors not directly related to the magnitude of health and environmental threats. The nomination process and the rules for NPL site inclusion, however, do not eliminate the possibility that factors other than the specific environmental threats have an impact on cleanup priorities.

States nominate sites for inclusion on the NPL. Each state is entitled to have sites on the list in order that it may benefit from the Superfund program, which generates considerable employment and taxable income regardless of whether EPA or liable parties carry out cleanups. When EPA performs a cleanup, most of the actual work is performed by private contractors, whose work is merely overseen by federal government employees.

EPA ranks sites on the NPL according to the Hazard Ranking System, a means by which site contamination is qualitatively and quantitatively evaluated for its risks to human health and the environment. The system yields a numerical value representing the seriousness of a site's health and environmental threats. EPA also establishes the numerical-value cutoff point, below which inclusion on the NPL is not warranted at the time and above which a site is included on the NPL.

Hazard ranking is a highly imperfect science. Even when comparing sites that have similar conditions, it is difficult to quantify their health and environmental threats. Ranking sites at which threats and conditions differ greatly is like comparing apples and oranges. It is difficult, for instance, to say whether mercury bioaccumulation in fish poses a greater threat than does elevated soil levels of lead. Not only must the relative dangers posed by various contaminants be considered; EPA must also evaluate probable exposure pathways and future potential uses of the land and the ground water. The uncertainties in ascertaining exposure pathways, assessing health risks, and analyzing ecological effects compound the difficulties of hazard ranking.

Experience has indicated that previously utilized hazard-ranking methods did not reflect intuitive and "common sense" judgements about which Superfund sites should be cleaned up first. The ranking system used before 1991 resulted in the inclusion of some sites on the NPL that probably posed less risk than some sites that were not included. In particular, the old system incorporated a bias favoring inclusion of sites where hazardous substances, rather than pollutants or contaminants, were the primary concern, even though certain pollutants or contaminants at unlisted sites posed a much greater threat. In 1991, EPA promulgated a new Hazard Ranking System based on revised site-ranking methodologies. Whether the 1991 system provides more valid comparisons of the relative dangers posed by Superfund sites remains to be seen.

Except in the case of emergency removals and site assessments, NPL listing is a necessary prerequisite for the use of Superfund monies. The threshold finding for a removal action is that the site pose an imminent and substantial danger, and many such removals are completed before the hazard-ranking process is concluded. Inclusion on the NPL becomes critical at the *remedial* stage, however. If a site is not on the NPL, EPA is not allowed to use Superfund monies to undertake remedial action. A site's eligibility for NPL listing often determines whether it will receive long-term remediation under CERCLA. Although EPA may enter into agreements with potentially responsible parties for long-term remedial actions, liable parties have less incentive to come to the bargaining table if they know that EPA is not authorized to undertake remedial actions and bring suit for recovering cleanup costs at a later date.

CERCLA section 103(c) is intended to facilitate EPA's task of identifying hazardous sites by requiring owners of disposal facilities and transporters who selected those facilities to file reports with EPA regarding the location and operation of the disposal facilities and the nature of wastes received there. As a practical matter, EPA must often rely on tips from citizens or law enforcement personnel who suspect that chemical substances may have been disposed at a given site. A fire, explosion, or break-in at an abandoned factory often precipitates discovery of a hazardous-substance release.

In 1991 the NPL included 1,185 sites, of which 116 were federally-owned facilities, such as military installations. Figures 7.1, 7.2, and 7.3 show the distribution of NPL sites by state.

A listed site is removed from the NPL when remediation is completed, if new information causes EPA to reevaluate the site and the site is found not to warrant NPL inclusion, or if a court decision overturns EPA's placement of the site on the NPL. Several challenges to NPL listing decisions in the early 1990s resulted in court rulings that EPA's listing was not warranted by the evidence which EPA placed on the record.[9] In these cases, sites were deleted from the NPL by virtue of court decisions.

Until 1991, EPA required at least one five-year review of the a site's remediation before removing the site from the NPL. EPA changed the policy that year to allow deletion in advance of a five-year review, undoubtedly partly in response to severe criticism of the length of time EPA was taking to finish Superfund cleanups. This issue is discussed in section 7.3.

Choosing the Proper Remedy: Operable Units, Records of Decision, and Consistency with the NCP

Under CERCLA, short-term measures for mitigating immediate dangers are characterized as ''removal'' actions, whereas long-term measures intended to eliminate or permanently control facility conditions are considered ''remedial'' actions. When long-term remediation is contemplated, Superfund sites are usually broken down into ''operable units.'' Each operable unit is characteristically

■ **Figure 7.1**   Hazardous Waste Sites on the National Priority List by State, 1990

State	Total Sites	Rank	Percent Distribution	State	Total Sites	Rank	Percent Distribution
Total	1,207	(X)	(X)	Missouri	24	15	2.0
United States	**1,197**	**(X)**	**100.0**	Montant	10	34	0.8
				Nebraska	6	43	0.5
Alabama	12	27	1.0	Nevada	1	50	0.1
Alaska	6	43	0.5	New Hampshire	16	22	1.3
Arizona	11	29	0.9				
Arkansas	10	34	0.8	New Jersey	109	1	9.1
California	88	3	7.4	New Mexico	10	34	0.8
				New York	83	4	6.9
Colorado	16	22	1.3	North Carolina	22	17	1.8
Connecticut	15	24	1.3	North Dakota	2	48	0.2
Delaware	20	19	1.7				
District of Columbia ...	–	(X)	(X)	Ohio	33	12	2.8
Florida	51	6	4.3	Oklahoma	11	29	0.9
				Oregon	8	40	0.7
Georgia	13	26	1.1	Pennsylvania	95	2	7.9
Hawaii	7	42	0.6	Rhode Island	11	29	0.9
Idaho	9	38	0.8				
Illinois	37	10	3.1	South Carolina	23	16	1.9
Indiana	35	11	2.9	South Dakota	3	46	0.3
				Tennessee	14	25	1.2
Iowa	21	18	1.8	Texas	28	13	2.3
Kansas	11	29	0.9	Utah	12	27	1.0
Kentucky	17	21	1.4				
Louisiana	11	29	0.9	Vermont	8	40	0.7
Maine	9	38	0.8	Virginia	20	19	1.7
				Washington	45	7	3.8
Maryland	10	34	0.8	West Virginia	5	45	0.4
Massachusetts	25	14	2.1	Wisconsin	39	9	3.3
Michigan	78	5	6.5	Wyoming	3	46	0.3
Minnesota	42	8	3.5				
Mississippi	2	48	0.2	Guam	1	(X)	(X)
				Puerto Rico	9	(X)	(X)

Note: Includes both proposed and final sites listed on the National Priorities List for the Superfund program as authorized by the Comprehensive Environmental Response, Compensations, and Liability Act of 1980 and the Superfund Amendments and Reauthorization Act of 1986.

Source: Statistical Abstract of the United States, 1991, p. 211.

defined according to which medium (e.g., air, soil, ground water) or geographical portion of the site is being addressed by a particular remedial activity.

A normal procedure is to clean up the source of contamination first; this is known as *source control.* In some cases, cleaning up the operable unit that is the source of contamination alleviates the need for cleaning up other media. If the source of contamination is soils, for example, the soils may first be bioremediated, excavated, or capped to prevent exposure of human beings or animals to the hazardous substances contained therein. Then other media such as ground water will be sampled or monitored to ascertain whether further treatment at the site is required. At this kind of site, the soils would be considered one operable unit and the ground water another. Breaking the site down into operable units helps

■ **Figure 7.2**   Distribution of Superfund Sites, June 1986

• Superfund site

Source: U.S. Environmental Protection Agency. Copyright © 1987 by The Conservation Foundation. Reprinted with permission.

to ensure that only the work that is necessary for remediating the site conditions is performed.

For each operable unit, EPA issues a "record of decision" (ROD) that documents why it is choosing a particular remedy. The ROD evaluates possible alternative courses of action; analyzes the drawbacks, benefits, and costs of each; and documents the rationale for selecting one remedy over the others. CERCLA enumerates the factors that EPA must consider in selecting remedial actions and spells out general rules or preferences for remedial-action selection.[10]

CERCLA favors remedial actions that permanently and significantly reduce the volume, toxicity, or mobility of hazardous substances. It disfavors offsite transportation and disposal of hazardous substances and mandates that EPA consider long-term effectiveness and overall costs. A remedy is considered effective if it restores environmental media to conditions that are protective of human health and the environment. In sum, a selected remedial action must protect human health and the environment, be cost-effective, and to the extent possible, effect a permanent solution while utilizing alternative treatments or resource-recovery technologies. More often than not, these objectives conflict with, rather than complement, each other. EPA usually specifies the required level of cleanup in numerical terms in the ROD. For instance, at a site contaminated by lead, EPA may specify that soils containing lead in excess of 300 parts per million be capped with clay.

Once construction of the remedy is complete, ongoing operation sometimes remains to be done. Some remedies, such as capping of soils, consist only of a

■ Figure 7.3   Hazardous Waste Sites, June 1990

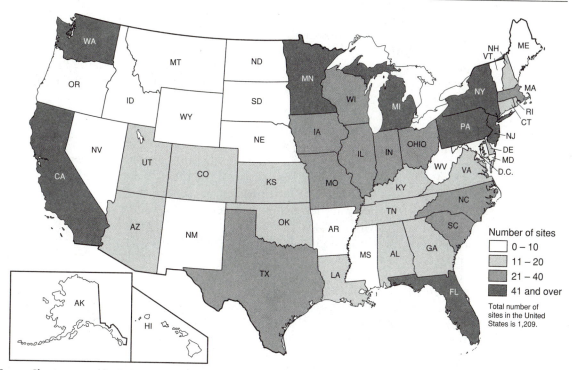

Number of sites
- 0 – 10
- 11 – 20
- 21 – 40
- 41 and over

Total number of sites in the United States is 1,209.

Source: Chart prepared by U.S. Bureau of the Census. *Statistical Abstract of the United States, 1991,* p. 211 (U.S. Dept. of Commerce).

construction phase that can be completed in a relatively short time. Other remedies, such as bioremediation, require an operation phase of up to ten years after construction is complete. In such cases, the operation phase is considered an integral part of the remedy.

After the remedial phase, an operation and maintenance phase (referred to as O&M) is often conducted. O&M activities are required at some sites to ensure that the effectiveness of the remedy is maintained, and they commonly entail ground-water monitoring and other sampling activities. EPA specifies the period of O&M in the ROD, and it may be as long as thirty years.

Administrative Orders and Sanctions: Ordering Cleanups

CERCLA section 106(a) permits EPA to issue orders to responsible parties "as may be necessary to protect public health and welfare and the environment."[11] The prerequisite for issuing a section 106(a) abatement order is a determination "that there may be an imminent and substantial endangerment to the public health or welfare or the environment because of an actual or threatened release of a hazardous substance from a facility."[12] Abatement orders may be issued to any person who is liable for response costs under CERCLA section 107. As pointed out earlier, however, parties may not challenge EPA's determination of liability prior to complying with the abatement order.

A person who complies with a section 106 order and is later found not liable for response costs is entitled to be reimbursed from the Superfund for reasonable costs of his or her compliance. Therefore, EPA must use its authority judiciously so as to avoid having to reimburse a nonliable party. Furthermore, EPA must ensure that the response action it orders is warranted by CERCLA and the National Contingency Plan. A party who is otherwise liable for response costs may be reimbursed for the reasonable costs of complying with an abatement order if it is found that EPA selected a response action in an "arbitrary," "capricious," or otherwise unlawful manner. Reimbursable costs include attorneys' fees and court costs and thus present EPA with considerable incentive to use its administrative-order authority prudently.

Failure to obey an abatement order can make a party liable for fines of up to $25,000 for each day it fails to comply with the order. If a party believes it is not liable for response costs, its remedy is not to disobey the order, but rather, to complete the work and then petition for recovery of its response costs from the Superfund. Likewise, a liable party that believes EPA ordered it to perform an improperly chosen response action cannot seek judicial review of EPA's choice of response action before complying with the order. However, it is entitled to reimbursement for amounts it expends over and above what would have been warranted.

As an alternative to enforcing a cleanup order through a court injunction, CERCLA permits EPA to perform the cleanup. In that case, CERCLA authorizes the assessment of punitive damages in an amount at least equal to but not in excess of three times the costs EPA must expend to perform the cleanup itself. Treble damages can be assessed against any liable party who fails "without sufficient cause" to obey an abatement or cleanup order. Although a court might find that a party's lack of CERCLA liability constitutes sufficient cause for failing to obey an abatement order, the party failing to obey the order runs the considerable risk of an adverse ruling and treble damages. In *United States v. Parsons*,[13] a Court of Appeals decided that under the treble damages provision, the United States could recover up to four times the amount it expended for the cleanup. That is, the United States remains entitled to its cleanup costs *and* may also collect punitive damages up to three times the cleanup amount.

The provision that a party subject to an abatement order cannot seek judicial review of its liability before complying with the order is an important one. Without this limitation on preenforcement review and stiff penalties for failure to comply, cleanups under abatement orders would be hopelessly delayed by litigation. Sanctions for liable parties that disobey abatement orders are designed to ensure that parties clean up first and litigate later. Unfortunately, even with these provisions, cleanups are often delayed by litigation.

Cost Recovery: CERCLA's Scheme of Strict, Joint, and Several Liability

In the event that EPA must perform a cleanup itself, CERCLA allows EPA to recover its reasonable costs from any or all liable parties under a scheme of joint and several liability. CERCLA specifies several categories of parties that are liable for response costs:

1. present owners or operators of the facilities,[14]
2. owners or operators of the facility at the time of hazardous-substance disposal,[15]

3. generators of hazardous substances or others who arranged for disposal or treatment at the facility,[16] and

4. transporters who accepted hazardous substances for transport to the disposal or treatment facility and selected that facility for disposal or treatment.[17]

Any person, including corporations and governmental entities, that falls into one of these categories is strictly, jointly, and severally liable for response costs at facilities from which hazardous substances are released or threaten to be released. The same parties may be subject to a section 106 abatement order.

Response costs for which responsible parties may be liable include expenditures required:

- to remove, treat, contain, or dispose of hazardous substances;
- to remedy threats or conditions associated with those substances;
- to monitor or evaluate risks associated with hazardous substances; and
- to repair or redress harm to human health or the environment attributable to those hazardous substances.

Response costs also include expenditures for such items as:

- security fencing;
- provision of alternative water supplies;
- temporary evacuation or housing;
- permanent relocation of homes and businesses;
- emergency assistance;
- segregation of reactive wastes;
- dredging or excavation;
- collection of leachate;
- confinement of hazardous substances by clay cover, dikes, or trenches; and
- other measures deemed necessary to minimize risks associated with hazardous substances.

Notwithstanding the statute's broad provisions, courts are not in full agreement as to what activities are properly considered response actions for which expended costs are recoverable under CERCLA. For example, the court in the *Daigle* case agreed that CERCLA response costs include the cost of monitoring health effects arising from efforts to contain and clean up hazardous substances, but it disagreed with other courts that had construed response costs as including long-term medical monitoring of health effects from exposure to hazardous substances released into the environment rather than from containment and cleanup activities.

CERCLA liability for response costs is strict, joint, and several. *Strict liability* means that a party who falls under one of the categories listed in CERCLA section 107(a) is liable without regard to fault. It does not matter whether a party acted with good or wrongful intent nor whether the party was diligent or negligent in its disposal or handling of hazardous substances. For example, a court held in 1992 that a contractor who excavated and graded city property that contained hazardous substances qualified as an "operator" and "transporter" under CERCLA and, as such, could be sued for contribution to response costs by the person who had owned the property at the time of disposal.[18] Indeed, under CERCLA, a person *need not even know* that a substance he or she is handling is hazardous in order to be held liable for response costs.

Moreover, CERCLA imposes liability without regard to the source or concentration of a hazardous substance. Even if one arranged for the disposal of only a very small portion of the hazardous substances present at a facility, one may still be liable. CERCLA does permit EPA to reach expedited settlements for a proportional share of liability with such *de minimus* or *de micromis* parties, however.

Joint and several liability arises when more than one party is liable at a site. Where the activities of more than one party have resulted in the release of hazardous substances, each such party is considered jointly and severally liable. Only if a liable party can establish that the harm it caused is divisible from the harms caused by other parties will it be able to escape liability for the entire cleanup. Normally, this entails a demonstration that the substances it disposed of can be identified and accounted for separately. In the rare instances when a defendant can prove this, its liability may be limited to the actual extent of the damages it caused but the burden rests with the defendant to prove that the harm is divisible.

If the harm is not divisible, each and every liable party is presumptively liable for the entire cost of cleanup regardless of its relative contribution to the release or threatened release of hazardous substances. The government or another party that has incurred response costs may sue any or all of the potentially liable parties. Upon obtaining a court judgment, the plaintiff in a CERCLA cost-recovery case is entitled to collect the entire amount of the judgment from any one or combination of the liable parties.

A defendant that pays the judgment or settles for the entire amount of liability may sue others for contribution. In a contribution action, the defendant (now called the *contribution plaintiff*) may sue other liable parties (*third-party defendants*) and may recover from each of them a share of the damages.[19] The share of damages allowed to be recovered from each third-party defendant is the share of harm caused by that defendant's activities. The court determines each defendant's contribution liability in a process called *apportionment of liability*.

The standard of joint and several liability places the burden upon defendants, rather than plaintiffs, to prove that the harm is divisible or to seek contribution from other liable parties. Although it may seem unfair to place the entire liability for response costs on a party whose actions accounted for only a fraction of the damages, the only alternative would be to place upon the innocent plaintiff the burden of proving which defendant was responsible for what part of the harm. Since defendants, rather than plaintiffs, are the ones whose activities led to the release of hazardous substances and consequent damage to the environment, it is more fair to place the burden of apportioning liability on defendants than on plaintiffs. Under joint and several liability, the government or another party that has incurred response costs need only prove which parties shipped hazardous substances to the site in order to render any of them jointly and severally liable for the total cost of cleanup.

The imposition of joint and several liability is particularly necessary in the environmental context. First, it prevents any one party from delaying cleanup by first asserting a right to pursue and collect contributions from other potentially liable parties. Second, it relieves the EPA of the often impossible burden of proving causation of environmental harm from particular sources or substances. The nature of hazardous substances virtually mandates that the liability for their release be joint and several. Many sites that qualify for cleanup under CERCLA are large tracts of land where leaking drums of chemical wastes have been buried, mountains of incinerator ash containing known carcinogens have accumulated, liquid wastes have been poured into unlined pools, and solid wastes have been dumped. As in the *Murtha* case, the number of companies that have disposed of their wastes at a site can number in the dozens or hundreds. At such sites, various chemicals leach into the soil and ground water and mix, sometimes producing explosions, fires, or vapors that burn exposed flesh within minutes. Any attempt to inventory and trace such substances and their effects to individual generators under these circumstances is remarkably difficult, if not impossible.

Even when it is possible to "fingerprint" the various defendants through their wastes, it is rarely possible to attribute specific environmental injuries or cleanup costs to particular wastes. Generally, it is not feasible to apportion removal or treatment costs according to specific waste streams when such streams have intermingled over time. Nor are the costs of evaluating, monitoring, and treating affected soil and ground water merely a function of the volume and toxicity of various wastes; variations in the persistence, mobility, and reactivity of different waste streams all affect cleanup costs.

In several early CERCLA cases, defendants proposed that liability be determined volumetrically. Under volumetric assessment, each generator bears a percentage of cleanup costs corresponding to the percentage of total volume it has contributed to the site. Indeed, defendants who agree to perform Superfund cleanups often agree amongst themselves to apportion their respective payments in this manner in order to save themselves the cost of determining with greater certainty which response costs are attributable to each identified waste stream. Nevertheless, courts that presided over early CERCLA litigation were not persuaded to adopt volume as a controlling standard for all cases. Jointly liable parties may voluntarily agree among themselves upon any apportionment formula, including a volumetric standard, in settling their respective contributions toward Superfund cleanups, but courts have rejected the imposition of that standard upon unwilling parties.

In rejecting the volumetric standard for apportioning liability, the courts noted that it could relieve some parties of their fair share of cleanup costs and shift those costs unfairly to others. Because some hazardous substances are more toxic, mobile, or persistent than others, the volume of a waste stream often bears little or no relationship to its environmental hazards or to the cost of cleaning it up. This is especially true for municipal solid waste, which is present in very high volumes at common dumpsites but contains relatively low concentrations of hazardous substances and does not pose nearly the difficulties that concentrated toxic chemical and industrial wastes do.

Moreover, placing the burden on the government to determine and prove the extent of harm each defendant caused in a situation where the harm also resulted from a combination of their activities would eviscerate the entire purpose of Superfund legislation—that is, to force polluters, not taxpayers, to pay for cleaning up hazardous waste sites. Indeed, in some cases it would cost the government far more to discover and prove which waste generator caused which damages than to finance the cleanup itself. Finally, if the government were forced to prove causation for each defendant, the environment and human health would be further jeopardized. Removal and remedial actions could not take place until the government had conducted an intensive "fingerprinting" analysis of the site. Instead, the government can now rely on documentation to prove which defendants shipped their wastes to a particular facility and can sue all or some of them jointly for the total cost of cleanup.

The *Goodrich* case illustrates some of the difficulties of identifying the harm caused by individual generators at a single Superfund site. In that case, literally hundreds of private businesses and local governments had dumped at a common landfill, where many different kinds of wastes had mixed, migrated, and changed chemically over time. Settlement of contribution claims among the many defendants for response costs could proceed only on grounds that were admittedly inexact.

In limited circumstances, CERCLA empowers courts and EPA to adjust or apportion response costs among potentially liable parties. That discretionary power does not remove the presumed joint and several liability of all liable parties, however, nor does it require EPA to prove each party's proper proportionate contribution as a condition of negotiating separate settlements with them or of ordering one of them to conduct the entire cleanup.

CERCLA facilitates adjustments of apportionment of response costs among jointly liable parties in two basic ways.[20] For liable parties whose relative shares of response costs are deemed minor, CERCLA authorizes EPA to negotiate administrative settlements with them for payment of an agreed share of response costs. As part of such settlement, they are released from further liability to the government and to other parties seeking to assert claims for contribution against them. For parties who are ineligible or unwilling to negotiate a voluntary settlement with EPA for cost contribution, CERCLA authorizes courts to determine their respective contribution liabilities on the basis of "equitable factors."

> Appellant municipalities are not without recourse to avoid inequitable and disproportionate burdens that may arise from their liability as third-party contributors. Courts have the authority to "allocate response costs among liable parties using such equitable factors as the court determines are appropriate." § 9613(f)(1). An array of equitable factors may be considered in this allocation process, including the relative volume and toxicity of the substances . . . , the relative cleanup costs incurred as a result of these wastes, the degree of care exercised by each party with respect to the hazardous substances, and the financial resources of the parties involved. Consequently, the amount of liability imposed will not necessarily be a function solely of the total volume of municipal waste disposed of in the landfills, but rather will be a function of the extent to which [a party's] dumping of hazardous substances both engendered the necessity, and contributed to the costs, of cleanup.
> . . . . [from the *B. F. Goodrich* opinion, excerpted below.]

The *Cannons* case illustrates the application of these CERCLA provisions.

Flexible discretion using these "factors" to determine contribution liability is necessary, because any of the factors may distinguish between parties to reach just results in some cases but unjust results in others. For example, cleanup costs are affected to some extent by the volume of wastes and to some extent by their toxicity, concentration, persistence, and mobility. Thus the use of a volumetric formula for cost assessment is appropriate in some circumstances, as was held in the *Cannons* case, and inappropriate in other circumstances, as in *United States v. Monsanto Co.*[21] As noted in *Monsanto* and in the *Goodrich* opinion, unless a court decides that it is unreasonable to assume that factors other than volume substantially affect cleanup costs, a volumetric standard for apportioning liability may be rejected.

Outline of Major Statutory Provisions

The outline here sketches CERCLA's major statutory provisions. The abridged text of selected provisions appears in the appendix to this chapter.

Hazardous Substance Identification

Designation of hazardous substances	§ 102(a)
Reportable quantities (which, if released, trigger reporting obligations under § 103)	§ 102(a),(b)

Release Reporting

Definition of *release*	§ 101(22)
Release reporting requirements	§ 103(a)

Hazardous Substance Response Actions

Definitions:	
Response (any removal or remedial action)	§ 101(25)
Removal (a short-term, emergency response)	§ 101(23)
Remedy (a long-term, final solution)	§ 101(24)
Presidential authorization to undertake response actions	§ 104(a)(1)
Removal must contribute to final remedy	§ 104(a)(2)
National Contingency Plan	§ 105(a)
Selection of remedial actions:	
criteria (technical standards and cost-effectiveness)	§ 121(a),(b)
cleanup levels (must be protective of human health	
and environment)	§ 121(d)
Abatement orders (cleanup orders)	§ 106(a)
Fines for failure to comply	§ 106(b)(1)

Identifying and Evaluating Facilities

Hazard ranking system (used to rank sites)	§ 105(c)
National Priorities List	§ 105(a)(8)

The "Superfund"

Appropriations	§ 111(p)(1)
Use of fund	§ 111(a)(c)

Liability

Definitions:	
facility	§ 101(9)
hazardous substance	§ 101(14)
owner or *operator*	§ 101(20)
person (includes municipalities)	§ 101(21)
Cost recovery:	
scope of liability	§ 107(a)
defenses	§ 107(b)
Superfund lien	§ 107(l)
"Innocent landowner" defense:	
Definition of *contractual relationship* (in innocent-landowner	
defense)	§ 101(35)
innocent-landowner defense	§ 107(b)(3)
Settlements	§ 122(a)
Effect of settlement (settlors cannot be sued for contribution)	§ 122(c)

Information-Gathering Authorities

EPA has site access and may gather information on suspected releases	§ 104(e)

Judicial Actions

No preenforcement review	§ 113(h)
Contribution	§ 113

Illustrative CERCLA Cases

DAIGLE V. SHELL OIL CO.

972 F.2d 1527 (10th Cir. 1992)

[In this case the court held that the costs of monitoring the health effects of exposure to hazardous substances during cleanup of contaminated site are not recoverable under CERCLA.]

This case arises from the cleanup effort at the Rocky Mountain Arsenal, a federally controlled CERCLA site in Colorado. Residents of the area seek "response costs" from Shell Oil and the federal government for medical monitoring. . . . The monitoring is designed to detect the onset of any latent disease that may have been caused by exposure to toxic fumes stirred up during the cleanup. . . .

. . . The residents instead seek redress in Section 107(a)'s private right of recovery for "response costs." Whether Section 107(a) response costs include medical monitoring is an issue of first impression in the courts of appeals, although several district courts have decided the issue.

. . . Congress enacted CERCLA to facilitate the expeditious cleanup of environmental contamination caused by hazardous waste releases. Section 107(a) is designed to further the overall objective of shifting liability for cleanup costs to the responsible parties. It provides that certain responsible parties may be sued for "(A) all costs of removal or remedial action . . . (B) any other necessary costs of response incurred by any other person . . . ." It is undisputed that Shell and the government are responsible parties. At issue is whether the residents' monitoring claims fall within the subsection (B) private right of recovery for "any other necessary costs of response."

The drafters did not directly define the phrase "any other necessary costs of response" as a whole, opting instead to define only the term "response." Under 42 U.S.C. 96019(25) a "response" is a "removal action" or "remedial action." "Removal actions" are actions designed to effect an interim solution to a contamination problem. "Removal" means the cleanup of released hazardous substances from the environment, and "such actions as may be necessary to monitor . . . the release or threat of release of hazardous substances, the disposal of removed material, or the taking of such other actions as may be necessary to prevent, minimize, or mitigate damage to the public health or welfare." . . . "Remedial actions," on the other hand, are designed to effect a permanent solution to the contamination problem. Remedial actions include "any monitoring reasonably required to assure that such actions protect the public health an welfare and the environment . . . ." . . .

The residents note that both definitions refer to "monitoring" in the "public health and welfare" context. They argue that this clearly covers the monitoring costs they seek, citing *Brewer v. Raven*, 680 F. Supp. 1176, 56 LW 2523 (D.C. M. Tenn. 1988), and several cases that cursorily arrived at the same result. *Williams v. Allied Automotive*, 704 F. Supp. 782 (D.C. N. Ohio 1988); *Adams v. Republic Steel Corp.*, 621 F. Supp. 270 (D.C. W. Tenn. 1988). Applying what it considered the plain language of the definitions, *Brewer* held that "removal" and "remedial" costs encompass medical monitoring as long as the monitoring is "conducted to assess the effect of the release or discharge on public health or to identify potential public health problems presented by the release."

The residents correctly assert that certain monitoring costs are recoverable as "removal action" or "remedial action" "response costs." We think, however, that the residents and the *Brewer* court go awry in affording a broad sweep to the "public health and welfare" language. Several district courts have expressly rejected *Brewer* as too broad, basing their conclusion on an examination of the plain language of the definitions in context with the overall structure and history of CERCLA. *Woodman v. U.S.*, 765 F. Supp. 1467 (D.C. N. Fla. 1991); *Bolin v. Cessna Aircraft Co.*, 759 F. Supp. 692, 59 LW 2568 (D.C. Kan. 1991).

Turning to the context of the "monitoring" and "health and welfare" language, both definitions are directed at containing and cleaning up hazardous substance releases. For example, the monitoring allowed for under the "removal action" definition relates only to an evaluation of the extent of a "release or threat of release of hazardous substances." . . . And the "remedial action" definition expressly focuses only on actions necessary to "prevent or minimize the release of hazardous substances so that they do not migrate to cause substantial danger to present or future public health or welfare or the environment."

The residents, however, concentrate on the additional . . . phrase referring to "other actions as may be necessary to prevent, minimize, or mitigate damage to the public health or welfare . . . ." They contend that this should be read broadly to cover any type of monitoring that would mitigate health problems. Medical monitoring would mitigate the potential individual health problems of the residents, but the general provision for prevention or mitigation of "damage to public health or welfare" must be interpreted consistently with the specific examples . . . enumerated in the definition. The specific examples all prevent or mitigate damage to public health by preventing contact between the spreading contaminants and the public. Although the statute provides that "removal" costs are not limited to the specific examples, it is reasonable . . . to conclude that any other recoverable costs must at least be of a similar type. Long term health monitoring of the sort requested by residents clearly has nothing to do with preventing contact between a "release or threatened release" and the public. The release has already occurred.

The legislative history is consistent with this interpretation.

The facts and procedural history of the next case, Northeastern Pharmaceutical, appear in the portion of the opinion presented in Chapter 6.

■   UNITED STATES v. NORTHEASTERN PHARMACEUTICAL   ■

810 F.2d 726 (8th Cir. 1986)

II. DISTRICT COURT DECISION

The district court found that dioxin, hexachlorophene, TCP, TCB (1,2,3,5-tetrachlorobenzene, also found at the Denney farm site), and toluene have high levels of toxicity at low-dose levels and are thus "hazardous substances" within the meaning of . . . CERCLA . . . . The district court also found there was a substantial likelihood that the environment and human beings would be exposed to the hazardous substances that had been disposed of at the Denney farm site. . . .

* * *

B. CERCLA Findings

CERCLA § 104, . . . authorizes the EPA to take direct "response" actions, which can include either short-term "removal" actions or long-term "remedial" actions or both, pursuant to the NCP, with funds from the "Superfund,"[2] and to seek recovery of response costs from responsible parties pursuant to CERCLA § 107, . . . in order to replenish the Superfund. The EPA can also use CERCLA § 106, . . . to seek injunctions to compel responsible parties to clean up hazardous waste sites that constitute an "imminent and substantial endangerment" to health and the environment. . . .

The district court applied CERCLA retroactively, . . . but held the government could not recover response costs incurred before the effective date of CERCLA, December 11, 1980. . . . The district court also held CERCLA imposes a standard of strict liability, . . . and that

responsible parties can be held jointly and severally liable, ...

The district court also found NEPACCO liable as an "owner or operator" pursuant to
CERCLA § 107(a)(1), ... With respect to the
individual defendants, the district court found
Mills liable as a "person who . . . accepted any
hazardous substances for transport to disposal
. . . sites selected by such person," pursuant to
CERCLA § 107(a)(4), ... The district court
also found Lee liable as an "owner or operator"
pursuant to CERCLA § 107(a)(1) . . . and as a
"person who by contract, agreement, or otherwise . . . arranged with a transporter for transport for disposal . . . of hazardous substances,"
pursuant to CERCLA § 107(a)(3). . . . The district court found Michaels liable as a person
who arranged for the transport and disposal of
hazardous substances pursuant to CERCLA §
107(a)(3). . . . The liability of NEPACCO, Lee,
Michaels, and Mills was joint and several. . . .

The district court further found the government's right to recovery of response costs was
very broad and included litigation costs, attorney's fees, future response costs, and prejudg-
ment interest, and that the defendants in an
action by the government for recovery of response costs had the burden of proving that the
government's response costs were inconsistent
with the NCP. . . . NEPACCO, Michaels and Lee
have appealed. . . .

III.   CERCLA—RETROACTIVITY

A.   Application of CERCLA to Pre-1980 Acts

Appellants first argue the district court erred
in applying CERCLA retroactively, that is, to
impose liability for acts committed before its effective date, December 11, 1980. CERCLA §
302(a) . . . provides that "[u]nless otherwise
provided, all provisions of this chapter shall be
effective on December 11, 1980." Appellants
argue that CERCLA should not apply to pre-
enactment conduct that was neither negligent
nor unlawful when committed. Appellants argue that all the conduct at issue occurred in the
early 1970s, well before CERCLA became effective. Appellants also argue that there is no
language supporting retroactive application in
CERLCA's liability section, CERCLA § 107 . . .
or in the legislative history. Appellants further
argue that because CERCLA imposes a new
kind of liability, retroactive application of

CERCLA violates due process and the taking
clause. We disagree.

. . . We acknowledge there is a presumption
against the retroactive application of statutes.
. . .

Although CERCLA does not expressly provide for retroactivity, it is manifestly clear that
Congress intended CERCLA to have retroactive
effect. The language used in the key liability
provision, CERCLA § 107, 42 U.S.C. § 9607, refers to actions and conditions in the past tense:
"any person who at the time of disposal of any
hazardous substances owned or operated," . . .
"any person who . . . arranged with a transporter for transport for disposal," . . . and "any
person who . . . accepted any hazardous substances for transport to . . . sites selected by
such person," . . . .

Further, the statutory scheme itself is over-
whelmingly remedial and retroactive. CERCLA
authorizes the EPA to force responsible parties
to clean up inactive or abandoned hazardous
substance sites, . . . and authorizes federal, state
and local governments and private parties to
clean up such sites and then seek recovery of
their response costs from responsible parties,
. . . . In order to be effective, CERCLA must
reach past conduct. CERCLA's backward-
looking focus is confirmed by the legislative
history. . . . Congress intended CERCLA "to initiate and establish a comprehensive response
and financing mechanism to abate and control
the vast problems associated with abandoned
and inactive hazardous waste disposal sites." *Id.*
at 22, 1980 U.S. Code Cong. & Ad. News at
6125.

The district court also correctly found that
retroactive application of CERCLA does not
violate due process. . . . Appellants argue
CERCLA creates a new form of liability that is
designed to deter and punish those who, according to current standards, improperly disposed of hazardous substances in the past. We
disagree.

It is by now well established that legislative
Acts adjusting the burdens and benefits of
economic life come to the Court with a presumption of constitutionality, and that the
burden is on one complaining of a due process violation to establish that the legislature
has acted in an arbitrary and irrational way.

[L]egislation readjusting rights and burdens is not unlawful solely because it upsets otherwise settled expectations. This is true even though the effect of the legislation is to impose a new duty or liability based on past acts. . . .

"Provided that the retroactive application of a statute is supported by a legitimate legislative purpose furthered by rational means, judgments about the wisdom of such legislation remain within the exclusive province of the legislative and executive branches. . . ." . . .

Appellants failed to show that Congress acted in an arbitrary and irrational manner. Cleaning up inactive and abandoned hazardous waste disposal sites is a legitimate legislative purpose, and Congress acted in a rational manner in imposing liability for the cost of cleaning up such sites upon those parties who created and profited from the sites and upon the chemical industry as a whole. . . .

Appellants also summarily argue retroactive application of CERCLA constitutes an unconstitutional taking of property. We disagree. First, because appellants do not have a property interest in the Denney farm site, we question appellants' standing to raise a taking issue. Second, we hesitate to characterize the government's cleanup as a taking at all; the government's cleanup of the Denney farm site has not deprived the property owner of any property interest. . . . Instead, the government's cleanup of the site abated an "imminent and substantial endangerment" to the public health and the environment, thus eliminating a public nuisance and restoring value to the property by removing the hazardous substances. . . .

B.   Application of CERCLA to Pre-1980 Costs

Related to the question of CERCLA's application to pre-1980 acts is the question whether the government can recover response costs incurred prior to CERCLA's effective date. . . . The district court held that the government could not recover its pre-enactment response costs. NEPACCO, . . . The government argues a close examination of the statutory language and scheme, legislative history and legislative purpose supports retroactive liability from pre-enactment costs. . . .

* * *

After the present case was decided, this issue was exhaustively examined and resolved in favor of recovery of pre-CERCLA response costs in *United States v. Shell Oil Co.,* . . .

In *United States v. Shell Oil Co.* the federal government sued under CERCLA . . . to recover the costs it had incurred and will incur in cleaning up the heavily contaminated Rocky Mountain Arsenal located outside of Denver, Colorado. The Rocky Mountain Arsenal has been owned by the United States since 1942 and was used by the United States Department of the Army for manufacturing and handling various chemicals and munitions. In addition, since 1947, Shell Oil and its predecessors had leased part of the Arsenal for the manufacture of pesticides, herbicides and other chemicals. The Army's wastes and all or some of Shell's wastes were disposed of through waste disposal systems built and operated by the Army. The waste disposal systems repeatedly failed and released the commingled wastes into the environment, severely contaminating the Arsenal and threatening the surrounding environment. In 1975 the Army began to clean up the Arsenal. By December 1, 1983, before CERCLA was enacted, the Army had incurred about $48 million in response costs and, by January 1984, had proposed four alternative cleanup programs, with estimated future response costs ranging from $210 million to $1.8 billion, and recommended the program estimated to cost $360 million. Shell argued, among other things, that CERCLA did not authorize recovery of the Army's pre-enactment response costs.

The *Shell Oil* court disagreed and held CERCLA authorized recovery of pre-enactment response costs. . . . First, the *Shell Oil* court agreed with the district court in the present case that "congressional intent to either impose or withhold liability for response costs incurred before CERCLA cannot be divined from the verb tenses in [CERCLA] . . . The *Shell Oil* court examined the grammatical structure of CERCLA § 107(a), 42 U.S.C. § 9607(a), and concluded that each party's argument cancelled the other out. . . .

* * *

At the opposite end of the spectrum are those sites . . . where the danger to the public health and welfare and to the environment was so imminent that the United States proceeded with cleanup without a special fund of money for that purpose and without assurance that it would be repaid by the persons responsible for the contamination. It was sites containing this magnitude of public danger that prompted Congress to enact CERCLA.

Construing section 107(a) to preclude recovery of pre-enactment response costs would carve out an exception to the general retroactive scheme of the statute for those most severe situations where ... the government's response commenced prior to the enactment of the statute. ... Congress could [not] have intended to protect the public fisc by imposing liability on the responsible parties, yet except the sites where response had already commenced because the situations were the most imminently threatening. Such an interpretation would penalize the government for prompt response and provide an undeserved windfall to the parties who had created, then abandoned, some of the most egregious sites.

* * *

V. Scope of Liability

The district court found NEPACCO liable as the "owner or operator" of a "facility" ... and as a "person" who arranged for the transportation and disposal of hazardous substances .... The district court found Lee liable as a "person" who arranged for the disposal of hazardous substances ... and as an "owner or operator" of the NEPACCO plant ... by "piercing the corporate veil." ... The district court also found Michaels liable as an "owner or operator" of the NEPACCO plant ....

* * *

Appellants argue (1) they cannot be held liable as "owners or operators" of a "facility" because "facility" refers to the place where hazardous substances are located and they did not own or operate the Denney farm site, (2) Lee cannot be held individually liable for arranging for the transportation and disposal of hazardous substances because he did not "own or possess" the hazardous substances and because he made those arrangements as a corporate officer or employee acting on behalf of NEPACCO, and (3) the district court erred in finding Lee and Michaels individually liable by "piercing the corporate veil." ...

The government argues Lee can be held individually liable without "piercing the corporate veil," under CERCLA § 107(a)(3), ... For the reasons discussed below, we agree with the government's liability arguments.

A. Liability under CERCLA § 107(1)(1), ...

First, appellants argue the district court erred in finding them liable under CERCLA § 107(a)(1), ... as the "owners and operators" of a "facility" where hazardous substances are located. Appellants argue that, regardless of their relationship to the NEPACCO plant, they neither owned or operated the Denney farm site, and that it is the Denney farm site, not the NEPACCO plant, that is a "facility" for purposes of "owner and operator" liability under CERCLA § 107(a)(1), ... We agree.

CERCLA defines the term "facility" in part as "any site or area where a hazardous substance has been deposited, stored, disposed of, or placed, or otherwise come to be located." ... The term "facility" should be construed very broadly to include "virtually any place at which hazardous wastes have been dumped, or otherwise disposed of." *United States v. Ward,* ... (definition of "facility" includes roadsides where hazardous waste was dumped); .... In the present case, however, the place where the hazardous substances were disposed of and where the government has concentrated its cleanup efforts is the Denney farm site, not the NEPACCO plant. The Denney farm site is the "facility." Because NEPACCO, Lee and Michaels did not own or operate the Denney farm site, they cannot be held liable as the "owners or operators" of a "facility" ....

B. Individual Liability under CERCLA § 107(a)(3), 42 U.S.C. § 9607(a)(3)

CERCLA § 107(a)(3) ... imposes strict liability upon "any person" who arranged for the disposal or transportation for disposal of hazardous substances. As defined by statute, the term "person" includes both individuals and corporations and does not exclude corporate officers or employees.... [C]onstruction of CERCLA to impose liability upon only the corporation and not the individual corporate officers and employees who are responsible for making corporate decisions about the handling and disposal of hazardous substances would open an enormous, and clearly unintended, loophole in the statutory scheme.

First, Lee argues he cannot be held individually liable for having arranged for the transportation and disposal of hazardous substances under CERCLA § 107(a)(3), . . . because he did not personally own or possess the hazardous substances. Lee argues NEPACCO owned or possessed the hazardous substances.

The government argues Lee "possessed" the hazardous substances within the meaning of CERCLA § 107(a)(3), . . . because, as NEPACCO's plant supervisor, Lee had actual "control" over the NEPACCO plant's hazardous substances. We agree. It is the authority to control the handling and disposal of hazardous substances that is critical under the statutory scheme. The district court found that Lee, as plant supervisor, actually knew about, had immediate supervision over, and was directly responsible for arranging for the transportation and disposal of the NEPACCO plant's hazardous substances at the Denney farm site. We believe requiring proof of personal ownership or actual physical possession of hazardous substances as a precondition for liability under CERCLA § 107(a)(3), . . . would be inconsistent with the broad remedial purposes of CERCLA. . . .

Next, Lee argues that because he arranged for the transportation and disposal of the hazardous substances as a corporate officer or employee acting on behalf of NEPACCO, he cannot be held individually liable for NEPACCO's violations. Lee also argues the district court erred in disregarding the corporate entity by "piercing the corporate veil" . . . .

The government argues Lee can be held individually liable, without "piercing the corporate veil," because Lee personally arranged for the disposal of hazardous substances in violation of CERCLA § 107(a)(3), ... We agree. . . . Lee can be held individually liable because he personally participated in conduct that violated CERCLA; this personal liability is distinct from the derivative liability that results from "piercing the corporate veil." "The effect of piercing a corporate veil is to hold the owner [of the corporation] liable. The rationale for piercing the corporate veil is that the corporation is something less than a bona fide independent entity" . . . . Here, Lee is liable because

he personally participated in the wrongful conduct and not because he is one of the owners of what may have been a less than bona fide corporation. . . .

We now turn to Lee's basic argument. Lee argues that he cannot be held individually liable for NEPACCO's wrongful conduct because he acted solely as a corporate officer or employee on behalf of NEPACCO. The liability imposed upon Lee, however, was not derivative but personal. Liability was not premised solely upon Lee's status as a corporate officer or employee. Rather, Lee is individually liable under CERCLA § 107(a)(3), . . . because he personally arranged for the transportation and disposal of hazardous substances on behalf of NEPACCO and thus participated in NEPACCO's CERCLA violations.

A corporate officer is individually liable for the torts he [or she] personally commits [on behalf of the corporation] and cannot shield himself [or herself] behind a corporation when he [or she] is an actual participant in the tort. The fact that an officer is acting for a corporation also may make the corporation vicariously or secondarily liable under the doctrine of respondeat superior; it does not however relieve the individual of his [or her] responsibility.

* * *

VII. BURDEN OF PROOF OF RESPONSE COSTS

The district court found appellants had the burden of proving the government's response costs were inconsistent with the NCP, . . . and that response costs that are not inconsistent with the NCP are conclusively presumed to be reasonable and therefore recoverable, ... Appellants argue the district court erred in requiring them to prove the response costs were inconsistent with the NCP, not cost-effective or unnecessary. Appellants further argue the district court erred in assuming all costs that are consistent with the NCP are conclusively presumed to be reasonable. Appellants note that the information and facts necessary to establish consistency with the NCP are matters within the possession of the government.

. . . CERCLA § 107(a)(4)(A) . . . states that the government may recover from responsible parties "all costs of removal or remedial action . . . not inconsistent with the [NCP]." The statutory language itself establishes an exception for costs that are inconsistent with the NCP, but appellants, as the parties claiming the benefit of the exception, have the burden of proving that certain costs are inconsistent with the NCP and, therefore, not recoverable. . . . Contrary to appellants' argument, "not inconsistent" is not, at least for purposes of statutory construction and not syntax, the same as "consistent."

. . . In comparison, CERCLA § 107(a)(4)(B), 42 U.S.C. § 9607(a)(4)(B), provides that "any other person," referring to any "person" other than the federal government or a state, can recover "any other necessary costs of response . . . consistent with the [NCP]." That statutory language indicates that *non* governmental entities must prove that their response costs are consistent with the NCP in order to recover them. The statutory scheme thus differentiates between governmental and nongovernmental entities in allocating the burden of proof of whether response costs are consistent with the NCP. . . .

* * *

Because determining the appropriate removal and remedial action involves specialized knowledge and expertise, the choice of a particular cleanup method is a matter within the discretion of the EPA. The applicable standard of review is whether the agency's choice is arbitrary and capricious. As explained in *United States v. Ward,*

[i] [appellants] wish the court to review the consistency of [the government's] actions with the NCP, then they are essentially alleging that the EPA did not carry out its statutory duties. The statute provides liability except for costs "not inconsistent" with the NCP. This language requires deference by this court to the judgment of agency professionals. [Appellants], therefore, may not seek to have the court substitute its own judgment for that of the EPA. [Appellants] may only show that the EPA's decision about the method of cleanup was "inconsistent" with the NCP in that the EPA was arbitrary and capricious in the discharge of their duties under the NCP.

Here, appellants failed to show that the government's response costs were inconsistent with the NCP. Appellants also failed to show that the EPA acted arbitrarily and capriciously in choosing the particular method it used to clean up the Denney farm site.

* * *

---

[2]CERCLA establishes two funds: CERCLA § 232, 42 U.S.C. § 9641, establishes the Post-Closure Liability Trust Fund, which is funded through taxes on hazardous substances disposed of at qualified disposal facilities, and the "Superfund," or Hazardous Substances Response Trust, which is funded largely by special taxes on the petroleum and chemical industries and also by general appropriations.

UNITED STATES V. CANNONS ENGINEERING CORP.

899 F.2d 79 (1st Cir. 1990)

[After the EPA identified four hazardous waste sites in Massachusetts and New Hampshire for cleanup, it notified some 671 parties as being potentially liable (PRPs) for the cleanup, and divided them into two classes; namely, contributors whose waste was minimal in volume and toxicity (DMC), and those not fitting the DMC classification. It then made administrative settlements with 300 waste generators in the DMC class. Suit was later brought by the United States and the host states against 84 PRPs. Consent decrees of liability were accepted and en-

tered, over the objection of seven defendants, against 47 major PRPs who where ineligible for administrative settlement and 34 parties in the DMC class who rejected prior administrative settlement. This opinion deals with the appeals of six parties who opposed the judgment against them.]

Selya, Circuit Judge

* * *

The government thereupon moved to enter the decrees. Seven non-settling defendants objected. After considering written submissions and hearing arguments of counsel, the district court approved both consent decrees and dismissed all cross-claims against the settling defendants. . . . The court proceeded to certify the decrees as final . . . . These appeals followed.

We approach our task mindful that, . . . a consent decree in CERCLA litigation is encased in a double layer of swaddling. In the first place, it is the policy of the law to encourage settlements. That policy has particular force where, as here, a government actor . . . has pulled the laboring oar in constructing the proposed settlement. . . .

Respect for the agency's role is heightened in a situation where the cards have been dealt face up and a crew of sophisticated players, with sharply conflicting interests, sit at the table. That so many affected parties, themselves knowledgeable and represented by experienced lawyers, have hammered out an agreement at arm's length and advocate its embodiment in a judicial decree, itself deserves weight . . . .

The second layer of swaddling derives from the nature of appellate review. Because approval of a consent decree is committed to the trial court's informed discretion, the court of appeals should be reluctant to disturb a reasoned exercise of that discretion. In this context, the test for abuse of discretion is itself a fairly deferential one. . . .

* * *

Originally, the EPA extended an open offer to all de minimis PRPs, including five of the six appellants, proposing an administrative settlement . . . . Settling PRPs paid their shares in cash and were released outright from all liability. They were also exempted from suits for contribution, ...

Following consummation of the administrative settlement, plaintiffs entered into negotiations with the remaining PRPs. These negotiations resulted in the proposed MP decrees (accepted by 47 "major" defendants) and the DMC decree. The terms of the former . . . do not bear repeating. The latter was modelled upon the administrative settlement, but featured an increased premium: . . . . The EPA justified the incremental 100% premium as being in the nature of delay damages.

* * *

III

* * *

Our starting point is well defined. The Superfund Amendments . . . authorized a variety of types of settlements which the EPA may utilize in CERCLA actions, including consent decrees providing for PRPs to contribute to cleanup costs and/or to undertake response activities themselves. . . . SARA's legislative history makes pellucid that, when such consent decrees are forged, the trial court's review function is only to "satisfy itself that the settlement is reasonable, fair, and consistent with the purposes that CERCLA is intended to serve." . . .

* * *

A.   Procedural Fairness

We agree with the district court that fairness in the CERCLA settlement context has both procedural and substantive components.

* * *

Appellants claim that they were relatively close to the 1% cutoff point, and were thus arbitrarily excluded from the major party settlement, avails them naught. Congress intended to give the EPA broad discretion to structure classes of PRPs for settlement purposes. We cannot say that the government acted beyond the scope of that discretion in separating minor and major players in this instance, that is, in determining that generators who had sent less than 1% of the volume of hazardous waste to the Sites would comprise the DMC and those generators who were responsible for a greater percentage would be treated as major PRPs. . . .

Nor can we say that appellants were entitled to more advance warning of the EPA's negotiating strategy. . . . At the time de minimis PRPs were initially invited to participate in the administrative settlement, the EPA, by letter, informed all of them, including appellants, that:

The government is anxious to achieve a high degree of participation in this *de minimis* settlement. Accordingly, the terms contained in this settlement offer are the most favorable terms that the government intends to make available to parties eligible for *de minimis* settlement in this case.

Appellants knew, early on, that they were within the DMC and could spurn the EPA's proposal only at the risk of paying more at a later time. Although appellants may have assumed that they could ride on the coattails of the major parties and join whatever MP decree emerged. . . . the agency was neither asked for, nor did it give, any such assurance in this instance. . . .

B. Substantive Fairness

Substantive fairness introduces . . . concepts of corrective justice and accountability: a party should bear the cost of the harm for which it is legally responsible. *See generally Developments in the Law—Toxic Waste Litigation, 99 Harv. L. Rev. 1458, (1986).* The logic behind these concepts dictates that settlement terms must be based upon, and roughly correlated with, some acceptable measure of comparative fault, ...

Even accepting substantive fairness as linked to comparative fault, an important issue still remains as to how comparative fault is to be measured. There is no universally correct approach. It appears very clear to us that what constitutes the best measure of comparative fault at a particular Superfund site under particular factual circumstances should be left largely to the EPA's expertise. Whatever formula or scheme EPA advances for measuring comparative fault and allocating liability should be upheld so long as the agency supplies a plausible explanation for it, ... Put in slightly different terms, the chosen measure of comparative fault should be upheld unless it is arbitrary, capricious, and devoid of a rational basis.

. . . [T]he agency must also be accorded flexibility to diverge from an apportionment formula in order to address special factors not conducive to regimented treatment. While the list of possible variables is virtually limitless, two frequently encountered reasons warranting departure from strict formulaic comparability are the uncertainty of future events and the timing of particular settlement decisions. Common sense suggests that a PRP's assumption of

open-ended risks may merit a discount on comparative fault, while obtaining a complete release from uncertain future liability may call for a premium. By the same token, the need to encourage (and suitably reward) early, cost-effective settlements, and to account . . . for anticipated savings in transaction costs . . . can affect the construct. Because we are confident that Congress intended EPA to have considerable flexibility in negotiating and structuring settlements, we think reviewing courts should permit the agency to depart from rigid adherence to formulae wherever the agency proffers a reasonable good-faith justification for departure.

We also believe that a district court should give the EPA's expertise the benefit of the doubt when weighing substantive fairness. . . .

In this instance, we agree with the court below that the consent decrees pass muster from a standpoint of substantive fairness. They adhere generally to principles of comparative fault according to a volumetric standard, determining the liability of each PRP according to volumetric contribution. And, to the extent they deviate from this formulaic approach, they do so on the basis of adequate justification. . . .

The argument that the EPA should have used relative toxicity as a determinant of proportionate liability for response costs, instead of a strictly volumetric ranking, is a stalking horse. Having selected a reasonable method of weighing comparative fault, the agency need not show that it is the best, or even the fairest, of all conceivable methods. The choice of the yardstick to be used for allocating liability must be left primarily to the expert discretion of the EPA, particularly when the PRPs involved are numerous and the situation is complex. We cannot reverse the court below for refusing to second-guess the agency on this score.

* * *

The last point which merits discussion . . . involves the fact that the agency upped the ante as the game continued, that is, the premium assessed as part of the administrative settlement was increased substantially for purposes of the later DMC decree. Like the district court, we see no unfairness in this approach. For one thing, litigation is expensive—and having called the tune by their refusal to subscribe to the administrative settlement, we think it not unfair that appellants, thereafter, would have to pay the piper. For another thing, rewarding PRPs who settle sooner rather than later is completely consonant with CERCLA's makeup.

* * *

1. *De Minimis Settlements.* In the SARA Amendments, Congress gave the EPA authority to settle with a de minimis PRP so long as (i) the agreement involved only a "minor portion" of the total response costs, and (ii) the toxicity and amount of substances contributed by the PRP were "minimal in comparison to the other hazardous substances at the facility." . . . The two determinative criteria are not further defined. Appellants, for a variety of reasons, question the boundaries fixed for the DMC class in this instance, ...

. . . We believe that Congress intended quite the opposite; the EPA was to have substantial discretion to interpret the statutory terms in light of both its expertise and its negotiating strategy in a given case. . . .

2. *Disproportionate Liability.* In the SARA Amendments, Congress explicitly created a statutory framework that left nonsettlors at risk of bearing a disproportionate amount of liability. The statute immunizes settling parties from liability for contribution and provides that only the amount of the settlement—not the pro rata share attributable to the settling party—shall be subtracted from the liability of the nonsettlors. This can prove to be a substantial benefit to settling PRPs—and a corresponding detriment to their more recalcitrant counterparts.

Although such immunity creates a palpable risk of disproportionate liability, that is not to say that the device is forbidden. . . . Disproportionate liability, a technique which promotes early settlements and deters litigation for litigation's sake, is an integral part of the statutory plan.

* * *

. . . When CERCLA was amended by SARA in 1986, Congress created an express right of contribution among parties found liable for response costs. . . . Congress specifically provided that contribution actions could not be maintained against settlors. . . . This provision was designed to encourage settlements and provide

PRPs a measure of finality in return for their willingness to settle. . . . Congress plainly intended non-settlors to have no contribution rights against settlors regarding matters addressed in settlement. thus, the cross-claims were properly dismissed; . . . .

The statute, of course, not only bars contribution claims against settling parties, but also provides that, while a settlement will not discharge other PRPs, "it reduces the potential liability of the others by the amount of settlement." . . . The law's plain language admits of no construction other than a dollar-for-dollar reduction of the aggregate liability. . . .

3. *Indemnity.* On a similar note, appellants bemoan the dismissal of their cross-claims for indemnity against the settling PRPs. We are unmoved. Although CERCLA is silent regarding indemnification, we refuse to read into the statute a right to indemnification and that would eviscerte § 9613(f)(2) and allow nonsettlors to make an end run around the statutory scheme.

* * *

4. *Notice.* The appellants also contend that the government's negotiating strategy must be an open book. We disagree. . . . In the CERCLA context, the government is under no obligation to telegraph its settlement offers, divulge its negotiating strategy in advance, or surrender the normal prerogatives of strategic flexibility which any negotiator cherishes. in short, . . . the EPA need not tell de minimis PRPs in advance whether they will, or will not, be eligible to join ensuing major party settlements.

5. *Exclusions from Settlements.* The CERCLA statutes do not require the agency to open all settlement offers to all PRPs; and we refuse to insert such a requirement into the law by judicial fiat. Under the SARA Amendments, the right . . . to structure the order and pace of settlement negotiations to suit, is an agency prerogative. . . . So long as it operates in good faith, the EPA is at liberty to negotiate and settle with whomever it chooses.

6. *Crown.* Appellant Crown raises an argument unique to it. . . . In 1986 and thereafter Crown failed to comply with EPA's requests for information and documents concerning the amount and nature of the waste it had sent to the Sites. . . .

Crown argues that it was unfairly subjected to a double penalty because withholding the information resulted both in its exclusion from the settlements and in the imposition of bad-faith penalties. We see nothing amiss. . . . Conditioning settlement eligibility on a PRP's compliance with an outstanding information request was a perfectly reasonable approach, especially since the data Crown refused to supply was the data necessary to verify the nature and amount of the wastes sent to the Sites, and thus provide a foundation for settlement.

* * *

Affirmed.

B. F. GOODRICH CO. v. MURTHA

958 F.2d 1192 (2nd Cir. 1992)

[Following successful actions by EPA and the State of Connecticut against B. F. Goodrich, Uniroyal, and other corporations for cleanup of two landfills designated as Superfund sites on the National Priorities List, B. F. Goodrich and the other corporations instituted a suit against Murtha and other owners and operators of the landfills. Murtha and the other landfill owners and operators, in turn, joined as additional defendants some 200 other parties (including 23 Connecticut cities and towns) that had also arranged for waste disposal and treatment at the landfills, claiming that they also were liable under CERCLA for cost contributions toward the landfill cleanups. The cleanup costs were estimated to approximate $47.9 million. The municipalities' claim that they were not liable for cleanup costs was rejected under the following opinion.]

* * *

Cardamone, Circuit Judge:

This appeal deals with the disposal of municipal solid waste that contains hazardous substances and as such is one piece of the national environmental problem. . . .

. . . [O]n this appeal we must carefully analyze the Comprehensive Environmental Response, Compensation, and Liability Act of 1980 (CERCLA or Act), . . . as amended by the Superfund Amendments and Reauthorization Act of 1986 (Superfund Amendments), . . . and while remaining aware of the interaction of CERCLA with other federal environmental statutes—in this case primarily the Resource Conservation and Recovery Act (Resource and Recovery Act or RCRA), . . . —determine what CERCLA defines as hazardous substances, and whether CERCLA imposes liability on a municipality which arranges for the disposal or treatment of municipal solid waste that contains primarily household waste.

At the center of this litigation lie the Beacon Heights and Laurel Park landfills, . . . designated as Superfund sites on a National Priority List by the Evironmental Protection Agency (EPA). . . .

* * *

The focus of our inquiry is the question of municipal liability under CERCLA for arranging for the disposal or treatment of municipal solid waste. . . . Appellants do not seriously dispute . . . that plaintiffs raised a genuine issue, . . . as to the existence of CERCLA-defined hazardous substances in the municipalities' solid waste. . . . Rather the municipal defendants argue that CERCLA provides plaintiffs no grounds for relief . . . .

At the center of our discussion is the subject of municipal solid waste which, while possibly containing material from commercial and industrial sources, is primarily composed of household waste. . . . Despite the tremendous volume of household waste, surveys generally reveal that it contains very low concentrations—less than 1 percent by weight—of substances the EPA considers hazardous . . . . Yet, even though household waste has a low concentration of hazardous substances, . . . the costs of cleanup at municipal landfills may be greater . . . due to household waste's greater volume . . . .

. . . The EPA is authorized to commence "response actions" to abate any actual or threatened releases of hazardous substances, § 9604(a)(1), and a federal Superfund exists to pay for mandated cleanups. Response actions include remedial efforts to prevent or minimize releases as well as attempts to remove hazardous substances entirely. . . .

* * *

Responsible Party

. . . [I]t is clear that a municipality may be liable as a potentially responsible party if it arranges for the disposal of hazardous substances. CERCLA expressly includes municipalities, states, and other political subdivisions within its definition of persons who can incur such liability . . . . Where, as an "owner or operator," a municipality acquires ownership or control of a facility involuntarily as a result of its sovereign function, . . . or where a municipality acts in response to an emergency caused by the release of hazardous substances from a facility owned by another party and does not act with gross negligence or willful misconduct, . . . no liability attaches. These express exceptions to liability are strong evidence that municipalities are otherwise subject to CERCLA liability.

* * *

CERCLA defines as hazardous any substance so designated by the EPA pursuant to § 9602 or by any of four other environmental statutes. . . .

* * *

Similarly, the definition makes no distinction dependent upon whether the substance's source was industrial, commercial, municipal or household. Whether the substance is a consumer product, a manufacturing byproduct, or an element of a waste stream is irrelevant. Quantity or concentration is not a factor either; when Congress wanted to draw distinctions based on concentration or quantity, it expressly provided as much. . . .Thus, the concentration of hazardous substances in municipal solid waste—regardless of how low a percentage—is not relevant in deciding whether CERCLA liability is incurred.

Against this backdrop, the municipalities nonetheless contend that CERCLA's silence regarding municipal solid waste is evidence that Congress aimed to have it excluded from the

definition of hazardous substances. Alternatively, the municipalities argue that Congress intended an exemption for household hazardous waste found in the Resource and Recovery Act regulations to be incorporated, . . . thus excluding municipal solid waste from the definition of hazardous substances under CERCLA.

We disagree with both contentions. The Act's silence on the subject of municipal solid waste is not evidence that such should be excluded from the definition of hazardous substances. . . . Municipal waste need not be listed by name—instead of its constituent components—to fall within the Act. . . . When a mixture or waste solution contains hazardous substances, that mixture is itself hazardous for purposes of determining CERCLA liability. . . . Liability under CERCLA depends only on the presence in any form of listed hazardous substances. Hence, if a municipality arranges for the disposal or treatment of waste containing substances listed as hazardous in any of the four identified environmental statutes or in Table 302.4, it may be held liable for contribution or response costs under the Act if a subsequent release or threatened release requires cleanup efforts.

The municipalities strenuously insist further that the exemption for household hazardous waste—promulgated by EPA and subsequently confirmed in part by Congress—from certain regulatory requirements under the Resource and Recovery Act extends, through incorporation by reference, to the definition of hazardous substance under CERCLA. This latter argument, . . . is not persuasive. The Resource and Recovery Act is designed primarily to regulate on-going treatment, storage, and disposal of solid and hazardous wastes. . . . Pursuant to RCRA, EPA promulgated two distinct regulatory systems . . . one for *solid* wastes . . . and the other for *hazardous* wastes . . . .

"In regulations identifying and listing hazardous wastes subject to the RCRA Subtitle C regulations, EPA excluded for regulatory purposes certain solid wastes from the definition of hazardous wastes, *even though these wastes might otherwise be considered hazardous wastes.*" . . . The EPA included household wastes, . . .

among those wastes excluded from the Resource and Recovery Act's Subpart C hazardous waste regulations. . . .

The household waste exclusion was promulgated pursuant to a Congressional scheme that such waste not be subjected to the same stringent standards during the day-to-day management of transportation, storage and disposal. . . . This narrow RCRA exemption in no way limits the definition of hazardous substance under CERCLA. . . . To construe this exemption to apply also to CERCLA would frustrate that Act's broad remedial purposes . . . .

Congress and the EPA have carefully distinguished between *wastes,* to which the Resource and Recovery Act applies, and *substances,* to which CERCLA applies. . . . This statutory and regulatory distinction is a substantial one and should be preserved, absent a clear legislative intent to the contrary.

In addition, application of the Resource and Recovery Act's regulations turns in part upon threshold quantity or concentration requirements—considerations which are irrelevant in defining hazardous substances under CERCLA. . . .

Nor does including wastes that are not subject to . . . regulations under the Resource and Recovery Act within the definition of hazardous substances under CERCLA create a conflict between the two statutes. . . . RCRA is preventative; CERCLA is curative. . . .

Other courts have concluded that exemptions from Resource and Recovery Act coverage do not extend so far as to exclude those materials from the definition of hazardous substances under CERCLA. . . .

* * *

Although municipalities do not benefit in a proprietary sense from arranging for the disposal of municipal solid waste, their taxpayers do obtain a benefit—given the necessity of disposal of such waste. Thus, our refusal to exempt such waste from the definition of hazardous substance under CERCLA cannot be said to create an irrational and clearly unintended result. . . .

D. EPA INTERPRETATION

The municipalities next argue that the EPA interprets CERCLA to impose no liability on municipalities. . . . The EPA, they state, has created in a policy notice a "rebuttable presumption that generation and transportation of municipal solid waste and domestic sewage sludge would not be deemed to incur CERCLA liability." We concede that a court should defer to EPA's reasonable construction of CERCLA, ...

We do not dispute appellants' characterization of how EPA's interpretation should be treated. Rather, we disagree with appellants' characterization of EPA's interpretation itself. Here, in fact, the EPA interprets CERCLA to *impose* liability on municipalities arranging for the disposal of municipal waste at sites that release or threaten the release of hazardous substances. . . .

. . . The [CERCLA] statute does not forbid the EPA from selectively prosecuting only the major contributors to a hazardous response site. In exercising its enforcement discretion the agency routinely prosecutes only the largest contributors, or those with the greatest means to pay for the cleanup response costs, and leaves those defendants to seek, through third-party actions, contribution from any other liable polluters. The Interim Municipal Settlement Policy merely indicates that the EPA presently does not intend to pursue enforcement actions against municipalities generating or transporting municipal waste—regardless of whether hazardous substances are present—unless the total privately generated commercial hazardous substances are insignificant compared to the municipal waste. . . .

. . . The Interim Municipal Settlement policy expressly warns, "[n]othing in the interim policy affects any party's potential legal liability under CERCLA . . . [N]othing in the interim policy precludes a *third party from initiating a contribution action.*" . . . In a similar vein, the notice states that CERCLA "does not provide an exemption from liability for municipalities . . . [T]he statute does not provide an exemption from liability for municipal wastes." . . .

Other EPA pronouncements point out its unambiguous position and provide strong support for the argument that it does not believe Congress planned for municipal waste to be exempt from CERCLA. . . . We conclude consequently that the EPA emphatically construes CERCLA to impose liability on municipalities disposing of household waste that contains hazardous substances.

. . . We are aware that holding the municipal defendants as responsible parties and including municipal solid waste within the definition of hazardous substances will have far reaching implications for municipalities and their tax-payers. But burdensome consequences are not sufficient grounds to judicially graft an exemption onto a statute, ...

Appellant municipalities are not without recourse to avoid inequitable and disproportionate burdens that may arise from their liability as third-party contributors. Courts have the authority to ''allocate response costs among liable parties using such equitable factors as the court determines are appropriate.'' § 9613(f)(1). An array of equitable factors may be considered in this allocation process, including the relative volume and toxicity of the substances . . . the relative cleanup costs incurred as a result of these wastes, the degree of care exercised by each party with respect to the hazardous substances, and the financial resources of the parties involved. Consequently, the amount of liability imposed will not necessarily be a function solely of the total volume of municipal waste disposed of in the landfills, but rather will be a function of the extent to which [a party's] dumping of hazardous substances both engendered the necessity, and contributed to the costs, of cleanup.

. . . The municipal defendants are not entitled to summary judgment . . . .

The "Innocent Landowner" Defense

Of the few exceptions from liability allowed by CERCLA, the principal one is granted to an ''innocent landowner,'' which CERCLA defines as a party that can prove it was justifiably unaware that hazardous substances had been disposed of on its property when it acquired title or possession to the property. The innocent-landowner defense arose out of concerns that individuals—particularly residential property owners—who had no connection with the disposal of hazardous substances were being unfairly held accountable for cleaning them up. In order to understand the genesis of the innocent-landowner defense, it is helpful to recall the reasons CERCLA's legislative drafters imposed strict liability.

Contrary to common criticisms of CERCLA, its legislative history leaves no doubt that CERCLA's strict liability principles were not unprecedented. Rather, the scheme grew out of a common law doctrine that holds those who engage in ultrahazardous activities strictly liable for any harms that result. The common law viewed strict liability as fair because the harms resulting from ultrahazardous activity, such as the use of dynamite, could never be eliminated, even by the exercise of caution and due diligence. Rather, such harms are presumptively foreseeable. Since there is no way for a cautious party to avoid the risk of the inevitable harms resulting from its ultrahazardous activity, fairness requires that other parties, who derive no benefit from the activity, should not have to bear the risks associated with it. Thus, the common law deemed it fairer to impose the risk of loss upon parties that choose to engage in the ultrahazardous activity by making them liable for resulting harms regardless of their negligence or fault.

The drafters of CERCLA likewise intended that strict liability should attach to classes of persons who engage in or benefit from generating or disposing of hazardous substances. For instance, property owners who charged fees for dumping on their properties may fairly be deemed to have engaged in and benefited from dumping activities, as may the manufacturers of the hazardous substances. However, early experience showed that many property owners had no connection with and no reason to know of hazardous substances existing on their property.

Holding those owners liable did not serve CERCLA's goal of spreading cleanup costs among those who benefited from the creation of hazardous substances. Nor did it matter that EPA generally refrained from bringing suit against so-called innocent landowners, because other liable parties could still sue the owners for contribution. The "innocent landowner" defense was thus designed to remedy the inherent unfairness in imposing owner or operator liability upon a person who had not benefited from the hazardous-substance activities and had had no reasonable way to foresee or avoid the liability.

The "innocent landowner" exception to liability results from imposing the narrow definition of *contractual relationship*, found in section 101(35), in the context of the third-party defense, found in section 107(b)(3). The innocent-landowner defense is one kind of third-party defense available to one who can prove that the release of a hazardous substance and the resulting damage were caused *solely* by a third party who was not in a "contractual relationship" with the party asserting the defense. The party asserting this third-party defense must show lack of negligence or fault. Without the special definition of *contractual relationship*, however, purchasers of contaminated property would never be able to qualify for the third-party defense, because contracts, deeds, and other legal instruments transferring title or possession to land are considered "contractual relationships."

To provide an escape for these "innocent landowners," Congress amended CERCLA to exclude from the definition of *contractual relationship* certain land transfers occurring under circumstances where the purchaser either had no reason to know of the contamination or had acquired the property involuntarily. The "innocent landowner" defense excludes from liability these groups:

1. purchasers who, at the time of property acquisition, did not know and had no reason to know that hazardous substances were disposed of on the property;[22]
2. governmental agencies that acquired the property by an involuntary transfer, such as for failure to pay taxes or through the exercise of eminent domain by purchase or condemnation;[23] and
3. those who acquired the property by inheritance or bequest.[24]

To establish that it had no reason to know of the presence of hazardous substances, a defendant must demonstrate that it made "appropriate inquiry" into the previous use and ownership of the property in question. "Appropriate inquiry" is a level of inquiry consistent with good commercial or customary practice undertaken in an effort to minimize liability. Factors that are considered include:

- whether the purchaser possessed any specialized knowledge or expertise,
- whether the purchase price was so low as to indicate that the purchaser knew about or should have investigated possible contamination,
- the existence of commonly known or reasonably ascertainable information about the property, and
- the obviousness or likelihood of contamination on a property of its kind.

The innocent landowner defense requires the court to take a close look at the particular circumstances in each case and to ascertain whether those circumstances are consistent with the parameters of the defense as set out in CERCLA sections 107(b)(3) and 101(35). In this area, there are few hard and fast rules; the success or failure of the innocent-landowner defense generally turns on the particular facts of each case. It is safe to say, however, that home buyers are more likely to prevail than are institutional purchasers, because businesspersons are presumed to have greater real estate expertise and more resources for conducting investigations into prior uses.

Lender Liability

This subsection investigates the liability of a lender who maintains title to a property in order to secure repayment of monies by the purchaser or owner of the property. For example, a bank that lends money to someone purchasing real property usually holds a mortgage on the property to assure that it will be repaid for the loan. The property "secures" the mortgage loan, and the lender's interest in the property is termed a *security interest*. If the mortgage is not paid, the lender has the right to take title to the property (by a procedure known as a *mortgage foreclosure*) and to sell the property in an effort to recoup the amount of the loan.

In some cases the mortgage holder has *legal title* to the property for the duration of the loan; the person who has borrowed the money still has a legal interest in the property. To complicate matters further, a bank or other secured creditor who forecloses on a commercial property may for a time manage the affairs of the business in order to protect its security interest. If the secured property is contaminated or if hazardous substances at the business facility must be disposed of, the secured creditor may become entangled in the management of hazardous substances.

CERCLA explicitly excludes from the definition of *owner* an entity that, without participating in the management of a facility, holds "indicia" (indications) of ownership primarily for protecting a security interest in the facility. This means that a bank that holds legal title to a property that is managed by the equitable owner will normally not be liable for cleaning up contaminated property. Difficulties arise when a secured creditor seeks to foreclose on a property for the borrower's failure to repay a loan or when a secured creditor overtakes day-to-day management of a business that has defaulted on a loan in order to protect its security interest.

If a lender that has foreclosed on contaminated property loses its security-holder exemption from liability, its only other potential defense is the innocent-landowner defense. That defense is seldom available to commercial lenders, however, because an "appropriate inquiry" into a property's condition will usually turn up evidence of existing contamination. It is also questionable whether the second prong of the innocent-landowner defense, involuntary acquisition by a government entity, would be available to governmental agencies (such as the Resolution Trust Corporation) that foreclose on properties in securing repayment of monies owed to banks.

In the leading case on lender liability, *Fleet Factors*, the court framed the issue:

> The critical issue is whether . . . [the secured creditor] participated in management *sufficiently* to incur liability under the statute.[25]

The *Fleet Factors* court held that a secured creditor may be liable as an owner, even though it was not an actual operator, by participating in the financial management of a facility to a degree indicating that it had the capacity to influence the facility's treatment of hazardous substances.

Like the innocent-landowner exception, this standard involves a highly fact-sensitive inquiry. The difficult question facing lenders after *Fleet Factors* is what degree of involvement the courts will deem sufficient to eliminate the secured creditor's CERCLA exemption. Under the *Fleet Factors* decision, merely auditing a borrower's accounts without controlling them or providing financial advice to a waste handler would not be sufficient to affect a lender's CERCLA exemption. Foreclosing on a contaminated property so as to protect the lender's security interest, however, may in some circumstances render the lender liable for its cleanup.[26] As the Ninth Circuit Court of Appeals later noted, the question is not whether the secured creditor reserves a right to intervene in the borrower's business, but whether the lender actually exercises a degree of managerial control that destroys the exemption.[27]

In response to complaints that the "fear of the unknown" (concerning the potential extent of lender liability) was choking off business loans, some Congresspersons proposed legislation to broaden the lender exemption from CERCLA liability. Other members of Congress, however, were divided on the propriety of these proposals. Since lenders derive economic benefit from loans they extend to CERCLA polluters, opponents of limiting lender liability have argued that holding lenders liable for participating in hazardous-waste management is consistent with CERCLA's goal of spreading cleanup costs among those who benefit from hazardous-substance activities. In addition, the prospect that lenders might have to surrender their interests in contaminated property in order to avoid CERCLA response costs could force lenders to investigate proposed security property before extending loans. This would further CERCLA's public policy goals.

In an effort to clarify the scope of lender liability, EPA issued a liability rule in final form on April 29, 1992, noting in the foreword to the rule:

> Uncertainty in this area has assumed particular importance because of the current difficulties faced by the lending industry [referring to the savings and loan crisis], and particularly by the Federal Deposit Insurance Corporation ("FDIC") and the Resolution Trust Corporation ("RTC"), both of which act as conservators and receivers of failing or failed insured depository institutions under the Federal Deposit Insurance Act . . . as amended, ... Consequently, these government entities are likely to own, possess, or have security interests in potentially contaminated properties transferred to them as a result of their appointment as the conservator or receiver of failed and insolvent lending institutions. . . . The government takeover of assets formerly held by private entities in this manner has raised pressing questions regarding the potential that these government entities may incur CERCLA liability as an owner or operator . . . and the availability of the "innocent landowner" defense . . . .[28]

EPA issued its final rule on lender liability as a revision of the National Contingency Plan (NCP). The rule specified the range of activities in which lenders could engage without risking CERCLA liability. It also specified which conservators and receivers would be considered "involuntary" owners. In the rule, EPA employed the following general test:

> . . . [A] holder would not be considered to be participating in management [so as to be liable under CERCLA] unless, while the borrower was still in possession, the [security] holder either (1) was exercising decisionmaking control over the borrower's environmental compliance, such that the holder had undertaken responsibility for the borrower's waste disposal or hazardous substance handling practices which resulted in a release or threatened release, or (2) was exercising control at a management level encompassing the borrower's environmental compliance responsibilities, comparable to that of a manager of the borrower's enterprise by establishing, implementing, or maintaining the policies and procedures encompassing the day to day environmental compliance decisionmaking of the enterprise.

The rule clarified that a lender (security holder) may conduct environmental compliance inspections to ensure that loans are not being secured by contaminated property and may foreclose on the security (property or assets) in order to wind up operations and liquidate (sell off) assets. Under the rule, a lender could continue operating a foreclosed enterprise without incurring CERCLA liability if it were taking reasonable actions to divest itself of the property promptly.

In early 1994, however, the District of Columbia Court of Appeals invalidated EPA's lender-liability rule in *Kelley and State of Michigan v. EPA,* an abridged version of which appears here. The court found that EPA's rule went far beyond an interpretative regulation, defining liability in a manner not authorized by Congress.

■   **KELLEY AND STATE OF MICHIGAN V. ENVIRONMENTAL**   ■
PROTECTION AGENCY

15 F.3d 1100 (D.C. Cir. 1994)

Opinion: Silberman, Circuit Judge: Petitioners challenge an EPA regulation limiting lender liability under CERCLA. We hold that EPA lacks statutory authority to restrict by regulation private rights of action arising under the statute . . . .

* * *

CERCLA also authorizes private parties and EPA to bring civil actions independently to recover their costs associated with the cleanup of hazardous wastes from those responsible for the contamination. . . . Section 107 of CERCLA generally imposes strict liability on, among others, all prior and present "owners and operators" of hazardous waste sites. . . . Congress created a safe harbor provision for secured creditors, however, in the definition of "owner or operator," providing that "such term does not include a person, who, without participating in the management of a vessel or facility, holds indicia of ownership primarily to protect his security interest in the vessel or facility." . . .

Conflicting judicial interpretations as to the scope of this secured creditor exemption opened the possibility that lenders would be held liable for the cost of cleaning up contaminated property that they hold merely as collateral. Lenders lacked clear guidance as to the extent to which they could involve themselves in the affairs of a facility without incurring liability and also as to whether they would for-

feit the exemption by exercising their right of foreclosure, which could be thought to convert their "indicia of ownership"—the security interest—into actual ownership. . . . In *United States v. Fleet Factors Corp.,* 901 F.2d 1550 (11th Cir. 1990) . . . the court, although adhering to the settled view that Congress intended to protect the commercial practices of secured creditors "in their normal course of business," . . . nevertheless stated that "a secured creditor will be liable if its involvement with the management of the facility is sufficiently broad to support the inference that it could affect hazardous waste disposal decisions if it so chose." . . .

This language, portending as it did an expansion in the scope of secured creditor liability, caused considerable discomfort in financial circles. Intervenor American Bankers Association points to survey data indicating that lenders curtailed loans made to certain classes of borrowers or secured by some types of properties in order to avoid the virtually unlimited liability risk associated with collateral property that may be contaminated. Some lenders, we are told, even chose to abandon collateral properties rather than foreclosing on them for fear of post-foreclosure liability.

EPA, responding to the understandable clamor from the banking community and in light of the federal government's increasing role as a secured creditor after taking over failed savings and loans, instituted a rulemaking proceeding, . . . to define the secured creditor exemption when legislative efforts to amend CERCLA failed. . . . In April 1992, EPA issued the final regulation, which employs a framework of specific tests to provide clearer articulation of a lender's scope of liability under CERCLA. The rule provides an overall standard for judging when a lender's "participation in management" causes the lender to forfeit its exemption. . . . A lender may, without incurring liability, undertake investigatory actions before the creation of a security interest, monitor or inspect the facility, and require that the borrower comply with all environmental standards. . . . When a loan nears default, the rule permits the lender to engage in work-out negotiations and activities, including ensuring that the collateral facility does not violate environmental laws. . . . The rule also protects a secured creditor that acquires full title to the collateral property through foreclosure, as long as the creditor did not participate in the facility's managment prior to foreclosure and undertakes certain diligent efforts to divest itself of the property. . . . Lenders still face liability under section 107(a)(3) and (4)—as opposed to liability as an "owner and operator" under section 107(a)(1) and (2)—if they arrange for the disposal of hazardous substances at a facility or accept hazardous waste for transportation and disposal. . . .

In response to comments . . . EPA stated that the regulation . . . "defines the liability of holders [of security interests] for CERCLA response costs in both the United States' and private party litigation." . . . The agency alternatively asserted that even if the rule were read as "a 'mere' interpretation of section 101(20)(A)," it would affect third-party litigation since "EPA guidance and interpretations of laws administered by the Agency are given substantial deference by the courts." . . .

. . . Petitioners are interested in the EPA rule because, as potential litigants under section 107, they do not want to be foreclosed from suing lenders. Petitioners argue that EPA lacks statutory authority to define, through its regulation, the scope of lender liability under section 107—an issue that they assert only federal courts may adjudicate. They also urge that the

substance of the regulation contradicts the plain meaning of certain statutory language.

II.

Although petitioners bring a general challenge to the authority of EPA to promulgate any substantive regulations under CERCLA, that issue is settled. We held in *Wagner Seed Co., Inc. v. Bush* . . . that the President had broadly delegated his statutory powers to EPA . . . However, we had previously recognized that with respect to any specific regulation, EPA must demonstrate "either explicit or implicit evidence of congressional intent to delegate interpretive authority." . . . EPA, for its part, contends that Wagner Seed went further and recognized EPA's general authority under section 115 of CERCLA to promulgate rules that a typical administrative agency would issue, rules that are "reasonably related to the purposes of the enabling legislation." . . .

The government overreads Wagner Seed. . . . We emphasized, however, that the language EPA interpreted did not bear directly on liability issues and, indeed, suggested that since Congress provided for de novo judicial review of the agency's "particularized decision respecting liability," deference as to those issues would be inappropriate. . . . Here we encounter an issue not squarely decided in Wagner Seed—whether the EPA can, by regulation, define and limit a party's liability under section 107. . . .

EPA looks to several different portions of CERCLA to find the specific authority we have required. The agency points to section 105 of CERCLA, which provides that the agency has responsibility to promulgate the national contingency plan . . . . It is argued that the broad language of section 105, authorizing EPA "to reflect and effectuate the responsibilities and powers created by this chapter," . . . gives it power to define section 107 liability . . . Although the mandate of section 105 does "provide the EPA with broad rulemaking authority to craft the NCP," it is hardly a specific delegation of authority to EPA to interpret section 107. We must still determine whether defining the scope of liability is among the "responsibilities and powers" Congress delegated to EPA under CERCLA.

EPA points to specific provisions of that section, paragraphs 105(a)(4) and 105(a)(3). The former authorizes the agency to prescribe "appropriate roles and responsibilities . . . of nongovernmental entities in effectuating the plan." . . . EPA claims that the lender liability rule accomplishes just that by defining the "role" of security creditors. That is an imaginative use of the word role, but . . . section 105 refers to the nature of actions parties must take in response to contamination—not their ultimate liability for the contamination set forth in section 107. If EPA's position were correct, Congress would have had no need to provide for a party's liability in section 107; EPA would have been authorized to develop those standards under section 105. For similar reasons, paragraph 105(a)(3) does not help EPA. That provision obliges the agency to issue "methods and criteria for determining the appropriate extent of removal, remedy, and other measures authorized by [CERCLA]," but it does not speak to liability. . . .

EPA also relies on those statutory provisions which grant it authority to seek enforcement. The agency may choose to contract to clean up a contaminated site (financed through the Superfund), and then bring action in federal court under section 107(a)(4)(A) to recover its costs from a liable party. It is argued that the agency must first decide whether a party is actually liable before bringing such an action. That is no different, however, than any government "prosecutor" who must in good faith determine for itself whether a civil action in federal court should be brought— . . . The court is, nevertheless, the first body to formally determine liability, and therefore a civil prosecutor typically lacks authority to issue substantive regulations to interpret a statute establishing liability. . . .

To be sure, the agency also has authority, when imminent danger of harm exists, to issue administrative orders under section 106(a) requiring private parties to clean up a site. . . . But, under the statute, a respondent must comply with such orders whether or not it is liable. Liability issues are resolved when the party

against whom the order was levied seeks reimbursement under section 106(b)(2). The statutory scheme might be described as requiring parties to shoot first (clean up) and ask questions (determine who bears the ultimate liability) later.

That brings us to EPA's strongest argument—that its role in implementing the reimbursement provisions of section 106(b)(2) implies authority to define liability. Under that section, a party that has cleaned up a contaminated site pursuant to an administrative order may petition the EPA for reimbursement of its reasonable costs. . . . By implication, EPA argues that it must decide these liability questions when it determines whether or not to reimburse.

A careful reading of that provision, and the entire subsection 106(b), leads us to a contrary view. Although a party must first petition EPA for reimbursement under subparagraph 106(b)(2)(A), that provision is completely silent as to what criteria EPA uses to grant reimbursement. If EPA denies reimbursement because the agency contends the party is liable, the party has a right to bring an action in federal court under subparagraph 106(b)(2)(B); if the party establishes that it is not liable by a preponderance of the evidence, . . . it prevails. EPA is, under that scenario, only a defendant; its preliminary conclusion that the party was liable is entitled to no consideration, let alone the deference afforded to the typical administrative agency adjudication. On the other hand, a petitioner who is liable may nevertheless seek review . . . to challenge the reasonableness of EPA's ordered response. In such a case, the party, "a petitioner," must establish that EPA's order was arbitrary and capricious or not in accordance with law, . . .

The drafters of subsection 106(b) appear to us to have quite consciously distinguished between EPA's role in determining the appropriate cleanup action (which is entitled to deference) from the agency's position on liability when a party disputes claims. Liability issues are to be decided by the court. . . .

That reading of section 106(b)(2) conforms with the provisions of CERCLA that provide for a private right of action in federal court by property owners or states to recover cleanup costs, . . . from those liable for the contamination. Questions of liability, accordingly, can be put at issue in federal court by disputing private parties—without any government involvement. Under these circumstances, it cannot be argued that Congress intended EPA, one of many potential plaintiffs, to have authority to, by regulation, define liability for a class of potential defendants. . . . Congress, by providing for private rights of action under section 107, has designated the courts and not EPA as the adjudicator of the scope of CERCLA liability. . . .

* * *

There remains the question of whether the regulation can be sustained as an interpretative rule. The preamble to the final regulation suggests that EPA attempted to straddle two horses—issuing the rule as a legislative regulation but asserting in the alternative that as an interpretative rule, it would still be entitled to judicial deference and therefore affect private party litigation. . . . Although we have admitted that the distinction between legislative and interpretative rules is "enshrouded in considerable smog," . . . it is commonly understood that a rule is legislative if it is "based on an agency's power to exercise its judgment as to how best to implement a general statutory mandate, ... and has the binding force of law. . . . By contrast, an intrepretative rule "is based on specific statutory provisions," . . .

The rule bears little resemblance to what we have traditionally found to be an interpretative regulation. EPA does not really define specific statutory terms, but rather takes off from those terms and devises a comprehensive regulatory regimen to address the liability problems facing secured creditors. This extensive quasilegislative effort . . . does not strike us as merely a construction of statutory phrases, ...

In any event, the same reason that prevents the agency from issuing the rule as a substantive regulation precludes judicial deference to EPA's offered "interpretation." If . . . Congress meant the judiciary, not EPA, to determine liability issues—and we believe Congress did—EPA's view of statutory liability may not be given deference. . . . Moreover, even if an agency enjoys authority to determine such a legal issue administratively, deference is withheld if a private party can bring the issue independently to federal court under a private right of action. . . . Petitioners are such private parties; they wish to preserve the right to sue lenders when, in petitioners' view, a lender's behavior transgresses the statutory test—whether or not EPA would regard the lender as liable. As we read the statute, Congress intended that petitioners' claim in such an event should be evaluated by the federal courts independent of EPA's institutional view.

Petitioners conceded that the regulation could be sustained as a policy statement that would guide EPA's enforcement proceedings across the country, but EPA has not asked that its regulation be so regarded. . . .

We well recognize the difficulties that lenders face in the absence of the clarity EPA's regulation would have provided. Before turning to this rulemaking, EPA sought congressional relief and was rebuffed. We see no alternative but that EPA try again. The petition for review is granted and the regulation is hereby vacated.

7.3   Appraisal of CERCLA's Regulatory Scheme

The Relationship betweeen CERCLA and RCRA

The Resource Conservation and Recovery Act (RCRA), discussed in Chapter 6, is designed to *prevent* the injuries of hazardous-waste pollution by regulating the ongoing activities of generators, transporters, and owners and operators of facilities that dispose of those wastes. In contrast, CERCLA aims not to regulate waste management as such, but to *rectify* the resultant conditions of past mismanagement of hazardous-substance disposal. It is more concerned with remediating hazardous releases and applies to closed or abandoned dumps as well as to actively managed dump sites. CERCLA aims primarily to regulate and enforce the cleanup and post-cleanup monitoring of hazardous dump sites. Although some of its liability provisions have the incidental, though significant, effect of deterring improper waste-management practices, its principal thrust is to repair and contain conditions that have already been created. CERCLA complements RCRA by addressing problems RCRA does not reach and by affording enforcement sanctions RCRA does not provide.

Certain sites may be subject to enforcement under both CERCLA and RCRA. In the *U.S. v. Colorado* case, extracted here, a federal facility that was the subject of an ongoing CERCLA cleanup was also the target of RCRA enforcement activities by state authorities under a state-authorized program.

U.S. v. State of Colorado

990 F.2d 1565 (10th Cir. 1993)

Baldock, Circuit Judge.

This case examines the relationship between the Resource Conservation and Recovery Act of 1976 ("RCRA"), . . . as amended by the Hazardous and Solid Waste Amendments of 1984 ("HSWA"), . . . and the Comprehensive Environmental Response, Compensation, and Liability Act of 1980 ("CERCLA"), . . . At issue is whether a state which has been authorized by the Environmental Protection Agency ("EPA") to "carry out" the state's hazardous waste program "in lieu of" RCRA, . . . is precluded from doing so at a hazardous waste treatment, storage and disposal facility owned and operated by the federal government which the EPA has placed on the national priority list, ...

I.

The Rocky Mountain Arsenal ("Arsenal") is a hazardous waste treatment, storage and disposal facility subject to RCRA regulation, . . . which is located . . . in the Denver metropolitan area. The United States government has owned the Arsenal since 1942, and the Army operated . . . until the mid-1980's. Without reiterating its environmental history, suffice it to say that the Arsenal is "one of the worst hazardous waste pollution sites in the country." . . . The present litigation focuses on Basin F which is a 92.7 acre basin located within the Arsenal where millions of gallons of liquid haz-

ardous waste have been disposed of over the years.

A.

Congress enacted RCRA in 1976 "to assist the cities, counties and states in the solution of the discarded materials problem and to provide nationwide protection against the dangers of improper hazardous waste disposal." . . . RCRA requires the EPA to establish performance standards, applicable to owners and operators of hazardous waste treatment, storage and disposal facilities "as may be necessary to protect human health and the environment." . . . The EPA enforces RCRA standards by requiring owners and operators of facilities to obtain permits. . . . and by issuing administrative compliance orders and seeking civil and criminal penalties for violations. . . . The EPA may authorize states to "carry out" their own hazardous waste programs "in lieu of" RCRA and to "issue and enforce permits for the storage, treatment, or disposal of hazardous waste" so long as the state program meets the minimum federal standards. . . . However, RCRA does not preclude a state from adopting more stringent requirements for the treatment, storage and disposal of hazardous waste. . . . Once the EPA authorizes a state to carry out the state hazardous waste program in lieu of RCRA, "[a]ny action taken by [the] State [has] the same force and effect as action taken by the [EPA]. . . ." The federal government must comply with RCRA or an EPA-authorized state program "to the same extent as any person. . . ."

* * *

II.

In November 1980, the Army, . . . submitted to the EPA part A of its RCRA permit application which listed Basin F as a hazardous waste surface impoundment. . . . In May 1983, the Army submitted part B of its RCRA permit application to the EPA which included a required closure plan for Basin F, . . . and the following month, the Army submitted a revised closure plan for Basin F. . . . In May 1984, the EPA issued a notice of deficiency to the Army regarding part B of its RCRA permit application and requested a revised part B application within sixty days . . . The Army never submitted a revised part B RCRA permit application to the EPA; rather, in October 1984, the Army commenced a CERCLA remedial investigation/feasibility study ("RI/FS").[9] Appellee's App. at 9, 30.

Effective November 2, 1984, the EPA, acting pursuant to 42 U.S.C. § 6926(b) (West Supp.1992), authorized Colorado to "carry out" the Colorado Hazardous Waste Management Act ("CHWMA"), . . . "in lieu of" RCRA. . . . That same month, the Army submitted its part B RCRA/CHWMA permit application to the Colorado Department of Health ("CDH") which is charged with the administration and enforcement of CHWMA. . . . Notably, the part B application was the same deficient application that the Army submitted to the EPA. . . . Not surprisingly, CDH found the application, specifically the closure plan for Basin F, to be unsatisfactory. . . .

Consequently, . . . CDH issued its own draft partial closure plan for Basin F to the Army, . . . and in October 1986, CDH issued a final RCRA/CHWMA modified closure plan for Basin F and requested the Army's cooperation in immediately implementing the plan. . . . The Army responded by questioning CDH's jurisdiction over the Basin F cleanup.

* * *

In September 1989, CDH, . . . issued a final amended compliance order to the Army, ...

The final amended compliance order requires the Army to submit an amended Basin F closure plan, ...

. . . [T]he United States filed the present declaratory action, ... The United States' complaint sought an order from the federal district court declaring that the final amended compliance order is "null and void" and enjoining Colorado and CDH from taking any action to enforce it. . . . Colorado counter-claimed requesting an injunction to enforce the final amended compliance order. *Id.* at 35–41. . . . [T]he district court . . . held that "[a]ny attempt by Colorado to enforce [ ] CHWMA would require [the] court to review the [Army's CERCLA] remedial action . . ." and that "[s]uch a review is expressly prohibited by [CERCLA] § 9613(h)." . . .

III.

. . . Colorado contends that § 9614(h) is not applicable to a state's efforts to enforce its EPA-delegated RCRA authority, that listing on the national priority list is immaterial, and that the district court's order amounts to a determination that CERCLA preempts a state's EPA-delegated RCRA authority contrary to well-settled principles. . . .

* * *

IV.

* * *

A.

Congress clearly expressed its intent that CERCLA should work in conjunction with other federal and state hazardous waste laws. . . . CERCLA's "savings provision" provides that "[n]othing in [CERCLA] shall affect or modify in any way the obligations or liabilities of any person under other Federal or State law, including common law, with respect to releases of hazardous substances or other pollutants or contaminants." . . . Similarly, CERCLA's provision entitled "relationship to other laws" provides that "[n]othing in [CERCLA] shall be construed or interpreted as preempting any State from imposing any additional liability or requirements with respect to the release of hazardous substances within such State." 42 U.S.C. § 9614(a) (West 1983). By holding that § 9613(h) bars Colorado from enforcing CHWMA, the district court effectively modified the Army's obligations and liabilities under CHWMA contrary to § 9652(d), and preempted Colorado from imposing additional requirements with respect to the release of hazardous substances . . . .

As a federal facility, the Arsenal is subject to regulation under RCRA. *See* 42 U.S.C. § 6961 (West 1983). More importantly, because the EPA has delegated RCRA authority to Colorado, the Arsenal is subject to regulation under CHWMA. . . .

. . . Congress' expressed purpose in enacting § 9613(h) was "to prevent *private responsible parties* from filing dilatory, interim lawsuits which have the effect of slowing down or preventing the EPA's cleanup activities." . . . Nonetheless, the language of § 9613(h) does not differentiate between challenges by private responsible parties and challenges by a state. Thus, to the extent a state seeks to challenge a CERCLA response action, the plain language of § 9613(h) would limit a federal court's jurisdiction to review such a challenge. . . .

Be that as it may, an action by a state to enforce its hazardous waste laws at a site undergoing a CERCLA response action is not necessarily a challenge to the CERCLA action. For example, CDH's final amended compliance order does not seek to halt the Army's Basin F interim response action; rather it merely seeks the Army's compliance with CHWMA . . . . Thus, Colorado is not seeking to delay the cleanup, . . . we cannot say that Colorado's efforts to enforce its EPA-delegated RCRA authority is a challenge to the Army's undergoing CERCLA response action.

* * *

While we do not doubt that Colorado's enforcement of the . . . compliance order will "impact the implementation" of the Army's CERCLA response action, we do not believe that this alone is enough to constitute a challenge to the action . . . .

* * *

. . . Thus, enforcement actions under state hazardous waste laws which have been authorized by the EPA to be enforced by the state in lieu of RCRA do not constitute "challenges" to CERCLA response actions; therefore, § 9613(h) does not jurisdictionally bar Colorado from enforcing the final amended compliance order.

V.

Even if an action by Colorado . . . would be a "challenge" to the Army's CERCLA response action, the plain language of § 9613(h) would only bar a federal court from exercising jurisdiction over Colorado's action. . . . Rather, Colorado can seek enforcement of the final amended compliance order in state court. Therefore, § 9613(h) cannot bar Colorado from taking "any" action to enforce the final compliance order.

* * *

VIII.

We REVERSE the district court's grant of summary judgement for . . . the United States. We REMAND to the district court with instruction to VACATE the order prohibiting Defendants-Appellants, Colorado and CDH, from taking any action to enforce the final amended compliance order and for further proceedings consistent with this opinion.

---

[9] While most of the President's CERCLA authority has been delegated to the EPA pursuant to 42 U.S.C. § 9615(West 1983), the President delegated his CERCLA response action authority under § 9604(a–b) with respect to Department of Defense facilities to the Secretary of Defense . . . The Army has since maintained that its CERCLA response action precludes Colorado from enforcing its EPA-delegated RCRA authority at the Arsenal.

That fact that RCRA and CERCLA sometimes cover sites concurrently (because many "hazardous substances" subject to CERCLA also constitute "hazardous wastes" subject to RCRA) should not blur important differences in their overall coverage and remedies. Whereas RCRA deals with the active management of solid and hazardous "wastes," CERCLA deals with the release of "hazardous substances," whether or not they fit any particular description of "waste," and without regard to how a hazardous substance came to be located at a particular site. CERCLA targets the nature of the substance itself, and not the activity of its handlers. Further, because the exceptions and exemptions arising under CERCLA and RCRA are not parallel, avoidance of one statute's proscriptions does not automatically satisfy the other's. For instance, a waste classified as "nonhazardous" by RCRA may qualify as a "hazardous" substance under CERCLA, subjecting municipally operated landfills to CERCLA cleanup liability. As the court observed in the *B. F. Goodrich v. Murtha* case,

> CERCLA was passed after RCRA and because the need to clean up hazardous sites was deemed impossible within the legal remedies then provided.

Another example of distinct coverage between CERCLA and RCRA is the regulation of petroleum. Petroleum disposal is covered by RCRA provisions, but petroleum is excluded from CERCLA's coverage of "hazardous substances."

Cleanup Technologies: Availability, Efficacy, and Cost

In setting environmental protection and cleanup standards under CERCLA, EPA is confronted with the limited state of scientific knowledge about the environment, about the treatment of environmental hazards and degradation, and about cause-and-effect relationships between hazardous substances and health and environmental conditions. One of the most difficult problems in CERCLA cleanups is determining how clean is clean *enough*. In every remedial decision EPA makes, it must determine what level of cleanup is sufficiently protective of human health and the environment. Moreover, EPA is always dogged by issues of "marginal utility," since each incremental increase in the level of cleanup usually costs more relative to its benefits than the previous increment. This puts great pressure on the agency to select remedies that are less, rather than more, protective in order to cut costs.

Even when scientific knowledge is available, EPA faces similar problems of engineering suitable technologies for achieving remediation goals. At best, the development of practical technologies from discoveries in the pure sciences takes time. At worst, knowledge gained in the pure sciences may not be readily convertible into effective technology.

The limited ability of science and technology to identify and predict the optimal targets and efficacy of particular cleanup measures in particular circumstances can, of course, support the argument for safe-side regulation as well as the argument for withholding remedial action that may be very costly and not totally effective. In any event, such choices must be made, because even a decision to take no action constitutes a decision that has costly environmental ramifications.

CERCLA section 121 authorizes EPA to select "appropriate remedial actions" that provide for "cost-effective response." As previously noted, section 121 is subject to myriad interpretations. The complexity and theoretical controversies surrounding cost-benefit analysis provides ample fodder for liable parties to challenge EPA's decisions. Under section 121, liable parties have often argued that the selection of the cleanup response should not be made solely on the basis of health and environmental standards; they argue that cost-effectiveness also should be a factor. Many states, on the other hand, have viewed cost-effectiveness as an appropriate consideration only when choosing between al-at 103 sites. Construction activities include such things as excavation, off-site transportation for disposal, capping, and drilling of treatment and monitoring wells. Many sites remain on the NPL after construction is completed because the chosen response action includes an ongoing operation, such as pumping and treating ground water or bioremediation, which will remove remaining contaminants only over a period of five, ten, or even thirty years.

One of former EPA Administrator William Reilly's particular areas of concern was EPA's "scorecard" for completing construction at NPL sites. Reilly committed EPA to reach these goals for construction completion:

130 sites by September 30, 1992
200 sites by September 30, 1993
650 sites by the year 2000

Approximately 1,185 sites were on the NPL in 1994. Since as many as 100 new sites can be added to the NPL yearly, EPA expects the list to total more than 2000 by the end of the century. Although reductions in the number of annual additions can be expected as better controls under RCRA begin to improve waste-management techniques, decades of effort will still be required to remediate only the nation's worst hazardous substance sites.

Many Superfund critics neglect to consider what the costs to society and the environment would be without Superfund. Those who argue that Superfund expenditures are not justified by the benefits achieved often fail to consider the costs that would have materialized had those sites not been cleaned up. Moreover, many critics overlook the reality that before CERCLA was enacted, virtually no market drove the development of hazardous-site remediation technologies. Consequently, trial and error has characterized Superfund program administration and cleanup technology development. New treatment technologies are being developed every year. Perhaps we have not yet begun to reap the most significant benefits of CERCLA—namely, the development of new technologies for managing the hazardous substances on which industrialized societies have become increasingly dependent.

CERCLA also advances the legal trend of forcing polluters to pay for environmental remediation and spreading the costs of environmental degradation among those who most benefit from it. It is precisely this trend—which has emerged only since the early 1970s—that created market incentives for industries' adoption of environmentally friendly production, packaging, recycling, source reduction, and disposal practices. The high costs associated with CERCLA have not only deterred unnecessary use and unwise disposal of hazardous substances; they have also induced companies and industries to reevaluate their production and disposal practices. The environmental and social benefits flowing from this dynamic are not easy to quantify, but they are no less significant because of that.

Nonetheless, the vast resources lost to transaction costs under the Superfund program cannot be discounted. It is important to remember that many of these transaction costs result from unnecessary or immoderate litigation on the part of businesses and insurance companies, many of which are ultimately found liable and are capable of committing substantial resources to cleanups. As Minnesota Senator David Durenberger, as the ranking minority member of the Senate Environmental Protection Subcommittee, saw it, allegations of excessive spending on Superfund litigation are "the manifestation of a campaign by the insurance industry to shift the costs."[30]

Some commentators suggest that many large corporations are dragging small-business owners and municipalities into Superfund litigation as part of a system-

ternative methods of achieving the identical cleanup leve
standards. EPA has indicated that where no clearly estat
environmental-cleanup standard exists, cost-effectiveness may
selecting remedial alternatives. A pending lawsuit brought by a n
raises precisely this issue; in that litigation, states are disputing th.
a proper consideration in choosing between remedies that rei
cleanup levels.

Superfund Reauthorization Issues: Is Superfund Woi

CERCLA comes up for Congressional reauthorization in 1995. Variou
tries most adversely affected by CERCLA's operation have vigorously
Congress to reconsider CERCLA's basic liability scheme. The last CERCLA
thorization was accomplished by a last-minute attachment to the 1991 b.
bill, which avoided legislative battles such as those that accompanied the
year-long reauthorization fight in 1986.

CERCLA opponents—including the petrochemical, insurance, and finano
lending industries—point to the slow completion rate and enormous costs assc
ciated with Superfund remedial actions as justifications for dismantling or re·
vamping CERCLA. Superfund spending could reach $1 trillion, much of that for
legal costs of enforcing the Superfund program. Legal fees account for 30 to 60
percent of Superfund-related spending. Studies by the Rand Corporation and the
Office of Technology Assessment, a federal agency, project that Superfund-
connected legal costs will ultimately reach $300 billion. According to an assistant
administrator and general counsel to the EPA, by 1992 it had taken an average
of ten years to clean up a Superfund site. Too much Superfund money was going
to consultants and lawyers and too little to remediation work; thus the benefits
of billions of dollars of Superfund expenditures had been very small relative to
other possible uses of those funds to improve the environment.[29] Figure 7.4
details Superfund-related expenditures through 1992 and shows the breakdown
between cleanup and administrative costs and litigation costs.

Although only about 35 Superfund sites had been fully cleared from the National Priorities List by July 27, 1992, response construction had been completed

■ **Figure 7.4**   Estimated Superfund-Related Expenditures, Fiscal Years
1981–1992, in Billions

	Cleanup and Administrative Costs	Litigation Costs	Total
Federal government	$ 6.8	$0.9	$ 7.7
Business and other organizations* held responsible for hazardous-waste cleanup	3.5	0.9	4.4
Insurance companies	0.2	1.2	1.4
Additional state cleanup costs	0.1	—	0.1
Total (public and private)	**10.6**	**3.0**	**13.6**

*Such as state and local government, nonprofit organizations, etc.
Source: Congressional Budget Office.

atic strategy to undermine CERCLA. Such tactics may have the effect of enlisting support from municipalities for changes in Superfund liability. A New Jersey Deputy Attorney General was quoted as saying:

> I have seen people sued—and settle—for waste no more hazardous than cardboard. The strategy is to make the entire Superfund system so ineffective that one way or another, Congress is going to be forced to scrap it.[31]

Law firms representing responsible parties have considerable financial incentive to extend litigation, to challenge governmental determinations of liability, and to file suit against as many potential contributors as possible. This course of action produces far more billable hours for legal services than would settlement of the case with other major players. Under present norms, such a course of action is arguably ethical so long as there exist some liability or contribution issues, even if those issues are not compelling.

When the regulated community takes a highly litigious stance, government regulators are forced to expend ever-increasing resources to document liability, to draft precise, loophole-free regulations and administrative orders, and to anticipate a barrage of possible objections and defenses that liable parties may have. Thus, unnecessary litigation results in increased administrative costs.

Amendments to CERCLA have been proposed for:

- eliminating joint and several liability,
- creating a fund to settle disputes between polluters and their insurers and to shield insurers from further liability,
- eliminating liability for disposal prior to 1987 (the year many insurers began excluding coverage for hazardous-waste cleanups),
- imposing new taxes on industry or insurers to pay for greater shares of cleanups,
- introducing nongovernmental arbitration,
- granting government officials greater flexibility to individualize cleanup standards suited to expected future uses of a site,
- exempting purchasers of abandoned urban property from liability.

It remains to be seen which of these proposals will be enacted into law.

7.4 Selected Issues in Hazardous Substance Cleanups

Municipal Liability

It is clear that Congress intended to exempt municipalities from CERCLA liability when they acquire a facility involuntarily or respond to an emergency created by others:

> Under CERCLA, . . . a state or local government that has involuntarily acquired title to a facility is generally not held liable as the owner or operator of the facility. Rather, the statute provides that in the case of any facility, title or control of which was conveyed due to bankruptcy, foreclosure, tax delinquency, abandonment, or similar means to a unit of State or local government [its owner or operator] is any person who owned, operated or otherwise controlled activities at such facility immediately beforehand.[32]

An exemption is also granted where the government unit acquires contaminated property while exercising the governmental powers of condemnation or tax or debt collection:

> Where a municipality acquires ownership or control of a facility . . . as a result of its sovereign functions . . . or where a municipality acts in response to an emer-

gency caused by the release . . . from a facility owned by another . . . and does not act with gross negligence or wilful misconduct . . . no liability attaches.[33]

However, when a municipality has owned, operated, or contributed wastes to a CERCLA site, it is considered a "person" liable for response costs under CERCLA.

The Superfund National Priorities List includes more than 300 sites at which municipal wastes were disposed; many of these sites were also municipally owned or operated. CERCLA poses a serious dilemma for local governments and their taxpayers. Although industrial entities may have been the primary contributors of hazardous substances at common dumpsites, joint and several liability permits them to pass on some cleanup costs to all parties that contributed even minuscule amounts of hazardous substances. Local governments that have disposed of residential and commercial trash, which typically includes small quantities of detergents and insecticides, are customarily targets for contribution claims.

Appeals to Congress and the courts to exempt municipalities from the potentially crushing burden of joint liability have thus far failed.[34] Nor would an administrative decision to refrain from pursuing municipalities that were not the principal source of hazardous substances protect them from third-party suits for a contribution of cleanup costs.

The *Goodrich* case is but one illustration of a growing trend of suits by corporations against municipalities for contribution to cleanup payments. For instance, Du Pont, Rohm & Haas Co., and Texaco, Inc., joined some 50 New Jersey municipalities in a contribution suit; General Electric and Polaroid corporations filed actions against 12 municipalities in Massachusetts; Occidental Petroleum, Lockheed, and Proctor & Gamble filed actions against 29 suburbs of Los Angeles; and Special Metals Corporation and Cheeseborough-Ponds USA made contribution claims against 603 defendants, including 44 municipalities in New York state.[35] Traces of hazardous substances found in consumer products provide third-party plaintiffs with a basis to draw municipalities into CERCLA lawsuits. These suits allege that in order to clean up their hazardous substances, liable companies must dispose of tons of intermixed municipal garbage. The theory and impact of such suits were summarized as follows:

> Their primary weapon is garbage. Some [corporations] . . . argue that they will have to treat tons of municipal solid waste to get to the hazardous material they are to clean up. Others contend that even seemingly innocuous trash is laced with hazardous substances found in everyday products.[36]

Government attorneys and officials complain that such suits unfairly pit experienced, well-financed corporate lawyers against municipalities that can afford neither high litigation costs nor the prospect of potentially ruinous judgments. The evident strategy of contribution litigation tactics is to extract negotiated contributions from municipalities that exceed what is fairly due. Moreover, apportionment of liability on a volumetric basis, if accepted by the court, makes municipalities, whose wastes are least toxic, accountable for the greatest part of the cleanup costs.

Given the questionable outcomes of some cases under current standards of liability, Congress will be challenged to devise legislation that will mitigate the burdens presently imposed on municipalities. One proposal is to limit the total municipal share at any one site to a small percentage of total costs unless other factors indicate that municipal waste at the site is more toxic than conventional municipal waste. It remains to be seen, however, whether a scheme that would relieve municipalities as a class is politically or legally viable.

Special Liability Problems of Small Businesses

CERCLA's liability standards also encourage strategic litigation against small businesses, which usually find it impractical to resist such claims or to pay the legal costs of a defense. In one reported case, two large corporations sued a two-table takeout-pizza business for contribution of $3,000 toward a $9 million cleanup bill. The lawsuit alleged that the proprietor had contributed hazardous waste to the landfill. Although the corporations' attorneys weren't certain what kind of waste the pizzeria sent to the landfill, they "surmised" that the trash included empty cleanser cans or pesticides.

Although the corporations demanded $3,000 contribution, they offered to settle for $1,500. Since it would have cost the pizza shop owner more than that to defend the case, she settled. The wonder is that the plaintiffs' attorney did not add to the list of 603 defendants every household whose trash went to the Superfund site, on the assumption that it too contained hazardous substances, in whatever minuscule amounts. This case also raises questions about the practices of the law firm representing the corporations; the attorneys' fees for preparing the papers against the pizza business might have cost their clients more in attorneys' fees than the expected recovery. Such cases give credence to the characterization of CERCLA as a lawyers' employment act.

Until Congress discovers a satisfactory alternative to the present system for apportioning cleanup contribution costs, the potential for abuse through litigation threats and tactics will remain. The assumption that overburdened courts will scrutinize and ensure the fairness of such settlements is not so clear as to dispense with seeking more satisfactory alternatives to current contribution practices.

Insurance Coverage

The relative novelty of CERCLA liability has generated serious disagreements concerning the coverage provided by traditional liability insurance policies. Insurance companies have come to spend almost as much money to deny their duty to indemnify or defend their policyholders as they have to pay or defend CERCLA claims.

A myriad of technical, complex issues arises when an insured seeks CERCLA indemnification from an insurer under a general liability policy. When an insured files a claim, the first issue is whether the policy covers environmental liabilities. Even if the policy expressly acknowledges that environmental liabilities are covered, insurers wrangle over which event triggers insurance coverage—for instance, the actual release of a hazardous substance or the issuance of a cleanup order—and whether the triggering event occurred during the term of policy coverage. In addition, insurance companies that acknowledge their obligation to indemnify and defend clients in environmental contamination suits often opt for extensive litigation to deny the insured's liability or to contest the amount of contribution sought. The stance of "millions for defense, but not one cent for tribute" dedicates more insurance company funds to litigation than to cleanups. The disparity between funds spent directly by companies for cleanups, and funds spent by their insurance companies to resist the imposition of cleanup liability reveals that insurance companies have spent almost as much money to dispute their insureds' CERCLA liability as to settle their liability claims.

The prevailing pattern of litigation to contest coverage under different insurance policies remains a serious obstacle to the spreading of costs sought by

CERCLA. Since interpretation of insurance policies is largely a matter of state law, clarification of insurance coverage in Superfund cleanups cannot be resolved by current federal statutes. From state to state, courts interpret similarly worded policies in radically different ways. This serves to encourage forum-shopping (filing suits in courts which have already ruled favorably on disputed issues) and further clouds the disposition of related CERCLA issues.

Much remains to be done, therefore, to render the liability and cost-spreading policies of CERCLA effective. Until more acceptable legal arrangements, voluntary or mandated, are developed to expedite the determination of contribution liability and the availability of insurance coverage, private funds will continue to be misdirected to litigation rather than to cleanups.

Bankruptcy

Bankruptcy presents a special set of issues and problems in CERCLA enforcement. In recent years, record numbers of bankruptcy filings have been made by companies subject to liability under several environmental statutes, particularly CERCLA. A number of cases have addressed the conjunction between CERCLA and the Bankruptcy Code, but conflicts among the federal courts continue to raise questions as to the proper interpretation and application of federal environmental laws to entities seeking protection under bankruptcy laws. Because the protection afforded debtors by insolvency statutes presents unique and difficult challenges to the enforcement of federal environmental laws, it is necessary to review the core principles of federal bankruptcy statutes here.

A debtor who files for bankruptcy protection may seek either to liquidate or to reorganize. In liquidation proceedings, all of the debtor's assets are sold to pay off a portion of each creditor's claim; after this liquidation, the company ceases to exist. In reorganization proceedings, the company reorganizes as a new entity, which is considered a successor of the debtor but is free of the liabilities of the bankruptcy debtor. As in liquidation, reorganization entails a plan of partial payment of creditors' claims. The amount each creditor receives in satisfaction of its outstanding claim depends on when the debt was incurred and whether collateral secured the debt.

A debtor's object in bankruptcy is twofold:

1. By filing for bankruptcy, the debtor receives the protection of the automatic stay, which prevents anyone who holds a claim against it from suing it in any other forum or taking other action to collect the debt, such as placing a lien on its property. Instead, anyone with a claim against the debtor must file the claim with the bankruptcy court.
2. The debtor obtains a *discharge* of most of the claims against it—that is, a release from those obligations—in exchange for paying a certain portion of its debts in accordance with the plan of reorganization or liquidation approved by the bankruptcy court. After bankruptcy proceedings are closed and the debts discharged, further suits for any claims that arose before the bankruptcy petition was filed are prohibited.

Bankruptcy presents difficult problems when an insolvent company is liable under CERCLA. Three different scenarios are possible:

- The debtor may already be subject to an abatement order.
- The government or a liable private party may already have brought suit to recover response costs incurred before the bankruptcy filing.

■ The government or another party may not yet have incurred response costs or issued an abatement order at the time the company files for bankruptcy but may be contemplating such action.

Under all of these scenarios, bankruptcy courts have held, and higher courts have affirmed, that potential and actual enforcement and cost-recovery actions under CERCLA are "claims" for bankruptcy purposes, and that the provisions and policies of bankruptcy statutes for discharging debtors from past legal obligations govern CERCLA claims and empower bankruptcy courts to discharge CERCLA liabilities.

What has not been uniformly decided is how these claims should be classified and treated relative to other creditors' claims. Bankruptcy law establishes the priority in which creditors' claims are to be paid. Courts in different circuits have used various tests to determine which CERCLA claims are subject to discharge, which are to be treated as administrative expenses (which are paid before other claims), and which are to be treated as unsecured debts. Initially, EPA argued that discharge of CERCLA claims in bankruptcy was counter to CERCLA's policy of making the polluter pay and was inappropriate in light of the remedial nature of the statute. Moreover, actions brought by the government in the exercise of inherent governmental functions—the so-called police power—are generally not barred by the automatic stay. EPA has argued that CERCLA claims fall within this exception. In addition, EPA has argued that potential CERCLA actions for recovery of response costs not yet incurred should not be considered "claims," because no cause of action arises under CERCLA until response costs are incurred.

Over the years, EPA has lost all three of these arguments. Bankruptcy courts have decided that incurrence of response costs under CERCLA is not necessary to render a claim subject to discharge in bankruptcy. Having determined that a claim under CERCLA arises for bankruptcy purposes even before the government has spent any money on cleanup, courts have been left with the thorny issue of precisely what triggers a CERCLA claim. *When* the claim arises is particularly significant, as it determines whether the debt is subject to discharge and what priority it will be afforded. Some courts have said that a CERCLA claim arises at the time of the release of hazardous substances; others have held that a CERCLA claim arises when the federal government has reasonable notice of the existence of a hazardous-substance release.

Consequently, many CERCLA plaintiffs have fallen in the least-favored class of creditors. Many bankruptcy decisions have effectively relieved bankrupt companies of substantial CERCLA obligations. By rejecting EPA's argument that CERCLA's manifest intent to hold polluters accountable for cleanups should prevent cleanup liability discharge, these cases have left EPA with drastically diminished leverage against a liable party that is under bankruptcy-court protection.

In suits against bankrupt entities, the remedies available to the federal government and other parties that have incurred CERCLA response costs are limited. In some proceedings, certain classes of creditors are paid only cents on the dollar. In other cases, there are no significant cash assets for distribution and creditors must settle for shares in the newly reorganized company. Adverse rulings have induced EPA to settle multimillion dollar claims for its cleanups of numerous sites around the nation, sometimes for shares in a reorganized company that has emerged from bankruptcy legally clear of all past CERCLA liability. EPA often has little choice but to accept these reorganization plans, since rejecting them would result in liquidation of the debtor business and produce even poorer recovery for EPA.

Another aspect of bankruptcy law that impedes environmental enforcement efforts is the provision of the bankruptcy code that permits a debtor to abandon property that is burdensome to the bankruptcy estate. Contaminated real property often falls into this category. In egregious cases, however, courts have not permitted property to be abandoned when doing so would present an imminent threat to public health or welfare. The leading case exemplifying this is *Midlantic National Bank v. New Jersey Dept. of Environmental Protection*.

MIDLANTIC NATIONAL BANK v. NEW JERSEY DEPT. OF ENVIRONMENTAL PROTECTION

474 U.S. 494 (1986)

[Quanta Resources, the operator of two waste-oil facilities, one in New Jersey and the other in New York, violated environmental law and permits by accepting PCB-contaminated oil for processing. Shortly after New Jersey authorities discovered its violations of environmental laws, and shortly before the discovery of similar violations at the New York plant, Quanta initiated bankruptcy proceedings in the New York federal court. The Trustee sought to abandon the properties in both states, claiming authority to do so under the bankruptcy law. Authorities in both states, however, wanted to force the Trustee to clean up the contaminated sites, and thus opposed the proposed abandonment as a violation of federal and state environmental law and of the bankruptcy-law provision requiring the Trustee to manage a bankrupt's property "according to the requirements of the valid laws of the State in which such property is situated." In considering the disputed operation and the interaction of the different laws, the Supreme Court, by a close 5 to 4 vote, ruled that a bankruptcy trustee may not abandon property in violation of a state law intended to protect public health and safety without imposing conditions of abandonment that will adequately protect public health and safety. The complexity of reconciling bankruptcy law with environmental law is apparent in this excerpt from the majority opinion.]

Justice Powell delivered the opinion of the Court.

These petitions . . . present the question whether § 554(a) of the Bankruptcy Code, 11 U.S.C. § 554(a) [11 U.S.C.S. § 554(a)], authorizes a trustee in bankruptcy to abandon property in contravention of state laws or regulations that are reasonably designed to protect the public's health or safety.

* * *

After trying without success to sell the Long Island City property for the benefit of Quanta's creditors, the trustee notified the creditors and the Bankruptcy Court for the District of New Jersey that he intended to abandon the property pursuant to § 554(a). No party to the bankruptcy proceeding disputed the trustee's allegation that the site was "burdensome" and of "inconsequential value to the estate" within the meaning of § 554.

The City and State of New York (collectively New York), . . . nevertheless objected, contending that abandonment would threaten the public's health and safety, and would violate state and federal environmental law. New York rested its objection on "public policy" considerations reflected in applicable local laws, and on the requirement of 28 U.S.C. § 959(b) that a trustee "manage and operate" the property of the estate "according to the requirements of the valid laws of the State in which such property is situated." New York asked the Bankruptcy Court to order that the assets of the estate be used to bring the facility into compliance with applicable law. After briefing and argument, the court approved the abandonment, noting that "[t]he City and State are in a better position in every respect than either the Trustee or debtor's creditors to do what needs to be done to protect the public against the dangers posed by the PCB-contaminated facility."

Upon abandonment, the trustee removed the 24-hour guard service and shut down the fire-suppression system. It became necessary for New York to decontaminate the facility, with the exception of the polluted subsoil, at a cost of about $2.5 million.

On April 23, 1983, shortly after the District Court had approved abandonment of the New

York site, the trustee gave notice of his intention to abandon the personal property at the Edgewater site, consisting principally of the contaminated oil. The Bankruptcy Court approved the abandonment on May 20, over NJDEP's objection that the estate had sufficient funds to protect the public from the dangers posed by the hazardous waste.

* * *

A divided panel of the Court of Appeals for the Third Circuit reversed.

* * *

. . . Accordingly, the Court of Appeals held that the Bankruptcy Court erred in permitting abandonment, ...

* * *

Before the 1978 revisions of the Bankruptcy Code, the trustee's abandonment power had been limited by a judicially developed doctrine intended to protect legitimate state or federal interests.

* * *

Thus, when Congress enacted § 554, there were well-recognized restrictions on a trustee's abandonment power. In codifying the judicially developed rule of abandonment, Congress also presumably included the established corollary that a trustee could not exercise his abandonment power in violation of certain state and federal laws.

* * *

Neither the Court nor Congress has granted a trustee in bankruptcy powers that would lend support to a right to abandon property in contravention of state or local laws designed to protect public health or safety. As we held last Term . . .

* * *

[W]e do not question that anyone in possession of the site—whether it is [the debtor] or another in the event the receivership is liquidated and the trustee abandons the property, or a vendee from the receiver *or the bankruptcy trustee*—must comply with the environmental laws of the State of Ohio. Plainly, that person or firm may not maintain a nuisance, pollute the waters of the State, or refuse to remove the source of such conditions.

Congress has repeatedly expressed its legislative determination that the trustee is not to have carte blanche to ignore nonbankruptcy law. . . . As we held nearly two years ago in

the context of the National Labor Relations Act, "the debtor-in-possession is not relieved of all obligations under the [Act] simply by filing a petition for bankruptcy."

* * *

Despite the importance of [the automatic stay under] § 362(a) in preserving the debtor's estate, Congress has enacted several categories of exceptions to the stay that allow the Government to commence or continue legal proceedings. It is clear from the legislative history that one of the purposes of this exception is to protect public health and safety:

> "Thus, where a governmental unit is suing a debtor to prevent or stop violation of fraud, *environmental protection*, consumer protection, *safety, or similar police or regulatory laws*, or attempting to fix damages for violation of such a law, the action or proceeding is not stayed under the automatic stay." HR Rep No. 95-595, supra, at 343 (emphasis added); S Rep No. 95-989, supra, at 52 (emphasis added).

* * *

Title 28 U.S.C. § 959(b) provides additional evidence that Congress did not intend for the Bankruptcy Code to pre-empt all state laws. Section 959(b) commands the trustee to "manage and operate the property in his possession . . . according to the requirements of the valid laws of the State." The petitioners have contended that § 959(b) is relevant only when the trustee is actually operating the business of the debtor, and not when he is liquidating it. Even though § 959(b) does not directly apply to an abandonment under § 554(a) of the Bankruptcy Code . . . the section nevertheless supports our conclusion that Congress did not intend for the Bankruptcy Code to pre-empt all state laws that otherwise constrain the exercise of a trustee's powers.

* * *

. . . we find additional support for restricting that power in repeated congressional emphasis on its "goal of protecting the environment against toxic pollution."

* * *

In the face of Congress' undisputed concern over the risks of the improper storage and disposal of hazardous and toxic substances, we are unwilling to presume that by enactment of

§ 554(a), Congress implicitly overturned long-standing restrictions on the common-law abandonment power.

* * *

The Bankruptcy Court does not have the power to authorize an abandonment without formulating conditions that will adequately protect the public's health and safety. Accordingly, without reaching the question whether certain state laws imposing conditions on aban-

donment may be so onerous as to interfere with the bankruptcy adjudication itself, we hold that a trustee may not abandon property in contravention of a state statute or regulation that is reasonably designed to protect the public health or safety from identified hazards. Accordingly, we affirm the judgments of the Court of Appeals for the Third Circuit.

* * *

Given the current state of the law, it is not surprising that many companies, particularly in the chemical industry, institute bankruptcy proceedings primarily to avoid environmental liabilities, including ones arising under CERCLA. In many cases, the same management that incurred substantial CERCLA liability for the company due to poor waste management remains at the helm of the newly reorganized company—which is relieved of its cleanup obligations and is given a fresh start. In such cases, bankruptcy law dramatically thwarts CERCLA's principle purpose of making polluters pay and spreading the costs of cleanups. Rather than spreading costs, bankruptcy law results in a shifting of costs, sometimes to other liable parties, but as likely as not, to taxpayers.

Other issues and policies implicated by bankruptcy laws and the bankruptcy process itself have elicited much criticism from those familiar with them. Among other difficulties, the tortuous progress of bankruptcy proceedings often drains the bankruptcy estate of much-needed resources. Particularly alarming are the large sums paid to debtors' attorneys as priority administrative expenses, before most other creditors, including environmental enforcement agencies, can be paid.

The Petroleum Exclusion

Petroleum is expressly excluded from CERCLA's definition of *hazardous substance* even though its characteristics and effects on the environment are not materially different from those of the substances covered by CERCLA. The petroleum exclusion resulted from effective lobbying by the petroleum industry, which knew that some petroleum was likely to be found at many Superfund sites. The petroleum exclusion has created interesting legal questions about CERCLA's applicability where petroleum products which contain other hazardous substances are released into the environment. As a general rule, the exclusion applies only to unadulterated (pure) petroleum products and not to petroleum products which are contaminated with other hazardous substances. Determining whether petroleum is adulterated with other hazardous substances often demands a fact-sensitive inquiry, however, and adulteration can be difficult to establish.

The Oil Pollution Act of 1990 (OPA), enacted after the *Exxon Valdez* oil spill in 1989, covers some releases of petroleum by imposing liability for oil spills and for resulting natural resource damage. However, it should be noted that the petroleum exclusion under CERCLA still eliminates from CERCLA liability parties responsible for petroleum releases at hazardous-waste sites. Thus, parties responsible for having disposed of petroleum products at Superfund sites need not enter into agreements with other responsible parties or risk joint and several liability for the cleanup—a decisive advantage to petroleum manufacturers at sites where numerous liable parties face cleanup costs amounting to millions of dollars. From this vantage point, OPA liability is considerably narrower than Superfund liability.

Emerging Cleanup Technologies

Some relatively new cleanup technologies offer hope for tackling massive hazardous substance sites in simpler, more cost-effective ways. Among them are bioremediation techniques, which use a combination of biochemical processes to convert complex organic compounds into nontoxic materials. The following article details the bioremediation revolution.

. . . In [the] search for new ways to tackle environmental Goliaths, EPA has also begun recruiting its own Davids: the bacteria, fungi, and other microorganisms that live everywhere around us. . . .

. . . In nature, [biochemical] processes help clear the environment of dead matter; for example, fungi help decompose dead trees by feeding on cellulose in the wood, thereby promoting the breakdown of the wood fiber. Scientists are trying to apply similar principles to convert hazardous chemical wastes to nontoxic or less-toxic materials. This approach is called *bioremediation*.

. . . By establishing conditions in which everyday microorganisms can flourish— for example, by adding nutrients or moisture to contaminated soil—scientists stimulate faster reactions in which toxic organic compounds are converted into water, carbon dioxide, and other safe materials.

Similar principles have been used for many years in treating waste water . . . . The technology moved into the public spotlight in 1989 when Exxon and EPA worked together to assess the effectiveness of biological treatment in cleaning up the *Exxon Valdez* oil spill in Prince William Sound, Alaska.

Traditional methods called for spraying hot water at high pressure onto the rocky shoreline to wash the spilled oil back into the water, where it was collected by skimming and vacuuming. EPA scientists supplemented this treatment by applying fertilizer to parts of the coast to stimulate natural oil-degrading bacteria. . . . Subsequent treatment showed that this treatment caused oil to degrade twice as fast as the oil in untreated areas. . . .

. . . In one recent study, [Office of Research and Development scientists] applied white rot fungus, a common wood-degrading fungus, to soil samples contaminated with pentachlorophenol (PCP) and other toxic compounds. . .

. . . Preliminary results from the study show that PCP concentrations of up to 1,000 parts per million (ppm) were reduced by 85 to 90 percent. . . . [T]he fungus accounted for the significantly greater share of the reduction in the treated plots, converting the PCP to carbon dioxide and nonhazardous organic matter.

At a Texas site, researchers treated petrochemical wastes with a process that began with the injection of air into the liquid to encourage aerobic degradation— that is, reactions involving bacteria that function in the presence of oxygen. Nutrients were added, centrifugal pumps were used to emulsify the wastes, and subsoil was mixed in with a hydraulic dredge.

Within 120 days, volatile organic compounds in the waste were reduced from 3,400 ppm to 150 ppm, benzene concentrations from 300 ppm to 12 ppm, and vinyl chloride levels from 600 ppm to 17 ppm. The process cost $47 million, in contrast to estimated costs of $63 million to $167 million for other options evaluated. . . .

As the experts readily admit, the current techniques have drawbacks. They do not destroy heavy metals that may be present in many sites, such as areas around former mining sites. Unlike incineration, bioremediation is a slow process, and it does not remove all quantities of a contaminant from treated soil.

On the other hand, the technology has a number of attractive features. It provides a less costly alternative to traditional cleanup methods, in which tons of soil have to be excavated and either incinerated or otherwise processed to remove contaminants. In addition, by converting toxic chemicals to other materials, bioremediation actually removes those toxics from the environment, rather than merely separating them for disposal in a later step. . . .[37]

Fungal technologies in particular are creating quite a stir among researchers.[38] Fungi, lower plants that lack chlorophyll, obtain nourishment from organic materials by secreting enzymes into the surface on which they are growing. The enzymes digest nutrients contained in the material, which are then absorbed by the fungi. The white rot fungus mentioned in the "New Davids" article breaks down not only PCBs, but also DDT, dioxins, cyanides, dyes, creosote, wood preservatives, coal tars, and explosives, including TNT, into relatively harmless substances such as carbon dioxide. In contrast to other waste treatment technologies such as incineration, fungal technologies are safe and have few, if any, detrimental impacts. After the site is cleaned up, treatment with nutrients that boost fungal activity is stopped. The fungi die off from lack of nutrition, leaving no hazardous by-products at the conclusion of treatment.

■ Problem Set Exercises

Part 1

On the site of Tully's operations, a two-square-mile area known as the Trench was used from 1960 to 1980 for dumping some of the waste and by-products resulting from the firm's research and production operations. Tully employees incinerated solid wastes and piled the ashes into heaps. They pumped liquid wastes into steel drums and buried the drums in the Trench.

Many of the drums buried in the Trench have now corroded and are leaking. There is no cover on the ash heaps to prevent the ash from becoming airborne. Nor are there any liners to prevent the ash from leaching into the ground. Liquid and incinerated wastes at the site are known to contain hazardous substances.

1. Is the Trench a CERCLA facility? Why?
2. Under what circumstances could EPA order Tully to undertake an emergency removal of the drums and ash?
3. In ordering the cleanup of the Trench, what guidelines would EPA be required to follow?
4. What would be the potential consequences for Tully if it failed to obey an EPA cleanup order?
5. What arguments might Tully make in attempting to mitigate its liability?

Part 2

From 1970 to 1975, Tully permitted another chemical company, Tam & Howe, to dispose of paints and solvents in the Trench. The paints contained lead and cadmium, both of which are listed as hazardous substances. None of Tully's wastes at the Trench contain cadmium.

EPA determined that the Trench must be cleaned up. Before undertaking the work itself, it offered to let Tully and Tam & Howe perform the removal action. Tam & Howe, however, has filed for bankruptcy reorganization and claims it cannot perform any part of the removal. Tully declines to undertake the removal itself.

1. If EPA issues the abatement order to both parties, can Tully refuse to clean up the cadmium at the Trench?

2. What options will EPA have if both Tully and Tam & Howe refuse to do the work?

3. EPA has now decided to perform the removal using Superfund monies. In a cost recovery action, who must EPA sue? What can it recover?

4. Assume that you are Tully's general counsel. Tully CEO, Bill Miller, asks you to explain the firm's options in defending against the ten-million-dollar lawsuit EPA has brought to recover its response costs at the Trench. Specifically, he'd like to know: (a) why Tully may be liable for the whole cleanup, even though Tam & Howe dumped its wastes there, too; (b) what Tully must show in order not to be liable for the entire cleanup; and (c) what action Tully may take against Tam & Howe. What do you tell him?

Part 3

Prior to 1960, Tully dumped wastes on an adjacent six-acre parcel, now the homesite of Hunter Brown. Mr. Brown worked for Tully as a chemical engineer for waste disposal at the time he purchased the property. Mr. Brown is now trying to sell his home so that he can move to a retirement community. The Wilsons, rare book dealers, are interested in purchasing the property. (Assume that hazardous substances from Tully's waste-dumping activities are still present on the Brown property.)

1. If EPA's investigations lead it to conclude that Hunter Brown's property also should be cleaned up, could Tully be held liable for the removal and remedial costs on the Brown property as well?

2. Is Hunter Brown a potentially liable party? Is the innocent-landowner defense likely to be available to him?

3. If there is no visible contamination on the property and the Wilsons buy the property, unaware that Tully formerly used the parcel as a waste dump, might they be held liable in a cost recovery action? What would they need to prove in their defense?

4. Before Hunter managed to sell his house, he defaulted on his mortgage payments. The bank foreclosed and took possession of his home. Might the bank, which now owns the property, be held liable for cleanup costs?

Part 4

Not all of Tully's wastes are dumped in the Trench. Some of them are hauled away by an independent contractor, Nelson Enterprises. Tully utilizes Nelson's hauling services because of its competitive rates.

One day en route to the Fairbank landfill, a Nelson truck carrying drummed liquid wastes containing hazardous substances collided with an XYZ truck carrying radioactive plutonium wastes. Several drums rolled off the Nelson truck and split open, spilling the contents near the ninth hole at Bellevue Country Club.

1. Under what circumstances could Nelson be held liable for the costs of cleaning up the spill? Could a provision of CERCLA be used in a suit against XYZ?

2. For five years, Nelson has hauled Tully's wastes, including hazardous substances, to the Fairbank landfill, which has a contract with Tully and which just last year had the distinction of appearing on the National Priorities List. Will Tully be liable when EPA sues to recover cleanup costs at Fairbank? Will Nelson be liable?

3. If it is determined that the Fairbank landfill poses an imminent and substantial endangerment to public health, can EPA issue an abatement order against Tully? Against Nelson?

Appendix—Chapter 7

Selected Statutory Sections—The Comprehensive Environmental Response, Compensation, and Liability Act (Codified at 42 U.S.C. § 9601)

CERCLA § 101   Definitions

(9) . . . "facility" means (A) any building . . . equipment, pipe or pipeline . . . well, pond, . . . landfill, storage container, motor vehicle . . . or (B) any site or area where a hazardous substance has been . . . stored, disposed of, or placed, or otherwise came to be located . . . .

(11) The term "Fund" or "Trust Fund" means the . . . Superfund established by [law and codified in the Internal Revenue Code]

(14) The term "hazardous substance" means any substance [designated by the Administrator under the provisions of § 102 or any substance designated by virtue of a number of other federal environmental laws]. The term does not include petroleum, including crude oil or . . . [natural or synthetic gas].

(20) (A) The term "owner or operator" means . . . (ii) in the case of any person owning or operating [the] facility and (iii) in the case of any facility, title or control of which was conveyed [by legal judgment or abandonment] . . . any person who owned or operated or otherwise controlled activities at such facility immediately beforehand. Such term does not include a person who, without participating in the management of a . . . facility holds . . . ownership primarily to protect his security interest in the facility (B)(C) [The term "owner or operator" shall mean a common or contract carrier during such transportation of a hazardous substance, but a carrier who completed delivery to a facility without release shall not be considered to have caused or contributed to any release at the delivery site that resulted solely from circumstances beyond his control. The shipper who hired the transportation contractor to transport a hazardous substance shall not be considered to have caused or contributed to any release during transportation that resulted solely from circumstances beyond his control.]

(D) The term "owner or operator" does not include a . . . state or local government which acquired [title or control of a facility involuntarily; e.g., through foreclosure]. The [foregoing] exclusion . . . shall not apply to any State or local government which . . . caused or contributed to the release . . . of a hazardous substance, and [in such cases] such a State or local government shall be subject to . . . this chapter . . . to the same extent . . . as any nongovernmental entity, including liability under . . . this title.

(21) The term "person" means any individual, firm, corporation, association, partnership, consortium, joint venture, commercial entity, United States Government, State, municipality, commission, political subdivision of a state, or any interstate body.

(22) The term "release" means any . . . [discharge or escaping of a hazardous substance into the environment, whether voluntary or involuntary].

(23) The term "remove" or "removal" means the cleanup . . . of released hazardous substances from the environment, action . . . necessary to monitor, assess and evaluate the release or threat of release . . ., or the taking of such other actions necessary to prevent . . . or mitigate damage to the public health, . . . welfare or . . . the environment. . . .

(24) The term "remedy" or "remedial action" means those actions . . . to prevent or minimize the release of hazardous substances so that they do not migrate to cause . . . danger to present or future public health, . . . welfare or . . . the environment . . . [including storage, confinement, perimeter protection by excavations, cover and neutralization, cleanup of hazardous substance and contaminated materials, recycling, diversion, repair of defective containers, outside treatment and incineration, and provision of alternative supplies, and protective monitoring. Also included are costs of relocation of persons, businesses and facilities where the President deems such relocations to be more cost-effective and environmentally preferable to alternative remedial actions].

(25) The term "respond" or "response" means . . . removal . . . and remedial action. . . .

(33) The term "pollutant or contaminant" [means] . . . any . . . substance or mixture . . . which . . . upon exposure . . . . [by] any organism, . . . either directly from the environment or indirectly through food chains, . . . may reasonably be anticipated to cause death, disease, . . . behavioral abnormalities, cancer, genetic mutation, . . . or physical deformations in such organisms or their offspring . . . except that [such] term shall not include petroleum . . . .

(35) (A) The term "contractual relationship" . . . includes contracts, deeds or . . . instruments [of transfer of] title or possession, unless the . . . property on which the facility . . . is located was acquired by the [party] after the . . . placement of the hazardous substance on . . . the facility and [unless] the defendant [proves one of the following circumstances]:

(i) At the time . . . [he] acquired the facility, the defendant did not know and had no reason to know that any hazardous substance . . . was disposed of in, on, or at the facility.

(ii) The defendant is a government entity which acquired the facility by invol-

untary transfer . . . or . . . eminent domain . . . .

(iii) The defendant acquired the facility by inheritance . . . .

In addition . . . the defendant must establish [compliance with] . . . section 107(b)(3)(a) . . .

(B) To establish [the innocent-landowner defense above referred to] the defendant must have undertaken . . . appropriate inquiry into the previous ownership and uses of the property . . . . [T]he court shall take into account any specialized knowledge or experience of the defendant, the relationship of the purchase price to . . . the property [value] if uncontaminated, . . . reasonably ascertainable information about the property, [and] . . . the ability to detect such contamination by appropriate inspection.

(C) [A defendant with actual knowledge of a threatened release of a hazardous substance at such facility who subsequently transferred the property to another person without disclosing such knowledge shall be liable, and no defense shall be available to such defendant.]

CERCLA § 104   Response Authorities

(a) Removal and other remedial action . . . ; applicability of national contingency plan; response by potentially responsible parties; public health threats; . . . exception

(1) [Whenever there is a release or substantial threat of release of a hazardous substance or pollutant or contaminant into the environment which may present an imminent and substantial danger to the public health or welfare, the President is authorized to act, consistent with the national contingency plan to provide for remedial action which the President deems necessary protect the public health or welfare or the environment. The President may allow the owner or operator or other responsible party to carry out remedial action only if that party agrees to reimburse the Superfund for costs incurred by the President in connection with the oversight or arrangement for remedial action.]

CERCLA § 105   National contingency plan

(a) Revision and republication

. . . [T]he President shall, after notice and opportunity for public comments, revise and republish the national contingency plan for the removal of hazardous substance . . . . Such revision shall include . . . the national hazardous substance resource plan which shall establish procedures and standards for responding to releases of hazardous substances, pollutants, and contaminants, which shall include . . . :

(1) methods of discovering and investigating facilities at which hazardous substances have been disposed or otherwise come to be located;

(3) methods and criteria for determining the appropriate extent of . . . remedy, and other measured authorized by this chapter;

(7) means of assuring that remedial action measures are cost-effective over the period of potential exposure . . .

(8)(A) criteria for determining priorities among releases or threatened releases throughout the United States for the purpose of taking remedial action . . . . Criteria . . . shall be based upon relative risk . . . to public health or welfare the environment . . . .

(B) . . . [T]he President shall list national priorities among the known releases or threatened releases throughout the United States and shall revise the list . . . [at least] annually . . . . [E]ach State shall . . . submit for consideration . . . priorities for remedial action . . . in that State . . . . To the extent practicable [the top one hundred priority facilities on the President's list shall include at least one site from each State, with the State allowed to designate its highest-priority facility only once].

(10) standards and procedures by which alternative . . . technologies can be determined to be appropriate for [use in] response actions. . . .

CERCLA § 106   Abatement actions

(a) Maintenance, jurisdiction

. . . [W]hen the President determines that there may be an imminent and substantial endangerment to the public health or welfare or the environment, because of actual or threatened release of a hazardous substance . . . he may require the Attorney General . . . to secure . . . relief as may be necessary to abate such danger . . . and the [appropriate federal district court may] . . . grant such relief. The President may also . . . take other action under this section including, but not limited to, issuing such orders as may be necessary to protect public health and welfare and the environment.

(b) Fines; reimbursement

(1) Any person who . . . willfully violates . . . any order of the President . . . may, in an action bought to enforce such order, be fined not more than $25,000 for each day . . . [of] violation. . . .

(2)(A)(B) [If a nonliable party responds to an abatement order, that party may petition the President for reimbursement from the Superfund for the reasonable costs of such action, plus interest. If the petition is denied, he may seek reimbursement through a lawsuit.]

CERCLA § 107   Liability

(a) Covered persons; scope; recoverable costs and damages; interest rate; comparable maturity date

(1) the [present] owner or operator of a facility,

(2) any person who at the time of disposal of any hazardous substance owned or operated a facility . . . ;

(3) any person who by contract, agreement or otherwise arranged for disposal or treatment, . . . or arranged for transport for disposal or treatment, of hazardous substances . . . ; [or]

(4) any person who accepts or accepted . . . any hazardous substance for transport to disposal or treatment facilities . . . from which there is a release or threatened release which causes the incurrence of response costs . . . shall be liable for—

(A) all costs of removal or remedial action incurred by the United States Government or a State . . . ;

(B) any other necessary costs of incurred by any other person consistent with the national contingency plan;

(D) the costs of any health assessment or health effects study.

The amounts recoverable under this section shall include interest. . . . Such interest shall accrue from . . . the date payment is demanded or . . . the date of expenditure [whichever is later] . . . .

(b) Defenses

There shall be no liability . . .for a person . . . who can establish . . . that the release or threat of release of a hazardous substance and the damages resulting therefrom were caused solely by—. . .

(3) an act or omission of a third party other than . . . one whose act or omission occurs in connection with a contractual relationship . . . with the defendant . . . if the defendant establishes . . . that . . . he exercised due care with respect to the hazardous substance concerned, . . . and . . . he took precautions against foreseeable acts or omissions of any such third party . . . .

(c)(3) If any person who is liable for a release or threat of release of a hazardous substance fails without sufficient cause to properly provide removal or remedial action upon order of the President . . . , such person may be liable to the United States for punitive damages in an amount at least equal to, and not more than three times, the amount of any costs incurred by the Fund as a result of such failure to take proper action. . . .

CERCLA § 111   Use of Fund

(a) . . . The President shall use the money in the Fund for the following purposes:

(1) Payment of governmental response costs . . . .

(2) Payment of any claim for . . . response costs incurred by any other person as a result of carrying out the national contingency plan . . . .

■ Chapter 7 Endnotes

1. These italicized terms are defined in CERCLA § 101 and are discussed more fully later in the chapter.
2. A. Macbeth, *Superfund: Impact on Environmental Litigation* (American Bar Association Committee on Environmental Law, 1982–83).
3. *State of the Environment—A View toward the Nineties* (The Conservation Foundation, 1987), p. 170.
4. See *American Bar Association Journal,* September 1992, p. 30.
5. F. Grad, ''Remedies for Injuries Caused by Hazardous Waste: The Report and Recommendation of the Superfund 301(e) Study Group,'' 14 *Environmental Law Reporter* (1984), pp. 10105–10107.
6. CERCLA § 101(14).
7. CERCLA § 105.
8. 40 Code of Federal Regulations (C.F.R.), Part 300.
9. See, for example, *Anne Arundel County, Maryland v. EPA,* No. 91-1210 (D.C. Cir., 1 May 1992), and *National Gypsum Company v. EPA,* No. 90-1574 (D.C. Cir., 19 June 1992).
10. CERCLA § 121.
11. 42 U.S.C. § 9606(a).
12. Ibid.
13. *U.S. v. Parsons,* 936 F.2d 526 (11th Cir. 1991).
14. CERCLA § 107(a)(1).
15. CERCLA § 107(a)(2).
16. CERCLA § 107(a)(3).

17. CERCLA § 107(a)(4).

18. *Kaiser Aluminum & Chemical Corp. v. Catellus Development Corp.*, 976 F.2d 1338 (9th Cir. 1992).

19. CERCLA § 113(f).

20. CERCLA §§ 113(f) and 122(g).

21. *U.S. v. Monsanto Co.*, 858 F.2d 160 (4th Cir. 1989).

22. CERCLA § 101(35)(A)(i).

23. CERCLA § 101(35)(A)(ii).

24. CERCLA § 101(35)(A)(iii).

25. *United States v. Fleet Factors Corp.*, 901 F.2d 1550 (11th Cir. 1990); emphasis added.

26. *Guidice v. BFG Electroplating and Manufacturing Co.*, 732 F. Supp. 556 (W.D. Pa. 1989).

27. *In re Bergsoe Metal Corp.*, 910 F.2d 668 (9th Cir. 1990).

28. 40 C.F.R. 300.1100.

29. E. Elliott, "Superfund: EPA Success, National Debacle?" *Natural Resources and Environment* (1992), no. 3, p. 11; and T. Garrett, "Superfund Liability and Defenses: A 1992 Primer," p. 3 in the same issue.

The following comments by the Chairperson of the Oversight Subcommittee, House of Representatives Ways and Means Committee, fairly summarized criticisms leveled at the Superfund law:

> The costs of the Superfund program are staggering. The average cost to clean up a Superfund site is in the range of $25 to $30 million. This figure could go even higher as more complex sites are readied for cleanup. The revenue to be raised by the Superfund taxes . . . is only a down payment on an enormous cleanup bill, and still not come close to paying for the cleanup costs of the Nation's toxic waste sites.
>
> * * *
>
> In my view, we haven't gotten much in the way of cleanup for the $11 to $12 billion spent so far on the Superfund program. Most of the sites on the National Priorities List are stuck in the Superfund pipeline, and years pass while the sites are studied and restudied, evaluated and reevaluated.
>
> On average, over 9 years elapses between the time the remedial investigation is first performed . . . and the time the site is finally cleaned up, and the average time taken to clean up a site is on the increase.
>
> * * *
>
> . . . The trust fund was intended to be a sort of revolving fund that would be replenished . . . from the parties responsible for the pollution.
>
> Trust fund moneys would not be recoverable in instances where there was an "orphan site," where no responsible parties could be found. According to figures supplied by the Congressional Budget Office, of the $12 billion in trust fund receipts, less than 5 percent, or about $546 million have resulted from cost recoveries from responsible parties.
>
> Moreover, EPA has done a poor job managing its accounts receivable. Last year, according to the Inspector General, 90 percent of the receivables were delinquent. In some instances, EPA did not even know it was owed money until it received a check from a responsible party.

(From "Administration of Superfund by the Environmental Protection Agency," Hearing, H.R. Subcommittee on Oversight of the Committee on Ways and Means, 103rd Cong., 1st Sess. (Serial 103–38), July 26, 1993)

30. Quoted in "U.S. Lawmakers Call for Review of Superfund," *San Francisco Chronicle*, 7 June 1991, p. A12.

31. Quoted in *The Wall Street Journal*, 2 April 1992, p. A1.

32. *United States v. Fleet Factors Corp.*, n. 25, supra.

33. *B. F. Goodrich Co. v. Murtha*, 958 F.2d 1192, at p. 1199.

34. See, for example, the *Goodrich* opinion in section 7.2.

35. *The Wall Street Journal*, 2 April 1991, p. A1.

36. Ibid.

37. E. W. Breethauer, "New Davids to Tackle Environmental Goliaths," *EPA Journal* (May/June 1992), p. 51–52.

38. See, for example, "Tests Show Woodland Fungus Can Destroy Hazardous Wastes," *Philadelphia Inquirer*, 10 February 1984, p. A21.

PART IV

MEDIA SPECIFIC PROTECTION

Part II reviewed laws dealing with specific contaminants that have been identified as harmful to the environment. Those pollutant-specific laws are intended to control the production, disposal, and release of specified categories of pollutants into the environment. This Part, in contrast, examines laws that deal directly with the quality of two environmental media, water and air. Soil, the other environmental medium, also suffers from the effects of pollution and degradation, but Congress has not enacted a major statute for protecting the quality of soils or land—perhaps because soils and land are not as homogenous as water and air. There are, however, land-use statutes that seek to maintain or improve the quality of land and to regulate public and private uses of public lands. Those statutes are examined in Chapter 10.

The Clean Water Act and Clean Air Act regulate many activities that are also subject to the pollution-specific statutes, discussed in Part II, for pesticides (FIFRA), toxic chemicals (TSCA), and hazardous wastes (RCRA). Although pollution-specific regulation provides some protection for environmental media, it fails to protect their overall quality. The legal mechanisms formulated to regulate polluting discharges to air and water from various sources are quite distinct from those that deal with specific pollutants.

A natural medium's particular characteristics must be clearly understood in order to devise effective media-specific regulation for it, but the interconnectedness of the three environmental media cannot be ignored. Land, water, and air are sometimes referred to as *sinks*, a term that might imply that they are final depositories of substances. As Barry Commoner has noted, however, there is no ultimate "sink" for untreated pollution: everything is connected with everything else; everything must go somewhere; and there is no such thing as a free lunch.[1] Specific environmental media are but intermediate sinks, as pollutants continuously migrate to other geographical places and other environmental media. The pollution of one medium adversely impacts others; for instance, air pollution affects the quality of lake and stream water through precipitation, and soil contamination can volatilize to impair air quality. The interconnectedness of land, air, and water complicate attempts to prevent the degradation of a single medium. Polluting emissions and discharges to air and water also create differing hazards depending upon the geography, climate, biochemical conditions, and organisms of specific environmental niches.

Nonetheless, Congress chose to address pollution problems that are peculiar to air and water with separate statutes. Certain key concepts and regulatory approaches that are hallmarks of media-specific regulation are common to both the Clean Water and Clean Air Acts. For example, both acts are in varying degrees technology-driven; many of their regulatory standards are based upon the perceived availability of existing pollution control technology. Both laws implicitly assume that natural media can absorb certain loads and levels of particular pollutants without resultant serious harm to the environment. To what extent this is so is widely debated. The Clean Water and Clean Air Acts do not prohibit all releases of pollutants, but only those in excess of legally established thresholds for given classes of pollutants and for different regions or bodies of water. Under the Clean Water and Clean Air Acts, EPA and state agencies (and to a lesser extent, local governments) are responsible for the often difficult task of setting effluent and emissions limits for pollutant discharges to air and water. Through lobbying efforts and litigation, affected industries have had considerable influence in the process by which effluent and emissions limitations are determined.

The Clean Water and Clean Air Acts deal with diverse categories of water and air pollutants and sources. Both statutes differentiate between new and existing sources of pollution and between conventional and toxic classes of pollutants. Both statutes also reflect political and economic compromises in provisions that authorize consideration of cost factors in setting effluent or emissions limitations. Both Acts employ considerable administrative flexibility in affording EPA wide discretion to promulgate specific requirements for particular pollutants and polluting sources and in permitting state and local governments to choose from among various options for achieving federal water and air quality standards.

CHAPTER 8

Clean Water Act (CWA)

A Technology-Driven Model

Outline

8.1 Causes of Water Pollution

The waterways of the United States—its extensive coastline, the Great Lakes, its millions of miles of rivers and streams, its lakes, basins, wetlands, and estuaries—are precious resources that support vital uses by humans and many plant and animal organisms. It is well known that many pollutants now threaten these vast, diverse bodies of water. Therefore, the need for regulating polluting discharges through law poses a complex challenge. In this section the major kinds and sources of pollution of the various water resources are explained. This will furnish a framework for examining water quality protection under the Clean Water Act (CWA).

Water-quality data are available for only a third of the nation's rivers, half of its lake acreage, and three fourths of estuarine waters. Scientists continue to learn more about hydrology and to discover interrelationships among water resources and ecosystems that were previously thought to be discrete systems. Also the predominant sources of water pollution have changed over time, partly as a consequence of pollution-control legislation and partly due to economic trends. For example, in recent years pollution resulting from untreated or poorly treated sewage wastes and from industrial discharges has diminished, primarily as a result of more stringent controls under the CWA and other legislation.

Many environmental statutes deal with special water problems, among them the Safe Drinking Water Act and the Marine Protection Act, and with specific water areas, such as the Great Lakes. The CWA, however, applies generally to all activities that affect waterways falling under federal jurisdiction.

Categories of Water Resources

How water quality is affected by pollution depends partly upon the nature of the water resource. Water resources do not fit into neat and precise categories. For instance, estuarine marshes can also be characterized as wetlands. However, resources within a broadly defined category manifest similar symptoms in response to pollution. This subsection describes the major kinds of water resources in the United States and the primary effects of pollution upon them.

Rivers and Streams

The United States has more than 2 million miles of rivers and streams. That figure includes intermittent streams—those that flow only in wet weather—as well as major waterways. Rivers and streams directly connect other types of water resources, such as lakes, estuaries, ground water, and oceans. Pollution in rivers and streams affects the aquatic life within them as well as downstream habitats and uses. Therefore, whole watersheds must be considered in assessing water quality. The term *watershed* designates a geographic area in which water, sediments, and dissolved contaminants drain to a common outlet. The leading causes of river and stream pollution are agricultural runoff, municipal discharges (including indirect discharges from factories), hydrologic modifications (dredging, dams, etc.), mining, and petroleum drilling.

Lakes and Reservoirs

The United States has 40 million acres of lakes, ponds, and reservoirs. In nature, lakes undergo an evolutionary process called *eutrophication*. Eutrophication occurs when sediments and organic materials accumulate in a lake, causing its depth, oxygen level, and water clarity to be reduced and its biological productivity to be altered. Human activity can greatly accelerate eutrophication, leading to a lake's untimely death. Acid rain, acid mine drainage, and contamination by metals such as mercury also contribute to lake pollution.

The Great Lakes contain one fifth of the world's fresh water, but they are highly polluted. Of the 94 percent of total Great Lakes shoreline miles assessed in 1990, only 3 percent were found capable of fully supporting designated human uses. The presence of PCBs, DDT, and mercury originating from atmospheric deposition (e.g., polluted rain) and industrial discharges in the lakes has necessitated the issuance of fish-consumption advisories for nearshore waters of the Great Lakes. In addition to industrial discharges, landfill leachate has been a major source of Great Lakes contamination.

Estuaries, Bays, and Coastal Waters

An estuary is a semienclosed coastal water body where outflowing river water meets sea water. Estuary waters exhibit varying degrees of salinity and are affected by ocean tides and river currents. Estuaries are some of the most productive terrestrial ecosystems, supplying unique habitats for numerous plant and animal species. They are characterized by the growth of submerged sea grasses, salt marsh plants, algae, and phytoplankton. Organisms that inhabit estuaries include: bottom-dwellers such as oysters, clams, and lobsters; fish, including sea trout, striped bass, and flounder; and many bird species such as gulls and pelicans. Salmon and shrimp species use estuarine waters as nurseries. Many fish species, in particular, are dependent upon estuary systems for survival. There are 36,000 square miles of estuaries in the United States.

Sediments and organisms in coastal waters near large urban areas exhibit high, and in some places, increasing, levels of toxic pollutants. Most estuarine-dependent finfish and shellfish populations have been reduced to historic lows as a result of overfishing, habitat impoverishment, and water-quality degradation. Pathogen (disease-causing) contamination has forced the closure of many shellfish beds throughout the country. Shellfish are filter-feeders; they extract food from water that they draw into their bodies. Bacteria and viruses that accumulate on their gills and in their digestive tracts pose serious health risks to human consumers.

Other marine resources display similar declines. In the Chesapeake Bay, catches of migratory fish species declined 82 percent between 1960 and 1990. Maryland oyster stocks have been ravaged by overharvesting and, more recently, by diseases, the spread of which may be partly attributable to increased pollution—which often decreases organisms' resistance to disease. Northwestern rivers continue to experience losses of salmon species; the populations of several species having fallen to less than one fifth of former levels. Fish kill events in coastal areas have also been on the rise. In more than 40 percent of these kills, a low level of dissolved oxygen is the culprit.

Wetlands

The U.S. Fish and Wildlife's 1979 definition of wetlands encompasses "lands transitional between terrestrial and aquatic systems where the water table is usually at or near the surface or the land is covered by shallow water." Marshes, swamps, bogs, and other areas lying between water and dry land that are periodically saturated by water during the growing season are all considered wetlands. Wetlands play host to a variety of plant species adapted to wet conditions and particular soil types and are considered a vital link between land and water.

Wetlands display considerable variety depending upon their location, regional hydrology, vegetation, soils, topography, climate, and water chemistry. Because wetlands vary so much from region to region, they are difficult to define precisely. The scientific complexity of defining wetlands has enabled politicians and regulators to alter the degree of environmental protection for them by redefining the *legal* concept of what constitutes a wetland.

Wetlands can be roughly divided into two categories: coastal and inland. Coastal wetlands are closely linked to estuaries and include estuarine or coastal marshes and mangrove swamps. Coastal marshes are characterized by colonies of certain grasses and grasslike, halophytic (salt-loving) plants. Mangrove swamps are comprised of halophytic shrubs and trees.

Inland wetlands, which occur on floodplains, at the edges of lakes and ponds, and in isolated depressions surrounded by dry land, include: inland saline and alkaline marshes, riparian wetlands, wet meadows, bogs, North Carolinian pocosins (upland swamps), bottomland hardwood forests, prairie potholes, cypress-gum swamps, playa lakes, Californian vernal pools, Alaskan wet tundra, and Hawaiian tropical rainforests. Marshes and wet meadows are characterized by the growth of grasses and herbs, whereas wooded swamps harbor trees. Figures 8.1 and 8.2 show the acreage of U.S. wetlands by category and their distribution.

Now recognized as some of the earth's most unique and productive biosystems, wetlands were once regarded as undesirable swamps that would be better

■ **Figure 8.1**   Wetlands in the Lower 48 States, 1986

Wetland Types	Millions of Acres
Coastal Wetlands	5.2
Inland Marshes and Wet Meadows	28.4
Inland Shrub Swamps	10.6
Inland Forested Wetlands	49.7
Other Inland Wetlands	5.0

Adapted from: U.S. Environmental Protection Agency, from OPA-87-016.

■ **Figure 8.2**   U.S. Wetlands Acreage Distribution, 1989

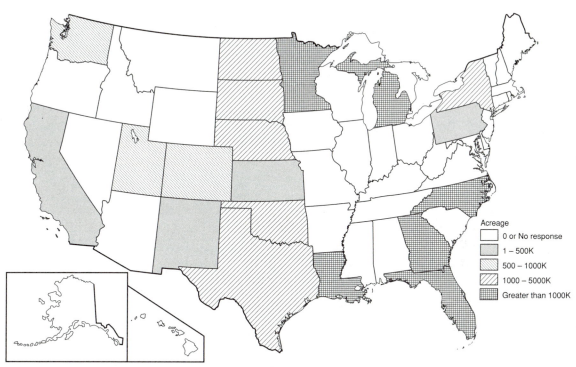

Source: U.S. Environmental Protection Agency, EPA 440/4-90-005, May 1990.

used for agricultural purposes or development. This point of view underlay passage of the federal Swamp Land Acts in the 1800s, which granted the states 65 million wetland acres to be converted to agricultural uses. Less than half of the more than 200 million acres of wetlands that existed when Europeans colonized America remained by the 1970s, as shown in Figure 8.3. Available data indicates

■ **Figure 8.3**   Wetlands Acreage: Original and Remaining Acreages in the Lower 48 States

	Percent
Remaining	46.0
Lost	54.0

Source: U.S. Environmental Protection Agency, OPA-87-016.

■ **Figure 8.4**   States with Wetlands Losses of Over 50 Percent

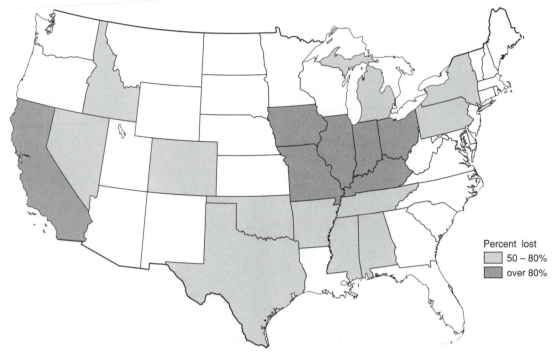

Note: Data is from 1780s through mid 1980s.

Source: U.S. Department of the Interior, Fish and Wildlife Service, *Wetlands: Status and Trends in the Conterminous United States, Mid-1970s to Mid-1980s* (Washington, D.C.: FWS, 1991), page 2, reported in CEQ, *Environmental Quality,* 22d Annual Report (1991), p. 196.

that from the mid 1950s to the mid 1970s, wetlands conversion averaged more than 450,000 acres per year, causing total losses for the period of 11 million acres—an area three times the size of New Jersey. More than two and a half million wetland acres were lost between the mid 1970s and the mid 1980s. The map in Figure 8.4 shows where the heaviest U.S. wetlands losses have occurred.

The fertility of wetlands' soils has made their conversion to farmland highly attractive. This accounted for most wetland losses until recently. In the 1980s, conversion of wetlands to agriculture slowed due to agricultural recessions, which made conversion less profitable, and to the Swampbuster provisions in the 1985 and 1990 Farm Bills, which eliminated farm subsidies for recently converted wetlands acreage. Oil, gas, and mineral deposits exist beneath some wetlands, making mining in wetlands another financially attractive but destructive prospect.

Today, commercial and residential development are primarily responsible for wetlands conversions. Wetlands continue to be lost to pollution, stream channelization, grazing, clearing, mining, highway construction, and draining and filling operations.

Disappearing as well are many of the numerous animal species that rely upon wetland areas for sustenance and shelter. Wetlands produce enormous volumes of food in the form of plants and they harbor a rich, diverse assortment of plant and animals species, including fish, birds, reptiles, and mammals—valuable components of food chains that ultimately support human life. Nearly half of the animal species and over a quarter of the plant species listed as threatened or endangered under federal law depend upon wetlands habitats during their life cycles.

Loss of habitat is an economic concern as well as an environmental concern. Coastal wetlands provide nursery and spawning grounds for 60–90 percent of all commercial fisheries. Government data indicate that 70 percent of the commercially harvested fish and shellfish in the United States depend upon wetlands habitats. In some areas such as the Southeast, that figure is nearly 100 percent. The U.S. Fish and Wildlife Service estimates that destruction of wetlands habitats between 1954 and 1978 accounted for lost fisheries income of $208 million *annually*. Wetlands losses also endanger economically and biologically significant waterfowl and fur-bearing animal populations that use wetlands as breeding and wintering grounds. Most of North America's ducks, for instance, use prairie potholes as breeding grounds.

Development has contributed heavily to a nearly complete loss of such unique wetlands habitats as California's submerged aquatic seagrass beds. The current rate of coastal wetlands conversion appears to be highest in the Mississippi River delta.

Wetlands serve other important functions besides providing habitat for plants and animals. They act as nature's water-purification system by filtering toxins and suspended solids and by processing pollutants far more efficiently than state-of-the-art water-purification plants. When wetlands are filled in, the streams to which they are connected become more polluted. As wetlands filter water, they also recharge ground-water supplies, a critical source of public water in many parts of the country. Wetlands have been used to process sewage, and scientists have begun to construct artificial wetlands for use as water-purification systems.

Wetlands are also valuable in controlling floods and storm surges and in preventing erosion along rivers and fragile shorelines. Most floodplain acreage is wetlands. Wetlands act as sponges, slowing flood waters and regulating water quantity by absorbing water during wet seasons and releasing it through springs during dryer seasons. Some wetlands plants, such as sphagnum moss, can hold up to 15 times their weight in water. River sediment is deposited on floodplains over time, preventing a rise in the height of the river. This also mitigates the danger and intensity of future floods.

The value of wetlands in flood control became very clear in the summer of 1993 when the upper Mississippi valley experienced a series of devastating floods. In many areas along the Mississippi, the landscape had been artificially altered by the construction of levees, flood walls, dikes, and diversion channels that cut the river off from its floodplains. These structures prevented the occasional minor flooding of the floodplains, where wetlands plants had previously slowed and absorbed the flow of the excess water. The structures also forced waters from heavy rains into an artificially narrow channel. Instead of gradually spreading over natural floodplains along its course, the swollen river finally broke through the levees in great waves. Afterward, the levees prevented floodwaters from returning to the river.

It is impossible to estimate the extent to which wetlands losses contributed to the damage caused by the 1993 floods. One study performed by a biologist at the U.S. Fish and Wildlife Service concluded that the more than 17 million acres of wetlands that had been destroyed in the Mississippi and Missouri River basins could have absorbed the volume of water contained by an area the size of 1,000 football fields with a depth of four and a half miles.[2]

Urban development not only destroys wetlands along river banks, but it also increases the rate and volume of surface-water runoff and consequently the possibility of flood damage. In a flood protection study for the Charles River area near Boston, the U.S. Army Corps of Engineers estimated that destruction of surrounding wetlands would cost an average of $17 million annually in flood damage. It determined that the most efficient flood-protection alternative in that locale was to preserve and protect the wetlands. Other communities are also finding that restoring and preserving wetlands is a cost-efficient method of flood control in the long run.

Wetlands plants also serve to control erosion. The roots of wetlands vegetation bind the soil, and its foliage slows and regulates water movement that would otherwise wash away the soil. In coastal areas, wetland plants slow wave movement and prevent the erosion of shorelines. Coastal erosion is a critical problem in many shore communities and was the catalyst for the state regulations that were challenged in *Lucas v. South Carolina Coastal Council,* a 1992 Supreme Court case that is discussed later in Section 8.5. Some kinds of wetlands, especially bogs, also play a role in climate control by storing carbon in decaying plants and reducing the amount of carbon dioxide that is released into the atmosphere.

Scientists and government agencies still have much to learn about wetlands ecosystems. A 1991 study by the National Oceanic and Atmospheric Administration (NOAA) found that 63 percent of coastal wetlands are forested and scrub-shrub areas, about which very little is known. Salt marshes and tidal flats, ecosystems that have received considerably more study, collectively account for only 20 percent of coastal wetlands.

Even as science enlarges its understanding of the many vital ecological purposes wetlands serve, these areas continue to be lost or degraded beyond repair. Some developers and farmers advocate "mitigation banking" as a regulatory solution to the tensions between economic interests and environmental concerns. Mitigation banking would allow future development of wetlands sites only in exchange for restoration of wetlands acreage elsewhere. In 1993 the EPA and the Army Corps of Engineers released a draft study concluding that in certain instances, mitigation banking is an ecologically sound means of compensating for wetlands losses.[3] However, the mitigation banking concept reflects a notion that is widely discredited among environmental scientists, the notion that science can create wetlands in "more convenient" locations to serve the same purposes as those being destroyed. As a U.S. Fish and Wildlife official put it, "Trying to recreate a wetland is like taking this vein in your arm and moving it to where there is not a vein. It may look like a vein, but it does not function as one."[4] The locations of particular wetlands are inextricably related to their functions; riverine bottomland, for instance, can provide flood control only if it is located alongside the river. It follows that not all wetlands are of equal ecological significance and that wetlands are simply not interchangeable commodities. An additional problem with mitigation banking is that the methodology of wetlands restoration remains undeveloped. A North Carolina wetland that had undergone an ostensibly successful restoration was found to be producing only one sixth of the living matter that a similar natural marsh produced.

The available information is sufficient to convince most scientists and environmentalists that wetlands ecosystems are priceless resources worthy of considerable legal protection. Some of the legal mechanisms for slowing wetlands conversion are discussed later in this chapter.

Groundwater

The vast majority of the earth's fresh water supply is not found in lakes and rivers; it is underground. Fully 96 percent of the earth's fresh water is ground water which is stored in *aquifers*, geological formations of saturated permeable rock, sand, or gravel. Ground water moves slowly (a few inches per year) in areas contained by impermeable clay layers, and more quickly (800 feet or more yearly) in sand and gravel strata. Consolidated ground-water movements are referred to as *plumes*. Aquifers are recharged by precipitation (e.g., rainfall) seeping into the ground or by connected surface waters. Ground water is naturally discharged to springs or streams. Figure 8.5 illustrates ground water and land use in the hydrological cycle.

Half of the U.S. population relies upon ground water for drinking and household use. Unfortunately, ground-water contaminants can concentrate in moving plumes whose speed and direction are affected by an area's geological characteristics. Once contaminated, ground water is exceedingly difficult or impossible to clean up because of the movement of the plumes. Major sources of ground-water contamination include leaking underground storage tanks, septic tanks, landfill leaching, hazardous waste sites, agricultural pesticide runoff, irrigation, and feedlot activity.

Kinds of Water Pollution

Water becomes polluted in various ways, both by discharges of hazardous or toxic substances into lakes and streams and by runoff. This subsection briefly outlines the various kinds of water pollution with which the United States must cope.

Nutrients

Eutrophication, the process by which lakes evolve into swamps, occurs naturally, but soil runoff and the inflow of waters polluted with nutrients—such as phosphates from detergents and nitrates from agricultural fertilizers—greatly accelerate the natural process. Excess nutrients stimulate the growth of algae, which consume dissolved oxygen and block the flow of light to deeper waters. This affects the respiration of fish and aquatic invertebrates and eventually decreases plant and animal diversity.

Silt/Suspended Solids

During periods of precipitation, silts and sediments run off plowed fields, construction and logging sites, urban areas, strip mines, and eroded streambanks. When they reach surface waters, these sediments impair fish respiration and plant productivity.

Pathogens

Inadequately treated sewage, storm water, and livestock-habitat runoff may be contaminated by pathogens such as bacteria and viruses that cause typhoid; cholera; and respiratory, intestinal, and skin diseases. Fecal coliform bacteria, although not the most dangerous of these pathogens, often indicate the presence

■ **Figure 8.5**   Ground Water and Land Use in the Water Cycle

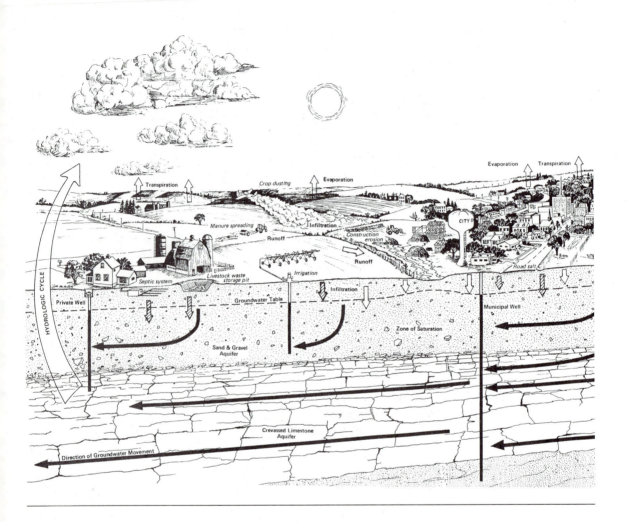

of more hazardous organisms, which is why their presence or absence is often used in ascertaining water quality. When ingested orally or through the skin, such pathogens can cause illness or death to humans and animals.

Toxic and Hazardous Chemicals and Metals

Industrial point-source discharges, runoff from mining sites, and leachate from landfills often contain hazardous and toxic substances or heavy metals that pose dangers to humans and other organisms. Toxins and metals may accumulate in the tissues of fish and shellfish, kill off aquatic organisms, disrupt reproduction and food chains, and make fish and shellfish unfit for human consumption. Toxic substances that accumulate in the sediment beds of streams, lakes, and estuaries may continue to contaminate the surrounding waters and adversely affect aquatic organisms, especially bottom-dwellers, for many years after the polluting discharges have ceased. When harbors and channels are dredged, contaminated sediments are stirred up, polluting the entire waterway.

■ **Figure 8.5**   Continued

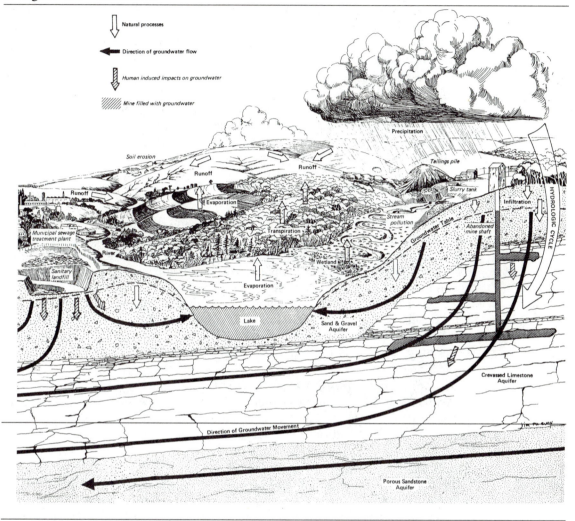

Source: EPA publication *Protecting Our Groundwater* (1990). Artwork courtesy of Wisconsin Department of Natural Resources.

Organic Wastes

Organic wastes include sewage, household garbage (discarded vegetable and animal products), and runoff from livestock feedlots and pastures. Organic wastes are decomposed by bacteria that feed off them. Excessive discharges of organic wastes into a water body raise its bacteria level and can make the water unsafe for bathing and drinking. An overload of organic wastes also reduces the level of dissolved oxygen, which supports aquatic life. Many species of fish and bottom-dwellers cannot survive in oxygen-depleted waters.

When dissolved oxygen is depleted, decomposition occurs anaerobically; that is, without oxygen. Methane and hydrogen sulfide are released into the water and the atmosphere during anaerobic decomposition, and these releases, in turn, create other ecological imbalances.

Pesticides and Herbicides

Agricultural runoff is the major source of pesticide and herbicide contamination of the water. Pesticides are highly persistent in the environment and, like metals, they can bioaccumulate in fish, shellfish, and wildlife. This interferes with reproduction and disrupts food chains.

Heat "Pollution"

Water used to cool machinery and equipment at industrial plants is commonly discharged into nearby waterways. The discharged water raises the temperature of the natural waterway, which can reduce its dissolved-oxygen content and thus accelerate the growth of algae. These changes cause imbalances in the aquatic environment that adversely affect fish and other aquatic life.

Salinization

Irrigation runoff, brines used in oil extraction, and road de-icing salts are saline (salty) pollutants that contribute to the salinization of fresh-water supplies. Sea water can also increase the salinity of ground water, reducing soil fertility and contaminating drinking-water supplies. Sea water intrusion often results when ground water is pumped from an aquifer at a rate exceeding the rate at which the aquifer is recharged by precipitation. Continued pumping of a depleted aquifer creates a kind of vacuum that pulls nearby sea water into the aquifer. In this way, domestic and industrial overconsumption of the ground water supply can lead to salinization of ground water.

Acid Rain, Acid Runoff, and pH Imbalance

Acid rain and runoff from abandoned mines modify the pH (acidity versus alkalinity) balance of soils and ground water. This affects the toxicity of other dissolved chemicals and can make lakes and streams uninhabitable.

Petroleum

Petroleum contains a number of substances known to endanger human health and the environment, including benzene, toluene, ethylene, and xylene. Oil spills and discharges from oil tankers and freighters have wreaked havoc on oceanic and coastal ecosystems for decades. They have destroyed or irreversibly modified habitats; killed off significant numbers of birds, fish, and mammals; and polluted vast areas of water and shorelines. The *Exxon Valdez* spill is a particularly spectacular example of the kind of devastation wrought by petroleum pollution.

Sources of Water Pollution

Unless adequate measures are taken to prevent contaminants from reaching surface and underground waters, these things can be expected to result in water pollution:

- the movement of water over (runoff) or through (leaching) contaminated soils or pavement;
- the direct discharge of industrial wastes into waterways; and
- the discharge of imperfectly treated waste water from treatment plants.

The most common sources of water pollution are described in this subsection.

Industrial Processes

Most manufacturing and industrial plants generate some waste by-products. Until the Clean Water Act (CWA) mandated specified levels of treatment for industrial wastes before discharge, businesses disposed of their wastes in nearby waterways without restraint. At common law, downstream users of such waters, such as municipalities and fisheries, could do very little to prevent or limit such industrial discharges unless they could establish some legal right to a particular water source or could show that polluting discharges constituted a nuisance under state law.

Industrial discharges are a type of "point source" pollution. A *point source* is defined as any discernable conveyance, including a drainage pipe or ditch, from which pollutants may be discharged. The CWA definition of point source specifically excludes agricultural runoff.

Agricultural Runoff

In the course of rainfall or crop irrigation, water runs off the land and drains into receiving waters such as lakes and streams. Runoff carries soil, sediments, and animal wastes with it. Where chemical pesticides or fertilizers have been used, agricultural runoff contains those substances as well. Runoff from pastures, feedlots, rangeland, and cropland carries wastes to other waterways and locales and generally occurs over a large, undefinable area. Hence, it is considered "nonpoint-source" pollution.

Storm Sewers and Combined Sewers

Dirt, garbage, animal excrement, spilled oil, gasoline, transmission fluids, and other wastes dropped or left on streets and sidewalks enter storm sewers during rainfall or street cleaning. If the storm-sewer system is not channeled to a sanitary-sewer system, these substances enter the receiving waters untreated. Even if the storm-sewer system does carry the contaminated runoff to a water treatment plant, however, many municipal treatment systems cannot process excess stormwater effectively. When a municipal treatment plant receives overflows or types of waste it is not designed to treat, both sewage and stormwater flow into the receiving waters without being fully treated. Leakage from septic tanks is another source of polluting runoff.

Municipal Treatment Plants

Many municipal treatment plants lack the capability to filter or treat numerous organic and inorganic pollutants and contaminants discharged by industrial plants, households, and combined storm- and sanitary-sewer overflow. Small, publicly owned treatment works, in particular, commonly lack the financial resources to implement technical improvements for treating certain classes of contaminants and elevated discharge volumes. Pollutants that overtax municipal treatment-plant capacity, and are released untreated, are referred to as *excursions*.

Silviculture

Timber harvesting, especially clear-cutting, can dramatically increase soil erosion because it involves removing tree roots and vegetation, which bind soils and moderate the effects of precipitation. Road construction for logging activities also increases soil runoff by uprooting soil-protecting vegetation and displacing large volumes of soil.

Construction

Residential and commercial development and highway construction create erosive effects similar to those of silviculture activities. Because the natural landscape is disrupted, the volume of soil runoff is increased.

Mining and Petroleum Drilling

Runoff from solid-ore mining sites introduces dangerous pollutants into water supplies. Leaking underground storage tanks are also a major culprit of ground- and surface-water contamination. Crude-oil extraction, petroleum processing, and transport spills all release hazardous and toxic constituents into water supplies.

Land Disposal

As explained in Chapters 6 and 7 on RCRA and CERCLA, respectively, landfills are the source of many hazardous constituents of ground water. As rainfall and other precipitation percolates through uncovered and unlined landfills, contaminants leach into ground water and run off into surface waters.

Hydrologic Modification

Hydrologic modification encompasses channelization, dredging, dam construction, and streambank modification. Such activities are undertaken to improve navigation, fill waterlogged areas for residential and commercial construction, and create reservoirs. In spite of the benefits of these activities, they can have detrimental impacts on surrounding water quality.

8.2   Legislative History and Overview of the Clean Water Act

Origins and Development of Federal Water-Pollution Law

Federal water-pollution legislation has its roots in the Refuse Act of 1899, which made the discharge of refuse into navigable waters without a permit illegal. Originally, the Act's purpose was to prevent discharges that would obstruct navigation. For six decades, no court or official construed the Refuse Act to apply to water pollution not affecting a waterway's navigability.

In 1960, Representative Henry S. Ruess of Wisconsin compiled a list of companies in his state that were discharging pollutants into rivers and streams and sent the list to the U.S. Attorney's office to test the Refuse Act's applicability to industrial-waste discharges. As a result, four companies were prosecuted and convicted of violating the Act. Based upon the plain language of the statute, the U.S. Supreme Court upheld application of the Refuse Act to discharges of pollutants into navigable waterways. In 1970, however, the Nixon Administration issued an instruction to the Department of Justice that shelved the use of the Refuse Act as a pollution abatement statute, directing that the Refuse Act should be used only:

> . . . to punish or prevent significant discharges which are either accidental or infrequent, but which are not of a continuing nature resulting from the ordinary operations of a manufacturing plant . . . . [C]ivil and criminal actions against manufacturing plants which continuously discharge refuse into the navigable waters of the United States are not among the types of actions which the United States Attorneys may initiate on their own authority.[5]

The ostensible reason for the guideline was to prevent the use of the Refuse Act "as a pollution abatement statute in competition with the federal water pollution act [of 1948, as amended in 1956 and 1965] . . . "[6]

At that time, the Federal Water Pollution Act was an ineffective piece of legislation which used ambient water-quality standards to specify acceptable pollution levels in interstate waters. The law granted states (with limited federal intervention) the authority to designate uses, including waste disposal, for particular waterways within their territories and mandated notice periods and highly cumbersome federal–state enforcement conferences before the federal government could take enforcement action. In order to take an enforcement action, governmental authorities needed to demonstrate that a particular polluter had caused degradation of water quality in a specific waterway. Given the numerous sources of pollution of major waterways at the time, this evidentiary standard was nearly impossible to meet.

The law was so ineffective in controlling water pollution that an Ohio river, whose designated use was "waste disposal," caught fire in 1969. In 1972, when the Senate Committee on Public Works declared that "the Federal water pollution control program . . . has been deficient in every vital aspect," only *one* enforcement case under the federal statute had been brought in more than 15 years.

When Congress passed the Federal Water Pollution Control Act Amendments of 1972 (FWPCA), it adopted a permit program based upon technology-based effluent limitations that set ceilings on the amount of pollution point sources could discharge into the nation's waterways. The Act did not entirely discard the water-quality approach but the new legislation subordinated that approach to the permit system. The permit system was designed to ensure that individual polluters achieve the greatest possible pollution reductions using available technologies. The effluent discharge limitations—to be promulgated by EPA for different industries on the basis of available pollution treatment technologies—removed the burden that government entities previously carried to determine which polluters were most responsible for degrading water quality in a particular waterway. These effluent limitations made all dischargers subject to uniform national standards. The permit system effected a translation of general effluent limitations into specific limits on the amount and concentration of enumerated pollutants an individual permitee could discharge, thereby facilitating enforcement of the statute. The statute made *all* point-source discharges of pollutants illegal without a permit; therefore, every discharger was required to obtain a permit.

The 1972 Act adopted a tiered approach to industrial discharges by requiring that sources utilize the best technology currently available by 1977 and the best technology economically achievable—a stricter standard—by 1983. In 1977 and again in 1987, amendments extended those deadlines and made applicable standards less stringent. Under the 1972 Act and subsequent amendments, the standards for public treatment works were generally more lenient and the standards for new sources remained somewhat more strict. For each class and category of industrial sources, EPA was required to promulgate regulations specifying what limits could be achieved using the technological standards specified by Congress in the statute. EPA's translation of the statutorily specified technological requirements into numerical pollution limits for each class and category of industrial sources has furnished ample litigation fodder for affected industries.

Water-quality standards remain a part of federal water pollution regulation and are to be imposed upon dischargers if applicable water-quality standards cannot be achieved through technology-based effluent limitations. The 1972 FWPCA set the federal goal of achieving "fishable, swimmable waters" nationwide by 1983, and of eliminating *all* pollutant discharges into "navigable waters" by 1985. These overly optimistic goals were relaxed and extended by later amendments. The 1987 Water Quality Act required states to adopt specific numerical criteria for addressing toxic pollutant discharges, to report the nonattainment of water-quality standards for particular waterways, to determine which point-source discharges were preventing attainment, and to develop individual statewide control strategies for particular waterways to achieve water-quality standards. It remains to be seen how effective these provisions will be.

In 1990 a court summarized the CWA as follows:

> Under the Act, the EPA must impose and enforce technology-based effluent limitations and standards through individual National Pollution Discharge Elimination System [NPDES] permits. These permits contain specific terms and conditions as well as numerical discharge limitations, which govern the activities of pollutant dischargers. Through the Clean Water Act, Congress has directed the EPA to incorporate into the permits increasingly stringent technology-based effluent limitations.[7]

Statutory Usage of Technical Terms

The FWPCA and its subsequent amendments are now generally referred to as the Clean Water Act (CWA). The CWA contains a number of technical terms that significantly affect its coverage. The central (though not comprehensive) meanings of some of those terms are given here.

Direct dischargers are those who discharge effluent directly into natural waterways such as rivers, streams, and lakes.

Indirect dischargers are those who discharge effluent into publicly owned treatment works (POTWs) for treatment before later discharge into surface waters.

Effluent means a material whose content or characteristics pollute or contaminate water.

Effluent limitations means restrictions imposed by law on the quantities and concentrations of pollutants that may be discharged into waters of the United States. All pollutants are divided into three categories: "toxic," "conventional," and "nonconventional." Effluent limitation standards also incorporate technology standards that apply to different sources of discharge. Thus, effluent limitations are based upon the type of pollutant and the category of the discharger.

Navigable waters of the United States is a term of art that has little to do with a waterway's actual use for navigation. The CWA governs any location, wet or dry, that has a colorable possibility of being used for or affecting interstate navigation. Most waterways of the United States thus fall within the jurisdiction of federal water-protection statutes, since they can be made navigable through construction and diversion techniques. In numerous public-works projects throughout the country, the Army Corps of Engineers has demonstrated that virtually any body of water can be made navigable.

Point source refers to any discernable conveyance, including a drainage pipe or ditch, from which pollutants are discharged into waterways. Federal water legislation classifies various kinds of point sources and specifically excludes agricultural runoff from the definition of point source.

Nonpoint source generally means sources of pollution discharge other than point sources; runoff of surface waters is an example. A 1987 study reported: "As industries and municipalities succeed in cleaning up their wastewater discharges, nonpoint sources have become the major source of water pollution in many parts of the United States."[8]

Publicly owned treatment works (POTWs) include public treatment facilities, such as municipal water and sewage plants.[9]

Overview of the Clean Water Act

The CWA has been aptly described as "a good old horse which over the years has periodically received new legs and new teeth."[10] Section 101 of the act declares that its objective is "to restore and maintain the chemical, physical, and biological integrity of the Nation's waters." The central prohibition of the CWA is found in its section 301, which bans the discharge of *any* "pollutant" by *any* "point source" into a navigable water without a permit. The permitting system is known as the *National Pollution Discharge Elimination System (NPDES)*, under which all point sources of water pollutants are required to have and comply with a NPDES permit. States are authorized to administer the permit program after receiving EPA approval, and most of them now do so. Section 505 of the CWA authorizes citizens to initiate enforcement suits in two circumstances; namely, to sue a party that is violating and likely to continue violating CWA effluent standards[11] and to sue the EPA Administrator for failure to carry out nondiscretionary duties that the law obliges him or her to perform.

Effluent limitation standards have been set for three classes of pollutants (conventional, nonconventional, and toxic) and are based on the availability of pollution-control technology. The various amendments to the CWA provide different time deadlines for adoption of the prescribed technologies. For instance, the law originally required use of the "best technology currently available" by industrial point-source dischargers by 1977 and use of the "best technology economically achievable" (a stricter standard) by 1983. Later amendments have imposed stricter effluent limitations on "new" point sources on the assumption that it is more feasible to install up-to-date pollution-control technology in new or expanded industrial plants than in older ones. All effluent-limitation standards are based upon the availability of pollution-control technology, whether widely used or merely technologically feasible.

Salient points of more recent amendments include these:

a. In setting new effluent-limitation standards for conventional pollutants, EPA must consider not only technological feasibility, but also the cost-benefit factors of attaining effluent reductions.

b. EPA is authorized to extend compliance deadlines and to waive statutory requirements in certain circumstances.

c. With regard to Publicly Owned Treatment Works (POTWs), EPA may extend the statutory deadlines for secondary-treatment requirements if a POTW's failure to meet the deadline results from the unavailability of federal construction funding.

d. States may not reduce federal effluent limitations even though they may designate uses for their waterways. This provision countered the threat that powerful industries would induce states to adopt relaxed water-quality standards in designating the use of state waterways. Nevertheless, the act allows greater effluent-limitation variances for municipal wastewater-treatment plants than it does for other direct dischargers.

e. States must establish programs for dealing with "nonpoint" discharges, such as runoff from agricultural and urban areas.

Although the CWA requires EPA to monitor federally approved state permit programs, EPA has limited incentive to do so. If EPA were to find a state's permit program inadequate, it would be required to expend its own limited resources to administer the NPDES program in that state. Therefore, even if a state is not administering the NPDES program with sufficient vigor, EPA may be reluctant to take over those functions.

Wetlands and Estuary Protection

As explained in section 8.1 (and exemplified by *U.S. v. Riverside Bayview Homes* in section 8.3 and *Lucas v. South Carolina Coastal Council* in section 8.5), development and other human activities can destroy wetlands and estuary ecosystems, which are now recognized as critical ecological resources. Wetlands and estuaries associated with navigable waters are protected under CWA. Unless a permit has been granted for it, the CWA prevents the disposal of any pollutant, including dredge or fill material, into any water of the United States. CWA section 404 gives the Army Corps of Engineers the authority to grant permits for the disposal of dredged or fill materials into "waters of the United States."

Initially, the Corps' regulations construed the CWA as granting it authority only over waters that were navigable in fact. In regulations issued in 1975, however, the Corps redefined "waters of the United States" to include tributaries and nonnavigable intrastate waters whose use or misuse could affect interstate commerce, and wetlands adjacent to all waters covered by the CWA. EPA had reached the same conclusion in regulations it promulgated two years earlier. In 1985, in *United States v. Riverside Bayview Homes*, the U.S. Supreme Court upheld the Corps' interpretation of "waters of the United States." The Court found that the Corps' inclusion of adjacent wetlands in its definition was reasonable, given the role which wetlands play in drainage, purification, flood control, and erosion prevention, all of which benefit navigable waters.[12]

It is fairly settled that when a wetland adjoins a lake, stream, or coastal area, the federal government has jurisdiction under the CWA to prevent dredging or filling activities.[13] The primary basis for federal CWA jurisdiction over U.S. waters is the Commerce Clause of the U.S. Constitution. Waters that potentially affect interstate commerce are therefore a proper subject for federal regulation pursuant to the Commerce Clause. Wetlands connected to navigable waters also fall under federal jurisdiction since activities affecting such wetlands can have a potential impact on navigability and quality of associated waterways. It is less clear, however, whether the federal government can regulate dredging and filling activities on "isolated" wetlands, that is, on wetlands not physically connected to navigable waters. If activities that affect isolated wetlands do not impact interstate commerce, the federal government does not have regulatory jurisdiction. If the isolated wetlands are habitats for migratory birds or other species that are an object of interstate commerce, however, they can be regulated by the federal government under the CWA.[14] Furthermore, isolated wetlands are often linked to navigable waters through the hydrological cycle; if destruction of isolated wetlands has a potential impact on the navigability or quality of such waters, that connection may be a sufficient basis for federal regulatory jurisdiction.

Under CWA section 404, the Corps has the authority to regulate discharges of dredge and fill materials for development and construction purposes as well as for "disposal," an interpretation that courts have upheld. Although the Corps is the primary permit authority, EPA may veto such permits. The Corps can bring penalty actions and has the authority to compel restoration of areas that have been dredged or filled without a proper permit. Criminal prosecutions under the CWA, including that of John Posgazi, who ignored repeated directives to discontinue his landfilling activities,[15] have attracted considerable media attention.

In addition, the 1977 amendments to the CWA empowered the states to establish permit programs for dredge and fill activities in nonnavigable waters. EPA can object to the issuance of state permits. General, rather than specific, permits can be granted by the Corps or by the states to allow certain classes of dredging and filling activities.

Environmental groups have challenged Corps regulations governing grants of general permits. In settling one lawsuit brought by these groups, the Corps agreed to tighten its requirements to assure that these general permits were granted only in situations where filling in wetlands would have little environmental impact. In November 1989, the Corps and EPA entered into a memorandum of understanding under which the Corps agreed to exercise its authority to review section 404 permit applications so as to minimize any loss of wetlands. This memorandum is the basis for what became known as the "no net loss of wetlands" policy.

In a 1991 report, EPA's Inspector General (IG) criticized EPA for undermining the protection of the nation's wetlands by inconsistently implementing wetlands programs. In particular, the IG focused on regional implementation of basic wetlands-program elements, concluding that enforcement, programming, and strategic initiatives varied in emphasis and that this had led to unpredictable and inconsistent regulation. According to the IG's report, EPA regional officers failed to coordinate their efforts with those of the Army Corps of Engineers to identify illegal discharges of dredged or fill materials and to take enforcement actions. The IG's report also criticized EPA for failing to make good use of limited resources by identifying and prioritizing wetlands according to value and vulnerability and informing the public as to which areas were most threatened.

EPA has also been criticized by developers, whose commercial, industrial, and residential construction projects are frequently delayed or impeded by permit requirements. In response to criticism and pressure from businesses and industry groups, many of which allied to form the National Wetlands Coalition, the Bush administration sought to narrow the definition of wetlands so as to alleviate impediments to commercial and residential development in some areas. To that end, the Bush administration proposed a new wetlands policy in 1992 that would have redefined wetlands to exclude more than half of the nation's remaining wetlands—including more than half of the Southeastern hardwood swamps, approximately one fourth of the Everglades, 80 percent of the South's Great Dismal Swamp, most freshwater wetlands near the Chesapeake Bay, most Northeastern and Midwestern bogs, almost 40 percent of North Dakota's prairie potholes, and many coastal high marshes. Major waterfowl winter habitats, breeding grounds, migratory stops, and feeding areas, particularly in the Pacific and Central flyways, would have been affected by the proposed regulations.

Under wetlands regulations in effect prior to, and since, the 1992 proposal, a host of criteria are used to determine if an area is a wetland, including plant inventories and frequency and duration of ground-water saturation sufficient to support vegetation adapted to saturated conditions. Environmental officials are required to look at the totality of the hydrogeological and biological evidence in determining if an area should be considered a wetland because very few wetlands exhibit the same duration of ground-water saturation every year. Instead, wetlands appear to undergo long-term, cyclical variation in the degree of saturation, which varies widely depending upon a large number of environmental factors.

In seeking to open previously protected wetlands to development, the Bush administration did not withdraw its "no net loss of wetlands" policy. Rather, it sought to narrow the legal definition of what constitutes a wetland. Nonetheless, the practical effect of the proposed redefinition would have been the same, and would have permitted the ecological destruction of significant acreages previously recognized as wetlands. Under this proposal, which EPA published for public comment prior to the November 1992 elections, an area would not have been considered a protected wetland unless it met a rigid set of criteria, including ground-water saturation for a minimum number of consecutive days per year. Many areas that scientists would agree are wetlands would not have qualified for protection under the proposal, which would have required quantified evidence based on inflexible standards. The proposed policy came under heavy criticism from scientists and environmentalists. Prior to its adoption, however, President Clinton took office, and it remains to be seen what position the Clinton administration or Congress will take on wetlands when the CWA is reauthorized. The Clinton administration convened a special panel, known as the *White House Task Force on Wetlands*, to develop a position on wetlands. The panel's focuses are private property rights and "takings" issues (discussed later in the chapter) and issues related to expanding existing protections for wetlands. The panel will make recommendations to a Congress that is divided over wetlands issues as it considers CWA reauthorization legislation.[16]

Other federal laws now encourage wetlands protection by eliminating certain incentives that have negatively impacted wetlands. The 1985 and 1990 Farm Bills included "Swampbuster" provisions, which deny agricultural subsidies to farmers who plant crops on newly converted or altered wetlands. The Tax Reform Act of 1986 eliminated favorable capital-gains treatment for improving lands by drainage. The Coastal Barrier Resources Act of 1982 eliminated federal insurance and other subsidies that had had the effect of promoting development on barrier islands, which was destroying their associated wetlands.

The federal government also provides financial incentives for protecting wetlands. Tax laws now allow charitable deductions for those who sell or donate wetlands to a government agency or a conservation organization. The federal government acquires wetland acreage or purchases conservation easements with monies from the Migratory Bird Hunting Stamp program, funded by duck hunters who are required to purchase duck stamps. The 1990 Farm Bill and the Water Bank Act established voluntary easement programs, which offer lease payments to landowners who grant easements of a minimum duration to maintain or restore wetlands. The federal Coastal Zone Management Act has given states incentives to implement programs for reducing the rate of coastal wetlands conversion. States also maintain their own wetlands protection programs, most of them aimed at preserving coastal, rather than inland, wetlands.

A related issue, estuary degradation, is beginning to receive some attention under the National Estuary Program (NEP), established pursuant to the CWA.[17] Utilizing a watershed approach, the NEP asks states to nominate estuaries of national significance that are being threatened by pollution, development, or overuse. This is part of a national demonstration program that seeks to characterize problems and identify solutions through management conferences with representatives of affected industries, conservation organizations, and state officials. The federal Coastal Zone Management Act also affords some measure of estuary protection.

Whenever private property owners are constrained from using their property in certain ways by government regulation, constitutional "takings" issues may arise. In the case of wetlands and other environmental resources, significant public policies are also implicated. Issues related to environmental regulation of private property are discussed more fully in section 8.5.

8.3   Structure and Workings of CWA

Outline of Major Statutory Provisions

The general scheme of the CWA is succinctly restated by the Supreme Court opinion in *P.U.B. No. 1 v. Washington Dept. of Ecology* which is reproduced later in this section. The major prohibition against discharges of pollutants into waters of the United States is found in CWA section 301(a) which prohibits discharges of virtually all materials, including substances not generally thought to be pollutating, without a permit. For instance, in the early 1980s the governor of Puerto Rico brought suit under the Clean Water Act to enjoin the U.S. Navy's accidental and intentional discharges of military ordnance into waters off the coast of Vieques Island. Although an injunction was not issued, the Supreme Court found that the Navy's discharge of ordnance into the sea was a technical violation of the CWA.[18]

Section 402 establishes the National Pollution Discharge Elimination System (NPDES), under which EPA may issue permits to point-source dischargers of polluting effluents. Section 404 establishes the Army Corps of Engineers' authority to issue permits for discharge of dredge or fill materials into navigable waters of the United States and specifies the situations under which permits are required. Section 404 is the primary wetlands protection provision of the CWA.

NPDES permittees must comply with technology-based limitations and conditions specified in the sections listed here.

Technology-Based Limitations

Timetables	§ 301(b)
Modification of timetable	§ 301(c),(g),(i)
Innovative technology	§ 301(k)
No modification for toxics	§ 301(l)
Fundamentally different factors	§ 301(n)
National performance standards	§ 306
Toxic effluent standards	§ 307(a)(2),(4)
Pretreatment standards	§ 307(b)(1)

The CWA also contains water-quality standards.

Water Quality Standards

Water-quality-related effluent limitations	§ 302(a)
State water-quality standards	§ 303(a)(2),(3)
State rankings	§ 303(d)(1)(A),(C)
Maximum daily load	§ 303(d)(1),(3),(4)
Water-quality criteria	§ 304(a)
Effluent limitation guidelines	§ 304(b)
Secondary-treatment guidelines	§ 304(d)(4)
Nonpoint-source pollution	§ 304(f)

CWA section 311 prohibits the discharge of oil or hazardous substances in harmful quantities into navigable waters and shorelines. Section 309 specifies mechanisms by which the CWA and the permits issued thereunder are to be enforced. Citizens can also bring suit to enforce provisions of the CWA pursuant to CWA section 505.

Illustrative Cases

The following opinion excerpts illustrate the general operation and some special problems of the CWA.

P.U.D. No. 1 v. Washington Dept. of Ecology

114 S. Ct. 1900 (1994)

Justice O'CONNOR delivered the opinion of the Court.

Petitioners, a city and a local utility district, want to build a hydroelectric project on the Dosewallips River in Washington State. We must decide whether respondent, the state environmental agency, properly conditioned a permit for the project on the maintenance of specific minimum stream flows to protect salmon and steelhead runs.

I

This case involves the complex statutory and regulatory scheme that governs our Nation's waters, a scheme which implicates both federal and state administrative responsibilities. The Federal Water Pollution Control Act, commonly known as the Clean Water Act, 86 Stat. 816, as amended, 33 U.S.C. § 1251 *et seq.*, is a comprehensive water quality statute designed to "restore and maintain the chemical, physical, and biological integrity of the Nation's waters." . . . The Act also seeks to attain "water

quality which provides for the protection and propagation of fish, shellfish, and wildlife." . . .

To achieve these ambitious goals, the Clean Water Act establishes distinct roles for the Federal and State Governments. Under the Act, the Administrator of the Environmental Protection Agency is required, among other things, to establish and enforce technology-based limitations on individual discharges into the country's navigable waters from point sources. . . . Section 303 of the Act also requires each State, subject to federal approval, to institute comprehensive water quality standards establishing water quality goals for all intrastate waters. §§ 1311(b)(1)(C), 1313. These state water quality standards provide "a supplementary basis . . . so that numerous point sources, despite individual compliance with effluent limitations, may be further regulated to prevent water quality from falling below acceptable levels." . . .

A state water quality standard "shall consist of the designated uses of the navigable waters involved and the water quality criteria for such waters based upon such uses." . . . In setting standards, the State must comply with the following broad requirements:

"Such standards shall be such as to protect the public health or welfare, enhance the quality of water and serve the purposes of this chapter. Such standards shall be established taking into consideration their use and value for public water supplies, propagation of fish and wildlife, recreational [and other purposes.]" . . .

A 1987 amendment to the Clean Water Act makes clear that § 303 also contains an "antidegradation policy"—that is, a policy requiring that state standards be sufficient to maintain existing beneficial uses of navigable waters, preventing their further degradation. Specifically, the Act permits the revision of certain effluent limitations or water quality standards "only if such revision is subject to and consistent with the antidegradation policy established under this section." . . . Accordingly, EPA's regulations implementing the Act require that state water quality standards include "a statewide antidegradation policy" to ensure that "[e]xisting instream water uses and the level of water quality necessary to protect the existing uses shall be maintained and protected." 40 C.F.R. § 131.12 (1992). At a minimum, state water quality standards must satisfy these conditions. The Act also allows States to impose more stringent water quality controls. . . .

The State of Washington has adopted comprehensive water quality standards intended to regulate all of the State's navigable waters. See Washington Administrative Code (WAC) 173-201-010 to 173-201-120 (1990). The State created an inventory of all the State's waters, and divided the waters into five classes. 173-201-045. Each individual fresh surface water of the State is placed into one of these classes. 173-201-080. The Dosewallips River is classified AA, extraordinary. 173-201-080(32). The water quality standard for Class AA waters is set forth at 173-201-045(1). The standard identifies the designated uses of Class AA waters as well as the criteria applicable to such waters.

In addition to these specific standards applicable to Class AA waters, the State has adopted a statewide antidegradation policy. . . . As required by the Act, EPA reviewed and approved the State's water quality standards. . . . Upon approval by EPA, the state standard became "the water quality standard for the applicable waters of that State." 33 U.S.C. § 1313(c)(3).

. . . In addition to these primary enforcement responsibilities, § 401 of the Act requires States to provide a water quality certification before a federal license or permit can be issued for activities that may result in any discharge into intrastate navigable waters. . . .

II

Petitioners propose to build the Elkhorn Hydroelectric Project on the Dosewallips River. . . . The project would divert water from a 1.2-mile reach of the River (the bypass reach), run the water through turbines to generate electricity and then return the water to the River below the bypass reach. Under the Federal Power Act (FPA), 41 Stat. 1063, as amended, 16 U.S.C. § 791a *et seq.*, the Federal Energy Regulatory Commission has authority to license new hydroelectric facilities. As a result, the petitioners must get a FERC license to build or operate the Elkhorn Project. Because a federal license is required, and because the project may result in discharges into the Dosewallips River, petitioners are also required to obtain State certification of the project pursuant to § 401 of the Clean Water Act, 33 U.S.C. § 1341.

. . . The Dosewallips supports two species of salmon, Coho and Chinook, as well as Steelhead trout. As originally proposed, the project was to include a diversion dam which would completely block the river and channel approximately 75% of the River's water into a tunnel alongside the streambed. . . . Respondent undertook a study to determine the minimum stream flows necessary to protect the salmon and steelhead fisheries in the bypass reach. On June 11, 1986, respondent issued a § 401 water quality certification imposing a variety of conditions on the project, including a minimum stream-flow requirement of between 100 and 200 cfs depending on the season.

* * *

III

The principal dispute in this case concerns whether the minimum stream flow requirement that the State imposed on the Elkhorn project is a permissible condition of a § 401 certification under the Clean Water Act. To resolve this dispute we must first determine the scope of the State's authority under § 401. We must then determine whether the limitation at issue here, . . . falls within the scope of that authority.

A

There is no dispute that petitioners were required to obtain a certification from the State pursuant to § 401. Petitioners concede that, at a minimum, the project will result in two possible discharges—the release of dredged and fill material during the construction of the project, and the discharge of water at the end of the tailrace after the water has been used to generate electricity. Brief for Petitioners 27–28. Petitioners contend, however, that the minimum stream flow requirement imposed by the State was unrelated to these specific discharges, and that as a consequence, the State lacked the authority under § 401 to condition its certification on maintenance of stream flows sufficient to protect the Dosewallips fishery.

If § 401 consisted solely of subsection (a), which refers to a state certification that a "discharge" will comply with certain provisions of the Act, petitioners' assessment . . . would have considerable force. Section 401, however, also contains subsection(d), which expands the State's authority to impose conditions on the certification of a project. Section 401(d) provides that any certification shall set forth "any effluent limitations and other limitations . . . necessary to assure that *any applicant*" will comply with various provisions of the Act and appropriate state law requirements. 33 U.S.C. § 1341(d) (emphasis added). The language of this subsection contradicts petitioners' claim that the State may only impose water quality limitations specifically tied to a "discharge." The text refers to the compliance of the applicant, not the discharge. Section 401(d) thus allows the State to impose "other limitations" on the project in general to assure compliance

with various provisions of the Clean Water Act and with "any other appropriate requirement of State law." Although the dissent asserts that this interpretation of § 401(d) renders § 401(a)(1) superfluous, *infra*, at 1916, we see no such anomaly. Section 401(a)(1) identifies the category of activities subject to certification—namely those with discharges. And § 401(d) is most reasonably read as authorizing additional conditions and limitations on the activity as a whole once the threshold condition, the existence of a discharge, is satisfied.

Our view of the statute is consistent with EPA's regulations implementing § 401. The regulations expressly interpret § 401 as requiring the State to find that "there is a reasonable assurance that the *activity* will be conducted in a manner which will not violate applicable water quality standards." . . . EPA's conclusion that *activities*—not merely discharges—must comply with state water quality standards is a reasonable interpretation of § 401, and is entitled to deference. . . .

Although § 401(d) authorizes the State to place restrictions on the activity as a whole, that authority is not unbounded. . . . The State asserts that the minimum stream flow requirement was imposed to ensure compliance with the state water quality standards adopted pursuant to § 303 of the Clean Water Act, 33 U.S.C. § 1313.

We agree with the State that ensuring compliance with § 303 is a proper function of the § 401 certification. Although § 303 is not one of the statutory provisions listed in § 401(d), the statute allows states to impose limitations to ensure compliance with § 301 of the Act, 33 U.S.C. § 1311. Section 301 in turn incorporates § 303 by reference. See 33 U.S.C. § 1311(b)(1)(C); . . . As a consequence, state water quality standards adopted pursuant to § 303 are among the "other limitations" with which a State may ensure compliance through the § 401 certification process. This interpretation is consistent with EPA's view of the statute. . . . Moreover, limitations to assure compliance with state water quality standards are also permitted by § 401(d)'s reference to "any other appropriate requirement of State law." We do not speculate on what additional state laws, if any, might be incorporated by this language. But at a minimum, limitations imposed pursuant to state water quality standards adopted pursuant to § 303 are "appropriate" requirements of state law. Indeed, petitioners appear to agree that the State's authority under § 401 includes limitations designed to ensure compliance with state water quality standards.

B

Having concluded that, pursuant to § 401, States may condition certification upon any limitations necessary to ensure compliance with state water quality standards or any other "appropriate requirement of State law," we consider whether the minimum flow condition is such a limitation. . . . In imposing the minimum stream flow requirement, the State determined that construction and operation of the project as planned would be inconsistent with one of the designated uses of Class AA water, namely "[s]almonid [and other fish] migration, rearing, spawning, and harvesting." . . . The designated use of the River as a fish habitat directly reflects the Clean Water Act's goal of maintaining the "chemical, physical, and biological integrity of the Nation's waters." 33 U.S.C. § 1251(a). Indeed, the Act defines pollution as "the man-made or man induced alteration of the chemical, physical, biological, and radiological integrity of water." § 1362(19). Moreover, the Act expressly requires that, in adopting water quality standards, the State must take into consideration the use of waters for "propagation of fish and wildlife." 33 U.S.C. § 1313(c)(2)(A).

. . . According to petitioners, the State may not require them to operate their dam in a manner consistent with a designated "use"; instead, say petitioners, under § 303 the State may only require that the project comply with specific numerical "criteria."

We disagree . . . . Under the statute, a water quality standard must "consist of the designated uses of the navigable waters involved *and* the water quality criteria for such waters based upon such uses." 33 U.S.C. § 1313(c)(2)(A) (emphasis added). The text makes it plain that water quality standards contain two components. . . . Accordingly, under the literal terms of the statute, a project that does not comply with a designated use of the water does

not comply with the applicable water quality standards.

Consequently, pursuant to § 401(d) the State may require that a permit applicant comply with both the designated uses and the water quality criteria of the state standards. . . .

EPA has not interpreted § 303 to require the States to protect designated uses exclusively through enforcement of numerical criteria. In its regulations governing state water quality standards, EPA defines criteria as "*elements* of State water quality standards expressed as constituent concentrations, levels, or narrative statements, representing a quality of water that supports a particular use." § 40 C.F.R. 131.3(b) (1992) (emphasis added). The regulations further provide that "[w]hen criteria are met, water quality will *generally* protect the designated use." *Ibid,* (emphasis added). Thus, the EPA regulations implicitly recognize that in some circumstances, criteria alone are insufficient to protect a designated use.

Petitioners also appear to argue that use requirements are too open-ended, and that the Act only contemplates enforcement of the more specific and objective "criteria." But this argument is belied by the open-ended nature of the criteria themselves. . . . In fact, under the Clean Water Act, only one class of criteria, those governing "toxic pollutants listed pursuant to section 1317(a)(1)" need be rendered in numerical form. See 33 U.S.C. § 1313(c)(2)(B); . . .

Washington's Class AA water quality standards are typical in that they contain several open-ended criteria which, like the use designation of the River as a fishery, must be translated into specific limitations for individual projects. . . .

Petitioners further argue that enforcement of water quality standards through use designations renders the water quality criteria component of the standards irrelevant. We see no anomaly, however, in the State's reliance on both use designations and criteria to protect water quality. The specific numerical limitations embodied in the criteria are a convenient enforcement mechanism for identifying minimum water conditions which will generally achieve the requisite water quality. And, in most circumstances, satisfying the criteria will, as EPA recognizes, be sufficient to maintain the designated use. See 40 C.F.R. § 131.3(b) (1992). Water quality standards, however, apply to an entire class of water, a class which contains numerous individual water bodies. . . . While enforcement of criteria will in general protect the uses of these diverse waters, a complementary requirement that activities also comport with designated uses enables the States to ensure that each activity—even if not foreseen by the criteria—will be consistent with the specific uses and attributes of a particular body of water.

Under petitioners' interpretation of the statute, however, if a particular criterion, such as turbidity, were missing from the list contained in an individual state water quality standard, or even if an existing turbidity criterion were insufficient to protect a particular species of fish in a particular river, the State would nonetheless be forced to allow activities inconsistent with the existing or designated uses. We think petitioners' reading leads to an unreasonable interpretation of the Act. . . .

The State also justified its minimum stream flow as necessary to implement the "antidegradation policy" of § 303, 33 U.S.C. § 1313(d)(4)(B). When the Clean Water Act was enacted in 1972, the water quality standards of all 50 States had antidegradation provisions. These provisions were required by federal law. . . . By providing in 1972 that existing state water quality standards would remain in force until revised, the Clean Water Act ensured that the States would continue their antidegradation programs. . . . EPA has consistently required that revised state standards incorporate an antidegradation policy. And, in 1987, Congress explicitly recognized the existence of an "antidegradation policy established under [§ 303]." . . .

. . . The Solicitor General, representing EPA, asserts, . . . and we agree, that the State's minimum stream flow condition is a proper application of the state and federal antidegradation regulations, as it ensures that an "existing instream water us[e]" will be "maintained and protected." 40 C.F.R. § 131.12(a)(1)(1992).

Petitioners also assert more generally that the Clean Water Act is only concerned with water "quality," and does not allow the regulation of water "quantity." This is an artificial distinction. In many cases, water quantity is closely related to water quality; a sufficient lowering of the water quantity in a body of water could destroy all of its designated uses, be it for drinking water, recreation, navigation or, as here, as a fishery. In any event, there is recognition in the Clean Water Act itself that reduced stream flow, *i.e.,* diminishment of water quantity, can constitute water pollution. First, the Act's definition of pollution as "the man-made or man induced alteration of the chemical, physical, biological, and radiological integrity of water" encompasses the effects of reduced water quantity. . . . Moreover, § 304 of the Act expressly recognizes that water "pollution" may result from "changes in the movement, flow, or circulation of any navigable waters . . . including changes caused by the construction of dams." . . . This concern with the flowage effects of dams and other diversions is also embodied in the EPA regulations, which expressly require existing dams to be operated to attain designated uses. . . .

Petitioners assert that two other provisions of the Clean Water Act, §§ 101(g) and 510(2), . . . exclude the regulation of water quantity from the coverage of the Act. Section 101(g) provides "that the authority of each State to allocate quantities of water within its jurisdiction shall not be superseded, abrogated or otherwise impaired by this chapter." 33 U.S.C. § 1251(g). Similarly, § 510(2) provides that nothing in the Act shall "be construed as impairing or in any manner affecting any right or jurisdiction of the States with respect to the waters . . . of such States." 33 U.S.C. § 1370. In petitioners' view, these provisions exclude "water quantity issues from direct regulation under the federally controlled water quality standards authorized in § 303." . . .

This language gives the States authority to allocate water rights; we therefore find it peculiar that petitioners argue that it prevents the State from regulating stream flow. In any event, we read these provisions more narrowly than petitioners. Sections 101(g) and 510(2) preserve the authority of each State to allocate water quantity as between users; they do not limit the scope of water pollution controls that may be imposed on users who have obtained,

. . . a water allocation. . . . Moreover, the certification itself does not purport to determine petitioners' proprietary right to the water of the Dosewallips. . . . The certification merely determines the nature of the use to which that proprietary right may be put under the Clean Water Act, if and when it is obtained from the State. . . .

IV

Petitioners contend that we should limit the State's authority to impose minimum flow requirements because FERC has comprehensive authority to license hydroelectric projects pursuant to the FPA, 16 U.S.C. § 791a *et seq.* In petitioners' view, the minimum flow requirement imposed here interferes with FERC's authority under the FPA.

The FPA empowers FERC to issue licenses for projects "necessary or convenient . . . for the development, transmission, and utilization of power across, along, from, or in any of the streams . . . over which Congress has jurisdiction." . . . The FPA also requires FERC to consider a project's effect on fish and wildlife. . . . In *California v. FERC, supra,* we held that the

California Water Resources Control Board, acting pursuant to state law, could not impose a minimum stream flow which conflicted with minimum stream flows contained in a FERC license. We concluded that the FPA did not "save" to the States this authority. . . .

No such conflict with any FERC licensing activity is presented here. . . . Indeed, at oral argument the Solicitor General stated that both EPA and FERC were represented in this proceeding, and that the Government has no objection to the stream flow condition contained in the § 401 certification. . . .

. . . because any conflict with FERC's authority under the FPA is hypothetical, we are unwilling to read implied limitations into § 401. . . .

In summary, we hold that the State may include minimum stream flow requirements in a certification issued pursuant to § 401 of the Clean Water Act insofar as necessary to enforce a designated use contained in a state water quality standard. The judgment of the Supreme Court of Washington, accordingly, is affirmed.

So ordered.

AMERICAN MEAT INSTITUTE v. EPA

526 F.2d 442 (7th Cir. 1985)

[This review of industry challenges to EPA methods of developing effluent limitations for meat-processing indicates the kinds of technical issues that arise under the Clean Water Act. Specifically, this suit centered on EPA authority to ignore or consider certain factors in setting effluent limits; the receiving waters' capacity to absorb pollution discharges without proven damage to those waters, the costs of employing feasible water-treatment technology, and the environmental impacts (other than upon water quality) that would result from EPA water-treatment requirements.]

TONE, Circuit Judge

* * *

The regulations classify slaughterhouses and packinghouses into the following four subcategories:

(1) simple slaughterhouses, which slaughter animals and perform a limited number, usually no more than two, by-product processing operations . . . ;

(2) complex slaughterhouses, which slaughter animals and perform several, usually three or more, by-product processing operations . . . ; and

(3) low-processing packinghouses, which not only slaughter animals but process meat

from animals killed at that plant . . . ; and (4) high-processing packinghouses, which not only slaughter animals but process meat from both animals killed at the plant and animals killed elsewhere (§§ 432.40–432.46).

For existing sources in each subcategory, the regulations set forth "[e]ffluent limitations guidelines" for 1977, ... The same is true of the 1983 standards.. . .

The regulations limit the discharge of "BOD5," "TSS," and ammonia, in addition to other pollutants not involved in this proceeding. Two of these terms require explanation:

BOD5. The initials "BOD" stand for "biochemical oxygen demand" and describe pollutants which, when they decompose, deplete oxygen necessary to support aquatic life. BOD5 is BOD measured over a five-day period.

TSS. The initials "TSS" stand for "total suspended solids," which are particles of organic and inorganic matter suspended in the water or floating on its surface.

The regulations permit the discharge of certain amounts of BOD5 and TSS per 1,000 pounds (or per 1,000 kilograms) of live weight killed. . . . The 1983 ammonia standard is set in terms of milligrams of ammonia per liter of effluent (mg/l), which shows the concentration of ammonia in the effluent. The regulations challenged in this case are the existing source limitations for 1977 and 1983 relating to BOD5 and TSS, and those for 1983 relating to ammonia.

* * *

AMI's first challenge is directed at the 1977 effluent limitations, which require application of "the best practicable control technology currently available." . . .

This, we think, is a reasonable view of the Administrator's responsibility. The "best practicable technology" will normally be defined based on the average performance of the best existing plants. If, however, the Administrator concludes that present practices in an industrial category are uniformly inadequate, he may require levels of control based on technology not presently in use . . . , if he determines, by applying the criteria listed in § 304(b)(1)(B), that this technology can be practicably applied throughout the category. One of these criteria

is the cost of applying the proposed technology in relation to the resulting effluent reduction. With these principles in mind, we turn to AMI's challenges to the 1977 standards.

It appears . . . that the 1977 effluent limitations are based primarily on the technology of biological treatment through a three-lagoon system. This is considered "secondary" treatment, that is, treatment which takes place after the waste water has passed through "primary," in-plant treatment systems. In a three-lagoon system, waste water from the plant flows first into the anaerobic lagoon, where organic matter in the effluent is partially consumed by anaerobic bacteria (bacteria that do not require free oxygen). To increase oxygen levels in the waste water, it is then mechanically aerated in the aerated lagoon. The water then flows to the aerobic lagoon, where most of the remaining organic matter is consumed by aerobic bacteria (bacteria that do need oxygen). After being held there for a relatively long period, the waste water is discharged.

* * *

AMI's first argument, . . . is that, while the proposed lagoon system qualifies as practicable, it cannot achieve the limitations on a year-round basis because of seasonal and climatic effects. Winter conditions, according to AMI, impair the efficiency of both anaerobic and aerobic lagoons, while algae growth in the summer increases BOD5 and TSS.

(1) The Effect of Winter Temperatures on the Anaerobic Lagoon

The optimum temperature for an anaerobic lagoon is approximately 90°F. Cold temperatures cause it to function less efficiently by slowing bacterial activity. The issue is the magnitude of this effect. AMI relies on an authority which says that removals are reduced to 70%. It conceded in its submittal to the agency, however, that the effect of winter temperatures on the anaerobic lagoon is small.

EPA argues that winter temperatures are counteracted by the heat of incoming waste water (80–100°F.) and by the insulating grease cover that forms over the pool. An article concerning the Wilson plant . . . reports that the grease cover on the anaerobic pool, after taking some time to build up, insulated the effluent and maintained satisfactory temperatures. The anaerobic pond at that plant operated at a 92% level of efficiency in February 1970. EPA's conclusion is also supported by data on other plants . . . which show, for example, that at one plant the anaerobic temperature on two dates in January 1972 was 77–78°F.

* * *

We conclude that there is firm record support for EPA's conclusion . . . .

(2)   The Effect of Winter Temperatures on the Aerobic Lagoon

Like anaerobic lagoons, aerobic lagoons operate less efficiently in winter. Cold temperatures inhibit aerobic microorganisms, and ice and snow covers reduce the oxygen content of water. EPA argues that these difficulties can be ameliorated by increasing detention time, thereby giving the microorganisms more time to work, by using additional aerobic ponds, or by using submerged aerators. We agree with AMI that EPA's argument . . . is inadequately supported by the record.

The record does suggest, however, that winter conditions do not make compliance with the 1977 standards impossible, since some plants have succeeded in complying with the BOD5 standards in winter. One such plant was the Wilson plant at Cherokee, Iowa, which maintained a 45% level of aerobic removal of BOD5 in February. The American Beef plant at Oakland, Iowa, also met the BOD5 limitations during the winter months, as did several other plants. AMI's argument that some of these plants should be disregarded because they did not discharge in some winter months is unsound. As counsel for EPA pointed out . . . a plant which does not discharge during a given period may be continuing its operations while storing its effluent. Our examination of the record confirms that the plants in question continued operations during periods when they did not discharge. The time of release is unimportant, so long as the effluent is successfully treated before release.

* * *

(3)   The Effect of Summer Weather on Aerobic Lagoons

Warm weather promotes the growth of algae. On the basis of comments in the record by industry representatives, state pollution authorities, and others about the effect of algae on aerobic lagoons, AMI argues that algae growth increases TSS and BOD5 counts. . . .

EPA states that the Illini Beef plant at Genesco, Illinois, and the Swift plant at Glenwood, Iowa, were able to meet the standards during summer months, as was the Routh plant at Sandusky, Ohio. AMI does not respond directly to these assertions, and, from our examination of the record we conclude that data from these plants fail to show the correlation between summer weather and TSS predicted by AMI.

With respect to BOD5, EPA cites data from five plants that complied with the 1977 effluent limitations during the summer. AMI does not contest the figures regarding summer performance for two of these plants . . . but argues that Illini Beef and another plant should be disregarded because EPA itself, as shown in the Final Development Document, excluded them from consideration. The fifth plant was not mentioned or relied on by EPA in the Final Development Document. AMI also points out that a sixth plant, American Beef, failed to meet the standards during the summer. Nevertheless, the ability of even two plants using the proposed technology to meet the BOD5 and TSS standards in summer demonstrates that the standards are attainable in warm weather . . . .

In summary, we find sufficient basis in the record for the Administrator's conclusion that temperature changes do not render the 1977 effluent limitations unattainable by the 1977 technology he designated.

■   **WEYERHAEUSER CO. V. COSTLE**   ■

590 F.2d 1011 (D.C. Cir. 1978)

[This opinion excerpt discusses the reasons Congress adopted a new mechanism of effluent limitations in its 1972 amendments and outlines the factors EPA must consider when issuing effluent-limitations regulations. The opinion also points up the ability of regulated industries to challenge specific regulations on numerous grounds.]

McGOWAN, Circuit Judge

. . . By these consolidated petitions, members of one such industry, American pulp and paper makers, challenge the validity of EPA regulations limiting the 1977–83 effluent discharges of many pulp, paper, and paperboard mills. . . .

* * *

. . . Some of these challenges concern the Agency's refusal to consider receiving water quality, while others concern EPA's manner of assessing the factors that all agree must be considered: cost and nonwater environmental impacts. We uphold the Agency's interpretation and application of the statute against both sets of challenges.

1.

Some of the paper mills . . . discharge their effluent into the Pacific Ocean. Petitioners contend that the ocean can dilute or naturally treat effluent, and that EPA must take this capacity of the ocean . . . . They urge . . . that because the amounts of pollutant involved are small in comparison to bodies of water as vast as Puget Sound or the Pacific Ocean, they should not have to spend heavily on treatment equipment, or to increase their energy requirements and sludge levels, in order to treat wastes that the ocean could dilute or absorb.

EPA's secondary response to this claim was that pollution is far from harmless, even when disposed of in the largest bodies of water. . . . Even if the ocean can handle ordinary wastes, ocean life may be vulnerable to toxic compounds that typically accompany those wastes. In the main, however, EPA simply asserted that the issue of receiving water capacity could not be raised in setting effluent limitations because

Congress had ruled it out. We have examined the previous legislation in this area, and the 1972 Act's wording, legislative history, and policies, as underscored by its 1977 amendments. . . . They make clear that based on long experience, and aware of the limits of technological knowledge and administrative flexibility, Congress made the deliberate decision to rule out arguments based on receiving water capacity.

The earliest version of the Federal Water Pollution Control Act was passed in 1948 and amended five times before 1972. . . . At the end of that period, Congress realized not only that its water pollution efforts until then had failed, but also that reliance on receiving water capacity as a crucial test for permissible pollution levels had contributed greatly to that failure. Based on this experience, Congress adopted a new approach in 1972. Under the Act, "a discharger's performance is . . . measured against strict technology-based effluent limitations— specified levels of treatment—to which it must conform, ..."

* * *

Moreover, by eliminating the issue of the capacity of particular bodies of receiving water, Congress made nationwide uniformity in effluent regulation possible. Congress considered uniformity vital to free the states from the temptation of relaxing local limitations in order to woo or keep industrial facilities. In addition, national uniformity made pollution cleanup possible without engaging in the divisive task of favoring some regions of the country over others.

More fundamentally, the new approach implemented changing views as to the relative rights of the public and of industrial polluters. Hitherto, the right of the polluter was pre-eminent, unless the damage caused by pollution could be proven. Henceforth, the right of the public to a clean environment would be pre-eminent, unless pollution treatment was impractical or unachievable. . . .

* * *

The Act was passed with an expectation of "mid-course corrections," and in 1977 Congress amended the Act, although generally holding to the same tack set five years earlier. . . . Except for a provision specifically aimed at discharges from "publicly owned treatment plants," section 301(h), Congress resolved in the recent amendments to continue regulating discharges into all receiving waters alike.

* * *

. . . Historically, the paper industry itself, . . . avoided the impact of regulation because of the difficulty of proving that its discharges adversely affected receiving water.

Under the new statutory scheme, Congress clearly intended us to avoid such problems of proof . . . .

* * *

2.

Petitioners also challenge EPA's manner of assessing two factors that all parties agree must be considered: cost and non-water quality environmental impacts. They content that the Agency should have more carefully balanced costs versus the effluent reduction benefits of the regulations, and that it should have also balanced those benefits against the non-water quality environmental impacts to arrive at a "net" environmental benefit conclusion. . . .

Section 304(b)(1)(B) identifies the factors bearing on BPCTCA in two groups. . . .

The first group consists of two factors that EPA must compare: total cost versus effluent reduction benefits. We shall call these the "comparison factors." The other group is a list of many factors that EPA must "take into account": age, process, engineering aspects, pro-

cess changes, environmental impacts (including energy), and any others EPA deems appropriate. We shall call these the "consideration factors." Notably, section 304(b)(2)(B), which delineates the factors relevant to setting 1983 BATEA limitations, tracks the 1977 BPCTCA provision before us except in one regard: in the 1983 section, *all* factors, including costs and benefits, are consideration factors, and no factors are separated out for comparison.

Based on our examination of the statutory language and the legislative history, we conclude that Congress mandated a particular structure and weight for the 1977 comparison factors, that is to say, a "limited" balancing test. In contrast, Congress did not mandate any particular structure or weight for the many consideration factors. Rather, it left EPA with discretion to decide how to account for the consideration factors, and how much weight to give each factor. In response to these divergent congressional approaches, we conclude that, on the one hand, we should examine EPA's treatment of cost and benefit under the 1977 standard . . . . On the other hand, our scrutiny of the Agency's treatment of the several consideration factors seeks to assure that the Agency informed itself as to their magnitude, and reached its own . . . considered conclusion about their bearing. More particularly, we do not believe that EPA is required to use any specific structure such as a balancing test in assessing the consideration factors, nor do we believe that EPA is required to give each consideration factor any specific weight.

CHEMICAL MANUFACTURERS ASSOCIATION v. NATURAL RESOURCES DEFENSE COUNCIL, INC.

470 U.S. 116 (1985)

[In this case, the Supreme Court Justices split 5 to 4 on the interpretation of related CWA provisions. The four dissenters would have ruled that the act prohibited EPA from granting exceptions from its effluent-limitations regulations. This excerpt from the majority opinion reveals the hasty manner in which Congress enacted the CWA amendments and the majority's grounds for reconciling provisions pointing to two potentially inconsistent goals; namely, to forbid exceptions to water-quality standards, and to allow case-by-case "variances" from those standards.]

Justice *WHITE* delivered the opinion of the Court.

These cases present the question whether the Environmental Protection Agency (EPA) may issue certain variances from toxic pollutant effluent limitations promulgated under the Clean Water Act.

I

. . . [R]espondent Natural Resources Defense Council (NRDC) sought a declaration that § 301(l) of the Clean Water Act, 33 U.S.C. § 1311(l), prohibited EPA from issuing "fundamentally different factor" (FDF) variances for pollutants listed as toxic under the Act. Petitioners EPA and Chemical Manufacturers Association (CMA) argued otherwise. . . .

The Clean Water Act, the basic federal legislation dealing with water pollution, assumed its present form as the result of extensive amendments in 1972 and 1977. For direct dischargers—those who expel waste directly into navigable waters—the Act calls for a two-phase program of technology-based effluent limitations, commanding that dischargers comply with the best practicable control technology currently available (BPT) by July 1, 1977, and subsequently meet the generally more stringent effluent standard consistent with the best available technology economically achievable (BAT).

Indirect dischargers—those whose waste water passes through publicly owned treatment plants—are similarly required to comply with pretreatment standards promulgated by EPA under § 307 of the Act, 33 U.S.C. § 1317(b), for pollutants not susceptible to treatment by sewage systems or which would interfere with the operation of those systems. Relying upon legislative history . . . and pursuant to a consent decree, EPA has set effluent limitations for indirect dischargers under the same two-phase approach applied to those discharging waste directly into navigable waters.

Thus, for both direct and indirect dischargers, EPA considers specific statutory factors and promulgates regulations creating categories and classes of sources and setting uniform discharge limitations for those classes and categories. Since application of the statutory factors varies on the basis of the industrial process used and

a variety of other factors, EPA has faced substantial burdens in collecting information adequate to create categories and classes suitable for uniform effluent limits, a burden complicated by the time deadlines it has been under to accomplish the task. Some plants may find themselves classified within a category of sources from which they are, or claim to be, fundamentally different . . . . As a result, EPA has developed its FDF variance as a mechanism for ensuring that its . . . rough-hewn categories do not unfairly burden atypical plants. Any interested party may seek an FDF variance to make effluent limitations either more or less stringent if the standards applied to a given source, because of factors fundamentally different from those considered by EPA . . . are either too lenient or too strict.

The 1977 amendments to the Clean Water Act reflected Congress' increased concern with the dangers of toxic pollutants. The Act, as then amended, allows specific statutory modifications of effluent limitations for economic and water-quality reasons in §§ 301(c) and (g). Section 301(l), however, added by the 1977 amendments, provides:

> "The Administrator may not modify any requirement of this section as it applied to any specific pollutant which is on the toxic pollutant list under section 307(a)(1) of this Act."

In the aftermath of the 1977 amendments, EPA continued its practice of occasionally granting FDF variances . . . .

* * *

II

Section 301(l) states that EPA may not "modify" any requirement of § 301 insofar as toxic materials are concerned. EPA insists that § 301(l) prohibits only those modifications expressly permitted by other provisions of § 301, ... Section 301(l), it is urged, does not address the very different issues of FDF variances. This view of the agency charged with administering the statute is entitled to considerable deference; and to sustain it, we need not find that it is the only permissible construction that EPA might have adopted but only that EPA's understanding of this very "complex statute" is a sufficiently rational one to preclude a court from substituting its judgment for that of EPA. . . . Of course, if Congress has clearly expressed an intent contrary to that of the Agency, our duty is to enforce the will of Congress. . . .

A.

NRDC insists that the language of § 301(l) is itself enough to require affirmance of the Court of Appeals, since on its face it forbids any modifications of the effluent limitations that EPA must promulgate for toxic pollutants. . . . As NRDC does and must concede, . . . § 301(l) cannot be read to forbid every change in the toxic waste standards. The word "modify" . . . is the proper subject of construction by EPA and the courts. NRDC would construe it to forbid the kind of alteration involved in an FDF variance, while the Agency would confine the section to prohibiting the partial modifications that § 301(c) would otherwise permit. Since EPA asserts that the FDF variance is more like a revision permitted by § 307 than it is like a § 301(c) or (g) modification, and since . . . we think there is a reasonable basis for such a position, we conclude that the statutory language does not foreclose the Agency's view of the statute. We should defer to that view unless the legislative history or the purpose and structure of the statute clearly reveal a contrary intent on the part of Congress. NRDC submits that the legislative materials evince such a contrary intent. We disagree.

B.

. . . The 1972 amendments to the Act added § 301(c), which allowed EPA to waive BAT and pretreatment requirements on a case-by-case basis when economic circumstances justified such a waiver. . . . In 1977, the Senate proposed amending § 301(c) by prohibiting such waivers for toxic pollutants. . . . At the same time, the Senate bill added what became § 301(g), which allowed waivers . . . where such waivers would not impair water quality, but which, like § 301(c), prohibited waivers for toxic pollutants. . . . The bill did not contain § 301(l). That section was proposed by the Conference Committee, which also deleted the toxic pollutant prohibition in § 301(c) and redrafted § 301(g) to prohibit water-quality waiv-

ers for conventional pollutants and thermal discharges as well as for toxic pollutants. While the Conference Committee Report did not explain the reason for proposing § 301(l), Representative Roberts, the House floor manager, stated:

> "Due to the nature of toxic pollutants, those identified for regulation will not be the subject to waivers from or modification of the requirements prescribed under this section, *specifically, neither section 301(c) waivers . . . nor 301(g) waivers based on water quality considerations shall be available.*" Leg. Hist. 328–329 (emphasis added).

Another indication that Congress did not intend to forbid FDF waivers as well as §§ 301(c) and (g) modifications is its silence on the issue. Under NRDC's theory, the Conference Committee did not merely tinker with the wording of the Senate bill, but boldly moved to eliminate FDF variances. But if that was the Committee's intention, it is odd that the Committee did not communicate it to either House, ...

* * *

C.

Neither are we convinced that FDF variances threaten to frustrate the goals and operation of the statutory scheme set up by Congress. The nature of FDF variances has been spelled out both by this Court and by the Agency itself. The regulation explains that its purpose is to remedy categories which were not accurately drawn because information was either not available to or not considered by the Administrator in setting the original categories and limitations. 40 C.F.R. § 403.13(b) (1984). An FDF variance does not excuse compliance with a correct requirement, but instead represents an acknowledgment that not all relevant factors were taken sufficiently into account in framing that requirement originally, and that those relevant factors, properly considered, would have justified—indeed, required—the creation of a subcategory for the discharger in question. As we have recognized, the FDF variance is a laudable corrective mechanism, . . . It is, essentially, not an exception to the standard-setting process, but rather a more fine-tuned application of it.

We are not persuaded by NRDC's argument that granting FDF variances is inconsistent with the goal of uniform effluent limitations under the Act. . . .

NRDC concedes that EPA could promulgate rules under § 307 of the Act creating a subcategory for each source which is fundamentally different from the rest of the class under the factors the EPA must consider in drawing categories. The same result is produced by the issuance of an FDF variance for the same failure properly to subdivide a broad category. Since the dispute is therefore reduced to an argument over the means used by EPA to define subcategories of indirect dischargers . . . these are particularly persuasive cases for deference to the Agency's interpretation. . . .

* * *

EPA and CMA point out that the availability of FDF variances makes bearable the enormous burden faced by EPA in promulgating categories of sources and setting effluent limitations. Acting under stringent timetables, EPA must collect and analyze large amounts of technical information concerning complex industrial categories. Understandably, EPA may not be apprised of and will fail to consider unique factors applicable to atypical plants during the cate-

gorial rulemaking process, and it is thus important that EPA's nationally binding categorical pretreatment standards for indirect dischargers be tempered with the flexibility that the FDF variance mechanism offers, a mechanism repugnant to neither the goals or the operation of the Act.

III

Viewed in its entirety, neither the language nor the legislative history of the Act demonstrates a clear congressional intent to forbid EPA's sensible variance mechanism for tailoring the categories it promulgates. . . .

Here we are not dealing with an agency's change of position . . . but rather with EPA's consistent interpretation since the 1970's. NRDC argues that its construction of the statute is better supported by policy considerations. But we do not sit to judge the relative wisdom of competing statutory interpretations. Here EPA's construction fairly understood, is not inconsistent with the language, goals, or operation of the Act. Nor does the administration of EPA's regulation undermine the will of Congress.

* * *

ARKANSAS V. OKLAHOMA

112 S. Ct. 1046 (1992)

[The EPA issued the City of Fayetteville, Arkansas, a permit to discharge half of the effluent from its new sewage-treatment plant into a stream that enters the Illinois River 22 miles upstream from the Arkansas–Oklahoma border. The State of Oklahoma and a group of Oklahoma residents challenged the validity of the permit, claiming that the Fayetteville discharge violated Oklahoma water-quality standards and that EPA's contrary determination that the discharge would not produce a detectable violation of the Oklahoma standards was unlawful. Arkansas argued that the Clean Water Act did not require it to comply with Oklahoma's water-quality standards.

This Supreme Court opinion reviews the CWA's permitting scheme.]

JUSTICE STEVENS delivered the opinion of the court.

* * *

III

The Clean Water Act anticipates a partnership between the States and the Federal Government, animated by a shared objective: "to restore and maintain the chemical, physical, and biological integrity of the Nation's waters." . . . Toward this end, the Act provides for two sets of water quality measures. "Effluent limitations" are promulgated by the EPA and restrict the quantities, rates, and concentrations of specified substances which are discharged from point sources. . . ."[W]ater quality standards" are, in general, promulgated by the States and establish the desired condition of a waterway. . . . These standards supplement effluent limitations "so that numerous point sources, despite individual compliance with effluent limitations, may be further regulated to prevent water quality from falling below acceptable levels." *EPA v. California ex rel. State Water Resources Control Board,* 426 U.S. 200, 205, n. 12, ...

The EPA provides States with substantial guidance in drafting of water quality standards. See generally 40 C.F.R. pt. 131 (1991) (setting forth model water quality standards). Moreover, § 303 of the Act requires, *inter alia,* that state authorities periodically review water quality standards and secure the EPA's approval of any revisions in the standards. If the EPA recommends changes to the standards and the State fails to comply with that recommendation, the Act authorizes the EPA to promulgate water quality standards for the State. . . .

The primary means for enforcing these limitations and standards is the National Pollution Discharge Elimination System (NPDES), enacted in 1972 as a critical part of Congress' "complete rewriting" of federal water pollution law. . . . Section 301(a) of the Act, . . . generally prohibits the discharge of any effluent into a navigable body of water unless the point source has obtained an NPDES permit. Section 402 establishes the NPDES permitting regime, and describes two types of permitting systems: state permit programs that must satisfy federal requirements and be approved by the EPA, and a federal program administered by the EPA.

Section 402(b) authorizes each State to establish "its own permit program for discharges into navigable waters within its jurisdiction." 33 U.S.C. § 1342(b). Among the requirements the state program must satisfy are the procedural protections for downstream States . . . . Although these provisions do not authorize the downstream State to veto the issuance of a permit for a new point source in another State, the Administrator retains authority to block the issuance of any state-issued permit that "is outside the guidelines and requirements" of the Act. . . .

In the absence of an approved state program, the EPA may issue an NPDES permit under § 402(a) of the Act. (In this case, for example, because Arkansas had not been authorized to issue NPDES permits when the Fayetteville plant was completed, the permit was issued by the EPA itself.) The EPA's permit program is subject to the "same terms, conditions, and requirements" as a state permit program. . . . Notwithstanding this general symmetry, the EPA has construed the Act as requiring that EPA-issued NPDES permits also comply with § 401(a). . . . Section 401(a)(2) appears to prohibit the issuance of any federal license or permit over the objection of an affected State unless compliance with the affected State's water quality requirements can be insured.

IV

The parties have argued three analytically distinct questions concerning the interpretation of the Clean Water Act. First, does the Act require the EPA, . . . to apply the water quality standards of downstream States? Second, even if the Act does not *require* as much, does the Agency have the statutory authority to mandate such compliance? Third, does the Act provide . . . that once a body of water fails to meet water quality standards no discharge that yields effluent that reach the degraded waters will be permitted?

In this case, it is neither necessary nor prudent for us to resolve the first of these questions. In issuing the Fayetteville permit, the EPA assumed it was obligated by both the Act and its own regulations to ensure that the Fayetteville discharge would not violate Oklahoma's standards. . . .

Our decision not to determine at this time the scope of the Agency's statutory *obligations* does not effect our resolution of the second question, which concerns the Agency's statutory *authority*. Even if the Clean Water Act itself does not require the Fayetteville discharge to comply with Oklahoma's water quality standards, the statute clearly does not limit the EPA's authority to mandate such compliance.

Since 1973, EPA regulations have provided that an NPDES permit shall not be issued "[w]hen the imposition of conditions cannot ensure compliance with the applicable water quality requirements of all affected States." 40 CFR § 122.4(d) (1991); .... Those regulations—relied upon by the EPA in the issuance of the Fayetteville permit—constitute a reasonable exercise of the Agency's statutory authority.

Congress has vested in the Administrator broad discretion to establish conditions for NPDES permits. ... Similarly, Congress preserved for the Administrator broad authority to oversee state permit programs:

> "No permit shall issue ... if the Administrator ... objects in writing to the issuance of such permit as being outside the guidelines and requirements of this chapter." ...

The regulations relied on by the EPA were a perfectly reasonable exercise of the Agency's statutory discretion. ...

* * *

... Congress, in crafting the Act, protected certain sovereign interest of the States; for example, § 510 allows States to adopt more demanding pollution-control standards than those established under the Act. Arkansas emphasizes that § 510 preserves such state authority only as it is applied to the waters of the regulating State. Even assuming Arkansas's construction of § 510 is correct, ... that section only concerns *state* authority and does not constrain the *EPA's* authority to promulgate reasonable regulations requiring point sources in one State to comply with water quality standards in downstream States.

For these reasons, we find the EPA's requirement that the Fayetteville discharge comply with Oklahoma's water quality standards to be a reasonable exercise of the Agency's substantial statutory discretion. ...

* * *

UNITED STATES V. RIVERSIDE BAYVIEW HOMES, INC.

106 S. Ct. 455 (1985)

[In this case the Supreme Court decided the statutory authority of the United States Corps of Engineers to classify low-lying land as "wetlands" and to regulate construction on it.]

Justice WHITE delivered the opinion of the Court.

This case presents the question whether the Clean Water Act, 33 U.S.C. § 1251 et seq. [33 U.S.C.S. §§ 1251 et seq.], together with certain regulations promulgated under its authority by the Army Corps of Engineers, authorizes the Corps to require landowners to obtain permits from the Corps before discharging fill material into wetlands adjacent to navigable bodies of water and their tributaries.

I

... [A]ny discharge of dredged or fill materials into "navigable waters"—defined as the "waters of the United States"—is forbidden unless authorized by a permit issued by the Corps

of Engineers pursuant to § 404, 33 U.S.C. § 1344 [33 U.S.C.S. § 1344]. After initially construing the Act to cover only waters navigable in fact, in 1975 the Corps issued interim final regulations redefining "the waters of the United States" to include not only actually navigable waters but also tributaries of such waters, interstate waters and their tributaries, and nonnavigable intrastate waters whose use or misuse could affect interstate commerce. ... More importantly for present purposes, the Corps construed the Act to cover all "freshwater wetlands" that were adjacent to other covered waters. ...

* * *

II

The question whether the Corps of Engineers may demand that respondent obtain a permit before placing fill material on its property is primarily one of regulatory and statutory interpretation: we must determine whether respondent's property is an "adjacent wetland" within the meaning of the applicable regulation, and, if so, whether the Corps' jurisdiction over "navigable waters" gives it statutory authority to regulate discharges of fill material into such a wetland. In this connection, we first consider the Court of Appeals' position that the Corp's regulatory authority under the statute and its implementing regulations must be narrowly construed to avoid a taking without just compensation in violation of the Fifth Amendment.

We have frequently suggested that governmental land-use regulation may under extreme circumstances amount to a "taking" of the affected property. . . . Moreover, we have made it quite clear that the mere assertion of regulatory jurisdiction by a governmental body does not constitute a regulatory taking. . . . A requirement that a person obtain a permit before engaging in a certain use of his or her property does not itself "take" the property in any sense: after all, the very existence of a permit system implies that permission may be granted, leaving the landowner free to use the property as desired. Moreover, even if the permit is denied, there may be other viable uses available to the owner. Only when a permit is denied and the effect of the denial is to prevent "economically viable" use of the land in question can it be said that a taking has occurred.

If neither the imposition of the permit requirement itself nor the denial of a permit necessarily constitutes a taking, it follows that the Court of Appeals erred in concluding that a narrow reading of the Corps' regulatory jurisdiction over wetlands was "necessary" to avoid "a serious taking problem." . . .

III

Purged of its spurious constitutional overtones, the question whether the regulation at issue requires respondent to obtain a permit before filling its property is an easy one. The regulation extends the Corps' authority under § 404 to all wetlands adjacent to navigable or interstate waters and their tributaries. Wetlands, in turn, are defined as lands that are "inundated *or saturated* by surface *or ground water* at a frequency and duration sufficient to support, and that under normal circumstances do

support, a prevalence of vegetation typically adapted for life in saturated soil conditions." 33 F.R. § 323.2(c) (1985) (emphasis added). . . .

. . . In deleting the reference to "periodic inundation" from the regulation as finally promulgated, the Corps explained that it was repudiating the interpretation of that language "as requiring inundation over a record period of years." 42 Fed. Reg. 37128 (1977). . . .

Without the nonexistent requirement of frequent flooding, the regulatory definition of adjacent wetlands covers the property here. The District Court found that respondent's property was "characterized by the presence of vegetation that requires saturated soil conditions for growth and reproduction," . . . and that the source of the saturated soil conditions on the property was ground water. There is no plausible suggestion that these findings are clearly erroneous, and they plainly bring the property within the category of wetlands as defined by the current regulation. In addition, the court found that the wetland located on respondent's property was adjacent to a body of navigable water, since the area characterized by saturated soil conditions and wetland vegetation extended beyond the boundary of respondent's property to Black Creek, a navigable waterway. Again, the court's finding is not clearly erroneous. Together, these findings establish that respondent's property is a wetland adjacent to a navigable waterway. Hence, it is part of the "waters of the United States" as defined by 33 C.F.R. § 323.2 (1985), and if the regulation itself is valid as a construction of the term "waters of the United States" as used in the Clean Water Act, a question which we now address, the property falls within the scope of the Corps' jurisdiction over "navigable waters" under § 404 of the Act.

An agency's construction of a statute it is charged with enforcing is entitled to deference if it is reasonable and not in conflict with the expressed intent of Congress. Chemical Manufacturers Assn. v. Natural Resources Defense Council, Inc. 470 U.S. 116, 125, 84 L.Ed. 2d 90, 105 S. Ct. 1102 (1985); Chevron, U.S.A., Inc. v. Natural Resources Defense Council, Inc. 467 U.S. 837, 842–845, 81 L.Ed. 2d 694, 104 S. Ct. 2778 (1984). Accordingly, our review is limited to the question whether it is reasonable, in light of the language, policies, and legislative history of the Act for the Corps to exercise jurisdiction over wetlands adjacent to but not regularly flooded by rivers, streams, and other hydrographic features more conventionally identifiable as "waters."

On a purely linguistic level, it may appear unreasonable to classify "lands," wet or otherwise, as "waters." Such a simplistic response, however, does justice neither to the problem faced by the Corps . . . nor to the realities of the problem of water pollution that the Clean Water Act was intended to combat. In determining the limits of its power to regulate discharges under the Act, the Corps must necessarily choose some point at which water ends and land begins. Our common experience tells us that this is often no easy task: the transition from water to solid ground is not necessarily or even typically an abrupt one. Rather, between open waters and dry land may lie shallows, marshes, mudflats, swamps, bogs—in short, a huge array of areas that are not wholly aquatic but nevertheless fall far short of being dry land. Where on this continuum to find the limit of "waters" is far from obvious.

Faced with such a problem of defining the bounds of its regulatory authority, an agency may appropriately look to the legislative history and underlying policies of its statutory grants of authority. Neither of these sources provides unambiguous guidance for the Corps in this case, but together they do support the reasonableness of the Corps' approach of defining adjacent wetlands as "waters" within the meaning of § 404(a). . . .

* * *

. . . Nonetheless, the evident breadth of congressional concern for protection of water quality and aquatic ecosystems suggests that it is reasonable for the Corps to interpret the term "waters" to encompass wetlands adjacent to waters as more conventionally defined. Following the lead of the Environmental Protection Agency, see 38 Fed. Reg. 10834 (1973), the Corps has determined that wetlands adjacent to navigable waters do as a general matter play a key role in protecting and enhancing water quality:

" . . Water moves in hydrologic cycles, and the pollution of this part of the aquatic system, regardless of whether it is above or below an ordinary high water mark, or mean high tide line, will affect the water quality of the other waters within that aquatic system.

"For this reason, the landward limit of Federal jurisdiction under Section 404 must include any adjacent wetlands that form the border of or are in reasonable proximity to other waters of the United States, as these wetlands are part of this aquatic system." 42 Fed. Reg. 37128 (1977).

We cannot say that the Corps' conclusion that adjacent wetlands are inseparably bound up with the "waters" of the United States—based as it is on the corps' and EPA's technical expertise—is unreasonable. . . .

This holds true even for wetlands that are not the result of flooding or permeation by water having its source in adjacent bodies of open water. . . . For example, wetlands that are not flooded by adjacent waters may still tend to drain into those waters. In such circumstances, the Corps has concluded that wetlands may serve to filter and purify water draining into adjacent bodies of water, . . . and to slow the flow of surface runoff into lakes, rivers, and streams and thus prevent flooding and erosion, . . . In addition, adjacent wetlands may "serve significant natural biological functions, including food chain production, general habitat, and nesting, spawning, rearing and resting sites for aquatic . . . species." . . . Again, we cannot say that the Corps' judgment on these matters is unreasonable, and we therefore conclude that a definition of "waters of the United States" encompassing all wetlands adjacent to other bodies of water over which the Corps has jurisdiction is a permissible interpretation of the Act. Because respondent's property is part of a wetland that actually abuts on a navigable waterway, respondent was required to have a permit in this case.

B

Following promulgation of the Corps' interim final regulations in 1975, the Corps' assertion of authority under § 404 over waters not actually navigable engendered some congressional opposition. The controversy came to a head during Congress' consideration of the Clean Water Act of 1977, a major piece of legislation aimed at achieving "interim improvements within the existing framework" of the Clean Water Act. . . .

* * *

The significance of Congress' treatment of the Corps' § 404 jurisdiction in its consideration of the Clean Water Act of 1977 is twofold. First, the scope of the Corps' asserted jurisdiction over wetlands was specifically brought to Congress' attention, and Congress rejected measures designed to curb the Corps' jurisdic-

tion in large part because of its concern that protection of wetlands would be unduly hampered by a narrowed definition of "navigable waters.". . .

* * *

We are thus pursuaded that the language, policies, and history of the Clean Water Act compel a finding that the Corps has acted reasonably in interpreting the Act to require permits for the discharge of fill material into wetlands adjacent to the "waters of the United States." . . .

* * *

8.4 Appraisal of CWA's Regulatory Scheme

The Permit Process

The CWA's permit scheme facilitates uniform enforcement of effluent limitations by translating general statutory directives into specific waste-treatment requirements for each discharge permittee. Under the CWA, EPA must establish national effluent limitations that subject similar dischargers to similar standards and obligations nationwide. However, one obvious weakness of the act is that it authorizes EPA and other government entities only to impose applicable effluent limitations and not to determine which polluters are most responsible for a diminution of water quality in a particular waterway. In other words, the CWA does not specify that enforcement priorities are to be based upon environmental risk assessments.

The permit system also contains sizable loopholes. As seen in the *Chemical Manufacturers* opinion in the previous section, the law allows EPA to grant variances from its effluent limitations in certain cases. Further, permit holders may generally discharge wastes into waterways regardless of the dischargers' adverse impact on water quality so long as they comply with permit conditions and applicable effluent limitations. "Federal courts lack authority to impose more stringent limitations . . . than those imposed by the agency charged by Congress with administering the comprehensive scheme."[19] Thus, as is often the case with licensing regulations, the permit scheme may allow a weakening, if not evasion of the statutory policy against harmful discharges.

Determination of Effluent Standards

Another drawback of the CWA's regulatory scheme is the considerable bureaucratic resources it demands for accomplishing its many purposes. Under the CWA, regulators must:

- categorize dischargers for the purpose of establishing effluent limitations,

- assess the availability of pollution-abatement technologies in innumerable industry categories and classes, and
- amend effluent limitations in response to new technologies.

This last task, in particular, seems less pressing than the others and tends to be postponed by an overburdened bureaucracy.

The CWA imposes upon EPA and other government agencies the heavy burden of developing appropriate effluent-limitation guidelines, which are critical to the success of water-quality regulation. Congress provided only very broad effluent-limitation guidelines in the CWA. It assigned EPA the responsibility for determining achievable numerical effluent limitations under each of the various CWA-specified technological standards for each class and category of discharger and for each type of pollutant. In order to derive enforceable limitations for pollution-producing industries across the nation, EPA is required to conduct extensive investigation into their myriad manufacturing and production processes as well as "end-of-the-pipe" pollution-control technologies, to investigate the availability and effectiveness of relevant control technologies for different classes of industrial activity (e.g., manufacturing, mining, power generation, food processing), and to consider the costs and benefits of all such technologies. These formidable tasks far outstrip EPA resources and partly underlie the broad deference the courts tend to give EPA judgments in suits challenging EPA determinations:

> Since application of the statutory factors varies on the basis of the industrial processes used and a variety of other factors, EPA has faced substantial burdens in collecting information adequate to create categories and classes suitable for uniform effluence limits, a burden complicated by the time deadlines it has been under to accomplish the task.[20]

Apart from EPA's lack of adequate resources for developing technology-based guidelines, the technology-based approach itself is criticized as being inefficient and inflexible. The CWA's technology-driven scheme acts as an economic deterrent to reduce pollution beyond the extent required and to develop more effective pollution-control technologies. Once adopted as the standard to set effluent limitations, the "best available technology" tends to remain impervious to improvement, even if it is less effective than newer but unproven technologies. Businesses are understandably reluctant to invest in research, development, and marketing of new technologies unless there is some marketplace incentive for doing so. The CWA fails to provide that incentive. "Because a technology-based approach makes environmental performance irrelevant, it cannot draw attention to the cases in which . . . more effort may be needed."[21]

The evolution of the Clean Water Act reveals tension between two policies that are not clearly resolved: the environmental goal of protecting public health and the environment, on one hand, and the goal of sustaining economic growth, which favors operational status quo and maintaining existing plant infrastructures, on the other. This tension is evident in environmental protection standards influenced by available technology and cost rather than by progressively stricter requirements that would provide the incentive for developing truly effective technologies even if it involved heavy short-term costs. The current accommodation of ends and means reflects a political compromise by Congress and EPA to balance competing environmental and economic interests. It may also represent but one stage in the evolution of environmental protection.

8.5 Selected Issues in Water Pollution Law

Wetlands and Regulatory Takings

The Due Process Clause of the Constitution's Fifth Amendment guarantees that private property will not be taken for a public purpose without due process and without just compensation to the owner. For instance, if a government entity appropriates real property for construction of a highway, the government must pay the owner the fair market value of the property. Similarly, if a governmental regulatory scheme so interferes with an owner's use of his or her real property as to deprive him or her of all beneficial or economically viable use, it is considered a *taking* and compensation must be paid. However, not all restrictions on the use of private property are considered constitutional takings.

Obviously, a regulation that prevents a private property owner from filling in wetlands or from building a permanent structure in a coastal zone impacts the range of economically beneficial uses available to the owner. In such a case, the constitutional issue is whether the restriction so interferes with the owner's use and enjoyment of the property and so diminishes its value as to require compensation by the government entity that is enforcing the restriction. It is important to keep in mind that the Constitution does not forbid regulatory legislation that results in takings. The Constitution merely requires that if the government enforces a regulation that results in a taking of private property, the government must compensate the owner. Thus, constitutional takings issues do not *legally* ban the enforcement of more stringent wetlands or estuary protection, but in an era of tight government budgets, the just compensation requirement tends to discourage enforcement of regulatory restrictions that would amount to takings.

The 1992 Supreme Court *Lucas* case on regulatory takings can be expected to affect the enforcement of wetlands regulations significantly.

■   LUCAS v. SOUTH CAROLINA COASTAL COUNCIL   ▨

112 S. Ct. 2886 (1992)

[This Supreme Court opinion discusses the controversial question of when an environmental protection regulation constitutes a noncompensable regulation of property use, and when it constitutes a regulatory "taking" that requires government compensation to the property owner.]

Justice SCALIA delivered the opinion of the Court.

In 1986, petitioner David H. Lucas paid $975,000 for two residential lots on the Isle of Palms in Charleston County, South Carolina, on which he intended to build single-family homes. In 1988, however, the South Carolina Legislature enacted the Beachfront Management Act, . . . which had the direct effect of

barring petitioner from erecting any permanent habitable structures on his two parcels. . . . A state trial court found that this prohibition rendered Lucas's parcels "valueless." . . . This case requires us to decide whether the act's dramatic effect on the economic value of Lucas's lots accomplished a taking of private property under the Fifth and Fourteenth Amendments requiring the payment of "just compensation." U.S. Const., Amdt. 5.

* * *

. . . Lucas did not take issue with the validity of the Act as a lawful exercise of South Carolina's police power, but contended that the Act's complete extinguishment of his property's value entitled him to compensation regardless of whether the legislature had acted in furtherance of legitimate police power objectives. Following a bench trial, [trial] the court agreed. Among its factual determinations was the finding that "at the time Lucas purchased the two lots, both were zoned for singlefamily residential construction and . . . there were no restrictions imposed upon such use of the property by either the State of South Carolina, the County of Charleston, or the Town of Isle of Palms." . . . The trial court further found . . . this prohibition "deprive[d] Lucas of any reasonable economic use of the lots, . . . eliminated the unrestricted right of use, and render[ed] them valueless." . . . The court thus concluded that Lucas's properties had been "taken" by operation of the Act, and it ordered respondent to pay "just compensation" in the amount of $1,232,387.50. . . .

The Supreme Court of South Carolina reversed. . . . The Court ruled that when a regulation respecting the use of property is designed "to prevent serious public harm," . . . no compensation is owing under the Takings Clause regardless of the regulation's effect on the property's value.

III

A

Prior to Justice Holmes' exposition in Pennsylvania Coal Co. v. Mahon, . . . it was generally thought that the Takings Clause reached only a "direct appropriation" of property, Legal Tender Cases, . . . or the functional equivalent of a "practical ouster of [the owner's] possession." Transportation Co. v. Chicago, ... Justice Holmes recognized in Mahon, however, that if the protection against physical appropriations of private property was to be meaningfully enforced, the government's power to redefine the range of interests included in the ownership of property was necessarily constrained by constitutional limits. . . . If, instead, the uses of private property were subject to unbridled, uncompensated qualification under the police power, "the natural tendency of human nature [would be] to extend the qualification more and more until at last private property disappear[ed]." . . . These considerations gave birth in that case to the oft-cited maxim that, "while property may be regulated

to a certain extent, if regulation goes too far it will be recognized as a taking. . . .

. . . In 70-odd years of succeeding "regulatory takings" jurisprudence, we have generally eschewed any "'set formula'" for determining how far is too far, preferring to "engag[e] in . . . essentially ad hoc, factual inquiries," . . . We have, however, described at least two discrete categories of regulatory action as compensable without case-specific inquiry . . . The first encompasses regulations that compel the property owner to suffer a physical "invasion" of his property. . . . For example, in Loreto v. Teleprompter Manhattan CATV Corp., . . . we determined that New York's law requiring landlords to allow television cable companies to emplace cable facilities in their apartment buildings constituted a taking, . . . even though the facilities occupied at most only 1-1/2 cubic feet of the landlords' property, ...

The second situation in which we have found categorical treatment appropriate is where regulation denies all economically beneficial or productive use of land. . . . As we have said on numerous occasions, the Fifth Amendment is violated when landuse regulation . . . *denies an owner economically viable use of his land.*" Agins, supra, . . .

We have never set forth the justification for this rule. Perhaps it is simply, as Justice Brennan suggested, that total deprivation of beneficial use is, from the landowner's point of view, the equivalent of a physical appropriation. . . .

On the other side of the balance, affirmatively supporting a compensation requirement, is the fact that regulations that leave the owner of land without economically beneficial or productive options for its use—typically, as here, by requiring land to be left substantially in its natural state—carry with them a heightened risk that private property is being pressed into some form of public service under the guise of mitigating serious public harm. . . . Morris County Land Improvement Co. v. Parsippany–Troy Hills Township, (. . . prohibition on filling marshlands imposed in order to preserve region as water detention basin and create wildlife refuge). . . . We think, in short, that there are good reasons for our frequently expressed belief that when the owner of real property has been called upon to sacrifice *all* economically beneficial uses in the name of the common good, that is, to leave his property economically idle, he has suffered a taking.

B

The trial court found Lucas's two beachfront lots to have been rendered valueless by respondent's enforcement of the coastal-zone construction ban. . . . The South Carolina Supreme Court, however, thought otherwise. . . .

It is correct that many of our prior opinions have suggested that "harmful or noxious uses" of property may be proscribed by government regulation without the requirement of compensation. For a number of reasons, however, we think the South Carolina Supreme Court was too quick to conclude that the principle decides the present case. . . .

The transition from our early focus on control of "noxious" uses to our contemporary understanding of the broad realm within which government may regulate without compensation was an easy one, since the distinction between "harm-preventing" and "benefit-conferring" regulation is often in the eye of the beholder. It is quite possible, for example, to describe in *either* fashion the ecological, economic, and aesthetic concerns that inspired the South Carolina legislature in the present case. One could say that imposing a servitude on Lucas's land is necessary in order to prevent his use of it from "harming" South Carolina's ecological resources; or, instead, in order to achieve the "benefits" of an ecological preserve. . . . Whether one or the other of the competing characterizations will come to one's lips in a particular case depends primarily upon one's evaluation of the worth of competing uses of real estate. . . . ("[T]he problem [in this area] is not one of noxiousness or harm-creating activity at all; rather it is a problem of inconsistency between perfectly innocent and independently desirable uses.") Whether Lucas's construction of single-family residences on his parcels should be described as bringing "harm" to South Carolina's adjacent ecological resources thus depends principally upon whether the describer believes that the State's use interest in nurturing those resources is so

important that *any* competing adjacent use must yield.

* * *

Where the State seeks to sustain regulation that deprives land of all economically beneficial use, we think it may resist compensation only if . . . the proscribed use interests were not part of his title to begin with. . . . It seems to us that the property owner necessarily expects the uses of his property to be restricted, from time to time, by various measures newly enacted by the State in legitimate exercise of its police powers; . . . In the case of land, however, we think the notion pressed by the Council that title is somehow held subject to the "implied limitation" that the State may subsequently eliminate all economically valuable use is inconsistent with the historical compact recorded in the Takings Clause that has become part of our constitutional culture.

Where "permanent physical occupation" of land is concerned, we have refused to allow the government to decree it anew (without compensation), no matter how weighty the asserted "public interests" . . . . We believe similar treatment must be accorded confiscatory regulations, i.e., regulations that prohibit all economically beneficial use of land: . . . .

* * *

The "total taking" inquiry we require today will ordinarily entail . . . analysis of, among other things, the degree of harm to public lands and resources, or adjacent private property, posed by the claimant's proposed activities, . . . the social value of the claimant's activities and their suitability to the locality in question, . . . and the relative ease with which the alleged harm can be avoided through measures taken by the claimant and the government (or adjacent private landowners) . . . .

* * *

The question, however, is one of state law to be dealt with on remand. We emphasize that to win its case South Carolina must do more than proffer the legislature's declaration that the uses Lucas desires are inconsistent with the public interest, or the conclusory assertion that they violate a common-law maxim such as sic utere tuo ut alienum non laedas. As we have said, a "State, by ipse dixit, may not transform private property into public property without compensation ...." ... Instead, ... South Carolina must identify background principles of nuisance and property law that prohibit the uses he now intends in the circumstances in which the property is presently found. Only on this showing can the State fairly claim that, in proscribing all such beneficial uses, the Beachfront Management Act is taking nothing.

* * *

The judgment is reversed and the cause remanded for proceedings not inconsistent with this opinion.

* * *

JUSTICE BLACKMUN, dissenting

* * *

The State of South Carolina prohibited petitioner Lucas from building a permanent structure on his property from 1988 to 1990. Relying on an unreviewed (and implausible) state trial court finding that this restriction left Lucas' property valueless, this Court granted review ....

* * *

I

A

In 1972 Congress passed the Coastal Zone Management Act. 16 U.S.C. § 1451 et seq. [16 U.S.C.S. §§ 1451 et seq.]. The Act was designed to provide States with money and incentives to carry out Congress' goal of protecting the public from shoreline erosion and coastal hazards. In the 1980 Amendments to the Act, Congress directed States to enhance their coastal programs by ... eliminating development and redevelopment in high-hazard areas." ...

* * *

B

Petitioner Lucas is a contractor, manager, and part owner of the Wild Dune development on the Isle of Palms. ... The area is notoriously unstable. In roughly half of the last 40 years, all or part of petitioner's property was part of

the beach or flooded twice daily by the ebb and flow of the tide. ... Between 1957 and 1963, petitioner's property was under water. ... Between 1981 and 1983, the Isle of Palms issued 12 emergency orders for sandbagging to protect property in the Wild Dune development. ...

* * *

IV

... From now on, there is a categorical rule finding these regulations to be a taking unless the use they prohibit is a background common-law nuisance or property principle. ...

* * *

... "[S]ince no individual has a right to use his property so as to create a nuisance or otherwise harm others, the State has not 'taken' anything when it asserts its power to enjoin the nuisance-like activity." ...

Ultimately even the Court cannot embrace the full implications of its per se rule: it eventually agrees that there cannot be a categorical rule for a taking based on economic value that wholly disregards the public need asserted. Instead, the Court decides that it will permit a State to regulate all economic value only if the State prohibits uses that would not be permitted under "background principles of nuisance and property law." ...

Until today, the Court explicitly had rejected the contention that the government's power to act without paying compensation turns on whether the prohibited activity is a common-law nuisance. ...

The Court rejects the notion that the State always can prohibit uses it deems a harm to the public without granting compensation because "the distinction between 'harm-preventing' and 'benefit-conferring' regulation is often in the eye of the beholder." ...

The threshold inquiry for imposition of the Court's new rule, "deprivation of all economically valuable use," itself cannot be determined objectively. As the Court admits, whether the owner has been deprived of all economic value of his property will depend on how "property" is defined. ...

* * *

Finally, the Court justifies its new rule that the legislature may not deprive a property owner of the only economically valuable use of his land, even if the legislature finds it to be a harmful use, because such action is not part of the "long recognized" understandings of our citizens." . . . These "understandings" permit such regulation only if the use is a nuisance under the common law. Any other course is "inconsistent with the historical compact recorded in the Takings Clause." . . . It is not clear from the Court's opinion where our "historical compact" or "citizens' understanding" comes from, but it does not appear to be history.

* * *

The Court makes sweeping and, in my view, misguided and unsupported changes in our taking doctrine. While it limits these changes to the most narrow subset of government regulation—those that eliminate all economic value from land—these changes go far beyond what is necessary to secure petitioner Lucas' private benefit. . . .

I dissent.

* * *

The *Lucas* opinion illustrates some of the tensions between constitutional protections of private property and public environmental law and regulation. Most, if not all, public environmental laws have some potential impact on the use and enjoyment of private property. Traditionally, however, takings jurisprudence has required a finding of *total deprivation of economically beneficial use* for a property owner to be constitutionally entitled to compensation. A salient feature of the *Lucas* opinion is its reliance on the trial court's finding that the legislative restriction prohibiting the erection of permanent habitable structures on Lucas's beachfront property deprived Lucas of all economic use of his property. The dissenting justices in the *Lucas* case strongly objected to the majority's reliance on this "implausible" factual finding. Arguably, the property could have supported a variety of uses that would not have contravened the restriction on erection of permanent, habitable structures. Depending upon the nature of state or local zoning or use restrictions, the property might have been used as a campground, bathing beach, boat dock, or nature preserve. Under precedent rulings cited by the *Lucas* court, it is irrelevant that these uses would not be as profitable as the construction of single-family beachfront homes. Indeed, in prior Supreme Court takings cases, use restrictions were rarely, if ever, found to result in a complete deprivation of all economic use of a property, even when the governmental restriction diminished the value of the property to a fraction of its preregulation market value.

The *Lucas* decision raises fundamental questions about the extent to which a landowner may be compelled to maintain the character of land in order to support the natural or ecological functions which that property serves. It has been pointed out that land serves a purpose in "the economy of nature" as well as in "the transformative economy."[22] *The transformative economy* here refers to a traditional concept of property that perceived undeveloped land and resources as serving no function until they are transformed by human technology to produce value in the marketplace.[23] The *economy of nature* refers to the ecological concept that land performs valuable functions in its natural state and that these functions are diminished by "development." In the transformative economy, wetlands are swamps harboring weeds and pests; they become valuable only when they are drained to permit, for example, the construction of residential subdivisions or the cultivation of crops. In the economy of nature, wetlands have inherent value as habitats for migratory birds, as sinks for flood waters, and as water purification systems. The *Lucas* decision relied upon traditional property concepts to limit governmental regulation that seeks to maintain a land's natural, ecological functions. It protects the right of property owners to engage in transformative activities, even those that are wholly incompatible with the land's ecological functions.

Drinking–Water Safety

Water pollution has long been known to impair the purity and safety of drinking water in many places in the United States. In 1974, Congress passed the Safe Drinking Water Act (SDWA) which mandated a nationwide program aimed at ensuring the safety of public drinking-water supplies. The Act did not set time-tables for EPA promulgation of drinking water standards, and the agency took little action. The SDWA was amended in 1986 in response to indications that U.S. drinking-water quality was declining, rather than improving. The amendments banned the future use of lead piping and solder in public drinking-water systems and required EPA to set national standards for 83 specified contaminants. EPA continued to ignore the statutory directives until a Portland, Oregon, citizens' group filed a series of lawsuits based upon the agency's failure to comply with the deadlines mandated in 1986. By 1993, EPA had promulgated practically all of the 83 national standards required by the 1986 amendments.

Primary Drinking–Water Standards

The SWDA addresses the two "primary" types of drinking-water contamination: microbiological contaminants, organisms that cause diseases, and chemical contaminants, which include metals and other substances identified as carcinogenic or toxic in high concentrations or through chronic exposure. Two substances commonly found in impure water are particularly troublesome because they pose immediate threats to human health. They are coliform bacteria from human and animal wastes—which can cause typhoid, cholera, infectious hepatitis, and dysentery—and nitrates, which cause an anemic condition in infants known as "blue baby" syndrome. In the first round of standard-setting mandated by the 1986 amendments, EPA was required to set enforceable *maximum contaminant levels (MCLs)* for coliform bacteria; elements such as arsenic and cadmium; organic substances such as insecticides, solvents, and fuel components; and radionuclides (species of atoms present in radioactive wastes). These MCLs constitute the EPA's primary drinking-water standards, which appear in Figure 8.6.

EPA is also required to issue *maximum contaminant level goals (MCLGs)*, which though unenforceable, are supposed to give water providers an idea of safe levels for certain contaminants. The law requires EPA to set the MCLs as close to the MCLGs as technologically and economically feasible. Alternatively, EPA may adopt a *National Primary Drinking Water Regulation* for a specific contaminant, which requires that a particular treatment method be used to reduce its level. This allows regulation of substances whose concentrations are not readily measurable. The treatment method, rather than sampling and testing, guarantees that the contaminant is not present in unsafe levels.

Several incidents in the early 1990s demonstrated that U.S. public water systems are not as safe as they should be. In the spring of 1993, Milwaukee's public water supply became contaminated with a microorganism that made many people ill and caused more than 40 deaths of persons with weakened immune systems. New York City had a water scare that summer, and Washington, D.C.'s water supply was found to be contaminated with fecal coliform bacteria in

■ **Figure 8.6**   Primary Drinking-Water Standards

Contaminant *Microbiological*	Health Effects	MCL[1]	Sources
Total coliforms (coliform bacteria, fecal coliform, streptococcal, and other bacteria)	not necessarily disease-producing themselves, but can be indicators of organisms that cause assorted gastroenteric infections, dysentery, hepatitis, typhoid fever, cholera, and others; also interfere with disinfection process.	1 per 100 milliliters	human and animal fecal matter
Turbidity	interferes with disinfection	1 to 5 NTU	erosion, runoff, and discharges
Inorganic Chemicals			
Arsenic	dermal and nervous system toxicity effects	.05	geological; pesticide residues, industrial waste; smelter operations
Barium	circulatory system effects	1	
Cadmium	kidney effects	.01	geological; mining and smelting
Chromium	liver/kidney effects	.05	
Lead	central and peripheral nervous system damage; kidney effects; highly toxic to infants and pregnant women	.05	leaches from lead pipes and lead-based-solder pipe joints
Mercury	central nervous system disorders; kidney effects	.002	used in manufacture of paint, paper, vinyl chloride; used in fungicides; geological
Nitrate	methemoglobinemia ("blue-baby" syndrome)	10	fertilizer, sewage, feedlots; geological
Selenium	gastrointestinal effects	.01	geological; mining
Silver	skin discoloration (argyria)	.05	geological; mining
Fluoride	skeletal damage	4	geological; additive to drinking water, toothpaste; foods processed with fluorinated water
Organic Chemicals			
Endrin	nervous system/kidney effects	.0002	insecticide used on cotton, small grains, orchards (canceled)
Lindane	nervous system/kidney effects	.004	insecticide used on seed and soil treatments, foliage application, wood protection
Methoxychlor	nervous system/kidney effects	.1	insecticide used on fruit trees, vegetables
2,4-D	liver/kidney effects	.1	herbicide used to control broad-leaf weeds in agriculture; used on forests, range, pastures, aquatic environments

[1]In milligrams per liter, unless otherwise noted. *Source:* EPA, *Is Your Drinking Water Safe?* (1989).

October. A 1993 report by the National Resources Defense Council, a citizens' group, documented more than 250,000 violations within a two-year period by 43 percent of U.S. public water systems, which collectively serve 123 million people.[24] The U.S. General Accounting Office has repeatedly criticized the EPA for failing to administer the SWDA effectively.

Most public water systems use chlorine, which may be carcinogenic, as a disinfecting agent. It is estimated that 10,000 to 12,000 cases of cancer may be attributable to chlorine in drinking water. Some public water plants have begun to treat drinking water with ozonation or granular-activated-carbon systems.

Secondary Drinking–Water Standards

EPA also sets secondary drinking water standards. These "standards" are actually unenforceable guidelines aimed at protecting the aesthetic qualities of drinking water, rather than reducing health risks. Figure 8.7 summarizes these guidelines.

■ **Figure 8.7**   Secondary Drinking-Water Standards

Contaminants	Suggested Levels	Contaminant Effects
pH	6.5–8.5	Corrosiveness
Chloride	250 mg/l	Taste and corrosion of pipes
Copper	1 mg/l	Taste and staining of porcelain
Foaming agents	0.5 mg/l	Aesthetic
Sulfate	250 mg/l	Taste and laxative effects
Total dissolved solids (hardness)	500 mg/l	Taste and possible relation between low hardness and cardiovascular disease; also an indicator of corrosivity (related to lead levels in water); can damage plumbing and limit effectiveness of soaps and detergents
Zinc	5 mg/l	Taste
Fluoride	2.0 mg/l	Dental fluorosis (a brownish discoloration of the teeth)
Color	15 color units	Aesthetic
Corrosivity	non-corrosive	Aesthetic and health related (Corrosive water can leach pipe materials, such as lead, into drinking water.)
Iron	0.3 mg/l	Taste and staining of laundry
Manganese	0.05 mg/l	Taste and staining of laundry
Odor	3 threshold odor number	Aesthetic

Secondary Drinking Water Standards are unenforceable federal guidelines regarding the taste, odor, color—and certain other non-aesthetic effects—of drinking water. EPA recommends them to the States as reasonable goals, but federal law does not require water systems to comply with them. States may, however, adopt their own enforceable regulations governing these concerns.

Source: EPA, *Is Your Drinking Water Safe?* (June 1989).

Protecting the Marine Environment

In the not-so-distant past, it was generally thought that the immense oceans could accommodate enormous quantities of polluting discharges without marine environments becoming degraded. Widespread contamination of the earth's beaches and coastal water, however, has made it abundantly clear that ocean dumping, even at considerable distances offshore, has serious deleterious effects on the global marine environment. In recognition of this, Congress passed the Marine Protection Research and Sanctuaries Act, also known as the Ocean Dumping Act, in 1972. This legislation prohibits most polluting discharges to the oceans within the nation's jurisdictional boundaries.

■ Problem Set Exercises

Tully Corporation is expanding its manufacturing facility by building a new chloromethanes plant. For its new plant, Tully purchased and cleared an adjacent property, formerly a swamp that local residents used as a dump for many years. The contractor for the project is Steve and Sons, which specializes in building on unstable sites. Steve and Sons is now ready to fill in the site to prepare it for construction.

1. Is a permit necessary? If so, must Tully or Steve apply for it? Who has the authority to grant the permit?
2. If the swamp is not adjacent to a river, lake, or other body of water classified as navigable, is a permit required? If this is the case and a permit is required, who would issue the permit?

Tully intends to build the plant alongside a small, unnamed creek that is a tributary of Adams Lake. In its current undredged state, the creek is not capable of carrying traffic. Tully plans to draw water from the creek to cool plant machinery and then return the water to the creek.

3. Will the discharged cooling water be considered a pollutant if it is not contaminated with a chemical substance?
4. Will Tully need a permit to discharge cooling water to the creek? Why or why not?
5. If Tully needs a permit, who will determine whether it should be granted? What must the permitting authority consider in ruling on the permit application?
6. What restrictions, if any, must the permitting authority place on the discharge of cooling water into the creek? What sections of the CWA govern this situation?

After Steve and Sons began filling in the swamp, Tully learned that medusa weed, a rare, delicate plant, previously thought to be native only to Brazil, is growing in the swamp. Researchers have speculated that medusa weed may be useful as a cure for a very rare, fatal disease. Medusa weed takes several years to germinate and needs a highly unusual habitat to grow and flower. Tully's development of the property would destroy the plant's habitat, which cannot be artificially created elsewhere. The Unique Habitats for Human Uses Act forbids the destruction of unique habitats that support potentially medicinally useful species. The FDA, which enforces this statute, has issued an order to Tully to cease any activities that would destroy the medusa weed's habitat.

Tully has already expended large sums of money on its chloromethanes plant project and does not want to wait and see if medusa weed is deemed a medicinally useful species—which would make it an extremely valuable commodity. You are hired as Tully's legal counsel to contest the FDA order.

7. Does the FDA order issued under the Unique Habitats for Human Uses Act constitute a taking of Tully's property? Why or why not?

8. Is Tully entitled to compensation for its inability to build on the swamp? If so, what measure of compensation is appropriate? If so, should a court consider the potential commodity value of medusa weed in determining whether, and how much, compensation should be paid to Tully?

Appendix—Chapter 8

Selected Statutory Sections—The Clean Water Act (Codified at 33 U.S.C. § 1251 *et seq.*)

CWA § 301   Effluent Limitations

(a) Illegality of pollutant discharges except in compliance with law

Except as in compliance with this . . . [subchapter], the discharge of any pollutant by any person shall be unlawful.

(b) Timetable for achievement of objectives

In order to carry out the objective of this chapter there shall be achieved—

(1)(A) not later than July 1, 1977, effluent limitations for point sources, other than publicly owned treatment works, (i) which shall require the application of the best practicable control technology currently available as defined by the Administrator . . . , or (ii) in the case of a discharge into a publicly owned treatment works . . . ; and

(B) for publicly owned treatment works . . . effluent limitations based upon secondary treatment . . . ; or,

(C) not later than July 1, 1977, any more stringent limitation, including those necessary to meet water quality standards, treatment standards, or schedules of compliance, established pursuant to any State law or regulations . . . , or required to implement any applicable water quality standard . . . .

(2)(A) . . . [for toxic and nonconventional pollutants], effluent limitations for categories and classes of point sources, other than publicly owned treatment works, which (i) shall require application of the best available technology economically achievable . . . , which will result in reasonable further progress toward the national goal of eliminating the discharge of all pollutants . . . . Such effluent limitations shall require the elimination of discharges of all pollutants if the Administrator finds . . . , that such elimina-

tion is technologically and economically achievable . . . .

* * *

(E) for conventional pollutants, as expeditiously as practicable but in no case later than . . . March 31, 1989, compliance with effluent limitations for categories and classes of point sources, other than publicly owned treatment works, which . . . shall require application of the best conventional pollutant control technology . . . ;

* * *

(c) Modification of timetable

(1) The Administrator may modify the requirements . . . of this section with respect to any point source for which a permit application if filed . . . , upon a showing by the owner or operator of such point source . . . that such modified requirements (1) will represent the maximum use of technology within the economic capability of the owner or operator; and (2) will result in reasonable further progress toward the elimination of the discharge of pollutants.

* * *

(f) Illegality of discharge of radiological, chemical, or biological warfare agents, high-level radioactive waste, or medical waste

Notwithstanding any other provisions of this chapter it shall be unlawful to discharge any radiological, chemical, or biological warfare agent, any high-level radioactive waste, or any medical waste into the navigable waters.

(g) Modifications for certain nonconventional pollutants
(1) General authority

The Administrator, with the concurrence of the State, may modify the requirements . . . with respect to the discharge from any point source of . . . [certain nonconventional pollutants].

(2) Requirements for granting modifications

A modification under this subsection shall be granted only upon a showing by the owner or operator of a point source . . . that—

  (A) such modified requirements will [use best practicable control technology or meet water quality standards];

* * *

  (C) such modification will not interfere with the attainment or maintenance of that water quality which shall assure protection of public water supplies, and the protection and propagation of a balanced population of shellfish, fish, and wildlife, and allow recreational activities, in and on the water and such modification will not result in the discharge of pollutants in quantities which may reasonably be anticipated to pose an unacceptable risk to human health or the environment because of bioaccumulation, persistency in the environment, acute toxicity, chronic toxicity (including carcinogenicity, mutagenicity or teratogenicity), or synergistic propensities.

* * *

(i) Municipal time extensions

  (1) Where construction is required in order for a planned or existing publicly owned treatment works to achieve [applicable] limitations . . . , but (A) construction cannot be completed within the time required . . . , or (B) the United States has failed to make financial assistance under this chapter available in time to achieve such limitations . . . , the owner or operator of such treatment works may request the Administrator (or if appropriate the State) to issue a permit . . . or to modify a permit . . . to extend such time for compliance. . . .

* * *

(k) Innovative technology

In the case of any facility subject to a permit . . . which proposes to comply with the requi-

rements . . . by replacing existing production capacity with an innovative production process [or an innovative control technique] which will result in an effluent reduction significantly greater than that required by the limitation . . . and moves toward the national goal of eliminating the discharge of all pollutants, . . . or by achieving the required reduction with an innovative system that has the potential for significantly lower cost than the systems which have been determined by the Administrator to be economically achievable, the Administrator (or . . . [an approved state]) may establish a date for compliance . . . no later than two years after the date for compliance . . . , if it is also determined that such innovative system has the potential for industrywide application.

(l) Toxic pollutants

. . . , the Administrator may not modify any requirement of this section as it applies to any [toxic pollutants] . . . .

* * *

(n) Fundamentally different factors
(1) General rule

The Administrator, with the concurrence of the State, may establish an alternative requirement . . . for a facility that modifies the requirements of national effluent limitation guidelines or categorical pretreatment standards . . . , if the owner or operator of such facility demonstrates to the satisfaction of the Administrator that—

  (A) the facility is fundamentally different with respect to the factors (other than cost) . . . considered by the Administrator in establishing such national effluent limitation or guidelines or categorical pretreatment standards;

  (B) the application—

    (i) is based solely on information and supporting data submitted to the Administrator during the rulemaking for establishment of the applicable national effluent limitation guidelines or categorical pretreatment standard specifically raising the factors that are fundamentally different for such facility;

(ii) is based on information and support-ing data . . . the applicant did not have a reasonable opportunity to submit during such rulemaking;

* * *

(D) the alternative requirement will not re-sult in a non-water quality environmental impact which is markedly more adverse than the impact considered by the Admin-istrator in establishing such national efflu-ent limitation guideline or categorical pre-treatment standard.

* * *

CWA § 302   Water Quality Related Effluent Limitations

(a) Establishment

Whenever, in the judgment of the Admin-istrator . . . discharges of pollutants from a point source or group of point sources, with the application of effluent limitations . . . , would interfere with the attainment or maintenance of that water quality in a specific portion of the navigable waters . . . public water supplies, ag-ricultural and industrial uses, and the protec-tion and propagation of a balanced population of shellfish, fish and wildlife, and allow recre-ational activities in and on the water, effluent limitations (including alternative effluent con-trol strategies) for such point source or sources shall be established which can reasonably be expected to contribute to the attainment or maintenance of such water quality.

(b) Modifications of effluent limitations

* * *

(2) Permits
(A) No reasonable relationship

The Administrator, with the concurrence of the State, may issue a permit which modifies the effluent limitations . . . for pollutants other than toxic pollutants if the applicant demon-strates at such hearing that (whether or not technology or other alternative control strate-gies are available) there is no reasonable rela-tionship between the economic and social costs and the benefits to be obtained (including at-

tainment of the objective of this chapter) from achieving such limitation.

(B) Reasonable progress

The Administrator, with the concurrence of the State, may issue a permit which modifies the effluent limitations . . . for toxic pollutants for a single period not to exceed 5 years if the applicant demonstrates that such modified re-quirements (i) will represent the maximum de-gree of control within the economic capability of the owner and operator of the source, and (ii) will result in reasonable further progress . . . toward . . . [attainment of water quality].

CWA § 303   Water Quality Standards and Implementation Plans

(a) Existing water quality standards

* * *

(2) Any State which . . . has adopted, pursuant to its own law, water quality standards appli-cable to intrastate waters shall submit such standards to the Administrator . . . . Each such standard shall remain in effect, in the same manner and to the same extent as any other water quality standard established under this chapter unless the Administrator determines that such standard is inconsistent with the ap-plicable requirements of . . . [the pre-1972 CWA].

(3)(A) Any State which . . . has not adopted pursuant to its own laws water quality stan-dards applicable to intrastate waters shall . . . adopt and submit such standards to the Administrator.

* * *

(C) If the Administrator determines that any such standards are not consistent with the ap-plicable requirements of this Act . . . [the pre-1972 CWA] he shall . . . notify the State and specify the changes to meet such require-ments. If such changes are not adopted by the State within ninety days after the date of no-tification, the Administrator shall promulgate such standards . . . .

* * *

(d) Identification of areas with insuffi-cient controls; maximum daily load; cer-tain effluent limitations revision

(1)(A) Each State shall identify those waters within its boundaries for which the effluent limitations . . . are not stringent enough to implement any water quality standard applicable to such waters. The State shall establish a priority ranking for such waters, taking into account the severity of the pollution and the uses to be made of such waters.

* * *

(C) Each State shall establish for the waters identified in paragraph (1)(A) . . . , and in accordance with the priority ranking, the total maximum daily load, for those pollutants which the Administrator identifies . . . as suitable for such calculation. Such load shall be established at a level necessary to implement the applicable water quality standards with seasonal variations and a margin of safety which takes into account any lack of knowledge concerning the relationship between effluent limitations and water quality.

* * *

(D)(3) For the specific purpose of developing information, each State shall identify all waters within its boundaries [not already identified] . . . and estimate for such waters the total maximum daily load with seasonal variations and margins of safety, for those pollutants which the Administrator identifies . . . as suitable for such calculation and for thermal discharges, at a level that would assure protection and propagation of a balanced indigenous population of fish, shellfish, and wildlife.

(4) Limitations on revision of certain effluent limitations
  (A) Standard not attained
  For waters identified under paragraph (1)(A) where the applicable water quality standard has not yet been attained, any effluent limitation based on a total maximum daily load or other waste load allocation established under this section may be revised only if (i) the cumulative effect of all such revised effluent limitations based on such total maximum daily load or waste load allocation will assure the attainment of such water quality standard, or (ii) the designated use which is not being attained is removed . . . .

(B) Standard attained
For waters identified under paragraph (1)(A) where the quality of such waters equals or exceeds levels necessary to protect the designated use for such waters or otherwise required by applicable water quality standards, any effluent limitation based on a total maximum daily load or other waste load allocation established under this section, or any water quality standard established under this section, or any other permitting standard may be revised only if such revision is subject to and consistent with the antidegradation policy established under this section.

* * *

CWA § 304   Information and Guidelines

(a) Criteria development and publication
  (1) The Administrator . . . shall develop and publish . . . (and from time to time thereafter revise) criteria for water quality accurately reflecting the latest scientific knowledge (A) on the kind and extent of all identifiable effects on health and welfare including, but not limited to, plankton, fish, shellfish, wildlife, plant life, shorelines, beaches, esthetics, and recreation which may be expected from the presence of pollutants in any body of water, including ground water, (B) on the concentration and dispersal of pollutants, or their byproducts, through biological, physical, and chemical processes; and (C) on the effects of pollutants on biological community diversity, productivity, and stability, including information on the factors affecting rates of eutrophication and rates of organic and inorganic sedimentation for varying types of receiving waters.
  (2) The Administrator . . . shall develop and publish, . . . (and from time to time thereafter revise) information (A) on the factors necessary to restore and maintain the chemical, physical, and biological integrity of all navigable waters, ground waters, waters of the contiguous zone, and the oceans; (B) on the factors necessary for the protection and propagation of shellfish, fish, and wildlife for classes and categories of receiving waters and to allow recreational activities in and on the water; and (C) on the measurement and classification of water

quality; and (D) . . . on the identification of pollutants suitable for maximum daily load measurement correlated with the achievement of water quality objectives.

* * *

(4) The Administrator shall . . . publish and revise as appropriate information identifying conventional pollutants, including but not limited to, pollutants classified as biological oxygen demanding, suspended solids, fecal coliform, and pH. The thermal component of any discharge shall not be identified as a conventional pollutant under this paragraph.

(5)(A) The Administrator, to the extent practicable . . . , shall develop and publish information on the factors necessary for the protection of public water supplies, and the protection and propagation of a balanced population of shellfish, fish and wildlife, and to allow recreational activities, in and on the water.

* * *

(6) The Administrator shall . . . annually . . . publish and revise as appropriate information identifying each water quality standard in effect under this chapter or State law, the specific pollutants associated with such water quality standard, and the particular waters to which such water quality standard applies.

* * *

(8) Information on water quality criteria

The Administrator . . . shall develop and publish information on methods for establishing and measuring water quality criteria for toxic pollutants on other bases than pollutant-by-pollutant criteria, including biological monitoring and assessment methods.

(b) Effluent limitation guidelines

For the purpose of adopting or revising effluent limitations under this chapter the Administrator shall . . . publish . . . regulations, providing guidelines for effluent limitations, and, at least annually thereafter, revise, if appropriate such regulations. Such regulations shall—

(1)(A) identify, in terms of amount of constituents and chemical, physical, and biological characteristics of pollutants, the degree of effluent reduction attainable through the application of the best practicable control technology currently availa-

ble for classes and categories of point sources (other than publicly owned treatment works); and

(B) specify factors to be taken into account in determining the control measures and practices to be applicable to point sources (other than publicly owned treatment works) within such categories or classes. Factors relating to the assessment of best practicable control technology currently available . . . shall include consideration of the total cost of application of technology in relation to the effluent reduction benefits to be achieved from such application, and shall also take into account the age of equipment and facilities involved, the process employed, the engineering aspects of the application of various types of control techniques, process changes, non-water quality environmental impact (including energy requirements), and such other factors as the Administrator deems appropriate;

(2)(A) identify, in terms of amounts of constituents and chemical, physical, and biological characteristics of pollutants, the degree of effluent reduction attainable through the application of the best control measures and practices achievable including treatment techniques, process and procedure innovations, operating methods, and other alternatives for classes and categories of point sources (other than publicly owned treatment works); and

(B) specify factors to be taken into account in determining the best measures and practices available . . . to be applicable to any point source (other than publicly owned treatment works) within such categories or classes.

Factors relating to the assessment of best available technology shall take into account the age of equipment and facilities involved, the process employed, the engineering aspects of the application of various types of control techniques, process changes, the cost of achieving such effluent reduction, non-water quality environmental impact (including energy requirements), and such other factors as the Administrator deems appropriate;

(3) identify control measures and practices available to eliminate the discharge of pollutants from categories and classes of point sources, taking into account the cost of achieving such elimination of the discharge of pollutants; and

(4)(A) identify, in terms of amounts of constituents and chemical, physical, and biological characteristics of pollutants, the degree of effluent reduction attainable through the application of the best conventional pollutant control technology (including measures and practices) for classes and categories of point sources (other than publicly owned treatment works); and

(B) specify factors to be taken into account in determining the best conventional pollutant control technology measures and practices . . . to be applicable to any point source (other than publicly owned treatment works) within such categories or classes. Factors relating to the assessment of best conventional pollutant control technology (including measures and practices) shall include consideration of the reasonableness of the relationship between the costs of attaining a reduction in effluents and the effluent reduction benefits derived, and the comparison of the cost and level of reduction of such pollutants from the discharge from publicly owned treatment works to the cost and level of reduction of such pollutants from a class or category of industrial sources, and shall take into account the age of equipment and facilities involved, the process employed, the engineering aspects of the application of various types of control techniques, process changes, non-water quality environmental impact including energy requirements), and such other factors as the Administrator deems appropriate.

* * *

(d) Secondary treatment information; alternative waste treatment management techniques; innovative and alternative wastewater treatment processes; facilities deemed equivalent of secondary treatment

(1) The Administrator . . . shall publish . . . information, in terms of amounts of constituents and chemical, physical, and biological characteristics of pollutants, on the degree of effluent reduction attainable through the application of secondary treatment.

(2) The Administrator . . . shall publish . . . information on alternative waste treatment management techniques and systems . . . .

(3) The Administrator . . . shall promulgate . . . guidelines for identifying and evaluating innovative and alternative wastewater treatment processes and techniques . . . .

(4) For the purposes of this subsection, such biological treatment facilities as oxidation ponds, lagoons, and ditches and trickling filters shall be deemed the equivalent of secondary treatment. The Administrator shall provide guidance . . . on design criteria for such facilities, taking into account pollutant removal efficiencies and, consistent with the objectives of this chapter, assuring that water quality will not be adversely affected by deeming such facilities as the equivalent of secondary treatment.

* * *

(f) Identification and evaluation of nonpoint sources of pollution; processes, procedures, and methods to control pollution

The Administrator . . . shall issue to appropriate Federal agencies, the States, water pollution control agencies, . . . information including (1) guidelines for identifying and evaluating the nature and extent of nonpoint sources of pollutants, and (2) processes, procedures, and methods to control pollution resulting from—

(A) agricultural and silvicultural activities, including runoff from fields and crop and forest lands;

(B) mining activities, including runoff and siltation from new, currently operating, and abandoned surface and underground mines;

(C) all construction activities, including runoff from the facilities resulting from such construction;

(D) the disposal of pollutants in wells or in subsurface excavations;

(E) salt water intrusion resulting from reductions of fresh water flow from any cause, including extraction of ground water, irrigation, obstruction, and diversion; and

(F) changes in the movement, flow, or circulation of any navigable waters or ground waters, including changes caused by the construction of dams, levees, channels, causeways, or flow diversion facilities. . . .

* * *

CWA § 306 National Standards of Performance

(a) Definitions

For purposes of this section:

(1) The term "standard of performance" means a standard for the control of the discharge of pollutants which reflect the greatest degree of effluent reduction which the Administrator determines to be achievable through application of the best available demonstrated control technology, processes, operating methods, or other alternatives, including, where practicable, a standard permitting no discharge of pollutants.

(2) The term "new source" means any source, the construction of which is commenced after the publication of proposed regulations prescribing a standard of performance under this section which will be applicable to such source, if such standard is thereafter promulgated in accordance with this section.

* * *

(b) Categories of sources; Federal standards of performance for new sources

(1)(A) The Administrator shall . . . publish . . . a list of categories of sources which shall, at the minimum, include:

pulp and paper mills;
paperboard, builders paper and board mills;
meat product and rendering processing;
dairy product processing;
grain mills;
canned and preserved fruits and vegetables processing;
canned and preserved seafood processing;
sugar processing;

textile mills;
cement manufacturing;
feedlots;
electroplating;
organic chemicals manufacturing;
inorganic chemicals manufacturing;
plastic and synthetic materials manufacturing;
soap and detergent manufacturing;
fertilizer manufacturing;
petroleum refining;
iron and steel manufacturing;
nonferrous metals manufacturing;
phosphate manufacturing;
steam electric powerplants;
ferro alloy manufacturing;
leather tanning and finishing;
glass and asbestos manufacturing;
rubber processing; and
timber product processing.

(B) As soon as practicable . . . the Administrator shall propose and publish regulations establishing Federal standards of performance for new sources within such category. . . . The Administrator shall, from time to time, as technology and alternatives change, revise such standards . . . . In establishing or revising Federal standards of performance for new sources under this section, the Administrator shall take into consideration the cost of achieving such effluent reduction, and any non-water quality, environmental impact and energy requirements.

(2) The Administrator may distinguish among classes, types, and sizes within categories of new sources for the purpose of establishing such standards and shall consider the type of process employed (including whether batch or continuous).

(3) The provisions of this section shall apply to any new source owned or operated by the United States.

* * *

(d) Protection from more stringent standards

Notwithstanding any other provision of this chapter, any point source . . . which is . . . constructed . . . to meet all applicable standards of performance shall not be subject to any more stringent standard of performance during a ten-year period beginning on the date of completion of such construction or during the period of depreciation or amortization of such facility . . . whichever period ends first.

(e) Illegality of operation of new sources in violation of applicable standards of performance

After the effective date of standards of performance promulgated under this section, it shall be unlawful for any owner or operator of any new source to operate such source in violation of any standard of performance applicable to such source.

CWA § 307 Toxic and Pretreatment Effluent Standards

(a) Toxic pollutant list; revision; hearing; promulgation of standards; effective date; consultation

. . . The Administrator in publishing any revised list [of toxic pollutants], including the addition or removal of any pollutant from such list, shall take into account toxicity of the pollutant, its persistence, degradability, the usual or potential presence of the affected organisms in any waters, the importance of the affected organisms, and the nature and extent of the effect of the toxic pollutant on such organisms. . . .

(2) Each toxic pollutant . . . shall be subject to effluent limitations resulting from the application of the best available technology economically achievable for the applicable category or class of point sources . . . .

* * *

(4) Any effluent standard promulgated under this section shall be at that level which the Administrator determines provides an ample margin of safety.

(5) When proposing or promulgating any effluent standard (or prohibition) under this section, the Administrator shall designate the category or categories of sources to which the effluent standard (or prohibition) shall apply. Any disposal of dredged material may be included in such a category of sources after consultation with the Secretary of the Army.

* * *

(b) Pretreatment standards; hearing; promulgation; compliance period; revision; application to State and local laws

(1) The Administrator shall . . . publish proposed regulations establishing pretreatment standards for introduction of pollutants into treatment works . . . which are publicly owned for those pollutants which are determined not to be susceptible to treatment by such treatment works or which would interfere with the operation of such treatment works. . . . Pretreatment standards . . . shall be established to prevent the discharge of any pollutant through treatment works . . . which are publicly owned, which pollutant interferes with, passes through, or otherwise is incompatible with such works. If, in the case of any toxic pollutant . . . introduced by a source into a publicly owned treatment works, the treatment by such works removes all or any part of such toxic pollutant and the discharge from such works does not violate that effluent limitation or standard which would be applicable to such toxic pollutant if it were discharged by such source other than through a publicly owned treatment works . . . , then the pretreatment requirements for the sources actually discharging such toxic pollutant into such publicly owned treatment works may be revised by the owner or operator of such works to reflect the removal of such toxic pollutant by such works.

* * *

(d) Operation in violation of standards unlawful

After the effective date of any effluent standard or prohibition or pretreatment standard promulgated under this section, it shall be unlawful for any owner or operator of any source to operate any source in violation of any such effluent standard or prohibition or pretreatment standard.

* * *

CWA § 311 Oil and Hazardous Substance Liability

* * *

(b)(3) The discharge of oil or hazardous substances . . . into or upon the navigable waters of the United States, adjoining shorelines, or into or upon the waters of the contiguous zone, . . . or which may affect natural resources belonging to, appertaining to, or under the exclusive management authority of the United States . . . , in such quantities as may be harmful as determined by the President . . . is prohibited.

CWA § 402 National Pollutant Discharge Elimination System

(a) Permits for discharge of pollutants

. . . [T]he Administrator may, after opportunity for public hearing, issue a permit for the discharge of any pollutant, or combination of pollutants, . . . upon condition that such discharge will meet [national effluent-limitation standards].

(b) State permit programs

. . . [T]he Governor of each State desiring to administer its own permit program for discharges into navigable waters within its jurisdiction may submit to the Administrator a full and complete description of the program it proposes to establish and administer under State law . . . . The Administrator shall approve each submitted program unless he determines that adequate authority does not exist:

(1) To issue permits which—

(A) apply, and insure compliance with [national effluent-limitation standards] . . . .

(o) Anti-backsliding
(1) General prohibition

. . . [A] permit may not be renewed, reissued, or modified on the basis of effluent limitations . . . subsequent to the original issuance of such permit, to contain effluent limitation which are less stringent than the comparable effluent limitations in the previous permit. . . .

(3) Limitations

. . . In no event may such a permit to discharge into water be renewed, reissued or modified to contain a less stringent effluent limitation if the implementation of such limitation would result in a violation of a[n applicable] water quality standard. . . .

CWA § 404 Permits for Dredged or Fill Material

(a) Discharge into navigable waters at specified disposal sites

The Secretary [of the Army acting through the Chief of Engineers] may issue permits . . . for the discharge of dredged or fill material into the navigable waters at specified disposal sites. . . .

* * *

(c) Denial or restriction of use of defined areas as disposal sites

The Administrator is authorized to prohibit the specification . . . of any defined area as a disposal site . . . whenever he determines . . . that the discharge of such materials into such area will have an unacceptable adverse effect on municipal water supplies, shellfish beds and fishery areas . . . , wildlife, or recreational areas. . . .

CWA § 502 Definitions

* * *

(6) The term ''pollutant'' means dredged spoil, solid waste, incinerator residue, sewage, garbage, sewage sludge, munitions, chemical waste, biological materials, radioactive materials, heat, wrecked or discarded equipment, rock, sand, cellar dirt and industrial, municipal, and agricultural waste discharged into water. . . .

■   ## Chapter 8 Endnotes

1. B. Commoner, *The Closing Circle* (1971).
2. "Wetlands' Loss Haunts River Basin," *The Philadelphia Inquirer*, 1 August 1993, p. A10.
3. Environmental Law Institute, "Wetlands Mitigation Banking" (draft, June 1993).
4. R. Tiner quoted in "A Natural Treasure Imperiled," *The Philadelphia Inquirer*, 28 March 1993, p. A12.
5. U.S. Department of Justice, Guidelines for Litigation under the Refuse Act, paragraph 11 (1970).
6. Ibid.
7. *Rybachek v. EPA*, 904 F.2d 1276 (9th Cir. 1990).
8. *State of the Environment* (The Conservation Foundation, 1987), p. 361.
9. For fuller definitions of the many technical terms employed in environmental statutes, see J. King, *The Environmental Dictionary* (Executive Enterprises, 1989).
10. *Clean Water Handbook* (Government Institutes, Inc., 1990), p. 3.
11. See *Gwaltney of Smithfield v. Chesapeake Bay Foundation*, 484 U.S. 49 (1987).
12. *United States v. Riverside Bayview Homes*, 106 S. Ct. 455 (1985).
13. Ibid.
14. *Hoffman Homes Inc. v. Administrator, U.S.E.P.A.*, 999 F.2d 256 (7th Cir. 1993).
15. *United States v. Pozsgai*, 999 F.2d 719 (3d Cir. 1993).
16. See, for example, *Inside EPA*, 25 June 1993. For a detailed report of wetlands policy changes suggested (but not finalized) by the Clinton Administration, see Hearings, "The Administration's New Wetlands Policy," (9-28-93) before House of Representatives Subcommittee on Environment and Natural Resources, 103d Cong., 1st Sess. (Serial No. 103–62, U.S. Govt. Printing Office, 1994).
17. CWA § 320.
18. *Weinberger v. Romero-Barcelo*, 456 U.S. 305 (1982).
19. *Milwaukee v. Illinois*, 451 U.S. 304, 320 (1981).
20. *Chemical Manufacturers Assn. v. Natural Resources Defense Council*, 470 U.S. 116 (1985).
21. W. Pedersen, "Turning the Tide on Water Quality," 15 *Ecology Law Quarterly* 69 (1988).
22. J. Sax, "Property Rights and the Economy of Nature: Understanding *Lucas v. South Carolina Coastal Council*," 45 *Stanford Law Review*, 1433, at 1442 (1993).
23. Ibid.
24. National Resources Defense Council, *Think before You Drink* (September 1993), pp. 3, 4.

CHAPTER 9

The Clean Air Act (CAA)

A Technology-Forcing and Market-Incentive Approach

Outline

9.1 Air Quality and Related Issues

"Traditional" Air-Pollution Problems

Long before the era of modern environmental legislation, industrialized societies were intimately acquainted with the hazards of air pollution. Residents of industrialized urban areas have long suffered the health effects and unpleasant living conditions associated with emissions from smokestacks and tailpipes. The industrial revolution saw the rise of new occupational hazards in mining, textile production, chemical production, and other industries. Prior to comprehensive

319

public regulation, citizens seeking relief from air pollution had few options. Some of them invoked the law of nuisance in attempting to abate nearby sources of air pollution, but they were generally unsuccessful. Anglo-American jurisprudence traditionally favored laissez-faire economic principles and protected the health of the polluting industries, rather than that of the environment or of the public. Furthermore, people who lived in the vicinity of polluting industries were economically dependent upon them. Although comprehensive legislation has now been enacted to alleviate the most noticeable hazards associated with air pollution in the United States, concerns for human health and the environment and economic concerns are frequently at odds.

During the decade preceding the first Earth Day in 1970, air pollution problems in the United States became far less localized, largely due to the automobile and an increasingly mobile and suburbanized culture. In addition, the number of other sources of air pollution—such as utility plants, factories, waste incinerators, and oil refineries—continued to increase. Nonetheless, the Clean Air Act of 1970 (CAA) and its amendments have made inroads in decreasing some polluting emissions since 1970. In 1990, the Council on Environmental Quality's report on changes in polluting and toxic emissions from fixed sources (primarily industrial plants) and mobile sources (motor vehicles) over the previous 20 years indicated the following progress:

- The national annual emission of *lead* for 1970 totalled almost 204 million tons. By 1987 the rate [had] dropped to 8 million tons, largely due to the phaseout of leaded gasoline.
- The national annual emission of *particulate matter* in 1970 was 18.1 million tons. In 1987 it was 7 million tons.
- The national annual emission of *sulfur dioxide* in 1970 was 28.2 million tons. By 1987 it [had] dropped only modestly to 20.4 million tons.
- The national annual emission of *nitrogen oxide* in 1970 was 18.1 million tons. By 1987 it [had] increased to 19.5 million tons.
- From 1970 the national annual emission of *carbon dioxide* [had] dropped by 38%, but the volume of carbon dioxide (and hydrocarbon) emissions in many cities and areas still exceed[ed] national health standards.
- As of 1989, 110 urban areas of the country did not meet the national ozone standard.
- The continuing growth in population and attendant increase in consumption of products that add to air pollution aggravates the task of reigning it in. In the past two decades the United States population increased by about 45 million persons, a significant 22% increase. In that period its economy grew almost three times as fast as the population, with explosive growth of automobiles, (89 million in 1970 to 139 million in 1989), which are a prime generator of air pollution.[1]

Efforts to attain air quality through national legislation have produced mixed results. In certain discrete areas, such as reducing lead emissions, air-pollution regulation has yielded respectable results, but in others, particularly in the attainment of primary health-based air-quality standards, the performance has been dismal. Arguably, Congress's willingness to revise attainment deadlines—and its failure to require their enforcement consistently—has diminished the effectiveness of the technology-forcing aspects of clean-air legislation, and contributed to the persistence of the nation's air-pollution problems.

Emerging Global Issues

Most people think of air-quality problems in terms of pollution—emissions of toxins, carcinogens, and other substances that are harmful to human health and to plant and animal life. In recent years, two other air-quality problems have emerged: ozone depletion and the greenhouse effect. These problems arise from the release of substances that are not in and of themselves harmful to human health. The Earth's protective ozone layer in the upper atmosphere is being broken down by accumulations of chlorofluorocarbons (CFCs) and other ozone-depleting substances released into the atmosphere. CFCs are not toxic, but their effect on the ozone layer produces harmful effects to humans and other organisms. The greenhouse effect, also known as "global warming," is a phenomenon caused by releases into the atmosphere of carbon dioxide from the burning of fossil fuels and of other "greenhouse" gases. Again, the problem lies not so much with the nature of the substances themselves, but with the ecological imbalances caused by excessive releases of them. These issues are reviewed more extensively in section 9.3.

9.2   Overview of the Clean Air Act

Legislative History of the Clean Air Act

The origins of the Clean Air Act predate the modern era of environmental legislation. In 1955, Congress passed legislation that authorized a federal air-pollution-research program and offered technical and financial assistance to the states, but it instituted no regulatory regime. In 1960 and 1965, Congress passed laws that did little more than authorize the study of motor-vehicle emissions, and in 1963, it passed the Clean Air Act, which addressed only interstate pollution.

During the sixties, the California legislature confronted considerable smog problems by enacting strict emissions limitations. Other states soon followed suit. In 1967, however, Congress passed the Air Quality Act, which preempted state regulation of auto emissions (except for California law), even though that act placed the primary burdens of implementing air-quality standards on state governments. The Air Quality Act adopted a regional approach to air pollution regulation by directing the Secretary of Health, Education, and Welfare (HEW) to designate air-quality-control regions across the nation. Each region was to be defined as an area affected by a common air-pollution problem requiring uniform control activities. This regional approach to air quality-control has remained essentially unchanged under present-day laws.

During debates leading to passage of the Air Quality Act, Congress and President Johnson grappled with two policy questions which remain prevalent issues in media-specific environmental legislation. The first is whether air-quality standards should be based on the availability of practical pollution-control technologies (known as a *technology-driven* approach) or whether standards should be set at levels deemed to be protective of health and the environment regardless of the current availability and cost of pollution-control technology. In the absence of available effective technologies, the latter approach is known as a *technology-forcing approach* because it requires the development of new technologies to meet legal standards. The question of technology-driven versus technology-forcing standards is also common to the development of legislation on water-quality.

The second policy question Congress and the President confronted in 1967 debates was whether air quality and pollution emissions standards should be national or local in scope, a question that also arises in development of water-quality law, and one that Congress has resolved differently at different times. Under the 1967 Act, Congress leaned toward state control of emissions limitations. While it made the federal HEW secretary responsible for issuing air-quality *criteria* based on identified health and environmental impacts of particular levels of particular pollutants, it gave the states the authority to formulate their own air-quality *standards*. In doing this, the states were not to be constrained by the unenforceable federal air-quality criteria, and they were to be permitted to consider technological and economic feasibility as well as criteria in formulating air-quality standards. The Act mandated that each state prepare and submit a plan for implementing emissions standards for the sources of polluting emissions in its jurisdiction.

Under the 1970 Clean Air Act (as well as subsequent amendments in 1977 and 1990), Congress maintained the distinction between air-quality criteria and air-quality standards, but it shifted responsibility for formulating *enforceable standards* to the federal government. States were to retain responsibility for submitting implementation plans, subject to federal approval, but the federal government would now promulgate national emissions standards pursuant to legislated criteria. The 1970 act also favored a health-based technology-forcing approach.

Although the 1970 law was called the "Clean Air Act Amendments of 1970," it completely rewrote the prior legislation and was thus an amendment in form only. The 1970 law was enacted after it became apparent that the automobile industry would not voluntarily undertake technological reform. By that time, there was overwhelming evidence that automakers deliberately adopted tactics to delay implementation of controls on automobile emissions. In 1968, the Department of Justice uncovered a collusive cross-licensing agreement among members of the Automobile Manufacturing Association (AMA) who sought to eliminate competition for production and installation of emissions-control technology by pledging not to purchase devices produced independently by nonsignatories to that agreement. In conjunction with the AMA's stated internal policy of not initiating voluntary programs to install emissions devices, the agreement effectively eliminated a market for emissions-control devices. In the last days of President Johnson's Administration, the Department of Justice filed an antitrust suit against the major automakers, but the incoming Nixon Administration promptly settled the suit.

One of the very first tasks assigned to EPA upon its creation was to implement the Clean Air Act of 1970 (CAA). Title I of the Act called for national standards for ambient-air quality and uniform national emissions limitations for hazardous air pollutants based upon health and environmental factors. It directed EPA to promulgate those standards and limitations. In a departure from the overall health-based approach, it also mandated that *new sources* of pollution, such as factories and foundries, utilize the "best available technology." Title I required that state implementation plans (SIPs) achieve the national ambient-air-quality standards within three years' time and it gave the EPA authority to amend inadequate SIPs. Congress later diluted this requirement by granting extensions of deadlines for achieving national standards.

Title II of the 1970 act addressed mobile sources of polluting emissions (automobiles) and required EPA to regulate those auto emissions that contribute to air pollution identified as hazardous to human health. It mandated that certain emissions be reduced by 90 percent in five years' time. The 1977 amendments contained even more specific numerical requirements. However on several occasions since 1970, Congress has also extended the deadlines for achieving these air-quality standards relating to auto emissions. Moreover, EPA has frequently used the Act's waiver provisions and thus further frustrated achievement of air-quality goals and blunted the Act's technology-forcing impact.

The 1990 CAA amendments seek to address the most conspicuous deficiencies in air-quality control. These relate to: non-attainment of federal air-quality standards in more than 50 cities, ozone depletion, acid rain, motor-vehicle emissions, and toxic air pollutants. The 1990 amendments mandate multitiered phaseouts of production and emission of harmful substances and, once again, set timetables for percentage reductions in emissions over a period of several years.

The 1990 law affected a shift away from health-based, technology-forcing standards toward technology-driven standards. For instance, hazardous air pollutants are now regulated on the basis of "maximum available control technology," rather than health-based standards. Under a more evident market-oriented approach, the 1990 amendments grant certain pollution "allowances," to businesses which can buy and sell them nationally. Although localized markets for tradeable emissions rights existed before 1990, the 1990 amendments created a national market for emissions-reduction credits.

The 1990 amendments grafted new regulatory requirements and mechanisms onto the framework of earlier legislation, resulting in a statute which is highly detailed and remarkably complex. The 1990 amendments are subdivided into titles and subtitles that regulate on the basis of many criteria:

- class of polluter (large vs. small businesses, public vs. private entities, new vs. old sources, mobile vs. stationary sources);
- pollutant characteristics (chemical vs. physical);
- existence of environmental phenomena (acid rain, greenhouse effect, ozone depletion, carcinogenic gases); and
- availability of pollution-control technologies.

The uniquely complicated regulatory scheme of the 1990 amendments can be perplexing even to legal and technical experts.

Primary Features of the Clean Air Act and the 1990 Amendments

The Clean Air Act as amended in 1990 contains provisions for:

a. National health-based air-quality standards,
b. State plans for implementing the national standards,
c. National emissions standards for hazardous air pollutants (NESHAPs),
d. "New source" performance standards,
e. Permit requirements aimed at preventing significant deterioration of air quality in regions with good air quality,
f. Special requirements for regions that have not attained the national air-quality standards ("nonattainment areas"),
g. Motor-vehicle-emissions standards,
h. Sulfur dioxide controls and market-based trading of emissions allowances,

i.   Universal federal permit program for existing sources of pollution, and

j.   Phaseout measures for stratospheric-ozone-depleting substances.

These provisions are discussed in the following subsections.

National Ambient Air Quality Standards

Central to the regulatory scheme are national standards for air quality based upon health and environmental considerations. EPA is required to identify emissions that contribute to air pollution that endangers public health or welfare. EPA must then establish "air-quality criteria" for each identified pollutant that describe its health and environmental effects in varying quantities and under varying conditions. Based upon these criteria, EPA must formulate *national ambient air quality standards (NAAQS)* for specific pollutants and then oversee state compliance with the standards.

Ambient air, as used in the law, means freely moving air, not contained or enclosed, to which the general public is exposed. Whereas the air-quality **criteria** are *descriptive,* of health and environmental effects, ambient-air-quality **standards** are *prescriptive,* that is, they *prescribe* or dictate what must be achieved. Ambient-air-quality standards are expressed as concentrations of specific pollutants in the ambient air. States are free to adopt and enforce standards stricter than the NAAQSs.

The law contemplates two classes of NAAQ standards:

■   *primary* NAAQS, which must be protective of human health, and

■   *secondary* NAAQS, which are protective of plants and animals.

Primary ambient-air-quality standards must be set at levels that provide an "adequate margin of safety" to public health. The law requires EPA to review the NAAQSs every five years and to revise them if they are not sufficiently protective.

Air-quality criteria and NAAQSs have been promulgated for six of the most prevalent air pollutants. Known as *criteria pollutants,* they are carbon monoxide, nitrogen oxides, lead, sulfur dioxide, ozone (of which volatile organic compounds, VOCs, are precursors), and particulates. When a region fails to meet one or more of the standards for the six criteria pollutants, it is considered a *nonattainment area* under the Clean Air Act. No major U.S. city has ever met national air-quality standards for all six pollutants. Over 50 U.S. cities are nonattainment areas for these health-based standards. In the 1990 amendments, Congress addressed this basic deficiency with special provisions. They are discussed in a later subsection on nonattainment areas.

State Implementation Plans (SIPs)

Each state must submit for EPA approval a plan (referred to as a *state implementation plan or SIP*), which will implement and enforce the NAAQSs within its boundaries. States are subdivided into air-quality-control regions for this purpose. The federal government may designate interstate or major intrastate air-quality-control regions when necessary for attaining national standards. An air-quality-control region is generally drawn according to geographical and topographical attributes that cause it to have fairly uniform air quality. A valley, for instance, would be more or less uniformly affected by sources operating there, because the surrounding mountains would impede the movement of air and polluting emissions into and out of the valley.

States use data from emissions inventories and computer modeling to determine the emissions levels at which air-quality standards will not be violated. In drawing up its SIP, a state may use whatever mix of controls on stationary and mobile sources it chooses, provided that the projected emissions of the criteria pollutants will not cause any NAAQS to be exceeded. EPA must review the SIP to determine if the NAAQSs will be met by the emissions controls the state anticipates imposing. An EPA-approved SIP is enforceable by both state and federal authorities. If a SIP does not meet EPA approval, EPA is supposed to revise the SIP and to require the state to enforce it.

National Emissions Standards for Hazardous Air Pollutants

Before 1990, EPA was authorized to establish separate health-based *national emissions standards for hazardous air pollutants (NESHAPs)*. From 1970 to 1990, EPA designated only eight substances as hazardous air pollutants, and it set emissions standards for seven of them: arsenic, asbestos, benzene, beryllium, mercury, radionuclides, and vinyl chloride.

The 1990 amendments require EPA to set technology-based, rather than health-based (technology-forcing) standards for 189 hazardous substances designated by Congress. Emitters of any of the 189 hazardous air pollutants will be required to install *Maximum Available Control Technology (MACT)*, with the goal of reducing toxic air emissions by 75 percent by the year 2000. EPA was required to promulgate MACT standards for 41 *source categories* by 1992. EPA is further required to set standards for *area sources* (such as dry cleaners and gas stations) that will serve to reduce emissions of the most hazardous pollutants by 90 percent. Utility plants may be exempted from these standards if their compliance is not essential for achieving the mandated reduction. Under the newer *air toxics* program, major emitters of hazardous air pollutants must obtain a permit.

The provisions relating to hazardous air pollutants exemplify CAA regulations that are now at least partly technology-driven and reveal Congress's shift away from the health-based, technology-forcing standards previously utilized. The *National Resources Defense Council* case, excerpted later in this section, illustrates some of the difficulties EPA experienced in regulating hazardous air pollutants prior to the 1990 amendments.

"New Source" Performance Standards

The CAA authorizes EPA to establish technology-based *new source performance standards (NSPSs)* for major new stationary sources and for existing major sources that are undergoing substantial modification. NSPSs for various industry categories are required to reflect the best adequately demonstrated, continuous emission-reduction technology. This higher standard for new sources is warranted because designing and installing environmentally sound technologies is generally more technologically feasible and economical for a new plant than for an old one. The mandate also reflects a philosophy that favors incremental improvements in U.S. air quality without a massive overhaul of major industries and facilities.

When a major source makes substantial modifications in its operations, it is required to implement NSPSs. In some cases, however, sources are permitted to circumvent this requirement by reducing certain emissions elsewhere in the plant. This method of counting emissions for multi-source plants is referred to as *netting*. The rationale for allowing netting is that the operation's overall emissions after netting will be less than if an entirely new source were added while no other emissions at the plant were reduced. The drawback of netting is that it can in some circumstances result in a net *increase* in emissions from the plant.

Netting is a very popular trading device; it allows firms to avoid new-source performance standards for modified sources, as well as costs associated with obtaining new source permits.

Prevention of Significant Deterioration

Under the CAA, every state implementation plan must contain emissions limitations and other control measures aimed at preventing significant air-quality deterioration in regions where national air-quality standards are exceeded. This national antibacksliding provision is necessary to prevent industrial firms from relocating their plants to regions with good air quality in order to avoid installation of required pollution control technologies or production limitations in regions that have not attained national standards. Without this provision, air-quality improvements in nonattainment areas would be offset by increased pollution in unpolluted regions.

To prevent significant deterioration, the CAA employs a pre-construction permitting mechanism in attainment areas whereby a new major source must obtain a permit prior to construction and must demonstrate that it will use the *best available control technology* for each pollutant it will emit. Preconstruction permits help to ensure that new major sources use all pollution-control technologies that are currently available for particular industrial processes. This prevents a firm from using outmoded, end-of-the-pipe pollution-control measures and arguing after construction has been completed that installing other control technologies would have been too costly.

Non-Attainment Areas

The 1970 CAA's deadline for achieving national air-quality standards was 1975. When many areas of the country failed to meet the deadline, Congress extended it several times. As a consequence, states were generally not penalized for failing to attain the standards so long as they were making "reasonable further progress" toward achieving the NAAQSs. A major concern has been that no major U.S. city has to date achieved the promulgated air-quality standards.

To achieve air-quality standards, existing sources are required to limit their emissions by using *reasonably available control technology (RACT)*. New and modified stationary sources in nonattainment areas are subject to a much stricter standard of *lowest achievable emission rate (LAER)*. Moreover, new and modified sources must also offset their own emissions through reductions from other sources which effect an overall diminution of total emissions of nonattainment criteria pollutants in the air-quality control region. To do this, new and modified sources must purchase, trade, or otherwise acquire emissions credits from sources which have ceased operations or which have reduced their emissions below their legally permitted levels. This form of emissions trading, known as *offsets*, does not assure that total emissions will be reduced to NAAQS levels. In the 1977 CAA amendments, Congress instituted a requirement that offsets in nonattainment areas exceed new emissions by an amount that constitutes "reasonable further progress" toward attainment of air-quality standards.

In the 1990 amendments, Congress again addressed the nonattainment problem. Those amendments classify nonattainment areas in five categories ranging from "marginal" to "extreme" depending upon the severity of the area's noncompliance with NAAQSs. A new deadline—ranging from five to twenty years—for attaining the health standard for ozone was set for each nonattainment class. Thus, for example, "marginal" areas had until 1993 to comply; but the country's worst air-quality region, Los Angeles, is now required to meet the ozone standard by 2010. Mandated yearly reductions are built into these attainment deadlines. In ozone-nonattainment areas, emissions of volatile organic compounds (VOCs), precursors of ozone, must be reduced at a rate of 3 percent per year until the standard is achieved.

A major facet of nonattainment provisions is the requirement for establishing or upgrading vehicle inspection and maintenance programs in areas that do not meet the standards for ozone and carbon monoxide. EPA is also required to impose sanctions on states that fail to prepare and implement SIPS for attaining the mandated standards. Under the sanctions, a state may either lose some of its federal highway funds or be subject to a requirement that new industrial facilities demonstrate emissions offsets at a 2 to 1 ratio. Under the new nonattainment provisions, smaller sources of VOCs are now regulated as major sources. The cutoff for defining "major" sources is now graduated according to nonattainment classification; the more serious the nonattainment status, the lower the emissions level that will subject a source to major-source control standards.

Motor Vehicles

Motor vehicles account for a substantial share of U.S. air pollution. The 1990 amendments contain numerous provisions mandating the use of tailpipe emissions-reduction equipment in newly manufactured automobiles, sale of cleaner fuels in nonattainment areas, and improvements in pollution-control-technology in fleet vehicles.

Starting with 1994 models (Tier I) new restrictions applied to tailpipe emissions of hydrocarbons, carbon monoxide, and nitrogen oxides. At least 40 percent of the new vehicles sold in the United States in 1994 were required to reduce emissions of hydrocarbon and nitrogen oxide by 35 percent and 60 percent, respectively. By 1998, 100 percent of all new vehicles sold must meet these standards. Additional reductions (Tier II) of a 50 percent decrease below mid-1990s standards will go into effect in 2003 if necessary to meet air-quality standards. A pilot alternative-fuels program in California requires sale of 300,000 "clean-fuel" vehicles and the availability of clean fuels by 1999.

Reformulated, cleaner gasolines with lower VOC and sulfur content are required to be sold in the most serious ozone-non attainment areas. These fuels must have 15 percent lower emissions of VOCs and other identified toxic substances by 1995, and greater reductions will be phased in by 2000. Other fuel standards for oxygen, benzene, and aromatics will also apply. Starting in 1992, carbon-monoxide-nonattainment areas were required to sell fuels containing higher levels of oxygen (for example, fuels containing ethanol additives) during the winter months, when polluting emissions from starting cold engines are greater. In order to meet some of the fuel-content standards, distributors are allowed to utilize a credit program that essentially pools all gasoline sold in a covered area. In 26 cities, fleets of ten or more vehicles must meet California emissions standards (which are more stringent than those in the rest of country) by 1998. These provisions are directed at creating markets for cleaner fuels and better emissions equipment and at forcing automakers to modify or rebuild production lines to produce more environmentally sound motor vehicles.

Emissions Credits and Trading

The sulfur-dioxide-emissions credit program established under the 1990 amendments is designed to address acid rain—which has become an international as well as domestic environmental problem. For example, acid rain caused by U.S. emissions falls in Canada. Seventy-five percent of acid rain is caused by emissions of sulfur dioxide and nitrogen oxide from the burning of fossil fuels by electric utilities. The 1990 amendments established a two-phase program to reduce sulfur dioxide emissions by 10 million tons (about 50%) from the 1980 level. Emissions allowances for individual emitters of sulfur dioxide are set according to a formula designed to achieve the overall reduction goal.

The 1990 amendments authorize a private trading of emissions credits for sulfur dioxide (SO_2) emissions among power-generation utilities. Each utility is allotted a specified emissions allowance, expressed in tons per year, in accordance with the two-phase emissions-reduction program. A utility that has reduced its emissions to below its allowance through the use of more effective pollution-control technology can "bank" its credits or sell them to a company whose emissions exceed its allowance. This has created a commodities market in pollution allowances and emission credits.

On March 29, 1993, the Chicago Board of Trade (CBOT), the world's largest commodity market, ran the first auction of EPA pollution allowances (each allowance unit permitting the discharge of one ton of sulfur dioxide per year). More than 150,000 allowances were sold that day at prices ranging from $122 to $450 per allowance. In addition to credits given to utility companies, EPA released a smaller number of credits to be auctioned off. Anyone may bid for them. Some environmental groups did so and retired the credits without using them. The CBOT also plans to offer futures contracts on pollution credits.

The pollution trading system is intended to create an economic incentive to reduce utilities' emissions. Nonetheless, if all available allowances are purchased and used, the overall level of polluting emissions will remain constant at the targeted level. Critics charge that the lack of oversight mechanisms for assuring regionally proportionate reductions in emissions will hamper efforts to control acid-rain deposition in environmentally sensitive areas. In a 1993 suit by the state of New York and the Adirondack Council to challenge the emissions trading allowances, the plaintiffs alleged that Midwestern use of purchased allowances will cause continued acid-rain deposition in the Adirondack region. A few states have sought to regulate the sale by in-state utility companies of credits to upwind sources as a means of preventing disparate increases in acid-rain deposition within their territory. They have also asked EPA to consider placing geographic limitations on emissions trading, at least until proposed transregional sales can be reviewed to ensure equivalent reductions in acid-rain deposition in sensitive areas. EPA and other proponents of emissions trading oppose efforts to place geographical or regional limitations on market trading of allowances, arguing that such controls will impair the alienability (transferability) of allowances and, hence, the efficiency of the emissions trading market.

At least six other suits have been filed to challenge other aspects of EPA's emissions allowances rules. Particularly controversial are some loopholes in "substitution and compensating units" rules that inadvertently allowed utilities to claim credits for emissions reductions which they achieved prior to passage of the 1990 amendments. In response to such lawsuits, EPA has proposed clarifying rules to disallow credits for emissions reductions achieved before 1991. These amendments are necessary to achieve the reductions Congress contemplated in the 1990 amendments.

Emissions trading is not an entirely novel concept. The Clean Air Act provides for other forms of emissions trading, including *bubbles, offsets, netting,* and *banking.*

Since 1984, facilities with multiple point sources (such as smokestacks) have been able to use *bubbles,* which allow emissions increases at some point sources within the facility so long as facilitywide emissions do not increase. In essence, the entire plant is viewed as existing within a single bubble and is treated as a single source for permitting purposes. A bubble allows a firm to use a more cost-effective mix of controls to achieve the same emissions limitations for the entire facility. New sources seeking to operate in nonattainment areas or to comply with require-ments for preventing significant deterioration are allowed to purchase or trade emissions allowances with existing sources in the same air-quality control region to *offset* their emissions. As explained earlier, firms undergoing modifications are allowed to use internal *netting* in order to avoid the more stringent limitations for modified sources.

Since the early 1980s, EPA has permitted communities to *bank* unused emis-sions allowances which result when a polluting source in a community ceases operations and polluting emissions fall below levels allowed by the SIP. State permitting authorities are authorized to determine what counties are entitled to emissions-reduction credits and how those credits may be distributed. All of the mentioned mechanisms—bubbles, offsets, netting, and banking—entail some form of emissions trading, whether within a single firm or with other firms in the same air-quality control region.

The 1990 amendments augmented and refined emissions trading by creating a national market for sulfur dioxide emissions and thus supplement the regional markets that already existed. The merits and drawbacks of treating emissions allowances as a marketable commodity are discussed further in section 9.4.

Permits and Enforcement

The 1990 amendments phase in a new national permit program for air emis-sions which is similar to the NPDES program under the Clean Water Act. Pre-viously, permits were required for only a few categories of sources; the new permit program is far more comprehensive. Under the 1990 CAA, states adopt and administer the permit program under EPA supervision, and EPA can veto any state permits that do not satisfy EPA standards. The new program regulates many major and smaller sources of pollution that were not covered by prior state permit systems.

The 1990 amendments impose stiffer penalties—up to $200,000 per violation of the act's provisions—and specify that knowing violations constitute felonies which carry criminal sanctions. Increases in civil penalties were clearly war-ranted; in many cases, the penalties assessed under prior versions of the CAA were less than the economic benefit the polluters derived from CAA violations. In some instances, it was more cost-effective for a business to continue to pollute than to install the appropriate pollution-control technology. The CAA also au-thorizes citizens' suits to seek penalties against violators, with the recovered mon-ies going to a Treasury fund supporting EPA enforcement activities.

Ozone Protection

Stratospheric ozone protection (an environmental issue with international ramifications) is discussed in Section 9.3 and in Chapter 11. The 1990 amend-ments limit the use of ozone-depleting substances such as chlorofluorocarbons (CFCs), hydrochlorofluorocarbons (HCFCs), carbon tetrachloride, and methyl chloroform. The amendments do not address bromines such as methyl bromide, a widely used pesticide, which also deplete stratospheric ozone.

Under the amendments, HCFCs are to be phased out completely by 2030. Recapture, recycling, and safe disposal rules were phased in, beginning in 1992, when a prohibition on venting refrigerants during equipment service or disposal became effective. The law created a national recycling program for CFCs used in refrigerators and air conditioners.

In May 1993, EPA issued a list of 130 ozone-safe chemical substitutes as part of the Significant New Alternatives Policy program. Under this program, manufacturers and importers must submit premanufacture notice of intent to sell or distribute CFC substitutes. EPA is then required to evaluate each chemical for potentially harmful environmental and health effects.

Illustrative CAA Cases

National Resources Defense Council, Inc. v. U.S. Environmental Protection Agency

824 F.2d 1146 (D.C. Cir. 1984)

BORK, Circuit Judge.

Current scientific knowledge does not permit a finding that there is a completely safe level of human exposure to carcinogenic agents. The Administrator of the Environmental Protection Agency, however, is charged with regulating hazardous pollutants, including carcinogens, under section 112 of the Clean Air Act . . . We address here the question of the extent of the Administrator's authority . . . .

Petitioner Natural Resources Defense Council ("NRDC") contends that the Administrator must base a decision under section 112 exclusively on health-related factors and, therefore, that the uncertainty about the effects of carcinogenic agents requires the Administrator to prohibit all emissions. The Administrator argues that . . . he is authorized to set standards that require emission reduction to the lowest level attainable by best available control technology whenever that level is below that at which harm to humans has been demonstrated. We find no support for either position in the language or legislative history of the Clean Air Act. . . .

I.

. . . The statute directs the Administrator to set an emission standard promulgated under section 112 "at the level which in his judgment

provides an ample margin of safety to protect the public health." Id.

This case concerns vinyl chloride regulations. Vinyl chloride is a gaseous synthetic chemical used in the manufacture of plastics and is a strong carcinogen. In late 1975, the Administrator issued a notice of proposed rulemaking to establish an emission standard for vinyl chloride. 40 Fed. Reg. 59,532 (1975). . . . Scientific uncertainty, due to the unavailability of dose-response data and the twenty-year latency period between initial exposure to vinyl chloride and the occurrence of disease, makes it impossible to establish any definite threshold level below which there are no adverse effects to human health. . . . The notice also stated the "EPA's position that for a carcinogen it should be assumed, in the absence of strong evidence to the contrary, that there is no atmospheric concentration that poses absolutely no public health risk.". . .

Because of this assumption, the EPA concluded that it was faced with two alternative interpretations of its duty under section 112. First, the EPA determined that section 112 might require a complete prohibition of emissions of non-threshold pollutants . . . . The EPA found this alternative "neither desirable nor necessary" because "[c]omplete prohibition of all emissions could require closure of an entire industry," a cost the EPA found "extremely high for elimination of a risk to health that is of unknown dimensions." . . .

The EPA stated the second alternative as follows:

> An alternative interpretation of section 112 is that it authorizes setting emission standards that require emission reduction to the lowest level achievable by use of the best available control technology in cases involving apparent non-threshold pollutants, where complete emission prohibition would result in widespread industry closure and EPA has determined that the cost of such closure would be grossly disproportionate to the benefits of removing the risk that would remain after imposition of the best available control technology.

. . . The EPA adopted this alternative. . . .

On October 21, 1976, the EPA promulgated final emission standards for vinyl chloride which were based solely on the level attainable by the best available control technology. . . .

The Environmental Defense Fund ("EDF") filed suit challenging the standard on the ground that section 112 requires the Administrator to rely exclusively on health and prohibits consideration of cost and technology. The EDF and the EPA settled the suit, however, upon the EPA's agreement to propose new and more stringent standards for vinyl chloride and to establish an ultimate goal of zero emissions.

The EPA satisfied its obligations under the settlement agreement by proposing new regulations on June 2, 1977. While the proposal sought to impose more strict regulation . . . . the EPA made it clear that is considered its previous regulations valid and reemphasized its view that the inability scientifically to identify a threshold of adverse effects did not require prohibition of all emissions, but rather permitted regulation at the level of best available technology. 42 Fed. Reg. 28,154 (1977). The EPA . . . took no final action for more than seven years. On January 9, 1985, the EPA withdrew the proposal . . . the EPA concluded that it should abandon the 1977 proposal and propose in its place only minor revisions to the 1976 regulations.

This petition for review followed.

* * *

III.

The NRDC's challenge to the EPA's withdrawal of the 1977 amendments is simple: because the statute adopts an exclusive focus on considerations of health, the Administrator must set a zero level of emissions when he cannot determine that there is a level below which no harm will occur.

. . . We find no support in the text or legislative history for the proposition that Congress intended to require a complete prohibition of emissions whenever the EPA cannot determine a threshold level for a hazardous pollutant. Instead, there is strong evidence that Congress considered such a requirement and rejected it.

Section 112 commands the Administrator to set an "emission standard" for a particular "hazardous air pollutant" which in his "judgment" will provide "ample margin of safety." Congress' use of the term "ample margin of safety" is inconsistent with the NRDC's position that the Administrator has no discretion in the face of uncertainty. The statute nowhere defines "ample margin of safety." The Senate Report, however, in discussing a similar requirement . . . under section 109 of the Act, explained the purpose of the "margin of safety" standard as one of affording "a *reasonable* degree of protection . . . against hazards which research has not yet identified." S.Rep. No. 1196, 91st Cong., 2d Sess. 10 (1970) (emphasis added). . . . And while Congress used the modifier "ample" to exhort the Administrator not to allow "the public [or] the environment . . . to be exposed to anything resembling the maximum risk" and, therefore, to set a margin "greater than 'normal' or 'adequate,'" Congress still left the EPA "great latitude in meeting its responsibility." . . .

Congress' use of the word "safety," moreover, is significant evidence that it did not intend to require the Administrator to prohibit all emissions of non-thresholded pollutants. As the Supreme Court has recently held, "safe" doest not mean "risk-free." . . .

. . . Had Congress intended that result, it could very easily have said so by writing a statute that states that no level of emissions should be allowed as to which there is any uncertainty. But Congress chose instead to deal with the pervasive nature of scientific uncertainty and the inherent limitations of scientific knowledge by vesting in the Administrator the discretion to deal with uncertainty in each case.

The NRDC also argues that the legislative history supports its position. To the contrary, that history strongly suggests that Congress did not require the Administrator to prohibit emissions of all non-threshold pollutants; . . . .

IV.

We turn now to the question whether the Administrator's chosen method for setting emission levels above zero is consistent with congressional intent. . . . The NRDC argues that this standard is arbitrary and capricious because the EPA is never permitted to consider cost and technological feasibility under section 112 but instead is limited to consideration of health-based factors. Thus, before addressing the Administrator's method of using cost and technological feasibility in this case, we must determine whether he may consider cost and technological feasibility at all. . . .

A.

On its face, section 112 does not indicate that Congress intended to preclude consideration of any factor. Though the phrase "to protect the public health" evinces an intent to make health the primary consideration, there is no indication of the factors the Administrator may or may not consider in determining, in his "judgment," what level of emissions will provide "an ample margin of safety." Instead, the language used, and the absence of any specific limitation, gives the clear impression that the Administrator has some discretion in determining what, if any, additional factors he will consider in setting an emission standard.

B.

The petitioner argues that the legislative history makes clear Congress' intent to foreclose reliance on non-health-based considerations in setting standards under section 112. We find, however, that the legislative history can be characterized only as ambiguous.

* * *

. . . Thus, we cannot find a clear congressional intent in the language, structure, or leg-islative history of the Act to preclude consideration of cost and technological feasibility under section 112.

* * *

D.

On the other side of this controversy, the EPA argues that the 1977 amendments of the Clean Air Act, . . . amounts to a ratification of the use of cost and technological feasibility considerations in setting standards under section 112. We think this overstates the significance of the legislative history leading up to the Clean Air Act Amendments of 1977. . . .

* * *

V.

Since we cannot discern clear congressional intent to preclude consideration of cost and technological feasibility in setting emission standards under section 112, we necessarily find that the Administrator may consider these factors. . . .

Our role on review of an action taken pursuant to section 112 is generally a limited one. Because the regulation of carcinogenic agents raises questions "on the frontiers of scientific knowledge," . . . we have recognized that the Administrator's decision in this area "will depend to a greater extent upon policy judgments" to which we must accord considerable deference. . . . We have also acknowledged that "EPA, not the court, has the technical expertise to decide what inferences may be drawn from the characteristics of . . . substances and to formulate policy with respect to what risks are acceptable," . . . and we will not second-guess a determination based on that expertise. . . . Despite this deferential standard, we find that the Administrator has ventured into a zone of impermissible action. The Administrator has not exercised his expertise to determine an acceptable risk to health. To the contrary, in the face of uncertainty about risks to health, he has simply substituted technological feasibility for health as the primary consideration under Section 112. Because this action is contrary to clearly discernible congressional intent, we grant the petition for review.

. . . [I]t seems to us beyond dispute that Congress was primarily concerned with health in promulgating section 112. Every action by the Administrator in setting an emission standard is to be taken "to protect the public health." In setting an emission standard for vinyl chloride, however, the Administrator has made no finding with respect to the effect of the chosen level of emissions on health. Nor has the Administrator stated that a certain level of emissions is "safe" or that the chosen level will provide an "ample margin of safety." Instead, the Administrator has substituted "best available technology" for a finding of the risk to health.

* * *

In the 1977 proposal to decrease the level of emissions, the Administrator did not determine the risk to health . . . . Nor did the Administrator explain why one standard was "safe" and the other was not. . . .

The absence of any finding regarding the relationship between the risk to health . . . is also evident in the Administrator's decision adopting the 1976 standards. Again, the Administrator mentioned the risks to health before and after regulation, . . . but did not provide any explanation as to whether the risk was significant, or whether the chosen standard provided an "ample margin of safety."

* * *

Thus, in setting emission standards for carcinogenic pollutants, the Administrator has decided to determine first the level of emissions attainable by best available control technology. He will then determine the costs of setting the standard below that level and balance those costs against the risk to health below the level of feasibility. If the costs are greater than the reduction in risk, then he will set the standard at the level of feasibility. This exercise, in the Administrator's view, will always produce an "ample margin of safety."

* * *

We find that the congressional mandate to provide "an ample margin of safety" "to protect the public health" requires the Administrator to make an initial determination of what is "safe." This determination must be based exclusively upon the Administrator's determination of the risk to health at a particular emission level. Because the Administrator in this case did not make any finding of the risk to health, the question of how that determination is to be made is not before us. We do

wish to note, however, that the Administrator's decision does not require a finding that "safe" means "risk-free," . . . or a finding that the determination is free from uncertainty. Instead, we find only that the Administrator's decision must be based upon an expert judgment with regard to the level of emission that will result in an "acceptable" risk to health. . . . In this regard, the Administrator must determine what inferences should be drawn from available scientific data and decide what risks are acceptable in the world in which we live. . . . This determination must be based solely upon the risk to health. The Administrator cannot under any circumstances consider cost and technological feasibility at this stage of the analysis. The latter factors have no relevance to the preliminary determination of what is safe. Of course, if the Administrator cannot find that there is an acceptable risk at any level, then the Administrator must set the level at zero.

Congress, however, recognized in section 112 that the determination of what is "safe" will always be marked by scientific uncertainty and thus exhorted the Administrator to set emission standards that will provide an "ample margin" of safety. This language permits the Administrator to take into account scientific uncertainty and to use expert discretion to determine what action should be taken in light of that uncertainty. . . . Thus, by its nature the finding of risk is uncertain and the Administrator must use his discretion to meet the statutory mandate. It is only at this point of the regulatory process that the Administrator may set the emission standard at the lowest level that is technologically feasible. In fact, this is, we believe, precisely the type of policy choice that Congress envisioned when it directed the Administrator to provide an "ample margin of safety." One "safety" is assured, the Administrator should be free to diminish as much of the statistically determined risk as possible by setting the standard at the lowest feasible level. . . .

We wish to reiterate the limited nature of our holding in this case because it is not the court's intention to bind the Administrator to any specific method of determining what is "safe" or what constitutes an "ample margin." We hold only that the Administrator cannot consider cost and technological feasibility in determining what is "safe." . . .

For the foregoing reasons, the petition for review is granted, the decision withdrawing the 1977 proposed rule is vacated, and this case is hereby remanded for timely reconsideration of the 1977 proposed rule consistent with this opinion.

It is so ordered.

AIR POLLUTION CONTROL DISTRICT OF JEFFERSON COUNTY, KENTUCKY V. EPA

739 F.2d 1071 (6th Cir. 1984)

[Jefferson County, Kentucky, on the Ohio river, is the location of the populous city of Louisville. Floyd County, Indiana, across the river, is sparsely populated and is the location of the Gallagher Power Station, whose air-polluting emissions were the cause of this suit. The two counties were designated by the EPA as the Louisville Interstate Air Quality Control Region. Jefferson County instituted proceedings under CAA section 126 to abate emissions from the power station. The county alleged that Gallagher's emissions violated CAA section 110, which prohibits emissions in one state that prevent the attainment or maintainance of national ambient air-quality standards (NAAQSs) in another state.

The *Jefferson County* case illustrates the inadequacy of the air-pollution law to address situations in which a state locates a power plant or other source of air pollution near a population center of a bordering state.]

ENGEL, Circuit Judge.

The Air Pollution Control District of Jefferson County, Kentucky, seeks review of an order of the . . . EPA . . . . That order denied Jefferson County's petition for interstate pollution abatement. . . .

The EPA denied Jefferson County's . . . petition . . . because it found that Gallagher did not 'substantially contribute' to the violation of NAAQSs [national ambient-air-quality standards] in Jefferson County.

. . . Each state is required by the Act to . . . submit to the Administrator for approval a SIP (state implementation plan) for enforcing the NAAQSs. . . .

. . . In this respect, the Clean Air Act has been described as "a bold experiment in co-operative federalism. . . ."

* * *

Nevertheless, the Act has generated much intergovernmental friction. Critics claim that the state-oriented structure of the Act ignores the realities of air pollution. Since any state's air at a given moment is at best transient, or in bureaucratic terms, "ambient," air pollution in one state inevitably affects the quality of air in surrounding states. Congress acknowledged that the 1970 version of the Act had proved "an inadequate answer to the problem of interstate air pollution" and in 1977 amended the Act to deal specifically with interstate pollution abatement. . . .

The Act, as now amended, provides that to approve any SIP or revision thereto, the Administrator must determine that:

(E) [The SIP] contains adequate provisions (i) prohibiting any stationary source within the State from emitting any air pollutant in amounts which will (I) prevent attainment or maintenance by any other State of any such national primary or secondary ambient air quality standard, ...

However, neither the Act nor its legislative history defines when the emission of a pollutant in one state will be deemed by the Administrator to "prevent attainment or maintenance" of the NAAQSs by another state. This uncertainty provides the basis for the present controversy.

* * *

Because the structure of the Clean Air Act is state-oriented, each state is charged with implementing national clean air standards within its own political boundaries. Thus, although Floyd County and Jefferson County are in the same air quality control region, each county is subject to the implementation plan adopted by its respective state. Initially this was not a problem, since Indiana and Kentucky had adopted identical emission limitations for the pollutant at issue in this case, SO_2.

* * *

This uniformity of emission limitations in Floyd County and Jefferson County did not last long. In 1974, Indiana adopted new SO_2 regulations for Floyd County that completely exempted Gallagher from the 1.2 lbs/MBTU emission limitation. . . . . In 1979, Indiana submitted a revision of the SO_2 portion of its SIP to the Agency. The new plan established an emission limitation for SO_2 of 6 lbs/MBTU heat input for most Indiana power plants, including Gallagher. . . .

Meanwhile, in Jefferson County the 1.2 lbs/MBTU emission limitation was generally enforced. . . . However, even with strict emission limitations, Jefferson County has yet to attain the NAAQSs for SO_2, ...

It can therefore be seen that a significant disparity exists between the permissible emission limits of power plants in Jefferson County, Kentucky, and the Gallagher plant in Floyd County, Indiana.

* * *

B.   Fairness and Uniformity in Criteria: Section 7601(a)(2)(A)

. . . Jefferson County argues that the EPA denied the section 126 petition without considering the "interstate inequities" that the interstate pollution provisions were designated to eliminate. . . . Although its argument is rather vague, the County apparently reads section 7601(a)(2)(A) as providing specific protections against "interstate inequities." . . .

* * *

. . . There is simply no indication in the statute that section 7601(a)(2)(A) establishes a substantive standard which requires similar or uniform emission limitations for all sources within a particular area as part of a section 126 determination. Such a reading of section 7601(a)(2)(A) is contrary to the federalist approach of the Clean Air Act: the Administrator is *required* to approve the emission limitations proposed by any state, so long as the require-

ments of section 7410(a)(2) are met, regardless of non-uniformity among the states. . . .

* * *

Consequently, Jefferson County's argument in this regard is not well taken.

C.   The "Margin for Growth" Argument

Jefferson County asserts that Kentucky's SIP was designed to create a margin of clean air in Jefferson County by setting stringent emission standards that would leave the air cleaner than the NAAQSs require. Creation of this margin of clean air would allow further industrial growth in Jefferson County without the NAAQSs being violated. Since the operation of Gallagher without controls could in certain parts of Jefferson County contribute 47% of the secondary NAAQS for SO_2, the County contends that the margin for growth contemplated by the Kentucky SIP has been stolen by Gallagher to the economic disadvantage of Jefferson County. . . .

* * *

The EPA contends that it is irrelevant to the petition brought by Jefferson County . . . whether Gallagher infringes on the margin for growth which the County asserts it needs for future industrial development. . . . Thus, in the EPA's view, the interstate pollution abatement provisions only protect against interference with national air quality standards, not with a margin for growth or any other "individually tailored" standard.

* * *

Under consideration of the statute and the relevant case law, we cannot say that the EPA's determination that the Act does not protect future margins for growth is unreasonable. Since Jefferson County has yet to achieve the NAAQSs for SO_2, any "interference" by Gallagher with the asserted margin for growth is necessarily conjectural. . . . We believe that the need for national uniformity in judicial interpretation of the Act is particularly important where, as here, the relationships between the states are at issue. Thus, we decline to disturb the EPA's holding that the Clean Air Act does not require an upwind state to alter an otherwise valid SIP solely because a downwind state that has yet to comply with the NAAQSs has requested such an alteration to protect an asserted margin for growth.

D.   The "Substantial Contribution" Test

* * *

. . . The EPA determined that Gallagher does not "substantially contribute" to NAAQS violations in Jefferson County and that consequently, section 126 does not require pollution abatement. For the purposes of this opinion, we decline to delve into the semantic distinctions between "substantial" and "significant" and choose to treat the terms as having the same meaning. We are convinced that the broad deference which we are statutorily required to accord to the findings of the Agency preclude our disturbing the EPA's determination, at least absent any other criteria established by the EPA, or found elsewhere in the Act, that would require a different result. . . .

V.   CONCLUSION

In a most practical sense, Jefferson County's concerns are understandable. There would appear to be a patent unfairness in an Agency policy which would tolerate so much higher a level of SO_2 emissions in one area than in another, especially given the high costs which Jefferson County has already incurred to reduce its own pollution. Nevertheless, we believe that the construction placed upon the statute by the EPA appears to be literally correct, even though arguably at odds with the important policy values represented by the 1977 amendments. This conclusion, and our strong preference to achieve an interpretation of the Act which is consistent among the several circuits, compels us to agree with the Agency here.

It may be that the problem of interstate air pollution abatement requires an effective regional regulative scheme rather than the present unsatisfying reliance upon state boundaries as the basic unit for pollution control. . . . However, we have neither the legislative authority to amend the statute nor the regulatory and technical expertise to set more specific technical standards. As long as the statute mandates that implementation plans be created and reviewed on the basis of state boundaries, there will be differences between the emission limitations imposed by neighboring states. No nationwide emission limitations appear to have been intended by Congress, and therefore, while we have considerable sympathy for the position of Jefferson County here, we conclude that we do not possess the statutory authority or regulatory expertise to grant any relief.

* * *

9.3   Selected Topics in Air-Quality Protection

The Ozone Layer

The ozone layer consists of a gas, ozone (O_3), which absorbs and forms a shield against ultraviolet radiation, specifically, short-wave ultraviolet beta rays. The layer forms 6 to 30 miles above the earth's surface, where ultraviolet rays strike oxygen molecules in the upper atmosphere (the stratosphere). The ozone layer has the same chemical makeup as ground-level ozone, which is formed by the interaction of hydrocarbons and sunlight. At ground level, ozone is a pollutant that has harmful effects on the human respiratory system and some crops. Stratospheric ozone, though, makes life on earth possible by filtering out ultraviolet radiation from the sun. Without the ozone layer's shielding effect, ultraviolet beta rays cause damage to DNA in plant, animal, and human cells, depress immune-system activity, and activate retroviruses. Exposure to excessive ultraviolet B rays causes skin cancers in humans and diminishes production of phytoplankton, a basic building block of food chains.

Every year in October and November a "hole" the size of the United States and Mexico combined forms in the ozone layer above Antarctica. Inside this hole, ozone is depleted by up to 50 percent in the winter (summer in the Southern

Hemisphere). The ozone layer is thinning in other localities as well. Since 1979, when the thinning was first observed, there has been a 4.5 to 5 percent loss of stratospheric ozone. EPA predicted in 1991 that over the next 50 years, 12 million Americans would develop skin cancer, up from previous estimates of 500,000 cancer cases for this timeframe.

Chlorofluorocarbons (CFCs) are nontoxic organic compounds, but when they are released into the atmosphere, they cause significant damage to the ozone layer. CFCs are used in refrigerators, air conditioners, and other industrial and consumer products, though less widely than they were when aerosols were commonly used in deodorants and hairsprays. The 1990 CAA amendments are expected to make production of CFC substitutes a billion-dollar industry. Some CFC substitutes, however, may contribute to heating of the atmosphere and melting of polar ice caps; they may also pose dangers to human health. Moreover, effective substitutes have yet to be found for substances such as halon, which is used in fighting fires.

International agreements mandate that CFC production cease by 1995 in developed nations and by 2005 in the rest of the world. Even with those controls, however, the ozone layer is expected to continue to thin until the early-to-mid 21st century. If the Montreal Protocol, an international agreement discussed in Chapter 11, has its intended effect of halting production of ozone-depleting chemicals, the ozone layer could stop thinning sometime after 2005.

No one knows the potential effects of continued use of ozone-depleting chemicals—such as the pesticide methyl bromide, which is allowed to be manufactured in the U.S. until 2000— and the continued improper venting of CFCs from old refrigerators and air conditioners. Moreover, increasing levels of carbon dioxide and methane in the atmosphere or volcanic eruptions could delay the thickening of the layer. Under optimistic estimates, the hole over Antarctica will not cover over until 2040.

Depletion of the ozone layer cannot be remedied by one nation alone. The ozone crisis affects the entire planet, illustrating that earth is one large ecosystem and that the actions of one nation can have far-reaching, international environmental consequences.

Global Warming and the Greenhouse Effect

The "greenhouse effect" results when atmospheric heat-trapping gases, such as carbon dioxide and methane, absorb and reradiate solar heat back to the earth's surface. Unaltered by excess atmospheric releases of heat-trapping gases, the greenhouse effect keeps global temperatures in a range that supports life. However, the burning of fossil fuels such as coal and oil releases large amounts carbon dioxide, the most significant greenhouse gas, into the atmosphere. Fossil-fuel combustion for energy production is currently releasing greater amounts of carbon dioxide into the atmosphere than ever before in history. For instance, in 1860, 90 million tons of carbon dioxide were being released annually. By 1990, the annual rate had increased to more than 5.5 billion tons.[2]

Deforestation also contributes 1 to 2.5 billion tons of carbon dioxide emissions annually.[3] Because trees absorb carbon dioxide and water vapor in photosynthesis, tree loss means that less atmospheric carbon dioxide is removed. Furthermore, when trees are burned or when they decompose, the carbon they have stored is released.

Many scientists, including those of the prestigious National Academy of Sciences, have warned that releases of greenhouse gases are preventing the reflection of a sufficient amount of solar heat back into outer space from earth; as a consequence, the temperature of the earth's surface may rise at an alarming rate. By the mid 21st century, the concentration of greenhouse gases in earth's atmosphere is expected to be twice that of preindustrial times. As early as 1896, Swedish chemist Svante Arrhenius, who later won a Nobel prize, predicted that a doubling of atmospheric carbon dioxide would raise average global temperatures by 9 degrees Farenheit. The National Academy's Committee on Science, Engineering, and Public Policy predicted in 1991 that global temperatures will increase 2 to 9 degrees Farenheit by the middle of the next century. In 1992, the United Nations' Intergovernmental Panel on Climate Change estimated a rise of 4.5 degrees. Scientists generally estimate an increase of 4 to 8 degrees Farenheit. At the upper end of those predictions, dramatic climate changes will result and could cause significant rises in sea level, massive coastal flooding, salt water intrusion, drought, and other catastrophes with significant ecological and economic impacts.

In its 1991 report, the National Academy of Sciences recommended that the United States reduce its emissions of greenhouse gases by 40 percent. It suggested the use of energy-efficient light bulbs, appliances, and heaters, and regulation to increase the fuel efficiency of automobiles by 30 percent. Many industrialized nations other than the U.S. have taken measures to reduce their carbon dioxide emissions in an effort to prevent the projected consequences of global warming.

Indoor Air Quality

In recent years, the issue of indoor, as opposed to ambient (outdoor), air quality has come to the forefront. The quality of air inside buildings and other enclosed structures where people live and work has a significant impact on human health, though not on the environment at large. EPA considers indoor air quality to be one of the largest inadequately addressed health risks in the United States.[4]

The concern for indoor air quality has coalesced over two controversial issues: the recognition of second-hand tobacco smoke as a health hazard and "sick-building syndrome." The latter is a relatively recent phenomenon; it arose when improvements in insulation for energy-saving purposes in the 1970s resulted in increased accumulations of indoor contaminants. During the 1970s, buildings were built or modified to incorporate more substantial insulation and permanently sealed windows in order to conserve energy and reduce heating and cooling costs. In many cases, this made building occupants completely dependent upon artificial heating, cooling, and ventilation systems for air flow and circulation. Such buildings must be maintained properly to account for the decreased airflow. If heating and cooling ducts and vents are not cleaned regularly, for example, contaminants such as bacteria, fungi, viral agents and synthetic toxins accumulate over time and recirculate continuously in the building's air. Some of these building ventilation systems draw in air from street level, bringing in vehicle fumes and concentrating them.

Some building materials (such as acoustical tiles, asbestos, paints, and adhesives), office furnishings and equipment, and carpeting emit substances that may be harmful immediately following installation. New buildings exhibit concentrations of chemicals such as xylenes, ethylbenzenes, decane, and undecane in concentrations up to 100 times greater than outdoor concentrations. These chemicals, which are used in paints and adhesives, may take up to a year to decline to concentrations typical in older buildings.[5] Indoor exposure to airborne pesticides may account for up 90 percent of total human exposure, and some pesticides found in studies of indoor environments have long been banned by EPA.[6]

Occupants of "sick buildings" report symptoms such as fatigue, headaches, eye and throat irritation, allergic reactions, and difficulty concentrating. One of the best-documented cases of sick-building syndrome was the outbreak of "Legionnaires' disease" at the old Bellevue Stratford Hotel in Philadelphia in 1976. The virus that causes the potentially fatal disease had developed in the hotel's air-circulation system, which drew in warm, moist air from nearby cooling towers. The system had not been cleaned on a regular basis before the outbreak.

Scientists have identified several types of indoor-air-quality problems. One is "multiple chemical sensitivity," defined as the manifestation of multiple symptoms to extremely low concentrations of chemicals following sensitization.[7] Multiple chemical sensitivity is difficult to identify and diagnose, as are other indoor air quality-related conditions.

Even though sick-building syndrome is difficult to characterize, the costs associated with it are not. Poor indoor air quality can cause significant damage to property, such as antiques and electronic equipment, as well as impairing human health. Medical costs associated with poor indoor air quality are estimated at hundreds of millions of dollars each year.[8] Lost worker productivity due to poor air quality is estimated to cost the United States billions of dollars annually.[9] Research has demonstrated that small initial investments in indoor-air-quality improvements can yield significant dividends in terms of avoided medical costs and property injuries and lower operating costs. Well-maintained buildings cost less to operate, prolong the life of expensive equipment, alleviate the need for repairs, and keep tenants from relocating.[10]

Indoor air quality is not directly addressed in the Clean Air Act. More than 20 federal agencies have some responsibility for indoor air quality.[11] The Occupational Health and Safety Administration (OSHA) has the most significant responsibilities for regulating indoor air quality pursuant to federal occupational health and safety standards. Although no federal statute directly covers the indoor air quality of residences, workplaces, or other buildings where OSHA regulations do not apply, it has become a matter of increasing concern for EPA as well as OSHA. One reason is the great amount of time that many Americans spend indoors. It has been estimated that citizens of industrialized nations spend about 90 percent of their time indoors. Thus indoor air quality may contribute far more significantly to overall human health than ambient-air quality, which is the CAA's focus. For many pollutants, small changes in indoor concentrations affect total human exposure more than do large changes in outdoor concentrations.[12]

Thus far, indoor air quality in nonindustrial work settings has not been subject to significant regulation. There are, however, good arguments for regulatory intervention in nonresidential buildings, such as office buildings, where occupants have little control over indoor air quality:

> . . . Typically, building managers are responsible for operation and maintenance of heating, ventilation, and air-conditioning (HVAC) systems. Occupants of the building, including both employers and employees, often have little or no direct control of temperature, fresh air input, and ventilation rate. Because HVAC systems are normally operated to minimize energy costs, the health and comfort of tenants rarely become an issue unless a significant number of complaints are reported.

Because health risks in this situation tend to be nonvoluntary, government may have a responsibility to safeguard public health by defining what constitutes acceptable indoor air and taking steps to ensure that those criteria are met. Examples of government actions that might be warranted include specification of minimum ventilation rates necessary to achieve healthful indoor air quality, establishment of emission limitations for building materials, and development of indoor air quality guidelines or standards for important contaminants.[13]

9.4 Appraisal of CAA's Regulatory Approaches

The CAA has employed a wide variety of regulatory techniques over the years, some of which have been underutilized or poorly tailored to environmental considerations or political realities.

Creating a Market in Air Pollution Allowances

We have noted several instances where the Clean Air Act gives pollution allowances without any penalty or sanction. In such cases, if a polluting source does not use its entire allowance, the law permits the remainder to be banked, sold, or traded. Theoretically, emissions trading encourages businesses to develop more efficient pollution-control technologies. The ''carrot'' is the polluter's ability to sell a portion of its right to pollute.

What the market trading mechanism does *not* accomplish is an overall reduction in the amount of pollution. Some industries will reduce their emissions so that they can sell their unused allowances, which will then be used by other industries. If demand does not exist for these allowances, industries will have no economic incentive to reduce their emissions. In addition, nationwide trading of allowances results in disparate regional impacts if no other mechanism exists to assure proportionate regional reductions in emissions.

Some environmentalists view market trading of emissions as an unsound environmental policy for two reasons. *First,* it enshrines a right to pollute in the environmental regulatory scheme. Emissions allowances are essentially treated as property rights that can be bought, sold, or traded on the market.* This is true even if the market is geographically limited. Laws are normative as well as positive in that they reflect a society's values as much as they influence behavior. The right to buy and sell pollution allowances establishes an *entitlement to pollute* the environment. In contrast, laws that mandate controls on pollution based upon health and environmental standards effectuate a presumption that pollution is not acceptable when it harms the environment and human health. Health-based and environment-based standards place public and environmental welfare above profit in the hierarchy of social and political values. They are evidence of the citizens' right to a clean and healthful environment.

Second, market trading of pollution allowances effectuates no overall reduction in the aggregate amount of pollution permitted by law. This stands in contrast to laws that mandate use of the best available technologies by all sources of

---

*We should note that the Clean Air Act specifies that emissions allowance provisions do not amount to a property right which could be constitutionally protected should the legislation be repealed at a future point in time. Nonetheless, for the period in which present legislation remains in effect, the emissions allowance is for all practical purposes very much like any property interest in that it can be alienated at the will of the holder.

polluting emissions. Clearly, if some sources are able to purchase unused emissions credits, the best available technology is not being employed by all sources. Similarly, technology-forcing regulatory mechanisms, which mandate protection of health and the environment despite economic cost, will reduce overall levels of pollution if they are properly enforced.

What can be said for emissions-credits trading as a regulatory mechanism is that it may spur the development of new technologies that will change the standards by which industries' polluting activities are evaluated. Thus, if new technologies are developed and prove to be effective and efficient, future legislation may grant fewer pollution allowances to particular industries. This effect will only be seen, however, if legislation continues to adjust downward the amount of aggregate pollution allowed. On the other hand, making pollution allowances marketable commodities may alter social perceptions of the acceptability of polluting behavior. This could make legislators reluctant to mandate increasingly lower levels of pollution allowances.

Spurring the Development of New Pollution-Control Technologies

The 1970 CAA's shift to federally enforced uniform national standards employing health-based, technology-forcing regulation stands in contrast to the Clean Water Act of 1972. That act employed primarily a technology-driven approach and placed regulatory emphasis upon the availability of pollution-control technologies and, in some instances, economic feasibility. Although the CAA was a technology-forcing statute *in principle* from 1970 to 1990, its lenient administration undermined that effect. Basically, the federal government's failure to penalize states for not implementing emissions controls to achieve national standards eviscerated the CAA's technology-forcing aspects. By letting the states continue to grant permits and allow sources to operate despite clear evidence that their emissions were the cause of nonattainment, Congress and successive presidential administrations failed to force polluters to develop appropriate technologies for achieving national standards.

The 1990 amendments effected a substantial shift away from the 1970 Act's technology-forcing scheme by enacting more provisions requiring the use of particular technologies—rather than requiring that polluting emissions be reduced to particular levels based upon health and environmental considerations. One example is the requirement for use of maximum available control technology (MACT). Congress softened the impact of the CAA's health and environmental mandates in order to minimize adverse economic effects. It was believed that more stringent application of the CAA would have resulted in decreased profits and the loss of jobs in certain sectors of the economy. This cost-mitigating approach continues to spawn controversy in political circles and lawsuits. Opposing parties dispute both the nature and gravity of the harms posed by particular emissions and the magnitude of the economic and social harms (lost jobs and business failures) that will ensue if polluters are forced to comply with proposed rules requiring new technology.

It is abundantly clear from the CAA's history that industries that emit harmful pollutants will not invest in better pollution controls unless they are legally compelled to do so. The automotive industry is a prime example. Many potentially useful alternative technologies have been available to that industry for years, but they have not been exploited because doing so would require substantial investments in research, development, and plant modification and the loss of vested capital in outmoded technologies. In addition, companies would have to forego short-term profits while they were developing, building, and marketing new products. The emphasis on short-term gain, which has come to be an integral part of the U.S. economic system, tends to work against technological upgrades in many industrial sectors. This can be counteracted only by legislation specifically designed to make it costly *not* to implement better technologies.

9.5   Policy Issues

Comparison with Schemes for Protecting Other Environmental Media

It is now clear that similar tensions have underlain development of the Clean Water Act and the Clean Air Act—namely, periodic shifts back and forth between technology-driven pollution limitations and media-quality standards based upon health and environmental considerations. Another similarity is that both acts focus on limiting emissions of specific contaminants in an attempt to improve the condition of the environmental medium. Likewise, air and water legislation have both been marked by alterations in the predominant regulatory methods employed, enforcement mechanisms, and the relationship between state and federal authorities.

Certain general conclusions can be drawn from a comparison of the regulatory techniques used by the CAA and the CWA since the 1970s:

1. Unless it is vigorously enforced, technology-forcing regulation is not effective. Revising compliance deadlines and failing to stringently enforce regulations eviscerate technology-forcing aspects of the law.

2. Under federal initiatives and requirements, states are not likely to develop and enforce stringent environmental regulations unless there are strong incentives for doing so. States have significant concerns about the economic impacts of regulations and about their ability to attract and retain revenue-producing industries. These concerns mitigate their willingness to enact and enforce strict federal standards.

3. Technology-driven regulation is more enforceable and, to that extent, may be more effective than technology-forcing regulation in reducing the worst polluting emissions. Technology-driven regulation does not spur the development of new technologies, however, and therefore results in diminishing returns.

4. There is often a regulatory tradeoff between cost-effectiveness and ecological effectiveness. The most economically efficient regulatory mechanisms—emissions trading being an example—rely to some extent on granting alienable rights to pollute and thus on adverse environmental consequences.

■   Discussion Questions

1. The 1990 CAA amendments provide for a "marketplace-oriented" approach to environmental regulation.
    a. What does the amendments' emissions-trading policy imply about the existence of citizens' rights to a clean environment?
    b. Does the policy give some industries a right to pollute?

    c. Do emissions allowances confer an economic benefit on certain industries or businesses? By whom? At whose loss or cost?

2. Although CFCs are no longer widely used as propellants in the United States, they are still manufactured in this country for use abroad.
   a. How might the lesser restrictions on CFC export be justified?
   b. Some of these exports are used for medical purposes in Third World Countries. Does this influence your views on the subject? How?

■ Chapter 9 Endnotes

1. CEQ, *Environmental Quality* 8–9 (1990).
2. G. J. Mitchell, *World on Fire* (Charles Scribner's Sons, 1991), p. 48.
3. M. Oppenheimer and R. H. Boyle, *Dead Heat: The Race against the Greenhouse Effect* (Basic Books, 1990), p. 57.
4. C. Haymore and R. Odom, "Economic Effects of Poor IAQ," 19 *EPA Journal,* no. 4 (October/December 1993), p. 28.
5. L. Wallace, "The TEAM Studies," 19 *EPA Journal,* no. 4 (October/December 1993), p. 23.
6. Ibid., p. 24.
7. K. Sexton, "An Inside Look at Air Pollution," 19 *EPA Journal,* no. 4 (October/December 1993), p. 10.
8. Haymore and Odom, note 4, supra.
9. Ibid.
10. Ibid.
11. B. Axelrad, "Improving IAQ: EPA's Program," 19 *EPA Journal,* no. 4 (October/December 1993), p. 17.
12. K. R. Smith, "Taking the True Measure of Air Pollution," 19 *EPA Journal,* no. 4 (October/December 1993), p. 7.
13. Ibid., p. 12.

PART V

SPECIAL ISSUES IN ENVIRONMENTAL REGULATION

Part V examines a number of broad subjects that are not fully addressed in previous chapters. These include environmental regulation on publicly owned and Indian lands, resource use and distribution, ecosystem management, and the global environment. Chapter 10 explores the laws and issues pertaining to environmental protection of federal lands, federal facilities, and tribal lands. Chapter 11 discusses the challenges of protecting the globally shared environment through international law.

CHAPTER 10

Environmental Regulation of Federal Lands, Federal Facilities, and Tribal Lands

Outline

10.1 Overview of Federally Owned Lands and Resources

In opening new territories to settlement and development, the federal government transferred ownership of much land to the states and to private parties such as railroads, homesteaders, ranchers, and loggers. The federal government retained as "public domain" vast territories variously reported as constituting from one fifth to one third of the U.S. land surface, most of it situated in 11 Western states and Alaska, and about two thirds of the total U.S. subsurface area.[1] The United States government holds title to these lands and is required to manage them for the benefit of the public. The map in Figure 10.1 indicates the scale and distribution of federal properties.[2]

The 1993 report of a Senate committee indicates the extent of public land ownership and of hazardous-waste-management problems on federal lands and at federally-owned and operated facilities:

> The Department of [the] Interior is the nation's largest landowner. The agency owns more than 440 million acres of public lands. Twenty percent of the surface area of the United States is managed by DOI. In addition, DOI holds about 62 percent of the nation's total subsurface area. The agency controls an additional 60 million acres, as a trustee for Indian tribes in the United States and in territories outside of the United States. Most of the public lands controlled by DOI are in the western United States.
>
> With about 75,000 full-time employees working at over 2,000 locations, DOI's specific responsibilities include managing: water and hydroelectric power projects in 17 western States; 359 national park system units; 490 national wildlife refuges; 78 fish hatcheries; and servicing over 500 Indian tribes and Alaska Native villages.
>
> As the primary steward of the nation's natural resources, the DOI also has several major environmental, safety and health responsibilities. They include:
>
> ■ management control of wastes on public lands in compliance with applicable laws and regulations;
> ■ preservation and restoration of natural resources on public lands controlled by DOI;

■ **Figure 10.1**   Federal Lands as Percentage of Total Area, by State, 1984

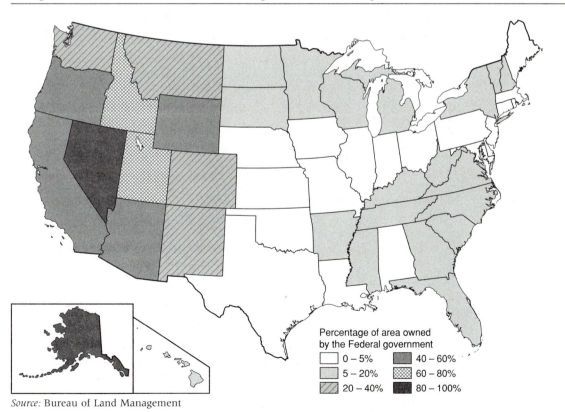

Source: Bureau of Land Management

- administration of the Surface Mining Control Act to assure the timely restoration of lands mined principally for coal;
- administration of a nation-wide system of parks and recreation; and
- protecting the health and safety of its employees.

Interior's traditional role of management of grazing, mining, oil and gas development, and timber harvesting began to change in the early 1980's when a growing number of hazardous waste problems started to emerge. In response, the DOI established under the Bureau of Land Management (BLM) the Hazardous Materials Management Program and then the Office of Environmental Affairs, which coordinates waste management across DOI's bureaus.

The growing number of environmental . . . problems that impact public lands have raised a major challenge to DOI. The agency must now incorporate as a priority . . . the handling of hazardous and solid wastes, and take proactive measures to avoid further contamination. Environmental . . . protection will also require the Department to reexamine its web of complex relationships involving an array of private interests, States, local government and even other nations.

HAZARDOUS MATERIALS PROBLEMS

In particular, the growing problem of hazardous materials on public lands is one of the largest, costly and most complex in the nation. There are several types of hazardous materials impacting public lands . . . . They include:

- mineral extraction and processing;
- oil and gas exploration and production;
- solid waste landfills;
- pesticide application, storage and disposal;
- hazardous-waste treatment, storage and disposal facilities;
- spills and leaks from vehicles, storage tanks and pipelines;
- underground injection wells; and
- illegal dumping of hazardous and solid wastes.

The Office of Environmental Affairs (OEA) provides oversight with respect to hazardous wastes. The OEA has six full-time employees at headquarters and 18 full-time employees in the field. . . . The DOI currently has 432 sites listed on the Federal Facilities Hazardous Waste Compliance Docket. As the following table indicates, DOI's environmental . . . problems cut across its many bureaus.

Bureau unknown	10
Geological Survey	2
Bureau of Indian Affairs	10
Bureau of Land Management	314
Bureau of Mines	5
National Park Service	35
Bureau of Reclamation	25
Fish and Wildlife Service	31
Total	432

* * *

INTERIOR'S ENVIRONMENTAL CLEANUP PROBLEM IS POTENTIALLY VERY LARGE AND VERY COSTLY

DOI's current number of entries on the Federal Facilities Hazardous Waste Compliance Docket indicates that hazardous waste site identification is still in an early stage. . . . The full magnitude of the Department's problems is not at all understood. Recently the DOI Office of Inspector General noted that "the potential number of sites is believed to be in the tens of thousands."

For example, as many as 10 million mining claims have been filed with the Interior Department since the 19th Century, and several hundred thousand acres of public land have been impacted by mining operations. . . . However, the agency lacks an accurate inventory of abandoned mine sites and the degree of hazardous wastes cannot be estimated with any reliability.

The total cost growth of DOI's environmental cleanup effort remains uncertain, but is potentially very high and could be in the billions-of-dollars. . . . Hazardous materials from U.S. military operations in refuge areas, Indian reservations, trust territories, and other public lands pose major potential liabilities for Interior. . . .

Between fiscal year 1988 and fiscal year 1992, the Department of Interior was litigating at least 13 cases in which DOI could be liable for site cleanup costs. However, according to the Department's Inspector General: "the total number of potential cases involving departmental liability may approximate several thousand." . . .

Some indicators of the costs associated with Interior's environmental problems can be found in the following situations:

- The Midnite Mine, a former uranium mine on the Spokane Indian Reservation in Washington is estimated to cost between $43 million and $107 million to cleanup.
- The National Forest Service has concluded that the cleanup of more serious contaminated sites may be $250 million. . . .
- The Department's Bureau of Indian Affairs is responsible for some 100 non-compliant landfills. The average annual operating and maintenance costs for these landfills to meet minimal environmental requirements could exceed $60,000 per landfill.

INTERIOR'S RESPONSE TO ENVIRONMENTAL PROBLEMS IS INADEQUATE

Unfortunately DOI's response to this enormous challenge has been slow, disjointed and wasteful.

* * *

According to the 1992 National Academy of Sciences report about hazardous wastes on public lands, Department employees of the Bureau of Land Management (BLM):

"Were directed to observe a 'hands-off' policy—to avoid all contact with known or suspected hazardous materials, report only known contaminated sites, and avoid any actions that could result in legal liability to the agency. . . . Current agency policy is that [environmental cleanup] activities should commence only after the land involved has been transferred . . . to some other entity."

* * *

More recently, a March 1993 audit of management of hazardous materials by the DOI's Office of Inspector General found that the Department:

". . . has made unsatisfactory progress in identifying, evaluating and cleaning up hazardous waste sites on public and Indian trust lands. . . .[3]

Besides the Department of Interior, the U.S. Forest Service, a branch of the Department of Agriculture, also has extensive landholdings of approximately 190 million acres. Environmental problems other than those relating to hazardous waste also have arisen from improper management of federal lands. For example, improper management of grazing, mining, logging, and other activities on federal lands has resulted in extensive degradation of soil, water, and habitat resources. These problems are discussed in later sections of the chapter.

All federal lands, including those used by private entities under federal government permits, remain subject to federal control, and federal laws supersede any contrary laws of the states where the lands are located. The Supreme Court decision in *Kleppe v. New Mexico,* excerpted here, established this important doctrine.

KLEPPE V. NEW MEXICO

426 U.S. 529 (1976)

[After a rancher, who grazed cattle under federal permits on Bureau of Land Management rangeland, complained that wild burros were molesting his cattle and eating their feed, the Livestock Board of New Mexico, acting under state law, entered the federal range, removed the burros and sold them at auction. The Bureau of Land Management demanded their recovery and return pursuant to the federal Wild Free-Roaming Horses and Burros Act. The State Board brought suit to challenge the constitutionality of the federal law and the Bureau's authority.]

* * *

The property Clause of the Constitution provides that "Congress shall have Power to dispose of and make all needful Rules and Regulations respecting the Territory or other Property belonging to the United States." U.S. Const., Art. IV, § 3, cl 2. In passing the Wild Free-Roaming Horses and Burros Act, Congress deemed the regulated animals "an integral part of the natural system of the public lands" of the United States, . . . and found that their management was necessary "for achievement of an ecological balance on the public lands."

According to Congress, these animals, if preserved in their native habitats, "contribute to the diversity of life forms within the Nation and enrich the lives of the American people." . . . Indeed, Congress concluded, the wild free-roaming horses and burros "are living symbols of the historic and pioneer spirit of the West." . . .

For these reasons, Congress determined to preserve and protect the wild free-roaming horses and burros on the public lands of the United States. The question under the Property Clause is whether this determination can be

sustained as a "needful" regulation "respecting" the public lands. . . .

* * *

. . . We have noted, for example, that the Property Clause gives Congress the power over the public lands "to control their occupancy and use, to protect them from trespass and injury and to prescribe the conditions upon which others may obtain rights in them. . . ." . . . And we have approved legislation respecting the public lands "[i]f it be found to be necessary for the protection of the public, or of intending settlers [on the public lands]." . . . In short, Congress exercises the powers both of a proprietor and of a legislature over the public domain. . . . Although the Property Clause does not authorize "an exercise of a general control over public policy in a State," it does permit "an exercise of the complete power which Congress has over particular public property entrusted to it." . . . In our view, the "complete power" that Congress has over public lands necessarily includes the power to regulate and protect the wildlife living there.

III

Appellees argue that if we approve the Wild Free-Roaming Horses and Burros Act as a valid exercise of Congress' power under the Property Clause, then we have sanctioned an impermissible intrusion on the sovereignty, legislative authority, and police power of the State and have wrongly infringed upon the State's traditional trustee powers over wild animals. The argument appears to be that Congress could obtain exclusive legislative jurisdiction over the public lands in the State only by state consent, and that in the absence of such consent Congress lacks the power to act contrary to state law. This argument is without merit.

* * *

. . . The Act does not establish exclusive federal jurisdiction over the public lands in New Mexico; it merely overrides the New Mexico Estray Law insofar as it attempts to regulate federally protected animals. And that is but the necessary consequence of valid legislation under the Property Clause.

Appellees' contention that the Act violates traditional state power over wild animals stands on no different footing. Unquestionably the States have broad trustee and police powers over wild animals within their jurisdictions. . . . But those powers exist only "in so far as [their] exercise may be not incompatible with, or restrained by, the rights conveyed to the Federal government by the Constitution." . . . We hold today that the Property Clause also gives Congress the power to protect wildlife on the public lands, state law notwithstanding.

IV

In this case, the New Mexico Livestock Board entered upon the public lands of the United States and removed wild burros. These actions were contrary to the provisions of the Wild Free-Roaming Horses and Burros Act. We find that, as applied to this case, the Act is a constitutional exercise of congressional power under the Property Clause. . . .

Appellees are concerned that the Act's extension of protection to wild free-roaming horses and burros that stray from public land onto private land, . . . will be read to provide federal jurisdiction over every wild horse or burro that at any time sets foot upon federal land. While it is clear that regulations under the Property Clause may have some effect on private lands not otherwise under federal control, . . . we do not think it appropriate in this declaratory judgment proceeding to determine the extent, if any, to which the Property Clause empowers Congress to protect animals on private lands or the extent to which such regulation is attempted by the Act. . . .

* * *

Economic and environmental regulation of federal land uses involves the perennial challenge of "sustainable development," which is explored in section 10.2. It is often observed that the United State's "native natural resources" (its grasslands, forests, minerals, and waterways) are the "bedrock" of its economic strength.[4] Conflicts between the economic interests of federal permitees who use and consume these natural resources, on one hand, and the interests of the general public, on whose behalf environmentalists seek to conserve the resources and ecology of federal lands, on the other hand, are a staple of environmental law. Federal agencies and officials are charged with mediating these political and legal disputes, since federal laws expressly require the government to pursue a policy of "multiple uses" of federal lands. These multiple uses include economic uses as well as recreation and aesthetic uses.

Federal law also exerts significant indirect influences upon state regulation of nonfederal lands.

> Through its management of these lands, the federal government is able to influence standards in natural resource conservation for the states and the private sector, which together control [the other] two thirds of the land in the United States.[5]

History of Federal Land Use Laws

Until recently, Congress made little attempt to harmonize federal laws which addressed various types of natural resources and various aspects of environmental protection for those resources. Earlier Congresses sought to solve isolated problems incrementally, by narrow laws addressed to special problems without reference to their interconnections with related economic and environmental issues. The impacts of separate laws at a given site are often confusing and sometimes conflicting.[6] Congress also created regulatory logjams by delegating different government agencies the authority to administer those uncoordinated laws, thereby occasioning jurisdictional conflicts with regard to a common government site or operation. Multiple-agency jurisdiction over particular sites and subjects has slowed the implementation of projects aimed at protecting publicly owned resources. The network of major federal environmental laws and federal agencies administering them are given here:

Endangered Species Act of 1973	16 U.S.C. § 1531
Federal Facilities Compliance Act of 1992	42 U.S.C. § 6901
Federal Land Policy and Management Act of 1976 (FLPMA)	43 U.S.C. § 1701
General Mining Law of 1872	30 U.S.C. § 21
Mineral Leasing Act of 1920	30 U.S.C. § 181
Multiple Use, Sustained Yield Act of 1960	16 U.S.C. § 528
National Forest Management Act of 1976 (NFMA)	16 U.S.C. § 1600
National Wildlife Refuge System Administration Act of 1966	16 U.S.C. § 668dd, 715s
Onshore Oil and Gas Leasing Reform Act of 1987	16 U.S.C. § 3148, 30 U.S.C. § 187 a–b
Public Rangelands Improvement Act of 1978 (PRIA)	43 U.S.C. § 1901
Refuge Recreation Act of 1962	16 U.S.C. § 460k
Taylor Grazing Act of 1934	43 U.S.C. § 315
Surface Mining Control and Reclamation Act	30 U.S.C. § 1201
Wilderness Act of 1964	16 U.S.C. § 1131

In recent years Congress has shown increasing awareness of the many environmental dimensions of its decisions on land uses. For instance, the Clean Air Act Amendments link transportation and land-use decisions with environmental-quality goals. The Coastal Zone Management Act amendments require that federal management of oil and gas leases and federal activities on the Outer Continental Shelf be consistent with coastal zone management plans of affected states where the federal activities affect state coastal resources.[7] These linkages of environmental issues with resource development offer hope for greater future cohesion of federal land management. However, the legacy of past uses of federal land without adequate environmental safeguards presents enormous challenges, as do the expectations created by the long history of private uses of publicly owned resources. These challenges are examined in greater detail in later sections of the chapter.

In order to encourage settlement and development of remote territories, early federal laws authorized liberal land grants and use permits, principally for railroad building, cattle grazing, logging, and mineral exploration and extraction. Before the end of the 19th century the U.S. government did not reserve substantial land areas for protecting wilderness areas, wildlife, endangered species, ecosystems, or water sources, national forests, national monuments, and parks. Even today, only about one tenth of the federal domain has protective designations, and most of those areas remain open to uses, such as recreation, that could damage the natural ecosystems.[8]

The minimal fees and regulations which federal laws originally set for private uses of federal lands remained substantially unchanged throughout the nineteenth century. Below-market fees for use of public resources, constituting federal subsidies, fostered expectations of continued cheap access to these resources for private use. These expectations persist to the present, and they explain the stiff resistance to proposals to increase federal permit fees for private extraction of publicly owned natural resources and to curtail economic development in order to restore and protect environments damaged by economic development.

The economics of federal land regulation implicate broad taxpayer concerns as well as environmental concerns. To the extent that permit fees for using natural resources do not recapture their fair value, public resources can be expected to be consumed disproportionately and at a greater rate than privately owned resources, with progressive losses of the public resource base and substantial losses to U.S. taxpayers. The failures to replenish depleted resources and to repair environmental damage caused by resource extraction have been partly due to inadequate federal regulation of private uses. Moreover, permit-fee revenues have not provided sufficient funds for conservation purposes. The present fee-revenue shortfall also delimits programs to develop federal lands for purposes that benefit wider segments of the general public. Ultimately, the burden of supplying necessary funds for these other purposes falls upon the taxpaying public.

Current fees for using some federally owned natural resources are undisputedly well below the market value of the taken resources, and often below the taxpayer's cost of maintaining the sites (which includes, for example, expenditures for surveying, road construction, fencing, and land restoration).[9]

Although the continuing controversy over fee reforms is examined more closely in section 10.2, an example is discussed here. The current grazing fee controversy typifies the seemingly intractable problem of bringing the economics of federal natural-resource development into line with environmental preservation.

In 1993 President Clinton proposed to raise the fees charged for permits to engage in grazing, timber cutting, and mining on federal lands. The proposed fees sought to better approximate the private-market value of the permits and to better cover the costs of managing the lands. Estimated to produce additional revenues of $1 billion over five years, the proposal had the added goal of helping to reduce the federal budget deficit. Predictably, the proposal raised a storm of protest from Western ranchers, loggers, miners, communities, and their state and federal legislators. They objected that the fee increases would devastate their resource-dependent economies and the workers and communities sustained by those economies. Pleas of "special hardship" in the name of small, independent ranchers, loggers, and prospectors, however, ill fit the profiles of the overwhelmingly dominant beneficiaries of below-market federal fees and federal subsidies. Large timber, mining and livestock corporations hold most of the federal lands under license for private development, and they enjoy the same low fee rates as small entrepreneurs, notwithstanding their significantly greater economic gain and adverse toll on natural resources and the environment. Small businesses and individuals whose livelihoods depend upon the use of federal lands and resources are caught in the middle of the controversy.

The political opposition to the President's initial fee proposals drove the administration into successive retreats. First it withdrew the request to effect fee increases through the federal budget process in order to avoid a threatened Senate filibuster. The administration then sought individual fee adjustments for different classes of natural resources. Its efforts to update logging and mining fees are discussed in later sections, but the grazing fees scenario illustrates the general pattern of special-interest opposition to altering the balance of economic and environmental priorities on federal lands.

As of 1990, the long unchanged grazing charge of $1.98 per month of grazing usage (e.g. by a cow and calf) was reportedly one fifth of the market rate for like grazing permits on privately-owned Western lands.[10] The administration's attempt to gain congressional approval of a grazing fee scale lower than its original proposal also failed in the face of an actual Senate filibuster. In response to that filibuster, the administration threatened to increase grazing fees without congressional support by administrative action of the executive branch, but that threat evaporated under persistent political heat and threats to challenge any such administrative action in court. The administration then fell to negotiating a compromise with the political opposition. In March 1994, it announced the negotiated proposal, which apparently satisfied the dominant leaders of the Western states, though it left many partisans from all camps unsatisfied. If adopted after public review and comment, the new regulation will provide graduated grazing-fee increases (per defined unit of monthly grazing) from the current $1.98 rate to $3.96 by 1997 (down from the $4.28 originally sought), but with a cap of $2.75 for ranchers who comply with specified environmental standards.[11] The proposed regulation vests state and local committees, rather than federal authorities, with the power to make important regulatory decisions and to specify the environmental conditions for eligibility for the reduced cap fee of $2.75. Environmentalists suspect that this could allow ranchers to gain the benefit of the modest $2.75 rate more easily than they would under total federal control. If the proposal is adopted without further changes, it is expected to take effect by 1995. Further court challenges to its final regulation form are likely, however, whether by dissatisfied ranchers or by dissatisfied environmental organizations.

Environmental Mandates for Federally Managed Lands

Two legal mandates dominate federal land management and sometimes collide with each other. They are the policy of encouraging multiple uses of the lands (as exemplified by the Multiple Use, Sustained Yield Act of 1960[12]) and the mandate to manage the lands so as to protect the natural environment (as exemplified by the Federal Land Policy and Management Act of 1976,[13] the Wilderness Act,[14] and the Endangered Species Act[15]). Approved multiple uses—that is, economic, social, recreational, and conservationist uses—must be somehow ranked and balanced. The task of integrating these varied uses is not eased by the fact that federal officials often find themselves in the unique position of being at one and the same time both a regulator and the regulated party. Thus a federal land-management agency is potentially both lawmaker and lawbreaker. This can pose equally unusual problems for implementing and enorcing general environmental laws on federal lands and at federal facilities.

Overlapping Jurisdiction of Federal Administrative Agencies

Under governmental immunity doctrines that are discussed in section 10.4, federal agencies are shielded from liability for violating federal laws—including environmental laws—unless Congress waives immunity by legislation. Since no one statute prescribes or waives governmental immunity for all purposes, there are no universal answers to the questions of whether and to what extent a federal agency may claim immunity for violating a particular environmental law. Each environmental statute must be consulted to determine if Congress has waived immunity with regard to it. Even where liability has not been waived by the environmental statute in question, the question remains whether a federal agency may still resist enforcement of that statute by another federal agency. Other statutes dealing with jurisdiction of different federal agencies also come into play. For example, Congress or the President may assign managerial or enforcement powers regarding a particular sphere of government action to more than one agency. In such a case, the authority of each agency must be harmonized with that of the other agency or agencies. Further discussion of agency overlaps and friction in administering environmental programs appears in section 10.4, but it is important to note here that administrative enforcement of environmental statutes is sometimes qualified or deflected by non-environmental statutes that generally govern the procedures and jurisdictions of administrative agencies.

10.2 Federal Land Management

As shown in Figure 10.2, the great bulk of federal lands is managed by the Bureau of Land Management (BLM), a part of the Department of the Interior, and by the Forest Service, a part of the Department of Agriculture. Other agencies within the Interior Department, the Fish and Wildlife Service and the National Park Service, manage specialized tracts, such as wilderness and national parks. The Department of Defense through the armed services manages lands operated for military purposes. This section deals primarily with the lands managed by the BLM and the Forest Service.

■ **Figure 10.2** Federal Land Management Agencies

Department	Agency	Land (million acres)
Interior	Bureau of Land Management	270
Agriculture	Forest Service	191
Interior	Fish and Wildlife Service	92
Interior	National Park Service	80
Defense	Army/Air Force/Navy/Marines	25
		658

Source: CEQ, *Environmental Quality,* Thirty-second Annual Report 168 (1991).

BLM oversees almost three fourths of public lands (about 270 million acres) while the Forest Service has charge of about 190 million acres. BLM manages most, though not all, federal rangelands, and sizable forest areas. The Forest Service manages most, though not all, federal forests and sizable rangeland and mining properties. The trend under modern laws

> is toward managing forests [and other lands] as complex ecosystems made up of interdependent communities of plants, animals, and microbes, rather than managing them for single outputs such as timber or game species [or livestock or minerals].[16]

Equally significant is the policy goal (since 1960) of managing federal lands in ways that sustain their productivity and suitability for many uses. These diverse objectives and the competing interests of groups that favor different uses spawn controversy over the proper balance of economic, recreational, and environmental elements in land management plans. The predominant conflicts involve federal rangelands, forests, and mining resources.

Rangelands and Livestock Grazing

The BLM administers about 171 million acres of rangelands on the lands it manages, while the Forest Service administers rangelands situated within National Forest boundaries. This subsection's discussion of BLM-managed rangeland generally applies also to rangelands managed by the Forest Service. Much of the information presented in this subsection was drawn from the five sources listed in the endnote.[17] Students are encouraged to consult those sources for fuller study of federal rangeland management.

Rangelands are semiarid, nonarable, and generally thought to be of little economic use except for livestock grazing. Over the course of many decades, ranchers overstocked, overgrazed, and gave little thought to preserving federal lands, and there was little or no regulatory restraint. That history presents a scenario similar to that of *The Tragedy of the Commons* which is discussed in Chapter 1.

> The unclaimed federal lands were an unregulated commons; no statute checked the human desire to take the grass before someone else did. Overgrazing destroyed much of the land's productive capacity. . . .
>
> In their race for available grass, the ranchers overstocked and itinerant sheep finished off the stubble. Grass production declined precipitously.[18]
>
> Much of this land, particularly the vast public domain, remains in desperate condition, as wind, rain, and drought have swept over them and eroded their exposed soils. Although the effect of overgrazing in rich pastures or prairies farmlands can be quickly corrected, the process is often irreversible on the limited soils and arid climate of much of the public lands.[19]

The degradation of rangelands and the collapse of their natural ecosystems remains unrectified in many places. In 1970, the BLM had "targeted 68 million acres for ecological restoration by the year 2009 . . ."[20]

The Taylor Grazing Act of 1934 imposed federal grazing controls, primarily to protect the livestock industry from the harmful economic effects of overgrazing during the depression. In 1978 Congress supplemented the Taylor Act with the Public Rangelands Improvement Act which declared that "vast segments of the public rangelands are producing less than their potential for livestock, wildlife, habitat, recreation, forage, and water and soil conservation benefits, and for that reason are in unsatisfactory condition." That Act increased funding for rangeland improvements. BLM administration of the Taylor Act and the National Environmental Policy Act (discussed in Chapter 3) is reviewed in the landmark *Morton* opinion.

■   **NATURAL RESOURCES DEFENSE COUNCIL, INC. V. MORTON**   ■

388 F. Supp. 829 (D.D.C. 1974)
Affd. 527 F.2d 1386 (D.C. Cir. 1975)

[In this suit brought against the Bureau of Land Management, six environmentalist groups charged that the BLM issued grazing permits without preparing an Environmental Impact Statement as required by the National Environmental Policy Act. After rejecting several other defenses and holding that the BLM grazing program was governed by NEPA, the court took up BLM's defense that its policy statements sufficed as a programmatic EIS to satisfy NEPA requirements. The opinion excerpts reprinted here explain the BLM management program on federal rangelands.]

FLANNERY, District Judge.

MEMORANDUM OPINION

This matter is before the court on cross-motions for summary judgment . . . . It presents important issues concerning the applicability of the National Environmental Policy Act (NEPA), . . . to the livestock grazing permit program of the Bureau of Land Management, United States Department of Interior. Five of the six plaintiffs are environmental organizations whose general objectives are to enhance and protect the environment and to insure proper resource management; . . . .

The Bureau of Land Management
Permit Program

The Bureau of Land Management (BLM) is charged with managing and protecting over 171 million acres of public or national resource lands located in 11 western states. These lands not only contain valuable environmental and recreational resources, but also provide grazing for an estimated 14 percent of all livestock in the United States during some parts of their lives. Livestock operators hold approximately 24,000 BLM licenses, permits, and leases to graze their stock on 150 million of the 171 million acres administered by the Bureau. The is-

suance and regulation of these licenses constitutes one of the main activities of the BLM. It also carries on activities such as vegetation control and the construction of fences and watering facilities designed to improve grazing and protect the land, and works closely with other federal agencies in such areas as watershed maintenance and soil conservation.

The Bureau's management of the public lands is carried out at three levels or stages of intensity. About 7 million acres are . . . managed in a merely custodial fashion due primarily to their scattered and isolated locations. Approximately 108 million acres are administered in a fashion the BLM describes as "the best management attainable within the limits of manpower and funding." It is, however, the goal of the BLM to bring 133 of the 171 million acres of public lands under the third category of management—intensive management—by the year 2000. Currently, however, only 25 million acres (18 percent) are under intensive management.

The 52 BLM grazing districts are the agency's basic management component. The procedures which these districts follow . . . are rather involved. Each district is divided into planning units and a unit resource analysis (URA) containing a detailed inventory of resources is prepared for each one. After public comment, a land use plan called a management framework plan (MFP) containing a set of "goals, objectives, and constraints" is prepared for each planning unit. Once the MFP is completed, more specialized plans known as program activity plans are prepared for each type of resource-related activity, such as timbering, recreation and grazing, in the unit. . . . The program activity plan for grazing is called an allotment management plan (AMP). A planning unit may contain a number of grazing allotments. . . . Before any AMP or other activity plan is implemented it is first determined whether an environmental impact statement is required for the plan. It is against the background that the court must examine the BLM's compliance with NEPA.

The National Environmental Policy Act

Section 102(2)(C) of the National Environmental Policy Act, 42 U.S.C. § 4332 (1970), requires that a detailed environmental impact statement (EIS) be prepared for every major federal action significantly affecting the quality of the human environment. This rather general legislative language has been explained and interpreted in guidelines published by the Council on Environmental Quality (CEQ) . . . . The CEQ Guidelines provide that the environmental assessment should be made as early as possible, and in all cases prior to agency decision concerning recommendations or favorable reports on proposals for major federal actions significantly affecting the environment. 40 C.F.R. § 1500.2(a) (1974). . . .

The BLM has prepared a draft programmatic EIS for its entire livestock grazing program. . . . The BLM contends that this statement will provide an overview of the cumulative impact of the grazing program and will serve as the foundation for subsequent environmental analyses and for supplemental impact statements . . . . The BLM does not indicate, however, under what circumstances it will be necessary to prepare supplemental statements.

Plaintiffs contend that the BLM has failed to comply with the provisions of . . . NEPA in that it has issued and renewed grazing permits in each year from 1970 to the present, and proposes to continue doing so, without preparing an EIS dealing with the actual environmental impact of such actions. Plaintiffs argue that the overall programmatic EIS for grazing does not suffice since it fails to consider the individualized, "on the ground" effects on local environments. They ask that the court declare the actions of the BLM to be violations of NEPA. . . . It should be noted that plaintiffs do not seek to enjoin the present issuance of licenses nor do they ask that impact statements be prepared for every license or permit. They ask rather that detailed individual statements be prepared on an appropriate district or geographic level to assess the actual impact of the issuance of federal grazing permits on local environments.

The Taylor Grazing Act

. . . Defendants-intervenors argue that NEPA does not require impact statements with regard to the licensing of public lands for grazing since the Taylor Grazing Act, 43 U.S.C. § 315 et seq. (1970), which established the licensing program is an operative and effective method of protecting the environment of the public lands . . . . Defendants-intervenors further argue that the BLM's rules, regulations and administrative procedures protect the environment and should apparently be considered the functional equivalent of an impact statement. . . . To call the Taylor Grazing Act purely environmental is to ignore its language and its history.

* * *

Federal defendants, unlike defendants-intervenors, concede that NEPA applies to the BLM grazing program but argue . . . that the Bureau is not in violation of the Act since the programmatic impact statement sufficiently complies with the intent of NEPA.

* * *

. . . Over the past four years the BLM has shown relatively slow progress in implementing a thorough management planning system which would assist in protecting the environment. As noted above, the BLM estimated that 8,320 AMP's are needed. Only 1,015 plans were implemented through fiscal year 1973, and completion of all AMP's is not estimated until the year 2000. Thus, in a substantial and practical sense there is a serious threat of injury to the public lands which lends urgency to plaintiffs' claims. While the court should always be reluctant to rule on issues before full and final agency determination, to wait until the filing of the final programmatic EIS would be a useless act and would thwart Congressional intent, reducing NEPA to a mere "paper tiger." Having considered the above, it appears to the court that there are no appropriate agency procedures which plaintiffs should be required to exhaust and that the situation dictates a decision by this court on the merits of the claim.

BLM's Programmatic Impact Statement

. . . Section 102 then establishes the requirement that impact statements be filed in all major federal actions significantly affecting the human environment. Thus NEPA makes environmental protection part of the mandate of every federal agency, compelling them to consider environmental issues just as they consider other matters within their mandates. . . . The courts have followed a strict interpretation of these provisions . . . . The Taylor Act is not purely environmental since it is aimed at promoting the highest use of the public lands; NEPA seeks to protect the environment. . . . These two purposes . . . are not the same, but are not in such conflict that a rigorous application of NEPA would give rise to violations of the Taylor Act.

. . . In the BLM grazing license program the primary decision-maker is generally the individual district manager, with his staff, who approves license applications. While the programmatic EIS drafted by the BLM provides general policy guidelines as to relevant environmental factors, it in no way insures that the decision-maker considers all of the specific and particular consequences of his actions, or the alternatives available to him. The proposed EIS does not provide the detailed analysis of local geographic conditions necessary for the decision-maker to determine what course of action is appropriate under the circumstances.

· Additionally, the programmatic EIS does not allow those who are not part of the decision-making process to adequately evaluate and balance the factors on their own. While NEPA does not require public hearings, it does provide a formalized procedure for such citizen input. . . . Even though the actual permits may be made public, that provides only information from the government to the citizens and does not allow information to flow from the citizens to the government. . . .

. . . While the BLM has certain licensing requirements, they relate mainly to the timing and duration of the allowable grazing period and the number of animals involved. The court has examined the Federal Range Code, 43 C.F.R. § 4110.0–2 et seq. (1973), portions of the BLM Manual, and sample licenses and finds them insufficient to fulfill the purpose defined

for an impact statement. They do not adequately assess the individual district or area situations so as to provide the local decision-maker with the data necessary to analyze the alternatives open to him and their consequences. A program statement may be very helpful in assessing recurring policy issues and insuring consideration of the cumulative impact that numerous decisions might have on the environment, but that does not mean that it will suffice to fulfill the NEPA mandate. The court is convinced that the BLM programmatic statement alone, unrelated to individual geographic conditions, does not permit the "finely tuned and 'systematic' balancing analysis" mandated by NEPA. . . .

While the BLM may decide in the future to prepare specific impact statements . . . , for the present grazing will continue on millions of acres without adequate individualized assessment of the impact of such grazing on local environments, and extensive environmental damage is possible. Indeed, the plaintiffs note that the BLM Budget Justification for fiscal year 1973 estimated that only 16 percent of the BLM managed grazing land was in good or excellent condition while 84 percent was in fair, poor or bad condition. In addition, plaintiffs present evidence from both private and governmental sources demonstrating that serious deterioration of BLM lands is taking or has taken place. In its first annual report, the Council on Environmental Quality reported that overgrazing had dramatically affected the public lands.

"Much of this land, particularly the vast public domain, remains in desperate condition, as wind, rain, and drought have swept over them and eroded their exposed soils. Although the effects of overgrazing in rich pastures or prairie farmland can be quickly corrected, the process is often irreversible on the limited soils and arid climate of much of the public lands." CEQ, *Environmental Quality* 182 (1970).

Unfortunately this situation has not been rectified since that date. A recent Bureau of Land Management report entitled Effects of Livestock Grazing on Wildlife, Watershed, Recreation and Other Resource Values in Nevada

(April 1974) documents the serious damage being wrought on the environment. The report, compiled by a team of BLM resource managers, states flatly that wildlife habitat is being destroyed. "Uncontrolled, unregulated or unplanned livestock use is occurring in approximately 85 percent of the State and damage to wildlife habitat can be express[ed] only as extreme destruction." *Id.* at 13. Overgrazing by livestock has caused invasion of sagebrush and rabbitbrush on meadows and has decreased the amount of meadow habitat available for wildlife survival by at least 50 percent. The reduced meadow area has caused a decline in both game and non-game population. *Id.* at 26. In addition, there are 883 miles of streams with deteriorating and declining wildlife habitat, thus making it apparent, according to the report, that grazing systems do not protect and enhance wildlife values. *Id.* at 14, 29.

While Congress has determined that public lands should be put to the best use possible, it has also demonstrated a strong interest in protecting the environment. In the present case over 100 million acres of public land are being leased for grazing although apparently no thorough analysis has been made of the specific impact of such activity. The court is, therefore, of the opinion that major federal actions having significant effects on the environment are being taken without full NEPA compliance, even though that Act has been in effect almost five years.

The court is aware that, like many agencies, the BLM has been given large scale tasks to be accomplished with limited manpower. That does not mean, however, that the agency may ignore or pay mere lip service to the NEPA requirements. . . .

For the above reasons the court will grant relief to the plaintiffs by entering a judgment declaring that the programmatic environmental impact statement prepared by the BLM, standing alone, is not sufficient to comply with the NEPA requirements. As noted above, plaintiffs have not sought an impact statement for each permit. The crucial point is that the specific environmental effects of the permits issued be assessed. So long as the actual environmental effects of particular permits or groups of permits in specific areas are assessed, questions of format are to be left to defendants. The court will maintain jurisdiction in order to facilitate future review . . . .

* * *

Though BLM critics acknowledge that the agency is not adequately funded, they find no excuse for its failure to set and collect fees for its grazing permits at a level that is needed to cover its costs of administering and maintaining rangelands. As previously noted, loose federal grazing controls tend to encourage overgrazing practices that enhance short-term profits but damage the environment in the long term. The argument that low fees are justified because some federal grazing land is extraordinarily "rugged," does not justify the same low rate for all federal grazing lands. Similarly, the fact that most holders of federal grazing permits are relatively small ranchers (less than 500 cattle) does not justify equally low charges for the large businesses that run huge herds over very large tracts of federal land. In 1988 these large cattle concerns received the largest BLM allotments, comprising 58 percent of the allotted 162 million acres.[21]

The law requires the BLM "to protect the range and minimize adverse impacts on environmental resources" by establishing appropriate terms and conditions for grazing permits, that is, by setting grazing schedules by time, place, and number and concentration of livestock in given areas; by excluding grazing from unsuitable areas, by rotating use and rest periods of pastures; and by performing required maintenance of fences and watering facilities.[22] In 1976, Congress enacted the Federal Land Policy and Management Act (FLPMA) which broadened the duties of BLM and other federal land management agencies. FLPMA requires

BLM to prepare master land-use plans consistent with the mandate of promoting optimum "multiple use" of federal lands:

> The term multiple use means the management of the public lands and their various resource values so that they are utilized in the combination that will best meet the present and future needs of the American people . . . a combination of balanced and diverse resource uses that takes into account the long-term needs of future generations for renewable and nonrenewable resources, including, but not limited to recreation, range, timber, minerals, watershed, wildlife and fish, and natural management . . . without permanent impairment of the productivity of the land and the quality of the environment with consideration being given to the relative values of the resources and not necessarily to the combination of uses that will give the greatest economic return . . . .[23]

Thus grazing is but one of many uses that are to be encouraged, and FLPMA bars single-purpose planning and single use for grazing in ways that render rangeland unsuitable for other uses by "the American people." It is clear that Congress intended BLM to consider all potential uses in making its grazing allotments and to impose grazing conditions that will promote land conditions to support multiple uses.[24]

The criticisms leveled by more recent literature against the BLM's rangeland management can be summarized as follows:

1. Almost all BLM land is already under grazing permits. . . . BLM remains committed to serving the livestock industry, and it gives priority to needs of livestock operators while ignoring environmental considerations. Statutory mandates and judicial orders have not overcome that pattern.
2. BLM often permits more grazing than is necessary, and overestimates available forage for grazing.
3. BLM has not completed resource management plans under the FLPMA for more than half of its resource areas, and those plans are largely ineffective non-plans and "do-nothing motherhood statements which offered neither managers nor users much useful guidance on future management."
4. BLM environmental impact statements are similarly useless generalities which provide scant environmental information and analysis.
5. BLM allotments and permits may run as long as ten years, and permit holders have priority to renew them over other permit applicants. BLM routinely renews grazing permits and has resisted public input on its permit decisions and foreclosed timely, practical public input. Permit protestors had to institute legal proceedings to gain a ruling of citizen right to hearing on permit renewals.[25]

Other statutes that significantly constrain rangeland management, such as those protecting endangered species and wilderness areas, are discussed in later sections. Relatively few disputes regarding BLM rangeland and the role of public participation in BLM planning and permitting proceedings have reached the courts. With the growing number of environmental organizations, however, future court actions to test BLM decisions are likely to appear in the foreseeable future.

Forests

The U.S Forest Service administers approximately 190 million acres in 156 national forests.[26] Much of the following discussion of Forest Service management is also pertinent to forest management by the BLM and by the Department of Defense, which manages 6 million acres of forestland of which 2.3 million acres support commercial use.[27] The political and environmental problems associated with managing federal forests are similar to those characterizing the history of federal rangelands. There are, however, distinctive features of forest resources that merit separate attention.[28]

Federal forest management involves multiple tasks:

> Forest ecosystems are vital to the health and welfare of the nation for such uses as recreation, watershed, wilderness and wildlife habitat, as well as for such commodity uses as timber, minerals, and range.[29]

The most significant issues in federal management of forest resources arise in three areas, each of which is reviewed in this subsection:

1. Timber cutting
2. Wildlife protection
3. Wilderness and water-rights protection

Timber Cutting

Since the turn of the century, the ... Forest Service ... sold over sixteen billion dollars' worth of timber, mostly from the Western states, and the [Forest Service] agency presently manages over one-half the nation's inventory of merchantable soft-wood sawtimber.[30]

Congress created the national forest system by statutes of 1891 and 1897 in order to preserve the nation's forests and to promote "a continuous supply of timber." The purposes remained unchanged until Congress significantly broadened the uses of national forests by enacting a series of modern-era laws:

- Multiple Use, Sustained Yield Act of 1960 (MUSYA),
- Wilderness Act of 1964,
- National Environmental Policy Act of 1969 (NEPA),
- Endangered Species Act of 1973 (ESA), and
- National Forest Management Act of 1976 (NFMA).

These laws mandate forest management that will achieve their multiple goals. To that extent, they remove timber harvesting as the sole or prime consideration in federal forest regulation.

NFMA, the principal statute now governing federal forest management, and its implementing regulations had the immediate effect of settling some formerly unresolved issues, notably: whether "clear-cutting" of timber areas (regarded by the Forest Service and the logging industry as the most economically efficient method of harvesting timber) is lawful, and whether loggers are limited to felling only trees determined to be suitable for cutting. Under NFMA, the Forest Service may permit clear-cutting if it determines that method to be "optimum" and consistent with other uses and goals contemplated by federal laws. Even so, the law limits the size of areas that may be clear-cut. Clear-cutting often wreaks environmental havoc in forest ecosystems by causing erosion, loss of habitat, and water pollution. Environmentalists vigorously oppose clear-cutting as a violation of protective statutes and have challenged clear-cutting on public lands without Environmental Impact Studies and Statements.[31]

NEPA requires the Forest Service to prepare an Environmental Impact Statement (EIS) before opening any area for logging that threatens to cause significant adverse environmental effects. A recent federal court decision virtually eliminated clear-cutting in national forests in Texas and substantially barred similar harvesting methods that had been challenged by environmentalists.[32]

In 1992 the Forest Service issued a policy directive that would limit clear-cutting as a general commercial harvesting practice. In order to avoid protracted litigation on listing the California spotted owl as an endangered species, the Forest Service announced in January 1993 that it would eliminate clear-cutting of timber in old-growth forests of the Sierra Nevada region. If fully implemented, that policy will reduce by half the annual volume of lumber logged on 5.3 million acres of national forests in the Sierras.[33]

NFMA addresses other broad issues of balancing economic and environmental interests. It limits the amount, types, and locations of timber to be cut in national forests and it limits harvesting to that "which can be removed . . . annually in perpetuity on a sustained-yield basis." Technically, it prohibits timber removal from forest areas that cannot be renewed and restocked with like timber within five years, and it prohibits tree cutting in areas where tree removal will irreversibly damage soil or mountain slopes, adversely affect rivers and streams, or unreasonably destroy local plant and animal habitats. The importance of creating off-limit zones was highlighted by Forest Service workers who petitioned the Service to expand the tree buffer zones near waterways from the existing standard of 100 feet to 300 feet.[34]

Current laws and Forest Service regulations require long-range plans for promoting all uses intended by FLPMA and MUSYA; these include "outdoor recreation, range, timber, watershed, and wildlife and fish." Such plans are also required to provide guidelines for determining suitable areas and methods for logging. In this regard, NFMA and Forest Service regulations distinguish three classes of woodlands:

Marginal woodlands are those deemed to be unsuitable for timber production and are therefore to be withdrawn from commercial logging.

Old-growth forests are those that contain very old trees with identified characteristics of tree size and density, canopy density, and forest-floor content and that have not been regularly harvested commercially.

These forests are subjected to special guidelines, and they remain the subject of heated conflict. Over 90% of the old-growth forests in the Northwest (the nation's only remaining old-growth region) have already been felled. Although old-growth forest timber has high commercial value, old-growth stands are critical to forest ecology and to the survival of certain endangered species. These forests do not host as many species as other forest habitats, but their unique biological habitats harbor species that cannot survive elsewhere.

Even-aged forests are those that do not qualify as "marginal" or as "old growth."

In contrast to BLM procedures, which were reviewed and disapproved in the *Morton* case, the NFMA and Forest Service regulations direct that forest management plans be guided by and tailored to local conditions, rather than by undifferentiated regional standards. Provisions for public notice and public opportunity to comment on Forest Service plans are designed to assure timely, meaningful public input to the planning process.

Another controversial economic issue with environmental consequences is the criticism that the Forest Service prices timber rights in federal forests below their actual market value and below the cost of providing the timber. According to a study reported to Congress in 1984, the Service was posting an annual loss of $1 billion at that time.[35] The Ouachita Watch League, an environmentalist group, estimated that the Forest Service lost $13 million in the Ouachita and Ozark–St. Francis National Forests in 1992 alone. In response to charges that taxpayers are being forced to pay for the destruction of their own forests, some members of Congress called upon the Service to develop a more adequate cost-accounting system for pricing timber sales.[36] Current laws do not specify which cost-accounting methods the Forest Service is to use.[37]

In response to federal agencies' failure to achieve market-based costing for all federally-owned natural resources, President Clinton directed the Forest Service to develop plans to address the issue of below-market logging fees. The Service thereafter proposed a plan to terminate logging in about 40 percent of the national forests and to reduce federal timber harvests within ten years from previous annual levels of seven billion board feet to less than four and a half billion board feet. The proposed plan would affect more than 60 million acres of forestlands in 23 states and would materially affect the supply and price of lumber.[38] Predictably, this stirred vigorous opposition from affected states and business interests. Whether that proposed plan will be finally adopted or will suffer the same fate as the grazing fee proposals discussed earlier cannot be predicted at this writing.

The ability of groups or citizens to challenge Forest Service operational (rather than planning) decisions by lawsuit has not been fully settled by the courts, due largely to "standing-to-sue" barriers. As explained in Chapter 2, standing doctrines have operated to deny many private organizations opportunities to challenge agency decisions. Although some courts have granted citizens' groups standing to challenge Forest Service decisions,[39] only a few courts have reviewed the standing issue under FLMA and MUSYA. One reason for this scarcity of court review arises from government officials' failure or refusal to make their rulings "final"—a prerequisite to court review under the administrative-law doctrine that a court will not hear an appeal from an agency ruling until all administrative proceedings have been exhausted. As explained in Chapter 2, this exhaustion doctrine translates into a bar to court appeal until the agency has made its ruling on an issue "final." This agency gambit to avoid court appeals has been noted and criticized in court opinions:

> The question of exhaustion arises because plaintiffs' Second Amended Complaint seeks judicial review of Forest Service Actions on which plaintiffs have pending administrative appeals. Final decisions on these appeals are three to five months overdue. . . . [T]he litigation history in this matter indicates that the Forest Service has developed a practice of making, withdrawing, and reinstating timber sales and forest policy decisions in a way that might forestall judicial review indefinitely if left unchecked. Such a result cannot be encouraged.[40]

In making timber harvesting decisions, government officials must comply with all laws that affect their way of proceeding as well as the principal NFMA and MUSYA statutes. For example, the Forest Service cannot satisfy NEPA's procedural requirements by complying with NFMA's procedural requirements, and it must also comply with the procedures of the Endangered Species Act before taking an action that is covered by that law.[41] The cumulative impact of these different statutes on a common forest site is further explained in discussions of the Endangered Species Act and the Wilderness Act in the following subsections.

Wildlife Protection

The Endangered Species Act (ESA) is one of the most formidable barriers to federal activities that have negative ecological impacts. Its broad reach is well established.

> Protection of wildlife is currently . . . invoked as a constraint on timber harvesting in virtually all the timber regions of the country: the Red-Cockaded Woodpecker in the southeast; the caribou in Maine; the gray wolf in Minnesota and Idaho; the Mexican Spotted Owl in the southwest; and the Northern Spotted Owl, Marbled Murrelet, and Fisher in the northwest.[42]

Figure 10.3 summarizes the growth in the number of wildlife and plant species listed as "threatened" and "endangered" between 1987 and 1991.

Official listing of species as endangered has caused tensions among individuals and groups favoring industrial, social, and preservationist uses of federal lands. These tensions have been resolved decisively in favor of species protection by explicit legislation, by court decisions, and by administrative agency policies. In brief, protection of listed "endangered" species is legally mandated and is not a matter of official discretion. Although parties may dispute particular means of protection, they may not dispute the duty to protect the species. The Supreme Court explained the subordination of economic interests to endangered-species protection in the landmark "snail darter" case, which enjoined completion of a federal dam because it threatened that fish:

■ **Figure 10.3**   Threatened and Endangered U.S. Wildlife and Plants, 1981–1991

	Threatened		Endangered	
Group	*1987*	*1991*	*1987*	*1991*
	Number (cumulative)			
Mammals	7	8	50	55
Birds	10	12	76	73
Reptiles	18	18	15	16
Amphibians	4	5	5	6
Fishes	30	34	47	54
Snails	5	6	3	7
Crustaceans	1	2	7	8
Insects	7	9	10	13
Arachnids	0	0	3	3
Clams	0	2	30	40
Plants	44	61	158	229
Total	126	157	404	511

Source: U.S. Department of the Interior, Fish and Wildlife Service, Division of Endangered Species and Habitat Conservation (Washington, DC: unpublished data). CEQ, *Environmental Quality* (1991), Table 80, p. 323.

> It may seem curious . . . that the survival of a relatively small number of three-inch fish among all the countless millions of species extant would require the permanent halting of a virtually completed dam for which Congress has expended more than $100 million. . . . We conclude, however, that the explicit provisions of the Endangered Species Act require precisely that result.[43]

Congress later enacted a special law to permit completion of the dam by preserving the threatened snail darter through relocating it to a new habitat away from the dam, but significantly, it left the ESA unchanged.

Under ESA all federal agencies must

> insure that actions authorized, funded, or carried out by them do not jeopardize the continued existence of such endangered species and threatened species or result in the destruction or modification of habitat of such species which is determined . . . to be critical.[44]

The U.S. Fish and Wildlife Service, a part of the Department of the Interior, is responsible for identifying and listing species that are "endangered." Proposals to list or not to list species understandably receive close attention in view of the major impact of listing decisions on access to protected species' habitats. The Forest Service, for example, may not proceed with a proposed timber sale until it has completed study proceedings with the Fish and Wildlife Service and has received the Wildlife Service's official opinion that the proposed sale will not violate ESA's protective provisions. By imposing this interdepartmental, interagency check, Congress made it clear that it intended species protection to be a paramount consideration and not merely one of several flexible factors to be considered in planning multiple uses of federal forests. This brake on timber sales constitutes a substantive rule as well as a procedural requirement. Even though the Secretaries of Agriculture (Forest Service) and the Interior (Fish and Wildlife) are appointed by and serve at the pleasure of the President, and thus have common Administration objectives, the ESA legally obligates the Wildlife Service to exercise independent judgment in the matter of species protection.

Courts have been more generous in allowing citizen standing to sue under ESA than they have under other environmental statutes. Environmental groups have been accorded standing to seek court injunctions against the use of timber management plans that allegedly violate the ESA[45] and to challenge alleged failures of the Fish and Wildlife Service to list threatened species and to designate their critical habitats.[46] The potential for such citizen suits may serve to encourage agency initiatives to save protected species. An example may be the Forest Service's voluntary adoption of a regulation for its own internal guidance that "habitat must be provided to support, at least, a minimum number of reproductive individuals and that habitat must be well distributed so that those individuals can interact with others in the planning area."[47]

Legal contests over forest habitats of endangered species are carried on in many forums and sometimes in several forums at once. The history of conflicts over logging in the Pacific Northwest, the home of the spotted owl, is illustrative. Following the listing of the spotted owl as "endangered," lawsuits were begun in 1990 to stop timber harvesting in their habitat. While court battles proceeded, Congress enacted what was popularly known as the *Northwest Timber Compromise* to provide temporary relief against the economic losses occasioned by halting all logging in old-growth forests of the Pacific Northwest. The Compromise law prescribed logging rules only for a limited period of time (until the end of fiscal year 1990) and only for limited areas of national forests.[48] Although it authorized specified quantities of timber sales by the Forest Service and the BLM, it prohibited timber harvesting in designated areas, and it did not affect ongoing litigation or court injunctions against other planned timber sales, such as those discussed in the following important case.

■   ■

SEATTLE AUDUBON SOCIETY V. MOSELY

798 F. Supp. 1484 (W.D. Wn. 1992)

[Environmental organizations sued the Assistant Secretary of Agriculture and the Forest Service, asking the court to enjoin the Forest Service from selling logging rights on 24 million acres of Northwestern national forest areas that it alleged sustained the northern spotted owl. This opinion, one of a series in the case, granted the plaintiff's request on findings that the Service violated NEPA and other environmental laws.]

In *Seattle Audubon Society v. Evans,* . . . the court of appeals summarized the relevant parts of the National Forest Management Act ("NFMA"), . . . and the implementing regulations as follows:

The NFMA requires the Forest Service to prepare management plans for its national forests to meet the multiple-use objectives of the national forest system. . . . In keeping with the statute's mandate, the Forest Service is required to promulgate regulations that will define how the management plans are to provide for a diversity of plant and animal communities. *Id.* . . . The Forest Service responded by promulgating the regulation at issue . . . . There are at least three major components to this regulation. First, the regulation establishes as its purpose management of the forest to maintain a "viable population" of existing species. . . . Second, the Forest Service must select "indicator species" for the purpose of evaluating wildlife decisions. . . . A third part of this regulation requires the Forest Service to identify habitats critical to threatened or endangered species and prescribe measures to prevent their adverse modification. . . . The Forest Service is also required to determine objectives for appropriate conservation measures for threatened or endangered species. . . .

NFMA was preceded by the Multiple-Use Sustained-Yield Act of 1960 ("MUSY"), in which Congress declared "that the national forests are established and shall be administered for outdoor recreation, range, timber, watershed, and wildlife and fish purposes." . . .

* * *

These public lands belong to the entire nation. In enacting NFMA Congress viewed them from the perspective not of a day but of generations. Many observers have noted the Forest Service's habit of maximizing timber production at the cost of the other statutory values. . . . But such a practice, no matter how long it may have gone on, cannot change what the statute requires.

NFMA and the regulations direct that the forests be managed so as to preserve animal and plant communities. Millions of acres of national forest lands in Regions Five and Six do not consist of spotted owl habitat and are suitable for logging. . . . Congress's mandate for multiple uses, including both logging and wildlife preservation, can be fulfilled if the remaining old growth habitat is left standing; it cannot be if the old growth in any national forest is logged to the point where native vertebrate species cease to exist there.

The records of this and other reported cases show that management of the national forests in compliance with NFMA is vital because other measures are inadequate for many species. Parks and wilderness areas alone are too small to permit the spotted owl to survive. . . . The efforts of the Fish and Wildlife Service ("FWS") under the Endangered Species Act ("ESA"), 16 U.S.C. § 1531 *et seq.*, come only after a species is threatened or endangered and fall short of systematic management of a biological community. . . . In this sense the national forests offer a last chance.

The Forest Service argues that it should not be required to conduct a viability analysis as to every species. There is no such requirement. . . .

The Forest Service also argues that the question of impact on other species will be dealt with in the individual forest plans. But those plans must be adopted in compliance with the regional guidelines and standards. . . . If the guidelines are illegal, the forest plans cannot fill the gap.

The agency also contends that the statement in the FEIS describing the impact on other species is merely a quotation from comments by the Scientific Panel . . . not the agency's own view. This is what makes this a NEPA question rather than one under NFMA at this stage. If the "low to medium-low" viability rating were admittedly the Forest Service's own rating, summary judgment under NFMA would be entered now. Full NEPA compliance may or may not lead to a plan different from Alternative B. Whatever plan is adopted, it cannot be one which the agency knows or believes will probably cause the extirpation of other native vertebrate species from the planning areas.

Finally, the Forest Service argues that SAS has pleaded only an NFMA violation, not a NEPA violation, as to the "other species" issue. However, the complaint sets forth the factual allegations on the issue and draws the agency's attention to both statutes. That is enough . . . .

* * *

The *Evans* findings establish that as of the date they were entered the spotted owl was threatened with extinction throughout its range; that the Forest Service estimated that an additional 66,000 acres of the bird's habitat would be destroyed if logging sales went forward to the extent permitted by the ISC Report over the next sixteen months; and that to allow this to happen, in the absence of a legally adopted conservation plan, would risk pushing the species past a population threshold from which it could not recover, . . . "Old growth forests are lost for generations. No amount of money can replace the environmental loss." . . .

The *SAS v. Evans* findings also established that logging sales outside owl habitat areas could be made during the period of an injunction; that the logging of sales already made could go forward; that the demand for wood products was flat; that additional timber supplies could be available from private sources and from restrictions on raw log exports; that the main reasons for mill closures and job losses over the past several years have been modernization of physical plants, changes in product demand, and competition from elsewhere; that job losses will continue regardless of whether the owl is protected; and that preserving old growth forests brings substantial economic benefits. . . .

* * *

The Forest Service now seeks to do the same thing it sought a year ago—to sell further logging rights in spotted owl habitat areas, consistent with the ISC Report, while the agency is in the process of arriving at a conservation plan. The question is whether the public interest and balance of equities today, as distinguished from May 1991, require injunctive relief.

. . . While some of the statistics have changed in the past year, the basic facts remain: Irreparable harm will occur if more owl habitat is logged without a plan in place; . . .

The agency points out that in 1992 it has the ISC strategy whereas in 1991 it had no plan. But the *SAS v. Evans* order called for a plan "as required by NFMA and its implementing regulations." 771 F. Supp. at 1096. NFMA incorporates the NEPA procedures, . . . and no plan as required by the 1991 order has yet been adopted. The Forest Service's request that it be allowed to sell logging rights without a legally-adopted plan in place must be considered in light of the agency's past statements that its proposals would allow the spotted owl to survive, followed by its later admissions that they would not. For example, the 1988 ROD assured the public that the since-abandoned "SOHA" concept "provides sufficient direction for planning habitat management to maintain population viability of spotted owls." 1988 ROD at 10. In the fall of 1990 the agency admitted that this was false. *SAS v. Evans,* 771 F. Supp. at 1089.

In the meantime, Congress had largely accepted the Forest Service's assurances in enacting a 1989 statute, Section 318, which allowed increased cutting in fiscal years 1989–90.

In *Portland Audubon Society v. Lujan,* 795 F. Supp. 1489 (D. Or. 1992), the district court in Oregon, issuing an injunction under NEPA, stated:

> The purpose of requiring a Supplemental Environment Impact Statement is to "ensure [ ] that the agency will not act on incomplete information, only to regret its decision after it is too late to correct." *Marsh v. Oregon Natural Resources Council,* [490 U.S. at 371], 109 S. Ct. at 1858. Going forward with timber sales without the preparation of a Supplemental Environmental Impact Statement or its equivalent is directly contrary to that purpose.

The same holds true here, and an injunction must be issued.

* * *

NEPA requires that an agency charged with preparing an environmental impact statement take a "hard look" at the environmental consequences of the project, and that it disclose the risks, present the alternatives, and respond with reasoned analysis to the opinions of reputable scientists concerning the hazards. . . . That requires here the adoption of an EIS which will cure the shortcomings identified in the May 28 order. . . .

* * *

The history of this matter shows the need for a timetable to assure prompt agency compliance. The Forest Service has been gathering and evaluating data on the spotted owl for years. In October 1989 Congress directed the agency to have a revised owl plan in place eleven months later. The Forest Service did not comply or attempt to comply.

In May 1991 this court ordered the adoption of a plan by March 1992; the net result was to give the agency a seventeen-month extension to finish the job that Congress had mandated be done by September 30, 1990.

While the Forest Service asked for a specific time allowance in *SAS v. Evans,* . . . it now contends that the court lacks the power to impose a timetable at all, and that none should be adopted. But the absence of a deadline could make an injunction meaningless; without a time for compliance, there could be open-ended delay. The interests of all concerned, including the timber industry, require the earliest possible resolution. . . . A timetable is necessary here, and one will be adopted as soon as the agency's time estimate and the other parties' comments are received in accordance with Section VII, below.

VII.

Injunction

For the reasons stated, it is ordered and adjudged that:

A.   The Forest Service is enjoined to prepare a new or supplemental EIS in compliance with NEPA. . . .

B.   The Forest Service is directed to file by July 14, 1992, its proposed schedule for completion of the steps required by paragraph A, above, and SAS and WCLA are directed to file by July 17, 1992, any comments on the schedule;

C.   The court will issue an order adopting a timetable after the agency's proposed schedule and the other parties' comments have been received; and

D.   The Forest Service is enjoined from auctioning or awarding any additional timber sales in Forest Service Regions Five and Six that would log suitable habitat for the northern spotted owl until revised standards and guidelines in compliance with NEPA and NFMA are adopted and in effect.

It should be noted that although the *Seattle Audubon* case does not involve or cover privately owned timberlands, private forests are also subject to the ESA and its incidental logging restraints.

In response to the economic effects of the *Seattle Audubon* decision, the Clinton Administration endeavored to fashion a new forest plan and Environmental Impact Study that would satisfy the plaintiffs' environmental demands and persuade Judge Dwyer to modify his injunction to permit logging in identified areas of Northwestern national forests. The administration's effort included supplemental proposals to grant federal financial assistance to logging industries, towns, and workers adversely affected by the logging restrictions. Following an administration-sponsored ''summit'' conference of interested parties in April 1993 and reports by an advisory group of private experts and officials of several federal agencies, public hearings were held on the proposed new plan. In February 1994 the President announced a ''final'' plan and Supplemental Environmental Impact Statement for logging federal forests in the Pacific Northwest and a planned governmental petition to Judge Dwyer to alter his outstanding injunction to permit logging in accordance with the new administration EIS and plan.[49] The new plan envisaged that certain areas of the forests would be set aside and protected from logging; that ''no-logging'' zones near waterways would be broadened; and that in areas where logging is permitted, timber harvesting would be subject to specified annual limits of about one fifth of the previous annual average harvest.[50] The President proposed to mitigate adverse economic effects of his proposal on local communities (including the loss of an estimated 9,500 jobs) by a federal aid program of $1.5 billion to provide economic development assistance, job training, and worker assistance. In June 1994, Judge Dwyer preliminarily ruled that the administration's proposal satisfied the ESA and lifted the injunction. It remains to be seen whether these proposals will

- satisfy other legal requirements and receive final approval by the court;
- start a new round of lawsuits to overturn the new proposal by dissatisfied industry, union, or environmental organizations; or
- trigger renewed attempts by dissatisfied parties or legislators to press for new laws to change or overturn the administration proposal.

Notwithstanding the failure to achieve widespread consensus in the *Seattle* case, the Clinton Administration has continued to encourage industry, labor unions, and environmental organizations to settle their differences by discussion and negotiation, rather than by costly court and legislative battles. This approach has gained some acceptance and results in fashioning federal land-use agreements that are tolerable to major adversaries. In March 1993, the Secretary of the Interior announced that the Administration would work with businesses and conservationists to develop plans to preserve the California Gnatcatcher, a threatened bird species in woodlands undergoing urban development. The parties planned to reserve areas needed for the bird's habitat by excluding new housing from specified zones. Similarly, in April 1993, the Georgia Pacific Corporation, the nation's largest timber company, agreed to protect the Red Cockaded Woodpecker in its privately owned forests, by leaving uncut ten acres of trees and brush surrounding each colony of the threatened species. In exchange, the Clinton Administration agreed not to raise an ESA challenge to the company's timber harvesting in that forest.[51] Other extralegal negotiated approaches to preserving endangered species on privately owned land include land exchanges, by which federal forest acreage is exchanged for privately owned forest acreage that harbors endangered species.[52]

Although the legality of such bargained arrangements has not been fully tested, their practical outcomes are likely to lead to increased acceptance of them over time.

The Migratory Bird Treaty Act[53] provides additional protection to migratory bird species. The Fish and Wildlife Service greatly expanded the list of birds classified as "migratory" to include such common species as crows, hawks, robins, and sparrows.[54] Theoretically, logging companies might be prosecuted for *directly* destroying even these common birds by cutting trees that contain their young, but the government has not pushed enforcement of the statute that far. Neither has it contended that migratory bird laws prohibit *indirect* harm to birds, such as removal of trees constituting part of their natural habitat. State governments may adopt wildlife protection laws more stringent than federal laws so long as they do not contravene federal law.

Private landowners may resist federal or state wildlife-protective regulations that deprive them of "all reasonable use" of their property on the ground that such regulations amount to a government "taking" without compensation, a violation of the Takings Clause of the Constitution. The *Lucas* case (excerpted in Chapter 8) established that a regulation that is economically restrictive or burdensome does not in itself deprive an owner of "all reasonable use" of a property. For this reason, private forest owners have not made serious attempts to defeat species-protection regulations as unconstitutional takings.

Wilderness and Water-Rights Protection

The Wilderness Act of 1964 authorizes the creation of a National Wilderness Preservation System and affords special protections to forest areas that are classified and reserved as wilderness. The act defines *wilderness* as a place "where the earth and its community of life are untrammeled by man . . ." and as an "undeveloped Federal land retaining its primeval character and influence, without permanent improvements or human habitation, which is protected and managed so as to preserve its natural conditions. . . ."[55] Under the Act, Congress may designate additional wilderness areas, and federal agencies must study, identify, and recommend lands for wilderness designation.

The Wilderness Act forbids human or commercial activities that are incompatible with preserving the character of the wilderness.[56] With limited exceptions, it prohibits the construction of infrastructure (such as permanent roads) for economic or commercial development of wilderness resources. Excepted from the ban on infrastructure development are service facilities that support Wilderness Act purposes (that is, "recreation, scenic, scientific, educational, conservational, and historic use"); facilities that preserve rights that were established before Congress designated the area as wilderness (for example, aircraft landing strips, grazing, motorboat use); and facilities that support conservation activities or wilderness conditions (such as control of fires, insects, and disease).[57] These exceptions do not preclude federal regulation of the excepted activities to minimize environmental damage.[58] Other Wilderness Act exceptions may be enacted to avoid constitutional questions. For example, it is unclear whether mining claims on tracts later designated as wilderness areas could "ripen" into property rights that could not be withdrawn without payment of government compensation.[59]

The management of wilderness lands under the Wilderness Act remains with the federal agencies that managed them before their designation as wilderness. Accordingly, wilderness lands are managed by the BLM, the Forest Service, the Fish and Wildlife Service, and the National Park Service. To date, Congress has designated some 361 reserves as part of the National Wilderness Preservation System. The BLM manages 61 million acres in 166 wilderness units (mostly in

Alaska), and the Forest Service manages 33.6 million acres, 80 percent of the wilderness areas in the 48 contiguous states.[60]

Although the Wilderness Act leaves the regulating agency discretion to decide which activities are consistent with preserving the character of the wilderness under its management, agency determinations are often challenged by environmental organizations. Courts have entertained such challenges even though the act does not expressly provide for judicial review of those agency determinations:

> We have determined that the Wilderness Act does provide limited guidelines by which courts may review the action or inaction of the Forest Service. As our opinion notes, judicial review extends to conduct of the agency that represents an abdication of its '. . . mandate to preserve the wilderness characteristics of the wilderness areas.'[61]

Courts will not overturn agency decisions unless the challengers make a clear showing of some immediate harm that a court has power to redress. With regard to an area that is being considered for wilderness designation, a court will find a violation of the duty to preserve its character only if it considers the managing agency's determination to be unreasonable.[62]

It remains unclear whether the Act empowers the government to restrain private activities in areas adjoining designated wilderness on the ground that the activity may damage or alter the character of the wilderness reserve.[63]

A major issue affecting public land environments, particularly in wilderness areas, is the extent to which the federal government has exercised its acknowledged right to reserve water flows in or needed for the support of federal land areas. It is sometimes difficult to determine whether and to what extent Congress intended to exercise its right to appropriate water from rivers and streams. Since water is so vital to the environmental and economic health of the Western states, this determination is crucial in deciding competing claims of state governments and citizens to appropriate waters from natural waterways. The *United States v. New Mexico* opinion excerpt illustrates the complex role of water law in preserving the resources and ecology of Western lands.[64]

UNITED STATES v. NEW MEXICO

438 U.S. 696 (1978)

[This suit was begun in a state court to determine the rights of farmers, miners, and other private parties to take water from the Rio Mimbres in New Mexico. The United States intervened to claim that Congress, by creating the Gila National Forest, reserved federal rights to use the river's water "as may be necessary for the purposes for which [the] national forest was created." In hearing the appeal of the case, the United States Supreme Court had occasion to note the complexity of laws governing rights to scarce water resources.]

Mr. Justice REHNQUIST delivered the opinion of the Court.

The Rio Mimbres rises in the southwestern highlands of New Mexico and flows generally southward, finally disappearing in a desert sink just north of the Mexican border. The river originates in the upper reaches of the Gila National Forest, but during the course it winds more than 50 miles past privately owned lands and provides substantial water for both irrigation and mining. In 1970, a stream adjudication was begun by the State of New Mexico to determine the exact rights of each user to water from the Rio Mimbres. In this adjudication the United States claimed reserved water rights for use in the Gila National Forest. The State District Court held that the United States, in setting the Gila National Forest aside from other public lands, reserved the use of such water "as may be necessary for the purposes for which [the land was] withdrawn," but that these purposes did not include recreation, aesthetics, wildlife preservation, or cattle grazing. The United States appealed unsuccessfully to the Supreme Court of New Mexico. . . . We granted certiorari to consider whether the Supreme Court of New Mexico had applied the correct principles of federal law in determining petitioner's reserved rights in Mimbres.

I

The question posed in this case—what quantity of water, if any, the United States reserved out of the Rio Mimbres when it set aside the Gila National Forest in 1899—is a question of implied intent and not power. In California v United States, . . . we had occasion to discuss the respective authority of Federal and State Governments over waters in the Western States. The Court has previously concluded that whatever powers the States acquired over their waters as a result of congressional Acts and admission into the union, however, Congress did not intend thereby to relinquish its authority to reserve unappropriated water in the future for use on appurtenant lands withdrawn from the public domain for specific federal purposes. . . .

Recognition of Congress' power to reserve water for land which is itself set apart from the public domain, however, does not answer the question of the amount of water which has been reserved or the purposes for which the water may be used. Substantial portions of the public domain *have* been withdrawn and reserved by the United States for use as Indian reservations, forest reserves, national parks, and national monuments. And water is frequently necessary to achieve the purposes for which these reservations are made. But Congress has seldom expressly reserved water for use on these withdrawn lands. If water were abundant, Congress' silence would pose no problem. In the arid parts of the West, however, claims to water for use on federal reservations inescapably vie with other public and private claims for the limited quantities to be found in the rivers and streams. This competition is compounded by the sheer quantity of reserved lands in the Western States, which lands form brightly colored swaths across the maps of these States.

The Court has previously concluded that Congress, in giving the President the power to reserve portions of the federal domain for specific federal purposes, *impliedly* authorized him to reserve "appurtenant water then unappropriated to *the extent needed to accomplish the purpose of the reservation.*". . .

* * *

II

A

The quantification of reserved water rights for the national forests is of critical importance to the West, where, as noted earlier, water is scarce and where more than 50% of the available water either originates in or flows through national forests. When, as in the case of the Rio Mimbres, a river is fully appropriated, federal reserved water rights will frequently require a gallon-for-gallon reduction in the amount of water available for water-needy state and private appropriators. This reality has not escaped the attention of Congress and must be weighed in determining what, if any, water Congress reserved for use in the national forests.

* * *

The Creative Act of 1891 unfortunately did not solve the forest problems of the expanding Nation. To the dismay of the conservationists, the new national forests were not adequately attended and regulated; fires and indiscriminate timber cutting continued their toll. . . . President Cleveland, in particular, responded to pleas of conservationists for greater protective measures by reserving some 21 million acres of "generally settled" forest land on February 22, 1897. President Cleveland's action drew immediate and strong protest from Western Congressmen who felt that the "hasty and ill considered" reservation might prove disastrous to the settlers living on or near these lands.

Congress' answer to these continuing problems was threefold. It suspended the President's Executive Order of February 22, 1897; it carefully defined the purposes for which national forests could in the future be reserved; and it provided a charter for forest management and economic uses within the forests. Organic Administration Act of June 4, 1897, . . .

* * *

The legislative debates surrounding the Organic Administration Act of 1897 and its predecessor bills demonstrate that Congress intended national forests to be reserved for only two purposes—"[t]o conserve the water flows and to furnish a continuous supply of timber for the people." . . .

* * *

Congress intended that water would be reserved only where necessary to preserve the timber or to secure favorable water flows for private and public uses under state law. This intent is revealed in the purposes for which the national forest system was created and Congress' principled deference to state water law in the Organic Administration Act of 1897 and other legislation. The decision of the Supreme Court of New Mexico is faithful to this congressional intent and is therefore affirmed.

* * *

A dissenting opinion (which does not appear in the excerpt) would have found that the federal government had reserved all waters needed to support the entire ecology of the wilderness areas, not merely the amount needed to support timber growth. The inconsistent patchwork of water-reservation statutes which Congress enacted on a piecemeal basis, and its failure to establish clear water policy for some areas creates uncertainty and controversy over the extent of reserved federal water rights.[65] Even where legislation is silent on water reservation, there are seemingly valid legal arguments for the President to claim priority of federal rights to water resources; for example, to protect the federal domain or to maintain military bases. However, the executive branch, like Congress, has only occasionally asserted this position, and the government's failure to press for decisive court rulings perpetuates fierce political and legal battles in the water-scarce West.[66]

Mineral Resources

Minerals on federal lands, including hard-rock minerals and mineral fuels (oil, gas, shale), may be mined only as permitted by law. A number of federal statutes deal with particular classes of minerals and mining methods; for example, the Mining Act of 1872, the Onshore Oil and Gas Leasing Reform Act of 1987, and laws dealing with coal mines and strip mining. Only the Mining Act of 1872, the major law affecting hard-rock mining on federal lands, is discussed in this subsection. The features of other mining statutes must be left to study elsewhere. Some sources of information on those laws are listed in the endnote.[67]

Mining operations generate huge amounts of pollution and wastes that degrade the mined land and the surrounding environment. Hard-rock mining creates several classes of debris which implicate different environmental hazards and which necessitate different environmental controls. These include:

Mine waste, the soil or rock that is removed from the earth in order to retrieve ore-bearing rock;

Tailings, the residual wastes of milling, a grinding process that separates ores from the ore-containing rock;

Slag, the waste produced by smelting, a heating process that separates particular metals in the ores; and

Leachate, the residue of liquids that have passed through mined materials.

According to a 1985 EPA Mine Wastes Study, mining operations were annually generating 706 million metric tons of mine waste, 481 million metric tons of tailings, 200 million metric tons of leachate wastes, as well as gases and other pollutants.[68] One example of adverse environmental impacts is the use of cyanide solutions to extract gold from low-grade ores. Called *heap leaching,* the process causes:

> . . . water contamination due to cyanide leakage and acid runoff . . . creation of arguably hazardous solid wastes, destruction of wetlands by mine dewatering, the need for reclamation of mined lands, . . . hazards to migratory birds and the endangered desert tortoise. . . .[69]

The Mining Act of 1872 addresses the mining of minerals other than oil, gas, coal, and oil shale. It opened federal lands to private mineral exploration and exploitation:

> Under the Mining Act of 1872 . . . a private citizen may enter federal lands to explore for mineral deposits. If the person locates a valuable mineral deposit on federal land, and perfects the claim by properly staking it and complying with other statutory requirements, the claimant "shall have the exclusive right of possession and enjoyment of all the surface included within the lines of their location" . . . although the United States retains title to the land. The holder of a perfected mining claim may secure a patent to the land by complying with the requirements of the Mining Act, and regulations promulgated thereunder, . . . and, upon the issuance of the patent, legal title to the land passes to the patent holder.[70]

This very old law thus allows an individual or a business to obtain a federal permit to mine valuable minerals on federal land without incurring an obligation to pay royalties for minerals taken from those lands. It also grants the permittee the right to file a claim and take absolute title to the land and its mineral resources at a nominal statutory cost (generally five dollars per acre) that bears no relation whatever to the value of the land or its minerals. Nor does the Mining Act provide for regulating mine wastes or for reclaiming abandoned mines. The National Park Service estimated that it would cost $50 million to reclaim 10,000 abandoned mines on federal lands.[71]

In one recent case, a company patented 910 acres of national forest near Bear Valley Creek outside of Boise, Idaho, for $2,277.50, and dredge-mined millions of pounds of rare-earth minerals and uranium. The mining operation buried chinook salmon spawning grounds 37 miles downstream with waste sediments. It also created a hazardous radioactive site which cost taxpayers two million dollars to clean up. In order to prevent further mining which would undermine the $2.8-million dollar Shoshone–Bannock Indian salmon-restoration project, the federal government was forced to repurchase the 910 acres from the company for $5.9 million.[72]

The environmental toll of unregulated mining and the annual "sale" of literally billions of dollars' worth of publicly owned minerals for almost no payment to the U.S. treasury has been deplored for years. As Secretary of the Interior Bruce Babbit observed in 1991,

> Hard-rock mining is the one area of federal resource law where the unrestrained giveaway, environment be damned attitudes of the 19th century have persisted.

... The time is long overdue to reform a law [that was] passed four years before the Battle of the Little Big Horn.[73]

In May 1994, Secretary Babbit was required, by court order in response to a suit brought under the Mining Act, to transfer to a Canadian mining company 1949 acres of federal mining lands reportedly containing 30 million ounces of gold in exchange for $5 per acre. (Refined gold was then valued at about $380 per ounce.) The Secretary called the transaction "the biggest gold heist since the days of Butch Cassidy."[74] Babbit was facing similar demands from hundreds of other mining companies at the time, each of them rushing to perfect their titles to federal mining lands lest Congress should suddenly stir itself to amend the Mining Law in ways that would prohibit such giveaways of federal lands and royalty-free mining. As of October 1994, the anticipated amendments to the Mining Act remained "unfinished business" for Congress.

In November 1993, the House of Representatives approved a bill that would:

1. require miners to pay the federal government royalties amounting to 8 percent of the gross value of hard-rock minerals extracted from federal lands,
2. end the ability of mining companies and prospectors to gain title to public mining properties,
3. authorize the Department of the Interior to deny mining permits for public lands that are unsuitable for mining activities, and
4. reserve the proposed royalties and other mining fees in a special fund for reclaiming abandoned mines.[75]

The bill represented a compromise between the 12.5 percent royalty rate sought by the President and the 2 percent rate of a Senate bill. It also constituted a compromise between stricter regulatory standards sought by environmentalists and the Administration and the looser standards advocated by mining interests and some Western senators. The considerable differences between the House and Senate bills must be reconciled by a House–Senate Conference Committee, and any bill proposed by the Conference must then be remanded to and approved by each chamber before it can become law. As of April 1994, however, the Conference Committee had not even been arranged or convened.

Given the opposition of some mining interests and their supporters in the Senate to the Administration's proposed mining fees and regulations, it is not possible to predict

-   when a bill will come out of the Congress,
-   what shape it will take,
-   whether it will be blocked or defeated by Senate vote or filibuster,
-   whether and when any enacted version will face court challenges by interest groups or organizations that disapprove of the final Congressional product.

To fill the void of regulation under the Mining Law, EPA has over the years endeavored to study and develop programs for regulating mine wastes under general environmental laws, such as the RCRA and Superfund statutes. These efforts have met resistance from several sources. Mining companies generally argue that state mining regulations and their own private solutions are preferable to EPA programs. The Bureau of Mines, a bureau of the Department of the Interior, advocated that a new RCRA subchapter be enacted to deal specifically with mine-waste regulation. Environmental organizations continue to complain of lax mining laws and regulations. Finally, many regulatory changes desired by the Clinton Administration cannot be effected by Executive Orders alone and require action by Congress to update or replace the Mining Act of 1872.

Although CERCLA (the Superfund law) provides mechanisms to enforce cleanup of mining wastes, many of which are "hazardous substances," polluted mining-waste sites often remain undiscovered until long after mining has ceased and long after responsible parties can be found to undertake or pay for such cleanups. Without laws to prevent mine-waste accumulation, the government and taxpayers will continue to shoulder the costs of such cleanups.

Other statutes that attempt to foster environmental protection of mineral lands include the Federal Land Policy and Management Act of 1976 (FLPMA), which is reviewed in section 10.1, and the National Environmental Policy Act (NEPA) which is reviewed in Chapter 3. FLPMA mandates federal officials "by regulation or otherwise, to take any action necessary to prevent . . . undue degradation of the lands.[76] NEPA furnishes procedural grounds to restrain environmentally harmful mining practices on federal lands that were not preceded by requisite NEPA environmental assessments and impacts studies.[77] Neither of these statutes, however, provides effective regulations for the day-to-day conduct of mining operations.

10.3   Native American Tribal Lands

The body of environmental law and regulation concerning the use of Indian lands is even more checkered than laws pertaining to other federal lands. The respective jurisdictions of the Indian tribes, the federal government, and state governments to regulate Indian lands are perennially contested in the courts. Unless Indian tribes have legally recognized jurisdiction over their lands, their lands may be regulated much the same as privately held lands. The legal status of different Indian tribes and different classes of Indian lands is unique and involves a maze of federal laws and treaties that govern various Indian tribes and the different categories of Indian lands.

> The tribes to be sure are "a good deal more than private voluntary organizations" and are aptly described as "unique aggregations possessing attributes of sovereignty over both their members and their territory". . . .
>
> * * *
>
> [J]urisdiction in "Indian country" . . . is governed by a complex patchwork of federal, state, and tribal law.[78]

This section presents a simplified sketch of the relation of federal and state environmental statutes to Indian lands. Publications that provide fuller studies of the relevant laws and issues on environmental regulation of Indian territory are listed in the endnotes.[79]

The law governing Indian tribes and Indian lands is founded principally upon three sources:

- doctrines governing Indian tribes' claims to independent nationhood and sovereignty;
- treaties between Indian tribes and the United States, and
- congressional authority to regulate Indian affairs.

Claims of Inherent Tribal Sovereignty

To the extent that the governance of an Indian tribe has not been ceded to or withdrawn by the federal government, Indian tribes retain part of their original independence and jurisdiction over their tribal affairs and activities on their tribal lands. It is equally settled that the federal government may dissolve tribal sovereignty, whether by conquest, treaty, or abrogation of prior treaties. Hence the critical questions: (a) has Congress by law preserved or withdrawn a given tribe's claimed independent power as a nation, and (b) does a disputed Indian action fall within or beyond the determined scope of that tribe's retained governing power and autonomy.[80]

Although Justices of the U.S. Supreme Court have acknowledged the retention of some tribal independence from outside regulation, they have often disagreed on the extent and effect of Indian sovereignty doctrines and on the limits of tribal control over tribal lands.

The Supreme Court has not directly decided the relationship of tribal sovereignty to environmental regulation of Indian lands, but some of its decisions strongly suggest that a tribe's sovereign authority is confined to matters involving its *internal affairs*—that is, to decisions that affect the members of the tribe, except where tribal control over nonmembers is necessary to preserve the tribe's political integrity, economic security, or health. Where Congress has not expressly withdrawn tribal sovereignty, there is room for argument over which kinds of concerns fall within the purview of the tribe's "internal affairs."

A variant of the "internal affairs" test of tribal authority involves a *territorial standard*, which considers the ownership of the affected Indian lands; specifically, whether the land is:

- held by the United States in trust for a particular tribe,
- owned absolutely by the tribe,
- owned individually by tribal members, or
- owned by parties who are not members of the tribe.

With respect to tribal members, the territorial classification is not decisive unless Congress withdraws tribal sovereignty over tribal members as well. However, when Indian lands have been opened to and acquired by the general public, tribal authority may remain if Indian control of the land is necessary for preserving the integrity of the tribe.

Where tribal authority to govern is acknowledged, a tribe may choose to surrender its authority for specified purposes or transactions. Examples of this include contracts or agreements with individuals that open Indian reservation lands to general public use or ownership and agreements with governments pertaining to particular activities on Indian lands. The rapid development of gambling casinos on Indian reservations throughout the country has given rise to many new agreements between tribes and state governments regarding their respective regulatory authority over different aspects of casino operations. It is not difficult to conceive situations where these agreements will implicate environmental concerns and raise jurisdictional conflicts on environmental regulation among tribes, the states, and the federal government.

Treaties with the United States

Although the federal government could by treaty vest a tribe with absolute authority over its tribal lands, the point is largely academic since Congress has never done so. To the contrary, Congress has abrogated many Indian treaties that could have barred federal and state environmental regulations in Indian lands. Indeed, several statutes that empower EPA to decide whether or not to delegate environmental regulatory power to Indian tribes suggest that Congress intended to deny Indian independence from federal environmental laws and thus to override any inconsistent tribal regulations. As explained in Chapter 2, the Supremacy Clause of the Constitution defeats laws that conflict with federal authority, and as previously stated, Congress may unilaterally withdraw Indian sovereignty.[81]

Congressional Delegations of Regulatory Authority to Tribes

The most meaningful source of tribal authority to regulate the environment, or to immunize Indian lands from federal or state regulation rests with the power of Congress to grant or deny tribe's authority to regulate reservation lands under congressionally specified conditions. In enacting environmental laws, however, Congress has not evinced a uniform policy on delegating regulatory jurisdiction over Indian lands.[82] This inconsistent and incomplete development of federal environmental policy is evident in the following review of pertinent environmental statutes.

When NEPA was enacted in 1969, Indian tribes did not consider themselves to be bound by it. A lower court ruled, however, that a tribe must produce at least a preliminary environmental assessment, if not a full environmental impact study, for any plan to develop reservation lands.[83] Some statutes permit tribes that meet specified conditions to regulate uses of reservation lands regardless of the nature of individual ownership of lands on Indian reservations. Under the 1990 amendments to the Clean Air Act, a tribe may be granted the same regulatory power that is given to an individual state if it submits an adequate implementation plan and shows adequate governing capacity to achieve the CAA's purposes. Similarly, under the 1987 amendments to the Clean Water Act, a tribe may be accorded the same regulatory authority that is granted to a state government for most purposes, if it receives government approval of satisfactory water-quality requirements. The Safe Drinking Water Act authorizes EPA to determine a tribe's regulatory jurisdiction on a case-by-case basis.

In contrast to the foregoing statutes, CERCLA and RCRA do not expressly permit federal agencies to delegate regulatory jurisdiction to tribes. CERCLA mentions specific situations in which tribes may arguably be permitted to exercise regulatory authority, but RCRA does not appear to do so, even though (as noted in the *Colorado* case, excerpted in section 10.4) RCRA policy favors delegating environmental regulation to state governments. Proposed amendments to RCRA would accord Indian tribes the same opportunities for delegated regulatory authority that are given the states. Those proposals had not yet been enacted by mid 1994. One commentator has suggested that a tribal regulation of hazardous waste that is more strict than RCRA or state law should be considered valid as consistent with, rather than contrary to federal law, even in the absence of a RCRA provision for delegation of regulatory authority to a tribe.[84] A contrary argument could be made that Congress intended RCRA regulation to be exclusive and to preempt all regulations that are not authorized by RCRA. Like RCRA, the Federal Insecticide, Fungicide and Rodenticide Act (FIFRA) contains no express provision to accord tribal governments regulatory authority.

Environmental disputes between state and tribal governments also hinge on the intent of federal laws, particularly whether a state regulation infringes on a federally recognized tribal right or is inconsistent with the operation of a federal environmental statute. Therefore, in any given case the question of whether a federal law preserves or subordinates tribal authority with regard to a state regulation turns ultimately upon the intention of the pertinent federal law. Such questions cannot be answered in the abstract, because the answers depend upon the impact of specific state regulations on specific Indian tribes and specific Indian lands. Thus a court could uphold an EPA decision that interpreted RCRA as precluding state regulation over Indian lands, either on grounds of tribal sovereignty or as a matter of federal policy for regulation of Indian lands.[85] The few lower-court decisions in this area are not decisive, and until such questions are clarified by Congress or the U.S. Supreme Court, lower courts are free to reach different conclusions regarding congressional intent concerning the authority of each tribe to regulate specific activities on various classes of its lands.

10.4 Environmental Compliance and Cleanup of Federal Facilities

By the end of 1987, federal agencies had identified approximately 5,400 possible federally-owned hazardous waste sites and an estimated 387,000 government owned buildings at 27,000 locations where hazardous waste might be found.[86] As this section points out, many of these properties are among the nation's worst hazardous and toxic waste sites, making the federal government one of the nation's worst polluters. Over the years several presidents urged federal agencies to adopt environmentally protective practices at the facilities they administer, but those directives have not stopped environmentally damaging practices at federal facilities.

The Legacy of Federal Environmental Violations

Deliberate disregard of hazardous-waste-management laws by operators of federal facilities has led to pressing environmental problems. Long-running violations at federal nuclear facilities and the crises they currently present are indicated in the following reports:

> On June 6, 1989, seventy agents from the FBI and EPA . . . entered the Department of Energy Rocky Flats nuclear weapons plant in Colorado. Capping a ten-month criminal investigation, the search exposed a wide range of environmental violations, including the secret incineration of hazardous wastes, false claims of compliance with ground water monitoring requirements, and intentional mixing of hazardous and radioactive wastes. The Rocky Flats incident is a particularly dramatic but nonetheless accurate reflection of the type of environmental problems created by federal facilities.[87]

> Engineers rushing to build nuclear bombs in the 1950s dumped millions of gallons of radioactive waste into the ground at the Hanford nuclear reservation near Richland, Washington . . . . But the Federal Government is still struggling to measure the level of contamination . . . . Wind, rain, birds, animals and underground water flow can all spread the radioactivity to the Columbia River. . . .[88]

At Hanford, nine reactors released millions of curies of radioactivity into the environment. During the 1950s, 127 millions of gallons of long-lived radioactive waste were dumped into trenches or injected into underground drainage systems, which filtered radioactive materials through the soil to an underground aquifer that flows to the Columbia River. Over the years, hundreds of underground storage tanks have leaked more than 500,000 gallons of higher-level radioactive wastes into the ground; those tanks continued to leak and pose a continuing risk of explosion. Plutonium that was discharged into the soil has the potential to clump together and spark a nuclear reaction. The Department of Energy is reportedly still discharging chemical and radioactive wastes into the ground at Hanford. The Hanford cleanup will require disposing of 30 million cubic feet of nuclear waste and perhaps 3 billion cubic feet of contaminated soil, at an estimated cost of $57 billion.

Rocky Flats and Hanford present only the most visible environmental disasters at federal facilities. The Department of Energy operates at least 16 major nuclear-weapons-production facilities, and the Department of Defense manages scores of facilities, military bases, and nuclear test sites where nuclear and nonradioactive hazardous materials and weapons have been tested and stored. As discussed in Chapter 6, huge quantities of radioactive materials—reactors, reactor rods, protective clothing, and contaminated soils for which no adequate treatment technologies are known to exist—remain in "temporary" storage at these facilities.

The legacy of poor environmental stewardship by government officials and government contractors is monumental. The costs of that legacy are impossible to quantify in material or psychological terms—whether in terms of damage to the environment, public health and welfare, natural-resource losses, cleanup costs, or in terms of the poor example that this legacy sets for private businesses and citizens. In flouting their own regulations, government agencies have manifested an attitude that complying with environmental statutes is secondary to carrying out the business at hand, such as developing military weapons or energy sources. The extent to which this attitude encourages the private sector to disregard environmental laws and discount environmental harms cannot be known, but it clearly provides a convenient excuse for engaging in similar environmental misconduct and thus undermines the effectiveness of environmental laws and regulations.

Obstacles to Environmental Enforcement against Federal Facilities

The principal legal difficulties encountered by EPA in regulating federal facilities arise from relationships between different governmental agencies. EPA's jurisdiction to impose and enforce environmental regulations at federal facilities is often contested by other federal departments. Conversely, the claims of those departments to immunity from environmental law enforcement are contested by EPA. EPA oversight of federal facilities management is impeded not only by disputes between EPA and other federal agencies, but also by disputes between EPA and state governments, and between EPA and environmental organizations, with respect to the proper enforcement roles of these parties under particular statutes.

When confronted with EPA enforcement attempts, federal facilities operators have argued that EPA cannot act against them because they have been designated by the President to manage a particular facility and EPA enforcement would undermine the President's constitutional authority to decide how the executive branch should carry out the laws. Managing agencies further argue that because all agencies in the federal executive branch, including the EPA, are part of the President's single "unitary executive," EPA proceedings against a sister agency of the same "unitary executive" are unconstitutional. These arguments have not been fully settled by the courts, but they have been invoked to deter EPA enforcement, whether by a President, the Department of Justice, or an agency targeted for EPA enforcement.

Perhaps the greatest hindrance to EPA enforcement efforts springs from the roles assigned to the U.S. Department of Justice (DOJ), namely, that of representing the various agencies of the executive branch. The DOJ must decide whether, when, and how to carry forward a request by one federal agency to institute legal action against another federal agency. EPA cannot itself initiate court actions but must ask the Department of Justice to do so on its behalf. DOJ, however, is charged with providing legal representation to other affected federal departments and agencies—such as the Department of Defense, whose facilities may be charged with environmental law violations. Thus DOJ may in one case commence enforcement proceedings on behalf of EPA, and in another case defend a federal agency against EPA orders or complaints.

When EPA requests DOJ to bring suit against another federal agency or official, DOJ faces two curious dilemmas: the *ethical* problem of trying to represent adverse parties, and the *practical* problem of allocating its resources to prosecute and defend the same legal action. Generally an attorney is not allowed to represent opposite sides of the same case, as this would violate the professional duty of undivided loyalty to the client. Although this conflict-of-interest rule does not legally bind DOJ, dual representation nevertheless raises important problems for legal representation—namely, the development of a legal strategy for attacking the weaknesses of the opponent's case while downplaying the weaknesses of the client's case. An attorney who represents both sides cannot help but expose or compromise the weaknesses of both sides, thus undermining the integrity of legal representation. In private law practice, the knowledge of one firm attorney is imputed to all other firm attorneys, since all firm members are considered allied to support the firm client. Unless the firm creates a "Chinese wall" or other mechanism for assuring that members representing opposing parties have no access to the other side's information or strategy, a conflict-of-interest is unavoidable.

In representing adverse government agencies, the DOJ is not actually required to ensure that information possessed by a DOJ prosecuting lawyer is not shared with the DOJ lawyer who is defending the target of prosecution in the same case. The possibility that information will be shared is an obvious disincentive for EPA to seek DOJ's assistance in bringing judicial suits in cases (not uncommon) where the case outcome may depend on the work-product of attorney and other agency personnel. The potential for factual, if not legal, conflicts-of-interest may alone suffice to undermine confidence in vigorous DOJ's representation. Moreover, DOJ has its own interest to consider in federal actions between sister agencies. DOJ must commit resources for both prosecution and defense and, as a matter of its own internal policy, may decide that its resources are not well spent prosecuting such actions.

EPA can attempt to avoid these problems by withholding direct legal action against the federal agency in charge of a government facility and, instead sue the private company that operates the facility under contract with the agency. However, many government contractors—particularly those that provide goods and services to the Department of Defense and the armed services—negotiate contracts terms that require the managing federal agency to defend them and to pay all defense costs and money judgments assessed against them by reason of activities they undertake in performing the government contract. In such cases, the government agency, rather than the private contractor, becomes the real party in interest, so that the DOJ may be called on to defend the contractor and thus face the same problems it would encounter if the managing agency were the named party defendant.

Even where a government facilities manager has no contractual obligation to defend its contractor, there is strong practical pressure for it to protect contractors, many of whom perform specialized services and are not easily replaced. The history of the government's persistent failure to force Rockwell International, one of its contractor operators, to rectify hazardous conditions at the Rocky Flats nuclear weapons plant typifies this scenario.

During EPA's investigation of illegal waste disposal at Rocky Flats, it became evident that high-ranking Rockwell and Department of Energy (DOE) officials were aware of serious environmental violations at the site. After collecting evidence from 110 witnesses over a period of two and a half years, an investigating grand jury recommended that federal criminal charges be brought against the Rockwell company, five Rockwell employees, and three DOE officials. This was done despite government prosecutors' instructions to the grand jury not to consider criminal charges against individual DOE officials because DOE as a whole had accepted (and implicitly condoned) the actions at Rocky Flats. DOJ also contended that Rockwell employees could not be charged. Notwithstanding the grand jury's recommendations, the government attorneys refused to return indictments against any Rockwell employees or DOE officials. The Rocky Flats grand jury responded by rejecting the prosecutors' limited indictment of the corporate entity and drew up its own indictments. The prosecuting attorney, in turn, refused to sign those indictments and did not issue any criminal indictment. Instead, DOJ filed a "criminal information" and accepted a plea bargain agreement that allowed Rockwell to settle the misconduct charges at Rocky Flats by paying a fine of $18 million. No government or corporate individuals were charged or fined. The grand jurors then wrote a report criticizing the government's handling of the prosecution, but the federal judge who supervised the grand jury proceedings refused to open the jury's report to public inspection and government officials threatened to prosecute grand jury members for violating the secrecy of grand jury proceedings. The U.S. House of Representatives Committee on Science, Space, and Technology Oversight conducted its own investigation of the Rocky Flats prosecution and concluded that DOJ had failed to prosecute the Rocky Flats case properly. The committee charged that the DOJ "failed to take the case seriously, hindered federal prosecutors in Denver, and blocked a federal grand jury investigation."[89]

DOJ prosecutions of environmental violations at other government sites have also been called into question. During the Rocky Flats investigation, the Energy and Commerce Oversight Subcommittee of the House of Representatives conducted hearings at which several EPA supervisors and investigators and an investigating official from the state of Washington testified that DOJ had accepted lenient "plea bargains" in connection with other government operations; had allowed major polluters to escape prosecution upon payment of minor penalties; had declined to prosecute cases where the evidence of criminal environmental violations was strong; and that high-ranking DOJ officials had suppressed investigations and prosecutions that DOJ staff attorneys and EPA officials had recommended pursuing.[90] Similar criticisms have been leveled against DOJ's conduct of civil proceedings to impose sanctions for environmental violations.

The Federal Facilities Compliance Act

Prior to 1991, prosecutions against federal facilities were clouded by uncertainty as to whether federal agencies could assert governmental sovereign immunity as a shield against liability for federal-law violations, and whether particular environmental statutes waived any such immunity. The enforceability of RCRA "cradle to grave" regulations at federal facilities remained unclear, especially when carried out by state agencies authorized to enforce them.[91] That Congress could waive federal immunity for environmental violations was never in doubt, but in examining each statute to determine Congressional intent to waive or not to waive liability, courts followed the rule that an intent to waive government immunity would not be found unless Congress used unequivocal language to indicate both the intent to waive governmental immunity and the intent that the waiver apply to the particular case in question.[92] Thus, the Supreme Court held that the RCRA and Clean Water Act (CWA) provisions for citizen enforcement suits against federal agencies did not express a Congressional waiver of DOE immunity from state-imposed fines for RCRA and CWA violations.[93]

Congress responded to the rulings favoring federal-agency immunity from environmental fines and penalties by enacting the Federal Facilities Compliance Act of 1992 (hereafter called the Compliance Act). The Compliance Act states in part:

> . . . The United States hereby *expressly waives any immunity* otherwise applicable to the United States with respect to any substantive or procedural requirement (including, but not limited to, any injunctive relief, administrative order or civil or administrative penalty or fine . . . .
>
> * * *
>
> The Administrator may commence an administrative enforcement action against *any department, agency, or instrumentality of the executive, legislative, or judicial branch of the Federal Government* pursuant to . . . this [Solid Waste] Act. The Administrator shall initiate an administrative enforcement action against such department, agency or instrumentality *in the same manner and under the same circumstances as . . . would be initiated against any person.*[94]

That Act thus made clear its intention that federal facilities and agencies are to be fully subject to all RCRA provisions, including penalties for RCRA violations. The Act incorporates a mechanism for encouraging compliance with RCRA in managing federal facilities. It provides that the violating department must pay all costs and penalties for RCRA violations out of its own departmental funds, rather than from other federal Treasury accounts.

In signing the Act, president George Bush confirmed that its aim was "to bring all federal facilities into compliance with applicable federal and state hazardous waste laws, to waive federal sovereign immunity under those laws, and to allow the imposition of fines and penalties" against offending federal agencies.[95] He also noted his adminstration's view that the Act would not apply to waive immunity where it might undermine national security or other paramount federal interests.

The Compliance Act covers storage and disposal of "mixed wastes" at federal facilities. It defines *mixed wastes* as "waste that contains both hazardous waste and solid waste . . . and special nuclear, or by-product material subject to the Atomic Energy Act . . . ," which clearly covers wastes produced by the Departments of Defense and Energy. DOE and DOD wastes account for the largest share of federal toxic waste accumulations. The Compliance Act took effect generally upon its signing, but for disposition of mixed waste its effective date was delayed for three years because of the lack of capacity to treat and dispose of mixed wastes at that time. The three-year delay was intended to allow federal facilities, particularly the DOE, the opportunity to develop adequate means of disposal. DOE then managed about 33 facilities in 15 states (not including its nuclear facilities at Hanford, Rocky Flats, and Savannah River) that had to be brought into compliance with the law on mixed-waste disposition. For practical purposes, therefore, the Act's waiver of sovereign immunity was delayed for three years so long as the affected facilities complied with approved plans for handling mixed waste in the interim.

In the Rocky Flats criminal proceedings, the DOJ sought to interpret the Compliance Act as relieving DOE from its storage violations for a three-year grace period, but that interpretation was publicly condemned as "grossly misleading" by a Congressional sponsor of the Compliance Act who asserted that the three-year delay provision had no application to criminal violations or to violations under cleanup agreements that had been made before the Act was passed.[96]

Though the Compliance Act lifted the *entity* immunity of federal government *agencies* from liability, it preserves the immunity of federal officials, agents, and employees from *personal* individual liability for *civil* RCRA penalties for actions which they took within the scope of their legally assigned duties. Criminal actions, however, cannot fall within the lawful scope of any government employee's work and they enjoy no such immunity. Government personnel thus remain liable to prosecution under criminal provisions of environmental laws.

In order to minimize disruptions at federal facilities, the Compliance Act requires the EPA Administrator to consult with an affected department before issuing final orders. Once made final, however, EPA rulings are enforceable against federal departments. In dealing with munitions, the Act requires the EPA Administrator to consult with appropriate military authorities and with officials of states where munitions are located, but such consultations do not affect the law's requirement that munitions regulations be issued no later than October 6, 1994.

A further important exception to the Compliance Act involves public vessels and operators (for example, ships of the U.S. Navy). They are excepted from general RCRA requirements for storage, inspection, and record keeping of hazardous wastes "until such waste is transferred to a shore facility." The Congressional Conference report on the Compliance Act stressed that this exception is not intended to have "public vessels become floating, unregulated hazardous waste storage facilities," and that public vessels should transfer wastes to shore facilities "as soon as . . . may be safely and feasibly accomplished."[97] It remains to be seen whether this open-ended requirement will undermine enforcement of hazardous-waste-management laws within the armed services.

With regard to federal water-treatment facilities, the Compliance Act permits the EPA Administrator to avoid closing a federal treatment facility that contains hazardous waste if he or she determines that the waste can be removed without closing it. The Act also excepts sewage in waste-water treatment from the general definition of hazardous waste. In effect, it allows federal waste-water facilities the same latitude that RCRA allows municipal water-treatment plants.

Cleanups at Federal Facilities

The government's burdens in complying with RCRA and the Compliance Act are dwarfed by its potential cleanup liability under CERCLA. Federal facilities may be potentially responsible parties (PRPs) subject to EPA cleanup orders and liability for cleanup costs (subject to the uncertain strictures on interagency prosecution discussed earlier). In 1992 there were 116 federal sites on the National Priorities List for Superfund cleanups, and federal facilities accounted for one third of 1,700 other sites listed for cleanup.[98] A recent court decision required EPA to evaluate more than 800 additional federal sites for possible inclusion on the NPL.[99] The escalating costs of federal-site cleanups are reflected in Figure 10.4, which shows the history of Congress's appropriations for those purposes.

A federal agency that was or is a past or present owner or operator of a hazardous-waste facility is subject to strict, joint and several liability for CERCLA response costs. In addition, it can be exposed to indirect CERCLA liability by reason of its contracts with a private party who is liable under CERCLA or by reason of its dealings with a liable private party who seeks joint-liability contribution from it.

When a federal facility is placed on the National Priority List, CERCLA requires the managing agency to develop an interagency agreement (IAG) with EPA for reviewing and selecting remedial actions. If the managing agency and EPA cannot agree on appropriate remediation, CERCLA authorizes EPA to determine what action must be taken. The IAG process has been hobbled in a number of ways. Where the President delegates Superfund compliance authority to the head of a facilities management agency by Executive Order, EPA encounters the previously discussed jurisdictional problems of enforcing compliance by another federal agency as well as the problems of enforcement prosecution by the Department of Justice. Indeed, some presidents have directed the Attorney General to resolve interagency disputes regarding a cleanup IAG and have authorized the Executive Office of Management and the Budget to resolve interagency monetary disputes under IAGs. Adding to the tangle of interagency jurisdiction, pres-

■ **Figure 10.4** U.S. Budget for Cleanup of Federal Facilities*

Federal Facility	1989 (Actual)	1992 (Enacted)	1993 (Proposed)	1992–1993 Change Dollar	Percent
Department of Energy	1,762	4,407	5,534	+1,127	+26%
Department of Defense	1,155	2,761	3,718	+957	+35
Department of Agriculture	8	38	39	+1	+3
Department of the Interior	41	70	80	+10	+14
Department of Transportation	29	54	59	+5	+9
NASA, DOJ, and DOC	28	41	58	+17	+41
Total	3,023	7,371	9,488	+2,117	+29
DOD anticipated supplemental	—	1,034	—	N/A	N/A

*In millions of dollars.

Source: Executive Office of the President, Office of Management and Budget, *Budget of the U.S. Government* (Washington, DC: U.S. Government Printing Office, 1992).

idential directives have the political effect of inviting agency resistance to EPA rules. The *Colorado* case, excerpted in this subsection, vividly illustrates how a federal agency can "stonewall" remedial action and maneuver to blunt environmental enforcement.

To avoid these obstacles and delays, EPA and environmental organizations have taken legal action against private contractors which operate federal facilities under agreement with managing agencies. These contractors typically bring the bypassed government agency into such lawsuits under contractual terms which oblige the government agency to defend and hold the contractors harmless from CERCLA response costs. In addition, the contractors may claim that the managing federal agency is directly liable, singly or jointly, for CERCLA response costs. In the face of these threats, managing federal agencies have been persuaded in some cases not to seek cover as a government agency, but to contribute toward CERCLA response costs.[100]

State governments may in some circumstances force federal-facilities cleanups under state environmental laws or pursuant to authority to enforce the federal law given them by EPA under the RCRA statute. The *Colorado* case opened this avenue of state enforcement that cannot be cut off by the Executive's manipulation of interagency operations.

■   **UNITED STATES V. STATE OF COLORADO**   ■

990 F.2d 1565 (10th Cir. 1993)

[After the U.S. Army Rocky Mountain Arsenal was placed on the National Priorities List, the State of Colorado ordered the facility to undertake corrective cleanup actions under the state-administered RCRA program. The lower court ruled that the State lacked authority to do this, but the Court of Appeals reversed that ruling and in the process resolved several thorny problems regarding the interaction of RCRA and CERCLA provisions.]

BALDOCK, Circuit Judge.

This case examines the relationship between the Resource Conservation and Recovery Act of 1976 ("RCRA"), . . . as amended by the Hazardous and Solid Waste Amendments of 1984 ("HSWA"), . . . and the Comprehensive Environmental Response, Compensation, and Liability Act of 1980 (CERCLA"), . . . as amended by the Superfund Amendments and Reauthorization Act of 1986 ("SARA"), . . . At issue is whether a state which has been authorized by the Environmental Protection Agency ("EPA") to "carry out" the state's hazardous waste program "in lieu of" RCRA, *see* 42 U.S.C. §

. . . is precluded from doing so at a hazardous waste . . . facility owned and operated by the federal government which the EPA has placed on the national priority list, . . . and where a CERCLA response action is underway. . . .

I.

The Rocky Mountain Arsenal ("Arsenal") is a hazardous waste treatment, storage and disposal facility . . . which is located . . . in the Denver metropolitan area. . . . Without reiterating its environmental history, suffice it to say that the Arsenal is "one of the worst hazardous waste pollution sites in the country." *Daigle v. Shell Oil Co.*, 972 F.2d 1527, 1531 (10th Cir. 1992) . . . . The present litigation focuses on Basin F which is a 92.7 acre basin located within the Arsenal where millions of gallons of liquid hazardous waste have been disposed of over the years.

* * *

. . . CERCLA otherwise applies to the federal government "to the same extent, both procedurally and substantively, as any nongovernmental entity." ...

II.

In November 1980, the Army, as the operator of the Arsenal, submitted to the EPA part A of its RCRA permit application which listed Basin F as a hazardous waste surface impoundment. ... In May 1983, the Army submitted part B of its RCRA permit application ... In May 1984, the EPA issued a notice of deficiency to the Army regarding part B of its RCRA permit application and requested a revised part B application .... The Army never submitted a revised part B RCRA permit application to the EPA; rather, in October, 1984, the Army commenced a CERCLA remedial investigation/feasibility study ("RI/FS"). ...

Effective November 2, 1984, the EPA, ... authorized Colorado to "carry out" the Colorado Hazardous Waste Management Act ("CHWMA"), ... "in lieu of" RCRA. ... That same month, the Army submitted its part B RCRA/CHWMA permit application to the Colorado Department of Health ("CDH") which is charged with the administration and enforcement of CHWMA. ... Not surprisingly, CDH found the application ... to be unsatisfactory.

Consequently, in May 1986, CDH issued its own draft partial closure plan for Basin F to the Army, ... and in October 1986, CDH issued a final RCRA/CHWMA modified closure plan for Basin F and requested the Army's cooperation .... The Army responded by questioning CDH's jurisdiction over the Basin F cleanup. ...

In response to the Army's indication that it would not implement CDH's closure plan ... Colorado filed suit in state court .... Colorado sought injunctive relief to halt the Army's alleged present and future violations of CHWMA and to enforce CDH's closure plan for Basin F. The Army removed the action to federal district court, and moved to dismiss Colorado's CHWMA enforcement action claiming that "CERCLA's enforcement and response provisions preempt and preclude a state RCRA enforcement action. ... at the Arsenal." ...

* * *

In October 1987, the Army advised Colorado that it was withdrawing its still pending part B RCRA/CHWMA permit application claiming that it was ceasing operations of all structures addressed in the application and that it intended to remediate Basin F pursuant to CERCLA. ...

... Thereafter, the Army ... completed the removal of eight million gallons of hazardous liquid wastes from Basin F, relocating four million gallons to three lined storage tanks and four million gallons to a double-lined holding pond. ...

In February 1989, the federal district court denied the Army's motion to dismiss Colorado's CHWMA enforcement action. The district court relied on several provisions of both RCRA and CERCLA, including CERCLA's provision for the application of state laws ... at federal facilities not listed on the national priority list. ...

In March 1989, the month following the district court's order, the EPA added Basin F to the national priority list. ., ... The Army immediately moved for reconsideration of the district court's order in light of the EPA's listing of Basin F on the national priority list.

In September 1989, CDH, ... issued a final amended compliance order to the Army, ... The final amended compliance order requires the Army to submit an amended Basin F closure plan, as well as plans and schedules addressing soil contamination, monitoring and mitigation, groundwater contamination, and other identified tasks ... required under CHWMA. ... The final amended compliance order also requires ... that the Army shall not implement any closure plan or work plan prior to approval in accordance with CHWMA. ...

As a result of the final amended compliance order, the United States filed the present declaratory action, ... The United States' complaint sought an order ... that the final amended compliance order is "null and void" and enjoining Colorado and CDH from taking any action to enforce it. ... Colorado counterclaimed requesting an injunction to enforce the final amended compliance order. ... On cross motions for summary judgment, the district court ... held that "[a]ny attempt by Colorado to enforce [ ] CHWMA would require [the] court to review the [Army's CERCLA] remedial action ... prior to [its] completion" and that "[s]uch a review is expressly prohibited by [CERCLA] § 9613(h)." . . . Based on this reasoning, the district court granted summary judgment to the United States . . . and enjoined Colorado and CDH from taking "any action to enforce the final amended compliance order." . . .

III.

. . . Colorado contends that § 9613(h) is not applicable to a state's efforts to enforce its EPA-delegated RCRA authority, that listing on the national priority list is immaterial, and that the district court's order amounts to a determination that CERCLA preempts a state's EPA-delegated RCRA authority contrary to well-settled principles. . . . the United States contends that CERCLA's provision, . . . bars Colorado from enforcing state law independent of CERCLA. . . .

* * *

IV.

. . . As the district court recognized, § 9613(h) expressly limits . . . jurisdiction by providing, . . . that "[n]o Federal court shall have jurisdiction . . . to review any challenges to removal or remedial action selected under section 9604 of this title. . . ." . . . However, contrary to the district court's reasoning, § 9613(h) does not bar federal courts from reviewing a CERCLA response action prior to its completion; rather, it bars federal courts from reviewing any "challenges" to CERCLA response actions. This is a critical distinction because an action by Colorado to enforce the final amended compliance order, issue pursuant to its EPA-delegated RCRA authority, is not a "challenge" to the Army's CERCLA response action. . . .

A.

Congress clearly expressed its intent that CERCLA should work in conjunction with other federal and state hazardous waste laws . . . . Similarly, CERCLA's . . . provides that "[n]othing in [CERCLA] shall be construed or interpreted as preempting any State from imposing any additional liability or requirements with respect to the release of hazardous substances within such State." 42 U.S.C. § 9614(a)

(West 1983). By holding that § 9613(h) bars Colorado from enforcing CHWMA, the district court effectively modified the Army's obligations and liabilities under CHWMA contrary to § 9652(d), and preempted Colorado . . . contrary to § 9614(a).

As a federal facility, the Arsenal is subject to regulation under RCRA. . . . More importantly, because the EPA has delegated RCRA authority to Colorado, the Arsenal is subject to regulation under CHWMA. . . . While the President has authority to exempt federal facilities from complying with RCRA or respective state laws . . . nothing in this record indicates that the Army has been granted such an exemption . . . .

* * *

Be that as it may, an action by a state to enforce its hazardous waste laws at a site undergoing a CERCLA response action is not necessarily a challenge to the CERCLA action. For example, CDH's compliance order does not seek to halt the Army's Basin F interim response action; . . . Thus, Colorado is not seeking to delay the cleanup, but merely seeking to ensure that the cleanup is in accordance with state laws . . . .

* * *

While we do not doubt that Colorado's enforcement of the final amended compliance order will "impact the implementation" of the Army's CERCLA response action, we do not believe that this alone is enough to constitute a challenge to the action as contemplated under § 9613(h). . . .

* * *

C.

Rather than challenging the Army's CERCLA remedial action, Colorado is attempting to enforce the requirements of its federally authorized hazardous waste laws and regulations . . . . While the decision to use CERCLA or RCRA to cleanup a site is normally a "policy question appropriate for agency resolution," . . . the plain language of both statutes provides for state enforcement . . . despite an ongoing CERCLA response action. Thus, enforcement actions under state hazardous waste laws which have been authorized by the EPA in lieu of RCRA do not constitute "challenges" to CERCLA response actions; therefore § 9613(h) does not jurisdictionally bar Colorado from enforcing the final amended compliance order.

V.

Even if an action by Colorado to enforce the final amended compliance order would be a "challenge" to the Army's CERCLA response action, the plain language of § 9613(h) would only bar a federal court from exercising jurisdiction . . . . Colorado, however, is not required to invoke federal court jurisdiction . . . . Rather, Colorado can seek enforcement of the final amended compliance order in state court. Therefore, § 9613(h) cannot bar Colorado from taking "any" action to enforce the final compliance order.

* * *

Despite the United States' concession . . . it argues that the listing of Basin F on the national priority list removes any doubt that Colorado's enforcement . . . at the Arsenal is precluded . . . . However, the national priority list is nothing more than "the list of priority releases for long-term remedial evaluation and response." . . . Placement on the national priority list simply has no bearing on a federal facility's obligation to comply with state hazardous waste laws . . . .

VII.

The United States alternatively contends that CERCLA's provision, which grants the President authority to select the remedy . . . bars Colorado from enforcing state law independent of CERCLA. This is a curious argument in light of §§ 9614(a) and 9652(d) which expressly preserve state RCRA authority, and we find it to be without merit.

* * *

B.

The United States also argues that to allow Colorado to enforce the final amended compliance order would violate CERCLA's provision that "[n]o Federal, State, or local permit shall be required for the portion of any removal or remedial action" . . . . The final amended compliance order does not require the Army to obtain a permit; rather, it merely requires the Army to maintain its interim status during the closure period as required by both RCRA and CHWMA. . . .

C.

* * *

. . . In our view, § 9622(e)(6) does not bar a state from exercising its EPA-delegated RCRA authority at a federal facility where a RI/FS has been initiated.

VIII.

We REVERSE the district court's grant of summary judgement for . . . the United States. We REMAND to the district court with instructions to VACATE the order prohibiting Defendants–Appellants, Colorado and CDH, from taking any action to enforce the final amended compliance order and for further proceedings consistent with this opinion.

Federal agencies that manage lands and natural resources encounter problems similar to those arising from the management of federal plants. As former or current owners of contaminated sites such as abandoned mines and oil fields, government land managers must deal with disposal and cleanup obligations. A 1986 Department of the Interior memorandum explicitly recognized that, as titular owner of public lands, the department could be a potentially responsible party under CERCLA.[101] When an agency voluntarily and knowingly acquires contaminated property, it cannot assert CERCLA's innocent-landowner defense.

10.5 Monetary Remedies for Natural Resource Damages

A wide range of natural resources—including natural objects, fish, wildlife, trees, plants, water resources, and crucial links of ecosystems—are exposed to environmental pollution and damage. To protect these assets, special legal remedies over and above those for preventing and cleaning up pollution are needed. One such remedy, monetary liability for natural-resource damages, serves two purposes: it pays for restoring or replacing resource losses and it serves to deter injurious activities. The compensation requirement vividly expresses the importance to society of commonly held natural resources, while the monetary value of the required compensation expresses the extent to which society values them.

Monetary remedies for natural-resource damage implicate two fundamental issues:

1. the extent to which liability should exist for natural resource damage, and
2. how the damage should be measured in monetary terms—by resource's market value, use value, cost of restoration or replacement, or by some other standard.

Three potential avenues exist for government entities to pursue compensatory remedies for natural resources injuries: state common-law principles, CERCLA natural resource damage provisions, and other federal statutes.

State law provides some nonstatutory grounds to support recovery for wrongful injury to natural resources. Under the common-law doctrine that a state holds public resources as a trustee for the benefit of the general citizenry, state governments may recover monies for damage to state natural resources as compensation for the public's loss of their benefits. Arguably, the federal government could assert the same doctrine for federally held natural resources. Additional nonstatutory grounds for monetary compensation might be found under contract law if federal contracts or permits specify that private users of federal lands will pay damages for any injuries they cause to the natural resources.

The trend, however, is toward creating statutory monetary liability for environmental injuries to natural resources, as exemplified by special provisions in CERCLA and in the Oil Pollution Control Act (OPA),[102] which is codified as part of the Clean Water Act. The following discussion focuses primarily on recoverable damages under those acts for injuries caused by wrongful releases of hazardous substances. CERCLA provisions adopt the rationale of the common-law "public trust" doctrine. Although the few court decisions in this area provide only limited guidance, the scholarly literature on natural-resource-damage theory is generous and it may hasten the development of stronger law by the courts.[103]

CERCLA sections 101(16) and 107(a) and (f) are pertinent. Section 101(16) defines *natural resources* as embracing only those resources owned or controlled by a government entity or quasi-government entity.[104] Section 107(a)(4)(C) makes parties liable for:

> damages for injury to, destruction of, or loss of natural resources, including the reasonable costs of assessing such injury [caused by a release of hazardous substances] . . . .[105]

Under CERCLA and the OPA, a number of difficult questions remain on the kinds, proofs, and measurement of resource damage. To cite a few examples:

- What kinds of injury to national resources are actionable?
- How strictly must the government prove causal relationships between hazardous-substance release and alleged damage to natural resources?
- What standard(s) of asset or use value should be used to assess the monetary compensation for natural resource damage?

The monetary measurement of natural-resource damages presents theoretical and technical issues of economics and law that are not fully addressed by current laws.[106] Among the alternatives advanced by various commentators, three stand out; namely,

> *use value* (value of the resource for material consumption),
> *existence value* (value of the resource for future as well as present uses), and
> *intrinsic value* (the need for and value of nature itself).

Valuation may include intangible as well as tangible elements, but commentators who purport to agree on a particular standard of valuation in theory often apply the standard differently.[107]

Economic theorists employ various yardsticks of value, principally,

> *restoration and replacement,*
> *market value,*
> *behavioral use* (change in the cost burden to see, use, or enjoy a natural object), and
> *contingent value* (public opinion of value derived through poll surveys).

The core of controversies over assessing the monetary loss of natural-resource injury is the conflict between the *anthropocentric* (*anthropo-*, "human"; *centric*, "centered") approach, which employs present value of physical resources on the market as the ceiling (maximum dollar amount) for monetary recovery, and the *biocentric* (*bio-*, "life") approach, which uses economic analysis to determine the "floor" (minimum) for recoverable damages and takes into consideration the natural resources' nonmaterial values to human society and to the natural world. At one extreme, the anthropocentric approach places greater emphasis on the *certainty* of valuation and tends toward an *exclusive measure*, that is, valuing only those resources that have existing, clear market values. Values not capable of fairly accurate market quantification are disregarded entirely. The opposite, biocentric position holds that because no single measure of value is reliable, *inclusive measures* are needed. In other words, capturing all relevant values is more important than certainty of valuation. Advocates of this approach favor the use of all available value measures, including those that are not readily quantifiable. Most participants in the valuation debate hold positions somewhere along the continuum that runs between the anthropocentric and biocentric poles. For them, the issue turns more on the relative emphases of the valuation elements than on inclusion or exclusion of particular elements.

The legislatures and courts have yet to settle these valuation issues, and no authoritative solutions are likely to emerge until greater experience with negotiated settlements and case opinions promotes a clearer consensus of opinion.[108] This excerpt from a leading case epitomizes the ongoing search for suitable monetary assessments for natural-resource inquiries.

STATE OF OHIO V. U.S. DEPT. OF THE INTERIOR

880 F.2d 432 (D.C. Cir. 1989)

WALD, Chief Judge, and SPOTTSWOOD W. ROBINSON III and MIKVA, Circuit Judges:

Petitioners are 10 states, three environmental organizations ("State and Environmental Petitioners"), a chemical industry trade association, a manufacturing company and a utility company ("Industry Petitioners"), who seek review of regulations promulgated by the Department of the Interior ("DOI" or "Interior") pursuant to § 301(c)(1)–(3) of the Comprehensive Environmental Response, Compensation and Liability Act of 1980 ("CERCLA" or the "Act") . . . The regulations govern the recovery of money damages from persons responsible for spills and leaks of oil and hazardous substances, to compensate for injuries such releases inflict on natural resources. Damages may be recovered by state and in some cases the federal governments, as trustees for those natural resources.

. . . State and Environmental Petitioners raise ten issues, all of which essentially focus on the regulations' alleged undervaluation of the damages recoverable from parties responsible for hazardous materials spills that despoil natural resources. Industry Petitioners attack the regulations from a different vantage point, claiming they will permit or encourage overstated damages. In addition, three public interest organizations("Environmental Intervenors") defend the regulations from the attacks of Industry Petitioners, and a collection of corporations and industry groups ("Industry Intervenors") defend the regulations from the attacks of State and Environmental Petitioners.

We hold that the regulation limiting damages recoverable by government trustees for harmed natural resources to "the lesser of" (a) the cost of restoring or replacing the equivalent of an injured resource is directly contrary to the clearly expressed intent of Congress and is therefore invalid. We also hold that the regulation prescribing a hierarchy of methodologies by which the lost-use value of natural resources may be measured, which focuses exclusively on the market values for such resources when market values are available, is not a reasonable interpretation of the statute. We remand the record to DOI for a clarification of its interpretation of its own regulations concerning the applicability of the CERCLA natural resource damage provisions to privately owned land that is managed or controlled by a federal, state or local government. . . .

B.   The Natural Resource Damage Assessment Regulations

Interior's responses to its assigned task of promulgating regulations for assessing natural resource damages was, to put it charitably, relaxed. In January 1983, *after* the original statutory deadline had come and gone, Interior issued an advance notice of proposed rulemaking soliciting comments from the public . . . A second advance notice of proposed rulemaking seven months later summarized the comments received in response to the first notice. . . . More than a year later, in January 1985, Interior published a notice inviting more

public comments and suggesting meetings with interested members of the public. . . .

In December 1985, five years after the enactment of CERCLA and three years after the statutory deadline, Interior published a proposed rule. . . .

Ultimately, on August 1, 1986, Interior published a final rule containing general natural resource damage assessment regulations. . . .

* * *

The August 1986 regulations were promptly challenged by state governments, environmental groups, industrial corporations and an industry group.

Shortly after the issuance of the August 1986 regulations, Congress amended CERCLA by enacting SARA. . . . In response to SARA, Interior issued revised rules . . . . A state government and an environmental group filed additional challenges to these revised rules . . .

* * *

III.   THE "LESSER-OF" RULE

The most significant issue in this case concerns the validity of the regulation providing that damages for despoilment of natural resources shall be "the *lesser of:* restoration or replacement costs; or diminution of use values." 43 C.F.R. § 11.35(b)(2) (1987) (emphasis added).

State and Environmental Petitioners challenge Interior's "lesser of" rule, insisting that CERCLA requires damages to be at least sufficient to pay the cost in every case of restoring, replacing or acquiring the equivalent of the damaged resource (hereinafter referred to shorthandedly as "restoration"). Because in some—probably a majority of—cases lost-use-value will be lower than the cost of restoration, Interior's rule will result in damages award too small to pay for the costs or restoration. . . . .

Interior defends its rule by arguing that CERCLA does not prescribe any floor for damages but instead leaves to Interior the decision of what the measure of damages will be. DOI acknowledges that all recovered damages must be spent on restoration but argues that the amount recovered from the responsible parties need not be sufficient to complete the job. . . .

Although our resolution of the dispute submerges us in the minutiae of CERCLA text and legislative materials, we initially stress the enormous practical significance of the "lesser of" rule. A hypothetical example will illustrate the point: imagine a hazardous substance spill that kills a rookery of fur seals and destroys a habitat for seabirds at a sealife reserve. The lost use value of the seals and seabird habitat would be measured by the market value of the fur seals' pelts (which would be approximately $15 each) plus the selling price per acre of land comparable in value to that on which the spoiled bird habitat was located. Even if, as likely, that use value turns out to be far less than the cost of restoring the rookery and seabird habitat, it would nonetheless be the only measure of damages eligible for the presumption of recoverability under the Interior rule.

After examining the language and purpose of CERCLA, as well as its legislative history, we conclude that Interior's "lesser of" rule is directly contrary to the expressed intent of Congress.

* * *

3. Congress' Rejection of the Premises Underlying the "Lesser-Of" Rule

CERCLA's legislative history undergirds its textual focus on recovering restoration costs as the primary aim of the natural resource damages provisions. Furthermore, it shows that Congress soundly rejected the two basic premises underlying Interior's "lesser of" rule—first, that the common-law measure of damages is appropriate in the natural resource context, and second, that it is economically inefficient to restore a resource whose use value is less than the cost of restoration.

A. CERCLA AND THE COMMON-LAW MEASURE OF DAMAGES.

DOI and Industry Intervenors argue that Congress intended that damages under CERCLA would be calculated according to traditional common-law rules. Accepting for the sake of argument the contention that the "lesser of" rule reflects the common law, support for the proposition that Congress adopted common-law damage standards wholesale into CERCLA is slim to nonexistent. . . .

B. CERCLA AND ECONOMIC EFFICIENCY.

Alternatively, Interior justifies the "lesser of" rule as being economically efficient. Under DOI's eco-nomic efficiency view, making restoration cost the measure of damages would be a waste of money whenever restoration would cost more than the use value of the resource.

* * *

The fatal flaw of Interior's approach, however, is that it assumes that natural resources are fungible goods, just like any other, and that the value to society generated by a particular resource can be accurately measured in every case—assumptions that Congress apparently rejected. Congress saw restoration as the presumptively correct remedy for injury to natural resources. To say that Congress placed a thumb on the scales in favor of restoration is not to say that it forswore the goal of efficiency. "Efficiency," standing alone, simply means that the chosen policy will dictate the result that achieves the greatest value to society. Whether a particular choice is efficient depends on *how the various alternatives are valued.*

Our reading of the complex of relevant provisions concerning damages under CERCLA convinces us that Congress established a distinct preference for restoration cost as the measure of recovery in natural resource damage cases. This is not to say that DOI may not establish some class of cases where other considerations—*i.e.,* infeasibility of restoration or grossly disproportionate cost to use value—warrant a different standard. We hold the "lesser of" rule based on comparing costs alone, however, to be an invalid determinant of whether or not to deviate from Congress' preference.

* * *

VI. THE HIERARCHY OF ASSESSMENT METHODS

The regulations establish a rigid hierarchy of permissible methods for determining "use values," limiting recovery to the price commanded by the resource on the open market, unless the trustee finds that "the market for the resource is not reasonably competitive." 43 C.F.R § 11.83(c)(1). . . .

Environmental petitioners maintain that Interior's emphasis on market value is an unreasonable interpretation of the statute, . . . While it is not irrational to look to market price as *one* factor in determining the use value of a resource, it is unreasonable to view market price as the *exclusive* factor, or even the predominant one. . . .

On remand, DOI should consider a rule that would permit trustees to derive use values for natural resources by summing up all reliably calculated use values, however measured, so long as the trustee does not double count. Market valuation can of course serve as one factor to be considered, but by itself it will necessarily be incomplete. In this vein, we instruct DOI that its decision to limit the role of non-

consumptive values, such as option and existence values, in the calculation of use values rests on an erroneous construction of the statute. . . .

* * *

We hold that the hierarchy of use values is not a reasonable interpretation of the statute.

* * *

■ Chapter 10 Endnotes

1. See, for example, "U.S. Department of the Interior: Environmental Problems and Issues," Committee on Governmental Affairs, U.S. Senate, 103d Cong., 1st Sess., September 1993, p. 8; CEQ, *Environmental Quality* (1991), pp. 167–172; and *Statistical Abstract of the United States* (1991), p. 203.
2. See also *State of the Environment* (The Conservation Foundation, 1987), p. 197.
3. Report, U.S. Department of the Interior, note 1, supra.
4. M. Rutzick, "Wildlife Constraints on Timber Harvesting," 5 *Natural Resources and Environment* 10, (no. 3, 1991).
5. CEQ, *Environmental Quality*, note 1, supra, p. 167.
6. See Report, Subcommittee on Federal Land-Use Law, 23 *The Urban Lawyer*, pp. 651 et seq. (no. 4, 1991).
7. Ibid.
8. CEQ, *Environmental Quality*, note 1, supra, p. 167.
9. Ibid., pp. 169, 170.
10. Report, "Sweeping Reversal of U.S. Land Policy Sought by Clinton," *The New York Times*, 24 February 1993, p. A1.
11. See report, "Babbit Unveils a New Version of Grazing Plan," *The Wall Street Journal*, 18 March 1994, p. A5.
12. 16 United States Code (U.S.C.) § 528.
13. 43 U.S.C. § 1701.
14. 16 U.S.C. § 1131.
15. 16 U.S.C. § 1531.
16. CEQ, *Environmental Quality* (1991), p. 101.
17. G. Coggins, P. Evans, and M. Lindberg-Johnson, "The Law of Public Range Land Management (I): The Extension and Distribution of Federal Power," 12 *Envl. L.* 535 (1982); G. Coggins and M. Lindberg-Johnson, "The Law of Public Range Land Management (II), The Commons and the Taylor Grazing Act," 13 *Envl. L.* 1 (1982); G. Coggins, "The Law of Public Range Land Management (III): A Survey of "Creeping Regulation, 1934–1982," 13 *Envl. L.* 295 (1983); G. Coggins, "The Law of Public Range Land Management (IV): FLPMA, PRIA, and the Multiple-Use Mandate," 14 *Envl. L.* 1(1983); H. Shepard, "Livestock Grazing in BLM Wilderness," 5 *J. of Envl. L. and Litig.* 61 (1990).
18. G. Coggins, P. Evans, and M. Lindberg-Johnson, "The Law of Public Range Land Management I," supra, pp. 547, 549.

19. *National Resources Defense Council, Inc. v. Morton,* 388 F. Supp. 852, 840 (D.D.C. 1974).

20. CEQ, *Environmental Quality,* (1991), p. 169.

21. See J. Feller, "Grazing Management on the Public Lands," XXVI *Land and Water Rev.* 571, 573 n. 19 (1991).

22. Ibid., p. 574 and numerous authorities there cited.

23. 42 U.S.C. § 1701(c).

24. G. Coggins, P. Evans, and M. Lindberg-Johnson, "The Law of Public Rangeland Management IV," 14 *Envl. L.* 1, 74–100); J. Feller, "Grazing Management on the Public Lands," XXVI *Land and Water L. Rev.* 573, 576 (1991).

25. *Feller v. Bureau of Land Management,* no. UT-06-89-02 (U.S. Dept. of the Interior, Office of Hearings and Appeals, Hearings Division, 13 August 1990). See, generally, G. Coggins, *Public Natural Resource Law* § 19.05[1] (1990); and J. Feller, note 21, supra, pp. 573, 576.

26. President's Private Survey on Cost Control (Report on the Department of Agriculture, 1983), p. 188; and CEQ, *Environmental Quality,* note 1 supra, p. 169.

27. See CEQ, *Environmental Quality,* note 20, supra, p. 183.

28. See, generally, S. Parent, "The National Forest Management Act: Out of the Woods and Back to the Courts," 22 *Envl. L.* 699 (1992); K. Barrett, "Section 6(k) of the National Forest Management Act; The Bottom Line on Below Timber Sales," 1987 *Utah L. Rev.* 373; D. Getches and K. Sheldon, "Recent Developments in Public Land Law," c. 722 ALI–ABA 403, part V (American Law Institute, 1992); and G. Coggins, "The Developing Law of Land Use Planning in the Federal Lands," 61 *U. Colo. L. Rev.* 307, 336–344 (1990).

29. CEQ, *Environmental Quality,* note 1, supra, p. 101.

30. Barrett, note 28, supra, citing J. Beuter, *Federal Timber Sales* 4–5 (15 February 1985).

31. *Sierra Club v. Forest Service,* 843 F.2d 1190 (9th Cir. 1988), *Wyoming Outdoor Coordinating Council v. Butz,* 484 F.2d 1244 (10th Cir. 1973).

32. *Sierra Club v. Lyng,* 694 F. Supp. 1260 (E.D. Texas 1988) (Under Endangered Species Act).

33. President's Private Survey, note 26, supra, p. 188.

34. "U.S. Forest Workers Seek Logging Limits at Streams," *The Philadelphia Inquirer,* 19 May 1993, p. A4; "Forest Service Workers Seek Salmon Protection," *The San Francisco Chronicle,* (19 May 1993), p. A4.

35. Barrett, note 28, supra.

36. Id. at p. 402; Hearings, H. Rep. No. 886, 98th Cong., 2nd sess. 1984, pp. 69–70.

37. Barrett, n. 28, supra.

38. "U.S. Would End Cutting of Trees in Many Forests," *The New York Times,* 30 April 1992, p. A1.

39. *Citizens for Environmental Quality v. United States,* 731 F. Supp. 970 (D. Colo. 1989).

40. See *Sierra Club v. Robertson,* 764 F. Supp. 546, 548, 550 (W.D. Ark. 1991).

41. *Seattle Audubon Soc. v. Robertson,* no. 89-160 (W.D. Wn. 1989).

42. Rutzick, note 4, supra, p. 12.

43. *Tennessee Valley Authority v. Hill,* 437 U.S. 153, 172, 173 (1978).

44. 50 Code of Federal Regulations (C.F.R.), part 402; *Sierra Club v. Lyng,* 694 F.Supp. 1260 (E.D. Texas 1988), rev'd on other grounds, 926 F.2d 429 (5th Cir. 1991).

45. *Seattle Audubon Society v. Evans,* 771 F. Supp. 1081 (W.D. Wn. 1991).

46. *Northern Spotted Owl v. Lujan,* 758 F. Supp. 621 (W.D. Wn. 1991).

47. 36 C.F.R. § 219.19 (1989).

48. See *Robertson v. Seattle Audubon Society,* 112 S.Ct. 1407 (1992).

49. See "Environment, Final EIA on Clinton Forest Plan Has Higher Estimate of Job Losses," 1994 *DER* 36 d41 (Bureau of National Affairs, 1994); "Tight Logging Limits Set in Northwest," *The New York Times,* 24 February 1994, p. A18.

50. Ibid.

51. "Accord Is Reached to Aid Forest Bird," *The New York Times,* 16 April 1993, p. A1.

52. See "Congress Allows Swaps of U.S. Land for Ancient Forest," *The Wall Street Journal,* 14 September 1993, p. A10.

53. 16 U.S.C. § 703.

54. 50 C.F.R. § 10.13.

55. 15 U.S.C. § 1131.

56. *Brown v. U.S. Dept. of Interior,* 679 F.2d 747, 750 (8th Cir. 1982) (mining prohibited); *Parker v. United States,* 448 F.2d 793 (10th Cir. 1971) (logging prohibited in wilderness area).

57. *Sierra Club v. Lyng,* 662 F. Supp. 40 (D.C. Cir. 1987) (tree cutting to control beetle infestation). See H. Shephard, "Livestock Grazing in BLM Wilderness and Wilderness Areas," 5 *Envl. L. & Lit.* 61 (1990.

58. *United States v. Weiss,* 642 F.2d 296, 299 (9th Cir. 1981).

59. Compare *United Nuclear Corp. v. United States,* 912 F.2d 1432 (Fed. Cir. 1990) (mining ban held to be a taking), with *Freese v. United States,* 639 F.2d 754 (Ct. Cl. 1981) (mining ban held not to be a taking).

60. CEQ, *Environmental Quality,* (1991), p. 172.

61. *Sierra Club v. Yeutter,* 911 F.2d 1405, 1422 (10th Cir. 1990) (concurring opinion).

62. *Voyageurs Reg. Nat'l Park Assn. v. Lujan,* 966 F.2d 424 (8th Cir. 1992) (upheld agency permission of snowmobiling as not permanently affecting prospective wilderness area); *Sierra Club v. Hodel,* 848 F.2d 1068 (10th Cir. 1988) (upheld agency right of way regulation), cf. *Friends of Boundary Waters Wilderness v. Robertson,* 978 F.2d 1484 (8th Cir. 1992) (disapproved agency permission for motorboating).

63. See D. Rohlf and D. Honnold, "Managing the Balance of Nature: The Legal Framework of Wilderness Management," 15 *Ecology L. Q.* 249 (1988).

64. For a good general reference on water law in the United States West, see M. Reisner, *The Cadillac Desert* (1993).

65. See Getches and Sheldon, note 28, supra, part V.

66. C. Coggins, P. Evans, and M. Lindberg-Johnson, "The Law of Public Rangeland Management I: The Extent and Distribution of Federal Power," 12 *Environmental Law* 535, 578 et seq. (1982).

67. See, for example, Mineral Leasing Act of 1920, 30 U.S.C. § 181 amended by Onshore Oil and Gas Leasing Reform Act of 1987, 30 U.S.C. § 16 U.S.C. § 3148; 30 U.S.C. § 187 a–b); Surface Mining Control and Reclamation Act, 30 U.S.C. § 1201; J. Laitos, "Paralysis by

Analysis in the Forest Service Oil and Gas Leasing Program," XXVI *Land and Water L. Rev.* 105 (1991); T. Sansonetti, and W. Murray, "A Primer on Federal Onshore Oil and Gas Leasing Reform Act of 1987," XXV *Land and Water L. Rev.* 375 (1990).

68. See also *State of the Environment*, note 2, supra, p. 108.

69. J. Draper and S. Fletcher, "Environmental Laws and Regulations Governing Gold Mining in the West—Current Issues," 36 *Rocky Mountain Mineral Law Institute* 5-1 (1990).

70. See *California Coastal Comm. v. Granite Rock*, 480 U.S. 572, 575 (1987).

71. "Current Developments," 23 *E.R.* 1553 (1992).

72. See R. Conniff, "Federal Lands," 185 *National Geographic* no. 2 (February 1994), p. 2.

73. As quoted in *The Washington Post*, 28 April 1993, p. A7. A history of failed attempts at federal regulation in this area is traced in J. Jacus and T. Root, "The Emerging Federal Law of Mine Waste: Administrative, Judicial, and Legislative Developments," XXVI *Land and Water L. Rev.* 461 (1991).

74. "Forced, U.S. Sells Gold Land for Trifle," *The New York Times*, 17 May 1994, p. A12.

75. "House Clears Bill to Impose Royalties for Hardrock Mining on Federal Lands," *The Wall Street Journal*, 19 November 1993, p. A4; "House Passes Measure to Limit Use of Public Lands for Mining," *The New York Times*, 19 November 1993, p. A1.

76. 43 U.S.C. §§ 1732(b), 1782(c).

77. *Sierra Club v. Penfold*, 857 F.2d 1307 (9th Cir. 1988) (enjoined mining practices that damage water sources).

78. See *Duro v. Reina*, 495 U.S. 676, 688, n. 1 (1990).

79. D. Brockman, "Congressional Delegation of Environmental Regulatory Jurisdiction: Native American Control of the Reservation Environment," 41 *Wash. U. J. of Urban and Contemp. L.* 133 (1992); W. Quinn, *Federal Environmental and Indian Law Confluent*, 29 *Ariz. Atty.* 19 (1992); P. Sly, "EPA and Indian Reservations," 20 *Envl. L. Rev.* 10429 (1990); R. Kovnat, "Solid Waste Regulation in Indian Country," 21 *N. Mex. L. Rev.* 121 (1990); W. Stern, "Environmental Compliance Considerations for Developers of Indian Lands," 28 *Land and Water L. Rev.* 77 (1993); R. DuBey et al., "Protection of the Reservation Environment: Hazardous Waste Management on Indian Lands," 18 *Envl. L.* 449 (1988).

80. *So. Dakota v. Bourland*, 113 S. Ct. 2309 (1993) (Indian/state dispute over authority to license hunting on Indian lands); *Duro v. Reina*, note 78, supra (no authority of tribal courts to try nontribal member for crime committed on Indian reservation); *Brendale v. Confederated Tribes, etc.*, 492 U.S. 408 (1989) (Indian authority to zone reservation land does not extend to land open to the public and owned by non-Indians).

81. *So. Dakota v. Bourland*, supra.

82. See Quinn, note 79, supra.

83. *David v. Morton*, 469 F.2d 593 (10th Cir. 1972).

84. See R. DuBey et al., note 79, supra.

85. *Washington, Dept. of Ecology, v. EPA*, 752 F.2d 1465 (9th Cir. 1985).

86. R. Davis and T. McCrum, "Environmental Liability for Federal Lands and Facilities," 6 *Natural Resources and Environment* 31, 66 (no. 1, 1991).

87. E. Cheng, "Lawmaker as Lawbreaker: Assessing Civil Penalties against Federal Facilities under RCRA," 57 *U. Chi. L. Rev.* 845 (1990).

88. "Wider Peril Found in Nuclear Waste from Bomb Making," *The New York Times,* 28 March 1991, p. A1.

89. "EPA Officials Criticize Justice Department," *The Washington Post,* 11 September 1992, p. A4.

90. Ibid.

91. R. Murchinson, "Reforming Environmental Enforcement: Lesson from Twenty Years of Waiving Federal Immunity to State Regulation," 11 *Va. Envl. L. J.* 179 (1991/1992); E. Cheng, note 87, supra.

92. *United States Dept. of Energy v. Ohio,* 112 U.S. 1627 (1992); *Mitzefelt v. Dept. of the Air Force,* 903 F.2d 1293 (10th Cir. 1990).

93. *United States Dept. of Energy v. Ohio,* supra.

94. 42 U.S.C. § 6901, as amended (emphasis added).

95. 1992 *U.S.C.C. & Am.* 1337-1; See also "Report of Committee of House and Senate Conference Committee" (H.R. Conf. Rep., 22 September 1992), pp. 102–886; 4 *U.S. Cong. & Admin. News* 1317 (1992).

96. Reported, in *States News Service,* 5 February 1993.

97. "Report of Committee," note 95, supra; 4 *U.S. Cong. & Admin. News* 1328 (1992).

98. A. Gaydosh, "The Superfund Federal Facilities Program: We Have Met the Enemy and It Is U.S.," 6 *Natural Resources and Environment,* 21 (no. 3, 1992).

99. *Conservation Law Foundation v. Reilly,* 743 F. Supp. 933 (D. Mass. 1990) rev'd, 950 F.2d 38 (1st Cir. 1991). See also CEQ, *Environmental Quality,* note 1, supra, pp. 87–94.

100. Davis and McCrum, note 86, supra, p. 33.

101. Ibid., p. 32.

102. As previously noted, CERCLA exempts petroleum products from its definition of hazardous substances.

103. See, for example, R. Kopp and V. Smith, eds., *Valuing Natural Assets* (1993); K. Russell, "A Research Guide to Natural Resource Damage under the Comprehensive Environmental Response Compensation and Liability Act," XXVI *Land and Water L. Rev.* 403 (1991), and the numerous publications there cited.

104. 42 U.S.C. § 9601 (16).

105. 42 U.S.C. § 9607 (a)(4)(C).

106. See, for example, "Natural Resource Damage Assessments—What Will the Second Generation Yield," 6 *Natural Resources and Environment,* 36 (no. 4, 1992); P. Campbell, "Economic Valuation of Injury to Natural Resources," 6 *Natural Resources and Environment,* 28 (no. 3, 1992); K. Russell, "A Research Guide to Natural Resource Damage," XXVI *Land & Water L. Rev.* 403 (1991); D. Hodas, "Natural Resource Damages: A Research Guide," 9 *Pace Envl. Rev.* 107 (1991); and B. Breen, "Citizen Suits for Natural Resource Damages: Closing a Gap in Federal Environmental Law," 24 *Wake Forest L. Rev.* 851 (1989).

107. See, for example, M. Jones, "Natural Resource Damage Assessment for Oil Spills," 1 *Vill. Envl. L. Rev.* 491 (1990).

108. Compare, for example, *Ohio v. United States Department of Interior,* 880 F.2d 432 (D.C. Cir. 1989), with *Idaho v. Bunker Hill Co.,* 635 F. Supp. 665 (D. Idaho 1986).

CHAPTER 11

International Environmental Law

Outline

11.1 Issues Affecting the International Environment

The subject matter of this chapter is examined in depth in the publications listed in the first endnote.[1] Those publications and the sources to which they refer are highly recommended for further study.

The international community has come to acknowledge that global environmental problems parallel those that each nation faces on its own lands. Untrammeled economic exploitation and consumption of the earth's resources are not environmentally sustainable, and human activities overwhelm the earth's capability to sustain and restore the ecological and material conditions required for human health and welfare.[2] As with domestic environmental movements, international environmental movements have been spurred largely by actual and threatened disasters that affect all nations. Examples include the Chernobyl nuclear explosion, global warming, the thinning of the ozone layer, and oil tanker spills. Governments and citizens' groups around the world have significantly influenced increased efforts to protect the international environment.

Comprehensive collective action to regulate the international environment is quite new. The first Earth Summit to address the topic of sustainable development was not convened until 1992. Familiar themes—that

environmental quality and economic health are inextricably linked; that the economic well-being of the Earth's people depends directly on the continued health of its natural resources''; [and that] [t]he choice between crisis and sustainable development is one [each] . . . nation shares with the rest of the world, and the only way to address it is through international cooperation . . . .[3]

—only gained urgency with the mounting evidence of threats to the international environment. The "external" effects of each nation's use of its natural resources (such as forests and rangelands) and of those that they share with other nations (oceans, airsheds) upon other nations' environments mandate international solutions. Excessive deforestation, overgrazing of rangelands, and improvident uses of chemical fertilizers and pesticides in one nation threaten vital habitats and resources of all nations. Pollution of the oceans—which cover almost three quarters of the earth's surface—affects myriad forms of marine life and the oceans' ability to supply free oxygen to the earth's atmosphere. When oceans are overloaded with excessive discharges of human wastes, their impaired functioning affects the entire planet.[4] Likewise, the degradation of air quality and the atmosphere from overloads of toxic and degrading man-made emissions affect all nations, regardless of the source of the pollution.

Unlike minor forms of localized transboundary pollution whose effects may be geographically confined, most threats to the international environment arise from the cumulative effect of many different activities in many nations. Traditionally, international law has not focused on regulating the worldwide environment. Earlier incremental programs carried out by a few nations to mitigate specific sources of pollution fell far short of systematically protecting the international environment. Modern problems are beyond the power of any single or small group of nations to solve. Hence the growing importance of environmental regulation in contemporary international relations.

> Environmental regulation does not, and should not, stop at state borders. Because both pollution and ecosystems cross state lines, a patchwork of national environmental regulations is ineffective and inefficient. Global environmental resources, such as rain forests, that lie within . . . a state that provides little environmental protection may be unnecessarily squandered; meanwhile, increased environmental protection in one country may simply drive polluting industries to other nations. These possibilities necessitate . . . some international environmental agreements.[5]

> The ecological truth that the nations of the world are bound together in an indivisible ecosystem . . . has begun to influence the discourse of international diplomacy. . . . The Scandinavian countries are contributing voluntarily to the control of pollution in Eastern Europe which affects the Baltic Sea and the Nordic forests. Dutch utility companies are investing in reforestation in the Amazon to offset the environmental effects of their operations. The Bush administration has given official . . . support to debt-for-nature swaps that effectively put U.S. wealth to work for the protection of ecosystems in Latin America.[6]

Although widespread recognition of the need for international action marks an essential first step, it is by no means the most crucial step that must be taken for international action.

11.2 Obstacles to International Environmental Regulation

The major obstacles to developing an international legal regime for protecting the environment are familiar to all law systems: the problems of establishing acceptance (both factual and political) of the need for protective laws on one hand, and the problems of formulating effective laws once their need is accepted, on the other.

The threshold and major obstacle to creating a body of international environmental law is the axiom that each juridically (legally) recognized nation is an independent sovereign entity that cannot be forced, but only persuaded, to accept international norms or agreements. According to the American Law Institute's *Restatement of the Law on Foreign Relations,* each nation has the right to govern its own affairs without outside interference according to these following principles:

§ 206. Capacities, Rights and Duties of States

Under international law, a state [nation] has:

(a) sovereignty over its territory and general authority over its nationals;

(b) status as a legal person with capacity . . . to make contracts and enter into international agreements, to become a member of international organizations, and to pursue and be subject to legal remedies;

(c) capacity to join with other states to make international law, by a customary law or by international agreement.

§ 451. Immunity of Foreign State from Jurisdiction to Adjudicatee: The Basic Rule

Under international law, a state [nation] or state instrumentality is immune from the jurisdiction of courts of another nation state, except with respect to claims arising out of activities . . . that may be carried on by private persons.[7]

Nations' reluctance to surrender or subordinate control over their territory, peoples, and affairs to external international authority must be confronted and overcome. Even when nations have joined in international agreements, many of them have appended "reservations" to preserve their right to decline to be bound by particular parts of the otherwise accepted agreement. The exercise of this power to reserve exceptions and exemptions weakens the total effectiveness of many international agreements.

Nations whose economic, cultural, and political aspirations are diverse—with differences being particularly evident between the industrially developed and still-developing, Third World nations—have competing objectives in international negotiations. Even where nations agree on the need for international programs, they tend to disagree on the propriety or fairness of the means to effectuate those programs—means that inevitably implicate economic or cultural sacrifices to some groups. Less-industrialized nations typically view as unfair environmental rules that would restrict their economic growth, while industrialized nations tend to resist proposals that would limit their development, use, and consumption of the earth's resources.

> As with human rights, the development of international rules concerning the environment has been hotly contested. Some third-world countries regard environmental concerns as problems for the rich and environmental regulation as another impediment to [their own] economic development. . . . Finally, environmental regulations may strike at the economic well-being of important industries and can even challenge cultural and social attitudes. . . .[8]

The scientific uncertainty regarding the seriousness and the causes of some environmental hazards also hinders international agreements.

> Whenever law is confronted with facts of nature or technology, its solution must rely on criteria derived from them. For law is intended to resolve problems posed

by such facts and it is herein that the link between law and the realities of life is manifest. It is not legal theory which provides answers to such problems; all it does is to select and adapt the one which best serves its purpose, and integrate it within the framework of law.[9]

When a nation is blamed for causing international pollution, it may dispute the factual or scientific evidence supporting the charge. For example, the United States government initially declined to acknowledge that its power-plant emissions were responsible for acid rain in Canada. It took measures to reduce the emissions only after overwhelming data proved that they were indeed causing the acid rain.

Further impediments to international agreement arise from issues of the proper allocation among nations of the costs for the necessary research and the requisite control regimes.

National self-interests motivate the challenges to international environmental regulation in the pursuit of a common international goal. Each nation seeks to minimize its burdens—fiscal, economic, political, and cultural—relative to those borne by other nation-parties. All nations expect to incur some costs in international programs, but their relative contributions and sacrifices vis-à-vis those of other nations is a chronic point of contention. On this point, two issues stand in sharp relief:

1. What share of global environmental harm is attributable to the economic and industrial activities of developed nations, and what share is attributable to improvident management of raw natural resources by less-developed nations?
2. To what extent should the disparate consumption of the world's resources (in the production and consumption of goods and services) by wealthier nations be weighed in assessing global environmental damage and resource depletion?

These issues are not amenable to objective scientific or political solutions, but they must be considered in negotiating international agreements. Developing nations continue to demand that economically advanced nations reduce their consumption of such resources as fossil fuels, which produces pollution and emits greenhouse gases. On the other hand, developed nations press poor nations to abandon the short-term expedients of excessive natural-resource removal—such as destroying the rain forests—because these resources are essential to preserving the earth's ecosystem. Relative faults aside, poor nations insist that they lack the necessary financial and technological resources to pursue desired environmental reforms and that wealthier nations that desire such reforms should furnish such resources through international assistance.

The clashes of national self-interest affect domestic politics, which color all international agreements. A nation's leaders may find it politically impractical or inconvenient to subordinate their country's domestic interests, even in the face of environmental imperatives. The later discussions of the Basel Convention and the Rio Earth Summit in section 11.4 provide clear examples of how special-interest groups within a nation can shift national positions and undermine international agreements, even when espoused by the nation's leaders or diplomatic missions.

The challenges to international cooperation are formidable but not insurmountable. When contemporary dangers to the global environment become critical for all nations and too important to sacrifice to national self-interest, the challenge of devising international law solutions that command international co-operation will be confronted and met, however haltingly.

11.3 Sources of International Law

International law has been succinctly described as "the body of rules and principles of action which are binding upon civilized states in their relations with one another.[10] The American Law Institute's definition reads:

> § 101. . . . International Law . . . consists of rules and principles of general application dealing with the conduct of [nation] states and of international organizations and with their relations . . . , as well as with some of their relations with persons [whether natural or fictitious; e.g., corporations].[11]

This definition embraces two branches of international law: "public" international law, which governs the relations among nation states and the international organizations to which they belong, and "private" international law, which governs the relations between a nation and citizens or corporations of other nations. This chapter deals primarily with government-to-government relations under public international law. It must be recognized, however, that such intergovernmental relations can produce international-law obligations for private parties.

By the mid twentieth century it was obvious that existing international law was ill-suited to emerging environmental issues. The unsatisfactory settlement of the 1987 Rhine River spill claims, discussed in section 11.4, resulted from the outmoded notion that national governments are responsible only for governmental actions and not for the actions of their respective subjects. That implicit lack of nation-to-nation responsibility for environmental injuries caused by private businesses and citizens is inherently incompatible with effective international regulation. Most older international-law decisions were equally limited in their focus on event-specific, localized harms; few of them addressed the continuing environmental injuries resulting from everyday private activities within many different nations. New international principles and rules are still needed for dealing with these continuing and widespread sources of environmental injury.

Branches of Public International Law

Public international law is derived from internationally recognized custom and international agreements:

§ 102. Sources of International Law
(1) A rule of international law is one that has been accepted as such by the international community of states
    (a) in the form of customary law;
    (b) by international agreement; or
    (c) by derivation from general principles common to the major legal systems of the world.
(2) Customary international law results from a general and consistent practice of states followed by them from a sense of legal obligation.
(3) International agreements create law for the states parties thereto and may lead to the creation of customary international law when such agreements are intended for adherence by states generally and are in fact widely accepted.
(4) General principles common to the major legal systems, even if not incorporated or reflected in customary law or international agreement, may be invoked as supplementary rules of international law where appropriate.[12]

Customary International Law

Customary international law is the oldest and the weakest foundation of international law. Custom cannot be taken as obligatory unless it has developed to the point where it is virtually universally adhered to. The lack of any long-established international customs regarding environmental problems provides little customary foundation to bind nations. Further, any custom that could be invoked would not bind a nation that has refused to adopt or follow it.[13]

Although scholars and commentators have attempted to beef up the "soft law" of international custom by arguing that resolutions and nonbinding actions of international organizations are evidence of customary international law, that argument has no entrenched acceptance in international law. The related argument that express international agreements are evidence of preexisting custom-based international law is equally problematic. Most treaties are too limited either in their covered topics or in the number of their signatory nations to manifest customary international acceptance of broad principles on the environment. The same objection applies to the argument that decisions of international courts are evidence of binding custom. Such decisions are too few in number and too narrow in scope to bind any nations other than those involved in the particular case.

Asserted principles of older customary law remain open to challenge. For example, the polluter-pays principle, or "nuisance" doctrine, that is well established in U.S. law was approved by some older international cases and in some international declarations.[14] In later years, however, that principle failed to gain full adoption by the U.N. International Law Commission on transboundary pollution.[15] The very fact that advocates of the polluter-pays doctrine continue to seek its formal adoption by written international agreement suggests that it is not firmly rooted in customary international law. In sum, customary international law is not sufficiently developed and has not generated significant solutions for modern environmental problems. Some commentators conclude that customary international law is "too vague to provide any guidance" for contemporary environmental problems and that modern international environmental law must be created by newly negotiated express international agreements.[16]

Express International Agreements

International agreements take many forms. They range from nonbinding unilateral declarations of intent, to joint proposed declarations of principles or goals, to firm agreements that create specific legal obligations. An international agreement may be called a *treaty*, a *charter*, a *convention*, an *accord*, a *protocol*, or some other term. International agreements are not confined to intergovernmental dealings. A nation may obligate itself in an agreement with an international organization or an agency of an international organization. Thus an agreement between the World Bank or the International Monetary Fund and a nation seeking a loan or grant for a specific project may, in setting forth the loan or grant terms, require the assisted nation to undertake specific environmental protection activities.

Major international agreements on the environment[17] employ a wide assortment of regulatory arrangements for structuring and monitoring environmental protection. In any agreement, the range of collective international actions is limited only by the imagination and political will of the participant nations. All such agreements, however, reflect the basic purposes of preventing and remediating environmental injury under an agreed upon system of environmental liability and enforcement. The examination of particular international agreements in the next section indicates the relative benefits of the various existing schemes of international regulation.

A common feature of many international agreements is the option of a nation to limit or condition its obligations by incorporating "reservations" regarding particular provisions or by attaching an "interpretive statement" as to its reading of the document.[18] Either device may exempt the "reserving" or "interpreting" nation from particular treaty obligations. As will be seen later in the chapter, these devices figured prominently in negotiations during the second Earth Summit and in the signing of the North American Free Trade Agreement. While selective reservations have the virtue of avoiding signatories' total rejection of a desired international agreement, they can also undermine an agreement's effectiveness when they are used excessively by parties to the agreement.

The Role of International Governmental Organizations

International governmental organizations are created by international agreements and are vested with powers to prepare and adopt international programs on specified subjects. Whereas some organizations such as the United Nations (U.N.) and the European Community (EC) perform a broad array of functions, others are highly specialized and directed to fairly narrow functions—the International Monetary Fund (IMF), the International Bank for Reconstruction and Development (IBRD; commonly called the *World Bank*), and various Joint International Commissions that implement single international projects being examples.

The structures and powers of international governmental organizations are not determined by any general norm of international law, but by the terms of the agreements that create them or assign tasks to them. For carrying out the terms of their agreements, nations may elect to rely upon specially created commissions, upon broadly chartered organizations, upon some combination of international organizations, or upon self-policing agencies of the signatory nations.[19] They may elect to submit a dispute to an outside international tribunal (such as the World Court and the European Community's Court of Justice, and Arbitration Commissions) or to the tribunal of a particular nation, or they may subject the parties to various internal and international tribunals at different stages of the dispute.

The impact and influence of international organization resolutions is sometimes direct, as when they promulgate rules that are made binding pursuant to formal treaty, contract, or by agreed conditions of international aid. More often the organizations' influence is indirect and persuasive, rather than binding, largely through educational and diplomatic activities. Respected organizations, such as the U.N., provide a forum and climate for encouraging nations to undertake environmental initiatives even where international law does not require them. Such specialized international organizations as the World Bank and the IMF have the leverage to induce environmental reforms in nations seeking their financial assistance, although they have sometimes promoted environmentally harmful industries and economic programs. For example, international aid packages may include contractual commitments or moral-obligation promises to use assistance grants or loans only in conformity with specified standards of environmental protection. Such conditions may also be negotiated independently of international organizations, as when a nation's grant agency, such as the United

States Agency for International Development (U.S. AID), and the recipient of its aid agree to follow an environmental-protection agenda.

International organizations and grant agencies have been criticized in the past for neglecting environmental issues and for unwittingly promoting projects that were environmentally damaging. For example, recent IMF loans to fund an expansion of the cattle raising industry in Brazil caused the displacement of people and the destruction of large areas of rainforest. However, the growing awareness of the potential adverse environmental impacts of poorly planned development projects and the increasing scrutiny of proposed aid projects by nongovernmental environmental organizations should lead to a higher priority to environmental concerns in the formulation of internationally assisted projects.

The Role of Nongovernmental Organizations (NGOs)

Nongovernmental organizations influence the formulation and administration of agreements among nations. Such NGOs as the World Conservation Union, the World Resources Institute, World Wildlife Fund, Friends of the Earth, Greenpeace, the Sierra Club, and the Wilderness Society, among many others, have sufficient expertise and political influence to command official consideration, if not endorsement, of their views.

NGOs provide centers for civic education and participation in official discussions of environmental programs. Many NGOs have acted as "shadow cabinets" and unofficial advisors at international meetings. Some have even received "consultative status" to governmental organizations that are directly involved in negotiating and implementing international agreements.[20]

> Never before UNCED [the United Nations Conference on the Environment and Development held in Rio de Janeiro, Brazil, in 1992] have NGOs been such active and material contributors to an international event. Only limited numbers of NGO representatives were admitted to the Riocentro [meeting of government delegates] but the UNCED proceedings were broadcast to the Global Forum on a twenty-foot television screen. . . . NGOs have animated most domestic and international issues for over twenty years. They served as "the soul and conscience of the [second Earth] Summit."[21]

At Rio, NGOs organized a Global Forum and conducted an "alternative Earth Summit" while monitoring the Summit proceedings. They sponsored numerous public events on the environment that were attended by thousands of people. NGOs were equally active in the negotiations of the North American Free Trade Agreement, and their officers have been appointed to official advisory bodies established under that agreement. The NGOs' advice and testimony are regularly sought by Congress and officials of the Executive branch, though they are not always welcome or accepted.[22]

11.4 International Environmental Law

International Custom

The *Trail Smelter Case*[23] illustrates the problems of developing customary international law in the environmental context. It arose out of a claim by the United States alleging that environmental injuries in Washington state were caused by emissions from a smelter plant across the border in British Columbia,

Canada. The U.S. and Canadian governments submitted the dispute to an international arbitration tribunal, which found Canada liable for the damage under customary international law. The tribunal stated that, although "[n]o case of air pollution dealt with by an international tribunal has been brought to the attention of the Tribunal nor does the Tribunal know of any such case," the "polluter pays" principle should apply. Since Canada did not contest the ruling, which extended unwritten international law principles to new ground, the *Trail Smelter* ruling could be construed narrowly as based on the parties' prior agreement to accept the tribunal's decision, rather than as an application of preexisting customary international law. While *Trail Smelter* has been cited favorably by some tribunals and publicists as authority for customary international law, its "polluter pays" principle has not been universally approved. Although some international declarations, which of themselves, are not legally binding, have espoused that principle, there is persisting division of opinion within the U.N. International Law Commission on the international obligation to refrain from transboundary pollution and on the effect of *Trail Smelter* in general international law.[24] As a standard of customary law, *Trail Smelter* may in time command wider international recognition, but only if the case is followed in other international forums.

International Agreements

No general agreement or recognized body of international principles governs the international environment universally. Modern international environmental law primarily consists of specialized international agreements dealing with specified environmental subjects.[25] It is far easier to achieve binding agreements on discrete environmental topics, especially among the nations directly affected by those topics, than it is to achieve widespread acceptance of omnibus regulation of all interconnected parts of the worldwide environment. Bilateral and regional agreements on specific environmental hazards far outnumber more ambitious, world-scale agreements. This specialized, incremental approach has fostered numerous accords among various coalitions of nations. Its successes are encouraging nations to consider expanded international efforts to cover a greater range of environmental regulation over wider geographic regions.

The currently favored approach to international deliberations is to prepare an agenda of acceptable topics in advance of an official conference. Proposals on the agenda item are then negotiated at the conference and are submitted to participant governments for their approval and joinder. Agenda proposals may include the creation of new norms of international law that supplement or alter existing laws or agreements. Examples of efforts to adapt prior international law to new environmental subjects and objectives include the 1972 Earth Summit, the 1972 London Dumping Convention, and the 1982 United Nations Convention on the Law of the Sea.[26]

The two-step "convention-protocol" process, which involves preliminary negotiation of a topical agreement (convention) followed by formal proposal (protocol) and its ratification (protocol), has gained increasing favor in world-scale conferences. It enables nations to attend and participate in the development of proposed conventions without being forced at that stage to accept or reject the adopted protocol. The decision is postponed to a later date. Through expanded nation participation in an open conference, more nations may be persuaded to accept the product of the conference deliberations. Further, by isolating the agenda topics for separate discussion and agreement, joinder by more nations in a greater number of protocols is more likely, since a comprehensive package of agreements would contain parts objectionable to many of them.

Proponents of the incremental convention-protocol approach point to the Montreal Protocol on Substances that Deplete the Earth's Ozone Layer (discussed in section 11.4) as a model of success. A drawback, however, is that it takes a long time to complete the convention-protocol process (agenda preparation, conference deliberation and formulation, postconference submission of protocols to nations for formal adoption and signature). The process often extends over a period of years, which may not be suitable for urgent problems that require prompt international responses.[27]

More than a dozen international conventions and treaties have been executed on wildlife, habitat, oceans, atmosphere, and hazardous substances. These include conventions on wetlands, endangered species, migratory wild animals, Antarctic marine life, marine pollution and ocean dumping, and the use and testing of nuclear materials and biological weapons.

Bilateral Agreements

Bilateral agreements typically address adjoining nations' transboundary environmental problems such as air and water pollution that cannot be solved by unilateral action.[28] Good-faith statements of intent or goals seldom satisfy any nation's desire to establish the obligations of other nations under international law. The following bilateral agreements between the United States and Canada and the United States and Mexico illustrate the environmental interdependence of neighboring nations and the control mechanisms that they may use.

United States-Canada Accords

The Great Lakes Water Quality Agreement of 1978, as revised in 1983 and 1987.   The Great Lakes system of inland seas contains 90 percent of the fresh surface water in North America. The lakes connect eight U.S. states and two Canadian provinces. Recognition of the need for international cooperation to protect the Great Lakes system led to one of the most comprehensive environmental ventures between the United States and Canada. It is also "one of very few . . . agreements to commit the signatories to an ecosystem-wide approach to solving water quality problems."[29] To assure comprehensive planning and regulation, the Agreement states that its mission is "to restore and maintain the chemical, physical, and biologic integrity of the waters of the Great Lakes Basin ecosystem," and it vests an International Joint Commission (IJC) of the United States and Canada with responsibility for carrying out that mission. The IJC recommends actions by each nation on all matters that affect the ecosystems of the Great Lakes and their abutting lands and feeder streams. Under the IJC administration, the lakes' water quality and ecosystems have substantially improved; the environmental stresses from air- and water-borne contamination and from eutrophication have materially diminished. Equally important has been the agreement's effect of fostering "an honest appraisal of the work that remains to be done" for continued protection of the Great Lakes.[30]

The United States–Canada Air Quality Accord of 1991.   This agreement followed years of discussion and debate on the causes and control of acid rain,[31] whose destructive impact in Canada was recently reviewed:

> . . . 14,000 Canadian lakes are . . . acidified with the loss of virtually all indigenous fish species; . . . one-third of the available Atlantic salmon habitat in Nova Scotia has been lost; more than 55 percent of forests in Eastern Canada . . . [are] in

areas where rainfall is acidic; even Canada's maple sugar industry is in jeopardy. . . . Fifty percent of the acid rain falling in Eastern Canada is manufactured in the United States and, thanks to prevailing winds and tall stacks, it is exported to Canada.[32]

The foregoing study noted that complete elimination of all acid-rain-causing emissions (sulfur dioxide) within either nation would not alone eliminate the problem, since pollution from the other nation would still produce damaging acid rain in both nations.

Before the Air Quality Accord, appeals to customary international law had been unavailing for controlling the acid rain problem. The agreement established firm obligations for emissions reductions for specific air pollutants and authorized air-quality-impact studies, research, and IJC recommendations for further cooperative initiatives by the two countries—obligations that are indispensable to meaningful progress.[33]

United States–Mexico Accords

The border separating the United States and Mexico is reportedly the longest border between a developed and a developing country, and the border region's environmental and economic importance can hardly be overstated:

> There are over 200 million crossings a year one way. It is distinguished by a map which is really a series of sister cities. . . . It is . . . a dozen sister cities across the border from each other in terms of where the people are.[34]

Severe water and sewage problems threaten the health of the region's populace and its economy.[35] Prior to the North American Free Trade Agreement (NAFTA) which is reviewed in section 11.5, the agreements between the United States and Mexico on their border environments were too modest in scale and obligation to have any material effect. Though NAFTA's primary focus is international trade, its demands for firmer environmental commitments and the debates over supplemental side agreements reflect the inadequacy of earlier bilateral agreements.

The *Colorado River Treaty of 1944* dealt with water supply sharing, and the saline degradation of Colorado river basin waters that vitally affect the United States and Mexico.[36] Nevertheless, the treaty had very limited goals, and the boundary commission (IBWC) it created confined its action to solving only narrow water problems. The IBWC made no attempt to implement a broad environmental program.[37]

The *La Paz Agreement of 1983*, "To Cooperate in the Solution of Environmental Problems in the Border Area,"[38] purported to address the air and water pollution that had become increasingly acute with the rapid urbanization of the border region—fueled by the influx of multinational corporations.[39] As an Executive Agreement between heads of state, *La Paz* had less momentum than a formally ratified treaty would have had. While *La Paz* declared the need for a framework of bilateral cooperation along a defined zone on both sides of the border and for a joint commission to monitor environmental programs, it failed to establish specific pollution-reduction targets (with a few exceptions). Its ineffective generality is apparent in the language of its Article 2:

> The Parties undertake, to the fullest extent practical, to adopt the appropriate measures to prevent, reduce and eliminate sources of pollution in their respective territory which affect the border area of the other. . . . Additionally, the Parties shall cooperate in the solution of the environmental problems of mutual concern in the border area, in accordance with the provisions of this Agreement.[40]

In 1991 the presidents of Mexico and the United States followed up *La Paz* by signing a Border Environmental Plan that called for special projects on water treatment, municipal waste collection, and industrial toxic wastes. The plan was criticized as being long on listed projects and short on concrete plans for controlling pollution,[41] and each nation failed to dedicate adequate resources for implementing border plans.

Although *La Paz* was cited in later NAFTA discussions as a model to be avoided,[42] experience under *La Paz* had the beneficial effect of sensitizing national leaders to the need for much stronger environmental commitments by both countries. The tasks envisioned by *La Paz* will now pass to official panels responsible for implementing NAFTA and its supplemental side agreements. It is hoped that the historic reserve and mistrust that impeded past U.S.–Mexico cooperation on environmental issues may give way to a better environmental outlook and performance under NAFTA. However, the serious environmental and health problems in Mexico's border *maquiladera* (factory) zone pose enormous challenges for NAFTA implementation.

Multilateral Regional Agreements

As with bilateral agreements, most multilateral regional agreements involve specific environmental concerns, very often concerns regarding international river basins. Agreements on international waterways in Europe date from the early nineteenth century, but they are now commonly found among nations of all continents.[43]

> There are now some 300 international agreements dealing with particular rivers, lakes or drainage basins, which together cover something less than half of the world's international drainage basins. . . . Many of these agreements . . . establish joint commissions or similar . . . institutions . . . .[44]

Rhine River Conventions

Agreements to protect the Rhine River include the *Berne Accord of 1963* (to protect it against pollution), the *Bonn Conventions of 1976* (to protect it against chemical pollution and chlorides), and the *Strasbourg Rhine Action Programe of 1987* (to protect it as an international river).[45]

The *Berne Convention* between France, Germany, Luxembourg, the Netherlands and the Swiss Confederation was expanded by the *Bonn Supplementary Agreement* to include the European Economic Community. It committed the parties to specific measures for reducing and eliminating discharges of specified pollutants into the Rhine and authorized a previously established international commission to propose maximum concentration limits for discharged wastes. *Berne* further provided for monitoring of river conditions in each nation and for arbitration of disputes arising under the agreements. It called upon the signatories to fashion their own national programs for achieving river restoration goals before specified time deadlines. The *Bonn Agreement* also covers preservation of the underground water sources that affect the condition of the Rhine.

The existence of these agreements did not prevent a catastrophic chemical spill at Basel, Switzerland, in 1987 that poisoned the entire length of the Rhine from Switzerland through West Germany, France, Luxembourg, and the Netherlands. That experience fixed the need for continued improvement of protective international regulations and demonstrated the inadequacy of postdamage liability rules of law to deter such mishaps. The spill occurred when firemen battling a blaze at a warehouse owned by the Swiss company, Sandoz S.A., washed tons of toxic chemicals stored there into the Rhine. The spill alert system that had been established by the International Commission for the Protection of the Rhine failed, because Swiss authorities did not issue the timely notices intended by that system that could have permitted the spill to be contained downstream. The resultant contamination cut off drinking and irrigation water supplies along the Rhine and decimated river ecosystems, fish kills were estimated at 500,000. Experts estimated that the Rhine would not recover from the spill for at least ten years.

Switzerland was not required as a matter of international law to pay for the spill's huge damage, and it did not do so. Instead, Switzerland and the other affected nations negotiated settlements of claims that the Sandoz company would pay.

> No trace of Swiss State responsibility can be found in the communiques from the conferences of the Rhine ministers held after . . . the accident. Nor did the European Community's Council of [environmental] ministers, meeting shortly after the disaster, breathe a word about State responsibility. Instead, both bodies spoke solely about Sandoz' civil liability. . . . Though there was undoubtedly unlawful action and omission by the Swiss Confederation and . . . authorities, so that, in principle, State responsibility is present, no riparian State has . . . called on the Swiss State for direct compensation for damage or restoration to the original state of the affected Rhine. The final communiques . . . of Rhine ministers carefully ignore the topic.[46]

Why the ministers of injured states avoided pressing the issue of state responsibility is a matter of speculation. Perhaps they regarded the prospect of national responsibility under international law as too fearsome a remedy and one that could one day be invoked against their own nations. If that be true, the need for preventive international regulations, as opposed to retrospective compensation, is all the more evident.

European Community Agreements

The European Community (EC) consisting of most, but not all, European nations evolved from a merger of transitional organizations and it remains a "still-developing entity". The EC functions as a sort of supranational entity through its parliament, Council of Ministers, European Commission, and European Court of Justice.[47] It promotes regional environmental protection through its commissions and directorates.

EC joinder in the above mentioned *Bonn Convention* signaled its growing involvement in regional agreements. The EC also joined a Convention on the Conservation of European Wildlife. Although many of the EC recommendations and regulations are not directly enforceable, their influence on the policies and attitudes of member nations, especially when endorsed by the EC Council of Ministers, is growing.[48] As noted in the next subsection, the EC's influence upon international agreements can be decisive. It has endorsed the polluter-pays principle.

> The Polluter-Pays Principle constitutes for Member countries a fundamental principle for allocating costs of pollution prevention and control measures introduced by the public authorities in Member countries.[49]

The respective jurisdictions of various EC offices and of its member nations are still being worked out, but the European Court of Justice has accorded legal significance to Community decisions in some cases.[50] As acceptance of the EC's recommendations grows, so may its regulatory authority on the European regional environment.

World Scale Agreements

The movement toward world-scale agreements on the global environment is relatively new and it is growing. Although some "holdout" nations still decline to attend world-scale discussions (because they lack conviction that international action is needed, they disagree with the structure of a particular conference, or they expect other nations to give them a "free ride" in solving international environmental problems), their numbers can be expected to diminish. Eventually the costs of environmental damage will hit them closer to home, and the pressure of international opinion favoring cooperation within the wider international community can only grow.

The Basel Convention on the Control of Transboundary Movements of Hazardous Wastes and Their Disposal

The conference that produced the *1989 Basel Convention on the Control of Transboundary Movements of Hazardous Wastes and Their Disposal* was convened by the United Nations Environment Programme to address problems caused by unregulated international trade in, and export of, toxic and hazardous wastes. The *Convention* forbids the export of hazardous waste to any country whose government does not agree in advance to accept it after receiving advance notification of the intended shipment from the government of the exporting country. Furthermore, it requires both the exporting and the importing nation to take the necessary measures to assure environmentally safe methods of disposal of the shipped wastes.[51] Delegates from Third World nations, which were suffering most from the dumping of hazardous-waste exports in their territories, had desired a total Convention ban on such exports. As of 1994, the *Convention* had been signed by 107 nations and ratified by 64 nations, and the EC Commission, and the United States had indicated its intent to support and ratify it.[52]

The first step toward U.S. ratification of the *Basel Convention* was taken in early March 1994, when the Swift–Synar bill was introduced in the House of Representatives. The bill sought to amend RCRA and implement the *Convention*.[53] President Clinton and the U.S. Chamber of Commerce supported the legislation.

On March 25, 1994, at a conference on the Basel Convention in Geneva, Switzerland, all attending nations—including all members of the Organization for Economic Cooperation and Development (OECD), which consists of 24 major industrialized nations including the United States—joined unanimously by consensus vote a "historic" resolution that was introduced and approved by the nation ratifiers of the Basel Convention. That resolution called for an *immediate and total ban* on hazardous-waste exports to countries outside the OECD. In addition, the resolution called for a phase-out by December 31, 1997 of hazardous-waste exports intended for recycling.[54] Although only those nations that had ratified the Convention would cast formal votes on the resolution, the unanimous support of the conference delegates was seen by some as binding on all nations that were represented, including those that had previously opposed a total ban. Even if not binding in international law without formal U.S. ratification and approval, the ban resolution will be difficult to resist, since it received prior official endorsement of the European Union Council of Ministers, which represents the major European exporters of hazardous waste.[55]

On May 18, in reaction to the foregoing resolution for a total ban on hazardous waste exports to non-OECD nations, the U.S. Chamber of Commerce withdrew its support and expressed U.S. industry opposition to the Basel Convention and to the Swift–Synar bill to implement it. By summer 1994, neither the Congress nor the Clinton Administration had arrived at a firm position on the matter, and the ultimate fate of the Basel Convention and of the 1994 consensus ban on exports to undeveloped nations cannot be predicted.

The Montreal Protocol on Substances that Deplete the Earth's Ozone Layer

The ozone layer, a gaseous layer of molecules which lies some 15 to 30 miles above the earth's surface, absorbs, and shields the earth from, certain forms of harmful ultraviolet radiation from outer space. The thickness of the ozone layer is closely associated with certain aspects of the earth environment, namely, climate and biodiversity. Without an adequate ozone shield, excessive penetration of ultraviolet radiation will alter the earth's climate systems and injure human, animal, and plant life—including the life of plankton, an integral link in aquatic food chains.

Changes in the earth's ozone shield and climate occur naturally from time to time and episodically due to exceptional natural events such as volcanic eruptions. These natural changes are aggravated, however, by emissions of some man-made substances, such as chlorofluorocarbons (CFCs). Scientists continue to study the processes and rate of ozone depletion and restoration in order to better understand the extent to which human activities deplete the ozone layer. They generally agree that ozone depletion has occurred since the 1970s, but they disagree as to the rate of depletion and the rate of ozone recovery. (Chapter 9 provides a fuller discussion of those issues.) The international community has acted to reduce the use of known ozone-depleting gasses, principally of chlorofluorocarbons (CFCs), which are widely used in manufacturing processes and in consumer and industrial products such as coolants, cleaners, and foams. These efforts are reported more extensively elsewhere.[56]

The *1985 Vienna Convention for the Protection of the Ozone Layer* and the *1987 Montreal Protocol on Substances that Deplete the Ozone Layer* (and its 1990 amendments) comprise the principal international agreements on the topic of ozone depletion.[57] The *Vienna Convention,* with United Nations sponsorship, was an attempt "to protect human health and the environment against adverse effects resulting or likely to result from human activities which modify or are likely to modify the ozone layer. . . ." Articles II and III of it called for systematic studies and exchange of information by the signatory nations and pledged the nations "to control, limit, reduce or prevent human activities under their jurisdiction" that adversely affect the ozone layer.

The *Montreal Protocol* advanced *Vienna* by establishing specific time schedules and control measures for limiting the use of listed ozone-depleting chemicals that, alone or in mixture with other atmospheric conditions, contribute to ozone destruction. The specificity of the controls undertaken in the *Montreal Protocol* assured concrete results in reducing industrial sources of ozone depletion. Even so, the later discovery that ozone-layer thinning was more extensive than was thought at the time of the Montreal meetings led 81 nations to press for an accelerated phaseout of chlorofluorocarbons production by the year 2000. The largest U.S. manufacturer of CFCs (Du Pont) voluntarily undertook to complete its phaseout of all CFC production by 1995.

Full achievement of the *Montreal* goals will require further international effort. Nations that did not sign the protocol may continue to emit ozone-depleting chemicals, and those that did sign it may still produce gases that were not outlawed by the Protocol but that also damage the ozone layer or impede its regeneration (for example, methane, carbon dioxide, and methyl bromide).

The 1990 Clean Air Act of the United States mandated that EPA develop a list of ozone-safe chemical substitutes for CFCs, and EPA issued a list of proposed substitutes in May 1993. Full use of CFC substitutes has been delayed while EPA assesses the environmental impacts of its proposed substitutes and while interim hearings are held for gathering public comments and objections. Environmental organizations have objected to some of the proposed substitutes as being environmentally dangerous and harmful.[58]

The Earth Summits of 1972 and 1992

The 1972 Earth Summit.   The *1972 United Nations Conference on the Human Environment,* also called the "first Earth Summit" and the "Stockholm Conference," convened pursuant to a resolution of the United Nations General Assembly:

> to provide a framework for comprehensive consideration within the United Nations of the problems of the human environment in order to focus the attention of Governments and public opinion on the . . . urgency of this question and also to identify those aspects . . . that can . . . be solved through international cooperation and agreement. . . .[59]

The conference was "the first . . . time that the global community came together to plan such a system" of international cooperation."[60] It was attended by some 114 governments and observed by many nongovernmental organizations, and it promptly disclosed the rift between developed and less-developed (Third World) countries:

- Southern Hemisphere and Third World nations argued that industrialized nations, as the principal generators and beneficiaries of global environmental damage, should undertake the primary burdens of environmental restoration—that they should scale back their environmentally damaging economic activities and consumption and their production of environmentally damaging products, and that they should underwrite the costs of restoring the global environment, providing financial and technological assistance to poor nations as needed to enable them to pursue environmentally sound economic activities.
- Developed nations argued that less-developed nations should modify their environmentally damaging practices, such as improvident land clearing, deforestation, overgrazing, and mining.

The Conference attempted to by-pass this fundamental conflict by supporting both positions under the ideal of environmentally compatible "sustainable development." It declared that environmental considerations should be part of the economic planning and development of all nations, and that economically advanced nations should assist poor nations to initiate environmental reforms, since they cannot afford to pursue them without such aid.

The Stockholm Conference produced three major documents: a Declaration on the Human Environment, which affirms human responsibility to preserve the environment; a Declaration of 26 Principles concerning the environment; and 109 Recommendations for follow-up action under United Nations auspices.[61] The two Declarations asserted important guiding principles but did little to change international law. The Recommendations had the important but limited value of providing a platform for continued international discussions.

The seminal ideas advanced by the Declaration of the Principles include the assertions of the human right to a safe environment; the responsibility of nations to preserve natural ecosystems, wildlife, and the earth's capacity to renew vital resources; the need to halt the releases of substances and heat beyond levels that are consistent with human health and the earth's capacity to absorb them safely; and the recognition that sound economic development is environmentally attainable with proper international cooperation and international financial assistance. The framers of the Declaration attempted to finesse the crucial challenge of these principles by affirming that each nation has a sovereign right to plan and control the economic development and exploitation of its natural resources as well as an obligation to prevent and abate extraterritorial environmental damage. The potential inconsistency in the Declaration may explain the hesitancy of many nations to commit to firm international environmental protection that would encroach upon their absolute autonomy. Less controversial were the Conference propositions advocating improved environmental education, applied science and technology, and improved international funding for the environment.

The Conference's 109 Recommendations covered a wide range of substantive and organizational topics. They are not legally binding and they leave to each nation the decisions of whether and how to implement them.[62] The Recommendations were referred to the United Nations Environment Programme for further action.

The 1992 Earth Summit.   On the twentieth anniversary of the first Earth Summit, the 1992 *United Nations Conference on the Environment and Development* (UNCED) convened in Rio de Janeiro, Brazil. The United Nations General Assembly had called the Conference to continue the work of the first Earth Summit. Representatives of some 117 countries attended the Rio Conference to consider a number of draft agreements and an "Earth Charter" which had been prepared for submission to UNCED.[63] The achievements and failures of the Rio proceedings are reported in several sources,[64] and were summarized as follows:

> Two conventions, the Framework Convention on Climate Change and the Convention on Biological Diversity, were negotiated before UNCED and signed there. Two aspirational documents were . . . concluded in Rio. They were a statement of guiding principles called the Rio Declaration and the 500-page "cookbook" for sustainability known as Agenda 21. Participating countries also agreed to a set of forest principles and to hold a conference for a future convention on desertification.
>
> The list of legal instruments is impressive . . . . The problem is that assent was reached through whittling away at somewhat better documents. . . . Typically, one party would let another relax its commitment in return for a similar easing of responsibility. . . . Much of UNCED, indeed, was an unseemly quarrel over money. Several of the developing countries plausibly apologized for their inability to stem deforestation . . . without financial help. Industrialized countries try to obscure their avoidance of promising aid to their have-not neighbors. . . .
>
> If Rio made a start on . . . the interconnected problems of sustainable development, there is surely doubt about whether it went as far as it should or could have. M. P. A. Kindall's view is that Rio failed at the most fundamental level. . . . Kindall, a member of the U.S. delegation to UNCED, corroborates that the . . . most intractable disagreements were between developing and developed countries.[65]

The U.S. Senate delegation's report to Congress outlined the goals and results of the Rio Conference in greater detail.

I.   BACKGROUND

A.

. . . the United Nations General Assembly adopted Resolution 44/228, calling for a major, comprehensive international conference on the global environment and development . . . .

. . . As outlined in the Resolution . . . , the primary issues to be addressed included:

> . . . Protecting human health and improving quality of life; Protection of the atmosphere by combating climate change, depletion of the ozone layer and transboundary air pollution; Protection of the quality and supply of freshwater resources; Protection of the oceans and other seas; Protection and management of land resources, including combating desertification, deforestation, and drought; Conservation of biological diversity and environmentally sound management of biotechnology; Environmentally sound waste management.

* * *

Three key documents resulted from the UNCED process.

> (1) Agenda 21—comprising some 40 chapters—is a comprehensive *but non-legally binding* action program designed to reconcile the goals of continued economic development and environmental preservation . . . . (Emphasis supplied.)
> (2) The Rio Declaration on Environment and Development" . . . [is designed] to guide world leaders in "Working towards international agreements with respect to the interests of all . . . .
> (3) The Statement of Principles for a Global Consensus on the Management, Conservation and Sustainable Development of All Types of Forests" is a *non-legally binding* statement addressing the multiple uses . . . of forest resources. (Emphasis supplied.)
> (4) Negotiations were also carried out . . . on . . . a global climate change convention and a biological diversity convention.

B.   Climate change convention

The [pre-Conference] negotiating . . . was initiated pursuant to UN General Assembly resolution . . . .

* * *

The Framework Convention was adopted . . . in February, 1992, and by June 14, the convention had been signed by 153 nations including the U.S. *Although specific commitments to targeted reductions in greenhouse gas emissions were sought by many parties . . . , the United States and some other countries successfully resisted inclusion of these* . . . . (Emphasis supplied.)

C.   Biological Diversity Convention

. . . . [It] called for the development of a legal instrument to protect the diverse biological resources of the planet.

. . . .[B]y June 14 the Convention had been signed by 153 states.

II.   Substantive Analysis of the Rio Agreements

A.   Agenda 21

. . . Agenda 21 puts forth several . . . action items that, if fully implemented, could prove to be quite significant. . . .

1.   Chapter 33. Financial Resources and Mechanisms: . . . it was agreed that: In general, financing will "come from a country's own public and private sectors"; . . . However, developed countries reaffirmed their "commitments to reach the . . . United Nations target of 0.7 percent of GNP [gross national product] for ODA [overseas development assistance]." It should be noted that the U.S. . . . [has] not . . . undertaken this UN commitment. Therefore, use of the word "reaffirm" *appears to exclude the U.S. from the terms of this provision.* (Emphasis supplied.)

* * *

2. Chapter 38. International Institutional Arrangements: This Chapter suggests means by which . . . various intergovernmental and United Nations agencies . . . may be better coordinated in order to further the objectives of Agenda 21. . . .

3. Chapter 34. Access to Environmentally Sound Technology: The activities proposed in this Chapter aim at "improving conditions and processes on information, access to and transfer of technology," . . . .

* * *

B.   Rio Declaration

This document was originally intended to be an "Earth Charter"—. . . to mark the beginning of a global partnership . . . to work toward sustainable patterns of development. Opposition . . . by some countries, including the U.S., however, combined with persistent calls by the developing nations for a recognition by the developed countries of: their disproportionate contribution to global environmental problems; a need to change consumption patterns . . . to stem further environmental destruction; and a need for developed countries to provide increased technical and financial assistance . . . resulted in an impasse. . . .

. . . [T]he Rio Declaration was . . . an attempt to reconcile contentious issues. . . . Several countries, including the U.S., issued interpretative statements expressing their respective understandings of the document's import.

C.   Statement of Principles on Forests

It was originally anticipated that a legally binding convention on the preservation of forests would be negotiated and agreed to . . . . Discussions toward that end proved highly contentious, . . . the U.S. initially insisted that the treaty should only apply to tropical forests, and . . . several developing countries resisted binding commitments on the grounds that they pose a threat to sovereignty and would unduly impede necessary development. Efforts to incorporate language calling for . . . negotiation . . . in the *non-legally binding Statement* . . . also failed.

The Statement of Principles does recognize that forests should be "sustainably managed to meet . . . needs of present and future generations." The statement also calls on all countries to take action "towards reforestation, afforestation and forest conservation," and to carry out environmental impact assessments. . . . Failure to agree on what is entailed in [these efforts] . . . raised concerns . . . that the Statement will not prove effective in preserving forest ecosystems.

D.   Framework Convention on Climate Change

The objective of the Convention . . . is to achieve "stabilization of greenhouse gas concentrations in the atmosphere at a level that would prevent dangerous anthropogenic interference with the climate system." Article 2 further specifies that such stabilization "should be achieved within a time frame sufficient to allow ecosystems to adapt naturally to climate change, . . . and to enable economic development to proceed in a sustainable manner." . . . Because developed, industrialized countries are responsible for the greatest share of anthropogenic greenhouse gas emissions and are best able, financially and technically, to stem those emissions, the undertakings . . . in the Convention differ for developed and developing country Parties.

* * *

. . . the United States, alone among industrialized countries, opposed . . . binding commitments to reduce greenhouse gas emissions. All other industrialized countries had . . . made commitments to reduce emissions . . . . . . *As a result,* other industrialized countries . . . ultimately accepted language that was *devoid of binding commitments* . . . .

* * *

. . . It is . . . fair to expect that follow-on Protocols, that will add binding commitment to the Convention, will be pursued—just as the Montreal Protocol and London Amendments added binding measures to the original framework outlined in the Vienna Convention.

E.   Convention on Biological Diversity

. . . [T]he objectives of the Conventions are: "the conservation of biological diversity, the sustainable use of its components and the fair and equitable sharing of the benefits . . . . [T]he Convention specifies actions aimed at conserving plant and animal biodiversity and at facilitating access to and transfer of relevant technology.

Conservation Provisions: . . . while the commitments are legally binding, *they are qualified,* and Parties are bound to fulfill them only "as far as possible and as appropriate."

* * *

The United States was alone among industrialized countries in declining to sign the Convention. . . . [W]e also took issue with provisions . . . dealing with intellectual property protections and with the treatment of modified living organisms. With regard to intellectual property protection, the White House believed the treaty could be read as calling for the subversion of such protections . . . .

* * *

The countries agreed to create a new Commission for Sustainable Development within the United Nations, to review the implementation of Agenda 21 . . . but its precise structure was left for future determination. They further agreed that additional funds to finance sustainable development in developing nations should employ all available resources, *but the industrialized nations refused to pledge the level of funding assistance which third world nations thought necessary to enable them to pursue the Rio objectives.* [Emphasis supplied][66]

Following his election, President Clinton essentially repudiated and reversed the positions of President Bush's administration regarding the Convention on Biological Diversity and the Framework Convention on Climate Change. On Earth Day (April 21) 1993, President Clinton announced that the United States would sign the Rio Treaty on Biological Diversity, but with an interpretive statement to protect U.S. industries from any obligation to share their technology and intellectual property with other countries. The interpretive statement reservations do not affect the Biodiversity Treaty provisions that foreign companies (including U.S. companies) share some of the profits they earn from products derived from native plant and animal species of developing countries (such as new pharmaceuticals and bioengineering products).

The biodiversity treaty contains important protective regulations on development of national strategies for coordinating economic planning with protection of plant and animal life and on inventorying, monitoring, and managing biological resources in terms of entire ecosystems as well as of individual species. The mixed reaction of environmental groups to Clinton's settlement of the biodiversity treaty impasse reflects a perennial environmental issue; is it necessary and desirable to seek negotiated compromises between environmental and business groups that accommodate their respective major concerns or should such compromises be opposed because they tend to dilute and postpone environmental reforms?[67]

With regard to the Convention on Climate Change, the Rio Conference reported that excessive emissions of gases (for example, carbon dioxide, CFCs, methane, and freon) create a "greenhouse" effect on the earth and consequent global warming and climate changes that portend dire harms to various forms of animal and plant life. Scientific uncertainty regarding the extent to which greenhouse gases and the substances that generate them interfere with natural climate variations justifies organized international studies. The 1990 World Climate Conference had urged world governments and nongovernment organizations "to treat climate change as a priority issue . . . [and] to increase understanding of all sources and causes of climate change . . . ."[68] Against that background, President Clinton announced that the United States would reduce its greenhouse gas emissions to 1990 levels by the year 2000.

11.5   Potential Conflicts between Trade Agreements and Environmental Agreements

International interdependence in solving global environmental problems is accompanied by international interdependence in liberalizing world trade, which is widely viewed as indispensable to all nations' economic welfare. In the trade sphere also, nations have resorted to regional and world-scale agreements in their efforts to eliminate barriers to free trade. The resultant trade agreements have done more than confront international trade frictions, however. In many cases they have aggravated the frictions between economic policy and environmental policy. Whereas the major world-scale trade agreement, the General Agreement on Tariffs and Trade (GATT), seeks free trade among all nations, many GATT member countries enjoy special regional trading preferences that serve to disadvantage nations in other regions. The trade blocs and agreements within the European Community and among Canada, Mexico, and the United States under NAFTA are cases in point. To the extent that regional trade agreements promote such trade preferences, they undercut GATT's free-trade ideal. These disparities in trade agreements in turn further complicate attempts to harmonize trade and environmental objectives worldwide. If environmental programs are not to be captive to shifting international trade arrangements, the international law on commerce must be harmonized with the international law on the environment, and means must be devised for resolving the inconsistencies in environmental and trade policies. In sum, international trade obligations and international environmental obligations cannot be considered in isolation of each other.

Trade-agreement obligations to grant access to certain nations' imports may clash with the importing nation's efforts to protect its own environment (and the international environment) by excluding imports whose content or method of production threaten those environments. Unqualified free-trade access for businesses operating in environmentally lax nations also creates unfair competitive advantages against nations with high environmental standards. When a nation attempts to remedy these cost and environmental disparities by imposing embargoes or tariffs, however, other nations invoke trade agreements that guarantee them free access to its markets.

Professor J. Jackson, a free trade expert and advocate, has summarized these dilemmas as follows:

- The policies of protecting the environment are vital to human welfare, but liberalizing international trade also is necessary for improving the lives of all peoples, particularly in impoverished nations.
- Imposing rules that restrict trade for environmental considerations defeats free-trade goals, while agreements that outlaw such restrictions prevent

nations from enforcing their own or internationally established environmental standards.

- Environmental and free trade policies may thus clash with each other, rather than harmoniously advance common human welfare goals.
- Trade and environmental rules need not necessarily be opposed, and they could be tailored in such ways that they strengthen each other.[69]

The task of adapting and integrating international agreements for free trade and environmental protection is far from finished. Among other things, it will require reformulating existing international agreements and structures and overcoming established cultures and mind sets of diplomats and technical experts whose training, concerns, and perceptions are focused only on one of the interrelated spheres of free trade and the environment. Further, there is no longer universal agreement that free trade policies will improve the quality of life in Third World nations, or their attempts to promote self-sufficiency. Many analysts question the desirability of free trade in the face of cooperative efforts that improve *regionally* self-sufficient communities. These critics charge that free trade operates to benefit richer nations, not impoverished ones, and that emphasizing regional and local self-sufficiency would be more effective for preventing further environmental degradation than would promoting worldwide free trade.

The General Agreement on Tariffs and Trade (GATT)

The *GATT agreement,* actually a series of agreements, refers to both a system of rules for international trade and the organization that oversees their implementation. As supplemented by numerous other trade treaties, GATT is the major international agreement on world trade. By agreement of its members, GATT will be replaced and succeeded in 1995 by the World Trade Organization (WTO). On April 15, 1994,

> The United States and more than 100 other countries . . . signed a historic agreement . . . to establish a new World Trade Organization to replace the General Agreement on Tariffs and Trade [in 1995]. . . . A total of 124 countries, plus the European Commission, . . . will automatically become members of WTO. Another 21 countries . . . have applied to join.[70]

This subsection's discussion of GATT applies generally to its successor WTO as well.

Although GATT establishes international trade rules and standards, it lacks independent authority to enforce them. The member nations generally (though not universally) comply with GATT decisions in the interest of preserving free trade opportunities.[71] Disputes arising under GATT are usually settled by negotiation or by GATT mediation.

The major frictions which GATT creates for environmental protection arise from its prohibition against excluding the products of member nations, even if those products or the exporting nation's production practices are environmentally damaging. GATT has thus tended to enforce trade access with a blind eye to environmentally harmful practices of businesses in exporting nations. The exception to this is products that *directly* harm the health or environment of the importing nation once those products reach the importing nation. Even then, however, nations may charge that this is trade discrimination, as in the case of complaints by foreign oil refineries that new U.S. requirements for reformulated gasoline discriminate against other countries' gasoline companies and their products.

GATT may find discrimination even where the businesses of an environmentally progressive importing country are placed at a competitive disadvantage against businesses of environmentally lax countries, which need not incur the costs of using environmentally sound materials, equipment, and processes in producing goods for international trade. Still, the fear exists that one nation's unilateral exclusion of foreign goods as an instrument for advancing its own environmental policies could create an unmanageable loophole for trade discrimination. This is referred to by some as "eco-imperialism," because one country through its trade laws would impose its own environmental policies on other nations. Such fears have led GATT to protect only free trade and not the environment.[72]

The lack of an adequate system for resolving free-trade/environmental protection conflicts became apparent when the United States imposed an embargo against the domestic sale (and importation) of tuna caught by "purse seine" nets, a practice the United States prohibited under its laws for protecting marine mammals. Fishing fleets using purse seine nets locate schools of dolphin on the ocean surface and cast large purse seine nets around them in order to capture schools of tuna, which tend to swim below the dolphin. This results in the death of the dolphins trapped in the giant nets. Mexico sought and obtained a GATT panel's ruling that the tuna embargo violated the GATT international trade rules.[73] The GATT Panel acknowledged the dilemma of pitting GATT trade rights against environmental policy, but insisted that its function was restricted solely to trade access.

The tendency of the tuna–dolphin decision to discourage environmental protection is obvious. If a nation is obliged to accept imports produced cheaply by environmentally destructive materials and methods, its own domestic industries suffer a competitive disadvantage. The consequence will be pressure to reduce environmental protection standards to the lowest common international denominator. The United States has appealed the panel's decision to a higher GATT tribunal, but environmental organizations have sought a moratorium on GATT proceedings in such cases, pending the organization of the new WTO,[74] which is scheduled to review GATT rules and revise them to accomplish a better linkage and reconciliation of trade and environmental protection.

At the April 1994 GATT meeting, the attending ministers approved the creation of a permanent committee on trade and the environment within the new World Trade Organization, with a broad mandate to investigate the linkages of trade and the environment. According to the director of GATT's division on technical trade and environment, the new committee is expected to

> look at problems, find solutions and, where necessary, propose changes to the world trading system, solutions to investigated problems and possible changes in the trading system.[75]

Among other things, the committee is expected to review the trade-related aspects of international environmental agreements (such as the Montreal Protocol and the Basel Convention) and the relationship between enforcement and dispute-settlement mechanisms of trade and environmental agreements. Investigation of such items could lead to incorporating environmental protection terms of international agreements into WTO's free-trade-access provisions as exceptions to free access obligations.

The effectiveness of the new permanent committee will, of course, depend upon adoption and ratification of its creation and of its final recommendations by WTO member nations. Since so many GATT members expressed preliminary support for creating the committee and have subscribed to international environmental agreements and conventions, the prospects for effectuating the committee's work seemed good in late 1994. The movement to make environmental protection an operative part of trade agreements is also gaining approval in regional pacts, such as the NAFTA agreement.

The North American Free Trade Agreement (NAFTA)

On December 17, 1992, Canada, Mexico, and the United States signed the lengthy (2,000-page) North American Free Trade Agreement (NAFTA). The document created a free trade market among the three nations by eliminating tariffs and other trade barriers. Among other things, NAFTA established a framework to supervise and implement its provisions including a Free Trade Commission, a Secretariat, and the use of arbitration panels. A suit was brought to invalidate NAFTA on the ground that it had been made without a prior environmental impact statement (EIS) in violation of NEPA (see Chapter 3). The deciding court, however, upheld the NAFTA agreement and rejected the argument that it was subject to NEPA requirements.[76]

It was understood, however, that NAFTA would not be submitted or considered for ratification by the U.S. Congress unless it were accompanied by satisfactory supplemental "side" agreements on subjects that were deemed to be crucial to NAFTA's success. Some side agreements resulted in minimal environmental protection (particularly with regard to Mexico) and labor-management policies within each trading nation, and cooperative management of surges of imported products during the initial operation of NAFTA that could otherwise disrupt the economy of any trading partner.

The development of a U.S. position on the terms of a side agreement on the environment produced heated controversies both within Congress and among and within major environmental organizations. Mexico's historical failure to enforce its own environmental laws, and the considerable disparity in the levels of wage and labor protection in the respective NAFTA nations begged for stringent and internationally enforceable prohibitions against substandard environmental and labor terms and conditions. But the refusal of Mexico and Canada to accede to controls deemed by them to interfere with their internal affairs and national sovereignty foreclosed any possible agreement of significant scope. While the U.S., Mexico and Canada agreed in general to pursue environmental and trade policies that are compatible with the new free trade zone created by NAFTA, the translation of those principles into international agreement required considerable compromise.

Against this background, the U.S. government, with the support of some but not all environmental NGOs (namely, World Wildlife Fund, National Wildlife Federation, Defenders of Wildlife, Environmental Defense Fund, National Audubon Society, Natural Resources Defense Council, Nature Conservancy) finally achieved side agreements on the above subjects. In November 1993, Congress approved the NAFTA package to take effect as of January 1, 1994, by enacting the North American Free Trade Agreement Implementation Act.[77]

As finally approved, NAFTA does not empower an international commission directly to enforce, enjoin, or penalize a signatory nation or its nationals for environmental offenses or for unfair labor standards. Rather, it directs the NAFTA agencies to press a nation-party to investigate complaints of environmental law or labor condition violations within the signatory nation's territory and then to take remedial action by reporting and making recommendations to the government and NAFTA agencies.

With regard to labor and wage control legislation, the lower wage structures and costs of companies operating in Mexico remain a concern to U.S.-based operations and workers. Unless the NAFTA nations devise means to diminish these disparities, the trade vs. environmental frictions discussed earlier in this chapter will impede full acceptance or achievement of NAFTA's free trade goals. In such an event, NGOs and labor organizations may revive their demands for firmer side agreements that will:

- Induce each member nation to adopt more effective laws and practice law enforcement;
- Set timetables for achieving the coordination of member nations' environmental laws;
- Adopt specific supplemental criteria for environmental harms or unfair trade practices and specific sanctions for such harms;
- Further include citizen and NGO participation on NAFTA advisory boards in each member country;
- Assure funding sources for NAFTA operations and for the creation of the necessary "infrastructure" facilities such as treatment plants and processing systems in order to manage pollution in border region environments, especially the region between the United States and Mexico;
- Clarify and improve NAFTA's effectiveness.[78]

The possibility of "snapback" tariffs to penalize NAFTA violations may also be revived, although opponents to such a remedy argue that such tariff remedies should be pursued under the general GATT framework.[79] Senator Max Baucus (D.-Montana) chairman of the Senate Environment and Public Works Committee, added an interesting spin on efforts to promote "green" NAFTA trade. Before completion of the final GATT (Uruguay Round) meeting in 1994, he suggested that any side agreement under NAFTA be included in a "green round" of GATT negotiations on the subject of the global commons and transboundary pollution.[80] It is too early to predict whether the implementation of NAFTA will require revisitation and/or negotiation of the foregoing suggestions.

■ Chapter 11 Endnotes

1. *Basic Documents of International Environmental Law—Volumes I–III* (Harold Hohman ed., 1992), hereafter cited as *Basic Documents*.
   L. K. Caldwell, *International Environmental Policy* (1990). Hereafter cited as *Caldwell*.
   B. Carter and P. Trimble, *International Law* (1991). Hereafter cited as *Carter*.
   "Developments in the Law—International Environmental Law," 104 *Harv. L. Rev.* 1484 (1991). Hereafter cited as *"Developments."*
   L. Kramer, *EEC Treaty and Environmental Protection* (1990).
   J. Jackson, "World Trade Rule and Environmental Policies: Congruence or Conflict," 49 *Wash. & Lee L. Rev.* 1227 (1992).
   F. Mathys, "International Environmental Law: A Canadian Perspective," 3 *Pace Yearbook of International Law* 91 (1992). Hereafter cited as *Mathys*.
   Trends in International Environmental Law (American Bar Association, 1992). Hereafter cited as *Trends*.

"United Nations Conference on Environment and Development (UNCED)," Symposium Issue, 4 *Colo. J. of Int'l L. & Policy* 1 (1993).

2. "1990 Bergen ECE Ministerial Declaration on Sustainable Development," *Basic Documents,* supra, pp. 558 *et seq.*

3. R. Train, "A Call for Sustainability," 18 *EPA Journal* (no. 4, 1992), p. 7.

4. Caldwell, pp. 257, 277, 283.

5. "Developments," supra, pp. 1487, 1550.

6. S. Gaines, "Taking Responsibility for Transboundary Environmental Effects," 14 *Hastings Int'l & Comp. L. Rev.* 781, 782 (1991).

7. *Restatement of the Law on Foreign Relations,* 3d ed. American Law Institute.

8. Carter, supra, 1145.

9. Judge Manfred Lacks of the International Court of Justice, as quoted in Carter, supra, p. 1110.

10. J. Brierly, *The Law of Nations* (1963).

11. *Restatement,* note 7, supra. See also Carter supra, pp. 1–7.

12. *Restatement,* note 7, supra, § 102.

13. Ibid., § 102, Comment b.

14. See, for example, the discussions of the *Trail Smelter* case and the European Community later in this chapter.

15. Carter, supra, p. 1160.

16. "Developments," supra, p. 1505, and *Trends,* supra, pp. 28 *et seq.*

17. See the compilation of agreements in *Basic Documents,* supra.

18. *Restatement,* note 7, supra, § 314 (Reservations and Understandings).

19. See, generally, *Developments,* pp. 1567–1604.

20. Carter, supra, pp. 459, 460.

21. D. Getches, "Foreword: The Challenge of Rio," 4 *Colo. J. Int'l L. & Policy* 2 (1993).

22. See, for example, Report of Hearings, NAFTA: Environmental Issues, (Subcommittee on Rules of the House of Representatives, 102d Cong., 1st Sess. 1992), p. 27.

23. III *U.N. Rep. Int's Arb. Awards* (1949).

24. Carter, supra, pp. 1150–1161.

25. Ibid., pp. 1147, 1148.

26. Mathys, supra, p. 91.

27. "Developments," supra, p. 1543.

28. The agreements are listed in *Basic Documents,* supra, and in chapter 5 of *Caldwell.*

29. CEQ, *Environmental Quality* (1990), pp. 332 *et seq.*; and *Basic Documents,* supra, pp. 1167–1213.

30. Ibid., p. 325.

31. Mathys, supra, 114.

32. Ibid., p. 107.

33. Mathys, supra, pp. 112–13.

34. Report of Hearings, *NAFTA Environmental Issues,* Subcommittee on Rules of the House of Representatives, 102d Cong., 1st Sess. (1992), pp. 34, 35.

35. Ibid., p. 37.

36. *Basic Documents,* supra, pp. 1237–1239.

37. Note, "The Environmental Cooperation Agreement between Mexico and the United States: A Response to the Pollution Problems of the Border Lands," 19 *Cornell Int'l L. J.* 112–121 (1986).

38. *Basic Documents,* supra, 1240–1260.

39. Note, 19 *Cornell Int'l L. J.*, 87–102 (1986).

40. *Basic Documents*, supra, p. 1240.

41. Reported in 16 *Int'l Environmental Reporter* 4 (1993).

42. Testimony of L. Williams, Director of the Sierra Club, in *NAFTA*, note 34 supra, p. 63.

43. *Basic Documents*, supra, pp. xii, xiii.

44. Carter, supra, 1188, citing Bilder, ''The Settlement of Disputes in the Field of the International Law of the Environment,'' 144 *Rec. des. Cours* 139 (1975–I).

45. *Basic Documents*, supra, 1092–1126.

46. H. U. J. d'Oliveira, ''The Sandoz Blaze: The Damage and the Public and Private Liabilities,'' in *International Responsiility for Environmental Harm*, 429–445 (Francioni & Scovazzi, eds., 1991).

47. Caldwell, supra, p. 135; L. Kramer, *EEC Treaty and Environmental Protection* (1990).

48. Caldwell, supra, pp. 138–39.

49. ''EC Council Recommendation, C(74) 223,'' *Basic Documents*, supra, p. 380.

50. Kramer, note 47 supra, p. 3.

51. 19 *Envl. Rep.* 2516 (1989).

52. *Basic Documents*, supra, 1585–1614; and ''Hazardous Waste, Basel Treaty Partners Agree to Ban Waste Exports to Nations Outside OECD,'' 1994 *DER* 58 d22 (Bureau of National Affairs, Inc., 1994).

53. Waste Export and Import Control Act of 1994, HR 3965 (also called the Swift–Synar bill.

54. ''Hazardous Waste,'' note 52, supra.

55. Ibid.

56. For more extensive surveys, see D. Caron, ''Protection of the Stratospheric Ozone Layer and the Structure of International Environmental Lawmaking,'' 14 *Hastings Int'l & Comp. L. Rev.* 755 (1991); and Caldwell, supra, pp. 262–263.

57. *Basic Documents*, supra, pp. 1691–1732.

58. Reported in ''EPA Lists Ozone-Safe Chemicals,'' *The Philadelphia Inquirer,* 6 May 1993, pp. C1, C5.

59. *U.N. General Assembly Resolution,* 3 December 1968.

60. ''Developments,'' supra, p. 1580, n. 4.

61. *Basic Documents*, supra, 21–47.

62. Ibid., Caldwell, supra, pp. 61–64, 84.

63. *Basic Documents*, supra, 1748–1762.

64. See ''United Nations Conference on the Environment and Development (UNCED),'' 4 *Colorado Journal of Int'l Envl. L. and Policy*, 1 (1993); ''United States Senate Delegation's Official Report,'' 138 *Congressional Record* S. 18236-01; ''United Nations Conference on Environment and Development,'' 31 *International Legal Materials* 814 (1992); ''Special Report,'' *Intern'l Environment Reporter*, 486 (July 15 1992).

65. D. Getches, ''Foreword: The Challenge of Rio,'' 4 *Colorado Journal of International Environmental Law and Policy*, 1 (1993).

66. *United States Senate Delegation's Official Report*, 138 Congressional Record S. 18236-01.

67. See *The New York Times,* 22 April 1993, pp. A1, A10.

68. See paragraph 6 of "U.N. Resolution 43/53: Protection of Global Climate for Present and Future Generations of Mankind, 6 Dec. 1988," in *Basic Documents,* supra, p. 525. See also Caldwell, supra, pp. 263–268.

69. J. Jackson, "World Trade Rules and Environmental Policies: Congruence or Conflict," 49 *Wash. & Lee L. Rev.* 1227, 1228 (1992).

70. "Over 100 Nations Sign GATT Accord," 11 *International Trade Reporter* 610, (no. 16 Bureau of National Affairs, Inc.).

71. Carter, supra, pp. 493–95.

72. J. Jackson, note 69, supra, p. 1241.

73. "Dispute Settlement Panel Report under General Agreement on Tariff and Trade—United States restrictions on Imports of Tuna," XXX *International Legal Materials,* 1594.

74. "Global Legislators Seek Moratorium on Challenges to Environmental Standards," 1994 *DER* 41 d22 (1994). Global Legislators is an international environmental organization.

75. "Accord Set among GATT Nations on Linking Trade, Environment," 1994 *DER* 70 d29 (1994).

76. Public Citizens v. U.S. Trade Representative, 5 F.3d 549 (D.C. Cir. 1993).

77. NAFTA, note 34, supra; 19 U.S.C. § 3301.

78. See "Current Report NAFTA," 16 International Environmental Reporter 88 (1993); "Daily Report for Executives," 1993 *DER* 85 (5 May 1993).

79. "Current Report," note 78, supra, p. 160.

80. "Daily Report," note 78, supra.

APPENDIX A

Selected Environmentally-Related Statutes

The following statutes are the more significant environmentally-related laws that could not be covered within this edition.

Emergency Planning and Community-Right-to-Know Act, 42 U.S.C. § 1101, *et seq.*

Marine Mammal Protection Act, 16 U.S.C. § 1361, *et seq.*; 16 U.S.C. § 1401, *et seq.*

Marine Protection, Research and Sanctuaries Act, 33 U.S.C. § 1401, *et seq.*; 16 U.S.C. § 1431, *et seq.*

Mining and Mineral Resources Research Institute Act, 30 U.S.C. § 1221, *et seq.*

National Ocean Pollution Planning Act, 33 U.S.C. § 1701, *et seq.*

Noise Control Act, 42 U.S.C. § 4901, *et seq.*

Occupational Safety and Health Act (OSHA), 29 U.S.C. § 651, *et seq.*

Outer Continental Shelf Lands Act, 43 U.S.C. § 1331, *et seq.*; 46 U.S.C. § 1841, *et seq.*

Surface Mining Control and Reclamation Act, 30 U.S.C. § 1201, *et seq.*

APPENDIX B

Selected Suggested Readings

The following references are listed in two parts. Treatises, books, and monographs are shown in italics. Periodicals and reports are shown within quotation marks.

General References

Atlas of United States Environmental Issues, R. Mason & M. Mattson (1990).
The Closing Circle: Nature, Man, and Technology, B. Commoner (1971).
Environmental Law Handbook, 10th ed. (Govt. Inst. Inc., 1989).
Federal Public Land and Resources Law, Coggins and Wilkinson (1987).
Guide to Benefit-Cost Analysis, E. Gramlich (1990).
Guide to Federal Environmental Law, R. Zoner (P.L.I., 1981).
Guide to State Environmental Programs, D. Jessup (BNA, 1988).
Hornbook of Environmental Law, 2d ed., W. H. Rodgers, Jr. (1994).
Rights of Nature: A History of Environmental Ethics, R. Nash (1989).
A Sand County Almanac, Aldo Leopold (1968).
Selected Environmental Law Statutes (West Publishing Co., Annual Editions).
Silent Spring, R. Carson (1962).
State of the Environment, The Conservation Foundation/World Wildlife Fund
    (1987).
Statistical Record of the Environment, A. Darnay, ed. (Gale Research Inc., 1992).
Tragedy of the Commons, G. Hardin (1968).
Treatise on Environmental Law, F. Grad (1989).
U.S. Environmental Laws, BNA (1993).

"EPA Journal," published bi-monthly by the U.S. Gov't Printing Office.
"Environmental Quality," Annual Reports of the Council on Environmental
    Quality (CEQ).
"Environmental Coverage," Am. Bar Assn., 1991.
"Environmental Law Reporter," Environmental Law Institute.
"State by State Environmental Data Summaries—A Research Paper," The Conservation Foundation/World Wildlife Fund (1987).

International Environmental References

A Collection of Bibiolographical and Research Sources, "International Environmental
    Law," Vol. 2 (1990).
EEC Treaty and Environmental Protection, L. Kramer, ed. (London, 1990).
International Environmental Policy, L. Caldwell (1990).

"International Environment: Briefing Book on Major Selected Issues," Cong. Research Service Report For Committee on Foreign Affairs, U.S. House of Representatives (U.S. Govt. Printing Office, 1993).

"Global Dumping Ground," companion volume to PBS "Frontline" television program, by Bill Moyers and the Center for Investigative Reporting (Seven Locks Press, 1990).

"Trends in International Law," Am. Bar Assn. (1992).

"United Nations Conference on Environment and Development 1992—Documents," XXXI International Legal Materials (Am. Society of International Law, 1992).

APPENDIX C

Environmental Terminology: Selected Dictionaries and Acronym Definitions

Dictionaries and Glossaries

J. King, *The Environmental Dictionary* (1989).

E. Lindbergh, *Modern Dictionary of International Legal Terms* (1993).

N. A. Robinson, *Environmental Law Lexicon* (1992).

N. Stoloff, *Environmental Law Dictionary* (1993).

T. Sullivan, *Environmental Regulations Glossary*, 6th ed. (1993).

Acronyms

APA	Administrative Procedures Act
BACT or BCT	Best conventional control technology
BADT	Best available demonstrated technology
BAT	Best available technology
BLM	Bureau of Land Management
BPT	Best practical technology
CAA	Clean Air Act
CERCLA	Comprehensive Environmental Response, Compensation, and Liability Act
CEQ	Council on Environmental Quality
CFC	Chlorofluorocarbon
C.F.R.	Code of Federal Regulations
CWA	Clean Water Act
DOI	U.S. Department of Interior
DOJ	U.S. Department of Justice
EA	Environmental assessment
EC	European Community
EIS	Environmental Impact Statement
EPA	U.S. Environmental Protection Agency
ESA	Endangered Species Act
FIFRA	Federal Insecticide, Fungicide, and Rodenticide Act
FWPCA	Federal Water Pollution Control Act (See CWA)
HAP	Hazardous air pollutant
IJC	International Joint Commission
MACT	Maximum achievable control technology
NAAQS	National Ambient Air Quality Standards
NCP	National Contingency Plan
NEPA	National Environmental Policy Act
NGO	Non-governmental organization
NPDES	National Pollutant Discharge Elimination System

NPL	National Priority List
NSPS	New Source Performance Standards
OMB	Office of Management and Budget
OPA	Oil Pollution Act
OSHA	Occupational Safety and Health Administration
PCBs	Polychorinated biphenyls
POTW	Publicly-owned treatment works
PRP	Potentially responsible party
RACT	Reasonably available control technology
RCRA	Resource Conservation and Recovery Act
SIP	State Implementation Plan
TSCA	Toxic Substances Control Act
USDA	U.S. Department of Agriculture
UST	Underground storage tank
VOCs	Volative organic compounds

APPENDIX D

Listing of Selected Environmental Organizations

U.S. Nongovernmental Organizations

Earth First!

Earthwatch

Environmental Defense Fund

Friends of the Earth

Greenpeace

National Audubon Society

National Wildlife Federation

Natural Resources Defense Council

Nature Conservancy

Nukewatch

Sierra Club

Wilderness Society

World Conservation Union

World Resources Institute

World Wildlife Fund

International Organizations

See "Representative Listing of International Organizations and Programs Concerned with Environmental Issues," in L. Caldwell, *International Environmental Policy,* Appendix A, p. 339 *et seq.* (1990).

INDEX